W9-BGM-333

Shorthanded: The Untold Story of the Seals

Hockey's Most Colorful Team

by

Brad Kurtzberg

Bloomington, IN   Milton Keynes, UK

authorHOUSE™

AuthorHouse™
1663 Liberty Drive, Suite 200
Bloomington, IN 47403
www.authorhouse.com
Phone: 1-800-839-8640

AuthorHouse™ UK Ltd.
500 Avebury Boulevard
Central Milton Keynes, MK9 2BE
www.authorhouse.co.uk
Phone: 08001974150

First published by AuthorHouse 02/07/06

I)ISBN: 1-4259-1028-9 (sc)

Printed in the United States of America
Bloomington, Indiana

This book is printed on acid-free paper.

TABLE OF CONTENTS

duction ix

ard xiii

PART I: WHO OWNS THE SEALS?

pter 1: The Van Gerbig Years 3

pter 2: Puck Inc. Takes Over—Sort Of 12

pter 3: Trans National Communications: Celebrity Ownership 14

pter 4: The Charlie Finley Error 17

pter 5: The League Takes Over 29

pter 6: Mel Swig, At Last 31

Part II: THE PLAYERS REMEMBER

pter 1: The Early Years: 1967–68 to 1969–70 37

Billy Harris 37

Kent Douglas 39

Larry Cahan 41

Larry Popein 42

Bob Baun 43

Wally Boyer 46

Charlie Burns 47

Aut Erickson 49

Charlie Hodge 50

Alain Caron 52

Ron Harris 53

Tracy Pratt 55

Tom Thurlby 57

Bill Hicke 58

Mike Laughton 61

Gerry Ehman 63

John Brenneman 64

Ted Hampson 66

Coach Fred Glover 68

Earl Ingarfield 72

Bryan Watson 74

Gerry Odrowski 75

Brian Perry 77

Bob Dillabough 79

Dick Mattiussi 80

Doug Roberts 82

Chris Worthy 84

Gene Ubriaco 86

Wayne Muloin 88

Gary Smith ....
George Swarbrick ....
Francois Lacombe ....
Joe Szura..
Howie Menard...
Joe Hardy..
Harry Howell...
Tony Featherstone ....
Bert Marshall...
Don O'Donoghue ....
Gary Jarrett...
Norm Ferguson..
Carol Vadnais ....
Other Early Seals ....
    Ron Boehm..
    Bob Lemieux ....
    Jean Cusson ....
    Terry Clancy ....
    Len Ronson..
    Barry Boughner ....
    Neil Nicholson..
Chapter 2: The Middle Years: 1970-71 to 1973-74 ....
    Dennis Hextall...
    Ron Stackhouse ....
    Ernie Hicke..
    Tommy Williams ....
    Dick Redmond...
    Tom Webster..
    Lyle Carter..
    Coach Vic Stasiuk ....
    Gary Croteau 1
    Gerry Pinder 1
    Bobby Sheehan...1
    Wayne Carleton 1
    Paul Shmyr...1
    Ivan Boldirev..1
    Stan Gilbertson 17
    Rick Smith..18
    Reggie Leach..18
    Hilliard Graves 18
    Pete Laframboise..19
    Marv Edwards 19
    Ted McAneeley 19
    Darryl Maggs..198

Terry Murray 199
Craig Patrick..201
Walt McKechnie..204
Bob Stewart 207
Joey Johnston 210
Marshall Johnston...214
Morris Mott 218
Gilles Meloche 221
Barry Cummins 226
Ray McKay...229
Paul Shakes..231
Rick Kessell..233
Stan Weir 235
er Middle Seals 239
Bob Sneddon 239
Del Hall 239
Ken Baird 239
Lyle Bradley 240
Al Simmons..240
Hartland Monahan..240
Jim Jones 240
Ron Serafini..241
Pete Vipond 241
Gary Coalter 241
Frank Hughes 241
Brent Meeke 242
Ted Tucker..242
Paul Andrea 242
Gary Kurt..243
Bob Champoux..243
Chapter 3: The Late Years: 1974-75 to 1975-76...244
Mike Christie..244
Al MacAdam 247
Brian Lavender 250
Larry Patey 252
Butch Williams...254
John Stewart 257
Dave Hrechkosy 259
Dave Gardner 262
Fred Ahern..265
George Pesut..267
Wayne King...269
Gary Simmons..271
Spike Huston 275

Len Frig...
Jim Neilson..
Jim Moxey...
Gary Holt...
Rick Hampton...
Charlie Simmer...
Frank Spring...
Bob Girard...
Bob Murdoch..
Gary Sabourin...
Jim Pappin...
Ralph Klassen...
Tim Jacobs...
Wayne Merrick...
Dennis Maruk...
OTHER LATE SEALS...
Greg Smith...
Bruce Greig..
Glenn Patrick..
Larry Wright...
Tom Price...
Krazy George—Cheerleader..
Postscript..
About the Author...

players were young and unrestrained. These stories were meant to celebrate the Seals and illuminate and entertain the reader. I hope they will all be taken in that light.

I have a lot of other people to thank for their help with my efforts and I'm sure I'll leave somebody out by accident. Thanks to Len Shapiro, April Earle, Ron Riesterer, Tiffany Bunke, the Seals Booster Club, Ty Toki, many members of the Hockey Researchers Association, Frank Selke, Jr., the NHL Alumni Association, Jackie, Josh and Haley, David Barish, Joel Kurtzberg, Ron Marshall, Peter E. Lamoureux, Brian O'Sullivan, Kathy DiPietro, Jerry Hearing, Linda and Ira Kurtzberg and all the players, owners and employees of the Seals who took the time to speak with me.

Finally, this book is first and foremost a labor of love. I hope my readers will have at least half as much fun reading this story as I did writing it and putting it together, and that, after reading this book, you will all understand why I chose to tell the story of the Seals, who—even though they were shorthanded—are hockey's forgotten treasure.

Brad Kurtzberg
Long Island, New York

November 22, 2005

Forward

By Len Shapiro, former Seals Assistant PR Director

The Seals were born in the 1967 National Hockey League expansion and died after the 1975-76 season. In between, the Seals played nine fruitless seasons filled with more stories, events and characters then most Original Six NHL teams could muster over the preceding 50 years.

The franchise was in trouble from the start. Barry van Gerbig's ownership made all the wrong moves. With the team not drawing fans and hopeless on the ice, money quickly vanished from the ownership groups' pockets. The team was always dealing with one foot in the penalty box of business operations.

Seals management drafted unknown American Hockey League players instead of Western Hockey Leaguers. WHL players might not have been as talented, but were known to Bay Area fans. Why have Joe Szura, when you could have had Wayne Connelly, who was an ex-WHL Seals goal scorer? Why have Billy Harris, when you could have had Seattle defenseman Larry Hale? Why didn't the Seals develop a minor league system instead of trading No. 1 picks? It made no sense!

Author Brad Kurtzberg has meticulously connected all the fateful dots in the Seals short NHL life, from van Gerbig to undercapitalized TransNational to short-lived Puck Inc. (with George Gillette, who now owns the Montreal Canadiens) and Oakland A's owner Charlie Finley to NHL ownership and, finally, Mel Swig, who should have been the original owner. Brad has simply covered it all.

In this book you will follow all the owners' blunders over the nine less-than-perfect seasons. How could Frank Selke trade a No. 1 pick? How could Finley let Bill Torrey go?

You'll read players' accounts of what actually happened during those nine fateful campaigns. Check out WHA defections, Bert Olmstead's closed Thanksgiving Day practice, Morris Mott's New York fan club, Rick Hampton's struggles, Mike Christie's meeting with the Broad Street Bullies and, of course, the Streaker.

Brad has gotten many players to let it all hang out about the team, teammates and front-office management.

I covered the Seals for the first six and half years of their existence and got to work with the club for the final two and half years in Oakland.

It was on February 1, 1976, when I came to the office and none of the top management could be found. PR secretary Loretta Marcus, the only nine-year veteran of the front office and I checked out President Munson Campbell's desk for a clue. To our dismay, we found a note that said "Book the Cleveland Hilton." Then Loretta and I knew it was over. The rumors of the last nine years, which had the team moving to Vancouver, Denver, Phoenix and Cleveland, were coming true. The Seals pulled up sticks and skate sharpeners and headed for the Richfield Coliseum, now known as the "mistake on the lake." When goalie Gary Simmons stepped on the ice for his first practice and saw the ice littered with dead flies, he said, "They all committed suicide because they were in Cleveland."

Even in Cleveland the Seals, now renamed the Barons, couldn't escape their legacy. After two terrible seasons, the Barons folded and merged with the Minnesota North Stars. The Seals were officially dead.

I would like to acknowledge the front office and media personnel, who suffered along with the players and franchise, and my public-relations predecessors—Tim Ryan, Bob Bestor, Frank Sanchez, Mark Freter and Shep Goldberg, who gave me a job—who all worked with one arm tied behind their respective backs. My ad budget for the last year in Oakland was $5,000. I blew it all on trying to get somebody to buy season tickets in August and September.

Broadcasters Ryan, Roy (Shot on Goal) Storey, and Joe (What a Bonanza) Starkey, who had to describe some of the worst games played in NHL history. Just ask Starkey about some of those blowouts he had to sit through against the Islanders, Buffalo and the Rangers, Sports Reporters

Spence Conley, John Porter, Fran Tuckwiller, Nelson Cullenward, Ken Miller, Hugh MacDonald, Dick O'Connor (Ranger fan), Dick Drapper and Jack Fiske, who help me get the PR job, who had to write stories about the hapless Seals.

And of course, we have to thank Brad for taking three years out of his life to sit down and write this book. He contacted as many Seals players as possible to give fans a true "bay window" into club operations during the strange journey of 698 regular season and 11 playoff games. If you weren't a Seals fan before, you will be after reading this great team biography.

Len Shapiro
San Francisco, California
November 2005

PART I:

WHO OWNS THE SEALS?

Chapter 1:
The Van Gerbig Years

From 1942 until 1967 the National Hockey League had only six teams. The so-called "Original Six" were located in Montreal, Toronto, Boston, Chicago, Detroit and New York. The league was stable and the owners were making profits but, with only six franchises, its influence and revenue streams were limited. While the owners of football and baseball franchises were making large amounts of money from national television contracts, the NHL could not get a major television deal in the United States with only four teams located there. By the mid-'60s the owners were finally persuaded to expand by the promise of hefty expansion fees and the strong probability of a network television contract in the United States.

While the NHL had only six teams, minor league hockey was played in many markets in the United States and Canada. Leagues such as the American Hockey League, International Hockey League, Eastern Hockey League, Central Hockey League and Western Hockey League provided hockey fans in local markets access to both up-and-coming prospects and professionals who were not quite good enough to be one of the 120 players in the NHL.

There was minor league hockey in the San Francisco Bay Area as early as the 1948–49 season, when a team called the San Francisco Seals played in the WHL. The team ceased operations after just two seasons, but a new franchise adopted the same name and joined the WHL in 1961. The Seals played their home games in Daly City, just outside of San Francisco, at the Cow Palace, a rickety old building originally built for rodeos and livestock fares—but it had a certain minor league charm.

The Seals drew good crowds at the Cow Palace, averaging nearly 7,000 fans per game between 1961 and 1966. The club was successful on the ice as well. Coached by Bud Poile, who later had a hand in the building of the Philadelphia Flyers, the club won back-to-back WHL championships in 1962–63 and 1963–64. Star players included Charlie Burns, Len Haley, Nick Mickoski and Wayne Connelly.

The club was owned by a group of investors led by Coley Hall and Mel Swig. They developed a loyal cult following in the Bay Area, but did not penetrate the region's consciousness like major league teams such as the San Francisco Giants, San Francisco 49ers, Oakland Raiders and San Francisco Warriors did. Hall began to lobby for the NHL to expand and to include the Bay Area. "The time has come for the NHL to realize that Los Angeles and San Francisco can't wait," Hall said in 1964. "Our hockey fans are just as major league-conscious as fans of baseball and football and feel they should be up there. An angry feeling is developing." Still, the NHL was reluctant to act.

The Seals had a working agreement with the Boston Bruins and were partly owned by the parent club. The Bruins sent players from their organization to stock the Seals. The prevailing state of mind was that those players sent to the WHL were not top prospects. The majority of the Bruins' top minor league players in the mid-60s were either playing for the Hershey Bears of the AHL or in the developmental league in Oklahoma City. Players sent to the WHL were, with a few exceptions, going to remain career minor leaguers as long as the NHL had only six teams.

When the NHL finally decided to expand beyond the Original Six in the mid-'60s, the Bay Area was high on the list of desirable locations. The minor league Seals had been successful and San Francisco was considered one of the country's major markets. In fact, when CBS announced a national television deal with the NHL in the United States, one requirement was that a franchise be placed in the Bay Area.

By 1966 it was clear that expansion was finally on the horizon. The potential earnings from American television were too good to pass up. League president Clarence Campbell announced that the NHL would double in size and six new teams, dubbed the West Division, would be added for the 1967–68 season: the Minnesota North Stars, Philadelphia Flyers, Pittsburgh Penguins, St. Louis Blues, Los Angeles Kings and the California Seals. The six established clubs would all play in the East Division.

Even before they were created, the California Seals were different from other NHL teams. Most NHL clubs were owned by one man or by a small group of partners who had a controlling interest in the team. Jack Kent Cooke, for example, owned the Los Angeles Kings and the Snider family owned the Philadelphia Flyers. The Seals, however, were owned by a uniquely structured group of owners consisting of more than 50 partners—none of whom held a majority interest in the team. The titular head of this partnership was 29-year-old Barend (Barry) van Gerbig.

Van Gerbig was born with the proverbial silver spoon in his mouth. His father-in-law was acting legend Douglas Fairbanks Jr. and crooner Bing Crosby was his godfather. Van Gerbig had some background in hockey before becoming involved in the ownership of the Seals. He played on Princeton University's varsity team and was later named a goaltender on the 1962 U.S. National Team.

Barry van Gerbig had a regal air about him. Jim Lingel, the club's vice president for marketing, recalled, "I remember his wife was a lady-in-waiting for the queen of England," Lingel said. "One time the van Gerbigs, the Ryans (team broadcaster Tim Ryan and his wife) and I went out to a restaurant and all had a few drinks, and I kept making Barry and his wife laugh by saying, 'Ladies and gentlemen, the queen.' "

When it came time for the NHL to select an owner for the new Bay Area franchise, van Gerbig had two indispensable qualities: he had contacts among the owners of the Original Six franchises and he had a lot of money (he owned a piece of both Union Carbide and Standard Oil).

"I had been very close to Bruce Norris of Detroit and Bill Jennings of the New York Rangers. I also knew Charlie Adams in Boston and his lawyer, Charlie Mulcahy, was a friend of my father," van Gerbig recalled. According to van Gerbig, it was Mulcahy who first broached the subject of owning an NHL team with him. "Charlie Mulcahy and I were both working on Wall Street in 1965," said van Gerbig. "One day, we were playing golf when Mulcahy mentioned that the Bruins organization owned an interest in the San Francisco Seals [of the WHL] and that they were looking for a partner to take over their interest when the NHL expands."

Of course there was more to it than that. *Oakland Tribune* hockey-beat writer Spence Conley recalled, "Mel Swig and Collie Hall were the co-owners of the WHL San Francisco Seals. Swig was very active in making his presence known; he was elegant, and open to reporters. Swig was truly a class act and was one of the nicest men in hockey. Swig also had the political connections in San Francisco to make things happen; there were allegations of anti-Semitism when he didn't get the Bay Area franchise."

Looking back, van Gerbig agreed that not keeping Swig involved was a mistake. "A bunch of good people led by Mel Swig owned a minority stake in the minor league franchise," van Gerbig said. "Swig was a good man and well connected in San Francisco. The league said to us that Mel Swig and his group were 'not acceptable partners'. Mel Swig was a prince of a man. We should have kept him involved in the ownership of the team. There were apparently some [negative] feelings between the Bruins and the Swig group. I think, in hindsight, that was one of the things that prompted the Bruins to approach me about owning the team in the first place."

The original five partners in the Seals were Barry van Gerbig, his brother Mickey van Gerbig, George Coleman, singer Bing Crosby and senior partner Virgil Sherrill. Frank Selke Jr., who served as president of the Seals in their first NHL season, recalled that "there were some 52 initial investors in the Seals at various financial levels." They included San Francisco 49ers quarterback John Brodie, Marco Hellman (the owner of Hellman's mayonnaise) and publishing magnate Nelson Doubleday (who would later be co-owner of baseball's New York Mets). Selke recalled that the members of the group ponied up the $2 million franchise fee plus an undetermined amount to cover start-up costs, player salaries and promotional expenses.

Van Gerbig remembered how the group quickly grew in size: "As soon as we had the inside track on the team, our friends came out of the woodwork. Our friends all saw sellouts in the Original Six buildings and we had guys who really wanted to be a part of it. The five of us owned over 50 percent of the team. I was the president, the figurehead, and I represented the team at NHL governors' meetings." With more than 50 partners to answer to, however, van Gerbig would have a lot of difficulty getting the authority to make important decisions.

The first problem the group faced was where to play its home games. "The minor league Seals played in the Cow Palace for four or five years and had a very successful run," *The Oakland Tribune*'s Conley recalled. "Ticket prices were very low and attendance was very high." Still, the Cow Palace, opened in 1941, was hardly an NHL-caliber rink, even by 1967 standards.

Seals vice president for marketing, Jim Lingel, remembered some of the major reasons why. "The Cow Palace had about 13,000 to 14,000 seats. However, between the goal lines there were only about 15 rows. Most of the seats were in the corners for hockey. It was like a big, square barn and it had terrible sight lines. The rink was also 15 feet short of the regulation 200 feet long. It was originally designed for rodeo."

Future Seals coach Fred Glover also disliked the Cow Palace. "It was the worst arena," Glover said. "The nets at each end were smaller at the bottom than at the top. They were bent in and couldn't fit on the pegs. The seats were up against the bench. There was just no room."

One fan recalled that the Cow Palace "always smelled like the rodeo was there." Like many old buildings, it had its own quaint "charms" and idiosyncrasies.

Even if the Seals owners wanted the team to play in the Cow Palace, the league was not going to permit it. Barry van Gerbig recalled that the members of his group went out there and realized there was no major league indoor facility in the Bay Area. "NHL president Clarence Campbell came to us and told us a new building was going up in Oakland, and that nobody gets a franchise in the Bay Area unless they agree to play in that new, state-of-the-art building. It only seated 12,500. That's when we should have walked away."

Although van Gerbig and his partners knew they would start the franchise in Oakland, they planned all along to move the club to downtown San Francisco as soon as a suitable arena could be built. "I got some assurances from some people who were well connected with the city government in San Francisco that if we got a hockey team, we would have the impetus for a new arena in downtown San Francisco," van Gerbig said. "I thought that we would be well placed. We would start the franchise in Oakland and then move to San Francisco when the new arena was built and we could maintain our fan base."

The Oakland Coliseum Arena was completed in 1966 and hosted its first WHL game on November 9, 1966. The Seals defeated the San Diego Gulls 6-5. Van Gerbig's group bought the WHL Seals prior to its final season in the WHL (1966-67). They quickly realized there was a problem with the new arena's location. Most Seals fans Seals came from San Francisco, San Jose and the outer suburbs. Very few fans came from the city of Oakland itself. Despite playing in a brand-new arena, the WHL Seals' attendance actually dropped by just over 1,000 fans per game after the team moved to Oakland. Of the five major partners, only Bing Crosby lived in the Bay Area, but the new owners realized they had a problem on their hands well before the NHL team even took the ice.

"We learned quickly that Oakland was just across the bay from San Francisco, but people from San Francisco don't cross the bay for anything," van Gerbig said. "If Jesus Christ came on a donkey over there, they wouldn't come."

Bay Area resident Jim Lingel concurred. "There was a psychological barrier to San Franciscans," he said. "Oakland was like nowhere to them. Anything in Oakland was considered second- or third class. The people in San Francisco were so smug and pseudo-sophisticated." Unfortunately for the Seals, the franchise would never be able to overcome the "stigma" of playing in Oakland during its nine- year history.

The team's name was also an issue. The club was initially called the California Seals because Oakland was considered "minor league" and the club hoped to draw fans from all over the Bay Area. Both the name and the marketing of the team would soon change.

Now that an arena was chosen, van Gerbig and his partners had two major tasks to accomplish before the Seals could begin play: they needed to hire somebody to run the club's hockey operations and they needed to begin marketing the team and selling tickets. As fate would have it, the franchise ran into problems in both areas.

Rudy Pilous was the coach of the WHL Seals. Pilous had extensive coaching experience and was behind the bench when the Chicago Black Hawks won their last Stanley Cup in 1961. While Pilous was considered good enough to coach the minor league Seals, van Gerbig had second thoughts about keeping Pilous on as the team entered the NHL. "Rudy Pilous was much older and much more laid back," van Gerbig recalled. "We felt we really needed a disciplinarian, and Bert Olmstead fit the mold. He had so much credibility as a player—he had an aura about him. We felt minor league players would respond to him as they wouldn't to Rudy."

Selke recalled Pilous as "a well-liked management type." Before Selke was hired in May of 1967, Pilous was already dismissed as general manager. "Part of Bert's deal was that Rudy had to go," Selke recalled. Seals broadcaster Tim Ryan also felt that Olmstead wanted Pilous out: "Bert Olmstead used to think Rudy Pilous was a clown, or a buffoon. Bert had him dismissed, and he brought in Gordie Fashoway as an assistant coach."

The choice of Olmstead as coach and GM caused some problems for Ryan in his role as team broadcaster and publicist. "Rudy was great with the press. He was gregarious and open with the media," Ryan said. "Olmstead was a hero because of who he was in Canada, but by nature he was a shy, inward-looking guy who put a lot of pressure on himself to do well. Bert was always short-tempered with 'stupid' questions from the press." Eddie Dorohoy, who worked with Olmstead during his days in the WHL, characterized the coach's attitude toward the press by saying, "If Olmstead did public relations for Santa Claus, there wouldn't be any Christmas."

The Oakland Tribune's Conley, who had to interview Olmstead often, also found him to be reserved and almost hostile to the press. This was the last thing an expansion team in a new market needed from a coach and general manager. "Bert didn't want you to know too much about the game or else I think he was afraid you would second-guess him—sort of like Bill Parcells in football. It's complete bullshit to think that if you never played the game, you can't become an expert at it."

Olmstead's attitude toward the media made establishing a positive relationship with the press more difficult and probably cost the team some badly needed publicity and good will early on. In fact, Frank Selke Jr. recalled that Olmstead and assistant coach Fashoway had "limited contact with the rest of the [Seals] organization—almost operating in secrecy at times. The very capable Tim Ryan, PR director, was often denied access to basic player information. Olmstead preferring to decide what would be released and to whom."

The expansion draft for the six new franchises was set for June 6, 1967, in Montreal. Because he was hired later, Olmstead had less time to prepare for the draft than his fellow expansion GMs. In fact, Olmstead had only a month to prepare for the expansion draft. This didn't help the Seals select players.

While Olmstead and Fashoway began preparing to select players from the pool made eligible by the existing clubs, the Seals organization began the arduous task of selling NHL hockey in what was certainly a nontraditional hockey market. "Our marketing strategy was simple," van Gerbig recalled. "The minor league team had a nucleus of about 8,000 fans. The strategy was 'we are bringing an NHL team to town and that is a step up. Chicago and Bobby Hull will be coming to town. Detroit and Gordie Howe will be, too'."

Unfortunately for van Gerbig and the rest of the Seals ownership, tickets to see an NHL expansion team were a lot more expensive than tickets to see the WHL team. Furthermore, van Gerbig claims the NHL made significant changes in the draft formula at the last minute. "We were told by the

NHL there would be a very generous draft formula," van Gerbig said. "Existing teams would protect eight skaters and a goalie. We would draft a player and the teams would fill a player. We scouted the Central Hockey League, which had mostly rookies at that time. One month before the draft they came up with each team protecting 14 players and one goalie and they rammed this down our throats. We had already paid $1 million and we ended up with the last guys on the bench in the NHL. The fans realized that the 'minor league team' may have been better than the 'major league team.' We spent a lot of money to promote, but everywhere we went people said, 'Why should we pay X more dollars to see your team play than we did to see the Seals in the Cow Palace?' They were right. We were charging major league prices for a minor league product." This problem—plus the team's move from San Francisco to Oakland—limited the enthusiasm of many of the WHL Seals' fans.

In addition, there was a pervasive attitude around the NHL that expansion was going to be easy. Frank Selke Jr. stated, "It has been my belief that just about everyone associated with expansion in 1967—all six owner groups, media players, fans, the Original Six clubs and the NHL itself—felt that expansion was a 'license to print money,' an expression I heard often at the time. Unfortunately, I felt the same. I had been witness to 20 years of great successes in Montreal, the league had solved its problems in Boston and Chicago and there was every reason to believe we were headed for increased interest in North America that would translate into instant success in six new cities. The truth is, we weren't prepared to manage the downside." Unfortunately, doubling the league's size would not be so simple, and the Seals would come to personify the downside of expansion for the NHL.

The next major task facing the Seals was to promote the club and sell tickets. For this task they hired Jim Lingel, who had been working for the WHL Seals. "I had worked for the minor league team," Lingel recalled. "Everybody knew expansion was coming. They asked me who would sell the tickets, and it ended up being me. My title was vice president for marketing and I was also running the ticket office."

The marketing plan for the Seals ticket office placed a heavy emphasis on season tickets and group sales. Tickets were selling much slower than expected. "We sold about 1,000 season tickets and 1,000 to 1,500 per game in group sales," Lingel recalls. Curiously enough, there was little effort made to sell single-game tickets. "After the season started, we didn't do much advertising for individual games," Lingel recalled. "Our entire advertising was geared toward selling season tickets and groups."

This meant that ticket sales were not being marketed to the new or casual fan, which constituted most of the people in the Bay Area at that time. Instead of encouraging individuals or families to check out the new NHL team, the club was emphasizing selling large numbers of tickets at a time. This strategy prevented the team from adding new fans to their fan base and made introducing hockey to the masses more difficult.

Selke said that when he arrived in Oakland in May of 1967, "the marketing was in place and in full bore. As I recall, some $750,000 had been budgeted for ticket sales, promotion, billboard and print advertising. It was good material—well produced—and I felt it would be effective."

"The guy who did the billboards was fascinated by hockey equipment and he drew a stylized sketch of a player with gloves, pads and skates. I also remember Tim Ryan helping me with the television spots," said Lingel. Selke added: "The material looked good, but it didn't have the desired effect." Plainly put, Seals tickets just weren't selling. Selke, Ryan and Lingel tried everything they could to promote the team. "I made a few speeches at luncheons, showed films, answered questions, hoped for the best and prepared for the worst," Selke recalled.

The team's broadcaster, 26-year-old Ryan, attempted to get more media coverage: "For example, we tried to get the papers to send reporters on the road with the team at the team's expense. We did between-periods promotions like Score-O. ['Peanuts' comic-strip creator] Charles Schulz was helpful. He did two or three program covers for us for free. He also came onto the ice for charity giveaways. Barry tried to get more money from the investors, but they were reluctant. Most of them were his golf buddies, not hockey people."

Ryan's job included encouraging the local media to write about the Seals and cover them. He recalls competing with the Oakland Oaks of the American Basketball Association for media attention. "Basketball was more popular," Ryan admitted. "Getting coverage from the outlying suburban papers was a problem. It was tough to ask them to drive to Oakland. When they did send people, they were not very knowledgeable about hockey so they wrote a lot more about the team's money problems and not about the game." Of course, many of the team's potential fans came from outside of the cities, and the limited coverage of the team in those newspapers further hurt attendance.

Even the local media could be indifferent to the team at times. Selke recalled a preplanned game viewing with the sports editor of *The Oakland Tribune.* "This would give me the chance to explain the game, talk about the players and give him some insight on hockey," Selke said. "After a few minutes, Raiders coach John Madden joined us. They talked football for the rest of the game. Selke and hockey were forgotten."

The Seals management felt it needed a fast start on the ice to help sell the team. "Like everyone else," Selke said, "I pinned my hopes on the team's early success. We looked good on paper, so training camp would provide some answers.

The Seals first training camp was held in Port Huron, Michigan. It was clear from the beginning that Bert Olmstead was going to work the players hard. *Oakland Tribune* writer Conley remembered one practice in particular: "One morning … I had breakfast with a writer from a French hockey publication. We noticed there were large ruts in the ice—it was in very poor condition. Bert Olmstead caused that by having the team do two or three hours of stops and starts, so the team was digging their skates down deeper into the ice. I asked Bert, 'Why did you do that?' He replied, 'They can't skate their lanes, but they can go back and forth'."

Seals forward Billy Harris recalled how Olmstead reacted when he was not pleased with the team's effort in an exhibition game. "We found out quickly how serious Bert Olmstead was about hockey. We tied the Buffalo Bisons, an AHL team, 4-4 in an exhibition game. Bert Olmstead was disgusted that a minor league team could tie an NHL team. The next day we had a two-hour practice with no pucks on the ice. He let us know we would be punished for poor play. We knew it wasn't going to be fun."

In addition to Charlie Hodge and Gary Smith, the two goalies the Seals selected in the expansion draft, another goalie was at camp with the club: Jacques Plante. Plante was officially considered a "goaltending consultant," but some people felt he was competing for a job with the club. In fact, rumors were circulating around the league that Plante had won the starting goaltending job. However, there were potential problems with Plante playing for the Seals. For one thing, the Seals did not posses Plante's rights as a player. Plante had retired from the NHL after the 1964-65 season, when he was with the New York Rangers. The Rangers claimed that they still owned Plante's rights as a player and therefore, the Seals could not sign him. The league did an investigation and determined that Plante was still the property of the New York Rangers. Shortly thereafter, the great goalie left the Seals camp.

Seals president Selke recalls Plante's short-lived tenure with the Seals and remembers that he left for a different reason, "Jacques Plante was in camp for a very short time and left before camp ended. He was very perceptive. He evaluated the team and its chances and decided he didn't want to be part of it. I think the final straw was getting bombarded in an exhibition game. He knew before anyone else that the team wasn't very good. He packed up and left."

It became clear to other people around the team that there were problems with the quality of the club and Coach Olmstead was growing frustrated. Selke remembers the scene when he first saw the team in Port Huron: "When I arrived, the mood of the players left little doubt that we were in for a difficult year. While camps are generally physically demanding and not much fun, Bert early decided that if his team didn't have much talent, they'd at least be in shape, and he drove them hard. After a couple of weeks there were no happy campers, and even Bert's former teammates were disgruntled and discouraged. Bob Baun had been elected as the team representative, and even Bert failed to resolve the wide gulf between Bert's 'plan' and the skill reality of the squad. On Bert's side, there was major disappointment in the performance of several players he had counted on, and he came out of camp frustrated and somewhat disillusioned, in my opinion. I'm sure after the draft he expected to have a good team. After training camp, I'm sure he felt otherwise."

Baun entered camp as Olmstead's biggest supporter. But even he did not have fond recollections of training camp. "I remember doing lots of stops and starts. I was going to stick the whistle in Bert Olmstead's ass. It was a tough camp that made Punch Imlach look like a schoolboy. Everybody worked hard."

The Seals finished the exhibition season with a 2-3-4 record. J.P. Parise scored the first ever goal for the Seals in a preseason game. Parise had a strong preseason and was sure he would be with the Seals. "I'm the second high scorer, so basically I had the team made," Parise recalled. Unfortunately, Parise had a falling out with Olmstead during one of the club's final exhibition games. Parise remembered the incident: The Seals were holding a one-goal lead and he had the puck. He saw a teammate breaking down the right side, "so I challenged and made the rink-wide pass." The pass was intercepted and a flustered Parise took a penalty in the defensive zone. The Seals let in a goal during the power play and the game was tied. According to Parise, Olmstead lit into him and called him "a little freaking frog" and threatened to ship him "back to Quebec." Parise didn't take kindly to the ethnic slur and responded to Olmstead using some colorful language. Olmstead had seen enough. Within 12 hours, Parise was traded to Toronto for Gerry Ehman. At the time, Parise thought his NHL career was over. "I destroyed my life and career," Parise remembers thinking. "I'm 25 years old. It's over." Fortunately for Parise, he was back in the NHL by the half way mark of the season and he went on to have a solid career, appearing in two All-Star Games and the 1972 Summit Series. He never did play a regular season game for the Seals, however.

While many members of the Seals brain trust had their doubts about the club's talent, the team headed to Oakland for the opener and hoped for the best. Attendance at the opening game was a disappointing 6,886—a mere 55 percent of capacity. Lingel recalled one reason why: "Barry van Gerbig gave me the job of setting up a banquet after the game. I invited investors, club officials and some season-ticket holders. I remember the guy who ran the banquet was with the teamsters union. He promised to take 5,000 tickets and sell them. He took the tickets, but he didn't sell them."

Despite the disappointing attendance, there was a carnival atmosphere at the game. Bing Crosby was in attendance, crooner John Gray sang the national anthem and a Dixieland band played during stoppages in play and between periods. The Seals responded with a strong performance, a 5-1 win over the their expansion brethren, the Philadelphia Flyers. Kent Douglas scored the first goal in Seals history and Ron Harris collected the game-winning goal. Bill Hicke scored twice, while goalie Charlie Hodge made 24 saves to earn the win.

"At the banquet, I remember Barry van Gerbig said to Bert Olmstead that he had never seen a hockey team so well prepared," Lingel recalled. It would be one of the last times the investors and season-ticket holders would be celebrating the California Seals.

Although the Seals started off 2-0-1 in their initial home stand, they quickly went into a 13-game winless streak. The team never really recovered from this slump, either on or off the ice. Rumors began to circulate almost immediately that the Seals would be leaving the Bay Area. Vancouver, a city with a strong minor league tradition that just missed out on the first NHL expansion, was the most frequently mentioned destination. In fact, there was some substance to these rumors. The van Gerbig group was losing money on the team and was thinking of selling it.

"Labatt's made a hell of a deal for us to move the club," van Gerbig admitted. "I had to say, 'I'm listening.' I went to see the new building in Vancouver [the Pacific Coliseum]. Labatt's offered to buy 51 percent of the team and would let me maintain 49 percent. Once that hit the papers, we had problems. We were a minor league team masquerading as a major league team and now the owners were looking to leave town. It sure as heck hurt our ticket sales."

The rumors began when the season was just a few games old. "It started after only three or four games," Lingel recalled. "Some of the guys under me were saying, 'How can we sell tickets if we are going to move?' Frank Selke was beside himself."

Indeed, Selke recalled the situation well. "Ownership was quietly investigating whether a move to Vancouver via a sale to Labatt's, a Canadian brewery in competition with Molson [who owned the Canadiens]. Bert Olmstead was aggressively pushing the project, but the NHL wouldn't budge. They wanted Vancouver for future expansion and, of course, were not prepared to admit defeat in the first year of expansion. A failure in Oakland would be a disaster, an NHL 'black eye,' and couldn't be allowed. So the league loaned the investors enough money to pay the bills, keep the club alive, and began looking for a new, more stable ownership structure." CBS also opposed any move out of the Bay Area. Vancouver was a much less attractive market to CBS than the United States' fourth most populated metropolitan area.

The van Gerbig group as it was structured was clearly having problems. One man who was involved in the group was Potter Palmer, an Illinois businessman who had a small stake in the original ownership. "Warren Hellman is a friend of mine," Palmer said. "I'd known him since 1957 when we went to Harvard Business School together. I got him involved in a group that originally bought the Milwaukee Braves and moved them to Atlanta. He returned the favor and introduced me to Barry van Gerbig." Palmer recalled that his initial investment in the Seals was a small one, "approximately $50,000. We had 52 partners and there was a lot of discontent. I attended a meeting of the partners. I think it was in New York. The consensus was to sell the team." The problem was finding a buyer.

Meanwhile, Selke had to try to stop the team's financial bleeding. "When it became apparent the advertising-promotion campaign was not producing, we drastically cut back about one third of the budget, as I recall. There weren't many other ways to trim costs otherwise." Palmer also remembered promoting with a "skeleton staff," and that the owners were "trying to keep costs down."

Lingel tried other ways to increase attendance. The team introduced ladies' nights. "I also tried to market to singles," said Lingel. "We had a singles section and tried to promote that a bit." Lingel also sought advice from employees of other expansion teams. "My counterpart with the Flyers said they were having their players speak at Lions Clubs and Rotary Clubs," Lingel recalled. "I went to Bert Olmstead and asked him about that and he said, 'No, I don't want our guys getting big heads.' I didn't understand that."

Less than two months after playing its first NHL game, the team changed its name. Originally, the club was known as the California Seals in an attempt to draw fans from all over the Bay Area. When that didn't have the desired effect, the team switched its name to the Oakland Seals, in an attempt to reach out to residents of its home city. "We felt we were better off pitching to Oakland fans," Tim Ryan said. Unfortunately, the name change did not help the team's performance on the ice or at the box office.

Despite the best efforts of Selke, Lingel, Ryan and company, the Seals managed an average of only 4,960 fans per game in the 12,500 seat Oakland Coliseum Arena. The team finished the season with a 15-47-17 recorded, mired in last place in the new West Division, which was made up of the six new expansion teams. As hockey-beat reporter Conley said, "I think I had the greatest collection of losing bylines in the newspaper business."

As the season progressed, Olmstead had trouble dealing with the continued losses. Winless steaks of 14 and 11 games didn't help. Olmstead's frustrations showed, and he took it out on his players at various times during the season. "They're just not trying," Olmstead said of the Seals during one losing streak. "I've tried everything to get them to snap out of it. I've insulted and I've threatened. But they've just quit." During another difficult time, Olmstead berated his players again. "If I were a player, I don't even know whether I'd want to be associated with this bunch," the coach yelled to a reporter. "I'd be tossing a few of them out of that dressing room on their cans. They have no pride. A lot of them are getting the chance of a lifetime, and they're reacting like playing in the NHL is a prison sentence." Late in the season, Olmstead stepped down as coach and let Gordie Fashoway take over behind the bench. The atmosphere around the team eased a bit, but the losing continued.

It was clear that changes would be made after a disastrous first season. The van Gerbig group wanted out in the worst way. They were denied permission to move the team to Vancouver by an 8-4 vote of the Board of Governors. Olmstead was "thoroughly frustrated and disgusted," recalled Selke. At the end of the club's first season, Olmstead, assistant coaches Gordie Fashoway and Ken Wilson, and trainer Bill Gray all stepped down.

Quickly, ownership hired Selke as the new GM. "With Olmstead gone, I was asked by the board if I would consider becoming GM in his place, relinquishing the presidential title and some salary," Selke said. "I agreed on both counts for several reasons, not the least being my conviction we could be better even if I wasn't so sure about selling more tickets."

Chapter 2:
Puck Inc. Takes Over—Sort Of

Another change took place in ownership. Potter Palmer, a minority owner in team's first season, stepped forward along with Colorado businessman George Gillett (now owner of the Montreal Canadiens) and Palmer's brother-in-law John O'Neil to take over the running of the club. Palmer recalled that the situation took him by surprise. "George Gillett was a mystery to me at the time. He was not an original partner. I think one of the original partners got a call from George and was told that George and I were interested in buying the team. I had never discussed it with him until then, but we decided to pursue it further."

The Palmer-Gillett-O'Neil group became known as Puck Inc. The three principal partners also owned the Harlem Globetrotters at the time and had an interest in baseball's Atlanta Braves and the Miami Dolphins of the AFL.

George Gillett recalled, "We had the best promotion staff in the business with the Globetrotters and we figured we could take that marketing team to the Seals and work on advertising and promoting. We negotiated a purchase agreement with an option to purchase and put our team to work. Barry van Gerbig still owned the team; we just had an option. We were not involved in the day-to-day running of the team; we were just involved in the marketing."

Although the Puck Inc. group only had an option to purchase the team, their faces are featured prominently in the 1968–69 Seals media guide and home programs as the club's "new owners." O'Neil is described as the "chairman of the Oakland Seals Board of Directors", Gillett as the "vice chairman" and Potter Palmer as the Seals "president and member of the National Hockey League Board of Governors."

Still, it was not completely clear, even to the participants, who had control over what. "We started to spend a lot of time with lawyers," Palmer recalled. "We started to attend league meetings but van Gerbig was also still attending them. I remember my lawyer attended these meetings and made a disclaimer speech before each meeting started stating that my being there didn't mean that I owned the team and what have you. I don't think I had a vote on league issues."

Slowly, the young Seals owner began to see things through more cynical eyes when dealing with his fellow owners. "I remember at the governors' meetings, Stafford Smythe would talk about how he screwed the fans. He would shut off the water fountains in the arena so fans would have to go to the concession stands. The owners were out for themselves, not for the good of the league or the fans or the sport. Unbeknownst to them, I was tape recording a lot of the governors' meetings. That came in handy later on when I had to commence the antitrust action."

The lawsuit brought by van Gerbig and the Seals original owners claimed that the NHL violated the Sherman Antitrust Act by prohibiting the Seals owners from moving the team from Oakland to Vancouver. The case was finally decided by the United States District Court in California on July 18, 1974. Although the court held that the Sherman Antitrust Act *did* apply to professional hockey, it held that NHL clubs were not actually in economic competition with each other and, therefore, the league's restrictions on territorial moves were not an illegal attempt to monopolize trade. [For those of you who want to look up such things, the citation is 379 F.Supp 966 (C.D. Cal. 1974).] The commencing of the lawsuit increased hostility between the van Gerbig group and the league. It also almost guaranteed that the Seals would not leave the Bay Area until the case was settled, as the league would be unable to explain why they let the team move during the litigation after refusing to let van Gerbig transfer the team before the case began.

One thing Puck Inc. did off the ice was hire Bill Torrey to work with Frank Selke Jr. on the hockey side of things. His title was executive vice president. Torrey had prior experience scouting for the Red Wings organization and as publicity director and business manager of the AHL's Pittsburgh Hornets.

Torrey's introduction to the Seals and the club's training camp in September 1968 was a rude one. "We stayed at a rather rundown hotel in the middle of Oshawa, Ontario," Torrey recalled. "During the night, in my rather sumptuous room, I was confronted by one of the largest rats I've ever seen." It was a scary beginning to Torrey's tenure with the club and an omen of things to come.

On the ice, the Seals, led by new coach Fred Glover, finished in second place in the West Division with a 29-36-11 record. Still, attendance was only 4,584 per game. Gillett recalled that his group's efforts resulted in "some improvement in attendance [over the course of the season], but it was not enough to go forward with the sale." Overall, despite the improvement on the ice, attendance actually dipped by almost 400 fans per game from the previous season. Puck Inc. decided not to exercise their option to buy the team.

"They couldn't pay the debt," van Gerbig recalled, as to why the deal didn't go through. "They thought they would use the Globetrotters to fund the losses until they got it going. We kept the franchise as collateral and we ended up having to take it back." For van Gerbig and his partners, the Seals were now like a stray cat that kept coming back despite all efforts to send it away.

After the move to Vancouver failed and the Puck Inc. group decided not to purchase the team, the van Gerbig group attempted another sale to a group called Niagara Frontier Hockey, headed by Seymour and Northrup Knox of Buffalo, New York. Palmer recalled having "some meetings with the Knox brothers. After a while, we were all just trying to get out of this thing."

Van Gerbig recalled that the Knox brothers did buy a percentage of the team, on the condition that they could move it to Buffalo within two or three years. This helped reduce the debt a little bit. "We kept running the team in the interim," said van Gerbig. "In the end, the league refused to let them move the team." Selke recalled why. "The NHL wanted to preserve the Buffalo territory so it could sell another [expansion] franchise along with Vancouver. The Buffalo deal vanished quickly. The Seals stayed in Oakland."

Although the deal fell through, van Gerbig recalled the Knox brothers as "honorable men with honest intentions. They got an expansion franchise [the Sabres] out of the deal." Of course, by awarding expansion franchises to Vancouver and Buffalo, the league added another $12 million to its coffers, money it would not have received had they let the Seals relocate to either of those cities. After two seasons of bad attendance and three attempts to sell the team, the van Gerbig group still owned the Seals and the team's debt was growing significantly. Tim Ryan saw the mess and left the team to take a job in New York. He went on to broadcast hockey, football and the Olympics for different networks. With the antitrust suit pending in court, the league wasn't about to move the team, so they looked for new owners to take over the club.

Chapter 3:
Trans National Communications:
Celebrity Ownership

Early in 1969, the NHL orchestrated a sale to Trans National Communications, a group headed by TV producer Bill Creasy and businessmen Ellis "Woody" Erdman, along with such celebrities and athletes as NFL broadcaster Pat Summerall, Yankees pitching legend Whitey Ford and former New York Giants defensive back Dick Lynch.

TNC was founded by Woody Erdman, then 42 years old. Erdman grew up in Pennsylvania Amish country and became a businessman with a reputation for making something out of nothing. Erdman owned a group of radio stations in upstate New York that carried New York Giants games; then he started to branch off into other ventures.

The idea for TNC got started shortly after Giants defensive back Lynch moved into Erdman's neighborhood and Erdman noticed how both kids and adults wanted to be around the football player. He wondered, "If 60,000 people will shiver and freeze and get soaking wet to see guys like Lynch, isn't there some way we could harness all that electricity?"

Erdman put together a team of businessmen and athletes and then decided to find some investments for the group to manage. TNC owned everything from farms to film companies and, eventually, the Oakland Seals.

"TNC was formed in 1968," recalled Bill Creasy, who had previously worked for CBS as a producer of NFL, Major League Baseball and NHL games. He had produced the first two Super Bowls for CBS and was a longtime hockey fan since living in Montreal during part of his childhood. The Westchester, New York, native was 38 when TNC purchased the Seals. "It was me, Pat Summerall, Woody Erdman, Dick Lynch and a bunch of lawyers and accountants," Creasy recalled. "My job was to get new properties. Somehow, the subject of the Seals came up and I said to Woody, 'What would you think of owning a hockey team?' I had known Clarence Campbell, Stafford Smythe, Bruce Norris and John Ziegler through my work on NHL TV broadcasts. We paid Barry van Gerbig approximately 80 percent of what he paid for the team. Perhaps it was $1.6 million, plus we assumed a lot of debt—approximately $3 million."

The debt was something the new owners would not be able to overcome. "There was immediate pressure to get money," Creasy admitted. "The attitude was, 'Let's get a winning team so we can get money for the shareholders.' " So Creasy went to work trying to improve attendance. "My job was to fill the seats," Creasy recalled. "I decided to try advertising my way. I wanted a whole new marketing plan. I hired an ad agency and we placed newspaper ads, started a radio advertising campaign and got the team on the local ABC radio affiliate. We put bumper stickers on cars and send out mailers. We tripled our season ticket sales. Unfortunately, there were only 300 or so season-ticket holders when TNC took over the club."

In fact, a well-known story said that a woman called the Seals offices identifying herself as a season-ticket holder and asking what time tomorrow's game started. "What time can you get here?" Bill Torrey reportedly answered. He was almost serious.

Creasy switched the marketing emphasis of the team and concentrated on selling tickets to the business community in San Francisco, what he referred to as "Wall Street West."

"My idea was to romance the San Francisco fan," Creasy said. "I tried to get them to cross the bridge. I spoke to Kiwanis clubs and businesses. I always wanted to put the team in the Cow Palace. We were drawing only 2,000 to 6,000 people per game in Oakland; the arena seemed cavernous. If we were in the Cow Palace, 'Wall Street West' would have packed the place. There was no meaningful attendance from San Francisco while we played at the Oakland Coliseum."

Once again, Mel Swig entered the picture. "Mel Swig and I became friends," said Creasy. "He spoke of building an arena in San Francisco. It was all done in secret since we had a contract with the Oakland Coliseum. The complex we were going to build would have an arena and an office building and so on. It would have been a terrific arena. George Ross, the sports editor of *The Oakland Tribune,* got wind of the plan and he wrote a lot of columns saying 'don't move the team or you'll get sued.' We tried to move the Seals to the Cow Palace but the NHL refused."

Another problem under TNC's management was internal. The new owners did not see eye to eye with the team of Selke, Glover and Bill Torrey, who were running the team's hockey operations.

"Torrey, Selke and Glover reacted negatively to us coming on board," Creasy said. "They had things their own way before we came along. I left it to Selke, Torrey and Glover to run the team. I ran the franchise."

Director of group sales Frank Sanchez also recalled the schism in the front office. "It was the traditional Canadian guys against the innovators," Sanchez said. Director of PR and marketing Bob Bestor added, "Frank Selke was the most vocal and was contemptuous of everything Bill Creasy was trying to do. There was a certain Canadian hardheadedness. They said, 'This is the way it was always done and so there can be no good new ideas.' "

The divisions in the front office aside, the biggest problem the Seals had under TNC was a familiar one: lack of money. Woody Erdman, who had founded TNC, had a reputation for being a bit of a schemer. In fact, an SEC administrative judge later described Erdman as "a very clever confidence man—i.e., a person who swindles using a confidence game." In his lifetime, the court indicated Erdman "was the subject of numerous legal proceedings both state and federal." It also indicated that Erdman was accused of securities fraud and had "multiple judgments totaling several million dollars and federal tax liens of over $1 million."

Bill Creasy described his former partner as "very bombastic. His personality was very aggressive and he was a born salesman. He could sell ice to Eskimos," Creasy said of Erdman. "He was always positive and he could convince you that Eskimos would buy ice. He was a bit of a bully. Erdman was trying a get-rich-quick thing—'Let's own a big-time franchise.' There was a lot of strutting going on. It was a mess."

Selke remains skeptical of TNC, even 30 years later. "TNC prided itself on its executive makeup and its ownership of the New York Jets radio rights," Selke recalled. "In addition, TNC owned the Bank of Philadelphia—in a tiny upstate village, Philadelphia, New York (population: 870). It also owned a vegetable farm in Florida. It claimed in its prospectus that 'if all the radishes they grew were placed end to end, they'd reach from Florida to New York!' In reality, the company had little or no money. Dick Lynch figured he could teach us how to market the team and was none too diplomatic in the process. Bill Creasy was a television producer who was a front man with nothing to back it up, and the others made one visit to announce their ownership and then disappeared. Under TNC, we had less operating cash than ever. They had radishes maybe, but cold cash, nope."

Selke remains frustrated by his experience with TNC. "TNC was a cruel hoax, further proof that the NHL would try anything to keep up appearances without any consideration for the fans, the players, their families and the organization. The less said about TNC, the better."

With the Seals economic fortunes continuing in a downward spiral, strange things started to happen at the club's offices. "Whitey Ford came into the office," recalled Frank Sanchez. "I met him, but he didn't seem to be in a very good mood. I later learned that he was there to make payroll. I think he laid out $30,000 so the club could make payroll that month."

"Later, a big press conference was called to announce that [NFL QB] Earl Morrall was coming on board," Creasy said. "It was really all publicity and I'm not sure, but I think they paid Morrall so they could use his name. It was a mess. TNC turned out to be a house of cards. Woody Erdman and Dick Lynch were taking box-office receipts. Lynch once held me out the window because I wouldn't give him the money from a playoff game's receipts. That money belonged to the league. We were once so deep in debt that we bought the Boston Celtics just to get their assets on our books. I remember part of the deal was that Ballentine Beer could use Pat Summerall in their advertising."

As the Seals floundered under TNC, *The Oakland Tribune* was unsure how to deal with the team's problems. "When Woody Erdman owned the team," recalled Spence Conley, "he didn't have the financial strength to stick it out. The *Tribune's* official policy was to help him stick it out because we wanted the team to stay. But the question was, was he the right owner?"

Larry Marshall, the Seals comptroller from 1968-71, recalled that the team needed to average approximately 6,000 fans per game to break even. In fact, although attendance increased to 6,225 per game, the debts remained and there were no funds to pay them off. TNC collapsed under the weight of its own debt; Erdman's shell game was over. "They didn't have any money," Barry van Gerbig added. "We had to take the team back again."

Creasy's job description suddenly changed from selling tickets to keeping a sinking ship afloat. "We had so many creditors, we were literally fighting them off," Creasy said. "I remember looking at a list of creditors that was two or three pages long and single-spaced. Eventually, the banks foreclosed and the league turned on us. I spent days in court holding off the creditors and nights trying to raise more money."

Comptroller Larry Marshall recalled how desperate things were getting. "We couldn't pay the airlines or the payroll taxes," Marshall said. "As the financial officer, I always cashed my paycheck first before giving the others out."

Bob Bestor recalled the irony that Creasy, a former television producer, couldn't get television coverage for his club. "We bought radio time," Bestor said. "I did color and Rick Weaver, who later called Miami Dolphins games, did play-by-play. There was no appetite to televise games in the Bay Area. It was a huge frustration for Bill Creasy. Nobody wanted the product. We couldn't afford to buy time to put the games on television either."

With the team in financial ruin, the Seals were forced to file for bankruptcy. Larry Marshall said, "I was called into [bankruptcy] court and I had to bring the books. I had boxes of them at the courthouse." Bill Torrey added, "The team was in bankruptcy and the judge decided that it was better for the league to choose who should own the team than a judge who knew nothing about hockey."

The league was fed up with van Gerbig's group and they clearly wanted out. NHL president Clarence Campbell expressed the league's dissatisfaction with the Seals original owner. "Unfortunately, the original error was our own," Campbell said in 1974. "We gave the team to a schoolboy who played good golf and wore a Princeton tie. If we had proper management there from the start, we wouldn't be doing missionary work today." Despite it's previous errors, the NHL was once again in a position to choose who the next owner of the Seals would be.

Chapter 4:
The Charlie Finley Error

Eventually, two potential owners came forward. One was a group headed by Roller Derby tycoon Jerry Seltzer, a Bay Area native, and the other by Charles O. Finley, the colorful and controversial owner of baseball's Oakland A's. Finley was a baseball maverick who courted attention and controversy, and always did things his way. A self-made millionaire based in Chicago, Finley was born into poverty, then made millions of dollars selling insurance.

In 1961 he purchased the downtrodden Kansas City Athletics baseball franchise. Finley, a lifelong baseball fan, had a new toy. He introduced all kinds of gimmicks, including an electronic rabbit to bring new baseballs to the umpire and a mule for a mascot that was fittingly named Charlie O. Depending on whom you ask, Finley was either an innovator who was ahead of his time or an egomaniac who was out to promote himself at the expense of his team. In actuality, Charles Oscar Finley was a little bit of both—and a whole lot of things in between as well.

The Athletics continued to lose games and attendance did not increase, so Finley moved his team to Oakland in 1968. Many people in Kansas City felt that Finley deliberately ran the team into the ground in order to move them, and local media and politicians accused Finley of negotiating in bad faith. When he moved the A's to Oakland, Finley became the first sports-team owner, but by no means the last, to be denounced on the floor of the U.S. Senate. Missouri Senator W. Stuart Symington called Finley "one of the most disreputable characters ever to enter the American sports scene" on the Senate floor and placed it in the *Congressional Record*.

Once in Oakland, Finley continued to alienate a lot of people with his unique brand of showmanship and his affinity for self-promotion. The Athletics suddenly became "The Amazin' A's" or "The Swinging A's." Instead of baseball's traditional white home flannels and gray road jerseys, Finley outfitted his team in kelly green and gold uniforms. He also introduced white shoes and initiated or suggested changes to the game, such as the designated hitter, using yellow baseballs for night games and playing World Series games at night to improve television ratings. Needless to say, the staid and traditional "lords of baseball," who viewed their game as something like a sacred national institution, were shocked by what they felt were Finley's outrageous attempts to rock the boat—even as they adopted some of his ideas.

Finley knew baseball and acted as his own general manager. Under Finley's guidance, the A's quickly improved in the standings. Oakland acquired young talented players like Vida Blue, Jim "Catfish" Hunter, Joe Rudi and Reggie Jackson. Finley quickly gained a reputation for being tight with money and for changing managers almost as often as he changed socks. Despite the turmoil, the A's won five consecutive American League West titles from 1971 to 1975 and three consecutive World Series from 1972 to 1974.

Finley's introduction to the world of NHL hockey came in 1969 through Munson Campbell. Campbell was a Yale graduate and successful advertising-agency executive. One of his classmates at Yale was Bruce Norris, whose family owned the Detroit Red Wings and had an interest in the Black Hawks and Rangers as well. Norris and Campbell were good friends and Norris once described Campbell as being "like one of the family." A client of Campbell's ad agency was trying to sell white shoes made out of imitation leather to Finley's A's. During one business meeting in Chicago, the subject of hockey came up. Munson Campbell described this rather innocent discussion to Herb Michelson in his 1975 book Charlie O:

"I was getting impatient at this session," Campbell recalled. "I had to meet [Black Hawks owner] Bill Wirtz and Bruce [Norris] to go to a hockey game and the matter of hockey came up. I asked Finley if he knew anything about it and he said he thought he liked it but he really didn't know if he did. He said that he'd been to one hockey game in his life. Mr. Finley knew *nothing* about hockey. Mr. Finley didn't know how to tape a hockey stick."

Through his friendship with Norris and Wirtz, Campbell was aware of the financial problems the Seals were experiencing and that the team was up for sale. He told Finley that as the owner of the A's, Finley was in a unique position to save money if he purchased the Seals. "I sat down and drew up a master plan for a 12 month a year administrative operation," Campbell said. "Finley could hire the top people in the country for front office work and pay them better than anybody else, because, in effect, they'd be doing two jobs. He could have group and season ticket incentive plans and special sales promotions combining the two teams … He could have become a total sports czar in the Bay Area following this plan."

Suddenly, Finley had instant access to Bill Wirtz and Bruce Norris, two of the most influential owners in the NHL. Campbell made the introductions to the "lords of hockey" while Finley turned on the charm.

Munson Campbell remembered how Finley operated. "I think the members of the Board of Governors assumed—and I think Finley led them to believe—that I would be in the forefront of the franchise, so they need not worry about him. And he was a different person when I took him to meet Wirtz, Norris and several of the other team owners. I think Finley's always different when he's insecure … Then he's just peaches and cream—totally charming. All he would keep saying in these meetings with these men was, 'Yes, I'm vitally interested in hockey. Yes, I'm going to move to Oakland if I get the Seals.' … He gave them all the right answers … Mr. Charles O. Finley can be a remarkably smooth salesman when he wants to be."

But not all of the NHL's owners were thrilled with the prospect of having Finley join their ranks. Sid Salomon III, the owner of the St. Louis Blues, was opposed to Finley partly because of his friendship with the aforementioned Missouri Senator Symington, who was still angry with Finley for the A's abrupt departure from Kansas City. Salomon contacted his old friend Jerry Seltzer and persuaded Seltzer to put together a group to bid on the Seals.

If ever there was a person who was a sharp contrast to Charlie Finley, it was Jerry Seltzer. While Finley was a conservative Midwestern businessman, Seltzer had long hair and wore colorful sports jackets. He was known for owning and promoting Roller Derby (his father founded it), which, as Frank Selke said, many viewed as "pro wrestling on wheels."

"Initially, I met with a great deal of resistance in trying to get a group together to bid for the franchise," Seltzer remembered. "Many of the people I talked with in the Bay Area couldn't see hockey having any possible success in Oakland—no matter who was running it. But, I felt, if there was a representative team and good promotion, hockey could be a huge success because even as [poorly as] it was being run, it was outdrawing the [NBA's] Warriors. As time went on, getting the Seals became quite a challenge to me."

Like Finley, Seltzer was not a big hockey fan. "I'm still not," Seltzer admitted when he was interviewed for this book. "When the Oakland Coliseum opened in 1966-67, the first event was a [WHL] Seals hockey game on Wednesday night. At the first hockey game, there were only 8,000 fans. For the Roller Derby, we had 11,000. I never really had a feel for the team or the game, but sometimes, people who are emotionally involved in a sport can't run the business end of it properly."

Slowly, Seltzer began to put a viable group together. "I got a call from George Ross, editor of *The Oakland Tribune*," Seltzer said. "He wanted to set up a meeting for me with some people including Wayne Valley, who was a developer who owned a large part of the Oakland Raiders. Bay Area car dealer John Buono was also interested."

"The franchise was in trouble and the NHL wanted stability in ownership," Seltzer recalled. "My record in the Bay Area was good and they [Valley and Ross] thought I could put together a local group and make the team successful." According to Seltzer, other owners of AFL football franchises were also getting involved through Valley, although they did so quietly. Lamar Hunt, owner of the Kansas City Chiefs; Bud Adams, owner of the Houston Oilers, and Buffalo Bills front man Ralph

Wilson were all involved as investors. Although these people had lots of money and had run successful sports franchises, their involvement was kept low-key. "The AFL owners kind of scared people and we couldn't use their names," Seltzer said. He also recalled that "Wayne Valley was in the midst of selling his company to Singer [sewing machines] so he also sought to maintain a low profile." So, Seltzer became the group's front man.

While there were two groups trying to buy the Seals, it wasn't exactly clear who was selling them. Both the van Gerbig group and TNC claimed the right to sell the club. Each group of potential buyers attempted to leverage one of the Seals ownership groups to maintain support for their respective bids. Through Munson Campbell, Finley dealt with Barry van Gerbig, who once again owned the team when TNC ran out of money and defaulted. Seltzer, meanwhile, chose to deal with TNC and Bill Creasy, who still wanted to be a part of the next Seals ownership group.

"The minute I met Charlie Finley, I liked him," admitted van Gerbig, who recalled meeting Finley on Bruce Norris's boat. "Charlie said to me, 'Listen, Junior. You've done everything you can with this team and these guys are kicking your ass. I have a major promotions department with the A's. If I can't sell this team, nobody can!' "

Creasy recalled that he and Seltzer were an "unlikely coupling. I wore a conservative button-down gray suit; he wore a loud suit, if he wore any suit. He was Jewish. I loved him and we started to work together on the Seals thing."

The two groups made presentations to the league in late June of 1970 at a hotel near New York's Kennedy airport. Seltzer was confident going in that his superior presentation would sway the NHL owners toward his group. "We put together a ... proposal which described in detail how we could build a fan base, do promotions and get on television," Seltzer recalled. "We made a deal with local TV to go into partnership with them. These are things that later became standard in sports but weren't then. We also planned to do an outreach program to sell tickets to different cities all the way to Sacramento. We could have done cross-promotions with the Raiders as well. I think it would have taken a year or two to fill the arena to capacity."

Seltzer got a lot of local support for his bid. "All of the Bay Area newspapers came out in favor of our bid," Seltzer said. "The Oakland Coliseum management said we would be the preferred new owners of the team even though Finley owned the stadium and the A's."

Seltzer also claims his group outbid Finley's. "Our bid was $4.3 million and Finley's was $4 million," Seltzer said. "I think the vote was rigged. The chairman said one group had bid more money but that Mr. Finley had come up with the difference so we could judge the two groups equally. Somebody obviously told Finley about our bid."

Seltzer also remembered NHL owners' attempting to take "bribes" for their vote. "The Rangers representatives told us they would vote for us if we let them have Carol Vadnais [who was then the Seals' best player]. I sort of danced around that."

The experience was a frustrating one for the Roller Derby magnate. "We had a 120-page proposal, while Charlie Finley's was one page," Seltzer said. "Finley also told the owners, 'I'm like you, a single proprietor,' as opposed to our group. We also had connections with the AFL and the old guard sort of identified more with Finley," Seltzer said, in retrospect. "He was one of them, a sole proprietor and a WASP. They felt they could control one man more easily than our group."

Frank Selke Jr. felt that the NHL governors "didn't want the Roller Derby influence and instead opted for the devil they felt they could control, C. O. Finley. A great many mistakes were made in Oakland over the years and this may have been the biggest. Despite their Roller Derby affiliation, father and son [the Seltzers] were highly respected in Bay Area media circles and well recognized as good corporate citizens—the complete opposite of carpetbagger Charlie. It's a personal opinion that the Seltzers would have been a far superior choice in every respect. By the time the NHL and Finley settled their legal differences, the NHL might have agreed."

Bill Torrey felt that Seltzer's association with TNC hurt his chances of acquiring the Seals. "It seemed ludicrous to the Board of Governors that Trans National Communications was trying to promote a successor [Seltzer] after not being able to run their own shop. Jerry's affiliation with TNC killed any chance he had of getting the franchise." The NHL owners voted to sell the Seals to Finley.

Immediately after being awarded the Seals, Bill Torrey recalled, "Charlie went up to his [hotel] room and spent the next two and a half hours telling the Bay Area media how happy he was about getting the franchise. Then he finally hung up the phone, he turned to me and said, 'Now how the fuck do I get out of Oakland?' To me, his intentions were very clear: he wanted to move the franchise." The Charlie Finley era had begun. The Seals and the NHL would never be the same again.

You could love him or hate him but you couldn't ignore him. Although many people disliked Finley's style, it was impossible to say that the Seals franchise was dull after Charlie O. took over its ownership. Prior to Finley's taking over, the Seals were not much different from most of their expansion brethren, even if attendance was low and ownership was shaky. The Seals qualified for the playoffs in two of their first three seasons in the league, a mark exceeded only by the St. Louis Blues among the "second six."

The Seals also had a solid and respected management team led by Selke, Torrey and Glover, and what could be described as decent on-ice talent. By the time Finley's three-and-a-half-year ownership was over, the Seals would be a laughingstock on the ice and practically beyond hope as a franchise off of it. Despite running the franchise into the ground, Finley did it in his own unique and colorful way and somehow managed to make a profit doing it.

Munson Campbell, who was instrumental in getting Finley the Seals, recalled that "as soon as he got the franchise, his whole tone changed. Before then, *I'd* be conducting meetings. Now, he was. He started going around me to people. The authority shifted to him. You can tell when the complexion is changing by the tone of his voice: it becomes arrogantly authoritative instead of just, 'I'm selling insurance.' "

So Finley started to do things his way. So what if he didn't know a thing about hockey? There was work to be done.

"On the day he was awarded the franchise, Finley called us in Oakland and spoke individually to Bill Torrey, Fred Glover and me," recalled Frank Selke, Jr. "He asked each of us if we were 'willing to work *with* him as opposed to working *for* him,' and of course we all agreed, despite having no knowledge of our contractual standing. We learned quickly where we stood: on very thin ice."

The biggest problem, according to Selke and many others, was Finley's refusal to listen to his employees. "Charlie was first and foremost a bully," Selke said. "He was a brilliant baseball mind. His marketing skills were nonexistent but you could not influence his thinking or change his mind on even the most minor issues. Having a mule for a mascot of the A's says a lot about his mind-set. While admitting he didn't know much about hockey, its operating policies, traditions, structures and so forth, he wasn't inclined to listen to his staff."

One of the new owner's first projects was a change in the team's uniforms. Selke recalled, "On his first visit to the office, he gave each of us a Photostat outline of Carol Vadnais on 8"-by-10" paper. We were instructed to come back in a few days with a variety of designs and colors, including a new crest. It was a childish exercise; any of the manufacturers could have provided professional makeups in 24 hours. Charlie wanted to show his authority so we wasted a few hours to satisfy his ego."

Bob Bestor recalled: "We talked about designing new uniforms almost all day. Torrey, Selke and Glover talked about uniforms. You thought the group had come to a consensus, but Charlie typically would do what he wanted to anyway." Finley chose kelly green and California gold, the same colors as his baseball club. His logo was the script word *Seals.*

Bestor recalled that one of the proposed designs said *Oakland Seals* on the jersey. "Finley said his jerseys would not say Oakland because Oakland was nothing but niggers.'"

Artist Denny McGee drew the final design that Finley picked. "The Seals didn't have an art staff," McGee recalled. He was put in touch with Finley through Paul Giovannoni, a salesman who had worked with McGee at the Gilmore Envelope Corporation. "Charlie said he needed a hockey-player illustration for the back of the season-ticket–plan folder," McGee continued, "and he practically needed it overnight. I remember doing that artwork in a panic from some photographs of current players on the team. Paul picked up the finished artwork that I had worked on most of the night and headed for Mr. Finley's office, but since price hadn't been mentioned, he asked me how much to charge for the artwork. Since I hadn't done much freelance artwork at that time, I told him if he could get $75 for it that would be OK with me. Paul took it into Finley's office and before he could say anything about the fee, Charlie yelled out, 'Those damned artists charge too much. I'm not paying any more than $150!' Obviously, I was thrilled when I got the check." The finished product, a stylized sketch of Carol Vadnais, was used on the season-ticket brochures, stickers, buttons and both the 1970-71 and 1971-72 yearbooks.

Finley wanted the team's name to change so it would not be so closely associated with Oakland but he was not sure of what the new name should be. The final decision was between two choices but Finley couldn't make up his mind. The season was fast approaching and the team did not have an official name.

"I got a call from Charlie Finley at 5 a.m.," Frank Sanchez recalled. "We had taken out a full-page ad in *The Oakland Tribune* and there was a 'small typo.' The typo was that the ad said 'Oakland Seals' and Charlie had not yet picked a name. He didn't like calling it Oakland and he kept switching from Bay Area Seals to California Golden Seals." The decision was finally made at the last possible moment. In fact, it was made so late that the team's 1970-71 yearbook simply read "The Seals, the Bay Area's Hockey Team." Eventually, Finley settled on California Golden Seals, although everyone in the hockey community still referred to the team as Oakland.

Finley also wanted to make opening night special—his way. "Finley insisted that we get a live seal as a mascot and introduce him to the crowd opening night, which we did," Bill Torrey remembered. "The only problem was that this trained seal preferred the cold ice and all he did in front of the crowd was lie down and sleep on the ice. End of mascot!" Unfortunately for the Seals, it was another bad omen.

In addition to a live, trained seal, Finley wanted additional entertainment on opening night. "Finley wanted skating girls," Sanchez said. "He also wanted me to find a skating mule, like the mule he had at his baseball games. I started calling different ice shows and, finally, two guys from the Ice Follies said they had a horse costume and they could fix it up to look like a mule. I hired them and we had the skating girls between periods. Then, 'Charlie O' the mule comes out on skates and all the fans started to boo. The next day in the papers, the press described it as 'Finley's Follies Hit the Ice.' "

A bigger folly that opening day had to do with tickets. Employees estimated the team had about 3,000 season-ticket holders. The very first thing that Finley did was to alienate them. "Two to three days after he bought the team, Finley called a press conference," recalled ticket manager Sam Russo. "He said the team was so bad he was cutting the price of tickets in half. The season-ticket holders [who had already paid for their tickets] lit up the switchboard. They wanted a refund." Of course, Finley gave his employees no advanced warning of his policy and Russo remembered having no answer for the team's most loyal fans.

Finley did make an effort to attract new fans but, naturally, he did it in his own style. "Finley printed up a big, elaborate, four-color brochure for season tickets," Bill Torrey said. "He spent a ton of money on it and we got a huge mailing list. But then he wouldn't let it be mailed out until late August. He just kept making changes on it for the sake of making changes and the brochure went out too late to have any value."

Although he took great care to get his ticket brochure just right, Finley skimped when it came to his staff. The A's were known to have the smallest front-office staff in baseball and now that he owned two Bay Area sports teams, Finley had many A's employees doing double work, treating them almost like slaves. Chaos resulted.

"Finley used the same ticket manager he had with the A's for the Seals," Jerry Seltzer remembered. "The first game, nobody had their tickets yet. They all had to pick them up at the game." Of course, the season opener against the Boston Bruins was a rare sellout, but the line of fans was even larger than normal because nobody had their tickets in advance.

Charlie wanted employees to do double work," Sanchez recalled. "I remember one time, the play-by-play announcer of the A's came in while we were stuffing envelopes. He had to join us and help us out." Of course, Finley never gave his employees extra pay for their extra work.

Another innovation that Finley introduced was putting the players' names on the back of their sweaters, making the Seals the first team in the NHL to do so. Frank Sanchez recalled coming up with the idea, which drew opposition from GM Frank Selke, Jr. and the more traditional hockey men in the organization.

"He [Selke] was convinced it would cut down on program sales," Sanchez remembered. "He was a traditionalist and that just wasn't the way things were done in the NHL." Of course, ruffling the feathers of sports traditionalists was one of Finley's favorite pastimes—even if the traditionalists in question worked for him.

Many other NHL owners were also afraid that putting the players' names on their sweaters would reduce program sales and therefore hurt revenues. Howard Ballard, the controversial owner of the Maple Leafs, was perhaps the most vocal opponent of the idea. As a result, the Seals carried two sets of sweaters with them on the road, one with the names on the back and one without.

"In Toronto once, they didn't want us to wear the jerseys with the names on them," recalled team trainer Barry Keast. "I had the team put them on at the noon skate-around. The managers of the Leafs were scared." The Seals did not wear the names on their sweaters at game time. (The Leafs, incidentally, were the last NHL team to put players' names on their sweaters, holding out until 1977-78, when the league mandated it. Even then, Ballard ordered his trainers to sew blue letters on the Leafs' road blue sweaters so the names would be impossible to see).

Finley also wanted the Seals to wear white skates to parallel the white cleats his A's were wearing. "I tried to convince Charlie that white skates on white ice wouldn't look near as good as his white baseball shoes did on green grass," Bill Torrey said. "He finally had to admit that I was right, and that's when he decided to go with green and gold skates." The white skates were put on hold, at least for one season. Meanwhile, some other teams like the St. Louis Blues and Pittsburgh Penguins also introduced skates in team colors, copying Finley's idea. Thankfully, the trend was short-lived.

Another problem Finley's employees faced was his constant interference with their work. The boss often got involved in the minutest details of their jobs. PR director Bob Bestor recalled one particular incident early in Finley's tenure as Seals owner. "One night, I remember we were sitting around, working on a mailing. We were sending out materials to agencies in San Francisco. I was working on a letter to go out, trying to figure out the content. Finley came up from behind me and asked what sized envelope I was going to use and what kind of labels I would be putting on them. He insisted on 'Avery labels' and told me the size and exact stock number. Going home that night, I knew this job wasn't for me."

Finley also failed to reward employees for their help. Munson Campbell was instrumental in getting Finley the Seals, yet according to Campbell, Finley never compensated him for his hard work and efforts on his behalf. Campbell recalled that Finley never gave him "a dime of expense money for my traveling." Worse yet, Campbell felt that Finley misled him with regard to what would happen after Finley purchased the team. "In conversations with Finley, I was led to believe that if I could get him this franchise at a very low price, that I would expect in return from him an interest in the franchise.... He leads you to believe that he's agreeable and I assumed he was." He wasn't.

In fact, Campbell was completely omitted from the team's 1970-71 yearbook, the club's first under Finley's ownership. "I was putting together the yearbook," Frank Sanchez recalled. "Munson Campbell was sort of Charlie's right-hand man on hockey issues. Campbell was a very distinguished-looking and proper guy. I was busy writing bios for the yearbook and I asked Charlie what to put in for Campbell's biography. Finley looked at me and just said, 'Screw him!' Munson Campbell was not in the yearbook at all that year."

Finley inherited the front-office team of GM Frank Selke Jr., vice president Bill Torrey and coach Fred Glover. It was a distinguished and highly–thought-of team. Selke was well known and respected throughout the hockey world both for his family connections, his experience in the sport and his work on *Hockey Night in Canada*. He had practically grown up around hockey, working for the Forum in Montreal with his father. Torrey was an up-and-coming front-office man who had successfully led the AHL's Pittsburgh Hornets to a championship in 1967 and would soon build the expansion Islanders into a dynasty that would win four straight Stanley Cups in the early '80s. Glover was a respected and tough AHL player who was named the NHL's coach of the year by the *Sporting News* when he turned the Seals from a last-place team to second-place team in his first year behind the bench (1968-69). Despite having this distinguished group of hockey men, Finley immediately set out to change things.

The first problem Finley created was contractual. He needed his GM to sign all the players for the upcoming season. This, of course, was made difficult by the actions of Charlie Finley. "Charlie had slashed the budgets," Selke recalled. "Despite my very difficult negotiations with some players and lots of uncertainties, of which the players were aware, we [Selke and Torrey] kept our word and brought the team back from Oshawa [training camp] ready to play." Of course, these negotiations did nothing to improve team morale.

The bigger problem for Selke and Torrey, however, was Finley's refusal to abide by their existing contracts. "Bill Torrey and I had at least one more year on our contracts," Selke said. "Finley insisted the courts awarded him the franchise and the player contracts only—not management and coaching. So, Finley was under no legal obligation to us in his mind. The NHL provided no support or information. We had to accept Finley's word, like it or not."

Eventually, Finley started to bully both of his hockey experts. "When Charlie Finley purchased the team, he promised me that he would not interfere with the running of the team; that he was advised by all the other governors that I knew what I was doing and should be left alone," Torrey recalled. "He did that for about two weeks and then started to interfere."

In addition to constant interference, Selke also faced a serious problem on the issue of his salary. "In ongoing negotiations, I insisted Charlie live up to the terms of my initial contract," Selke recollected. "He refused and offered me one year and about two thirds of what I felt I was due." It was then that Selke saw how Finley operated to put pressure on his employees. Selke said, "One day, after we'd returned from training camp and were getting ready to start the season, Finley asked me if I was going to accept his offer. I told him I was still thinking about it. In a very fatherly gesture, he put his arm around my shoulder and said—as best as I can recall—'Son, you are a nice young man. I've met your wife and kiddies and you have a nice family. If you are thinking of legal action, let me tell you if you are going to get into a pissing contest with a skunk, I'm the biggest pisser in the U.S.A.' "

Selke felt there were other issues between he and Finley besides his contract. "Munson Campbell became increasingly involved with the team's day-to-day operation," Selke recalled. "He had Charlie's ear and convinced him to change the farm teams' locations without any input from Torrey or Selke. It became clear that Bill and I weren't subservient enough in insisting on our contractual rights. We were being shut out of key decisions—even some player evaluations were being questioned."

It didn't take long for the impasse between Selke and Finley to come to a head. "In early November, Finley called me at home from Chicago over the supper hour," Selke said. "In his best Simon Legree voice, he asked if I was going to accept his offer or not. I asked him, in response, if he was going to honor my contract. He said no, I said no and then he said, 'Get your ass out of my office by tomorrow. You're through.' He hung up and I finished my dinner."

With Selke gone, Bill Torrey took over as general manager but he, too, soon realized he could not get along with Finley. He found Finley wouldn't let him do his job. "He violated the non-interference clause in my contract so often that it got to the point where I had my lawyer talking to his lawyer," Torrey told Herb Michelson. "My lawyer told me that I could either keep letting Charlie interfere with me or go to court and get the matter resolved."

Torrey had a contract drawn up but Finley refused to sign it. Torrey threatened to take Finley to court. The new GM got a similar answer to the old GM. "Finley said, 'Well, there'll be a lot of publicity on this one. I won't mind that,' " Torrey recalled. "Then he said, 'Do you have your lawyer on a monthly retainer? Jesus, they're expensive.' He was, in a sense, trying to tell me that I couldn't afford to take him to court. He told me once that he'd never been sued by an employee and lost. He did in this case."

Torrey won his case against Finley and left the Seals in December 1970. The Seals finished an injury-riddled 1970-71 season in last place with the league's worst record. Approximately one year later, Torrey was hired as general manager of the New York Islanders, a new expansion team that started play in 1972-73. There, he quickly built the Islanders into an NHL powerhouse, drafting players like Denis Potvin, Bryan Trottier and Mike Bossy. By their third season, the Islanders made the NHL semifinals and came within one game of unseating the Flyers, the defending Stanley Cup champions. By their seventh year, the Isles had the league's best record. One year after that, they won their first of four consecutive Stanley Cups. Bill Torrey was inducted into the Hockey Hall of Fame in 1995, primarily for building the Islanders dynasty.

By the time the Islanders made the playoffs in 1974-75, Finley had destroyed the Seals and made them into the laughingstock of the league. By the time the Islanders won their first Stanley Cup in 1980, the Seals were nothing but a memory.

In 1971-72, Finley continued to play musical chairs with his front office. He hired former Bruins scout Garry Young to be his new general manager. Young cleaned house, trading away many of the Seals veterans for younger players, most of whom he had scouted or selected while working for the Bruins. Players like Ivan Boldirev, Reggie Leach and Bobby Sheehan made the Seals younger and faster. Then three games into the regular season, Finley fired coach Fred Glover and replaced him with former Flyers coach Vic Stasiuk. Unfortunately, the timing wasn't so good.

"Charlie Finley fired Fred Glover while Freddie was in the hospital," recalled John Porter, who took over as the Seals beat reporter for *The Oakland Tribune* in 1970. "I wrote a story about it and Finley called me on it. He was an early riser and he had somebody get him the early edition of the West Coast paper. He called me around 6 a.m. Chicago time, which was 4 a.m. or so California time. I remember for sure I was asleep. Finley had an unmistakable voice. He yelled at me, and I quote, 'John Porter, you should be taken out into the middle of the street and be publicly horsewhipped.' I found it best to reply with humor so I said, 'I'm glad you liked my story.' "

During his tenure with the Seals, Finley tried some offbeat yet inexpensive ways to try to promote the club. Frank Sanchez recalled Finley's idea for Barber Night. "He said to me, 'Tell me, Sanchez, who has the ears of all the men in this area?' It was the barbers. He asked me to go to barbershops and promote this idea. The barbers didn't want to talk to me because they all thought I was selling something. I told them it was free and that helped bring some of them in. Still, on Barber Night Finley was mad at me because there weren't enough barbers in attendance."

John Porter also recalled Barber Night. "He thought if he got the barbers enthused and talking about the Seals, they'd all tell their customers. Well, all that happened was the barbers took advantage of the open bar and got drunk on Charlie's liquor. I don't want to think about his face when he got the bar bill." Needless to say, Barber Night did not result in a significant increase in Seals home attendance.

While Finley was enthused about Barber Night, he opposed other ideas for promotions that might have made more sense. "Charles Schulz, the creator of the 'Peanuts' comic strip, was a big fan and a great guy," recalled Sanchez. In fact, Schulz was a rarity, a Seals season-ticket holder. "Every game, Mr. Schulz would sit in the stands and sign autograph after autograph," said Sanchez. Schulz later opened an ice-skating rink in his hometown of Santa Rosa and had many Seals players appear in a hockey game there to raise money for charity. "I wanted to have a 'Peanuts' Night," recalled Sanchez, "but Charlie O. was against it. He didn't want anybody to compete with him for attention."

John Porter agreed with Sanchez's assessment. "Finley was always trying to make himself the center of attention," Porter recalled. One example of this behavior occurred when Finley took his team to a fancy dinner party. "After he bought the team, Charlie sent invitations for a big party and dinner at the Elegant Farmer restaurant," Sam Russo recollected. "The players and staff were all invited. The women went to the regular part of the restaurant while the guys were in the party room in the back. The guys got a dinner of shrimp cocktail and two-pound T-bone steaks. Charlie said he separated the women from the men because 'women couldn't eat that much and he didn't want all that good food to go to waste.' " Frank Sanchez was also there. "It was like a scene out of a movie," he recalled. "If Charlie laughed, we all laughed. When we were sitting there, he'd tell us news before it broke, like a trade that was upcoming or how much money he signed [A's shortstop] Bert Campanaris for. He knew nobody would tell because he had his spies all around."

According to Sanchez, Tom Massey was one of Finley's "spies" although Massey didn't recall his job description in exactly that way. Massey found a most unusual way of joining the staff of a major league sports team.

"I met Charlie Finley on an airplane," Massey said. "I was the flight service director and my job was to convert revenue from other airlines. Charlie was on a flight from Los Angeles to Chicago with his wife and there was a one-hour delay, so I was working the crowd on the airplane. If Charlie liked you, he'd take you in like a stray dog." Finley took a liking to Massey. "Finley hired me to work for the A's and the Seals," Massey recalled. "I actually lived in Charlie Finley's apartment in Oakland with Seals coach Fred Glover. It was a penthouse suite overlooking Lake Merritt in downtown Oakland."

Massey admitted that when he was hired by Finley, he "knew absolutely nothing about hockey. I didn't know a stick from a basketball." He traveled with the team at first, but was "not exactly sure what my job was." Eventually, he did some PR work under Frank Sanchez.

Like many employees of Finley, Massey had a "love/hate relationship" with his boss. "Finley was one hard-nosed son of a bitch and extremely close-minded, but he was also a bright guy and there was something everybody liked about him," Massey said. "Part of me despised him for being so narrow-minded and egotistical, but he could also be endearing. He would go into a restaurant and have the entire place eating out of his hand. Yet, when he came in from Chicago, nobody wanted to be around him because he treated people like shit."

Massey also remembered that when Finley was at his home in Chicago, "he would have somebody call him on the telephone and give him complete play-by-play of the Seals and A's games over the telephone."

He also remembered how Finley liked to push his weight around. "Charlie came into the Bay Area to get his son into Stanford," Massey said. "He set up a meeting with the dean of the business school. I don't know what was exactly said in the meeting, but when he came out Finley said to me, 'I made him an offer he couldn't refuse.' His son got into Stanford too."

Eventually, Massey left the Seals and A's. "I left after about 14 to 15 months there," Massey said. "Finley found another stray dog and I felt like I had no direction there."

Another employee who had an unusual experience working for Charlie Finley was broadcaster Joe Starkey. Starkey recalled how he was hired prior to the 1972-73 season. "I got the job by inventing a road trip for myself," Starkey said. "I went to Chicago and I asked if Mr. Finley would see me. I played a game tape I made sitting [in the stands] at a game and he hired me on the spot. Before I even left his office, he had fired me. I had a background in employee satisfaction and I told him I could help him with his employee turnover problems. He took it personally and I was immediately fired. To get the job back, I had to make an end run. I went to the radio station and played the tape for them, and they hired me to call the games." Starkey went on to a productive career as a broadcaster and now does play-by-play for Cal football and the San Francisco 49ers. His "Oh, what a bonanza!" call, which he uttered after every Seals goal, became his trademark.

It didn't take Finley long to alienate and dismiss all of his inherited employees. "One time, I came back from an out-of-town meeting and Charlie noticed I had golf clubs in my car," Sanchez remembered. "Now, I hadn't used those clubs for over three months but Charlie was on my case. 'I'm paying you good money to represent my team and you have time to play golf?' Finley said. I took those clubs out of the car that night."

When PR director Sam Russo left, Sanchez took on that job while still maintaining his post as group sales director. Sanchez figured he was due a raise for his additional responsibilities. "I asked Charlie for a raise and he said, 'Talk to me in the middle of the season,'" Sanchez recalled. "So, New Year's comes around and I asked Finley about the raise. He said, 'How's your wife doing?' He would always remind me that he had a stack of résumés in his office of people who wanted to do my job. I knew right then and there I was done in Oakland."

Ironically, Sanchez must have thought Finley was following him when he finally did leave the Seals to take a position with the ABA's Denver Rockets. When he informed Finley he had taken a position with the Rockets, Finley responded, "Oh, I just bought the Memphis Pros" (which Finley would rename the Memphis TAM's). "It seemed like I would never get rid of him," said Sanchez.

By midway through the 1971-72 season, even Munson Campbell was gone, temporarily taking his leave of hockey to return to the relative sanity of the business world. Campbell recalled, "The league became painfully aware that Mr. Finley had no intention of trying to build hockey at all and, in essence, was letting the franchise deteriorate because he wanted to move it. In no way was the board of governors going to let the Seals leave the Bay Area." In fact, they couldn't let the Seals leave since Barry van Gerbig's antitrust suit was still pending at that time in a California Federal Court. Finley wanted to move the Seals to Indianapolis but the league said no. The NHL tried to find somebody—nearly anybody—who would step in and run the Seals. They even approached Jerry Seltzer again to see if he was still interested. However, there were no immediate takers.

While the league looked for answers, Finley continued to run the team his way. Despite earlier protests from Bill Torrey, Fred Glover and just about all of the players on the Seals, Finley unveiled all-white skates for 1971-72. Most of the players hated the skates, although they did attract attention. There was one major problem with the white skates: they wouldn't stay white. Team trainer Barry Keast had the unenviable task of maintaining the white skates. "They would rub against the boards and other skates," Keast remembered. "We used to whitewash them, and we had to start early in the morning." After every game, the skates had to be touched up and repainted. "They got a little heavy after a while," assistant trainer Gerry Dean recalled.

Finley also had the Seals farm teams in Salt Lake City and Columbus, Ohio, wear the white skates. Dean recalled the first time he had to prepare them in Columbus. "Charlie Finley came to Columbus to see the home opener," Dean said. "The skates arrived and had to be painted white for the next day. We arrived in Columbus at 2 a.m. from a road trip. GM Chuck Catto and I painted the skates all night. By the end of the first period, they were black again." Despite these problems, Finley insisted the team stick with the white skates.

Sam Russo recalled the players' reaction to the white skates, which were then only worn by figure skaters. "I remember Carol Vadnais telling Finley that other teams would think we were sissies, wearing white skates," Russo said. In the macho world of NHL hockey, the comparisons to figure skating were not welcome.

On the ice, 1971-72 was the best season the team had under Finley's ownership. Young stars such as rookie goalie Gilles Meloche, speedy center Bobby Sheehan and team-scoring leader Gerry Pinder kept the Seals in the thick of the playoff race until the final week of the regular season. Unfortunately, the young squad slumped down the stretch, losing its final six games and missing the playoffs by a mere six points.

It was then that the Charlie Finley era took a drastic turn for the worse. Prior to the 1972-73 season, a group of renegade millionaires led by Dennis Murphy and Gary Davidson formed the WHA, a rival pro-hockey league that would compete with the NHL for both fans and players. In the summer of 1972, Chicago Black Hawks superstar Bobby Hull signed with the new league, giving it instant credibility and making Hull the first hockey player to sign a million-dollar contract. Soon, other star players like Bernie Parent, Derek Sanderson and Gerry Cheevers jumped to the rival league. NHL teams scrambled to sign their players to new contracts before they signed with the WHA. Player salaries increased instantly and dramatically. The only team that refused to pay increased salaries to its players was the California Golden Seals. The idea of paying his players more than he thought they were worth infuriated Finley. GM Garry Young had his hands tied, as Finley refused to authorize additional funds to keep his players. As a result, the Seals lost nine players to the rival league, more than any other NHL team. What seemed to be a promising young team in 1971-72 was gutted. Five of the Seals six leading scorers from 1971-72 left the club prior to the 1972-73 season. The Seals suddenly had less talent than many of the teams that had been formed after them, including the expansion Atlanta Flames.

GM Garry Young was the next employee with whom Finley interfered. First, a controversy arose with regard to the contract of forward Hilliard Graves. Finley, in an attempt to save money, tried to force Graves to retire rather than accept assignment to the team's minor league affiliate. "Finley made Garry Young take a lie-detector test regarding the contract of Hilliard Graves," John Porter said. "It depends who you ask as to whether or not Young passed the test, but that was humiliating."

At the beginning of the 1972-73 season, Young had taken over both the coaching and general manager's duties. Fred Glover recalled that "Charlie Finley was not too happy with what went on the year before. He told me that Garry Young told him to get rid of Vic Stasiuk, so Charlie said to him, 'You want to get rid of him; you're the coach.' " Young had no NHL coaching experience at that point but was suddenly faced with the prospect of coaching the Seals.

The last straw for Young was the contract of defenseman Dick Redmond, one of the few promising young players who did not leave for the rival league. Apparently, Young signed Redmond to a contract for more money than Finley had authorized.

According to Chuck Catto, who served as GM in Columbus and as a scout for the Seals organization, Young was his own worst enemy. "Garry Young was a bright guy, a very good hockey scout, but a lousy general manager," Catto said. "He could never say no. He lied, man. He lied and really believed in what he was saying. Most of all, Garry wanted to be liked and respected by his peers."

Catto remembers that Young had Dick Redmond sign three or four copies of his contract. "Garry then put in false figures, less then what he and the kid agreed upon. When Dick started to get his paycheck and multiplied it by the months that he'd be playing, wow … the shit really hit the fan. Dick took it to Alan Eagleson. Garry had given Dick a copy, the NHL had a copy and our main office had a copy. Garry Young had hidden the contract with the figures on it that the kid [Redmond] and he had agreed upon."

"I found the contract," Fred Glover said. "It said $70,000 for the first year and $100,000 for the second year. That was a big raise from $15,000. I know Charlie didn't authorize that." Finley refused to pay Redmond the amount he had signed for. Instead, he started to pay him what he thought he was worth: $30,000 per year. NHL Players' Association director Alan Eagleson told his client not to cash his checks. Eagleson and Finley had some tense meetings. The result: Garry Young was fired and Redmond was traded to Chicago for Darryl Maggs. The team fell deeper and deeper into turmoil. Finley replaced Young with Fred Glover after Young had coached all of 12 games.

In roughly a year, Glover had gone from being fired as coach to rejoining the team as interim coach and general manager. It seemed Glover was one of the few people who knew how to handle being employed by Finley. "Working for him was a piece of cake," Glover said. "I can't say enough about the man. I talked to him differently than other people did. He knew when I said no it was no. I told him off twice. He respected people who weren't afraid to stand up to him." Despite Glover's return behind the bench, the talent-depleted Seals finished in last place in the West Division in 1972-73. Only the expansion New York Islanders, who set an all-time record for NHL futility, finished with a worse record than the Seals.

Seals broadcaster Joe Starkey remembered how tough a season 1972-73 became for the franchise. "During my first year calling the team's games, the club was awful," Starkey said. Perhaps the lowest moment was an 11-0 loss at the Maple Leaf Gardens that Starkey called "so ugly it was fascinating! It was a game so boring that [Leafs] goalie Jacques Plante claimed he was sick after two periods leading 6- or 7-0 because it wasn't worth having to be in such a one-sided game."

The Seals had bad luck both during and after the game, which only prolonged their agony. "Twice, shots broke the glass and each delay took at least 20 minutes to repair after the game was long settled," Starkey said. "Then fog made the half-hour flight to Detroit take two hours. Before we landed the pilot said, 'Fog is very low and conditions are marginal, but you guys had a rough night, so let's give it a try.' " The plane landed safely.

Starkey also recalled an awkward moment on air late in the season. "With five or six weeks left in the season, I was doing a live, between-periods interview with Walt McKechnie. The team was out of the playoffs already but there was plenty of season left. I asked McKechnie what he does to stay sharp and psych himself up for the remaining weeks of the season. He said, 'I don't have any, I wish the season was over today and, next year, I hope they send me somewhere else.' Where do you go from there? The interview was dead after that. As a rookie announcer, it was a tough moment."

Prior to the 1973-74 season, the Seals lost a few more players to the WHA. The franchise hit rock bottom both on and off the ice. The Seals finished the 78-game season with just 13 wins and 36 points, a stunning 52 games under .500. The Seals winning percentage was a dreadful .231, below that of even the 1962 New York Mets in baseball. Finley refused to spend any money to improve the team on the ice or to promote it off the ice. The owner even went as far as to provide no local television or radio coverage during the season. The only way to follow the Seals in 1973-74 was to buy a ticket to a game. Nobody was buying tickets. The fans were staying away in droves.

"The team had awful ratings," recalled play-by-play announcer Joe Starkey. "It was a bad team and we got no help from Charlie Finley. KEEN radio carried Finley's A's so they agreed to do hockey [often tape delayed during the 1972-73 season], but then they decided it just wasn't worth it."

The Seals became the most invisible professional sports team in more than 20 years. Attendance fell to just 4,850 per game, it's lowest rate in five years. With no buyers on the horizon, the NHL stepped in and bought the club back from Finley. In February of 1974, the sale was finalized and the board of governors bought out Finley for approximately $6.5 million. Charlie O. even claimed to have made a profit on the deal, telling a reporter, "The league not only gave me a good price, but they also met all my expenses for this year. Let's put it this way, I didn't lose anything on the Seals." The NHL wished it could say the same.

Sam Russo, who now works for the NBA's Charlotte Hornets summed up his experience of working for Finley when he said, "I learned more from Charlie Finley than anybody else. Do the opposite of what Charlie said and you'll succeed. He was a fun guy and a great jokester who loved pranks. He certainly had a different approach for running his business." But for the Seals, it had been the wrong approach.

Chapter 5:
The League Takes Over

The NHL now owned the Seals (which was in violation of its own bylaws) and the league had to decide what to do with the team. Ironically, the board of governors appointed Munson Campbell as president of the club and Campbell hired Garry Young as director of player personnel. The following day, Fred Glover resigned as coach and defenseman Marshall Johnston was named the team's new man behind the bench. The Seals immediately ditched their white skates, finishing the season in traditional black. When the season ended, rumors abounded that the Seals would be folded. All hope seemed lost, but the league wasn't ready to give up on the Seals franchise just yet.

The NHL decided to continue to run the Seals while they searched for a buyer willing to keep the team in the Bay Area. The NHL established a committee that included Munson Campbell, Black Hawks owner Vic Wirtz and Bruce Norris, owner of the Red Wings. The league decided to run the team for the 1974-75 season until a buyer could be found.

In the summer of 1974 the committee hired former St. Louis Blues forward Bill McCreary as director of hockey operations. Since retiring as a player after the 1971-72 season, McCreary had coached and helped found the Blues farm team in Denver before coaching both the Blues and the Canucks for part of one season each.

"The NHL had taken over the Seals and Jim Cullen, who was counsel of the NHL, called me asked me if I was interested in working for the Seals," McCreary recalled. He agreed to take the job.

McCreary faced a daunting task. He took over a team with no owner, few paying customers in the stands and low morale and talent on the ice. "The Seals were like a really good AHL team before expansion," McCreary said of the team's talent level when he took over the club. "They were a free team and winning was just not all that important on their minds. They had good parts to the team but were limited. We were weak on defense and if we played a strong game, it took three to four days to get over it."

McCreary also faced constant rumors that the Seals would move or be folded (the Barry van Gerbig lawsuit was finally decided in the league's favor prior to the start of the 1974-75 season). Even if a new owner was found, he would likely bring in his own man to run hockey operations.

"It was tough to keep the players focused," McCreary admitted. "The biggest problem was the rumors about the team being purchased and moved. Money was also a problem. We had to stay under budget. The budget was a big thing. [The league] wanted the team to be competitive enough that somebody would buy them. We couldn't go out and get a player with a big contract. Things could also have been done faster if we didn't need five peoples' approvals."

Len Shapiro, who was hired by the team as PR director for 1974-75, recalled the effect of the NHL's ownership on the front office. "We really had a skeleton crew," Shapiro remembered, laughing. "There were all of eight people working there when I started. We had Munson Campbell, a ticket manager, Shep Goldberg and myself doing public relations, the coach, Marshall Johnston, GM Garry Young and Steve Howley. I think we did an admirable job with what we had to work with."

Still, the league's takeover of the team did improve the atmosphere around the franchise, especially after the neglect of the Charlie Finley era. "Morale was very positive when the league took over," Shapiro recalled. "There was a hope that good things would follow on and off the ice."

To address the team's on-ice weaknesses, McCreary traded center Ivan Boldirev to the Black Hawks for two young defensemen, Len Frig and Mike Christie. In addition to having youth and size, Frig and Christie had lower salaries than Boldirev. Hilliard Graves was dealt to Atlanta for speedy left wing John Stewart, while right wing Reggie Leach was traded to the defending Stanley Cup champion Flyers in exchange for young players that included rookie Al MacAdam. Veteran defenseman Jim

Neilson was also acquired as part of a three-way deal that sent center Walt McKechnie to Boston. In all, four of the club's five leading scorers from 1973-74 were no longer with the team prior to the start of the 1974-75 season. Unlike the mass defection to the WHA three years prior, at least the Seals got something in return.

The Seals also said goodbye to their kelly green, California gold and polar bear white sweaters. Munson Campbell was in charge of developing the new uniforms that were "pacific blue" (a sort of aqua) and gold. According to McCreary, the new uniforms were "liked in general." Either way, most people were happy to rid the team of any vestiges of the Finley era.

The Seals remained competitive early in the season. Because of a scheduling oddity, the team had most of its home games late in the season. After a solid January, however, a February slump followed. Bill McCreary fired coach Marshall Johnston and took over as coach of the team for the rest of the 1974-75 season.

"My relationship with Bill McCreary started out OK, but got strained after that," Johnston recalled. "I'm not sure why. He didn't hire me, but he didn't have the authority to fire me and bring in his own person. Some things went on between the GM and the coach that were unnecessary."

Somehow, McCreary and Johnston were never on the same page. A *Sports Illustrated* article recalled that McCreary set up walkie-talkies so he could communicate with Johnston during the game, something the coach couldn't have appreciated. Johnston remembered the first message he received early in the game. "Beep-beep. Cab to 66th and Seminary." The walkie-talkies were quickly discarded but the tension between Johnston and McCreary remained.

McCreary felt that Johnston's inexperience and closeness with the players led to his downfall. "Marshall was too big a friend with the players," McCreary claimed. "He left a great deal of training to the players' own will. You can do that on a good team but not on a team with lesser players. The less talent that is on a team, the more discipline is needed. I wouldn't knock Marshall, but his dismissal was something that had to be done."

Unfortunately, the team did not respond well to McCreary's stricter style and the Seals finished the season with an 8-20-4 record with their GM also serving behind the bench. "I wanted to see the team in the locker room," McCreary said. "I wanted to stay and make a contribution to the program. When you have less talent, you have to have more of other things. You have to get more sleep, eat properly, etc. I was criticized for being too tough. I have always said if you can't bring 100 percent to the game, you shouldn't be there."

McCreary felt the Seals made progress in 1974-75, but they really needed new ownership. "We had a small building [seating capacity: 12,500]. Prospective buyers were concerned that we would need high ticket prices [for the team to be profitable]." McCreary described some of the team's obstacles in finding a new owner: "Our attendance was up, but we couldn't raise prices because of the team. Sportswriters and media did a lot to support the team. Little money was spent on advertising and promotion. The promotional budget was basically zero. We'd put an ad in the paper for the next game, but we really relied on sportswriters and the media to promote. Munson Campbell's hands were tied. Everybody wanted something for nothing. That may work in Montreal or Toronto, but not in Pittsburgh or Oakland." Despite the difficulties, McCreary did feel the Seals had a future in the Bay Area.

Chapter 6:
Mel Swig, At Last

Prior to the 1975-76 season, a new owner was finally found. The key to the future was rooted in the past: the Seals were finally bought by San Francisco hotel magnate Mel Swig. To many people close to the team, Swig was the man who should have been awarded the franchise in the first place.

Swig took over ownership with high hopes and enthusiasm. "Hockey is the greatest sport in the world," Swig proclaimed. "That's why I made the investment." Swig also promised that the team would hold on to its first round draft choices and add some experienced players to their young roster.

Unfortunately for this snakebitten franchise, Swig's purchase came too late to save the team. On the ice things were improving but, off the ice, troubles continued to accumulate.

"Things didn't change that much," Bill McCreary said. "The budget was still small." How small was it? PR Director Len Shapiro recalled, "My advertising budget for the 1975-76 season was $5,000. We spent it all on season-ticket advertisements. I had to beg, steal and borrow and get money any way I could. Attendance actually picked up by 20 percent in the last season."

The Seals' attendance in 1975-76 was 6,949 per game, the highest in the club's nine-year history. Attendance was even higher during the second half of the season as fans saw new coach Jack Evans' club play an exciting brand of hockey with new stars like rookie center Dennis Maruk and the recently acquired Wayne Merrick.

McCreary hired Jack "Tex" Evans to coach the Seals in 1975-76. Evans had led the Seals top affiliate in Salt Lake to the CHL's Adams Cup title the previous year. "Jack was a solid citizen and gave 100 percent," McCreary said. "He won at Salt Lake and he knew the organization. He deserved an opportunity."

Evans was 47 when he was hired to coach the Seals. He had played 12 NHL seasons as a tough defenseman for Chicago and New York and was a member of the 1961 Stanley Cup champion Black Hawks coached by Rudy Pilous. In 1966-67, Evans played for the WHL Seals in their final year of existence.

The new coach set to cut down the Seals goals against and helped bring a system to the Seals on and off the ice. "There are no tricks or gimmicks in my philosophy, just hard work," Evans said. While Evans was not very vocal, he did earn his players' respect. "When Jack tells you to do something," Seals forward Al MacAdam said, "you want to do it."

Other organizations also noticed the change in the Seals under Evans' guidance. Flyers coach Fred Shero said at the time, "Evans has the Seals working all the time. They skate hard and play the man." Bruins coach Don Cherry called the Seals a "different team" under Evans. He said the Seals were "an exciting team with good, young talent that can really skate." On the ice, the Seals seemed to be turning a corner.

Len Shapiro did everything he could to promote the Seals without spending money. "We would try to get on talk shows and get deals with fundraising groups," he said. "We were among the first to do postgame skates," Shapiro said. "For example, we tried to get the San Francisco firefighters to skate against the Oakland firefighters after the game. Each would have to buy 200 tickets to do that, though. We also had Sunday skates where two or three players would skate around with the fans, but we really couldn't advertise it because we had no budget."

For the club to remain viable Swig felt he needed additional capital from some minority owners and a new arena in San Francisco. Swig found some help with the investments from George Gund. Gund, a Cleveland native, owned a minor league hockey team in Sun Valley, Idaho, at the time. He was a lifelong hockey fan and film buff who met Swig through the many film festivals that they had both been involved with.

"I was originally told I was going to have a very small interest in the team, but it turned out to be much bigger," Gund recalled. "Mel told me he had a lot of people ready to invest in the team, including the Doobie Brothers. They never did get involved. I was initially focusing on things in Sun Valley. Shortly after I invested in the Seals, the cash calls started coming. I inquired why I was asked to put so much more money in so quickly. It was a harsh realization."

Politically, Swig and Gund were relying on Swig's political connections with San Francisco Mayor Joseph L. Alioto to get a new hockey arena built downtown. "Alioto was very helpful," Gund remembered. "He had hoped to put the team where the Moscone Center is now. It was very close to public transportation."

Regrettably for the Seals, Swig's timing was off. Alioto was leaving office and Swig supported the wrong man in the 1975 election. When George Moscone took office, the new arena died. "The new mayor put the new building on hold," Len Shapiro said. "He ran an investigation into the report and then said that the survey had to be resurveyed, so basically, it went nowhere. Then there were plans to remodel the Cow Palace but that never happened either." Once those two plans feel through, the Seals were finished in the Bay Area.

"After the new arena in San Francisco fell through, the league gave us the go-ahead to move the team," Gund remembered. "We looked at a lot of other places. We looked at Denver and Seattle-Tacoma. We ended up picking Cleveland because hockey was very popular there."

Rumors that the Seals would leave the Bay Area were almost as old as the team itself. The owners were quietly but aggressively looking over other locations. The NHL had planned expansion franchises for both Seattle and Denver, which were supposed to begin play in 1976-77. The new entries, though, were experiencing problems so moving the Seals to those cities was still a possibility.

Shapiro recalled when he first got an inkling the team might be leaving. "On February 1, 1976, I realized something might be up. I was in the office with Loretta Marcus [the team's secretary] and nobody else was there. I had no idea where anybody was. I looked at Munson Campbell's schedule and it said he was booked at the Cleveland Hilton. Then I knew something must be up."

George and Gordon Gund owned the Richfield Coliseum in Richfield, Ohio, where the NBA's Cleveland Cavaliers played. It was halfway between Akron and Cleveland, a location that would cause the franchise more problems in the future. In typical Seals fashion, even its exit was not smooth. The club participated in the July 1976 entry draft as the Seals and even started selling tickets for the upcoming season in Oakland.

At the 1976 entry draft, the Seals made history by becoming the first NHL team to use its first-round draft pick on a European player by drafting Swedish defenseman Bjorn Johansson. The team didn't make its intention to move officially known until August 26, 1976. It was announced that the team would move to Cleveland and take the name of the AHL franchise that played there for so many years, the Barons. Because of the late move, the Barons had a mere six weeks to sell tickets in their new home. Once again, the franchise started its new life behind the proverbial eight ball.

John Porter described the news that the franchise was moving as "a relief. I was actually tired of living with these stories and rumors about the team's demise." After nine crazy seasons in the Bay Area, the Seals became the first NHL team to move since the original Ottawa Senators moved to St. Louis in 1934 to become the St. Louis Eagles.

The Seals bad luck would follow them to Cleveland, where the team lasted only two seasons before being merged with the Minnesota North Stars. Attendance in Cleveland was even lower than it was in Oakland. During the 1976-77 season, Mel Swig suffered a heart attack that hampered his ability to run the team. By midseason the Barons failed to meet payroll and the players held a meeting before a home game to decide whether or not they should play that night. The Barons voted to play. Eventually Swig and the NHLPA each put in some money to get the team through the remainder of the 1976-77 season. The off-ice turmoil seemed to hurt the team's performance on the ice and they finished in last place again.

The following season, the Gund brothers bought out Mel Swig but attendance was no better. The Barons finished in last place again, and again played to mostly empty houses in the Richfield Coliseum, which ironically had the largest capacity of any rink in the league at the time. After the 1977-78 season, the Barons became the first NHL team since the Brooklyn Americans in 1942 to disband. As part of a "merger" deal, the Gunds acquired ownership of the Minnesota North Stars and the new club got the first chance to protect teams from the Barons roster. This is how Minnesota acquired players like Al MacAdam and Gilles Meloche, both of whom were significant contributors to the team's 1981 march to the Stanley Cup finals. Those players who were unclaimed were subject to a leaguewide dispersal draft. The Seals franchise became the only one of the "second six" expansion teams of 1967 to fail. A franchise that was shorthanded from day one and had limped through 11 seasons in the NHL was finally put out of its misery.

Part II:
THE PLAYERS REMEMBER

Chapter 1:
The Early Years: 1967–68 to 1969–70

Billy Harris

"The finest gentleman you will ever meet or that ever stepped on the ice."
—Seals forward Charlie Burns on Billy Harris

In the rough-and-tumble world of professional hockey, the word "gentleman" is not frequently used when discussing most hockey players. However, gentleman is the word overwhelmingly used to describe Billy Harris. It was clear that Harris was respected by his teammates both as a hockey player and as a man.

Harris came to the Seals in the expansion draft along with many other former Leafs who played on their Stanley Cup winning teams in the early to mid-'60s, such as Bob Baun, Gerry Ehman and Kent Douglas. Harris was 32 years old when the Seals selected him in 1967, and on the downside of a lengthy and productive NHL career. In fact, Harris had actually spent the 1966-67 season in the AHL with the Pittsburgh Hornets. He had a very good year, scoring 34 goals and 70 points to help Pittsburgh win the Calder Cup.

In Toronto, "Hinky" Harris had been an extra forward and a power-play specialist. Somehow, the Toronto native always seemed to find a way to score important goals for the Leafs. Harris described himself as "an average goal scorer but a good playmaker. Punch Imlach said I was a liability defensively, but I was always something like a plus-15 on the plus-minus chart."

Although Harris weighed only 157 pounds dripping wet, he was able to become an effective NHL player in the Original Six era. Harris's best statistical season was 1958-59, when he finished with 22 goals and 52 points in 70 games. It turned out to be his only 20-goal season in the NHL.

"I had mixed feelings," Harris said when he recalled his selection by the Seals in the expansion draft. "I had played the year before in the AHL for the Pittsburgh Hornets and I enjoyed Pittsburgh. I was hoping to be drafted by the Penguins. When I was drafted by Oakland, I tried to look on the bright side. We had nice weather out there and I had five or six former teammates on the team."

Harris admitted that the transition to playing for the Seals was tough for him. "It was different for me," Harris admitted. "I grew up in Toronto. I didn't need a pep talk or to be motivated if I had a blue and white sweater on. Oakland was not a hockey climate. The atmosphere was different—I had to give *myself* a pep talk. It was a big challenge."

Harris noticed the difference in atmosphere right away. For the Seals first home opener, Harris recalled, "there were a lot of empty seats. I had never seen that in Toronto. Opening night was always a big event in Toronto. It just didn't seem like the NHL with all those empty seats." Despite the sparse crowd, Harris played a strong game, adding two assists in a 5-1 California win over the Philadelphia Flyers.

In addition to the weather and lack of hockey atmosphere, Harris faced another challenge that all members of the Seals had to deal with: travel. "We started off the year with three home games and we went 2-0-1. I was tied for the league-scoring championship after three games. I thought it was going to be fun. Then, for the first time in hockey, we had a *seven*-game road trip. In Toronto we would play home on Saturday, in Chicago on Sunday and be home again by Monday. We went on this seven-game road trip and I think we were 0-6-1. Most games were competitive, but it was an uphill battle from there. Los Angeles was our only short trip. Everything else was two to four hours in the air."

There were other factors that made the 1967-68 season difficult for Billy Harris. First among them was his relationship with coach and former Maple Leafs teammate Bert Olmstead. For whatever reason, Harris became Olmstead's whipping boy. "As a teammate, Bert and I got along very well," Harris said. "As a coach, he challenged me on many occasions. I told him many times that if I were as good as he thought I should be at age 33, then I wouldn't be on an expansion team."

Bob Baun remembers how hard Olmstead was on Billy Harris. "All Bert could see was Billy Harris's weaknesses. He was light, but a heady hockey player. He scored goals and got assists when you needed them. He needed just a little pat on the back, though, and in Oakland, he didn't get it. [Assistant coach] Gordie Fashoway tore him apart." Rookie Tracy Pratt added: "It was hard for Billy to swallow being treated that way by an ex-teammate."

Harris tried to explain the issues he had with Olmstead: "That was the first time Bert was an NHL coach and he was very demanding. When Bert played in the NHL, nobody worked harder. He couldn't understand why everybody else didn't apply themselves like he did. Bert didn't understand that a player could be tired."

Harris recalled that, although Olmstead was a perfectionist, he was just as critical of himself as he was of his players. "Bert pointed fingers at different players over the course of the season but, deep down, I think he blamed himself," Harris said.

Harris recalled a particularly tough practice on Thanksgiving Day. "We practiced in the morning from about 10 to 11:30. We had a team meeting scheduled for noon. We all sat in the dressing room until 5 p.m.," Harris remembered. "Bert Olmstead came back at 5:00 and told us that all the secretaries had to work from 9 to 5, so his hockey players would have to do the same. We sat and looked at each other. We were all supposed to be home helping our wives with the turkeys." Olmstead finally unlocked the door and let the players go home.

In addition to having a tough time with his coach, Harris felt distracted by the controversy surrounding the club's future in Oakland. "We knew ownership wasn't happy in Oakland," Harris recalled. "By the second month, we were told we might move to Vancouver midseason. It was very unsettling. There was a feeling that maybe if we would have stayed in San Francisco, at the Cow Palace, we might have drawn better."

When Harris was feeling down, he would often speak to team president Frank Selke Jr. "He was terrific—a good hockey person. Many times after I spoke to Frank in his office, it brought back some sanity in my life. Frank always seemed to be the one saying things would get better."

There were bright spots for Harris during his season and a half in Oakland besides playing well early in the season. Harris recalls assisting on two goals to help beat one of the Original Six teams 3-2 on the road. "Gerry Ehman scored twice, I think, but the memory is vague," Harris said.

Harris also enjoyed playing in the Bay Area. "I loved the weather," Harris remembered. "We'd head to the driving range after winning a game. At the end of the season, I had three kids under 6 years old and we drove down the coast to Knott's Berry Farm and Disneyland. The fans were enthusiastic, and it's hard to be enthusiastic when your team is in last place."

Harris finished the 1967-68 season with 12 goals and 17 assists for the Seals after playing in 62 of the club's 74 games. The year left a bad taste in his mouth. "I played on three Stanley Cup teams and two Calder Cup teams. Finishing in fifth or sixth place was embarrassing."

Things didn't get much better for Harris the following year. Bert Olmstead stepped down as coach and Fred Glover took over. But Glover was not enamored with Harris as a player and the two did not get along well. Harris appeared in 19 games for the Seals in 1968-69 and picked up only four assists. He knew he was not playing well. The Seals traded Harris to Pittsburgh on November 29, 1968, for Bob Dillabough. Harris was "relieved" by the trade. "I didn't have many pleasant memories of Oakland in hockey and I looked forward to going back to Pittsburgh, where I knew the city and I knew a lot of the players."

Harris finished the 1968-69 season with the Penguins before retiring as an active player. He later went on to coach the Swedish National Team and the WHA's Toronto Toros. Harris was awarded the Howard Baldwin Trophy as the WHA's coach of the year in 1973-74 and was selected as the coach for the WHA All-Stars when they played against the Soviets in September 1974. Unfortunately, Harris's club did not fare well against the mighty Russians, going 1-4-3 in an eight-game series. Later in his life, he retired to Toronto and was president of the Leafs Alumni Association.

Billy Harris developed a rare form of leukemia in the late 1990s. He was in remission for a while, but he passed away at the age of 66 on September 20, 2001, a few months after being interviewed for this book. He left four children and five grandchildren.

Harris was remembered in the hockey world for his class, both on and off the ice. Tracy Pratt summed up the feelings of most of Harris's teammates by saying, "He was a good teammate and a great family man—a gentleman." Despite his frustrations, Harris brought class, stability and experience to the Seals during his tenure in Oakland. He will be missed.

Kent Douglas

"He had a mind of his own. He did what he wanted to do but he was all business on the ice."
—*Wally Boyer on Kent Douglas*

Kent Douglas was a bit of a rebel in the rather staid world of professional hockey during the era of the Original Six. Nobody would deny that Douglas had world-class talent, but it was his rebellious attitude that made his trip to the NHL a long one for the native of Cobalt, Ontario.

"I played in the Ontario League, then senior hockey for a year and then five years in the minors before getting to the NHL," remembered Douglas. "I thought I could play [in the NHL], or there was no point in staying. You couldn't get rich playing in the minors."

Douglas spent four seasons with Eddie Shore's Springfield Indians in the AHL, a time he remembers very fondly. "We won the Calder Cup three years in a row at Springfield. I don't think we would have been any worse than second in the NHL. In Springfield, we had players that other teams thought of as rebels, but you could be rebels there."

Douglas also had a great deal of respect for Eddie Shore, despite the fact that he was not always easy to play for. Although Shore's temper was legendary, he seemed to bring out the best in Kent Douglas. "Eddie Shore forgot more about hockey than anybody will ever know," Douglas exclaimed. "He never gets any credit. He wasn't the greatest teacher in the world. It was his way or no way. For example, when he skated, he wanted short, choppy strides."

Douglas also recalled how Shore trained his goalies to play his preferred stand-up style of goal. "We had a goalie named Henderson. In practice, Eddie Shore put a noose around his neck and tied it to the back of the goal. He told him, 'If you flop around, you'll hang yourself.' "

Billy Harris, who played with Douglas in both Toronto and Oakland, felt that Douglas "had a great relationship with Eddie Shore. Shore brought out the best in Kent Douglas."

Douglas finally broke into the NHL with the Toronto Maple Leafs during the 1962-63 season. He spent most of the next five seasons with the Leafs, although he had three stints with various minor league teams during this time. When expansion came along, Douglas was made available by the Leafs in the expansion draft. The Seals selected him in with their fourth selection in the expansion draft, the second pick that could be allocated for non-goaltenders.

Douglas noticed the difference between playing for an expansion team and his prior tenure with Toronto. "The confidence wasn't there," he recalled. "You look around the dressing room, and the guys weren't there. Bert Olmstead wanted to use the system from Montreal, but if you don't have the horses, you don't win the race. It was tough to play well and then lose or tie."

The other thing that Douglas noticed was that the Seals practice facility, located at Berkeley, was not regulation-sized. "Berkeley was the biggest ice surface I had ever seen," Douglas remarked. "It was like 100 feet by 220 feet. It was even bigger than Olympic-sized surfaces. It was like skating on a lake. It was tough to play defense there in practice. If you played the normal angles, forwards would just go around you. If not, they would go down the middle. It hurt us, especially when we would go into Boston and there would be no room."

Douglas helped the Seals get off to a fast start. He had the honor of scoring the very first goal in Seals history, although when interviewed for this book, he could not remember scoring it. Douglas got off to a hot start for the Seals. In fact, after three games Douglas was one of the top point-getters in the league. Unfortunately, he was not able to keep up that pace. In 40 games with the Seals, he finished with four goals and 11 assists to go with a team leading 80 penalty minutes.

Douglas described himself as a good defenseman. "I didn't carry the puck, but I made good passes," he said. "I was mean enough, I kept people away from the front of the net." His former teammates also remembered his physical style of play. "Douglas had a lot of talent," rookie defenseman Tracy Pratt remembered. "He used a big, thick stick and liked to cross-check people. He had a great shot and was a strong son of a gun."

Douglas also favored an offensive style of play that was rare for blueliners in the mid-'60s. "Speed is what makes the difference," Douglas said to Spence Conley of *The Oakland Tribune* in October 1967. "In my view, a defenseman has to move the puck to create offense and make the play."

Despite his ability, one of the things that often got Douglas into trouble was his off-ice behavior. Douglas had a reputation for working hard on the ice and playing hard off it. Former Seals goaltender Charlie Hodge recalled, "He liked his firewater. On a road trip, you couldn't say anything directly to him. Once, on a road trip, I was getting shell-shocked. I said, 'Kent, you have a good time and I pay for it the next night.' So the next night, he stayed home in bed and he played awful the next game. So I told him to do whatever it is he used to do."

Douglas also had some disagreements with team captain Bob Baun. Gary Smith recalled that Baun and Douglas were often at odds, often over seemingly minor things. "Baun wanted everybody to wear jackets and ties on road trips and Kent didn't like that."

Douglas and Baun also disagreed about Bert Olmstead's decision to lock the team in the locker room for a few hours on Thanksgiving Day after a particularly bad practice. "Boomer and I almost got into a fight over it," Douglas said. "He backed Bert Olmstead on that one."

To this day, Baun wonders what might have been had Douglas lived his life differently. "He was his own worst enemy," Baun recalled. "He's forgotten more about the game than most guys have ever known, but his life off the ice always cost him."

Whether it was due to his falling out with Baun, his rebel attitude or some other factor, Douglas' days in Oakland were numbered. On January 9, 1968, the Seals traded Douglas to Detroit for Ted Hampson, Bert Marshall and John Brenneman. The deal worked out well for the Seals as both Hampson and Marshall made long-term contributions to the club and eventually served as captain.

"I couldn't believe it," Douglas said, recalling the trade. "All three guys they got were younger than I was. They said they needed me in Detroit because Carl Brewer was hurt."

Douglas spent a season and a half in Detroit before returning to the AHL, first with the Rochester Americans and then with the Baltimore Clippers. In 1972-73, Douglas returned to major league hockey when he spent a season with the New York Raiders of the WHA. He continued as an active player in the AHL until the 1975-76 season.

Today, Douglas is retired and lives in Ontario. He is married and has two sons, and spends much of his time helping to care for his mother. The former Seals defenseman also plays plenty of golf. Tracy Pratt recalled that Douglas could play golf equally well left-handed and right-handed.

Billy Harris remembered Douglas as having "unbelievable potential. A great shot, great on the power play and rugged, but inconsistent."

Even today, when interviewed, Douglas was his own person. Full of wit and candor, he has remained a "rebel." Kent Douglas wouldn't have it any other way.

Larry Cahan

"My favorite. He was a comedian. He had a quick wit and was fun to be around. 'Hank' was a guy you wanted on your team."

—*Wally Boyer on Larry Cahan*

Larry (Hank) Cahan was one of the more popular players on the Seals in 1967-68, especially among his teammates. Cahan was 34 years old when the Seals selected him from the Rangers organization in the expansion draft. The stocky native of Fort William, Ontario, had already played in 383 NHL games before joining the Seals. Cahan made his NHL debut with the Maple Leafs in 1954-55. After one-and-a-half seasons with Toronto, Hank was selected by the Rangers in the intraleague draft prior to the 1956-57 season. Cahan spent parts of seven seasons with the Broadway Blueshirts, but also spent substantial time with the Vancouver Canucks of the WHL during those years. In his final two seasons in Vancouver, Cahan was named to the WHL postseason all-star team and won the 1967 Hal Laycoe Cup as the WHL's top defenseman. His coach was Bert Olmstead.

Cahan was a big man, an imposing 6'2" tall and, although he was listed at 220 pounds, many of his teammates thought he was closer to 250. Cahan also possessed great strength. Seals goalie Gary Smith, who played both with and against Cahan, recalled, "He was so strong, like Tim Horton was. If you were five feet from the boards, he could flick his wrist and you would hit the boards. He was a super guy and really old school."

Despite his imposing appearance, Cahan was a gentle giant and a practical joker off the ice. "He was a real character. He was like a storybook and had the greatest sense of humor," Bob Baun recalled. "Hank was like a big Saint Bernard. He just loved to put his arms around you. He was a Moose Vasko–type defenseman and had a lot of ability. He needed just a little more desire and a bit more of a mean streak, and he could have been a great hockey player."

Despite his lack of a mean streak, Cahan was strong and nobody wanted to mess with him. He was the Seals designated policeman in 1967-68, according to Charlie Burns. Kent Douglas said Cahan "marched to the beat of a different drummer. He was a big guy who took up a lot of room. He was about 250 pounds, a big strapping bugger. If he decided to take you out, you were out."

Mike Laughton recalled a run-in he had with Cahan in his WHL days with Vancouver. "When I first played in the WHL, he was the toughest guy in the league," Laughton said. "He said to me, 'Rookie, you want to get your face rearranged?' I said, 'Not particularly.' He was a jovial guy."

Aut Erickson, who was often paired with Cahan on defense that first season in Oakland, recalled that Cahan was "a good player and a big guy. If he'd have been mean with his size, he'd have scared the whole league. He was the mainstay of our defense in Oakland." In the 1967-68 season, Cahan appeared in all 74 games for the Seals and scored an NHL career-best nine goals and 24 points. He also added 80 penalty minutes.

While Cahan was a physical presence on the ice, off the ice he kept his teammates laughing with his mischievous actions. His teammates realized it was all in good fun. Ron Harris said, "We laughed at Hank all the time. He was a funny guy; he loved to have fun. A great man in the dressing room and off the ice."

Tracy Pratt acknowledged that Cahan was "a total leader in the sense that he taught you how to recognize authority, respect your teammates and your coaches. He was fun to be around and kept the guys loose. He was the biggest grizzly bear you ever saw in your life but he was tame. His heart was as big as the moon." Pratt then paused and started laughing as he said, "He just hated to have a good time. He was a big gregarious man who wanted to play the game he loved." Gerry Odrowski remembered Cahan as "the backbone of the team" and recalled, "He never got excited, he helped out and was good in practice. And he always spoke his mind."

Pratt also recalled an incident between Cahan and coach Bert Olmstead. "Once in Montreal, some of the guys went to pick up some booze at the duty-free. Bert Olmstead grabbed Larry Cahan and the two of them went to drink some whiskey together. Bert asked Cahan, 'Why don't the players like me?' Hank told Bert, 'Sometimes you gotta back off a bit, you're too macho.' The next day, we were in New York, where we played well but lost to the Rangers. Olmstead yells in front of the entire team, 'Cahan, if I ever catch you drinking the night before a game, I'll fine you, you SOB."

Offensively, the most memorable game Cahan had for the Seals came at the "Jewel Box" on Nov. 15, 1967. Cahan scored a goal and added an assist as the Seals defeated the Kings 4-1 to end a 14-game winless streak.

Cahan was also one of the players who checked Bill Masterton when he lost consciousness and fell into a coma. The hit was considered clean by everybody who saw it, including members of the North Stars.

Despite his leadership and steady play, the Seals did not protect Cahan in the intraleague draft after the 1967-68 season. The Canadiens claimed him and promptly traded him to the Kings three weeks later. Cahan spent the next three seasons with the Kings and was captain of the team in 1969-70, a position he held for two seasons. After spending the 1971-72 season with the Seattle Totems of the WHL, Cahan signed with the Chicago Cougars of the WHA. He retired as an active player after the 1973-74 season.

Unfortunately, Cahan did not have a long life after hockey. He died suddenly on June 25, 1992, at the age of 58. All of his teammates have fond memories of Cahan. Billy Harris said, "He provided 75 percent of the entertainment on the bench. He was a fun-loving, hard-working hockey player, a good player and a good person. I don't think he took Bert Olmstead too seriously. He did a good job in Oakland and he enjoyed life." It seems his teammates enjoyed life more when this gentle giant was around, too.

Larry Popein

"A real good skater and a great guy. A 100 percent hockey man who lived and died hockey."
—*Gary Smith on Larry Popein*

By the time he arrived in Oakland midway through the 1967-68 season, 37-year-old Larry Popein was already a veteran of professional hockey. He made his first appearance in the NHL with the New York Rangers in 1954-55 and played with the Broadway Blueshirts until 1960-61, when he was sent back to the minors. From 1960-61 until 1966-67, Popein played mostly for the Vancouver Canucks of the WHL. The 5'9", 170-pound native of Yorkton, Saskatoon, was known as a defensive center and penalty killer. Popein was a friend of Bert Olmstead's and Olmstead coached him in Vancouver just prior to expansion. The Seals acquired Popein's rights from the Rangers in a cash deal prior to their inaugural season. When the Seals struggled early in the year, Olmstead brought up the veteran Popein to add some character and leadership to his floundering club. Olmstead figured that Popein knew his system and knew what Olmstead expected of his players. He hoped Popein's work ethic would rub off on some of his less-experienced teammates.

Wally Boyer recalled Popein's call-up from Vancouver. "Bert Olmstead brought him in about halfway through the season. He was going to be our savior. He tried to do what Bert Olmstead asked him to do, but I don't think any one player could have saved us that year."

Aut Erickson added, "He was a hard worker and a good player who tried to keep us winning." Billy Harris revealed the reason why Olmstead likely sought to bring Popein up from the minors. "He took the game very seriously," Harris said. "He was a hard worker and a good defensive centerman."

Popein had a reputation as a thinking man's hockey player. Rookie Mike Laughton added, "He was thinking all the time and always rubbing his forehead."

Popein was also brought in to give leadership to the club's younger players. Tracy Pratt, then a rookie defenseman with a reputation for having fun off the ice, was selected to room with the veteran center. "He was a stone-faced disciplinarian-type hockey player," Pratt recalled. "He wanted everybody in bed early before a game. A man of little words, he was a good skater and puck handler. Bert Olmstead expected more from Larry Popein than he got from him. He was an honest hockey player."

When he arrived in Oakland, Popein saw action in 47 games, scoring five goals and adding 14 assists. Ron Harris, who Popein later coached in New York, remembered "Pope" as "a hard worker. He could skate and was a good penalty killer and a nice man." Goalie Charlie Hodge added that Popein was "a first-class gentleman. I can't say enough about him."

Popein appreciated Bert Olmstead's style of coaching and attempts at keeping the team disciplined. "I thought Bert was a fine coach," Popein told one reporter. "He even told us to stand smartly at attention during the national anthem and to come charging out on the ice from the dressing room … to show some pride in being a professional hockey player. I think that's right. I think hockey players should be proud."

After the 1967-68 season, Bert Olmstead left the Seals organization and Frank Selke Jr. took over as general manager. Shortly thereafter, Popein was traded back to the Rangers on May 14, 1968, in another cash deal. The following season, Popein was the player-coach of the Omaha Knights of the CHL. In his second year as coach, he led the Knights to a first-place finish and the Adams Cup title. Popein also had a successful stint as coach of the Rangers top affiliate, the Providence Reds. He was handpicked by Emile Francis to take over the Rangers coaching position in 1973-74, but the team went into a midseason slump and Popein was replaced in January. The main criticism against him was that he wasn't tough enough on the Rangers veteran players. Popein remained active in hockey as a scout and in various other capacities, although he never coached in the NHL again.

Although he was only with the Seals for a brief time, his teammates appreciated the effort and contributions of Larry Popein. Gerry Odrowski said Popein was "a real go-getter. He gave 110 percent all the time." Charlie Burns summed up Popein by saying, "He was old school. He came from the Rangers. He was a tremendous skater and a gentleman's gentleman."

Bob Baun

"He was a hard-nosed individual. He didn't know how to do anything else but win."

—Charlie Burns on Bob Baun

In the team's first season, Bob Baun was the foundation of the California Seals. He was the team's first captain and the first non-goaltender chosen by the Seals in the expansion draft. It was Baun who was expected to lead the expansion Seals and teach them how to win.

In Toronto, Bob Baun was almost the personification of old-time hockey. He earned a reputation as one of the hardest hitters in the league, despite the fact that he was only 5'9" and weighed all of 175 pounds. He played on four Stanley Cup winning teams with the Maple Leafs, including the last Leafs team to win the NHL title in 1967. The Lanigan, Saskatchewan, native was probably most famous for scoring the game-winning goal in game six of the 1964 Stanley Cup finals. Baun left the game in the third period with a broken bone in his leg but returned to the ice in overtime and to put the puck behind Terry Sawchuk to defeat the Red Wings. It was "The Goal" that guaranteed Baun's spot in Maple Leafs lore.

After the Maple Leafs won the 1967 Stanley Cup, Baun was left unprotected in the expansion draft. He was not surprised but "utterly disappointed" by the Leafs decision to make him available to the six fledgling teams. But one thing gave Baun hope: joining the Seals.

"It was exciting for me," Baun said, when recalling being selected by the Seals. "My mentor, Bert Olmstead, was there. I thought the world of him. Bert has forgotten more about hockey than most people in this country ever knew. He should be a sports guru for Canada. His people skills were not what they should be, but his knowledge of the game was second to none."

Now Baun would have the chance to be captain of an NHL franchise. "I had always wanted to be a captain," Baun said. "A captain of a hockey team is a very special person. I think I would have been a better assistant captain because my thinking on the ice is so far forward, so people have trouble keeping up with me sometimes. A captain has to be special, like George Armstrong was. I couldn't help Bert Olmstead the way he needed to be helped, probably because my thinking was so similar to Bert's."

Baun threw himself into promoting the new Bay Area franchise full-throttle. He was one of the few Seals players who bought a home in the Bay Area rather than renting one. He also recalls doing a lot of speaking engagements in the summer before the NHL Seals made their debut. "I spoke to school boards, Rotary, Kiwanis and Lions Clubs," the former Seals captain said. "I often went with Tim Ryan. A lot of the players didn't like doing these speaking engagements, so I did most of it. I wanted to be a part of the community."

Despite his initial enthusiasm, Baun soon discovered that there were some difficulties associated with playing hockey in Northern California as opposed to Toronto. "For me, the warm-weather aspect was a big problem," Baun explained. "It was tough getting yourself psyched for hockey. I used to go into my living room, turn on the fireplace and stare at this winter landscape painting I had. Eventually, I would come to my senses and look out the window at the Bay Bridge and the Golden Gate Bridge."

Another obstacle Baun sought to overcome was the lack of fans at the Oakland Coliseum Arena. Baun recalled, "Small crowds were demoralizing. When you're a performer, you start to second-guess yourself. I always thought I should play every game like it was my last and give 100 to 110 percent every game. But without people to perform in front of, it's harder to take your game to the highest level."

Perhaps the biggest adjustment the ex-Leaf defenseman had when joining the Seals was the difference in culture and attitude between an expansion team and an established club. "When you play with true professionals and people who lived hockey, it is different. I would say 60 to 70 percent of the players never really changed teams from year to year in the days of the Original Six. All we talked about was hockey. The attitude of a lot of the minor leaguers or the 30 percent that did move around, their attitude was so different from ours. After practice, they'd head to the pub every day, take a six-pack home, stay up late and watch Johnny Carson. It was no fault of their own. They just lived like gypsies. They always rented a place and moved after the hockey season was over. It was certainly different."

To Baun, this difference in attitude coupled with Olmstead's short temper and superior knowledge of the game made things even more difficult for his new club. "I loved the guys, but I couldn't get my head around that attitude. You can imagine telling someone five or six times what to do on the ice, but the sixth or seventh time, that kills you. Once you start thinking about the game of hockey, it's too late. It has to be automatic. The guys thought this was mumbo jumbo and they refused to listen. Bert had superior knowledge and retention of the game … He simply laid things out like tic-tack-toe. I had no trouble following him, but some of the other guys must have."

The player-coach relationship put a temporary strain on Baun and Olmstead's friendship. In fact, Bob Baun's memory of the first-ever Seals game was tainted somewhat by the tension between him and his mentor. In the early fall of 1967, Baun was named as interim president of the NHL Players' Association. Olmstead did not approve of this position, likely feeling that it would distract Baun's attention from hockey. "Bert Olmstead was fining me $1,000 per day every day I stayed as president of the NHLPA," Baun recalled. The fine reached $13,000 before Olmstead agreed to waive it. Baun signed his contract to play with the Seals on the trunk of his car the night of the opener. "My head was not in the right spot that night," Baun admitted. "I wasn't thinking too fondly of Bert at the time." Still, Baun played a strong game. Spence Conley's article in *The Oakland Tribune* said "Baun handed out body checks like a Tahoe blackjack dealer" during the Seals 5-1 win over the Flyers on opening night.

Later in the season, although the team struggled on the ice, Baun still received favorable reviews from management. Frank Selke Jr., then Seals president said, "Baun has given 110 percent to us each time he's played." At midseason Baun was selected to represent Oakland at the NHL All-Star game.

Maple Leafs owner Harold Ballard, perhaps unintentionally, showed he still respected Baun as a hockey player. In order to keep Baun's mind off of hockey before a game against his Leafs at the Oakland Coliseum, Ballard resorted to trickery. "Ballard pulled a fast one on me," Baun said. "He had loaned me some money for my farm. He had the bank call me up the day before our game with Toronto and call in the note. I had to fly to Toronto, pay off the note and fly back to Oakland for the game."

Baun tried to install a "first-class mentality" with the Seals, but his suggestions were not always met with open arms. Fellow defenseman Bert Marshall recalled that "we had to wear ties in practice when he was the captain. He tried hard, but you can't make chicken from chickenshit. He was an aggressive, outspoken guy and a good, solid defenseman."

Ron Harris remembered Baun as "our leader on defense," and added that "he was a hard-nosed guy. He'd get mad. When you didn't do your job, he'd give you hell."

While some teammates may have questioned Baun's methods, nobody ever questioned his dedication. Bill Hicke remembered how hard Baun worked on defense. "He tried hard and was an unbelievable defensive defenseman," Hicke said. "He blocked as many shots as our goalies did and he had the bruises to prove it."

Another former teammate recalled that Baun was a "great leader," but explained: "His skills were diminishing when he was with the Seals. He was not a great skater but his style fit in with the Leafs, who had enough talent on the ice to compensate for his lack of speed. On the Seals, people could get around him."

The Seals captain did have some fond memories of his season in Oakland, including Seals season-ticketholder Charles Schulz, creator of the "Peanuts" comic strip. "Charles Schulz spent a lot of time in the dressing room and was a joy to be with," Baun remembered. "He autographed things for everybody. I never kept the autographs for myself. I always gave them away to friends' kids."

Baun finished the 1967-68 season with three goals and 10 assists in 67 games played. He also amassed 81 penalty minutes. However, the lack of interest in hockey in Oakland and the constant losing got to Baun. When it was announced that Olmstead would not be back to coach the Seals in 1968-69, Baun asked Frank Selke Jr. to trade him, preferably back to an Original Six team. Baun and Ron Harris were traded to the Red Wings on May 27, 1968, in exchange for Gary Jarrett, Doug Roberts, Howie Young and Chris Worthy. After two-plus years with Detroit, Baun finished his career with the Maple Leafs, retiring after the 1972-73 season. After retiring as a player, Baun coached the Toronto Toros of the WHA before settling down to various business interests.

Today, Baun lives in Ajax, Ontario. He wrote a book about his life and career entitled *Lowering the Boom: The Bobby Baun Story,* which was published in 2000.

Despite all the difficulties he encountered, Baun enjoyed his time in Oakland. "I loved living in the Bay Area," Baun admitted. "It was a great year out there for the Baun family. My kids really enjoyed living out there. It was a great experience and the kids didn't want to move."

Baun also had the respect of his teammates, even in difficult times. Kent Douglas summarized Baun's career thusly: "He gave 150 percent every time he was out there. If he made a mistake, he made a mistake—but opponents had to have their heads up when he was out there." But perhaps longtime teammate Billy Harris put it simplest and best when he said, "Nobody worked harder than Bob Baun."

Wally Boyer

"He was a scrappy little bugger and a great penalty killer."

—Kent Douglas on Wally Boyer

Wally Boyer was typical of many players selected in the Expansion Draft of June 6, 1967. In the era of the Original Six, Boyer was a fringe player. He was a bit small for an NHL center, standing 5'7" and weighing only 160 pounds. But the Cowan, Manitoba, native had one thing going for him: he never quit.

Ask most of Boyer's former teammates, and they would describe him as quiet and a bit of a loner. But not one of them questioned his desire.

"I started late in the NHL," Boyer recalled. "I played four or five years in the minors before I was finally called up by the Maple Leafs. I got called up and did well my first few games, so they kept me there."

Boyer finished the 1965-66 season with the Leafs, scoring four goals and 21 points in 46 games. The following year, he was claimed by the Black Hawks in the intraleague draft and appeared in 42 contests.

When the expansion draft took place, Boyer was thrilled to go to Oakland. "I looked at all the cities that were in the expansion draft and all the players Oakland had selected. I thought we had a good chance of winning everything. We had a very good team on paper."

Interestingly enough, Boyer was one player who appreciated Bert Olmstead's style of coaching. "Olmstead coached the way he played," Boyer said. "He was all desire. He wanted to win in the worst way. Bert intimidated me all the time. I was a borderline player and a hard worker. I had my best year in the NHL in Oakland. I know I was angry at Bert a lot at the time, but when you look back, he was a good coach."

Boyer admitted that it was not always easy playing for Olmstead. "One time, I recall that Bert wouldn't let me leave the ice. I had a two- or three-minute shift and wanted to come off. Bert grabbed me by the scruff of the neck and threw me back onto the ice."

Boyer also recalled an odd occurrence on Thanksgiving. "I remember sitting in the dressing room on Thanksgiving Day when Bert Olmstead locked us all in there," Boyer said. "We were all just sitting there waiting for him to come back and open the door." The team spent all of Thanksgiving afternoon locked in their own dressing room until Olmstead let them join their families for dinner at about 5:00.

Wally Boyer finished his one season in Oakland with a career-best 13 goals and 33 points. He was one of only two players on the Seals to play in all 74 games in 1967-68.

Because the Seals were struggling, especially on offense, Boyer remembers that Olmstead switched the line combinations around "every two or three games if we weren't producing." Boyer recalled one combination in particular: "I played a bit with Gerry Ehman and Billy Harris. I was No. 6, Ehman was No. 7 and Harris was No. 8. We were the '6-7-8 line.' People would say, 'There goes 6-7-8'."

Although hockey did not succeed immediately in Oakland, Boyer remembered that the club did make a sincere effort to sell itself to the fans. "They brought out Dick Irvin. They were always promoting the team on radio. They were promoting baseball [the Oakland A's] at the same time they were promoting hockey. The A's stayed in the same hotel as we did. It was a tough selling point for hockey." Boyer always felt, however, that hockey would have thrived in the Bay Area if only the Seals could produce a winning team.

Playing hockey in California was a different experience for a man from Manitoba. "It was a different environment. It was not freezing with snow. It was more like a vacation. I enjoyed my season out there."

Despite enjoying his time in Oakland, Boyer saw two main drawbacks: travel and the constant losing. "We expected to be in first place," Boyer said. "I thought we'd at least make the playoffs. Because we weren't winning, Bert Olmstead kept everybody on edge all the time."

As for travel, Boyer stated, "You weren't in the right time zone and you weren't used to the weather. I don't think it bothered visiting players coming from the East Coast to Oakland as much. I think they looked at it as a vacation."

After the 1967-68 season, Boyer was traded by the Seals to Montreal, along with Alain Caron, in exchange for Norm Ferguson, François Lacombe and two other players. The Canadiens traded him to the Penguins less than a month later. Boyer spent three-plus seasons in Pittsburgh before finishing his professional hockey career with the Winnipeg Jets of the WHA. In 365 career NHL games, Boyer finished with 54 goals and 159 points.

After his hockey career was over, Boyer sold real estate and owned a hotel. Today he is retired and living in Midland, Ontario. The ex-Seals center is married and has two children and two grandchildren.

While never a major offensive force in the NHL, Wally Boyer was a solid player who gave 100 percent all the time. "He was more defensive-minded than offensive-minded," Tracy Pratt recalled. "And he was very reliable on the penalty kill."

Billy Harris added, "He was an honest worker and an honest hockey player. A good person and a good team player."

Charlie Burns

"He was a good assistant captain who spent time with the younger players. He brought a lot to the table; a good playmaker who set up his wingers."

—Tracy Pratt on Charlie Burns

Ask most of his former teammates about Charlie Burns and they'll tell you about how he was different from the "typical" hockey player in the 1960s and '70s. In an era where 98 percent of the players came from Canada, Burns was an American. In the '60s, when almost no players wore a helmet, Burns wore an unusual-looking leather helmet to protect his injured head. By the time Burns arrived to play with the NHL version of the Seals, he had already been a player-coach for the WHL Seals. But despite all of these surface differences, one thing Burns had from all of his teammates was respect.

Charlie Burns was born in Detroit, Michigan, on February 14, 1936. His family soon moved to Toronto, where Burns grew up as a fan of the Maple Leafs. He made his NHL debut with the Detroit Red Wings during the 1958-59 season. The following year he was selected by the Bruins in the intra-league draft. He spent the next four seasons in Boston as a checking line center. Burns never scored more than 15 goals and 41 points in any of his seasons with the Bruins.

The Bruins assigned Burns to their WHL affiliate the San Francisco Seals in 1963-64 and he remained in San Francisco until expansion came in 1967. Burns enjoyed his time in the Bay Area and in his final two WHL seasons; he was a player-coach, splitting duties first with Bud Poile and later with Rudy Pilous. The NHL Seals acquired his rights when the new NHL team's owners bought the WHL club in 1966.

Burns was happy to be staying in the Bay Area. "I loved playing in San Francisco. The fans were tremendous," Burns fondly recalled. "San Francisco was really where the team should have been. Oakland was considered to be strictly a football town. There was not a lot of acceptance on that side of the bay. A lot of people wouldn't come across the bay back then. There was a lot of animosity at the time."

When the Seals moved from the WHL to the NHL, Burns was no longer a player-coach. Now, he was just a player, but Burns didn't seem to mind. "I enjoyed what I was doing as a player-coach,"

Burns said. "It was tough to do two things at the same time. When I went to the NHL, I was able to concentrate on one."

Burns's coaching experience gave Burns some insight into Bert Olmstead's methods and the wily veteran forward respected the Seals first-year coach. "Bert was a good man. He was old school and a very tough individual who expected a lot from his players. He expected everybody to play like he did, giving 200 percent all the time. He also expected his players to be in shape."

Burns loved the Bay Area and playing for the Seals, but the transition to the NHL was not always easy. "It was tough for our team trying to live up to the standards of the NHL at that time," Burns remembered. "We had a lot of guys who had been there years ago and a lot of guys who never quite made it. We had to put them together and make an NHL club."

In the WHL, the 5'11", 170-pound Burns was a good if not great goal scorer. However, in the NHL Charlie Burns described himself as "a checker and a penalty killer—a defensive-style player. I did put the puck in the net in the WHL, but in the NHL I played more of a checking role."

In addition to his defensive skills, Charlie Burns was a good passer. In fact, he led the 1967-68 Seals with 26 assists. He also tallied nine goals for 35 points in 73 games.

The reason Charlie Burns was one of the few NHL players to wear a helmet was due to a head injury he suffered in juniors. The injury was nearly fatal. "He had a metal plate in his brain," Billy Harris said of Burns. "He was advised not to play hockey again but he found a way. He was a good skater and a winner." After the head injury, Burns played with a crude leather helmet that covered the sides of his head but not the top of it. It looked like a turn-of-the-century leather football helmet and it made Burns easily recognizable on the ice.

The small crowds in Oakland did have an effect on the team, according to Burns. "Anytime you play in front of a small crowd, it's different than playing in front of a full house," Burns explained. "There is some disappointment. You want to see a big crowd and you want the team to stay [in the Bay Area]."

Burns was not one to make excuses, however. While many players complained about the extensive travel West Coast teams had to endure, Burns refused to do so. "Everybody goes through ups and downs," Burns said. "People use [travel] as an excuse. Winning is a habit and so is waiting to win. Losing is a habit and so is waiting to lose."

While the Seals inaugural season was tough on all players, Burns started the year with a lot of optimism. "I remember the first game as one of the highlights," Burns said. "It was the first game for a new team and I was back in the NHL. Now I could stay in the same area and be in the NHL. It was great."

The toughest game for Burns came midway through the season. "I usually played a regular shift. One game, I had all my friends there and I spent the entire game sitting on my backside on the bench."

After the 1967-68 season, Burns was selected by the Pittsburgh Penguins in the intra-league draft. "I was totally heartbroken," Burns said. "I had been in San Francisco for a number of years and I had made a lot of friends there. You think you're going to be there forever, but I guess trades come with the territory in professional sports."

After scoring a career-high 51 points for the Pens, Burns spent the next four seasons with the Minnesota North Stars, including some time as a player-coach in 1969-70. He later coached the North Stars for half a season more after he retired as an active player.

Today, Burns works lives in Connecticut and works in the airline industry. He continues to coach youth hockey in his spare time and has now coached in some capacity for about 20 years.

Although he was a quiet man, Burns led by example and is remembered fondly by his teammates. Tom Thurlby described Burns as "one of the better guys I know; a very dedicated player. A good skater, he survived by working hard."

But perhaps it was the Seals captain Bob Baun who summed up best what Charlie Burns meant to the Seals in their inaugural season: "He was a good playmaker and a team player. He thought the game out and really lived the game."

Aut Erickson

"He was a good defensive defenseman. He could skate pretty good. His game didn't waiver much one way or the other."

—Tracy Pratt on Aut Erickson

Steady. Consistent. Reliable. These are the type of words used to describe Aut Erickson by his former Seals teammates. While Erickson's game was not flashy offensively and he didn't put up gaudy statistics, he was a respected member of the Seals first-year blue-line corps.

Autry Erickson was named after singer/actor Gene Autry and is a native of Lethbridge, Alberta. He made his NHL debut with the Boston Bruins in 1959-60. After two seasons in Boston, Erickson spent most of the next three seasons playing for the Buffalo Bisons of the AHL, with a few cups of coffee with the Chicago Black Hawks mixed in. By 1965-66, Erickson had settled down with the Victoria Maple Leafs of the WHL. He was called up by the Toronto Maple Leafs for the postseason in 1966-67 and appeared in only one playoff game with the Leafs, but it was enough to get his name on the Stanley Cup. Less than two months later, the Leafs made Erickson available in the expansion draft, where the Seals eagerly selected him.

Erickson recalled his reaction to being selected by the Seals. "I was happy," he said. "It was nice to go to the West Coast. It was kind of like a vacation with pay. I also knew some of the guys who were on the team from my time with the Leafs."

Because there were as many as nine former Maple Leafs on the first-year Seals, including captain Bob Baun, Billy Harris, Gerry Ehman, Kent Douglas, Terry Clancy and Coach Bert Olmstead, Erickson said, "I think there was some resentment of all the ex-Toronto players." The fact that the players had all come from different organizations seemed to cause a problem for the expansion team. It was one reason the Seals never developed much team chemistry in 1967-68.

Erickson had trouble adjusting to playing hockey in Northern California. The first problem Erickson saw was the team's practice rink. "We practiced at Berkeley which was a big old rink," Erickson said. "When things were going bad, we couldn't rectify it. The rink was wide and short and you couldn't get into the pattern of play that you wanted to."

Another problem Erickson had was the constant rumors that the team might leave town. "We were settled and didn't want to move," the 6'0", 180-pound defenseman recalled. "From day one, there were stories that there was not enough money and talk of moving the team. It bothered you."

Erickson had a good deal of respect for Coach Bert Olmstead. "He was a perfectionist," Erickson said. "I respected and admired him as a coach. [But] he was very demanding; he wanted a little more than some of us were able to give him." The demands of Olmstead were sometimes difficult for Erickson. "Bert practiced us for two or three hours until we could pass the puck right," Erickson said, recalling his least-favorite practice drill. "I would get so nervous that I couldn't make a good pass."

When he was playing in junior, Erickson was more of an offensive defenseman, but in the NHL, he was known more for his defense. In 1967-68 with the Seals, Erickson finished the season with four goals, 11 assists and 46 penalty minutes in 65 games. Offensively, that was his best NHL season. "I was pretty good, defensively," Erickson recalled. "I also had a reputation as somewhat of a fighter. I won some and I lost some. In retrospect, I wish I played more offensively so I had a little more to offer."

Erickson did keep to himself to an extent with the Seals, and some teammates remember him as a bit of a loner. Tom Thurlby recalled Erickson as "a minor leaguer who got the chance to play and played well when I was there. He was very self-conscious and stayed by himself all the time."

49

Erickson also had a reputation for helping out the younger players. Mike Laughton, who was a rookie in 1967-68, recalled that Erickson was a big help to him, even when they played together in the minors. "He took me under his wing in Victoria. He was very helpful," Laughton said. "It's too bad he really didn't get the chance to play in the NHL that long."

Ron Harris remembered that Erickson tried to keep the mood around the team light, but it was not an easy thing to do. "He was very funny sometimes," Harris said of Erickson. "But we were losing and there wasn't always much to laugh about."

The long road trips that were so new to NHL players were particularly hard on Erickson. "We had a lot of two- or three-week road trips," the former defenseman recalled. "It was tough. Some of those trips seemed to take forever. You do what you can. It cut into our practice time."

Despite the difficulties of playing losing hockey, Erickson looked back fondly on his time with the Seals. "It was great being in the NHL," he recalled. "Oakland had a new rink and it was a nice place. We all made more money than we did in the minors. I think I made about $20,000. Things went good until Christmas. After that, we couldn't win."

After the 1967-68 season, Erickson had time to reassess his hockey career. "I had some back problems for the last six or seven years," Erickson said. "They offered me the chance to go to the Phoenix Roadrunners of the WHL and eventually get a chance to coach. It was the job I wanted. Frank Selke Jr. offered to let me stay in Oakland, but I wanted the opportunity to coach. He was a nice, honest gentleman who did all he could."

Erickson played the following two seasons for the Roadrunners before moving into coaching. He also was called up to play one more game with the Seals during the 1969-70 season. Erickson coached the Roadrunners for two seasons—one of his players with Phoenix was ex-Seals teammate Gerry Odrowski. Later, Erickson worked in the Islanders organization, including a stint as an assistant coach in 1972-73. Eventually, he left hockey and worked as a manager for Cargo West Airlines in Los Angeles. He is now retired and splits his time between Canada and the Phoenix area.

Erickson's final NHL statistics include seven goals and 24 assists in 226 games; he added 182 minutes in penalties. He also got his name on the Stanley Cup.

Kent Douglas did a good job of summing up his teammates' view of Aut Erickson. "He moved the puck pretty well—a pretty good defensive defenseman who was smart and a good skater." Smart. Steady. Consistent. That was Aut Erickson.

Charlie Hodge

"One of the most dedicated, hardworking, quiet people. Nobody wanted to win more than Charlie did."

—Kent Douglas on Charlie Hodge

Charlie Hodge had the honor of being the first player selected by the California Seals at the expansion draft. The 5'6", 160-pound native of Lachine, Quebec, had a successful career with the Montreal Canadiens prior to joining the Seals. He won the Vezina Trophy as the league's top goalie twice, once in 1963-64 and then again in 1965-66 when he shared the honor with Gump Worsley. He was also an integral part of the Canadiens 1965 Stanley Cup winning team. Twice he was a postseason second-team all-star and three times he appeared in the NHL All-Star game.

Despite his success, Hodge was always fighting for a job in the six team NHL. Many coaches felt uncomfortable with Hodge's lack of size. First, he played behind the great Jacques Plante. Then Gump Worsley and, later, Rogie Vachon got the starting nod ahead of Hodge, who had to be frustrated with his lack of playing time.

Hodge described himself as both "excited and disappointed" when the Seals selected him in the expansion draft. The ex-Canadiens netminder was late in reporting to the Seals first training camp in Port Huron, Michigan, due to a contract dispute. Finally, with one week remaining before camp broke, Hodge signed on the dotted line. He remembered his first day of practice with the Seals. "Kent Douglas and Bob Baun were shooting on two goalies, one on each end. Then they switched. They shot pucks for 45 minutes and the rest of the guys skated between the blue lines for 45 minutes."

Hodge appreciated and enjoyed Bert Olmstead's coaching style. Like Olmstead, Charlie Hodge was a competitor. "I enjoyed Bert," Hodge said. "We played together in Montreal and I knew how badly he wanted to win."

Perhaps it was due to the fact that Hodge was always looking over his shoulder in the NHL, but the one trait most of his former teammates remembered about Charlie was that he was a worrier. Seals forward Gene Ubriaco recalled, "Charlie had a cast-iron stomach—he took a lot of 222's [a Canadian brand of aspirin]." Another teammate recalled that after every goal he gave up, Hodge seemed to be "calculating his goals against average."

Even in the minors, Hodge was a worrier. Billy Harris, who roomed with Hodge one season in the minors, remembered, "Once he woke up at 4 a.m. and was pacing back and forth across the room muttering to himself, 'I should have joined the Navy, I should have joined the Navy.' "

In 1967-68, the Seals inaugural season, Hodge was the starting goalie. He appeared in 58 games and finished with a 2.86 goals against average. He also had three shutouts, including the first-ever shutout in Seals history, a 6-0 win over the Minnesota North Stars in the club's second-ever game. Of the 15 games the Seals won that year, Hodge was the winning goalie in 13 of them, an astounding 86.7 percent of the team's victories. At the end of the season, Hodge was voted the Seals most valuable player.

Of course, it was not easy playing goal for the Seals in 1967-68. The team set an NHL record by scoring only 153 goals in 74 games, an average of 2.06 goals per game. The lack of offensive production left Hodge with little room for error. Hodge remembered the difference between playing for the Canadiens and the Seals. "In Montreal, we had to win. With the Seals, we had to stay alive."

On American Thanksgiving Day in November, Hodge recalled a practice held by Bert Olmstead. "Bert made a comment," Hodge remembered: " 'You guys are going to start acting like a regular working person; you would work the whole day.' So he called practice and we showered and he said we had to come back. So we came back at 1 p.m. on Thanksgiving Day and he made us just sit in the dressing room, doing nothing, until 4 p.m. We were waiting to go home for Thanksgiving dinner. We couldn't leave because Bert was in the next room."

Hodge's favorite game with the Seals came against his former team, the Canadiens. The diminutive netminder recalled, "We were playing Montreal in Oakland. John Ferguson and I were friends. John was being a smart aleck; he came by the front of the net and smacked me in the behind. He hit me so hard you could hear it throughout the building. Well, a penalty was called and I started laughing. Toe Blake chewed John out. The next time he came up against the glass, he stopped short. Anyway, we beat Montreal 2-1. I had the satisfaction of beating the best. I remember J.C. Tremblay congratulating me after the game."

Besides his tendency to worry, teammates remembered Hodge as a good teammate with a kind heart. Hodge even helped the people he was competing with for a job. "He was always great with me," said Gary Smith, who was Hodge's backup in 1967-68. "I used to get pissed and go to the airport and say I was quitting. Charlie would go and get me. He was great and tried to help me, which was gracious considering I was trying to take away his job."

Despite his success in 1967-68, the following year another young goaltender, Chris Worthy, was brought in and Hodge started the season in Vancouver in the WHL. Worthy had nothing but good things to say about Hodge. "I loved him," Worthy said. "I lived with him and his wife for the better part of a month. He tried to mentor me somewhat, but it was tough for him to do when I was challenging his job. I'm sorry I lead to the decline of his career. He was a first-class guy, a competitor and very smart and talented."

In addition to helping his fellow goaltenders, Hodge tried to help the skaters on the Seals as well. Rookie forward Mike Laughton remembered that Hodge would "stay out after practice with me and let me shoot. I really appreciated that. He was an immeasurable help."

While Hodge was considered tight with money by his teammates, they also all appreciated his generous spirit. "He wouldn't spend money in a restaurant," Ted Hampson recalled. "But he would invite you to his home and let you eat like a king."

When Fred Glover became coach of the Seals in 1968-69, Hodge's days as a starter were numbered. Glover explained his reasoning, saying, "Charlie figured that because of his experience, he should be the guy. That's not the way I thought. In my thinking, a smaller goaltender is always at a disadvantage. Smitty [Gary Smith] was big."

Of course, there was nothing Hodge could do to change his size. In his remaining two seasons with the Seals, Hodge appeared in only 28 games and never regained his starting position. Billy Harris explained, "[Hodge] was very talented, but on the small side. There is so much net behind a small goaltender and that gave the shooters a lot of confidence because they saw a lot of goal on either side."

When asked to describe his goaltending style, Hodge explained, "I was a stand-up goalie, not a butterfly goalie like today. I worked the angles because of my size. I tried to cut off as much of the net as possible."

Hodge maintains a self-deprecating sense of humor, even after all these years. He recalls that one time his wife picked him up after practice and asked him how he got so sunburned. Hodge replied, "That's from the red light going off so much."

Despite the many frustrations he had in Oakland, Hodge viewed his time in the Bay Area in a positive light. "It was an opportunity to get a full-time job in the NHL and you had to grab it," he said. "The family certainly enjoyed Oakland. We bought a house out there. The backyard was against a regional park and the kids loved it." Hodge also appreciated the fans in the Bay Area. "The fans were good fans—there just wasn't enough of them. We were invited out on Thanksgiving the first year we were there."

After playing three years with the Seals, Hodge was left unprotected in the 1970 expansion draft. The Vancouver Canucks grabbed him and Hodge again found himself with a brand-new team. "It wasn't really a surprise," Hodge said. "I was 36 and Gary Smith was about 27. Frank Selke Jr. told me Vancouver had showed an interest."

Hodge played one season with the Canucks and managed to have a winning record (15-13-5) despite playing for a first-year team that finished 22 games under .500. After his one season in Vancouver, Hodge hung up his pads and retired.

Today, Charlie Hodge is still active in hockey as a scout. He and his wife live in Langley, near Vancouver. They have three children and six grandchildren.

Perhaps Gene Ubriaco summed up Charlie Hodge best: "He was honest, sincere and smart. Pound for pound, he was a great goalie. He was an intelligent goalie, too." Hodge will forever hold the Seals club record for lowest goals against average in a season. He proved to be a little goalie with a big heart.

Alain Caron

"He had a hell of a shot. He didn't say very much. He could really fire the puck. You didn't see many slap shots like his."

—*Ron Harris on Alain (Boom-Boom) Caron*

By the time he joined the California Seals in 1967, 29-year-old Alain (Boom-Boom) Caron was already a legend in the minor leagues for his goal scoring. In 1962-63, the 5'9" 170-pound native of Dolbeau, Quebec, had scored 61 goals in 54 games with the St. Louis Braves of the EPHL. He finished the season playing for the Charlotte Checkers of the EHL and added another 10 goals in just 13 games. The following year, Caron led the CHL with 77 goals and 125 points. The 77 goals is a CHL record that stands to this day. In 1964-65, Caron had an off year for the Braves, scoring "only" 46 goals. Despite his impressive goal totals, Caron had never played a game in the NHL before the Seals selected him from the Black Hawks organization in the expansion draft. According to the Seals first media guide, "The Seals caused quite a stir at the draft when they announced, 'California selects Boom-Boom [pause]—Caron.' " Bernie Geoffrion was safe.

While Caron possessed one of the game's best slap shots, he needed time to release the shot—time he was not afforded in the NHL. Seals goalie Gary Smith recalled that Caron "had a big shot and was a very funny guy. He was a great minor leaguer but he struggled in the NHL. He had a great shot but no wheels, so in the NHL he had trouble getting his shot off." While Smith felt that Caron's skating was holding him back at the NHL level, teammate Billy Harris felt it was the quality of NHL goalies. "He scored a lot of goals in the minor leagues," Harris said of Caron. "When he stepped up to the NHL, he found it more difficult to score against the Halls, Plantes and Sawchuks."

In 58 games with the Seals in 1967-68, Caron scored nine goals and added 13 assists. His main role was as a power-play specialist and three of his nine goals came with the man advantage.

Defenseman Tracy Pratt recalled that Caron "had a great shot. His stick was no longer than a golf wedge. He could hit the top corner of the net from the red line consistently in practice. He was a great power-play specialist." Tom Thurlby recalled that "the fans would never notice Alain, but then you'd pick up the paper the next day and he scored two goals." Off the ice, Caron was a bit of a loner. Wally Boyer described Caron as "a quiet French kid who kept to himself."

After the Seals first season was over, Caron was traded to the Canadiens along with Wally Boyer and two future No. 1 draft picks for Norm Ferguson and Stan Fuller. Caron played two games for the Canadiens, spending the rest of the season with the Houston Apollos of the CHL, where he promptly scored 38 goals. He never played in another NHL game in his career. Caron remained a consistent 30-goal scorer in the minors until the birth of the WHA in 1972-73, when he joined the Quebec Nordiques. Caron had two straight seasons of more than 30 goals for Quebec before injuries and age started to slow him down. He split his final WHA season between the Nordiques and the ill-fated Michigan Stags/Baltimore Blades franchise. Caron perhaps saved his most spectacular season for his last one as an active player. In 1975-76, Caron played for the Beauce Jaros of the NAHL. Playing on a line with former Seals center Joe Hardy, Caron led the league with 78 goals in 73 games.

After his playing career ended, Boom-Boom worked as a representative of Labatt Breweries. Caron had a heart attack and passed away on December 16, 1986, at the age of 48.

Gerry Odrowski fondly recalled his days playing with Alain Caron. "He had one of the harder shots in the NHL and was a good right winger. He could put the puck in the net and he was fun, too." That was Alain Caron, the Seals "Boom-Boom."

Ron Harris

"A strong man and a super guy. He was steady and hard-nosed and didn't back down from anybody."

—Gerry Odrowski on Ron Harris

Ron Harris was never a big goal scorer in the National Hockey League, but he had three things that served him well during his eight-plus years in the NHL: strength, dedication and versatility.

The Verdun, Quebec, native was one of the first hockey players to use weights as part of his training regimen. Back in the '60s, weight training was simply unheard of in hockey. Harris stood only 5'9", 175 pounds, but was built solid as a rock. Former teammate Kent Douglas recalled that Harris used to put weights on his wrists, ankles and shin pads to build up his strength before practice. The result was that Harris became one of the strongest men in the league. Mike Laughton recalled an incident where Harris picked up Bob Woytowich of the Penguins and "threw him from the red line to the blue line. He was the strongest guy in hockey."

In addition to his strength, Harris had versatility. "I wanted to play a lot and gave 100 percent," Harris recalled. "I was always on the checking line or playing defense. I could play every position except goaltender." With the Seals, Harris was primarily used at forward, but occasionally saw time on the blue line. He also killed penalties.

Tracy Pratt remembered Harris as "a good teammate. He brought a lot to the table with his toughness," Pratt said. "He was a checking player who played steady up and down the wing."

The road to the NHL was not easy for Ron Harris. He was originally property of the Detroit Red Wings but appeared in only four NHL games for Detroit before being sent to the Boston organization. The Bruins assigned Harris to the San Francisco Seals of the WHL, where he played for two seasons. Harris was familiar with the Bay Area and expected to be selected by the Seals in the expansion draft.

"We had good and vibrant fans in San Francisco," Harris remembered. "We used to get 10,000 fans for WHL games. A lot of the San Francisco fans were mad because the team went to Oakland. If they built a new rink in San Francisco, the team would probably still be in the Bay Area today."

Harris liked the Seals home in Oakland, but recalled a small quirk about it. "The Oakland Coliseum was a nice rink," Harris continued. "The only problem was it had too many windows. You had to close the drapes or the ice would melt. It was hot as hell in there."

Harris started his Seals career with a flourish, scoring the game-winning goal in California's first-ever NHL game—a 5-1 win over the Flyers at the Oakland Coliseum Arena. It was Harris's most memorable game as a member of the Seals. He finished the 1967-68 season with four goals, 10 points and 60 penalty minutes in 54 games.

Off the ice, Harris was considered fairly quiet by many of his teammates. On one occasion, Harris sent a message to Jim Lingel, a club vice president, without saying a word. "Sometimes during my lunch hour, I would skate at the arena," Lingel recalled. "The team practice was at 1 p.m., so I would finish by then and the trainer let me use the shower. Well, one time I wasn't paying attention to the time and the players started to come out onto the ice for practice. I was skating behind the net and Ron Harris let a shot go that whizzed by my head. I took that as a message: get the hell off the ice."

The low point for Harris had to be the Bill Masterton incident that took place in Minneapolis on January 13, 1968. Harris was on the ice at the time; in fact, he was one of the players who hit Masterton as he crossed the blue line into the Oakland zone. Although nobody ever said the hit was dirty or outside of the rules, you could tell the incident still bothered Harris, even more than 30 years later. When asked about it, he paused for a moment and his voice got very quiet.

"Masterton got squashed between a couple of players and fell," Ron Harris said slowly. "He hit his head on the ice. We realized right away it was bad."

Billy Harris was also on the ice at the time. "Bill Masterton dumped the puck into our end. I came back to our end to get the puck and tried to figure out what the commotion was," Harris recalled. "My back was to the puck and he was on the ice. It looked like a bad concussion. He was on the ice for about 10 minutes and then they took him off on a stretcher. It was a clean check; they didn't call a penalty. They say Bill Masterton dumped the puck in and put his head down."

Wally Boyer added, "He came across the blue line and I moved out of the way. Ronnie Harris hit him when his head was down and he fell backwards onto the ice. It was not a dirty check; it was just the way he fell that caused the injury. We didn't know at the time, we just sat around and looked. They took him off the ice and I think he died two days later. It was sad; he was a nice guy."

Rookie defenseman Tracy Pratt also remembered the incident. "I was on the ice at that time. It was a funny type of play," Pratt said. "Larry Cahan and I were playing together. Ron Harris was back checking and Masterton was on the left wing skating down our right side. I went to stand him up, Ronnie came from behind and Masterton's skates came up from under him and his head hit the ice. We were kind of in awe. We saw some blood but the blood was thick and clotty, which would indicate that he had suffered a concussion the night before. I heard that he had a concussion the night before when the North Stars played Boston. We were waving our arms for the trainers and Masterton was not moving. He might have been convulsing. The doctors came out and took him off the ice. Ronnie Harris felt very bad about it but there was no way to really prevent it."

Masterton slipped into a coma and never regained consciousness. He died a few days later. To this day, it remains the only on-ice fatality in the history of the National Hockey League. The Masterton Trophy, awarded annually by the NHL for dedication to hockey, was named after Masterton.

For Harris, the best part about playing for the Seals was finally making it in the NHL. Still, he was not terribly upset when he was traded after the 1967-68 season to the Red Wings along with Bob Baun in exchange for Gary Jarrett, Doug Roberts, Howie Young and Chris Worthy.

"I felt pretty good about the trade because I knew a lot of people in the Red Wings organization since I played there for a few years," Harris recalled. "I knew that the traveling wouldn't be so bad anymore and that I was going back to an Original Six team. I would also be playing with Gordie Howe."

Harris spent four seasons in Detroit before being selected by the Atlanta Flames in the 1972-73 expansion draft. Later that season, he was traded to the New York Rangers. Harris spent more than three seasons in New York and played an integral role in the Rangers 1974 playoff win over Montreal. After scoring only two goals all season, Harris added three clutch goals in the playoffs, including two overtime winners. He also continued to stick up for his teammates and play both forward and defense when needed. An injury suffered early in the 1975-76 season ended Harris's playing career. He finished with 20 goals and 111 points in 474 NHL contests.

Today, Harris is still active in hockey as a scout. He lives in Beaconsfield, Quebec, when he's not out on the road working. Harris and his wife have four sons.

Wally Boyer did a good job of summing up what Ron Harris meant to the Seals that first season in Oakland: "He was a tough little guy and a good solid player. He hit everything that moved."

Tracy Pratt

"He was a big, strong individual, and very aggressive. He was good with the puck and had a good sense of humor."

—*Charlie Burns on Tracy Pratt*

Tracy Pratt grew up around hockey. His father, Babe Pratt, was a Hall of Fame defenseman for the Rangers and the Maple Leafs. In fact, Pratt was born in New York City when his father played for the Rangers. He grew up in British Columbia and recalls being a rink rat at the Queens Park Arena in New Westminster.

"I remember as a kid that I wouldn't let anybody touch my equipment," Pratt recalled. "I used to clean it thoroughly every Sunday. I took pride in my stuff. The game has to be learned and respected."

After three years in the CPHL and one in the WHL, Pratt was not confident that he had a future in the big leagues. But then expansion came along and Pratt was thrilled to get a chance. "I wasn't good enough to play in the Original Six," admitted Pratt. "I got my chance with expansion. It was the summer of 1967 and I was on my honeymoon. I was coming out of Wenatchee, Washington, and picked up the morning paper to see if I was drafted by an expansion team. I was elated. The first thing you think of is that you love to play the game. Also, money comes into it. The minimum wage back then was $7,500. I think the year of expansion it went up to $12,500, which is what I made. I thought to myself, 'Wow, here we go. Getting to the dance, the NHL, holy smokes!' There weren't too many players in the NHL from British Columbia back then."

Pratt started the 1967-68 season with the Seals top minor league affiliate, the Vancouver Canucks of the WHL. He was called up for the first time in late December. "When I first got called up to the

Seals from Vancouver, I was on my way to San Diego with the Canucks to play the Gulls," Pratt said. "When we landed in San Diego, I was told to head over to join the Seals. I had no coat and only two pair of underwear packed for the trip to San Diego. My first game as a Seal? It was played at the Forum in Montreal. I froze up there."

In his first game, Pratt quickly discovered the difference between the minors and the NHL. "I remember sitting on the bench waiting for my first shift, and Bert Olmstead said, 'Pratt, you're up next,' about midway through the first period. I said to him, 'Are you kidding me? Bert, they're moving so fast.' Olmstead replied, 'That's your job, to slow them down.' "

Pratt earned a reputation with the Seals as a tough guy on the ice and a guy who had a good time off it. He stood 6 feet tall and, at 185, was a big man for a hockey player in 1968. He used his size to add some much-needed toughness to the first-year expansion club.

Pratt developed a love-hate relationship with the coaching duo of Bert Olmstead and assistant Gordie Fashoway. "I got along pretty well with Bert and Gordie," remembered Pratt. "I was picked the most-improved player on the team that year. I brought brawn to the club. I handled myself pretty good. I was loquacious and brought some respectability to the team. I stuck up for my smaller teammates."

Pratt said that Bert Olmstead had "an exceptional hockey mind" but "he was not a humanitarian," while Fashoway was "a nice guy, but a follower. As Olmstead went, Fashoway went."

Pratt recalled one time that Fashoway tried to set him up. "The team was flying into St. Louis. Gordie said to me, 'You'll be a good boy, right, rookie? You know that there's a new Playboy club in St. Louis, but you won't miss curfew, will you, rookie?' I told him, 'I'm good, I won't miss curfew.' When he came to do the bed check, I was in bed drinking a Coke. He didn't look very carefully, I guess, because I was wearing my clothes under the covers. Five minutes later, I was out the door."

Another time, Pratt ran into Bert Olmstead in a bar when he was out with an injury. The rookie defenseman had had a little too much to drink. "We had practice the next day and Bert told me if I could drink, I could practice," Pratt said, chuckling. "He had me doing one-on-one drills for about two hours. I was puking on the ice. You just lose your edge."

Although Olmstead was respected and feared, his players did occasionally have some fun at their coach's expense. Pratt remembered one incident in particular. "My rookie season, they still had the old-style benches that were not attached to the floor. One game, Bert was particularly tough on us and Larry Cahan told us all to stand up at the same time when we scored a goal. Well, it was, like, 'One … two … three … up,' and the bench flew back and hit Bert in the shin. He was cursing us from behind the bench: 'You sons of bitches, you did that on purpose.' "

Pratt's favorite memory of his rookie season was a game against the Rangers in which he battled toe-to-toe with New York tough guy Reg Fleming. "We were going at it for almost 15 minutes," claimed Pratt. "We started in front of the goal and ended up at center ice. After the game, the Hells Angels were all around my car to congratulate me. I even met Sonny Barger, the founder of the Hells Angels."

Pratt only played 34 games with the Seals in 1967-68. He did not score a goal, but had five assists and a team-leading 90 penalty minutes. In addition, he was given an award as the Most Improved Player on the club. Despite the accolades, he started the 1968-69 season back in Vancouver, as new coach Fred Glover did not think as highly of Pratt as Olmstead did. On January 30, 1969, Pratt, George Swarbrick and Bryan Watson were traded to the Penguins for Earl Ingarfield, Gene Ubriaco and Dick Mattiussi. Pratt eventually realized the promise he showed in his rookie season and went on to play 580 NHL games in his career for the Seals, Penguins, Sabres, Canucks, Rockies and Maple Leafs. His career totals were 17 goals, 97 assists and 1,026 penalty minutes.

Pratt is certain that he cost himself some longevity as a hockey player. "I was always anti-management," he admitted. "I was never a diplomat. It cost me several years off my career."

Pratt summed up his career, saying, "I was a journeyman player that brought an awful lot of try every night. I had an all-out effort. Sometimes, going all-out, you don't accomplish anything. You'd come back to the bench exhausted. Experience teaches you. I was also tough in front of my own net."

Today, Pratt owns a bar called The Cabaret in Langley, British Columbia, about 40 minutes east of Vancouver. The ex-defenseman is also involved in property management. Clearly, he enjoys telling stories about his playing days and maintains his sense of humor. One thing has changed, however. Pratt says he has not had a drink in more than 15 years.

Mike Laughton called Pratt "a tough customer. He always stood up and was accounted for. He was carefree off the ice but all business on it." Gary Smith added, "Pratt was a good, stay-at-home defenseman and a very tough guy."

I'm sure his father would have been proud.

Tom Thurlby

"A steady defenseman. He was never flashy but he got the job done. A good man to have on your team, reliable."

—Gerry Odrowski on Tom Thurlby

Tom Thurlby's NHL career was both brief and unexpected. Thurlby was a steady defenseman from Kingston, Ontario, who played six seasons with the San Francisco Seals of the WHL, from 1962-1967. When the Seals future NHL owners took control of the WHL club in 1966, Thurlby's NHL rights were transferred to the Bay Area franchise.

In training camp, the veteran minor leaguer remembers that he was not in the big club's plans. "We had a combined camp with minor leaguers and the NHL team," Thurlby remembered. "It was nothing out of the ordinary. I regret that none of the minor leaguers had the chance to play in exhibition games. They had their guys already picked. The minor leaguers like me were there to get other guys in shape."

Thurlby started the season with the Seals top minor league affiliate in Vancouver. When the Seals started to go south in the standings, Bert Olmstead called for help and, much to his surprise, Thurlby was among the call-ups. "I never thought I would get the chance," Thurlby admitted. "I was pretty thrilled."

The jump from the WHL to the NHL was not an easy one for Thurlby. "The level of play was completely different," the 5'10", 175-pound defenseman recalled. "I was a defenseman but they put me up on the forward line. It was a big change. I coped for a while. There was a lot of pressure there because of where we were in the standings."

There were other differences, Thurlby noticed, between his six seasons playing minor league hockey in the Bay Area and his partial season playing in the NHL with the Seals. "It was much more serious in the NHL," the converted defenseman recalled. "You were scared to make a mistake or do anything wrong."

Off the ice, there was a different atmosphere as well. "There were very few fans in Oakland," Thurlby said. "We had more fans at the Cow Palace in San Francisco. The Oakland Coliseum was built in a slum area. People refused to go to Oakland. The fan level dropped the last year, when we played in Oakland in the WHL. It was a far trip over the Bay Bridge."

Still, Thurlby has fond memories of the hockey fans in the Bay Area. "The fans that were there were good fans," Thurlby recalled. "There were many old hands from the Cow Palace. I'm still in touch with some of the fans from the WHL days. But it was tough when Montreal would come to town and we had 5,000 to 6,000 people there in a brand-new building. The owners were always pushing tickets. Many of the tickets were freebies."

When asked how he would describe himself as a hockey player, Thurlby was modest. "I was a worker, a digger," Thurlby said. "There was not any part of my game where my talent stuck out. I was not even an all-star in the minors. I was a journeyman."

Still, Thurlby's brief NHL career had its highlights. His most memorable game was played in the Maple Leaf Gardens and involved a personal memory. "We played in Toronto. My father and brother came to see me play. I had a good game. At the time, my dad was very sick with cancer, but he got to see me play at the Maple Leaf Gardens."

Thurlby scored one goal in his 20-game NHL career. It came on November 25, 1967, at the Oakland Coliseum against the Pittsburgh Penguins. Thurlby beat Penguin netminder Hank Bassen for the first goal in a 2-2 tie. He still has the puck packed away as a keepsake. In 20 games with the Seals, Tom Thurlby finished with one goal and three assists, and received four penalty minutes.

Ex-teammate Ron Harris remembered Thurlby as a quiet man. "He never said too much," Harris said, "and he did his job. He worked hard and was a nice guy off the ice."

Thurlby remained in the minors for two more seasons before playing senior hockey in Ontario. He eventually settled down in Kingston with his wife and two children, and took a job with the local Parks Department. Today, he is retired and remains in Kingston.

Perhaps Tom Thurlby never did become a big star in the NHL, but he realized the dream of millions of young Canadians by making it to the big time. "The best part," Thurlby admitted, "was just being there, just playing in the NHL." It's something nobody can ever take away from Tom Thurlby.

Bill Hicke

"A dynamic player, he could really score. He shot left-handed and played the right wing, one of the first off-wingers. He was very smart and knew when to break and how to finish. He had lots of charisma."

—Ted Hampson on Bill Hicke

From a young age, Bill Hicke was ticketed to hockey stardom. He made the Regina Pats at age 15 and his club played in the Memorial Cup Finals three of the four years he was there. In his first professional season with the Rochester Americans in 1958-59, Hicke scored 41 goals and 97 points. The Montreal Canadiens owned Hicke's rights and their scouts touted him as the successor to Rocket Richard.

While Hicke never developed into the goal-scorer Richard was, he became a respectable NHL wing, reaching the 20-goal mark in his third NHL season. During the 1964-65 season the Canadiens traded Hicke to the Rangers, where he figured he'd get more ice time; that never really materialized. Hicke remembered the difference between Montreal and New York. "The Montreal organization was and is the classiest organization in the game. They look after their alumni. Going from Montreal to New York was like going from heaven to hell. I wasn't ready for New York. Ninety-nine percent of the people there didn't know a hockey stick from a broomstick, although it was nice going to Madison Square Garden because the fans there were really fanatics and Emile Francis was a class act."

One thing that seemed to always hold Hicke back was his health. He suffered from a mysterious respiratory ailment that sapped his strength and prevented him from taking long shifts. This hampered his progress with both the Habs and the Rangers and contributed to the Rangers decision to leave him unprotected in the expansion draft.

Hicke recalled his reaction to being selected by the Seals. "I was working for Molson in the summer of 1967 in Saskatchewan when I found out I had been picked in the expansion draft. I had asked Emile [Francis] to put me on the list. I had never been to Oakland before, but it was probably the best four years of my life, off-ice especially. I went sailing every day and there was plenty of sunshine. For older players like me [Hicke was 29 at the time], it gave us a new lease on life and extended your career."

In his first season in Oakland, Hicke led the team in goal scoring with 21 tallies. He was the club's only 20-goal scorer that year. Hicke also set a club record with 12 power-play goals for the season.

The Seals inaugural season was a tough one for Hicke. "The first year we had a good team," Hicke remembered. "We drafted well and were picked to finish first in the new division, but the chemistry just wasn't there between the coach and the players. We never jelled like we should have."

Hicke remembered the tough time the team had with Coach Bert Olmstead. "Bert was very respected when he played for Montreal," Hicke said. "He worked very hard and made the NHL through grit and determination and power. When he became coach, he expected that of everybody. He took very little for excuses. Once, in practice, I told Bert I didn't feel well. He said, 'Get back in there, you piss-pot and work.' Well, during that practice, I collapsed and was rushed to the hospital. I think Bert just expected too much from the guys we had. We were an expansion team, not the Montreal Canadiens. If he had coached two or three years, I think he could have handled it better and gotten through to the guys more."

Despite the difficult season, Hicke still had the respect of his teammates. Ron Harris called Hicke "one of our leaders on the ice. He was our goal scorer. It's too bad he got sick."

Hicke's respiratory problems flared up again during the 1967-68 season, so the Seals came up with a different solution: they sent him to Hawaii. Hicke missed 22 games that first season as a result of his breathing problems and the team's Hawaiian remedy. Despite that, he still led the club in goals. While the trip was a nice break for Hicke, it did not cure his illness.

Later on, Hicke became one of the first NHL players to develop a skin problem, known informally as "gunk," that became an epidemic in the league by the mid-'70s. Bert Marshall remembered that Hicke "had a really bad case. It got so bad that he couldn't even practice."

Still, looking back, Bill Hicke had many pleasant memories of Oakland. Hicke recalled his impression of what the students at Berkeley were thinking when the Seals showed up for practice in their jackets and ties. "We must have looked like the FBI to those people, walking in the rink in our suits and ties while all that free-love stuff was going on," he said.

In 1968-69, Fred Glover took over as coach of the Seals. Hicke had his finest NHL season, finishing with 25 goals and 61 points in 67 games. "Fred was an excellent choice," Hicke said. "Frank Selke Jr. chose him because he played with a lot of the players in the AHL. Fred Glover was kind of the Bert Olmstead of the AHL. He was a very hard worker but he was more calm than Bert and brought in a different atmosphere. We made two or three good trades before our second year and it paid off, as we finished in second place that year. I played on a line with Ted Hampson and Gary Jarrett."

Jarrett remembered his former linemate fondly. "He was a good player—one of the best offensive right wingers I played with," Jarrett said. "He was robust and full of self-confidence (and) he was an aggressive skater. He had that fire in his eyes when he got in on the goalie from the blue line. He was a bit like Rocket Richard in that regard, although I'm not saying he was as good as Richard."

Hicke also had the pleasure of playing on the same team as his younger brother Ernie when Ernie joined the Seals for the 1970-71 season. "I never expected it to happen," Bill Hicke admitted. "Ernie was 10 years younger than me. I left home when I was 19 and Ernie was about 9. He was a good skater, had a good shot and was tough. I was overjoyed when he joined the team."

Ernie recalled, "It was a great opportunity to play with him. I looked up to him for all those years. He was at the end of his career but it was a thrill to play with him. We had our run-ins, as brothers always do, but it was great."

Bill Hicke was also known as a carefree person off the ice. It was a bit upsetting to him that the team "had practically no notoriety off the ice." He recalled one incident that would have played out very differently today than it did in 1970. "I remember one time I was pulled over by a police officer after going out drinking with the guys," Hicke said. "He gets out of the car and asks me what I'm doing here with Saskatchewan plates on my car. I explained to him who I was and that I played hockey for the Seals and he let me go. When I got home, Ernie, who lived in the same complex at the time, told me that the same policeman had pulled him over, too, and told him that he'd heard all this stuff before. Today, something like that would have been all over the papers and we would have been arrested."

Hicke's flamboyant style and carefree attitude did rub some of his teammates the wrong way, especially when his skills started to fade a bit. Doug Roberts remembered that Hicke was "highly skilled, but he didn't take care of himself. I thought he was playing out the string. He was not consistent, especially on the road. He had a lot of skill and we all looked up to him from his days with Montreal."

Rookie Tracy Pratt said that Hicke was "an individualist who *thought* he was a prolific goal scorer." But even Pratt admitted that Hicke "scored clutch goals and provided leadership."

When Charlie Finley bought the Seals before the 1970-71 season, Hicke saw some things he never thought he'd see. When the Seals were given white skates to wear, Hicke realized the team had a problem. "Charlie Finley was innovative and white shoes worked in baseball," Hicke remembered. "But what Finley didn't realize was that in hockey, the puck touches the skates and the skates get blackened. By the end of the game, they'd look a mess. Poor Barry Keast, our trainer, had to be detoxed because he was putting so much paint on those things. In Detroit, fans whistled at us and called us 'pretty boys.' Then Finley gave us green and gold skates. They looked like mustard seed on your feet." It was just too much for an old-timer like Bill Hicke.

Hicke also recalled what it was like when Charlie O. showed up to watch the Seals. "I think he must have taken acting lessons because he screamed and talked loudly to everybody. He talked to us like we were deaf," Hicke said. "I remember one time he attended a road game in Boston, which we won, and he treated us like we were the best team ever and that this was the greatest victory ever. He yelled at me, 'Hicke, you're in charge.' Then he gave each of us $300 to buy new suits and alligator shoes. Tony the Tailor made $30 suits back then, so we all went there. Finley was quite a character."

After the 1970-71 season, Hicke found out what happened to players when they argued with Charlie Finley about money. "Finley called me up and said he was disappointed in the team and with me and he wanted me to sign for the same amount as the year before," Hicke remembered. "He said he'd put a $10,000 minor league clause in there. I told him I wouldn't sign that and I took him to arbitration, and I won. We had the arbitration hearings in the York Hotel in Toronto. I told Mr. Finley that I won and was told to go back to Oshawa [where the Seals had training camp] and meet Charlie there. Well, I went to eat lunch and when I got back to the front desk, there was a message from the GM saying I had been traded to Pittsburgh."

Hicke split the 1971-72 season between Pittsburgh and two minor league teams before spending the 1972-73 season with the Alberta Oilers of the WHA. It was his last season as an active player.

After retiring, Hicke later became co-owner of the Regina Pats for ten years but sold them in 1996. Soon thereafter, Hicke retired and he and his wife split their time between Regina and Scottsdale, Arizona. Hicke later developed cancer and fought a valiant seven year battle with the disease. Despite the fact that he was often in pain, he never stopped smiling. Hicke passed away on July 18, 2005 at the age of 67. After Hicke's death, Brent Parker, the current GM of the Regina Pats remarked, "He was a player, a coach, a general manager and an owner but most of all he was a first-class person who touched everyone around him."

Bill Hicke is third on the Seals all-time leading scoring list, with 180 points in 262 games played with the team. He is second all-time in franchise history in goals and second in assists. He is also in the Seals all-time top 10 in games played and penalty minutes.

Earl Ingarfield had this to say about Bill Hicke: "He is one of my best friends in hockey and a real character. He was a skilled player and a good person off the ice." For the expansion Seals, Hicke was their first real goal-scoring threat and their most colorful offensive player. He left his mark on the memories of hockey fans in the Bay Area.

Mike Laughton

"My figure-skating center iceman. He fooled a lot of people. He got in front of the net and nobody could move him."

—Seals Coach Fred Glover on Mike Laughton

Mike Laughton grew up in Nelson, British Columbia, with a dream to play in the NHL. He started figure skating at the age of 2, but was a latecomer to professional hockey. "I grew up a Maple Leafs fan," Laughton recalled. "They were on television and the radio with Foster Hewitt." As fate would have it, Laughton would become property of the Leafs and spent the 1966-67 season with the Leafs Victoria affiliate in the WHL. After one season in Victoria, the Seals selected Laughton in the expansion draft in June 1967.

Laughton was excited about his opportunity. "It was hard to break in with the six-team league," he said. "A lot of good players never got the chance. Expansion gave me a real chance to play in the NHL. I remember I was helping a contractor build a building. A newspaper guy said I had been drafted by the Seals [in the expansion draft]. I asked for the rest of the day off."

The big 6'2", 185-pound Laughton started the season with the Seals farm club in Vancouver, but was called up in midseason, when the Seals were having trouble scoring goals. In his first season, Laughton was just happy to be there. "It was pretty classy to deal with NHL players," Laughton remembered. "Bert Olmstead was a Hall of Famer and he was running the show. He knew all the ins and outs of the league. Olmstead was an excellent coach. I was young and he pushed me. I liked to play fairly tough and he liked it that way. He was a real help to me. He was a tough coach. We did a lot of extra skating under Bert. I also remember negotiating my first contract with Bert. In those days, we didn't have agents. Larry Cahan told me to ask for a certain amount. When I did, I saw the veins in Bert's neck start to pop out. He was, like, 'This is what you're getting,' and I signed for that amount. It was very different in those days."

In his first season, Laughton lacked confidence and was a little bit intimidated about being in the NHL. "I was a young guy and I wanted to do well," Laughton admitted. "I never wanted to have a bad practice. I was playing with guys who had done so well at this level and I found it tough sometimes to keep on an even plateau in games and in practice. I wouldn't even break in a new pair of skates in practice except at an optional practice because I didn't want it to affect my play."

Laughton remembered a time during his first season when the Seals were playing against Detroit. "I was about to face off against Alex Delvecchio," Laughton recalled. "He said to me, 'You'll never touch the puck, rookie,' and I never did."

Laughton finished the 1967-68 season with two goals and six assists in 35 games with the Seals. Despite his background in figure skating, most scouts felt that it was Laughton's skating that was preventing him from thriving at the NHL level. Charlie Burns, who was Laughton's teammate that season, remembered the center as "a big strong guy with limited skating skills who could put the puck in the net." Gary Smith also noted Laughton's lack of skating skills. "He was a plugger. He was a figure skater at one point, but he struggled when he skated and was anything but smooth." Bob Baun recalled Laughton as a "good, hard-nosed kid." The potential was clearly there, but Laughton needed some work.

The young center took the criticism to heart and set out to improve his skating and his overall game. Although Laughton started the 1968-69 season with the Seals farm team, the Cleveland Barons of the AHL, he was called up to the Seals on November 27, 1968, and remained with the big club for the rest of the year. The Seals brass noticed a difference in Laughton's play. General Manager Frank Selke told Fran Tuckwiler of *The San Jose Mercury News* that "Mike worked hard all summer and has matured as an athlete. He works hard all the time now. He isn't fancy and he has to work to force the play. When he does, he is very effective."

Laughton also learned to use his size to dig the puck out of the corners, run opposing players over and create havoc in front of the opposing team's goalie. Laughton enjoyed his best NHL season with the Seals in 1968-69. Despite playing in only 53 games, he scored 20 goals and 23 assists. He was named the Seals Most Improved Player for his efforts.

Gene Ubriaco, who came to the Seals during the 1968-69 season, remembered Laughton as a "hard worker and a good checker. He was big and strong and young, and willing to work."

For most of the season, Laughton centered a line between left wing Gary Jarrett and right wing Bill Hicke. The line's success was a major part of the Seals turnaround that season, improving from last in the NHL the year before to second in the West Division in 1968-69. Jarrett recalled that Laughton was "a good player and a hard worker. He was … a real grinder."

It was during the 1968-69 season that Laughton earned his nickname, "The King." Laughton was one of the first NHL players to wear a helmet. Fred Glover recalled, "Half the time, the helmet was over his eyes." His teammates felt that the helmet he wore looked more like a crown than proper hockey headgear and that's how The King was born.

When asked to describe himself on the ice, Laughton said, "I worked hard. I had an attitude and desire that was second to none. When I lined up, I felt nobody was going to beat me. I played tough, although I was not a big fighter. I was hard to move in front of the net and got most of my goals as 'garbage goals.' I was not a gifted scorer. I think forechecking was my forte. I was always playing against the other team's big line."

Laughton's most memorable game came on February 5, 1969, when the Seals defeated the visiting Canadiens 5-1. "I scored on Gumper [Gump Worsley] and we won the game. I got a few points that night," Laughton recalled. "A reporter from Montreal asked me if that was the best game I ever played. I said that everything just clicked. Some games, you play well and nothing goes in, sometimes everything you touch ends up in the net. That may have been my best game pointwise, but I think there were other games I played better in."

One game in which everything Laughton touched ended up in the net was January 25, 1970, at the Met Center in Bloomington, Minnesota. Laughton recorded his first and only NHL hat trick, against North Stars goalie Fern Rivard, in a 4-1 Seals victory.

As a whole, the 1969-70 season was a bit of a disappointment for Laughton and for the Seals. Laughton's offensive totals fell to 16 goals and 35 points, despite playing all 76 games. Oakland barely made the playoffs, falling to fourth place in the West Division. Still, he proved he belonged in the NHL as a regular. "Things were topsy-turvy … all year long and I don't know why," Laughton said. "We got to the playoffs but there was nothing there." The Penguins swept the Seals in four games.

The 1970-71 season was a difficult one for Laughton. He tore ligaments in his knee during training camp. The knee required surgery and Laughton started the season on the injured list. Even when he came back, he appeared in just 25 games for the Seals and scored only one goal. "After I hurt my knee, they had no use for me," Laughton said. "Montreal picked me up the next year and I was captain of their farm team in Nova Scotia, which won the AHL title."

Another former Seals player, Tony Featherstone, was Laughton's teammate with the Voyageurs. Featherstone recalled Laughton's sense of humor. "On the road, we all had to travel with jackets and ties. In Baltimore, I was mugged one time," Featherstone said. "I didn't have a tie on and Mike said, 'Oh, I see the mugger took your tie, too.' "

After a year in the AHL, Laughton returned to big-league hockey in 1972-73 with the New York Raiders of the WHA. He topped the 20-goal mark in 1973-74, playing for the same franchise—now renamed as the New York Golden Blades and, later, the New Jersey Knights. Still, the knee gave him trouble and, after one more year in the WHA with San Diego, he took a year off. He returned to play two years in the WHL before retiring from hockey after the 1977-78 season.

Laughton has fond memories of his time in Oakland and of the Seals fans. "They were tremendous," Laughton said. "They always say there were not too many fans, but I remember plenty of nights that were sold out. I always threw pucks in the stand after practice for the kids, and the kids were always waiting for me." Laughton also said the fans could be unpredictable: He recalled one game in Oakland when an overzealous member of the Hells Angels threw a chair at John McKenzie of the Bruins.

Today, Laughton lives in his hometown of Nelson, British Columbia, and owns his own business. He was previously in sporting goods, but he sold that and now owns a furniture business. He and was wife have two sons and one grandson. He still plays senior hockey whenever he can.

Norm Ferguson perhaps summed up Mike Laughton's tenure with the Seals aptly when he said, "Mike worked hard every night. He was a sort of unsung hero. He got more from his ability than anyone else on the team." That's how The King got his crown.

Gerry Ehman

"He was an old pro who played up and down his wing. His man almost never scored. He had a great shot and he gave it all he had. He hit a lot of posts when he was with us because he would cut things so fine—that's how much talent he had. He was an excellent professional and a great guy."

—Gary Smith on Gerry Ehman

When Gerry Ehman arrived in Oakland in October 1967, he was already 35 years old and a veteran of the AHL and the NHL. The 6', 190-pound native of Cudworth, Saskatchewan, made his first NHL appearance during the 1957-58 season with the Boston Bruins. He appeared in only one game and scored a goal. Ehman spent the rest of that season with the AHL's Springfield Indians and enjoyed a 40-goal season. After a brief stopover with the Detroit Red Wings, Ehman settled down in the Maple Leafs organization. He spent 2½ seasons with the Leafs and the rest of his time with the Rochester Americans of the AHL. Even when Ehman spent most of the regular season in the minors, the Leafs would often call him up for the playoffs. In the 1959 playoffs, "Tex" Ehman scored 13 points in 12 games for Toronto. He was also on the 1964 Stanley Cup winning team for the Maple Leafs, appearing in nine playoff games after spending most of the regular season in Rochester. Throughout the '60s, Ehman was a regular 30-35 goal scorer and 80-plus-points-per-season player for the Americans. Although he was not chosen in the expansion draft, the Seals acquired Ehman from the Maple Leafs on October 3, 1967, just eight days before their first regular-season game, in exchange for Bryan Hextall and J.P. Parise.

Ehman made the most of his opportunity to return to regular NHL duty. In the Seals inaugural season, Ehman was second on the club, with 19 goals, and led all Seals players with 44 points. Being a veteran, Ehman had the instant respect of his peers. He was a strong offensive player and he was among the better defensive players on the club.

Rookie Tracy Pratt called Ehman "a great, honest hockey player and a two-way specialist. He was a real student of the game and very reliable. If he said he had his man, he had him locked up. Gerry was a very well-coached player." Ron Harris remembered that Ehman was "quiet. He didn't say much but when he spoke, you listened."

Ehman also had the honor of scoring the very first hat trick in Seals history. On January 7, 1968, Tex tallied three times against Terry Sawchuk in a 6-0 Seals victory over the Los Angeles Kings at the Oakland Coliseum. Charlie Hodge earned a shutout in that game. It was the only hat trick scored by a member of the Seals during the club's first season in the NHL. Ehman was finally getting a chance to play in the NHL and he showed he belonged there. Bob Baun remarked that Ehman "had the talent to play in the NHL sooner than he did," but he was not really given a chance until late in his career.

In 1968-69, the Seals improved to second place in the West Division and Ehman had the finest offensive season of his NHL career. He finished with 21 goals and 45 points, breaking the 20-goal barrier for the first time in the bigs. He also added a pair of goals and four points in the Seals seven-game playoff series against the Kings.

Many teammates recall the wily veteran as helpful during practice and games. Gerry Odrowski remembered that Ehman "couldn't do enough to help you out. He was serious about hockey and wanted to win." Gary Jarrett felt that Ehman "had a calming effect on the team."

Defenseman Bert Marshall recalled Ehman's unique skating style. "I could actually hear him coming down the ice, the way he skated—you could hear him chopping down the ice. He was a good skater but not light on his feet. He was a good friend and a great player."

While Marshall recalled his skating style, Ted Hampson remembered Ehman's effective shot. "He could really shoot the puck. He had a great snapshot," Hampson said. "He tried to teach me to shoot for years, but I could never learn."

Ehman turned 37 during the 1969-70 season, but he remained in excellent shape, appearing in all 76 games for Oakland. He scored 11 goals and had 30 points. The Seals often used Ehman to defend against the opposition's top offensive threat, including players such as Black Hawks sniper Bobby Hull. Ehman also set an example for younger, less-experienced players by his consistent work ethic. Fellow veteran Harry Howell said that Ehman "worked hard every game and was a settling influence on younger players." Rookie Tony Featherstone simply recalled that Ehman "just did everything the right way."

Ehman rebounded in his final NHL season in 1970-71 to score 18 goals and 36 points. Again, he appeared in all of the Seals 78 games. It must have been difficult for a serious and dedicated hockey player like Ehman to adjust to the green and gold skates supplied by Charlie Finley and to the instability that surrounded the club that year. After the 1970-71 season, Ehman retired as an active player. He finished his NHL career with 96 goals and 214 points in 429 games.

Ehman remained in hockey both in a management capacity and as a scout. He was general manager of the St. Louis Blues for one season before working alongside ex-teammate Earl Ingarfield and ex-Seals vice president Bill Torrey for the New York Islanders. Ehman scouted predominantly in Western Canada for the Islanders for more than 20 years. Today, Ehman is retired and living in Saskatoon, Saskatchewan.

Ehman has left his mark on the Seals franchise record book. In addition to recording the first hat trick in club history, Ehman ranks second in franchise history in games played (297), fourth all-time in points (155), fourth all-time in goals (69) and recorded the fifth most assists in Seals history (86). More than all the records he earned in the AHL and in the NHL, Ehman earned the respect of his teammates. Dennis Hextall, who only a teammate of Gerry Ehman's in his final NHL season, summed up Tex by saying, "He worked hard. He had a lot of experience and wanted to win. I had a lot of respect for that man."

John Brenneman

" 'The Road Runner.' He could really skate. He had great speed and he worked hard. He always had a smile on his face."

—*Karl Ingarfield on John Brenneman*

John Brenneman was very fast on his skates. His skating speed and skills earned him a job in the NHL, but his lack of scoring ability never really allowed him to keep it. By the time Brenneman arrived in Oakland in January 1968, the 25-year-old was already a journeyman player. The 5'10", 175-pound left wing from Fort Erie, Ontario, got his first taste of NHL action during a 17-game stint with the Chicago Black Hawks in 1964-65. Later that season, Brenneman was traded to the Rangers as part of a seven-player deal that included Camille Henry and Wayne Hillman. He completed the 1964-65 season with the Rangers, scoring three goals and adding three assists in 22 games. In 1965-66, Brenneman remained in the Rangers organization, playing 11 games for New York and splitting the rest of the season between Rangers affiliates in Baltimore and Minnesota. He was claimed by the Maple Leafs in the intraleague draft prior to the 1966-67 season and played for both the Leafs and the Rochester Americans of the AHL. In 41 games with Toronto, Brenneman managed six goals and 10 points.

When expansion came, Brenneman was not protected by the Leafs and was selected by the St. Louis Blues. About a week into the season, before he even appeared in a game for St. Louis, Brenneman was traded to the Red Wings, where he added two assists in nine games before being sent down to the Fort Worth Wings of the CHL. Finally, Brenneman was traded to the Seals along with Ted Hampson and Bert Marshall in exchange for Kent Douglas on January 9, 1968.

After joining the Seals, Brenneman caught fire, scoring in three consecutive games. He scored his first goal as a member of the Seals in Minnesota on January 13, 1968, the game in which Bill Masterton was fatally injured. The following night, the Seals hosted the Flyers and Brenneman had a goal and two assists in a 6-3 loss. He then scored the only Oakland goal in a 1-1 tie with Pittsburgh on January 17. In 31 games with the Seals in 1967-68, Brenneman scored 10 goals (a career high) and added eight assists. He tended to be a streaky goal scorer. Twice he scored two goals in a game, including his best offensive game with Oakland, a two-goal, one-assist effort against the Penguins in Oakland on March 27, 1968.

Brenneman did impress some of his teammates during his brief but explosive first half season in Oakland. "He was a young guy full of vim and vigor," recalled Aut Erickson. "I thought he would be a great hockey player, but I don't know why he didn't turn out to be one."

Charlie Burns remembered that Brenneman was "solid and came to play every night. He always gave 100 percent." Gerry Odrowski called Brenneman "a good winger. He was fast and good with the puck."

If, on the ice, Brenneman was noted for his skating skills, off the ice he was known as fun-loving and an active bachelor. Wally Boyer remembered that the speedy Brenneman "loved to go out with the girls" during his stay in Oakland. Gary Smith also related that Brenneman earned the nickname "Tire Tycoon" among some of his teammates because he invested some money in a tire company.

Brenneman remained with the Seals at the beginning of the 1968-69 season under new coach Fred Glover. Glover appreciated Brenneman's skating skills, but had a problem with what he felt was Glover's lack of physical play. "He could skate like nobody could skate," Glover said. "He always had his feet going in the corners, but he was always afraid somebody would hit him. He had a slight build and body checking was not his thing."

Brenneman played 21 games for the Seals in 1968-69 and scored one goal and two assists before being demoted to the Cleveland Barons of the AHL. Seals captain Ted Hampson recalled that, "at times, Brenneman could score spectacular goals. He could really skate but he couldn't convert that to long-term results."

Brenneman was discouraged about playing in the minors again and he retired after the 1968-69 season. After spending a year out of hockey, he returned the following season and played for the Dayton Gems of the IHL. Although the Seals still owned Brenneman's NHL rights, they never called him up to Oakland again. After one year in Dayton, Brenneman retired again. His final NHL totals included 21 goals and 40 points in 152 games.

Although Brenneman could excite a crowd with his fast skating and brilliant moves, he was never able to score consistently on an NHL level. His hands could never catch up to his skates. Bryan Watson remembered that "he came highly touted, but it never worked out for him." Instead, Brenneman moved like a shooting star, briefly illuminating the Seals and then disappearing forever into retirement.

Ted Hampson

"Anybody would be happy to have Ted Hampson, a good guy and a hard worker. You might call him an overachiever but I don't think so; he had a big heart. I could use him on the power play, penalty kill and double shift him and he never said a word. He was a good leader, too."

—Seals Coach Fred Glover on Ted Hampson

If you were to choose a player to personify the Oakland Seals in the first four years of their existence, Ted Hampson would be as good a choice as anybody. Hampson stands second on the Seals all-time scoring list with 184 points, just one point behind all-time leader Joey Johnston. Hampson holds the all-time Seals records for assists (123), is sixth all time in goals scored and holds the single-season record for points scored in a season. He served as captain of the Seals from 1968-69 until he left the team during the 1970-71 season, and represented the Seals in the NHL All-Star game in 1969. But more than that, Hampson was the heart and soul of the early Seals clubs. Norm Ferguson described Hampson as "the hardest worker on the team, a great leader and an inspiration." Many of his teammates shared that view.

Ted Hampson broke into the NHL in 1959-60 with the Toronto Maple Leafs. He later played for the Rangers and Red Wings, mostly in a defensive or checking role. The biggest question surrounding Hampson was his size. The native of Togo, Saskatchewan, stood 5'8" and weighed 165 pounds. Despite his lack of physical size, nobody questioned his desire. "He was about 5'6" in stature but 6'5" in heart," former teammate Gary Croteau said of Hampson. Dennis Hextall, who played both with and against Hampson during his career, added, "He never quit. You could knock him down, but he'd get right up and go faster."

Hampson was traded to the Seals midway through the 1967-68 season, along with John Brenneman and Bert Marshall for Kent Douglas. "I was extremely disappointed," Hampson said of his reaction to the trade that sent him to Oakland. "I really liked playing in Detroit. The Red Wings were struggling because Doug Barkley had lost sight in one eye. They couldn't win on the road and they lacked a big presence. Sid Abel was the GM and coach. He called me up from Pittsburgh to kill penalties because Val Fonteyne and Bryan Watson were injured. I played a game in Boston and scored two goals. I was never sent back to the Hornets. I played on a line with Gordie Howe and Alex Delvecchio for 20 games. Dean Prentice, Andy Bathgate and Floyd Smith were among my other linemates. I had a good year and didn't expect to be traded."

When Hampson arrived in Oakland, he found the atmosphere very serious. The team was losing and, as Hampson described it, "pretty businesslike." He also had a few surprises. "The Seals were in tremendous shape when I arrived," Hampson recalled. "I thought I was in great shape in Detroit, but everyone in Oakland was in better shape than I was." Bert Olmstead's skating drills had apparently accomplished their goal.

Hampson also received surprising information about one of his future linemates. "Bert Olmstead told me that I'd have a right winger that I'd like as soon as he came back from Hawaii," Hampson said. "That turned out to be Bill Hicke, who was down there recovering from asthma. I couldn't believe they sent him to Hawaii."

Upon his return from Hawaii, Hicke and Hampson made a good combination. Olmstead gave Hampson more ice time than he ever got in New York or Detroit and Hampson finished the year with 27 points in 34 games for the Seals. "I enjoyed playing for Bert Olmstead," Hampson said. "He was a no-nonsense type of guy."

On March 13, 1968, at the Oakland Coliseum, Hampson got his first chance to show his former team what he could do. Hampson beat Roger Crozier of the Red Wings on a breakaway to give the Seals a 2-0 first-period lead. Unfortunately, Detroit scored four goals in the third period and downed the Seals 4-2.

The 1968-69 season was the most successful season in Seals history and the most successful on a statistical level for Ted Hampson. The club finished in second place in the West Division with 69 points, and Hampson had the most prolific offensive season of any member of the Seals. He totaled 26 goals, 49 assists and 75 points. For most of that season, Hampson was put on a line with veterans Gerry Ehman and Earl Ingarfield. The trio worked well together. Hampson recalled that Ingarfield gave him his nickname "The Tic" "because I latched on and never let go," Hampson said.

At the end of the season, Hampson was named the winner of the Bill Masterton Trophy as "the NHL player who best exemplifies the qualities of perseverance, sportsmanship and dedication to hockey." It was the only NHL postseason award a Seals player would earn in the team's nine-year history.

"We had a successful season," Hampson said of the 1968-69 Seals. "We won a lot of games against the Original Six. Things were positive. We may have gotten up for games against the Original Six more than we did for games against expansion teams." The Seals were 14-18-4 against the established teams that season while finishing 15-18-7 against their supposedly weaker expansion brethren.

Another fond memory for Hampson was the final game of the 1968-69 season against the Minnesota North Stars. Hampson recorded four assists in that game, but that's not what made the game memorable for him. "Earl Ingarfield and I tried to set up Gerry Ehman to get him his 20th goal," Hampson recalled. "He just wouldn't shoot the puck. We kept giving him the puck and he just wouldn't shoot. Finally, he got his 20th." It was the first time in his NHL career the 36-year-old Ehman went over the 20-goal mark.

Prior to the 1968-69 season, Ted Hampson was voted the second captain in Seals history, replacing the recently traded Bob Baun. "It was a great thrill for me," Hampson said. "I had been the captain of my teams a couple of places before. I was an old-style captain. I didn't say anything in the dressing room. I tried to give my best effort on the ice and hopefully get others to do likewise. I tried to bring the players together off the ice and not to exclude anybody. Today's captains are more vocal and demanding in the dressing room. For me, it was play together and play to win."

The younger players on the Seals seemed to really respect Hampson's leadership qualities. Rookie Ron Stackhouse saw that Hampson was "a veteran who was not resting on his laurels," while young Ernie Hicke remembered that "Ted helped me as captain when I was a rookie. He was a team player and he wanted to win more than anybody on the team. He was always there when I needed him."

After the 1968-69 season, the Seals met the Kings in the playoffs. Although the Seals held home-ice advantage and a 3-2 lead in the series, they were ousted in seven games. "It was a good series," Hampson recalled. "I think we had a letdown. Maybe Los Angeles was better than we thought they were. I remember Eddie Joyal played pretty well for the Kings. The loss may have had something to do with the changes that were made the following season. I never played on a line with Ehman and Ingarfield again."

Hampson fell off to a more pedestrian 17 goals and 52 points the following year when the Seals made the playoffs for the final time, finishing in fourth place in the West Division. It was good enough for Hampson to lead the team in scoring for a second straight year. Once again, the Seals were eliminated in the first round of the playoffs, this time by the Pittsburgh Penguins in a four-game sweep.

When asked to describe himself as a hockey player, Hampson replied, "Skating was easy for me. I came into pro hockey as a high scorer but I had to learn to be a checker in the NHL. In Oakland, I got the chance to play more offensively, take face-offs, kill penalties and did my share of checking. I liked to play with guys who liked to share the puck. Team play was important to me and the Seals had a lot of it. I gave it my best try to win every game."

Ted Hampson also recalled an amazing moment that Bruins defenseman Bobby Orr created at the Oakland Coliseum. "We were killing a penalty and Orr was out on the power play for Boston," Hampson recalled. "He's on right defense and I was on left wing, killing the penalty. We shot the puck out of our own end [and Orr picked it up]. Orr lost his glove at the red line. He went back, circled the net, came up-ice and we started retreating. He looked toward my side of the ice and worked his way back to the glove. He picked up his glove and never lost the puck."

In 1970-71, the Seals entered new territory when Charles O. Finley took over ownership of the club. Before the season was over, Finley had dismissed General Manager Frank Selke Jr. and his replacement, Bill Torrey. "Bill Torrey and Frank Selke were class people," Hampson said. "Things started to fall apart when Torrey and Selke left. It weighed on the players." After a while, playing for Charlie Finley took its toll on the Seals. "He was like a used-car salesman and we felt like the cars," Hampson said of the atmosphere that permeated the club that year.

Things didn't start out that badly under Finley, but they soon soured. "He was all gung ho when he came in," Hampson claimed. "We went into Boston and won. We pooled our money and bought a trophy to commemorate the victory. We had it inscribed to Mr. Finley for his first victory. It took a month for that trophy to be engraved and to get out to Oakland. By that time, we didn't like Mr. Finley so much anymore. We didn't know what to do with that trophy. Someone suggested we throw it in the garbage. We gave it to trainer Barry Keast and he put it in a closet somewhere. For all I know, it could still be there."

Later in the 1970-71 season, Hampson found out what happened when you disappointed Charlie Finley. "We were on the road and on our way to Minnesota," Hampson remembered. "We were in the Chicago airport and I was paged to pick up the courtesy phone. I thought it was a joke and I told the guys I wasn't going to fall for it. They said it was probably Mr. Finley calling. I said maybe it was and maybe it wasn't. I figured if it was Finley, he wanted to talk to me about the coach [Fred Glover]. I didn't want to say anything bad about the coach, so I didn't pick up the phone. One week later, I was traded to Minnesota."

On March 7, 1971, Hampson and defenseman Wayne Muloin were sent to the North Stars in exchange for Tommy Williams and Dick Redmond. Hampson played one more season with the North Stars before signing with the Minnesota Fighting Saints of the WHA. He retired as an active player after the 1975-76 season, although he did briefly return to active duty with the Oklahoma City Blazers of the CHL a few years later.

Hampson has remained involved in hockey as a scout. Until the 2002-03 season, he served as the director of amateur scouting for the St. Louis Blues. Hampson and his wife have three sons. His son Gordie played hockey at the University of Michigan, in the CHL and had a brief NHL stint with the Calgary Flames in 1982-83.

Two former linemates did a great job of summing up what Ted Hampson meant to the Seals. Bill Hicke described Hampson as "a real 3-D player: dedication, determination and desire. He gave 110 percent every night." Meanwhile, Earl Ingarfield called Hampson "the ultimate player for determination; a team player who gave his all every shift. He didn't know when or how to quit." Determination, hustle, effort, desire. Ted Hampson possessed all these qualities on the ice and they made him the heart and soul of the Seals.

Coach Fred Glover

"He was all heart. He did anything to win—anything. He'd put his face in front of a shot! He was a marked man; *everyone* took a shot at him. Freddie carried so much inside. He was one tough SOB, and I think he did a pretty good job of motivating the players."

—*Frank Sanchez on Seals coach Fred Glover*

The Seals played nine seasons in the National Hockey League. Former Cleveland Barons star Fred Glover coached the Seals for part of six of those seasons and also served stints as the team's general manager and executive vice president in charge of hockey operations. The Seals reached the playoffs only twice in their history, both times under Glover's guidance. Conversely, the team also had some of their worst years with Glover behind the bench. Through all the difficulties the Seals faced in their front office, Glover held the ship together and exuded his love of the game of hockey.

Fred Glover was a minor league superstar in the days when there were only six teams and 120 jobs in the NHL. Glover played 18 years of professional hockey, 15 of them with the AHL's Cleveland Barons. The 5'9", 160-pound native of Oakville, Ontario, retired as a player after the 1967-68 season, holding the AHL career record for games played, goals, points, assists, and penalty minutes. Glover was the AHL's MVP three times and was a seven-time AHL postseason All-Star. Marshall Johnston recalled Glover's playing reputation in the AHL: "He had been a hard-nosed player, a battler. He was a real successful AHL scorer with a Ted Lindsay type of reputation."

Despite his heroics in the AHL, Glover was never able to consistently break into the NHL. He appeared in only 92 NHL games in his career, with Chicago and Detroit, last appearing in an NHL contest in 1952-53. "I guess they figured I was too small and too slow for the NHL," Glover said. "I think I could have made it. After all, there is nothing more important than being able to put the puck in the net."

Glover spent his last six seasons in Cleveland as a player/coach and was successful at it. The Barons made the playoffs five of his six years as player/coach, and won the AHL championship once and lost in the finals another time. Glover cited Ott Heller and Bun Cook as two coaches who influenced him the most. "Ott Heller had energy like I couldn't believe," Glover said. "He was not a young man but he could outskate and 'out-energy' his players at any time. Bun Cook could teach you things you didn't know existed. He never really got upset about anything either. He was always calm, cool and collected and he kept his players like that."

According to Seals legend, General Manager Frank Selke Jr. hired Glover in April of 1968 after an interview on a park bench in St. Louis. Glover was sure Selke's father had a hand in his hiring. "When I was in Cleveland, we used to get some players from Montreal. Frank Selke Sr. had been GM in Montreal," Glover recalled. "I think Frank Selke Sr. recommended me to his son. When I spoke to him years later, he apologized to me for recommending me, but he didn't have to."

When Fred Glover took over as coach of the Seals, the team was at rock bottom. They finished their inaugural season under Bert Olmstead and Gordie Fashoway with the league's worst record, winning only 15 of 74 games. "The first season of expansion was hard on everyone except St. Louis," Glover recalled. "The team was under pressure all the time. The coached had expected the players to act the same as in the pre-expansion days. That wasn't always possible." The Seals became tense under Olmstead and felt constant pressure not to make mistakes. Fred Glover set out to change that.

"Fred had a fantastic reputation in the American Hockey League not only as a competitor, but a handler of men," Frank Selke Jr. said when asked why he hired Glover as coach. "We need that kind of man to put us back on our feet, to give those players we had a badly needed shot of confidence."

Glover responded to the challenge and his players responded to Glover's coaching. The Seals improved 22 points in the standings and enjoyed their most successful season ever in 1968-69, finishing in second place in the West Division with 69 points. Still, attendance was sparse and the team's future in the Bay Area was in doubt.

"Freddie brought a new atmosphere to the club," remembered broadcaster Tim Ryan. "He had an understanding of what we were up against and the team's financial problems were acknowledged. He knew he had to be fan-friendly. He got the players into the community. He was good with the media. It wasn't his personality, but he did it." Glover always made time for hockey fans and did his best to promote the team.

Praise for the new coach came from every corner of the organization that year. "It is truly amazing the difference one man made in our club," Selke exclaimed. Bill Torrey added that Glover's "competitiveness and intensity were his strengths. He was very good with young players and it was our young players who made a big impact on our team that year." *Oakland Tribune* beat writer Spence Conley also saw the difference Glover brought to the team. "Fred Glover was a better coach than

Bert Olmstead for this team. He was closer in age to the players and he had a better understanding of hockey at that time. Fred Glover had an entirely different viewpoint."

For helping turn the Seals around, Glover was named the NHL coach of the year by *The Hockey News* for 1968-69 (the Jack Adams Award for NHL coach of the year was not created until 1973-74). Glover felt a close camaraderie with his players that year. "The players were in the same situation I was," he recalled. "We had to prove something. I told them to play as best they could and they did."

The Seals opened the playoffs against the fourth-place Los Angeles Kings. Attendance remained sparse. The Seals led he best-of-seven series 3-2 but lost the final two games of the series, including the seventh game at home. Glover felt that was a big turning point in the team's off-ice fortunes. "If we would have won that seventh game, it would have made a hell of a difference as far as attendance [was concerned]. In those days, there were few chances to be on television. It was just Montreal, Toronto, the Rangers and St. Louis. People just couldn't see what the game was all about."

In 1969-70, the Seals again made the playoffs, although they fell back to fourth place and did not play as well as the previous year. The cast was mostly the same, but the Seals second-year coach sensed something was missing. "They had a taste going from last place to second and thought things would happen for them that didn't," Glover said about his team. "They thought their skills alone could get them there."

In the playoffs that year, the Seals were swept by the Penguins in a first-round series that Fred Glover simply called "a disaster." "Penguin rookie Michel Briere was a piece of work. He practically beat us by himself."

There were instances where Glover's reputation as a tough player caused trouble for the Seals. Selke recalled, "We played an exhibition game in Buffalo against the AHL Bisons—a team that Fred Glover had played against during his great AHL career at Cleveland. He was thoroughly despised by Bison fans and they gave him and the team a hard time of it all night. There was a lot of tough talk around the bench area and some pretty vicious heckling. It was a rousing game—lots of contact and lots to yell about. At game's end the crowd surged behind the team as it headed for the dressing room. Some brave souls even tried to get at Glover. In the pushing, shoving and yelling—the crowd so densely packed—fortunately no one could reach Freddie. I was about 20 feet or more behind him—at 5'7" not having much luck getting to the room. Right behind me was Spence Conley, *The Oakland Tribune* hockey writer and a former Denver University football star. Some punk in front of me recognized who I was and started yelling at me. Conley whistled a right arm over my shoulder—smacked the guy flush and then pushed me through the crowd to the room. Whether I was ever in danger is a question, but Spence's one-punch victory solved the issue very dramatically." The Seals, Glover and Selke made it out of Buffalo unscathed.

During his first two seasons as coach of the Seals, Fred Glover kept his team together despite the ever-present financial problems the team was facing. "The first couple of years, there was always something going on, but it was always explained to the players," Glover recalled. "We'd have a meeting and talk about what was happening. The players knew what they were up against. We told them it wouldn't be easy but we told them if we made the fans take notice, we could start something."

Glover also stuck up for the Seals organization and fans. Tim Burke of *The Montreal Gazette* reported that after a home game, a Seals fan got into a fight with another fan who was heckling the last-place Seals. Fred Glover rushed in to protect the Seals fan. Glover said, "The last thing we're going to do is let anything happen to one of our season-ticket holders. We have so few, we can't afford to."

When Charlie Finley took over ownership of the Seals before the 1970-71 season, many Seals employees had problems with the controversial new owner, but not Fred Glover. "Working for him was a piece of cake," Glover exclaimed of Finley. "I can't say enough about the man. I talked to him differently than other people did. He knew when I said no, it was no. I told him off twice. He respected people who weren't afraid to stand up to him. Finley was famous for chewing people out, but only if you didn't stand up to him."

Whatever Glover did, it worked. He survived the 1970-71 season, despite a last-place finish due in part to numerous injuries to key players. Mysteriously, Glover was fired just three games into the 1971-72 season with a record of 0-1-2. Garry Young, the general manager, took responsibility for firing Glover. "I believe in playing younger players in all circumstances. That's the only way they could learn," Glover said. "I put young defensemen on ice late in a game with the game tied. Sometimes we lost. I guess he didn't like that." Regardless of the reason, Glover was gone. He finished the 1971-72 season coaching the Los Angeles Kings. The following year, he was working as general manager for the Cleveland Crusaders of the WHA when Charles Finley called and invited him back. "I wasn't too keen on how [the Crusaders] were running things. Charlie Finley was looking for me. He told me he wanted me back as executive vice president and take over on top of everything, except salaries," Glover recalled. Glover quickly took over as coach after Gary Young was fired just 12 games into the season. Glover remained as coach as long as Charlie Finley owned the team, until February of 1974.

By the time he returned to coach the Seals, the team had been gutted of much of its talent, courtesy of the WHA. "Players were jumping from Oakland left and right," Glover recalled. "Players who could have stayed in the NHL went elsewhere because they were lured away. The talent had already been thinned by the original expansion."

Gradually, Glover started to lose the team. Some things Glover did that were overlooked when the team was relatively successful became problems when the team sank to the depths of the NHL standings. One issue was a nagging suspicion that Glover still wanted to play in the NHL. "Unfortunately, Freddie still wanted to play and was obsessed with the thought that somehow he could regain his playing rights and finally make it to the NHL," recalled Selke. "He practiced regularly in full equipment—acceptable for a time, but eventually becoming a problem. He was still feisty and the players were reluctant to mix it up with him. Often, they'd let him score in practice to give his ego a boost."

In fact, the players got to the point that when they wanted to end practice early, they knew what to do. "The other goalies and I figured out that if Fred scored, the practice was over," Gary Smith remembered. "If he didn't score, we could keep going for two hours or more. Eventually, we sort of figured out when to let him score." Two-hour practices became very rare in Oakland.

The losing took its toll on the Seals coach. Team broadcaster Joe Starkey remembered Glover as "moody" and recalled that he started "drinking heavily" as the losses piled up. Perhaps Glover was a little too intense and competitive for his own good. "Freddie carried so much inside," Frank Sanchez recalled. "He was one tough SOB."

Despite the losing and the lack of talent, Glover never stopped caring about his players, the fans or the game of hockey. Tom Massey, who worked for the Seals after meeting Charlie Finley in an airport, lived with Glover after being hired. "Fred Glover was a real gentleman," Massey said. "He studied the game hard and was a first-class man. He was very nice to me even though I knew nothing about hockey." Trainer Barry Keast called Glover "a man of his word, a super guy to work with. He was quiet off the ice but vocal on the ice." Off the ice, team comptroller Larry Marshall described Glover as "the sweetest guy you'd want to meet." He recalled how important hockey was to Glover. "Before he could walk, he was in skates," Marshall said.

Despite the tough times on the ice, Glover recalled some lighter moments. "I was in Chicago for a meeting with Charlie Finley," Glover said. "We were going to a restaurant, Garry Young, Mr. Finley, Mr. Finley's lawyer, Charlie's secretary and me. There was a cab in front of my hotel waiting for us. Just then, a newspaper delivery truck was there and the driver wanted Mr. Finley to meet his brother. We all went to the restaurant in the back of the delivery truck. His secretary said it wasn't the first time Mr. Finley did that."

Despite all the difficulties he faced—coaching an expansion team, low attendance, a team constantly on the verge of being moved and/or sold and a talent poor roster—Fred Glover persevered. He led the Seals to their greatest successes and kept them together through their toughest times. He genuinely loved coaching in Oakland despite facing so many problems. "The fans we had were great and I coached for two good guys in Barry van Gerbig and Charlie Finley," said Glover when asked what he recalled most fondly about coaching the Seals. He also loved his players. "I don't think I ever had a guy who played for me that I don't like," he said in retrospect. Today, it seems Glover's players respected him more after they were finished playing. "I liked Freddie," Ivan Boldirev said. "He was a good guy and a tough cookie."

The day the Seals were sold to the NHL, in February 1974, Glover resigned as coach of the Seals for the last time. He never coached again in the NHL. Glover settled down in Hayward, California, where he lived until his death from cancer in 2001.

Oakland Tribune beat writer John Porter summed up Fred Glover by saying, "Fred Glover deserved respect. He played the game himself with great intensity. He was put in a position to coach when the money the players were making was going off the scale. Suddenly, players that couldn't hold his jock were making more money than he ever saw. Freddie was also very loyal to Charlie Finely and visa versa."

Barry van Gerbig added, "Fred Glover had respect among the players on the team and he brought us respectability." Ticket manager Sam Russo added, "Freddie was a pretty decent coach considering what he had to work with in Oakland." There was no question, he loved and respected the game of hockey and always gave his all.

Earl Ingarfield

"He was one talented player—a finesse player who was always meticulous about his personal attire and how he played. He handled the puck with confidence and was a great passer."

—*Chris Worthy on Earl Ingarfield*

Earl Ingarfield was 34 years old when he arrived in Oakland late in the 1968-69 season. The 5'10", 165-pound native of Lethbridge, Alberta, broke into the NHL with the New York Rangers during the 1958-59 season. In nine seasons with the Broadway Blueshirts, Ingarfield topped the 20-goal mark twice and added stability to a Rangers club that often struggled to win hockey games. When Emile Francis started to improve the Rangers in the mid-'60s, Ingarfield was an important part of the equation.

Ingarfield was made available in the 1967 expansion draft and was selected by the Penguins in the first round that non-goaltenders could be selected. After a season and a half in Pittsburgh, Ingarfield was sent to the Seals along with Gene Ubriaco and Dick Mattiussi in exchange for Bryan Watson, George Swarbrick and Tracy Pratt on January 30, 1969. "I was happy to go," Ingarfield recalled. "Pittsburgh wasn't going too well. I had suffered a knee injury my first year there and wasn't playing as well as I wanted to. I knew I was near the tail end of my career. What better place to finish my career than in sunny California?"

There were some adjustments that had to be made for Ingarfield when he arrived on the West Coast. The first was travel. "We had 12- to 18-day road trips," Ingarfield said. "If you lost a few games, it was difficult to recover." The other big adjustment was playing in a building that was half empty. "When you go to the rink, it's bad if there's a quietness in the building. We seemed to play better against better teams when there were more fans at the games," Ingarfield remembered. "We tried to raise our level of play."

Ingarfield finished the 1968-69 season on fire. Due to injuries to a number of Seals players, Ingarfield played all three forward positions at various times. He also played the point on the power play. In 26 games with Oakland, Ingarfield managed eight goals and 23 points.

"He has stepped in and done an outstanding job in every place we've needed him," Seals coach Fred Glover said at the time. "That's because he's a first-class professional with top NHL ability." To Glover, the acquisition of Ingarfield was one of the keys to the Seals second-place finish in 1968-69.

"There was something different about him and something special," Glover said. "He changed our team the second half of the 1968-69 season."

Ingarfield's torrid offensive pace continued into the postseason. In the seven-game series with the Kings, the ex-Ranger led the Seals with four goals and 10 points. One of his goals was a game winner. Ingarfield is the Seals all-time leading scorer in the postseason with 11 points in 11 games.

Ingarfield described himself on the ice by saying, "I had good hockey sense and saw the ice well. I could skate fairly well and I guess I scored my share of goals. I put the team before individual goals. I respected my teammates and I'd like to think they respected me. I could check and play defense as well as offense. I was happy to play in the NHL."

For his teammates, especially the younger players, Ingarfield provided leadership. "Earl came to us very late in my first year there," said rookie Norm Ferguson. "He was very experienced and one of the best players we had. He was on the downside of his career, but he was a big help for us." Defenseman Dick Mattiussi recalled that Ingarfield was "an older player who tried to help people out all the time." Gerry Odrowski remembered that Ingarfield "was always joking off the ice. On the ice, he was serious."

In 1969-70, Ingarfield played in only 54 games due to injury. Despite missing roughly one third of the season, he still scored 20 goals for the final time in his career. Ingarfield finished the year with 21 goals and 45 points. He led the Seals with nine power-play goals and had the best shooting percentage and plus-minus rating on the team.

In the playoffs, the Penguins eliminated the Seals in four straight games. Ingarfield was very disappointed by the outcome. "Having played for Pittsburgh, I wanted to do well against them," he admitted.

In 1970-71, injuries really took their toll on the 36-year-old. He appeared in only 49 games and managed five goals and a paltry 13 points for the season. Even his teammates noticed that Ingarfield was slowing down. Ron Stackhouse, who was a rookie in Ingarfield's final season in Oakland, recalled him as "a heck of a nice guy who was at the end of his career. I think the organization had unrealistic expectations of him at that time." Brian Perry said that, for Ingarfield, "sometimes the energy was there and sometimes it wasn't."

Ingarfield himself realized the end was near. "I had injured my knee in Pittsburgh," Ingarfield said. "I hurt my wrist and my kneecap in Oakland. I was taking cortisone shots every two weeks just to be able to play. It was time." After the 1970-71 season, Ingarfield retired as an active player. He finished his NHL career with 179 goals and 405 points in 746 games.

Ingarfield did play one season for the Seals when Charlie Finley owned the club. When asked about his reaction to the team's green and yellow—and then white—skates, Ingarfield said succinctly, "I was not impressed." He didn't find Finley himself a distraction to the team. "He was not around a lot," Ingarfield said.

After retiring as a player, Ingarfield remained active in hockey. Today, he is still scouting part-time for the New York Islanders. He was a scout for the Islanders during their glory days when they won four Stanley Cups and served as interim coach of the Islanders for the second half of their inaugural season in the NHL, 1972-73. Ingarfield and his wife live in Lethbridge, and they have three children and two grandchildren. His son Earl Ingarfield Jr. also played professional hockey, including some stints with the Atlanta and Calgary Flames and the Detroit Red Wings in the early '80s.

Gary Smith described what Ingarfield was like as a teammate. "He was a real professional and a great guy. He brought a lot of experience to the team and took care of the younger players." That was Earl Ingarfield, a true professional.

Bryan Watson

"He was the ultimate team man. He gave you all he had and everything he did he did for the team. Even in practice, he would go all-out and take a run at his own teammates sometimes."

—Gary Smith on Bryan Watson

Nobody who played with or against Bryan (Bugsy) Watson would soon forget him. Although he scored only 17 goals in 878 career NHL games, Watson made a name for himself by hurling all of his 5'9", 170-pound frame at the opposition. "I came to play every night and would do whatever it took to win," Watson said when asked to describe himself on the ice. "I strongly believed in my ability and I loved hockey."

Watson grew up a Montreal Canadiens fan and his favorite player was Doug Harvey. "I met [Harvey when I was] a 12- or 13-year-old boy," Watson recalled. "I collected those Bee Hive cards and I remember telling him that I didn't get his card and it was one of the most disappointing things from my childhood."

Despite being offered some college scholarships, Watson chose junior hockey instead. "With six teams, college wasn't a way back to the NHL," he said. Watson's first coach in juniors was Scotty Bowman.

Watson was always a positive thinker. "I never thought I wouldn't play in the NHL," he said. "That's the way I think. Whenever I was traded, I never thought that the team I was leaving gave up on me, it's just that the team I'm going to wants me."

Watson's positive thinking and determination helped make his dreams a reality. He made his NHL debut with the Canadiens in 1963-64, then moved on to the Red Wings in 1965-66 and was sent back to the Habs in 1967-68. It was in Detroit that Watson earned the nickname Bugsy. "Gordie Howe and Andy Bathgate gave me that nickname," Watson said proudly. "I used to drive them crazy."

On June 10, 1968, the Seals acquired Watson and an undisclosed amount of cash from the Canadiens in exchange for the Seals first-round pick in the 1972 draft. This was the first of many first-round picks the Seals would deal away. With this pick, the Canadiens drafted goaltender Michel (Bunny) Larocque. Watson viewed his trade to Oakland as a great opportunity. "I knew I wouldn't stay in Montreal," Watson said. "I played in Houston [in the CPHL] and had a great year. I knew in Oakland I would play defense. I had played for Fred Glover and I knew Carol Vadnais from Houston. I was excited."

Many former Seals sensed a great deal of tension between Watson and coach Fred Glover, although both of the parties involved denied it. One ex-Seals player said that practice wasn't over until Watson and Glover got into a little scrum. Still, looking back, both men had praise for each other. "He was a hard-nosed player and expected everyone to play that way," Watson said of his former coach. "He was very strong and very fair." Glover, meanwhile, admired Watson's team ethic and courage. "He would have gone through a wall for you," Glover said.

After playing in hockey-mad Montreal, Watson had a big adjustment coming to the Bay Area. "We had a beautiful rink, but the problem was coming to a city where you are the low team on the totem pole in pro sports," Watson said. "Montreal was geared to win. Out West, it was difficult to stay focused on hockey when the rink is half full and nobody knows anything about the sport. The few fans we had were true blue." Watson eventually learned to love Northern California. For him, the best part of playing for the Seals was that he "got to play in the NHL, and to realize what a fantastic state California was and how nice the Bay Area is."

Watson recalled a funny incident involving teammates Carol Vadnais and Francois Lacombe. "The translation of *the Seals* from English to French is *les phoque,* which rhymes with truck. We were at the team party with the owners and it was '*phoque* this' and '*phoque* that'. We had to get somebody to translate it for them."

74

In 50 games with the Seals, Watson scored two goals and added three assists and 97 penalty minutes. In a short time, he left a lasting impression on his teammates. When the Seals played the Black Hawks, they would often use Watson to try to shadow superstar Bobby Hull, then the most dangerous sniper in the game. "Watson was an enigma for Bobby Hull to play against because he would shadow Hull and never let him relax for a minute," Ted Hampson recalled.

Fellow penalty killer Gerry Odrowski recalled, "Watson wouldn't back down from anybody. You never knew what he was going to do. In Montreal he went right after John Ferguson. Bugsy didn't lose any ground on him and we won."

Norm Ferguson recalled that Watson was "different and full of energy. He was go-go all the time. For his size, he was the toughest guy I ever saw." Besides his toughness, his teammates appreciated his leadership qualities. "He was a great team player," Brian Perry recalled. "When you were down, he'd get you up."

But management did not always see Watson's locker-room presence in a positive light. Fred Glover later claimed that the reason he traded Watson to Pittsburgh on January 30, 1969, was because he was having a negative influence on Carol Vadnais, "on and off the ice." Vadnais was the team's young rising star and best player. "That's why Bryan had to go," Glover claimed. Watson recalled having a run-in with Glover the day before he was traded. That was probably the last straw. Watson was packaged off to Pittsburgh with Tracy Pratt and George Swarbrick in exchange for Earl Ingarfield, Gene Ubriaco and Dick Mattiussi.

Watson spent the next five and a half seasons with the Penguins. In 1971-72 he led the NHL in penalty minutes with 212. One year after being traded off the Seals, Watson got a measure of revenge as the Penguins swept the Seals out of the 1970 NHL playoffs. "I remember I played well in that series," Watson recalled. "I always loved to shove it down their throats after they traded me."

Bryan Watson played in the NHL 10 more seasons after being traded off the Seals, playing for the Penguins, Blues, Red Wings and Washington Capitals. He finished his career in 1978-79, playing 21 games for the Cincinnati Stingers of the WHA. Watson retired with a total of 2,212 career penalty minutes in 878 NHL games. He was, briefly, the NHL's leader in penalty minutes before being passed for that "honor" by Dave Schultz. Today, Watson has fallen to 35th in NHL history in career penalty minutes.

After his retirement, Bugsy settled in Alexandria, Virginia, just outside of Washington, D.C. For almost 20 years he has owned and run Bugsy's Pizza Restaurant and Sports Bar. He is married and has two grown children.

Ted Hampson summed up what Bryan Watson meant to the Seals in 1968-69. "Bugsy was a real competitor. He was fierce to play against. For us, he played forward and killed penalties with Gerry Odrowski. We missed him in the dressing room when he left." Although he was not with the Seals long, Bryan Watson left his mark on his teammates and the fans in Oakland—and left more than a few marks on opposing players.

Gerry Odrowski

"A beauty—he was one of a kind. He gave 150 percent on every shift. I've never seen anybody sweat like him. He worked very hard and was deceptively quick."

—Kent Douglas on Gerry Odrowski

Ask any of his former teammates about Seals defenseman Gerry Odrowski and the first thing most of them will mention was his sense of humor. Odrowski knew how to keep his teammates loose. With the Seals struggling through their inaugural season, that quality became even more valuable.

Odrowski grew up in Trout Creek, Ontario. Among his earliest memories as a hockey fan was listening to Foster Hewitt call Maple Leafs games on "Hockey Night in Canada" on the radio.

Odrowski broke into the NHL in 1960-61, appearing in 68 games with the Detroit Red Wings that season. After two full seasons in Detroit, Odrowski settled down with the San Francisco Seals of the WHL for most of four seasons. His NHL rights belonged to the Bay Area expansion club when Barry van Gerbig and his group took over the WHL team in its final season of operation. Odrowski was not expected to be in the Seals plans when they joined the NHL, but his hard work in camp earned him a spot with the team.

Immediately, Odrowski noticed a difference between the days of the Original Six and the expansion Seals. "In the Original Six, you knew by Christmas if you would make the playoffs or not," Odrowski said. "The talent wasn't the same on expansion teams. We had talent in Oakland but we had to make it gel."

Odrowski also noticed a falloff in attendance when the Seals moved from the Cow Palace to the new Oakland Coliseum and entered the NHL. The veteran defenseman had some theories as to why. "In the Bay Area, there was a rivalry between San Francisco and Oakland. Oakland fans wouldn't go to San Francisco, and visa versa," Odrowski said. "There were a lot of die-hard fans but there were also a lot of people who didn't know much about hockey, and the team didn't try to educate them. The NHL ticket prices were also too high. People who used to bring their family to the WHL games couldn't bring them as much to NHL games."

The steady defenseman felt the small crowds at home did have an affect on the players' performance on the ice. "St. Louis fans, for example, were very loud. It gives the home team more incentive. If there's no noise in the background, it feels more like practice. You end up going through the motions."

Odrowski started the Seals first season with the parent club, but quickly found himself sent down to the WHL's Vancouver Canucks after a confrontation with assistant coach Gord Fashoway. "Once, we were on the bus heading to the airport," Odrowski remembered. "I said, 'Where is everybody?' Gordie said, 'What business is it of yours?' I asked him again and he got so angry, he sent me down to Vancouver."

Odrowski described himself as "an average hockey player." His specialty was killing penalties. "I wasn't known for scoring goals," Odrowski admitted. "I never really had the knack." His teammates recalled his bald head, his speed on skates and his effort. They nicknamed him "The Bald Eagle." Mike Laughton thought Odrowski "looked a little like Al Lewis, who played Grandpa on the television show 'The Munsters.' "

Odrowski's most memorable moment came against Gump Worsley and the Canadiens. "We were playing Montreal in Oakland. I was killing a penalty and stole the puck from J.C. Tremblay, and scored a shorthanded goal."

Killing penalties was Odrowski's forte and he was always a threat to score shorthanded. He scored nine goals in his two seasons with the Seals and five of them came with his team down a man. In 1968-69, the 5'10", 180-pound Odrowski scored all three of Oakland's shorthanded goals for the season.

"Charlie Burns and I killed penalties together a lot," Odrowski recalled. "One of us went into the zone and the other would stay back. It was a system designed to make the opposition take the puck up-ice." Ted Hampson added, "He was one of the best penalty killers and he could really skate. He handled the puck well and did a good job of getting it out of our zone."

The 1967-68 season was a rough one for Gerry Odrowski and his Seals teammates, as the team finished a distant sixth place with the worst record in the league. "There was a lot of pressure there because of Bert Olmstead," Odrowski said. "When Bert walked into the rink, he became a different man. There was just too much tension near the rink the first year and there didn't have to be."

When Fred Glover took over as coach the following year, things changed and the Seals finished second in the West. "Glover was a good coach," Odrowski said. "He tried to get you to play up and down your wing, stay with your man and don't get caught. He was that kind of coach."

While penalty killing was Odrowski's strong suit on the ice, off the ice his strength was keeping his teammates relaxed, especially on the long road trips the Seals had to endure. "The travel was worse than the games," Odrowski recalled. "We were never right on sleep."

Seals goaltender Gary Smith remembered one of Odrowski's favorite jokes. "He always sat on the last seat on the bus," Smith said. "There was a lot of movement in the back and he used to say he sat back there to get a hard-on. He'd say, 'Mother, soup's on.' " "He was a lot of fun," Ted Hampson recalled of Odrowski. "He kept us loose and on our toes. He gave the guys hotfoots."

After 1968-69, Odrowski was let go by the Seals. "I think my age had a lot to do with it," Odrowski said. He was 32 at the time. "They were trying to better themselves. It never bothered me. I wouldn't take any shit from them, they knew that. They aren't always right."

Defenseman Bert Marshall was one teammate who didn't understand why the team let Odrowski go. "He was a specialty player, a great skater and a good guy. He contributed when we were competitive and they let him go."

After three seasons in the WHL, Odrowski resurfaced in the NHL with the St. Louis Blues in 1971-72 before playing four seasons in the WHA for the Los Angeles Sharks, Phoenix Roadrunners, Minnesota Fighting Saints and Winnipeg Jets. When his hockey career was over, he worked with his brother, selling automotive parts and industrial supplies. Odrowski is now retired and living in Trout Creek.

Gerry Odrowski was respected by his teammates because he knew how to work hard and how to play hard. Billy Harris said, "He was a good team man, a good skater and rugged." The Bald Eagle always put a smile on everybody's face.

Brian Perry

"He should have gotten more recognition. He was a good hockey player."
—Norm Ferguson on Brian Perry

Brian Perry came to the NHL from the unlikely location of Aldershot, England, although he grew up in Canada and played junior hockey in Ontario. Perry later spent two seasons in the old Eastern Hockey League, first with the New York Rovers and then with the New Haven Blades. But it was as a member of the AHL's Providence Reds that Perry began to realize he could make it in the NHL. "There were only six teams in the NHL then. I could handle myself there [in the AHL], so there would be no problem moving up one level," Perry said.

In 1967-68, Perry scored 31 goals for Providence then added nine points in eight playoff games for the Reds. It was then that Perry caught the eye of Seals general manager Frank Selke Jr., who selected Perry in the intra-league draft in June 1968. "I was happy," Perry said when asked about his reaction to becoming a member of the Seals. "I was willing to go anywhere. I found out about it when a friend of mine read it in the paper. He told me so I went out and got a paper."

Little was expected of Perry during his first season in Oakland, but he made the Seals and appeared in 61 games, mostly as a third-line left wing. Perry scored 10 goals and added 21 assists for a respectable rookie season in the NHL. Seals coach Fred Glover was pleased by Perry's performance. "He was a big surprise," Glover admitted. "I thought he'd do all right, but he did even better than I expected."

"I was a lunch-pail guy," Perry said of his hockey abilities. "I went to work and worked hard. I'm glad I was there."

Most teammates recalled Perry's skating ability as his strength. Harry Howell said, "He wasn't a big guy, but he was a good skater." Chris Worthy also recalled that Perry was "a good penalty killer" when called upon. Perhaps the only thing missing from Perry's game was confidence. "He was a good player," Gerry Odrowski said of Perry. "He was surprised to be playing in the NHL. He often said he didn't know what he was doing here." Earl Ingarfield noted that Perry was "a follower, not a leader," but that "he had good speed and played hard."

Perry, who was nicknamed "Beep" by his teammates, played his best hockey with the Seals midway through his rookie season. In a 17-game span, Perry accumulated 23 of his 31 points that year. Included in the hot streak was, what Perry recalled, easily the highlight of his NHL career—a hat trick against the Chicago Black Hawks at the Oakland Coliseum on February 19, 1969. "Dennis DeJordy and Dave Dryden were the goalies," Perry recalled. "The third goal occurred after Mike Laughton passed the puck between Bobby Hull's legs. I got it in front and scored. We won the game 5-2. Norm Ferguson scored the other two goals for the Seals in that game. We were both rookies." Perry still has a plaque commemorating the hat trick.

After their second-place finish during the 1968-69 season, the Seals were upset in the first round of the playoffs by the Los Angeles Kings in seven games. "We should have beaten them," Perry said. "We were in second place. I can't put a finger on it as to why we didn't win. We were the better team." Perry scored a goal an added an assist in the series. He played in six of the seven games that postseason with Oakland.

The following season, things just weren't the same for the Seals and they stumbled to a fourth-place finish in the West division. "They got rid of team chemistry," Perry said. "In 1968-69, the guys liked each other and played hard for each other. Then the team was broken up. It made no sense." Perry was one of the casualties. He split the season between Oakland and the Seals AHL affiliate in Providence. With the Seals, he appeared in 34 games, scored six goals and 14 points. He was much more productive in Providence, where he scored 27 points in 24 games. Perry was with the Seals for the playoffs and appeared in two of the four games against the Penguins, who swept the Seals in four straight games. "Michel Briere just dominated," Perry said, recalling the Penguins rookie who was considered an up-and-coming star. A few months later Briere was in a car accident, slipped into a coma and died.

Perry claims his biggest problem in Oakland was his ongoing feud with GM Selke. "I couldn't get along with Frank Selke," Perry admitted. "There was something about me he didn't like and I brought out something about him that I didn't like." Perry also felt that coach Fred Glover "listened to Selke a little too much."

Ted Hampson felt that Perry "was a good skater, but not really a finisher at that point in his career. He didn't really establish himself with Freddie Glover."

Gene Ubriaco recalled an incident in which Perry took a hit to help produce a goal for the Seals. "We were playing the Kings," Ubriaco said. "Perry passed the puck and was hit over the boards by Larry Cahan, that big defenseman for L.A. Anyway, Cahan knocked Perry over the boards and into the penalty box. We scored a goal off the pass Perry made and he was sitting in the penalty box thumping on his chest, yelling how he deserved an assist. In the second period, Cahan missed a check on Perry and he went flying over the boards and into the Seals bench. They guys started to help him up but Freddie Glover said, 'Don't help him.' All Cahan could say was, 'Guys, I bet this looks great on TV.' "

After the 1969-70 season, Perry was left unprotected in the expansion draft; the Buffalo Sabres selected him. "I wanted to stay in Oakland," Perry recalled. "I really enjoyed the people I played with at that time, the city was beautiful and the weather was great. I also liked the coach." Perry only played one NHL game with the Sabres and spent the rest of the 1970-71 season with the Seattle Totems of the WHL. A year later he was back in Providence. Perry returned to major league hockey in 1972-73 when he played for the New York Raiders of the WHA. He stayed with the Raiders/Golden Blades/Knights/San Diego Mariners franchise until hanging up his skates after the 1974-75 season.

Today, Perry lives in Swastika, Ontario, with his wife and works for Siemens Westinghouse in a sales-related position; he has two children. It is clear that Perry enjoyed his time with the Seals. While he was never a superstar in the NHL, he made his mark on his teammates. Defenseman Dick Mattiussi said, "Beep was a good goal scorer and a good guy to be around." That was Brian Perry.

Bob Dillabough

"A fast player and a good skater. An exciting player who was really a nice guy."

—Gene Ubriaco on Bob Dillabough

It seems that every hockey team has one or two players that almost everybody has a story about. On the early Seals, that player was Bob Dillabough. Dillabough was a swift-skating left wing and center who specialized in penalty killing. The Belleville, Ontario, native made his NHL debut during the 1961-62 season when he played five games with the Red Wings. He finally became an NHL regular with the Bruins in 1965-66, two seasons before expansion doubled the size of the league. The Pittsburgh Penguins selected the 5'10", 180-pound Dillabough in the expansion draft and he scored seven goals and 19 points for the Pens in 47 games during 1967-68.

On November 29, 1968, Dillabough was traded to the Seals in exchange for Billy Harris. In 48 games with the Seals, Dillabough scored seven goals and 19 points. While he may not have scored often, many of his goals were clutch. Three of his seven tallies were game winners.

Seals coach Fred Glover remembered Dillabough as "a hell of a penalty killer. He could skate like hell. He didn't look smooth, but he was fast." In the 1969 playoffs against the Kings, Dillabough scored three goals, including one while the Seals were shorthanded.

To his teammates, Dillabough was a man who had a great sense of humor, lived life on his own terms and had a kind heart. He loved hunting and the outdoors. Unfortunately, his life was never easy.

Doug Roberts recalled that after he left camp one year, he went home with Dillabough. "He lived at MacArthur Mills in a small, rundown house. We raced through the woods shooting birds. He was a funny guy with a heart of gold. He had wheels to burn but he had a tough time handling the puck. He always lived for today."

While speed was Dillabough's No. 1 asset, his other hockey skills usually couldn't keep up with his skating. Gary Smith said, "Bob was very quick, really speedy. In fact, he would skate too fast and therefore couldn't score. He was actually skating faster than the puck sometimes."

"He had excellent speed and average hockey sense," veteran forward Earl Ingarfield recalled. "He was a penalty killer and a defensive type player. He was a good person but he wasn't one of the smartest people around. He had a big heart and was a nice guy."

Bert Marshall recalled that Dillabough "had a million-dollar set of wheels but he didn't put it together with the puck." Marshall also remembered that one of Dillabough's favorite sayings was "Look it up in the book."

According to Harry Howell, Dillabough was "one of the better skaters on the team and in the league but he had trouble putting the puck in the net. We had a few laughs together."

It seemed that almost every former teammate of Bob's had a story to tell about him. Ted Hampson remembered a particular incident that took place at a team gathering. "We had a barbecue at my place and we all ate off paper plates," Hampson recalled. "The guys all brought their own steaks and the host provided other things. Bob attacked his steak. He brought it, cooked it and ate it. He also ate the bottom of his plate. He said to me, 'I wondered what that white stuff was.' "

Wayne Muloin recalled another occasion when the Seals were in Boston. "Bob Dillabough was there and we had been given money to buy shoes. Bob bought a pair of alligator shoes. A friend of mine took Bob and I shooting. He wore the alligator shoes while hunting in the mud. The shoes got all curled up and he looked like an elf." Muloin added wistfully, "There are stories and stories about Bob. He was a funny guy. I could write a book about him alone."

Seals forward Mike Laughton called Dillabough "the best penalty killer in the NHL." He also recalled that Dillabough "always had money folded up in his pocket somewhere, but he couldn't see it too well. He had to hold the bill really close to his eyes to know how much it was."

There were stories that teammates recalled on the ice as well. Charlie Hodge remembered that "Bob had a rough night the evening before a game. During the game, he got a breakaway and scored a goal. I think it was even the winning goal. He skated back to the bench and said, 'I didn't think my legs would stand with me.' "

In 1969-70, Dillabough was again a penalty-killing specialist for Oakland. He appeared in 52 games and scored five goals and five assists. He also tied for the team lead in shorthanded goals that season. After the 1969-70 season, Dillabough was left unprotected by the Seals in the expansion draft and was chosen by the NHL's Vancouver Canucks. He never played for the Canucks, however, and spent the next two years in the minor leagues, predominantly in the AHL. In 1972-73, Dillabough signed on with the Cleveland Crusaders of the WHA. In 72 games with the Crusaders, the speedy left winger scored eight goals and eight assists. His last active season as a player was 1973-74, which he spent in the IHL before he hung up his skates for good. His final NHL statistics were 32 goals and 86 points in 283 NHL games. While those are hardly Hall of Fame numbers, Dillabough is represented at the Hockey Hall of Fame in Toronto—one of his sticks is there on display. In 1966-67, Dillabough lent his stick to a rookie teammate who scored his first NHL goal with it. The rookie's name: Bobby Orr.

Unfortunately, life after hockey was tough on Dillabough. Howie Menard remembered that Dillabough "worked in the uranium mines after his playing days were over." He was still an avid outdoorsman and went hunting and fishing when he could. Eventually, though, his health deteriorated. He died at the age of 55 on March 27, 1997.

To this day, every former player I spoke to had a soft spot for Dillabough and the very mention of his name put a smile on their faces. Gerry Odrowski summed up Dillabough accurately when he said, "He was one of the fastest men on ice. He was good with the puck and a funny guy. Unfortunately, he had a hard life."

Dick Mattiussi

"He was a good, steady ... defensive player, yet he also picked up some key goals for us."
—*Wayne Muloin on Dick Mattiussi*

Dick Mattiussi knew from a very young age that he wanted to be an NHL player. "I was a Maple Leafs fan since I lived in northern Ontario," said Mattiussi, a native of Smooth Rock Falls. "Television was just coming to northern Ontario back then and I used to watch the Leafs every Saturday night. My favorite players were Ted Kennedy and Bob Goldham." Mattiussi played for the Maple Leafs-sponsored club at St. Mike's before embarking on a successful AHL career with the Rochester Americans, Pittsburgh Hornets and Cleveland Barons. In fact, in 1966-67, the 5'10", 185-pound Mattiussi led all AHL defensemen with 54 points.

"When expansion hit, I figured I would get my chance to play in the NHL," Mattiussi recalled. He was right. The Penguins acquired his rights and Mattiussi appeared in 32 games with Pittsburgh in 1967-68 and another 12 games in 1968-69. On January 30, 1969, Mattiussi was traded to the Seals with Gene Ubriaco and Earl Ingarfield in exchange for Bryan Watson, Tracy Pratt and George Swarbrick.

Mattiussi was generally pleased with the trade. "I just wanted to play," he said. "I knew Fred Glover was coaching in Oakland and I had played for Freddie for five years in Cleveland. I thought I had a real chance to play. I knew Freddie and I liked him. He let you play," Mattiussi said of Glover's style of coaching. "He didn't punish you for making a single mistake. Now, if you made a mistake four or five times, you would hear about it. He let you use your skills to the best of your ability. If he had a weakness, it was that perhaps he should have said something a little sooner to the guys. He was a great coach and a great guy."

Mattiussi took advantage of the chance he was given in Oakland. In 24 games with the Seals in 1968-69, he scored one goal and added nine assists. On March 2, 1969, Mattiussi scored his first NHL goal off future Hall of Famer Bernie Parent in a 4-4 tie with the Flyers at the Oakland Coliseum.

During the first two seasons Mattiussi played for the Seals, the club's ownership situation was unsettled. At least three different groups were running the club at various times, with many minority owners also buying an interest in the club. Mattiussi, however, remained philosophical about the situation. "All you can do, especially in my situation as a journeyman player, is just to play as well as you can and try to stay in the league," Mattiussi said. "You have to try to put it out of your mind. I tried not to think about it much."

Mattiussi's most memorable game with the Seals took place on December 31, 1969, at the Maple Leaf Gardens. The Seals and Leafs skated to a 1-1 tie. Mattiussi scored the only goal for Oakland to even the score with just 4:14 remaining. "My parents were at the game," Mattiussi remembered. "That was the first game they saw me play live."

Mattiussi also enjoyed his stay in the Bay Area. "I always appreciated the fans. They always tried to encourage you. We had some really good people," Mattiussi recalled. He also remembered that Charles Schulz, the creator of the "Peanuts" comic strip, invited the team to practice at his rink in Santa Rosa a few times.

In 1969-70, Mattiussi had his most productive offensive season in the NHL, scoring four goals and 10 assists in 65 games. Mattiussi was bothered by injuries throughout his career. In Oakland, he suffered a shoulder injury that caused him to miss time during one season with the Seals. "I had a knee operation when I played in Pittsburgh and I wasn't really the same after that," Mattiussi said when asked to describe himself as a hockey player. "I don't like to do that … I was a good skater and could handle the puck well … It's hard to describe yourself."

Mattiussi's teammates had an easier time describing him. They recalled his strong work ethic and his often self-deprecating sense of humor. "He was a good, steady defenseman," Gary Jarrett said. "Dick was a lunch-pail kind of guy who worked hard and put in overtime." Seals captain Ted Hampson called Mattiussi "a likeable guy. He was very outgoing and he had a good sense of humor; he always made fun of himself. He wasn't a very fluid skater but he was a good skater. He gave you everything he had."

Gene Ubriaco, who was probably Mattiussi's best friend on the team, called him "a major cutup." Seals forward Mike Laughton recalled, "We pulled practical jokes on each other. I shaved his stick halfway through and, in retaliation, he nailed my new alligator shoes to the floor."

Prior to the 1970-71 season, the Seals left Mattiussi unprotected in the intraleague draft, although they pulled him back before another team selected him. He remained with the Seals and responded with a respectable season as the club's fourth or fifth defenseman. He scored three goals and had 11 points in 67 games while providing steady defense. Mattiussi had no trouble adjusting to the ownership of Charlie Finley that season. "Charlie Finley tried everything he could," Mattiussi recalled. "He gave us Bulova watches and alligator shoes. He once shipped in steaks from Chicago for the players and our wives. He did everything he could for the players."

Mattiussi was a bit confused by Finley's introduction of green and gold skates for the team to wear. "I remember the first time we wore those skates in Chicago," Mattiussi recalled. "The fans started whistling at us. It made you feel funny. You would ask yourself, 'What's going on here?' " Despite this uneasiness about Finley's colorful footwear, Mattiussi still has a pair of the green and gold skates today.

Following the 1970-71 season, there were significant changes in the Seals management. Both Frank Selke and Bill Torrey left the team before the season was over. The team became unsettled. "Frank Selke and Bill Torrey were very nice, human people. They always treated me well," Mattiussi said. "As a team, we had some very good hockey people. Along with Fred Glover, we had a real good management team."

Before the 1971-72 season, Garry Young was hired as the new general manager. He and Mattiussi did not see eye to eye and Mattiussi was quickly off the Seals. "I guess they found better and younger players," he said, refusing to divulge the specific quarrel he had with Young.

Mattiussi spent four more seasons in the AHL before retiring from hockey after the 1975-76 season. His final NHL career totals were eight goals and 31 assists in 200 games. He also added one assist for the Seals in eight playoff games. After his hockey career was over, Mattiussi returned to Smooth Rock Falls where he worked in a paper mill for 20 years. He is now retired and living in Branford, Ontario. He and his wife have two children and two grandchildren.

Earl Ingarfield described Mattiussi as "a good team man," but Ron Stackhouse summarized his fellow blueliner this way: "I respected him as a hardworking guy. He may not have had all the talent in the world, but he gave it all he had." Fellow rookie Tony Featherstone said it more precisely: "He was a good, strong, stay-at-home defenseman."

Doug Roberts

"He was a serious type. He moved the puck well. He was not a physical defenseman but he had very good hockey sense. He was more reserved and paid attention to the game; he was very determined."

—Earl Ingarfield on Doug Roberts

Doug Roberts took a very unusual route to the NHL. When he joined the Seals in 1968, Roberts was one of only two American-born and -trained hockey players in the NHL (the other being future Seals forward Tommy Williams). The Detroit, Michigan, native found a love of hockey at an early age and even served as a stick boy for the visiting teams at the old Olympia in Detroit. Instead of playing junior hockey, Roberts opted to attend Michigan State University.

"I turned down an offer from Jack Adams to join a junior team affiliated with the Red Wings," Roberts said. "The next time I saw him, he walked right by me at a Red Wings game and didn't say a word." At that time, very few NHL players played college hockey in the United States. "I didn't think I would make the NHL when I went to college," Roberts admitted.

After three successful years at Michigan State, Roberts was sent to Memphis and Fort Worth in the Wings organization in between cups of coffee with the big club. He played in 51 games with Detroit over three seasons before the Wings traded Roberts to the Seals in the deal that sent Bob Baun and Ron Harris to Detroit. The Seals received Roberts, Gary Jarrett, Chris Worthy and Howie Young on May 27, 1968. "I was looking forward to playing with my hometown team [the Red Wings], but this opened a door for me." Roberts said. "It was a chance to get a new lease on life and that was pretty exciting."

Roberts was shocked to learn upon his arrival in Oakland that instead of playing his customary position of right wing, he was now listed as a defenseman. "I had never played defense except for a few weeks in the minors," Roberts recalled. "I was surprised when I got there and they had me down as a defenseman. I never thought of myself as a defenseman. I was a right wing in college and in the minors. I guess my size, my range and my aggressive play made them take notice. Sometimes, when you don't think, you play well. Defense is a very instinctive position. I started to think about what to do one-on-one and that didn't help."

Seals coach Fred Glover remembered that he "spoke to Frank Selke and Bill Torrey and told them Roberts would make a heck of a defenseman, and he did." Glover also added, "We figured we'd know by Christmastime if we had a hockey player in Doug Roberts. We found out a long time before that." The Seals organization was sure Roberts would succeed as a defenseman when his first defense partner in Oakland, Bert Marshall, went down with an injury. Suddenly, Roberts found himself paired with the inexperienced Francois Lacombe. Roberts more than held his own and gained the confidence of his coach.

Roberts had an interesting relationship with coach Fred Glover. "I could understand him," Roberts said, in retrospect. "He was a small guy who played tough, carried his stick high and battled everybody. He took pride in the player that he was and was respected around the AHL. He thought he could play in the NHL and still scrimmaged with us. Bryan Watson ran him a few times [in practice] and he was gone. Freddie was a stern taskmaster, but we got along well and I understood him more than the other guys." At the same time, Roberts acknowledged that "communication was not a big part of [Glover's] manner. Frank Selke told me to speak to Freddie about some problems Freddie felt I had," Roberts recalled. "I wondered why Freddie didn't come to me if he had a problem with me. So we went to lunch together and Freddie just told war stories. That was it."

In his first season with the Seals, Roberts appeared in all 76 games. He scored one goal and 19 assists and added 79 penalty minutes. He added one assist in the Seals seven-game playoff loss to the Kings. "We had been building a rivalry," Roberts said about the Seals first playoff opponent. "They had a flamboyant owner, [Jack Kent Cooke]. It was two young teams trying to establish themselves."

Roberts was considered a serious person and studious player by most of his teammates. Most of this was likely due to the fact that he had a college degree and was an American. This made him a bit of an outsider at times. Still, his teammates generally liked and respected Roberts.

Dick Mattiussi, who was often paired with Roberts on defense, recalled Roberts as "an American player and a good player, a serious person and a hard worker. He was good with the puck." Harry Howell recalled that the 6'2", 200-pound Roberts was "big, rangy and hard to get around." While some of his teammates may have been intimidated by Roberts's college education, goalie Chris Worthy truly appreciated it. "We could talk about things other than hockey," Worthy said. "He knew different kinds of people and opened up new worlds for me."

Roberts' best season in Oakland was in 1969-70. He again appeared in all 76 games for the Seals and scored six goals and 25 assists. The 31 points placed him highest among all Seals blueliners for the year. Roberts also added 107 penalty minutes, placing him third on the club.

Despite his individual accomplishments, Roberts felt that the Seals unsettled ownership situation was creating problems for the club. Barry van Gerbig's group had sold the team to Trans National Communications. TNC ran out of money and the team reverted back to van Gerbig's group. "It created uneasiness and didn't help create stability," Roberts said. He knew more about the goings-on in management because he lived in the Bay Area in the summer and was hired by the team to speak to various organizations and sell tickets. "I got a kick out of the New York people who came in. They thought they would just push the buttons and it would happen. [Ex-New York Giant football player] Dick Lynch tried to speak to groups for a week and then he asked me, 'How the hell do you sell these things?' "

The 1970 playoffs against Pittsburgh were a particularly stressful time for Roberts. Management was putting more pressure on him to perform. "We felt like our backs were against the wall," Roberts admitted. "Frank Selke said he wanted me to be more of a leader. I felt like I played my heart out in that series. We needed to win that series to re-establish ourselves, but we were swept. My stomach was in a knot for two weeks after that."

If Roberts thought the management was unstable in 1969-70 under TNC, things got even more unsettled the following year when Charlie Finley bought the team. "I saw it before the others because I was working for the team that summer," Roberts said. "We spent the entire summer redesigning the uniforms. The players were an afterthought."

Roberts remembered the first time he got to meet Finley. "I went into his office to meet him. He sat on his desk and told me strategies for talking to people so you look like you have authority," Roberts said. "He said you should always be higher than the other person. He said hockey players had longer torsos and that's why they're so good. He thought he would have been a good player, and he showed me his torso."

Another change that Charlie Finley brought in for the 1970-71 season that Roberts didn't fully appreciate was the introduction of the green and gold skates. "I took it a little lighter than some of the guys," Roberts said. "It was an embarrassment around the league. We looked like a carnival. It made a mockery of the game. The other players busted our chops a bit."

The 1970-71 season was a frustrating one for Roberts on the ice as well. He scored four goals and only 13 assists in 78 games for the Seals. The team also fell out of the playoffs and into last place. Attendance dropped. "Not having big crowds was tough," Roberts admitted. "When he had bigger crowds, half of them were rooting for the Bruins or Rangers. We actually heard a lot of what the fans said because we only had 6,000 people in the building." The highlight of the 1970-71 season for Roberts had to be his selection to the 1971 NHL All-Star game. He and Carol Vadnais represented the Seals for the West that year.

On September 4, 1971, Roberts was traded to the Bruins for cash. "I saw it coming," Roberts said. "I was frustrated with how the season ended. Fred Glover took it out on everybody. We bought some liquor and were mixing it with some soda during a flight back to San Francisco from Los Angeles. There was a guru in the airport with some flower children. I walked over and shot the breeze with some of the kids and one of them gave me a flower. I walked onto the team bus, handed Fred Glover a flower and said, 'Love's what it's all about, baby.' Freddie didn't appreciate that. That summer, I got a 6 a.m. phone call from Milt Schmidt of Boston. That's how I found out about the trade. I was excited."

Roberts split the next three seasons between the Bruins and their top farm club, the Boston Braves. He later played for the Red Wings and the WHA's New England Whalers before spending a year in Finland. He retired as an active player after the 1977-78 season.

Shortly after retiring as a player, Roberts decided to try coaching at the collegiate level. He coached the men's ice hockey team at Connecticut College for more than 20 years and won over 235 games there before stepping down during the 2002-2003 season. He and his wife have three children and six grandchildren. One of his sons, David Roberts, played hockey at the University of Michigan and was a member of the 1994 U.S. Olympic team. The younger Roberts also spent time in the NHL, playing for the Blues, Oilers and Canucks.

When looking back at his career, Roberts recalled, "I was dedicated to getting the most out of my body. I wish I knew about weight training then. I see my son and what he does with his personal trainer today. I gave my best effort all the time."

Gerry Odrowski summed up Doug Roberts appropriately when he said, "He was a good defenseman, steady and hard-nosed. A good guy who was appreciated around the league." Hardworking, honest and straightforward, that was Doug Roberts of the Oakland Seals.

Chris Worthy

"He had just come up from the minors. He had a lot of potential and played well for us."
—*Gerry Odrowski on goaltender Chris Worthy*

To this day, former Seals goaltender Chris Worthy feels he never got a fair chance in the National Hockey League. The amazing thing is that many of his contemporaries agree with him. Worthy was born in Bristol, England, but grew up in Canada. He played junior hockey with the Flin Flon Bombers and was an all-star in 1967-68 with Flin Flon. Worthy remembers playing some summertime games against NHL players at 17 or 18 years old, and "I realized I could compete against them." He knew then that if he worked hard, he had a shot at playing in the NHL.

Worthy was originally property of the Detroit Red Wings, but was traded to the Seals in May 1968 in the deal that sent Bob Baun and Ron Harris to the Wings in exchange for Worthy, Gary Jarrett, Doug Roberts and Howie Young. Worthy found out about the trade in an unusual way. "My dentist told me about it," Worthy remembered. "I was getting dental work done and my dentist said, 'Congratulations! Detroit traded you to Oakland. I heard it on the radio this morning.' " Worthy was initially disappointed, having grown up a Red Wings fan. "Given my record in juniors the last two years," Worthy said, "I thought I was a candidate to be on the Red Wings club. They obviously didn't share that view. I also knew that Oakland had Gary Smith and Charlie Hodge, who were both good goaltenders."

Worthy became one of the first goalies to jump directly from the junior ranks to the NHL for an entire season. He was only 21 when he made the Seals for the 1968-69 season, more than a decade before 18-year-olds were eligible to be drafted. There was a big adjustment for the young netminder. "I only played 14 games," Worthy said. "In juniors, I played 100 games a year. I was a big guy [6'0", 180 pounds]. I needed to work a lot to achieve a confidence level. They thought I was erratic and I ended up being halfway to nowhere."

Style-wise, Worthy tried to pattern himself after one of his heroes when he was growing up, Terry Sawchuk. "I used a deep crouch and exploded to the puck on a save," Worthy recalled. "I *tried* to do that at least. I did not run off at guys to cut off angles. I didn't like that strategy and I was criticized for that."

Worthy had mixed memories about his time with the Seals. He fondly remembered his first NHL game, November 12, 1968, at the Forum in Inglewood, California, against the Kings. The Seals lost 3-1, but Worthy played well and made 30 saves. The following night, the Seals returned home and the rookie netminder earned his first NHL win in a 2-1 victory over Detroit. Gary Jarrett scored with 48 seconds left to put Oakland ahead, but Worthy remembers stopping Ron Stewart of the Red Wings on a breakaway with about 20 seconds left to preserve the win.

Worthy also had a part in games that were memorable to coach Fred Glover and GM Frank Selke Jr. Glover recalled a game played at Maple Leaf Gardens on February 8, 1969. "In the hotel before the game," Glover recalled, "I told people not to bet on the game because they could get their ass whipped. I didn't tell Chris he was starting until the last minute. Charlie Hodge always got nervous playing in Toronto, so I went with Worthy." Worthy made 39 saves in a 4-1 Seals win.

Selke recalled a narrow win over the Rangers. "Trying to get something going, we started Worthy in goal. He was sensationally brilliant. He stopped everything in a goaling display seldom seen at any level. In the final minute, Emile Francis, the Rangers coach, stood on the Rangers bench and joined the crowd's salute to the kid. It was the first and only time I've seen a rival coach publicly applaud the opposition."

Worthy also experienced some injuries while in Oakland. "We used to practice at Berkeley," the ex-goalie said. "I remember Joe Szura took a slap shot from about 15 feet out and hit me in the left cheekbone. He actually broke my cheekbone through the mask. There was swelling there immediately. Well, the next day we had a game at the Cow Palace and I was in my street clothes. Fred Glover came in and said, 'What's going on here? I want Worthy dressed!' I couldn't take warm-ups because I couldn't even get my mask on over the swelling in my face. Quickly, we were down 3-0 and Freddie said he wanted me to play. I had one eye closed and [trainer] Barry Keast had to tape my eye. Still, I finished the game and we lost something like 5-3."

Worthy's time in Oakland was not without humor, though. He recalled one of his first few games playing in Boston. "Instead of putting the puck behind the net, I would put it in the corner. Carol Vadnais kept going into the corner to get it and he kept getting hit. He said something in French which I didn't understand so then he said to me in English, 'If you put that puck in the corner one more time, I'll kill you!' "

In another game against the Bruins, Phil Esposito was trying to tie the single-season goal-scoring record. In the third period of the game, Esposito fell on top of Worthy during a scramble and said to Worthy, "Why don't you just let that last one go in?" Worthy did not yield the record-tying goal to the Bruins center.

After the 1968-69 season, Worthy grew a bit disillusioned with hockey. He decided to sit out 1969-70 and told Frank Selke Jr. that he didn't want to play hockey anymore. It was perhaps one of the more difficult things Worthy had to do late in the season when he called Selke back and asked to be reinstated. Worthy recalled the incident. "When I left the team for half a year, they forgot to put me on the suspended list. I knew I wasn't going to be paid for a full year, but I wanted credit for my pension. Fred Glover was cursing at himself for forgetting to place me on the suspended list. The club called Clarence Campbell, the league president, and he said—and I'll never forget these words—'Son, you're trying to be a lawyer. You should know better than that.' That was when I realized I didn't want to be with that element and that I had to do something besides hockey."

Worthy returned to the Seals for the 1970-71 season, but only saw action in 11 contests. This was the first season of Charlie Finley's ownership and Worthy saw a lot of changes that he didn't like. "Frank Selke knew the hockey business," Worthy said. "He knew how to put a team together. Bill Torrey was always competent and self-assured. All that changed when Charlie Finley came in." Finley dismissed both Selke and Torrey by midway through the 1970-71 season.

In 1970-71, Finley forced the Seals to wear green- and gold-colored skates. Worthy was not amused. "It was ridiculous," Worthy said, remembering the Seals new footwear. "Guys whistled at us. Putting colored skates on a guy like Gerry Ehman was an oxymoron."

Another time, Worthy remembered that Charlie Finley came to speak to his team during the second intermission. "We were losing badly, something like 7-1 after two periods. He came into the dressing room and spoke for a half-hour about his philosophy of life. We were late for the start of the third period. He told us why we should play better in the third period, how a higher power was watching us. He truly believed it, too. I think we lost 7-2 or 7-3."

Worthy remained elusive to many of his teammates, although nobody seemed to dislike him. Rookie defenseman Ron Stackhouse recalled that Worthy "didn't seem like the goalie type. He was much more normal."

After the 1970-71 season, Worthy was selected by the St. Louis Blues in the intra-league draft. He spent a year playing for the Blues minor league affiliate in Kansas City and a year with the Denver Spurs of the WHL before joining the Edmonton Oilers of the WHA in 1973-74. He remained with the Oilers for three seasons before hanging up his skates for good.

After he retired, Worthy tried to get as far away from hockey as he could. He did not keep in touch with anybody in the sport and did not become involved in NHL Alumni activities. "I cut myself off from the hockey world," the ex-goalie admitted. "I needed to accomplish something on my own."

Today, Worthy is a successful businessman in the Vancouver area and owns his own investment company. He and his wife have two sons. Worthy seems very happy away from the ice and apparently has no regrets. He appears to have learned a lot from his NHL experience, and it helped him find his way in life.

It's ironic that Worthy never felt he got enough of a chance to show what he could do in the NHL. Fred Glover, who was Worthy's coach with the Seals, said this when asked of Chris Worthy: "He could have been one hell of a goalie. Until we sent Charlie Hodge to Vancouver, we had three goalies. We should have used Chris as the primary backup. When he played, he played well." He just didn't play enough.

Gene Ubriaco

"Our little pepper pot. He was always talking and working. He seemed shorter than he was because he skated so low to the ice."

—*Gary Jarrett on Gene Ubriaco*

Ask any former Seals about Gene Ubriaco and the three things you'll almost always hear about are his sense of humor, his lack of size and his great work ethic. It seems that nobody can mention "Ubie" without a smile coming across his face. The 5'8", 157-pound left winger left an indelible impression on those he played with.

Ubriaco was born in Sault Ste. Marie, Ontario, the same place the Esposito brothers called home. "From the day I put on my skates, I knew I wanted to play in the NHL," Ubriaco admitted. Ubriaco grew up as a Red Wings fan and admitted that if he had one player to build a team around, it would be Gordie Howe. "He could beat you in so many ways and beat you up in so many ways."

Gene Ubriaco started playing junior hockey for St. Michael's in 1954-55 and then bounced around the AHL, making stops in Rochester, Pittsburgh, Hershey and Baltimore. "I played in the AHL until I was 27 or 28," Ubriaco recalled. "I never gave up the dream of playing in the NHL. Now, guys give up at 22 or 23. They dream the dream, but not really. I wanted it so badly, had I not made it, I would have been distraught."

Ubriaco finally made his long-awaited NHL debut with the Pittsburgh Penguins in 1967-68. He finished the season with 18 goals and 33 points in 65 games. "I tried to work hard," Ubriaco responded when asked to describe himself as a hockey player. "I was a scorer. Back checking, well, I did my share, but I was not known for it. I went hard to the net despite being a smaller guy. I feel good about what I did."

On January 30, 1969, Ubriaco was traded to the Seals with Earl Ingarfield and Dick Mattiussi for Bryan Watson, George Swarbrick and Tracy Pratt. Ubriaco has fond memories of his time in the Bay Area. "Going to the Bay was great," Ubie recalled. "We had more fun as a team. We made second place and had a great bunch of guys. The booster club out there was great. Fan clubs are very important to keeping a team going. I started up a number of hockey teams and I always started a fan club first. I learned that from my time in Oakland."

The other thing Ubriaco remembered fondly about Oakland was his teammates. "We had a great bunch of guys. When I see those guys, I pick up the conversation where we left off 30 years ago. We knew each other very well back then, not like today. We used to go to the Cactus Room restaurant," Ubie recalled. "We were even friends with some of the Raiders back then. I was friends with George Blanda."

Coach Fred Glover made a positive impression on the Sault Ste. Marie native. "Fred was passionate, really passionate. He was a player's player," Ubriaco recalled. "He loved the game so much. As a coach, he never could separate himself as a player. He never gave up as a player and he instilled that in us when he coached."

Ubriaco played in 26 games with the Seals in the 1968-69 season. He scored four goals and added seven assists, giving him a career-best 19 goals on the year. In the season finale, the Seals were taking on the North Stars in Oakland. "I had 19 goals on the season. I had a $1,000 bonus clause in my contract if I made 20 goals," Ubriaco said. "Lou Nanne was playing defense for the North Stars and Cesar Maniago was in net. We were winning 4-1 with about five minutes left in the game. I needed one more goal for 20 and the guys all knew it. Lou Nanne would say to me, 'Go to the left. Go to the outside.' He was trying to help, but this only made it more difficult for me. I said, 'Lou, would you play normal here?' Even Maniago would have given me the goal, but I never got it." Bert Marshall remembers the team trying to get Ubriaco his 20th goal, "but he was snakebitten."

The Seals made the playoffs that year and faced the Los Angeles Kings in a series that went seven games. Ubriaco scored twice for the Seals in the series but the Seals fell short, losing the seventh and deciding game at home. "I know we were good enough," Ubriaco said, recalling the series. Like the rest of the Seals organization, the loss was disappointing for Ubriaco.

Ubriaco was back with the Seals at the start of the 1969-70 season, but there were changes being made and they did not bode well for Ubie. First, new ownership in the form of Trans National Communications took over. "Whitey Ford came in with new owners at the end of my first year there and said everything was fine. A lot of promises were made," Ubriaco said. "Hockey players are amazing though. Once the puck drops, nobody realizes that stuff. We just loved the game."

The second problem Ubriaco faced was trying to negotiate a new contract with the Seals. "I was the last player to sign a contract that year," Ubriaco remembered. "I had to walk in and negotiate with Fred Glover, Bill Torrey and Frank Selke Jr. They got mad at me after I held out. I didn't get a raise after scoring 19 goals [in the regular season] the year before. I was asking for $25,000 instead of $20,000. Frank Selke Jr. said I was way out of line, asking for a 25 percent raise. The most I ever earned in the NHL, including playoffs, was $35,000. Back then you never fought back. They tried to strip you of your dignity. As a result of the holdout, Fred hardly played me," Ubriaco said. Although Ubriaco remained with the team until the end of December 1969, he appeared in only 16 games, scoring once and adding one assist.

Just before he was traded to Chicago in December 1969, Ubriaco and his wife attended the Seals Booster Club's Christmas party. "After the party, my wife and I walked to San Francisco," Ubriaco recalled. "People were walking up to me and saying, 'Hello Gene, how are you?' We paid the toll and the toll taker said, 'Hello, Gene, how are you?' Total strangers, people I didn't even know kept saying that to me. I thought to myself, Wow, the team is really catching on now. Then I realized I left my name tag on from the Christmas party."

Shortly after the Christmas party, Ubriaco was traded to the Chicago Black Hawks for Howie Menard. He recalled that Seals wing Bill Hicke threw a party for him after he was traded. "Hicke was the MC," Ubriaco joked. "I think that stands for mental case."

Ubriaco appeared in 21 more games with the Hawks that season to conclude his NHL playing career. Although he was no longer playing, Ubriaco remained active in hockey. He started coaching at Lake Superior State University in Michigan in 1972-73. Later, the ex-Seals forward coached in the USHL, EHL, Central Hockey League and the AHL. He returned to the NHL as coach of the Pittsburgh Penguins in 1988-89, leading the Pens to a 40-win season and a win in the first round of the playoffs. He was let go as coach of the Penguins 26 games into the following season when the team got off to a slow start. "I had a good year in Pittsburgh," Ubriaco said. "Mario [Lemieux] only had 199 points." Ubriaco also coached the Italian Olympic Team at the 1992 games at Albertville, France.

Today, Ubriaco is the director of hockey operations and assistant general manager of the Chicago Wolves of the AHL. Under his guidance, the Wolves won two Turner Cups in three years while members of the now defunct IHL. In addition, Ubriaco invented and patented a new kind of hockey stick now being used by many NHL players. He joked, "It looks like I'm going to the NHL a third time. I love this game," Ubriaco said. "That's why I'm still in this business. Hockey is a great game, but a lousy business."

Even today, Ubriaco showed his sense of humor and an undying love for the game of hockey. Ted Hampson summed up his teammates' view of Ubriaco well. "Ubie could keep you loose," Hampson recalled. "He had lots of hustle and never stopped working." Nobody probably had more fun working in hockey all these years than Gene Ubriaco.

Wayne Muloin

"He had an unbelievable hip check. He was old school. He never tried to hurt people but he hit people when they weren't expecting it sometimes. An unbelievable hitter."

—Ron Stackhouse on Wayne Muloin

Wayne Muloin took the indirect route to the NHL. He was invited to Detroit's camp in 1958-59 and played three games for the Red Wings in 1963-64. After traveling around the EHL, the WHL and the CPHL, Muloin seemed to have found a home with the Providence Reds of the American Hockey League. The Dryden, Ontario, native spent four solid seasons as a stay-at-home defenseman with Providence. Then, he got a big surprise. "I was in Providence," Muloin recalled, "and they sent me to Oakland's camp. I was a little surprised that I stayed [on]. I was set to go back to Providence. My family was still staying there. But I had a good camp and there I was."

Perhaps the one thing holding Muloin back from the NHL was his size. Despite his physical style of play, Muloin stood only 5'8", 175 pounds, not exactly intimidating dimensions for a defensive defenseman.

Muloin had played against Seals coach Fred Glover in the AHL and Glover recommended his former foe to Seals management. "He was quite a guy on the ice, it was like warfare on ice," Muloin said of his battles with Glover. "I was surprised that when I got to know him, he was a pretty nice guy."

Muloin served as the Seals fifth defenseman for most of the 1969-70 season so, in practice, Glover would often be his defense partner. In his first full season in the NHL, Muloin appeared in 71 games for the Seals. True to form, he scored only three goals and six assists but added a physical element to the Seals blue line that the team sorely needed.

It didn't take long for Muloin to earn his teammates' respect. Veteran defenseman Harry Howell recalled Muloin as "a little guy and a devastating checker. He hit people when they didn't see him coming. He put some guys out of commission. I even had to watch for him in the practice rink."

Gary Jarrett vividly recalled Muloin's specialty, the long forgotten art of the hip check. "He had a bruising hip check," Jarrett said. "He sort of perfected it. He made some of the most spectacular hits—a short, fireplug type of guy. He'd put you in the air like you were a field goal." Mike Laughton called Muloin "the best hip checker outside of Leo Boivin. He was a real hard checker and a real competitor."

Muloin described himself as "a grinder, a blue-collar guy. I didn't have finesse but I got the job done the best way I could." When asked to describe his infamous hip check, Muloin said, "My hip check was damaging. Timing it was important. With my lack of size, it was a great way of bringing guys down. I also loved shot blocking. The first time I dropped in front of a Bobby Hull shot, the guys thought I was nuts."

While all of his teammates remember Muloin as a hard worker, he had some fun times, too. Howie Menard remembered the camaraderie he had with his teammates. "He called me 'Maynard' and I called him 'Muldoon.' I don't know why, probably because I didn't want to pronounce Muloin. He was a super guy. He could really hit even though he wasn't very big. He worked hard on and off the ice."

Two games really stood out in Muloin's mind as memorable. "One game, I was on the power play, although I don't know why. We were in Philadelphia. Ed Van Impe came to the point and just as I let a shot go, he went down. I knocked out all of his teeth," Muloin said. "He got repairs and came out again to finish the game."

"Another time, in Boston, we were outshot something like 69-19 and we won the game 2-0," Muloin said. "I remember somebody said, 'Let's get out of here before they realize what we are doing.' The Bruins were so mad, they were busting their sticks on the ice."

Muloin appeared in all four of the Seals playoff games against the Penguins, although he was held scoreless. "I remember it as a rough series with a lot of fighting," Muloin recalled. The Seals were swept in four straight games.

The following season was full of changes for the Seals and Muloin. Charlie Finley took over ownership of the club and, immediately, Muloin sensed a difference. He remembered some of Finley's attempts at promoting the Seals. "In his first year there, Finley had Barber Night. He invited barbers and beauticians and brought them steaks and flaming desserts. He tried to get them to spread the word about the team, but I don't think there was a big turnout."

Finley also gave the team yellow and green skates to wear. "I remember the opening game of the season in Detroit," Muloin said. "We got a lot of kisses blown at us—and not from women, either."

Another promotion Muloin recalled involved "Peanuts" comic-strip author Charles Schulz, who was a season-ticket holder of the Seals, despite the fact that he lived in Santa Rosa. "Charles Schulz packed his rink in Santa Rosa. Once he had some chimpanzees on the ice and one of them shot and scored on Gary Smith."

Muloin also remembered his most embarrassing moment on ice. "We were in Oakland and I was chasing the puck down. I thought it was icing and I just whacked it toward our goal. Gary Smith had to make a pad save. It was one of my better shots."

Muloin appeared in 66 games with the Seals in 1970-71. Although he didn't score any goals, Muloin added 14 assists and 32 penalty minutes. On March 7, 1971, Muloin and team captain Ted Hampson were sent to the North Stars in exchange for Tommy Williams and Dick Redmond. "I hated leaving," Muloin admitted. "I liked the Bay Area. We had a good bunch of guys. Everybody liked Oakland and I didn't want to go back to the cold weather."

After finishing the 1970-71 season with the North Stars, Muloin returned to the AHL to play for the Cleveland Barons the following year. When the WHA was born in 1972-73, Muloin remained in Cleveland and spent four seasons with the Crusaders. He also had a brief tenure with the Edmonton Oilers in 1975-76. After retiring from hockey, he settled in the Cleveland area and is now working in the construction field. Among the projects he worked on was the Gund Arena in Cleveland. Muloin and his wife have five children and one grandchild.

Ernie Hicke described Muloin this way: "He was the smallest guy on the team with the most heart. He would block shots and take the body. He was famous for his hip check."

Muloin never became a star in the NHL, but he proved that hard work and determination could take a little man far in a big man's game.

Gary Smith

"A real character and one of the all-time funniest guys I've ever met. Everybody loved him. When times were tough, he made it better for us."

—Bryan Watson on Gary Smith

The stereotype around the hockey world is that goaltenders are just a bit odder than most people; that they dance to the beat of a different drummer. Perhaps nobody personified that better than Seals netminder Gary Smith. Smith played for seven different teams in the NHL and two more in the WHA. Ask anybody who had the privilege of being Gary Smith's teammate and they will have a number of stories to tell about the big goaltender from Ottawa.

Smith broke into the NHL with the Toronto Maple Leafs in 1966-67. He appeared in only two games for the Leafs that season but could not break the starting lineup. "There were only 12 jobs for goaltenders in the NHL back then," Smith said. "I knew I wasn't going to make it."

Before he even played in the NHL, he earned the nickname "Suitcase" for his frequent travels. "I got that name back in my minor league days," Smith explained. "I was the property of the Maple Leafs and they had four minor league teams back then: one in Toronto, one in Victoria, one in Rochester and one in Tulsa. They would send me to whichever team had an injured goalie so I was always going from place to place whenever somebody got hurt. One of the local writers said I always had my suitcase ready and that sort of stuck." Smith also earned the nickname "The Ax" among his teammates because he liked to swing his goalie stick at players who invaded his crease.

While he only played in two games for the Maple Leafs, Smith left his mark on the NHL rule book in the process. In one of the games he played for Toronto, he carried the puck all the way up the ice and stickhandled across the opposing team's blue line in an attempt to become the first NHL goalie to score a goal. Although the crowd went wild, the NHL passed a rule the following season prohibiting goalies from crossing the red line. The rule was affectionately known around the NHL as "the Gary Smith rule."

Smith was the second goalie selected by the Seals in the expansion draft after Charlie Hodge. "To go from Eastern Canada to California was a big thrill," Smith recalled. "I had a chance to make the team and a chance to play in the NHL. I knew I could make a few thousand dollars more, which back then was a big deal. The $3,000 difference was a lot of money back then."

Smith has vivid memories of the Seals first training camp in Port Huron, Michigan. "I roomed with Jack McCartan, who played on the 1960 U.S. Olympic Team. I also remember that Charlie Hodge held out and we had Jacques Plante in camp. I read in the newspaper that Plante was there to help the young goalies, but he never talked to me and I was the only young goalie in camp. He must have been there trying out for a contract. He was unstoppable in practice although he never appeared in any games. I think he saw how bad our team was going to be and he didn't sign with us."

Smith also recalled what happened after the Seals lost an exhibition game against the AHL's Buffalo Bisons. "Bert Olmstead was livid. He said an NHL team should never lose to an AHL team. The next day in practice, we did two hours of stops and starts. After an hour, we were all exhausted and the ice was so worn out, but Bert yelled to us, 'You're halfway there.' "

Smith spent the 1967-68 season backing up Hodge in net. He appeared in 21 games for the Seals and finished with a 2-13-4 record and had 3.19 goals against average. He also earned his first NHL win and shutout that season. Playing for Bert Olmstead was a positive experience for Smith. "Bert was a real strict-type coach," Smith said. "I really respected him as a player and as a human being. He was always fair with me, but he was harder on his friends like Billy Harris, Kent Douglas and Bob Baun. He told Harris once to take off his stuff because he was a disgrace to the team. He said that in New York in front of the entire squad."

Like many goalies, Smith had his own set of pregame and between-periods rituals. Defenseman Doug Roberts remembered Smith's routine. "Gary Smith was the biggest character on the team. He kept people loose. He drank seven glasses of water between periods and then stripped naked. Once, he forgot his goalie skates. The trainer found some that were three or four sizes too big. Gary got a shutout in that game and after that, he wore skates that were three or four sizes too big every game." Ron Harris added, "The first time he took all his equipment off, we all thought he was quitting." Bill Hicke recalled that "every time we won, Gary put on a new pair of socks [over the old ones]. Once, we won a few in a row and Gary kept asking for new pairs of skates because they wouldn't fit him anymore over all the socks." Smith explained his reasoning for the rituals. "I think it made me feel more comfortable," he said. "My skates and uniform would get so loose so I would fix them up. I wanted my pads tighter. I think nerves had a lot to do with it."

In one of his first games with the Seals, Smith's wandering caused a problem for defenseman Kent Douglas. "He ran over me behind the goal once," Douglas said. "I had the puck and he just ran me over."

Smith also recalled getting adjusted to the travel that playing on the West Coast involved. "The traveling was tough," he said. We'd play nine games in 14 days and be away for both Christmas and New Year's. We had less practice time because of our travel schedule and, therefore, I think, more injuries. It is also hard to rebound if you started a road trip poorly. Lose the first three games of a nine-game road trip and it was easy to start a long skid."

Smith stood 6'4", 215 pounds, which was considered very large for a goaltender. When asked to recall his style of play, Smith had trouble describing it. "I have no idea," he admitted. "I got a tape of a game we played against the Leafs and I seemed to stay as far back in the net as I could to allow myself more time to stop the puck. The puck used to hurt back then when it hit you because our protection was so basic. Now, goalies are better than they were in those days because they don't get hurt every time the puck hits them. Also, we never had goalie coaches in my day so you just sort of had to figure things out for yourself."

Smith also took a liking to the fans in the Bay Area. "The fans we had were good fans," Smith recalled. "The Booster Club had about 100 members and they were great. The fans were very loud; 7,000 fans in Oakland could sound like at least 10,000."

In his second year with the Seals, Smith assumed the starting role. New coach Fred Glover preferred larger goaltenders and Smith fit the bill. Glover described Smith as "happy-go-lucky and nutty. I know he drove me nuts. He played well for me and I enjoyed working with him."

Smith responded to his new role of the Seals starting goalie. In 1968-69, he appeared in 54 games and set two franchise records: one by winning 21 games in a season, the other by recording four shutouts. He managed a very respectable 2.96 goals against average and led the Seals to a second-place finish in the West Division. The Seals lost a tough seven-game series to the Kings in the first round of the playoffs. Smith played reasonably well in the series, making all seven starts and having a 3.29 goals against average.

In addition to his performance on the ice, Smith also had a reputation off the ice. "He was oblivious of what anybody else thought or did, especially management," Chris Worthy said. "He just did what he wanted to do. Everybody loved him." Gene Ubriaco remembered that when he and Smith went out to a bar after practice, "Smith would joke to the guy next to him, 'How would you like to fight a guy who's 6'4"?' As a guy who was 5'9", I was scared." Harry Howell recalled Smith's attitude toward life. "Nothing phased this man. He had an attitude most goalies wish they had," Howell said. "He was a fun-loving, good guy. We spent a lot of time at the track together." Both Howell and Smith shared a passion for horse racing.

Smith's best game for the Seals probably came in Boston. Earl Ingarfield recalls a 2-1 win over the Bruins in which the Seals were outshot "something like 55-20," but Smith carried the team to an upset win over the Bruins.

The knock against Smith was usually consistency and concentration. Team GM Frank Selke once criticized Smith in a San Francisco newspaper. Smith was upset by the story. "It had to be the worst story I've ever read," Smith replied. "I wasn't concentrating, I'm immature, I don't take care of myself; all that jazz. I know sometimes I don't concentrate. It's something you don't realize you're not doing until it happens."

Some of Smith's teammates also questioned if his behavior off the ice didn't affect his play on the ice. "He was sometimes his own worst enemy," Dennis Hextall said. "Like a lot of goalies, I was not sure if his elevator went to the top floor, although sometimes he was facing 50 shots a night." Defenseman Bert Marshall added, "He was a pretty good goalie. When he had it going, he was as good as there was, but he couldn't keep it going. He loved to play, but didn't devote 100 percent effort to being a good player. He was happy-go-lucky."

Smith never denied his unique outlook on life. He had a reputation as a bachelor-about-town during his days in Oakland and as a fun-loving player. Tracy Pratt said of Smith, "He loved to have a good time after the game, but he came to play. He was a big, overgrown kid. If he would have matured sooner, he would have been a lot better than he was." Smith recalled a saying the players had in Oakland: " 'Do your best. If it's not good enough, get hammered.' " Even on the ice, Smith had a different way of acting. Seals comptroller Larry Marshall recalled one game against Chicago when "Bobby Hull came in on a breakaway. He took a slap shot and Gary Smith ducked. Luckily, the shot went wide."

After two productive seasons as the Seals starting goalie, in which he led the team to the playoffs, Smith entered 1970-71 full of anticipation. The club had a new owner in Charlie Finley and things seemed to be different. "I actually enjoyed Charlie Finley," Smith said. Smith had an unusual theory about Finley's ownership of the Seals, however. "I believe [Finley] was just a front for the Mafia. We had a guy named Munson Campbell who ran things. Finley was almost never there. Campbell was our governor and he was involved in a company based in Arizona that owned dog tracks and owned a lot of concession stands around the NHL called Sports Service. That company was controlled by the mob. I remember when I was in Winnipeg, owner Mike Gobuty ran into trouble. He owned a racetrack and I was at the track. So was Munson Campbell. He said his company gave people money to buy racetracks and then if they don't pay it back, we take back the track at reduced prices. The entire thing was a front for the mob."

Smith also had to get used to Finley's addition of green and gold skates for the Seals. "I didn't mind it so much, but I felt bad for Jim Pickard, our trainer, because he always needed to keep painting the skates," Smith explained. "The skates would get scuffed and then he'd have to paint them. It didn't affect my skates so much as a goalie because only the toes would get scuffed. But the other guys used to say that, eventually, the skates got heavy."

In 1970-71, Smith set a club record by appearing in 71 of the Seals 78 games. The Seals were beset by injuries and fell to last place in the West Division. Smith led the league in games played and minutes played. He also set an NHL record with 48 losses in a season. Unfortunately, the strain of playing so many games on a losing team became too much for Smith. Mike Laughton recalled that

Smith "faced a lot of shots. He would just look at me and shake his head." Rookie defenseman Ron Stackhouse recalled that Smith "was brilliant at times. In Toronto, I remember the Leafs had us pinned in our own end for about 12 minutes. Finally, Gary got the puck, stickhandled to center ice and shot it into their end. The crowd in Toronto went nuts."

When asked about Smith, Gary Croteau laughed, and said, "That poor guy. He was a real good goaltender. We just couldn't provide the offensive threat he would have liked. He was a great game player, although you figure he faced 50 shots in so many games. After one season with us, he literally needed some R&R."

Unfortunately, Smith needed a lot more than simple rest and recuperation. After the 1970-71 season, playing for the Seals literally made Gary Smith sick and he ended up in the hospital. "It was simply too many games to play," Smith admitted. "I had a nervous breakdown after the season. I felt bad when we lost. I was facing 50 to 60 shots per game, we were never winning and there was nobody in the stands. It seemed like the puck was always in our end. I was literally in the hospital and I thought I was going to die."

After suffering the nervous breakdown, Smith realized he needed to leave the Seals. The club obliged his wishes and sent Smith to Chicago on September 9, 1971, in exchange for Kerry Bond, Gerry Desjardins and Gerry Pinder. Desjardins was suffering from a broken arm and was unable to play, so a few weeks later Desjardins was returned to the Black Hawks and the Seals received Paul Shmyr and Gilles Meloche in return.

Smith is the Seals all-time leader in career wins by a goalie and career shutouts. He is also second all-time in franchise history in games played by a netminder and career goals against average.

Like many players, Smith responded well after leaving the Seals. He backed up Tony Esposito in Chicago and the duo proceeded to win the Vezina Trophy in 1971-72 for having the league's best goals against average. Smith said he learned more about goaltending in his two years playing with Esposito than he had previously in his career. After two seasons in Chicago, Suitcase Smith was traded to Vancouver. In 1974-75, he had his best individual season, playing in 72 games for the Canucks and leading them to a surprising division title. Smith later played for the Minnesota North Stars, Washington Capitals and Winnipeg Jets in the NHL and the Jets and Indianapolis Racers in the WHA. He retired as an active player after the 1979-80 season.

Today, Smith lives in the Vancouver area, still has a passion for racehorses and is involved in the business world. The vagabond goaltender looks back at his NHL career and time in Oakland fondly, despite the difficulties he faced. Brian Perry summed up Gary Smith by saying, "He was the ultimate; he was great. I never met anybody like him in my life. He was a great guy both on the ice and off." Now, all these years later, Smith's ex-teammates remember the laughter and the good times when they think of the big goalie who guarded the Seals nets.

George Swarbrick

"He was very flamboyant. He was small but stocky. He could shoot the puck and was a good skater."

—Charlie Burns on George Swarbrick

George Swarbrick took the long way to the NHL, but he did eventually make it. Swarbrick played for the Moose Jaw Canucks in the Saskatchewan Junior League. Reluctant to leave Moose Jaw, Swarbrick then spent a year in the Saskatchewan Senior League before joining the 1964 Canadian Olympic Team. Although Canada did not win a medal that year, Swarbrick had a good series, scoring three goals and six points in seven games. Swarbrick spent the next three seasons with the San Francisco Seals of the WHL where he scored more than 20 goals twice and hit the 30-goal mark in the final year before expansion, 1966-67. He was named WHL Rookie of the Year in 1965. Swarbrick's rights were awarded to the NHL Seals when their future ownership took over the WHL club in its last year of operation.

Few people expected Swarbrick to stay with the Seals when they joined the NHL, but "Snowy" Swarbrick found a way. The 5'10", 185-pound Swarbrick had a reputation for having a hard shot—and on a team that lacked scoring punch, that was a valuable commodity. In 1967-68, his first season in the NHL, Swarbrick was beset by injuries. At different times, he suffered a broken hand and a broken ankle and, as a result, appeared in only 49 games. He scored 13 goals and had only five assists and 62 penalty minutes. Swarbrick led all Seals players in shooting percentage that year, scoring on 15.1 percent of his shots. His main role was as a penalty killer and third- or fourth-line forward. Swarbrick was a familiar face for Seals fans who followed the team in their WHL days at the Cow Palace.

Teammates remembered Swarbrick's skating and shooting ability most. Aut Erickson simply said Swarbrick was "a worker, he could really skate." Kent Douglas recalled that Snowy was "a quick skater who could really shoot the puck."

Swarbrick also possessed a sense of humor that was appreciated both on and off the ice. Gary Smith remembered Swarbrick as "a real practical joker who played up and down the wing. I remember we used him to shadow Bobby Hull when we played Chicago. Somebody once asked him, 'Can you stay with Hull tonight?' and George said, 'I don't know. Tell me where he's staying; I have to ask my wife.' "

Swarbrick was assigned the task of shadowing Hull when the Seals recorded their first home sellout on February 21, 1968; 12,025 fans showed up at the Oakland Coliseum Arena to see the Seals host the Black Hawks. Frank Selke Jr. recalled that "Hull beat us in a really thrilling game. We had George Swarbrick on Bobby all night and he did a great job until Hull simply overpowered him late in the third." Hull scored the only goal of the game with 2:50 left on the clock in a 1-0 Chicago win.

Teammates had fun with Swarbrick off the ice as well. Seals captain Bob Baun recalled an incident that occurred during the Seals first season. "Once, George parked his car in front of somebody's house and the engine was stolen. He went to drive the car away and what was left of the engine fell on the floor." Tracy Pratt remembered Swarbrick as "a playboy" off the ice and "a good teammate who wouldn't back down from anybody" on the ice.

At times, Swarbrick struggled while adjusting to the NHL. Billy Harris felt that Snowy "didn't live up to Bert Olmstead's expectations," although that first season, very few members of the Seals did. Gerry Odrowski recalled that Swarbrick "was a good up and down winger. It was his first time in the NHL and he had a lot to learn."

In 1968-69, the Seals improved as a club and Swarbrick was used mostly as a penalty killer on the second unit with Bob Dillabough. In 50 games with the Seals, he scored three goals and 13 assists and was assessed 75 minutes in penalties.

On January 30, 1969, Swarbrick was traded to the Penguins along with Bryan Watson and Tracy Pratt for Earl Ingarfield, Gene Ubriaco and Dick Mattiussi. He spent the remainder of the 1968-69 season with Pittsburgh, but played only 12 games for the Pens the following season before being sent down to the Penguins farm team in Baltimore. Before the 1970-71 season, Swarbrick was traded to the Flyers. He played in two games for the Flyers and spent the rest of the year in the AHL. Swarbrick spent six more seasons in professional hockey, playing in the WHL, the CHL and the NAHL before retiring after the 1976-77 season. His final NHL statistics included 17 goals and 25 assists in 132 games. Swarbrick's son-in-law Greg Adams later played for several NHL teams in the '80s and '90s.

George Swarbrick only had a brief stop in the NHL. It is likely that without expansion, he would not have made it. But Swarbrick enjoyed his opportunity and won the respect of his teammates and Bay Area fans. Wally Boyer summed up Swarbrick by saying, "He was a hard-working winger and a tough kid. He skated up and down the wing and did his job." His job was to play hockey for the Oakland Seals.

Francois Lacombe

"A young guy who came from the Montreal organization in a trade. He was young, aggressive and could have had a good career. He was a pretty intelligent player as well."

—Gary Jarrett on Francois Lacombe

Francois Lacombe was a virtual unknown when he was acquired by the Seals from the Montreal Canadiens as part of the deal that brought Norm Ferguson to Oakland on May 21, 1968. The previous season, the 5'9", 185-pound native of Lachine, Quebec, was playing for the Montreal Junior Canadiens in a Junior B league. At the age of 20 he made the jump from Junior B to the NHL.

Coach Fred Glover recalled that Lacombe "was a real surprise. He played well for us. He was not very big, but not afraid to hit. I paired him with Doug Roberts and Doug played very well." Statistically, Lacombe played in 72 of the Seals 76 games, scoring two goals and adding 16 assists. In the playoffs that season, Lacombe scored one goal in three games against the Kings. He also managed to play well enough defensively to hold down a regular job during the Seals most successful season.

Lacombe scored his first NHL goal on December 15, 1968, during a 7-4 loss to the Black Hawks at Chicago Stadium. Dennis DeJordy was the victim. The other goal Lacombe scored came on February 12, 1969, during the Seals first-ever win against the Rangers. Lacombe beat Ed Giacomin to give Oakland a 2-0 lead in a game the Seals held on to win 3-2.

Mike Laughton remembered Lacombe as "a good, young defenseman." He also recalled a particular incident during an exhibition game. "Francois gave me a sucker pass in Sudbury and Bob Plager sent me into the next town during an exhibition game with the Blues," Laughton said, laughing.

Chris Worthy, who was also a rookie in 1968-69, said Lacombe "was a talented guy and I envied his playing time. He got more experience with every game. He had some tough times, but they stuck with him. Of course, as a goalie, I couldn't get away with any mistakes."

While Worthy remembers Lacombe's play improving as the season progressed, Bill Hicke remembered it differently. Hicke called Lacombe, "Freddie Glover's discovery. He played very well at the start of the season but other teams caught up with him as the year went along. He also didn't speak much English when he got here."

Doug Roberts was Lacombe's defense partner for part of 1968-69. "He was a very naive kid when he came up," Roberts said. "He was a good kid and he worked hard. I roomed with him for awhile. I remember once in Pittsburgh, we lost 3-2 on a late goal and the coach was really upset. My brother was down for the game and as Fred Glover came to check on us, my brother came into our hotel room with some beer. Francois got nervous and he said, 'Hey, Dougie, maybe we should go to bed.' "

Team comptroller Larry Marshall recalled that Lacombe was a young kid from a small town in Quebec. "Guys would kid him and say things like, 'Look at this jacket, it's perfect for you.' Francois would buy these outlandish things after the guys kidded him."

Eventually, the naive kid from Quebec earned the respect of his teammates. "He was a quiet guy," Earl Ingarfield remembered. "He was smaller for a defenseman but he handled the puck well and saw the ice well. He was more laid back."

The following year, the Seals brought in some more experienced defensemen. Harry Howell was acquired from the Rangers and Lacombe spent most of the 1969-70 season with the Seals top AHL affiliate, the Providence Reds. He was called up for a pair of games with the Seals and did not pick up any points. In Providence, Lacombe scored 11 goals and 50 points in 70 games. After the 1969-70 season, Lacombe was traded back to Montreal as part of the trade that sent the Seals first-round draft pick to the Habs in exchange for Ernie Hicke. Montreal used the pick to draft Guy Lafleur. Lacombe later played one game for the expansion Buffalo Sabres in 1970-71, but otherwise played mostly for the Salt Lake Golden Eagles of the WHL. In 1972-73, Lacombe signed with the WHA's Quebec Nordiques, which he played with for the next three years. After one year with the Calgary Cowboys, Lacombe returned to Quebec in 1976-77 and remained there until the demise of the WHA in 1979.

His final WHA totals are 38 goals and 177 points in 440 games. When the Nords joined the NHL the following season, Lacombe played in three games with Les Nordiques and spent most of the season with the AHL's Syracuse Firebirds. He retired as an active player after the 1979-80 season.

Lacombe remained involved in hockey after his playing days were over. He coached in the Quebec league and participated in some hockey schools in La Belle province. During 2001-2002, Lacombe even spent time coaching in Europe.

His teammates remember Lacombe fondly. He was the young Frenchman who came out of nowhere to grab an NHL job. Dick Mattiussi remembered Lacombe this way: "He was a good skater and a nice person. He gave everything he could."

Joe Szura

"He was a big centerman and a quiet type. He handled the puck well, was reliable, and big and strong."

—Earl Ingarfield on Joe Szura

Big Joe Szura came up through the Montreal Canadiens organization in the days of the Original Six, although he never appeared in a Habs uniform. Billy Harris recalled that the Montreal organization "had high hopes he was going to be another Jean Beliveau and they put a lot of pressure on him." Instead of starring with the Habs, Szura thrived with the Cleveland Barons of the AHL. From 1962-63 until 1966-67, Szura was a steady center for the Barons, scoring as many as 46 goals in a season and between 65 to 70 points per year. The Seals selected Szura from the Canadiens organization in the ninth round of the expansion draft and invited him to camp with the club in their first year.

According to his teammates, there were two things held Szura back during his first year with the Seals: his lack of skating speed and his refusal to play a more physical style of hockey despite his 6'3", 185-pound frame. Mike Laughton remembered Szura from the Seals first training camp. "We went to camp together and we were fighting for a job," Laughton said. "Joe was such a gentleman you hated to run over him. I remember we lost an exhibition game in Buffalo and we were doing skating drills after the game. I skated next to Joe because he was not the fastest skater."

Szura's strong points were his passing and playmaking. Kent Douglas recalled Szura as "a good, solid player. He was not the fastest skater, but he could pass the puck and hold onto it." Ted Hampson said that Szura "had size, strength and good hands. He could also win face-offs." What's more, Szura got along well with his teammates. Ron Harris recalled that the Fort William, Ontario, native "was a go-easy kind of guy. He always had a smile and all that."

Szura was a 28-year-old rookie with the Seals in 1967-68. He spent part of the year with the Oakland Seals and part of the year with the Buffalo Bisons of the AHL. In 20 games with the Seals, Szura scored one goal and added three assists. Charlie Burns recalled that during the Seals first year, Szura's "overall game was solid, but there was nothing spectacular about him." Wally Boyer called Szura "a very hardworking guy." Then he added, "If he could have skated a little faster, he could have been a superstar." Tom Thurlby remembered that Bert Olmstead was tough on Szura and, like all of the Seals players, he expected more from him. "[Szura] was frazzled up there," Thurlby recalled. "Bert Olmstead was on his ass. He told him he was facing the same guys he was playing against last year [in the minors]."

Good fortune smiled on Joe Szura prior to the 1968-69 season. His former teammate and coach with the Barons, Fred Glover, took over as coach of the Seals. "My man Joe," Glover recalled. "My protégé. I had him in Cleveland. He became an excellent player but he was an awkward skater." Glover gave Szura a real chance to play in the NHL and Szura responded. In 70 games with the Seals in 1968-69, Szura notched nine goals and 21 points. Norm Ferguson, who played on a line with Szura part of the year, recalled that Szura and he "complement each other well." Ferguson scored a Seals club record 34 goals that season. In the playoffs, Szura scored a pair of goals and five points in seven games. Gary

Jarrett remembered Szura's 1968-69 season this way: "He was our second-line center. I didn't know much about him before he came to the NHL, but he was a good centerman and playmaker."

The following year, however, the Seals sent Szura down to the minor leagues. Defenseman Bert Marshall didn't understand the move. "He was a good player," Marshall said. "In our best year, he played consistently and well but they let him go at the end of the year." Szura spent the next two years with the Seals farm team, the Providence Reds. He scored 21 goals both seasons and averaged about a point a game. Still, the Seals did not call him up. In 1971-72, Szura joined the Baltimore Clippers of the AHL and scored 38 goals and 76 points. A year later, Szura signed with the Los Angeles Sharks of the WHA. In 73 games with the Sharks, the 6'3" centerman scored 13 goals and 45 points. The following year, Szura was traded to the Houston Aeros and scored eight goals and 15 points in 42 games. In 1974-75, Szura finished his career as an active player with the Cape Codders of the NAHL. He played in only 10 games.

Today, Szura lives in Thunder Bay, Ontario. Many of his teammates feel that Szura was not given a fair chance to stay with the Seals after the 1968-69 season. Brian Perry said, "Joe was a big guy and a good centerman. We were all good that second year, but then Frank Selke broke up the team." The Seals certainly could have used a playmaker like Joe Szura in some of their later seasons. If only he could have skated faster.

Howie Menard

"A fast little player who could score. He was small, but tough, and never gave ground."
—Dick Mattiussi on Howie Menard

Howie Menard grew up in Timmons, Ontario. Because there were a lot of French Canadians in the area, he grew up following the Canadiens and idolizing Rocket Richard. In juniors, he won a Memorial Cup with the Hamilton Red Wings. His NHL rights were owned by Detroit and, after two consecutive invitations to the Wings camp, Menard thought he would get a chance to play in the NHL. In fact, his brother Hillary (Minnie) Menard played one NHL game for the Black Hawks in 1953-54.

The biggest obstacle facing Menard was his size. Menard was generously listed as 5'8", 160 pounds. To compensate for his lack of bulk, Menard concentrated on his skating. "I could really skate and, at my size, I *had* to skate," Menard said. "If I ever stopped, somebody would chop me to the ice. Gump Worsley once said, 'Put a lasso on that guy.' I was a good face-off guy and checker."

Menard made his NHL debut with the Red Wings in 1963-64, appearing in three games. That was his only appearance in the big league before expansion. He spent two seasons playing for Eddie Shore's Springfield Indians in the AHL before splitting the next two seasons between the Los Angeles Kings and their Springfield AHL affiliate.

Menard started the 1969-70 season with the Chicago Black Hawks but was traded to the Seals in exchange for Gene Ubriaco in midseason. "I was actually a little disappointed," Menard admitted when reflecting on the trade. "I liked Chicago. It was just before Christmas and I was pissed about that. I was going from playing with Bobby Hull and Stan Mikita to playing with the Oakland Seals. I had a lot of friends in Chicago, like Doug Mohns, and my brother knew Bobby Hull. It was a bit rough."

Seals winger Norm Ferguson recalled that Menard had a tough time adjusting to Oakland at first. "He was Bobby Hull's centerman in Chicago and he never let us forget that." After a brief adjustment period, however, Menard came to enjoy playing for the Seals. "I enjoyed being on the team and being with the guys," Menard said. "That's what I miss most. Playing hockey with the guys and then getting a beer."

Menard had a pleasant surprise when he walked into the Seals locker room for the first time. "I came into the locker room after I was acquired and I saw Bill Torrey sitting there with his bow tie on," Menard said. "I hadn't seem him since he worked for the Pittsburgh Hornets of the AHL. In

Pittsburgh, he was the PR man and we thought he knew nothing about hockey. He sort of whispered to me, 'I'm the executive vice president of the team.' I was shocked."

The Seals were not expecting a large offensive output from Menard. An article in a Seals home program profiling Menard quoted coach Fred Glover as saying, "He's doing just the job we hoped we would when we traded for him. He won't score a lot of goals, but he has been a demon forechecker and is a real battler."

Menard recalled two games in particular as his favorite moments with the Seals. The first was an individual effort in which he scored three points in one game. The other was a team highlight. "Once we beat Montreal in the Forum 1-0," Menard said. "Fred Glover couldn't believe it. He was like, 'How did we beat these guys?' "

The overall lack of hockey fever in the Bay Area was another adjustment for Menard. "The fans were good, but we were a tough draw," Menard admitted. "The A's and Raiders were doing well. There was just too much going on in the area. We had a base of about 8,000 fans. The more fans you have, the better. I think it's worth a goal per game at home."

Menard didn't always see eye to eye with Seals coach Fred Glover. "I played against Freddie in the AHL," Menard said. "He was a grouchy little bastard. He was a good player and good players aren't good coaches. He was tough and stubborn, but he wasn't one of the guys. He would put on the gear in practice and we would run him. We figured we might as well get one in while we had the chance."

Menard finished his only season in Oakland with two goals and seven assists in 38 games. His overall season totals were four goals and 14 points in 57 contests. Menard dressed for the first game of the Seals playoff series against the Penguins, but missed the rest of the series with an injury. "Duane Rupp caught me at center ice knee to knee, and that was it," Menard recalled. "I tore ligaments in my knee and was out for the series."

Despite his lack of offensive output, teammates recognized Menard's value to the team. "He wasn't afraid of anything," Brian Perry recalled. "He always gave his all." Defenseman Wayne Muloin called Menard "a good little hustler. I liked playing with him more than against him. He was like a horsefly. He would pick away at you until you broke down."

Menard briefly left the Seals prior to the 1970-71 season. "I was picked up by Buffalo in the expansion draft," Menard said. "I got off the plane and was at one game with the Sabres in Pittsburgh. Punch Imlach then said he had traded me back to Oakland. I called Frank Selke Jr. and he told me to go to Providence [the Seals AHL affiliate that year]. I asked him, 'How long?' and he told me he'd call me in a couple of weeks. I stayed there the entire year. I was disappointed. I wanted to play in the NHL. I didn't feel right in the AHL. I didn't play well; I was discouraged."

Although Menard remained an active professional hockey player until the 1975-76 season, he never appeared in another NHL game. He spent most of his time with the Baltimore Clippers, although he also played for the Providence Reds and Salt Lake Golden Eagles. He found it difficult situation to get used to not playing hockey anymore. "It was tough adjusting to life after hockey," Menard admitted. "I didn't know what to do. They did everything for you and just handed you a hotel-room key. I took two years off because I didn't know what to do. I had no advanced training and no trade. It was rough."

Despite the difficulties he faced, Menard found a way to become successful. Today, he works for Corby Distilleries, although now he's only there part time. He and his wife have three daughters. These days, he's only too happy to tell stories of his time with the Oakland Seals.

Although Menard only played in the NHL for a brief time, he left his mark on the people he played with and against. Seals forward Earl Ingarfield described Menard this way: "He was a gritty little guy. He was cocky and he stuck his nose into traffic. He was a smaller guy with not a lot of skill, but he worked very hard." That description would bring a smile to Howie Menard's face. He was a buzz saw on skates, and proud of it.

Joe Hardy

"He came out of the Quebec League and did quite well. He was a good puck handler and a skilled player. A taller guy, he was kind of happy-go-lucky."

—Earl Ingarfield on Joe Hardy

Joe Hardy signed with the Seals as a free agent prior to the 1969-70 season. "I played four years in junior and then went to New Haven of the EHL," Hardy said. "A Seals scout saw me and invited me to camp in Oshawa. I wanted to go to the AHL, but was offered an NHL contract. I couldn't believe it—the first time out, I made it. It was a dream come true. There were only three guys in the NHL who came from where I'm from: Pierre Pilote, J.C. Tremblay and me."

Hardy split the 1969-70 season between the Seals and their top affiliate in the AHL, the Providence Reds. In 46 games with Providence, he scored 11 goals and 38 points. Hardy played 23 games for Oakland and scored five goals and four assists. "Gypsy Joe" provided size and skating ability to the Seals. "He was big and strong," fellow rookie Tony Featherstone recalled about Hardy. The 6', 185-pound native of Kenogami, Quebec, was a good stickhandler as well. Norm Ferguson recalled that Hardy was "a slick centerman and a real dipsy-doodler, but he never passed the puck." Defenseman Harry Howell recalled that Hardy helped in his own zone and described him as "defensive-oriented."

At first, Hardy was a bit awestruck about being in the NHL. "I was now playing with Hicke, Howell and Ingarfield. I watched them play. I lacked experience. I was so young at the time; I was impressed by playing in Detroit and Chicago and against the players I saw on TV. I played in the OJHL, which was not as good as the OHA. The guys I used to play against were smaller and not as tough."

Hardy remembers his first game in Detroit very vividly. "We had a team meeting and a morning skate," Hardy recalled. "They told us it would be O'Donoghue, Hardy and Featherstone against Howe, Mahovlich and Delvecchio. I was watching the Wings skate around during warm-ups and Carol Vadnais said to me, 'Joe, you have to skate.' I only played one period against that line."

Frank Selke Jr. and Carol Vadnais, both from Montreal, proved to help the young center adjust to life in the NHL. Vadnais was the only other French speaker on the team at that time and he took the young Hardy under his wing. Selke was also a big help. "Frank Selke was real. He was friendly to me and my wife. My wife spoke no English and his wife was very helpful to us."

The most dramatic moment in Hardy's first season with the Seals came at the Oakland Coliseum Arena on March 25, 1970. The Seals were hosting the Flyers and were in the thick of a fight for the final playoff berth in the West Division with Philadelphia and Minnesota. The Seals were trailing the Flyers 2-1 late in the third period when Hardy stole the show. With 3:40 remaining in the game, "Gypsy Joe" set up Don O'Donoghue's goal to tie the score at 2-2. Then, with just 12 seconds left in the game, Hardy beat Bernie Parent and the Seals downed the Flyers 3-2 to gain two much-needed points. Oakland ended up tying the Flyers for fourth place in the standings, but qualified for the playoffs because they had more wins than Philadelphia. Hardy's contribution was critical to the Seals playoff drive.

Hardy also recalled scoring a shorthanded goal against the mighty Bruins. "Bobby Orr tried to pass to Fred Stanfield on the other point, but I got a breakaway and scored on Gerry Cheevers," Hardy said proudly. "After I scored, Orr cross-checked me in the back."

One problem Hardy encountered in Oakland was the language barrier, which often affected many French-speaking NHLers at the time. "He spoke broken English," Wayne Muloin recalled. "He was a good guy, a funny guy and a smooth player." Hardy remembered that Fred Glover told the players only to speak English in the dressing room. Dick Mattiussi also gave him a hard time about his English. "He killed me," Hardy said. "I said 'shpaghetti' instead of 'spaghetti.'"

Despite the language barrier, Hardy got along well with most of his teammates. "He was quiet off the ice but he got along with everybody," captain Ted Hampson said. "Big Joe was good with the puck. He had good size and one-on-one skills."

Hardy was held scoreless in the four-game sweep against Pittsburgh in the 1970 playoffs. "We should have beat them," Hardy said. "They were close games—close so far as play was concerned." "Gypsy Joe" felt that the Penguins intimidated the smaller Seals to win the series. "Carol Vadnais was our only tough guy and they had more tough guys like Bryan Watson."

Like many of his teammates, Hardy fell victim to the injury bug in 1970-71. He missed 38 games with a fractured wrist and didn't see action until the last half of the season. In 40 games, Hardy contributed four goals and 10 assists. Again, despite seemingly limited offensive numbers, Hardy scored some big goals. His best game that season came against the Red Wings on March 14, 1971, when Hardy scored twice in an 8-5 loss to Detroit.

The green and yellow skates that Finley introduced didn't bother Hardy at all. "I didn't care at the time. It was my dream to play in the NHL," he said. "Even if we wore pink skates, it didn't matter to me. Years later, when I was coaching in the Quebec junior leagues, people still asked me about those skates."

Looking back, Seals coach Fred Glover appreciated some of Hardy's skills with the puck. "He could fool anybody with his slick stickhandling. He was big. I don't think he really got a chance."

One thing many teammates noticed about Hardy was his laid-back nature. "I liked his attitude toward things," said Ron Stackhouse. "He didn't take things too seriously." Doug Roberts recalled Hardy as "an easygoing guy who played the same way."

In October 1971, the Seals decided Hardy was not in their plans and they traded the smooth-skating Quebec native to the Canadiens in a cash deal. Hardy spent the 1971-72 season with the Nova Scotia Voyageurs and helped lead them to the Calder Cup title. With the creation of the WHA the following year, Hardy signed with the Cleveland Crusaders. He spent three years in the WHA, and also played for the Chicago Cougars, Indianapolis Racers and San Diego Mariners. "He hurt himself by going to the WHA," Fred Glover said later, thinking that Hardy would have developed his skills further in the more-established NHL. Statistically, Hardy did well in "the other league," totaling 46 goals and 140 points in 210 games.

In 1975-76, Hardy played for the Beauce Jaros of the NAHL. He won the league-scoring title, netting 60 goals and adding an incredible 148 assists for 208 points in 72 games. He helped lead the Jaros to the league's best record in the regular season. Hardy split the 1976-77 season between Beauce and Binghamton, joining the latter after the Jaros folded on December 22, 1976. His final season as an active player was 1977-78 with the Binghamton Dusters of the AHL.

After retirement, Hardy coached for many years in the Quebec League and with Binghamton of the AHL and NAHL. He also worked for the Quebec Nordiques in advertising sales. Today, Hardy is working for the D&R Belly Paper Board Co. as the sales director. He lives in a suburb of Quebec City.

Although his stay with the Seals and in the NHL was brief, Hardy's teammates remembered him fondly. "He was a happy go lucky person who could score goals and get points," Dick Mattiussi recalled. That was Joe Hardy, briefly a big centerman for the Seals.

Harry Howell

"A real class act. A top defenseman who was very intelligent and good with the puck. He was big, strong and steady. Not an offensive type, but one of the best defensemen in the NHL … It was a pleasure to be his teammate."

—Earl Ingarfield on Harry Howell

Ask almost any NHL player who played with or against Harry Howell to describe the native of Hamilton, Ontario, and the words you will most likely hear are "classy" or "gentleman." Howell made his NHL debut with the New York Rangers in 1952-53 after playing only one game in the AHL. He spent the next 17 seasons with the Rangers as the mainstay of their blue line. To this day, Howell holds the Rangers franchise record for games played, with 1,160. He won the Norris Trophy as the NHL's best defenseman in 1966-67 right before a young kid named Bobby Orr won it eight straight times. Howell never put up gaudy offensive numbers. He was a classic defensive defenseman. Despite the fact that he only scored more than 10 goals a season once in his NHL career, and never had more than 40 points, Howell was an a shoo-in for the Hockey Hall of Fame. In fact, he is the only member of the Seals who has been inducted in the Hall of Fame for his services as a player.

The Seals purchased Howell from the Rangers in June of 1969. "It wasn't that surprising," recalled Howell. "Emile Francis saw me in the hospital. I had a bad back and the team doctor then liked to do back operations, so I was one of the many Rangers who had spinal fusions. Emile Francis told me they were changing the face of the Rangers and he gave me several options to stay in the organization, but not as an active player. I still wanted to play. He asked me where I wanted to go and I said that California sounded good to me. I knew either Oakland or Los Angeles were possibilities."

When he arrived in Oakland, Howell was still recovering from his spinal surgery and didn't make his debut with the Seals until December 1969. Howell did notice a difference between playing for the Rangers and the Seals. "Many of the Rangers teams I played for were made up of draftees. For example, there were six players who I played with in juniors at Guelph. In expansion, players came from six different organizations. We got along well, but it was just a different feeling."

Howell settled in and provided experience and leadership on the blue line, even if he was not the same player he was in his prime. Goalie Chris Worthy described Howell as "a talented guy—a prince of a guy—a quiet type leader that you need on a team. You could see the talent was still there and you could see what used to be there." Forward Brian Perry added, "He was our elder statesman and a complete gentleman. I always wanted to call him 'Mr. Howell.' "

Rookie defenseman Ron Stackhouse recalled playing with the veteran Howell. "You see him out there and you have to respect his presence. He was near the end of his career, but he was still a presence. He set an example by trying to do what he could."

Howell took a liking to Seals coach Fred Glover. He described Glover as "a player's coach." "I had a good relationship with Freddie," Howell explained. "As a player, he was hard-nosed and aggressive and wanted 100 percent all the time. He focused on that as a coach. He really liked to scrimmage with the team. He'd be banging and hitting out there."

Another thing that took getting used to for Howell was the travel involved in playing for a California team. "The first year I was there we had a 17-day road trip over Christmas and New Year's," Howell said. "We spent Christmas in Philadelphia and there isn't much open in Philadelphia on Christmas Day."

Goalie Gary Smith recalls that Howell tried to inspire his teammates during long road trips. "In warm-ups," Smith recalled, "I remember he would say 'Here we are, the opposition' whenever we were playing on the road. He always said we should try to put on a show for the 17,000 fans who came to see the other team."

In 1969-70, Howell appeared in 55 games for the Seals, scoring four goals and 20 points. He showed the poise of a veteran, however, as three of his four goals were game-winners.

The highlight of Howell's career with the Seals was the 1970 regular-season finale against the Kings in Los Angeles. "On Saturday afternoon, Philadelphia was playing. They needed to tie to make the playoffs but they lost 1-0, and we were in." The celebration was short-lived, however as the Seals were eliminated by the Penguins in four straight games in the first round of the playoffs. "We got knocked out fast," Howell said. "They were a hungrier team and they got the jump on us. In the playoffs, you just have to get hot for 10 days. We had a bad 10 days." Howell had one assist for Oakland in four playoff games.

Howell's contract expired after the 1969-70 season and he and defenseman Carol Vadnais were holding out. "The night before the season opener, we hadn't signed contracts yet," Howell recalled. I got a call from Frank Selke Jr. and Bill Torrey. They said they thought Charlie Finley wanted to call me. Well, Finley did call me. He said, 'You know, Harry, I don't care if you sign or not. We won't win anyway.' " Howell signed his contract and rejoined the team.

Another thing the veteran hockey player had to adjust to were the uniquely colored skates Charlie Finley introduced. "I hated every minute of it," admitted Howell. "We opened in Detroit. They turned off all the lights and put the spotlight on us. I was the first one out on the ice with the skates. The fans were whistling at us."

Howell kept himself in excellent shape. Rookie Tony Featherstone remembered that the 38-year-old Howell "had a physique that was just amazing. He was the fittest guy I ever met. He was a solid guy, a tough guy." Featherstone also remembered that Howell "once took a shot to the cup. A teammate said to me, 'I bet that made Harry howl.' "

The veteran defenseman had the respect of his teammates. The Seals young star at the time was Carol Vadnais, who quickly came to admire Howell. "He was a great veteran. I always wondered what was so great about him, but you had to play with him to see what a great skater he was." Doug Roberts, who had to make the transition from forward to defenseman when he joined the Seals, recalled, "He had class. We all looked up to him. He had a big adjustment coming from Manhattan to Oakland. I learned a lot from him." Joe Hardy added, "He was the king of all old men. He had gray hair when I played with him. He was a smooth skater and a great guy on and off the ice. Nobody wanted to hit him; he was respected by all."

Howell played 28 games for the Seals in 1970-71. It was an odd sight to see the dignified, gray-haired Howell wearing the "kelly green, California gold and white" sweaters that Charlie Finley had designed for the team.

On February 5, 1971, Howell received a surprise. "We played in Philadelphia and were heading home," Howell recalled. "We had to fly and make a stopover in Los Angeles. I was playing cards in the back of the plane. Fred Glover said he wanted to talk to me. He said, 'When we get to Los Angeles, it's a stopover. I want you to get off the plane and not get back on. We've traded you to Los Angeles.' It was a shock."

Howell played just over two years for the Kings before joining the WHA's New York Golden Blades as a player/coach in 1973-74. He spent three seasons in the WHA before retiring as an active player after the 1975-76 season. He later served as assistant general manager of the NHL's Cleveland Barons and briefly coached the Minnesota North Stars. Howell later became a scout and finally got his name on the Stanley Cup in 1990 when the Edmonton Oilers won their fifth Stanley Cup. Today, Howell is scouting for the New York Rangers and was honored as the Rangers 2001-2002 alumni of the year. He was elected to the Hockey Hall of Fame in 1979.

Fellow defenseman Wayne Muloin summed up Harry Howell by saying, "They don't come any better than him. He could cover the ice and cut the time in half; a perfect gentleman. I learned a lot by watching him." That was Harry Howell: classy, consistent and a leader on the and off the ice.

Tony Featherstone

"He was a good, young hockey player, a hard-nosed kid. He'd go through a brick wall for you."
—*Wayne Muloin on Tony Featherstone*

Toronto native Tony Featherstone was faced with an identity crisis in the NHL. What kind of player was he going to be? Was he going to be an enforcer and a fighter, or was he going to be more of a scorer and a checker? The Seals never really answered this question and, as a result, Featherstone's development as an NHL player stalled.

The Seals drafted Featherstone with their first-round pick in the 1969 draft, the seventh pick overall. The season before with the Peterborough Petes of the OHA, Featherstone scored 29 goals and had 67 points in just 54 games. He also added 167 penalty minutes. The 5'11", 187-pound Featherstone had the potential to do it all. Growing up, he was a Maple Leafs fan and his favorite player was future Seals forward Billy Harris.

Featherstone recalled being "elated and happy" when the Seals selected him in the draft. It was then that he knew he could play in the NHL. He was also pleased when the Seals drafted his good friend defenseman Ron Stackhouse in the second round. Featherstone spent most of his first professional season with the Seals top farm club, the Providence Reds of the AHL. In 55 games with the Reds, he scored 15 goals and 25 assists to go along with 78 penalty minutes. The Seals called him up for three short stays and he played in nine games and earned one assist. Featherstone made an impact in his first game in the NHL. It came against the Chicago Black Hawks, and Featherstone recalled skating against Bobby Hull on his first shift. Later in the shift, he knocked Keith Magnuson off the puck. Mike Laughton scooped up the loose disc and passed to Don O'Donoghue, who scored the winning goal in a 2-1 Seals win.

Featherstone remained with the Seals in the postseason and appeared in two of the four playoff games against Pittsburgh that year without scoring a point. "I was excited about it," Featherstone said about his first and only NHL playoff appearance. "It was a short series. Michel Briere played very well for Pittsburgh."

Featherstone made the Seals outright in 1970-71 and remained with the team all season. The rookie right wing started the year as an extra forward, but when Norm Ferguson was injured early in the season, Featherstone was inserted onto the club's first line with center Dennis Hextall and left wing Gary Croteau. The trio was dubbed the "Battle Line," as all three of its members were tough, physical players. The Battle Line quickly became the most productive trio on the Seals squad. There was nothing subtle about the way this line played. Seals coach Fred Glover said at the time, "Grace and style is not their forte. If they try to get fancy, then they're in trouble. None of them can accomplish anything without working his tail off."

All three members of the Battle Line were also known for their ability to throw punches. Linemate Gary Croteau recalled that Featherstone "was a great fighter. He was one of the few guys in the league with arms as long as his legs. He didn't go looking for fights, but he could handle himself. He would protect the other players on the team."

After Norm Ferguson returned from injury in late December, Featherstone was taken off the Battle Line and returned to being a third- or fourth-line player. Suddenly, there were questions about his role on the team. Featherstone's best friend on the team, Ron Stackhouse, recalled the quandary the rookie right wing was placed in. "Feather had to work so hard to get where he got, and nobody realized it. In Peterborough, he couldn't skate or shoot well enough to play Junior A. He stayed around because of his physical toughness but he worked so hard on his game. In Oakland, they wanted him to be a goon and that's not what Tony wanted. He had a few fights and lost some to the heavyweights. Tony wanted to be a hockey player, not a goon."

Featherstone's personality made him seem ill-suited for an enforcer. Norm Ferguson recalled that "off the ice, Feather wouldn't hurt a fly."

Some of his teammates speculated that one particular fight changed Featherstone's attitude toward being an enforcer. "He worked his butt off, a real tough kid," Dennis Hextall said of Featherstone. "Ronnie Harris finished him off. He put him in the hospital with just two punches. I think that took his heart out of it." Coach Fred Glover also recalled the fight as being a turning point for his rookie right wing. "He was a tough kid. He played well until he got into a fight. He had the guy, but he thought, 'What am I doing?' Then he got the shit beat out of him and he wasn't the same."

Despite the questions that surrounded his role with the club, Featherstone got along well with Glover. "He was a very quiet man with a strong will," Featherstone recalled. "I liked him. He insinuated more than he actually told you what he wanted you to do."

Featherstone recalled some memorable games he had with the Seals. "I remember my first NHL goal against Rogie Vachon in Los Angeles," he said. "I got it off a scramble in front of the net."

Featherstone was also witness to what may be the most unusual goal in NHL history, according to both Featherstone and former Bruins coach and CBC commentator Don Cherry. "I remember Bobby Orr scoring the most remarkable goal," Featherstone said. "He took a shot on Gary Smith. Smitty juggled it [in his glove] and Bobby Orr went behind the net and tipped it in from back there. I saw that again on a highlight film recently and I was amazed because I always thought I had dreamed it."

Orr was also responsible for Featherstone's most embarrassing moment with the Seals. "I remember chasing Bobby Orr around the net in Boston. We went around the net two or three times like a train."

Featherstone also had no problems with Seals owner Charlie Finley. "I was so young at the time that nothing bothered me. Charlie Finley was good to us. He didn't know much about hockey, but everybody liked him." The only minor problem Featherstone had with Finley was the green and gold skates he made the team wear. "I didn't think anything of it until we got to Chicago," Featherstone said. "Lou Angotti said to me, 'Feather, you look like a canary.' I was proud to wear them anyway."

Featherstone also enjoyed the fans in the Bay Area. "They were patient and faithful," Featherstone said. "I never remembered being booed."

Featherstone finished his only full season with the Seals with eight goals and eight assists in 67 games. He also added 44 penalty minutes. There were changes in management before the 1971-72 season and they didn't bode well for Featherstone's future with the Seals. "I didn't leave on good terms," Featherstone admitted. "I wasn't very happy. In camp, I wasn't getting along with Garry Young, the new general manager. There were no hard feelings, though."

On October 6, 1971, just two days before the start of the season, the Seals traded their former first-round pick to the Montreal Canadiens for minor league goaltender Ray Martyniuk. Featherstone spent the next two seasons with the Habs farm club, the Nova Scotia Voyageurs. In 1972-73, he had his best professional season playing for Nova Scotia and was named a first team AHL all-star. Featherstone scored 49 goals and totaled 103 points that year. He also led the AHL in playoff goal-scoring with 10 goals in 13 postseason games. The following season he was traded to the Minnesota North Stars, where he played his final NHL season. Featherstone spent two years with the WHA's Toronto Toros before retiring from hockey.

Today, Tony Featherstone lives in Toronto. He has worked for Allstate, selling insurance for the past 25 years. He and his wife have two sons and a daughter.

Nobody doubted Featherstone's effort or his integrity. When asked about Featherstone, Hall of Famer Harry Howell said, "He was a good checker and a hard-nosed guy." He was also a player who never quite found his niche in the NHL.

Bert Marshall

"We came to Oakland in the same trade. He was one of the best shot blockers in the game. A defensive defenseman, you could always count on him to get the puck out of our own end."

—Ted Hampson on Bert Marshall

Bert Marshall was a hockey player's hockey player. Perhaps the fans didn't notice him a lot because he was not flashy. He didn't make end-to-end rushes or score a lot of goals. But game in and game out, Marshall did his job: blocking shots and keeping the puck out of his own end. He came to the Seals as a 25-year-old youngster and by the time he left, he was a veteran leader and captain of the squad. In the nine-year history of the Seals franchise, no player appeared in more games than Bert Marshall. He is the only player in the club's history to appear in more than 300 regular-season games with the Seals and took part in six of the nine seasons the team was in Oakland.

Marshall was born in Kamloops, British Columbia. As a youngster, he fantasized about playing in the NHL but he didn't think that dream could come true until relatively late in his hockey development. "I didn't think I could make it until my second year of junior," Marshall admitted. "I was 19 years old. It was a fantasy, not a dream, when I was growing up. Growing up, you thought about it and you were a fan. I was fairly big, played on a good team and we won the Memorial Cup. I was a contributor. I had size and was a pretty good defenseman."

The dream finally came true for Marshall during the 1965-66 season. The Detroit Red Wings had his NHL rights and Marshall appeared in 61 games with Detroit that season. Although he did not score any goals, the 6'2", 195-pound Marshall recorded 19 assists. The following season he played in 57 games and registered 10 assists. Marshall tallied his first NHL goal with the Red Wings in 1967-68, but on January 9, 1968, he was traded to the Seals with Ted Hampson and John Brenneman for Kent Douglas. "Looking back, I think at that time I was immature at 21, 22 or 23," Marshall said. "I was making $7,500 per year and thinking it was a big deal. We were paid like a regular job. I was disappointed at being traded but you know, after expansion, you knew things would change."

By the time he joined the club, the Seals were already buried in last place in the West Division. Marshall admitted that playing hockey in the Bay Area was a different experience for him. "It was part of a new arena without any fan base," Marshall said. "They liked to say there was a fan base because so many Canadians lived there. That doesn't mean didly. Hockey is a subculture. Many Canadians have never been to a hockey game. All the fans ended up coming from San Jose. There was ongoing turmoil in the player personnel. Looking back on it, it wasn't like the Wings or the Islanders."

The other adjustment Marshall had to make when arriving in Oakland was travel. "Travel was a big deal," he admitted. "Practice time was hard to come by and that affects performance. We would go on the road, start a slump and it snowballs. If you have a six- or seven-game road trip and you lose the first two or three games, you can lose them all. I'd say because of travel, we practiced 20 percent less than other teams and we probably needed to practice 20 percent more than the other teams."

Quickly, Marshall realized that Seals coach Bert Olmstead was having problems reaching his players. "Bert was a little bit strange as a coach," Marshall commented. "Probably the kind of player he was—a power left wing, competitive, tough, mean and even a little nasty. He was trying to compete in the NHL with a hodgepodge of up-and-comers and career minor leaguers. The personalities just couldn't mesh with the guys he was trying to lead. It didn't happen fast enough."

Marshall played in 20 games for the Seals and assisted on four goals in 1967-68. He was hampered by a knee injury and missed almost 20 games. Despite the injury, Marshall's teammates quickly appreciated his value to the squad. "He was a big, strong individual," Charlie Burns said of Marshall. "He had limited skating skills, but he knew what to do with the puck." Wally Boyer added that Marshall "was a funny guy and a good defenseman. He was hard to get around." Veteran defenseman Bob Baun, who captained the Seals that first season, recognized that Marshall was "a pretty good young hockey player. He had good size and mobility and a good attitude." Bill Hicke, who claimed he had a nickname for everyone on the Seals, nicknamed the strapping young Marshall "Candle" because "when he would fight, it was one blow and he was out."

In 1968-69, the Seals had their most successful season on the ice. Part of the turnaround was due to the club's new coach, Fred Glover. "Fred was a survivor," Marshall said. "He came back to coach us three times. I got along fine with him. We didn't have enough horses to make good things happen on the ice. He was an old-style guy, but he worked hard and he wanted to be successful." Marshall appeared in 68 games and had three goals, 18 points and 81 penalty minutes. The three goals would be the highest total Marshall had in one season with the Seals. He was not known for his powerful shot. Mike Laughton joked that he "had to go out of the slot to tip Bert's shots." In the playoffs that season, Marshall suddenly found an offensive touch. He was red hot, picking up seven assists in seven games against the Kings. Still, the Seals lost the series in seven games after holding a 3-2 lead in the series.

By 1969-70, the Seals were under their third different ownership group in the three years that Marshall had been a member of the club. "We had a new owner every year. We had no problem getting owners, although some were probably shady deals or rocky business deals," Marshall said. "The people were fine, but the commitment to putting a product on the ice was lacking. There were some pretty good hockey people there, but you would get one problem area fixed and then have problems in other areas, and then we would have player turnover again. Mr. Selke was a classy guy and an old-style hockey man. Bill Torrey was a new guy coming in on the way up. They were both classy guys."

Despite all the difficulties Marshall experienced in Oakland, the time there was not without its lighter moments. "Munson Campbell at one time was Bruce Norris's left-hand man in Detroit. Munson was once voted most eligible bachelor in the East Bay. Anyway, Munson called one of the local patrolmen and told him he wanted to give all the guys living in the barracks some tickets. He thought all patrolmen lived in barracks."

Another incident Marshall recalled had to do with the local chapter of Hells Angels, whose members often attended games. "They requested preferred tickets, free parking, and that kind of thing. I told them they had asked the wrong guy."

In 1969-70, the Seals returned to the playoffs but performed below expectations. Marshall's role began to change. Instead of being one of the team's younger players, he gradually became more of a leader. He was named an alternate captain during his third season in Oakland. Rookie Tony Featherstone recalled, "I learned a lot about being in the NHL, as a person, from Bert." In 1969-70, the 26-year-old Marshall scored one goal and added 15 assists and a career-high 109 penalty minutes. Hall of Fame defenseman Harry Howell, who played with Marshall that season, recalled that "Bert made very few mistakes. He was a steady type. He covered for me when *I* made mistakes."

The Seals were swept in the playoffs by the Penguins that year but Marshall felt two things stood out for him about those games. "I remember how well Michel Briere played and that he was killed that summer, and that my daughter was born April 10, 1970, during those playoffs," Marshall said.

After the season, it was determined that Marshall had actually played the 1969-70 season with a hairline fracture of his wrist. Unfortunately, the team doctors were unable to detect it until just prior to training camp for 1970-71. Marshall needed surgery on his wrist and missed the first half of the season as a result. He played in only 32 games, scoring twice and adding six assists.

When he played for the Seals, the club's goalies certainly appreciated his efforts. "He was solid in front of you," Gilles Meloche said. "I think he blocked as many shots as I did." Chris Worthy called Marshall "a damn good defenseman; a tough guy with a good sense of humor." Gary Smith showed how he truly appreciated Bert Marshall. "I named my son Marshall after him," the big goalie admitted. "He was best man at my wedding and good at blocking shots."

By 1971-72, the Seals had introduced their white skates. Marshall was amazed at the contrast. "We went from Fred Glover as coach, who said I couldn't wear a helmet, to Charlie Finley, who put us in white skates. Imagine what must have been in Fred Glover's mind. We all laughed about it. Charlie

Finley was a different guy. Charlie ran things the way he wanted to and he owned us. We were like a horse stable and the players were his horses."

Marshall also had to deal with a new coach, Vic Stasiuk. "He was the first coach that ever benched me," Marshall said. "He was right in a way. If we were ahead, I would play, and if we were behind, I wouldn't. He was old school. He had a different way about him than Fred Glover, but he was out of the same school—the ex-player school of coaching. When we were good, he was jovial; when we were bad, he was not too pleasant to be around." Stasiuk genuinely appreciated Marshall's efforts, but spent some time trying to change his style. "He was big enough," Stasiuk said of his 6'2" defenseman. "I tried to get him to be a bit more twinkle toes, but he was not a great skater. He tied guys up in front of our net."

Late in the 1971-72 season, Seals captain Carol Vadnais was traded to the Bruins. The Seals named Marshall, the last player on the roster to play for the club in its inaugural season, as captain. "It was a big deal, in a sense," Marshall said, "but I came to be captain by default when Carol Vadnais was traded. If you told me I could be captain of an NHL team, I would have said no, but somebody had to be the captain and it was me. I was more of a support guy than a lead guy."

Marshall did add a personal touch as captain. Many teammates warmly remembered that after practice, Bert would drive his Winnebago around and invite the players in for some beers.

The 1971-72 season also provided Marshall with his most memorable and most embarrassing moments as a member of the Seals. Ironically, both came against the Boston Bruins. "We came into Boston and we beat them," Marshall remembered. "Gilles Meloche earned a shutout. Charlie Finley came in after the game and bought us all suits. We were outshot something like 60-15 and we won 2-0." Ironically enough, Finley called Marshall after the bills for the suits came in. "When he bought the team suits, I bought a few other things in the store," Marshall admitted. "He phoned me personally and asked, 'What's with this bill? I said one suit!' "

Later in the season, the Seals were hosting the Bruins in Oakland. "We were beating the Bruins 6-1 and they beat us 8-6," Marshall said. "Bobby Orr was killing a penalty and he had the puck. He lost his stick, picked up the stick and he kept the puck. He almost killed the entire penalty carrying the puck. I was on the power play. I shouldn't have been on the power play."

When asked to describe himself as a hockey player, Marshall said, "I was a good, solid defensive defenseman. I was a good support player. I could play for a good team and contribute, and could be a bad player on a bad team. I kept the puck out of the net. I had one of the top plus-minus ratings on the Seals and the Islanders."

Many of Marshall's teammates also respected his defensive abilities. "He was a steady defenseman," Paul Shmyr recalled. "One-on-one, you couldn't go around him. He was never caught up-ice." Craig Patrick said that Marshall was "a leader, our captain and a solid guy for us. He was not gifted offensively, but he knew the game well." Walt McKechnie added, "Bert was a veteran influence on the team and a real competitor. He would be blocking shots like it's the seventh game of the Cup finals in overtime." Marshall Johnston said that Marshall was "One of the smartest players I ever played with. He was first-class."

After the 1971-72 season, the Seals lost half their roster to the WHA. Marshall remained with the Seals, although very few fans know how close he came to being another key member of the Seals to jump to the new league. "When the WHA came, the New York Raiders called and offered me a contract," Marshall admitted. "The owner said he'd meet me at the Oakland airport but when I went there, he wasn't on the plane. He called and told me he had missed the plane and he made me the offer again, but I declined. That's how close I came to signing with the WHA."

In 1972-73, Marshall returned as captain of the Seals. The team was missing a lot of players who had signed with the WHA and the talent drain was taking its toll. It was particularly noticeable on defense as the Seals allowed the most goals in the West Division, 323. "Bert was one of the older guys on the team and he worked hard," Reggie Leach said. "He was one of the best shot blockers I've ever seen. He had marks all over his body from blocked shots. He was very disgusted with us for not coming back to help out defensively." Rookie Stan Weir recalled that during the 1972-73 season, Marshall was "a good leader of a bunch of guys that didn't know how to be led."

Statistically, Marshall played in 55 games for the Seals in 1972-73, collecting two goals and eight points. Then, like the three previous Seals captains before him, Marshall was traded. On March 4, 1973, the Seals sent Marshall to the New York Rangers for cash and future considerations. The Rangers were suffering with injuries to their defensive corps and desperately needed blue-line help. Marshall helped the club reach the Stanley Cup semifinals that year.

In typical Seals fashion, Marshall was told of the trade in an unusual way. "We were flying back to Oakland from Atlanta," Marshall recalled. "Fred Glover was sitting on the plane in front of me. When we got home, Fred called me up and told me I had been traded, on the telephone. He waited until I got home to tell me."

Bob Stewart remembered that Marshall was not pleased initially about the trade. "I went to his house the day after the trade," Stewart said. "He was devastated when he was traded to the Rangers. He loved the Bay Area and the team." "There was a big party at my house," Marshall recalled. "I really didn't want to get traded but in terms of my career, if it didn't happen, I would have been out of the game. It was the best thing that ever happened to me, but I really enjoyed my time out in Oakland."

A few weeks later, Rick Smith remembered Marshall's changed outlook about the trade. "Bert wrote the team a letter and the essence of the letter was that he had found hockey again and he was excited again, and that he loved going to the rink now. I never heard of a player doing something like that."

After finishing the 1972-73 season with the Rangers, Marshall was selected by the crosstown Islanders in the intraleague draft. He spent six productive seasons on Long Island and helped the Islanders go from a lowly expansion team to the team with the best record in the NHL the year of his retirement. He hung up his skates after the 1978-79 season, one year before the Islanders began their run of four straight Stanley Cups.

Marshall stayed active in hockey after his retirement as a player. He later coached the Islanders top affiliate in Indianapolis and the NHL's Colorado Rockies. Today, he lives in the Seattle area and is a scout for the Carolina Hurricanes. Marshall has two daughters, one from his previous marriage and one from his current one.

Ted McAneeley summed up what Bert Marshall meant to the Seals: "He was the most experienced player on the team and a stabilizing guy. He was a good defensive defenseman and the cornerstone and captain of the team."

Don O'Donoghue

"He had excellent wheels but average talent. He was a very cocky kid who had a fairly high opinion of himself. He worked hard and played hard. That cockiness helped get him into the NHL."
—Earl Ingarfield on Don O'Donoghue

The old adage in sports is that speed kills or that you can't teach speed. In hockey, speed can also be a major factor to a player's success. Hockey fans remember the quick skates of Yvan Cournoyer, who earned the nickname the "Roadrunner" and used his speed to win 10 Stanley Cups and a ticket to the Hall of Fame. Or Pavel Bure, whose speed earned him the nickname the "Russian Rocket" and made him one of the games most feared scorers in the '90s. In 1969, the Seals drafted their own potential speedster in the third round of the entry draft, 5'10", 180-pound Don O'Donoghue.

O'Donoghue, a native of Kingston, Ontario, joined the Seals immediately, making the club for the 1969-70 season. As a rookie, he played 68 games, netting five goals and 11 points. Perhaps the highlight of O'Donoghue's rookie season came on January 25, 1970, when he assisted on three goals in a 4-1 Seals win at Minnesota.

One problem facing O'Donoghue in his rookie season was his inexperience—he was just 20 years old. Like any rookie, O'Donoghue had to face his share of razzing from his teammates. "He was a quiet kid," Doug Roberts said of O'Donoghue. "He had great wheels but he was pretty naive. He was a little in awe of some of the guys on the team; he was serious about life and himself."

Mike Laughton recalled one incident in particular that happened on the ice. "We were playing in New York one night," Laughton said. "I cut to the outside and he cut to the inside and I was flattened [when we collided]. The Rangers bench was laughing at us. I told Don that was the hardest check he ever threw."

The other problem O'Donoghue faced was figuring out what to do with his exceptional speed. At that point in his career, many teammates felt he lacked the tools to put his wheels to work for him. "If you opened the gate, he'd be skating by the Bay," Carol Vadnais joked. Howie Menard, who was a teammate of O'Donoghue's during his rookie season, recalled that the first-year's nickname was "Crazy Legs." "I didn't know if he was coming or going," Menard exclaimed. "He could really skate. He just didn't know what to do with the puck once he got it."

In 1970-71, O'Donoghue had his most productive NHL season. He started the year with the Seals top affiliate in Providence, but when a string of injuries hit the big club, the speedster was recalled at midseason. In 43 games with the Seals, O'Donoghue scored 11 goals and 20 points. In fact, he led the Seals in shooting accuracy that year, scoring on 17.5 percent of his shots. He scored twice during an 8-3 Seals loss to the Kings at the Oakland Coliseum, his career high.

Seals coach Fred Glover appreciated some of the things his young wing brought to the table. "Don was a good player," Glover said. "He could skate and check. If he'd stayed around longer in the NHL, he'd have been better off." By 1970-71, O'Donoghue had found acceptance with his teammates. "He was more of a defensive player and a pretty good skater," captain Ted Hampson recalled. "Don was also a good guy off the ice."

Off the ice, O'Donoghue got married after the 1970-71 season. Bert Marshall recalled that O'Donoghue "married the daughter of the owner of the Elegant Farmer, which was a top restaurant in Oakland." He started the 1971-72 season with the Seals, but after 14 games in which he scored two goals and four points, new coach Vic Stasiuk sent O'Donoghue down to Baltimore of the AHL.

In February, O'Donoghue was traded to the Bruins along with Carol Vadnais in the deal that brought the Seals Reg Leach, Bob Stewart and Rick Smith. He finished the 1971-72 season with the AHL's Boston Braves and never played in another NHL game during his pro career.

In 1972-73, O'Donoghue became one of the many ex-Seals to sign with the WHA. O'Donoghue joined the Philadelphia Blazers and scored 16 goals and 39 points in 74 games. In fact, O'Donoghue assisted on the very first goal in Blazers franchise history. He stayed with the Blazers franchise for two more seasons after they relocated to Vancouver before spending part of the 1975-76 season with the Cincinnati Stingers. After two more seasons in the minor leagues, O'Donoghue retired as an active player after the 1977-78 season. He was only 28 years old.

Today, O'Donoghue is one of the few former Seals who remains in California. He owns a restaurant called O'D's Kitchen in Gilroy. His NHL career was brief, mainly because he never did learn how to effectively utilize his blazing speed. Gary Smith summed up Don O'Donoghue's NHL career by saying, "He had all kinds of speed, but he was actually too fast for his own good." But you can't teach speed.

Gary Jarrett

"A really nice guy. He was hardworking. I can't forget a guy like that. He was really trying to help our team and gave effort every night; that wasn't easy on our team."

—Ron Stackhouse on Gary Jarrett

Speedy Gary Jarrett grew up in Toronto idolizing the Maple Leafs. "I was born and raised in Toronto," Jarrett recalled. "It was a ritual every Saturday night to watch the Leafs play on TV or listen to Foster Hewitt on the radio until I fell asleep. My favorite players were probably Teeder Kennedy and Syl Apps. When they had a career day or people would ask me, 'What do you want to be when you grow up?' I would always say, 'An NHL hockey player or, if that didn't work out, a sports reporter.' "

In 1959-60, Jarrett played junior hockey for the Toronto Marlboros. The following season, he got a game callup to play for the team he grew up rooting for, the Toronto Maple Leafs. Jarrett spent the next five years playing for various minor league teams in the AHL, WHL and CHL, including stops in Rochester, Denver, Tulsa and Pittsburgh. The Leafs traded his NHL rights to Detroit after the 1964-65 season and he was called up for four games with the Red Wings in 1966-67. "Once expansion came, Jarrett said, "I had a regular shift with Detroit." In 1967-68, his first full season in the NHL, Jarrett scored 18 goals and 39 points in 68 games.

On May 27, 1968, Jarrett was traded to the Seals along with Doug Roberts, Howie Young and Chris Worthy in exchange for Bob Baun and Ron Harris. "I was OK with the trade," Jarrett said. "California is kind of fun; you know, sunny California. It was a new era in the NHL. There were six teams and then there were 12 teams overnight. It was a new ballgame. I was traded in the off season so at least I didn't have to uproot my family. At the time, we didn't have a great team in Detroit so we weren't going to win the Cup there anyway. I looked at it as an opportunity to be a better player on the team."

When Jarrett arrived in Oakland, he did realize there was something different about playing for an expansion team. "We were all from someplace else," Jarrett said. "In Toronto and Detroit, the players spent their entire lives in the organization. In Oakland, we were all from other places. That was different, but not necessarily bad. There never was a 'Seals culture,' although one might have developed if the team would have stayed. Just the same, back then, there was no Kings culture or Blues culture either."

Jarrett took an immediate liking to the Bay Area and he flourished there in his first season with Oakland. Still, Jarrett was not blind to some of the problems the franchise was facing. "They were trying so hard to make hockey work in the Bay Area. We had some pretty sparse crowds. I played junior hockey in front of 12,000 fans at the Maple Leaf Gardens for a Sunday doubleheader. In Oakland, we would sometimes draw 5,000 to 6,000 people. The fans we had were terrific but, too often, we had sparse crowds. We were always having giveaways and that was new at the time. We had 'buy two tickets, get one free' or 'family night.' That was peculiar to me. In other places, they never had to give away tickets. We also used to go to different functions to speak and tried to be a part of the community."

In his first year with the Seals, Jarrett recorded his first career, NHL 20-goal season. He finished the year with 22 goals and 45 points. Jarrett took a liking to his new coach in Oakland, Fred Glover. "My first year there, 1968-69, we had a very good team and it was Freddie's first year as coach. As a player, he was a career minor leaguer. He just didn't skate well enough to play in the NHL back then. His desire and determination were the best I've ever seen. He is one of the most dedicated hockey people I've ever met. Was his coaching responsible for us not being as good a team as we should have been? I'd have to say no. He was a good coach, but not a great one. I think he saw people playing for him who were not as good a player as he was. He was a pretty strong taskmaster and, in retrospect, not a happy person. I don't think I ever remember Freddie smiling that much. He gave everything he had to his job. Our practices were intense. Everything about Fred Glover was intense."

The 1968-69 season also gave Jarrett his most memorable game in a Seals sweater. On February 8, 1969, the Seals defeated the Maple Leafs 4-1. "We beat Toronto in Toronto on a Saturday night on national TV," Jarrett said. "For a Canadian boy growing up in Toronto, to go back there on a visiting team and have friends and family there to see it … I remember it was a good feeling when I was leaving the ice." Ironically enough, Jarrett did not figure in the scoring in that game.

Two of Jarrett's most memorable offensive efforts for the Seals came during the 1968-69 season. In his second game ever for the Seals, Jarrett scored twice and added an assist in a 4-4 tie against the Kings in Oakland. Both of Jarrett's goals came in the third period, including the tying goal, which he scored with just 1:08 left in the game. A month later, Jarrett got some measure of revenge on his former team when he beat Roger Crozier with just 48 seconds remaining in a 2-1 Seals win over Detroit.

Despite a sometimes serious nature, Jarrett was very popular with his teammates. "He had a great year for us and was a nice fellow," Gene Ubriaco recalled. "He did very well, and I think he could sell you the Brooklyn Bridge. He worked hard and hustled and was fast. He always repeated himself whenever he spoke. If he was on that old game show 'I've Got a Secret,' the first guy would say, 'My name is Gary Jarrett.' The second guy would say, 'My name is Gary Jarrett,' and then Gary would say, 'My name is Gary Jarrett, Jarrett.' " Bill Hicke added, "I called him 'Parrot' because he was talking all the time. He could skate. He's a nice guy with good skills."

Unfortunately, during his first year with the Seals Jarrett suffered a serious eye injury. "We were practicing at Berkeley and the place was so poorly lit," Jarrett said. "Mike Laughton took a shot and it deflected off a stick and hit my eye. It broke my macula." The stick belonged to defenseman Doug Roberts. "I had a puck tip off my stick and hit him in the eye," Roberts remembered. "I felt horrible about that. I have good memories of Gary." Norm Ferguson remembered that after "he got that horrible eye injury, Gary was never really the same."

Jarrett returned to the Seals in 1969-70, but offensively, he was not as effective. Wayne Muloin, who joined the Seals that season, still recognized Jarrett's effort. "He was a real hustler and an exciting player. He was not afraid to go to the net at 100 miles per hour." Jarrett scored 12 goals and 31 points in 75 games in 1969-70. The "Parrot" did have one memorable moment that season, however. On April 3, 1970, Jarrett tied a club record with 11 shots on goal in one game during a 4-1 Seals win over the Kings at the Oakland Coliseum. Like Carol Vadnais, whose record he tied, Jarrett scored one goal on 11 shots.

The following year, Charlie Finley took over ownership of the Seals. "Charlie Finley had peculiar promotions," Jarrett recalled. "I remember once we had barber night. All barbers get into the game for $1. Mr. Finley figures that barbers would talk to people while cutting their hair and that would sell more tickets. The night before, I got a couple of goals and Charlie Finley said, 'Young man, I'm proud of you,' and praised my play to whoever was there. The next night they had the reception for the barbers. If they came to the reception, they would get two tickets to the game of their choice. The players were invited too, so we could mingle with them. When I got there, Charlie Finley asked me where my barber shop was located."

To Jarrett, working for Finley was a different experience. "He was the Bill Veeck of hockey," Jarrett said. "He was trying to make the game more exciting to people who didn't grow up with the game. He was a real promoter and a flamboyant guy, always trying to do gimmicky things like introducing the white skates and the kelly green and gold skates. We were always wondering what was going to happen next. We had green and gold suitcases when we traveled on the road. We looked like a traveling minstrel show."

Jarrett's final season with the Seals was 1971-72. Three games into the season, Fred Glover was replaced as coach by Vic Stasiuk. Jarrett appeared in only 55 games and scored five goals and 15 points on the season. "Vic was a totally different type of guy," Jarrett said of Stasiuk. "He was fun-loving. He had an NHL career and was more easygoing, more humorous. He got to know you more as a person and not just as a player."

Despite Jarrett's decreased offensive production his final season in Oakland, he still had the respect of his teammates. Joey Johnston recalled that Jarrett was "a little older, but he worked hard and was in tip-top shape. If half of us were in his condition, we would have been a better team, but Garry Young was busy bringing in younger guys." Paul Shmyr remembered that Jarrett was "a small forward who was fast and could shoot. He was a team guy and sort of the straight man on the team. When we told him a joke, it sometimes took him a minute to get it. Eventually, he got used to the guys and loosened up." Seals center Bobby Sheehan recalled that Jarrett "was all business. He'd travel up and down his wing. He was quiet and a hard worker. He reminded me a bit of Claude Provost." Gerry Pinder recalled that as a veteran, Jarrett was always "good to the younger guys."

After the 1971-72 season, Jarrett had serious thoughts about retiring. "Charlie Finley was a generous man—except at contract time. I was playing less and less and still had lingering problems from my eye. I was not having as much fun as I used to and my contract was over. Charlie Finley was a firm believer in the one-year contract. I decided to retire and return to Evergreen, Colorado, where I had bought a house. I got a call in the summer from the WHA asking me if I was interested in playing for the new league. I said maybe. Chuck Catto came to see me. There were about 15 other Seals players who were interested in going to the WHA. None of them had contracts either. I was interested because I could stay with some of those guys. I think about five or six of us ended up in Cleveland together. With Charlie Finley, the most you would get would be a $1,500 raise, and people were not comfortable with that."

The decision to join the Cleveland Crusaders was a good one for Jarrett. In the WHA's first season, the 5'8", 170-pound Toronto native was a second-team WHA all-star, scoring 40 goals and 78 points in 75 games. The following year, Jarrett scored 31 goals for the Crusaders. He remained with Cleveland through the 1975-76 season before retiring as a player for good.

Today, Jarrett still lives in Evergreen, Colorado. Looking back, the Parrot has fond memories of his time with the Seals. "I still have a sweater," Jarrett admitted, "or maybe my daughter does. I still get more people sending me cards to sign, more Seals cards than from anywhere else." Jarrett also said that a few days before our interview, he caught a glimpse of the Oakland Coliseum in a blimp shot during a Raiders game. "It just put a big smile on my face the other day to see it," Jarrett said. "It was a wonderful facility; at that time, as good as there was. It was a nice place to play hockey. We had a group of fans that were just marvelous."

"He was an excitable kind of guy," Tony Featherstone recalled in summarizing Oakland's popular Parrot. "He worked hard and was a great skater. He had lots of energy and was always ready to go back onto the ice."

Norm Ferguson

"He scored 34 goals as a rookie. He had an easy way about him and he took good care of himself. He came to play night after night. Experience helped him. He was a little small and wouldn't have gotten a chance to play in the NHL without expansion."

—Doug Roberts on Norm Ferguson

Norm Ferguson was one of the few NHL players in his day to come from the Maritimes. The 5'8", 160-pound winger was from Sydney, Nova Scotia. Ferguson came to the Seals from the Canadiens organization along with Lyle Bradley and Francois Lacombe in exchange for Alain Caron and Wally Boyer on May 21, 1968. Despite the fact that Ferguson grew up rooting for Rocket Richard and the Canadiens, he was thrilled to go to Oakland. "I thought it was great," Ferguson recalled. "I was owned by the Canadiens and I knew I wouldn't play there. I came to Oakland and that was my chance. Fred Glover was the coach and he had coached me the year before in Cleveland of the AHL so I was happy.

Glover was my favorite coach. He took me to Oakland and gave me an opportunity to play in the NHL. His style probably wouldn't work today, there wasn't enough time spent on details. His attitude was like, 'You're here, you're good enough, let's go out and play.' "

Ferguson burst onto the scene for the Seals, scoring 34 goals in his rookie season. No Seals player ever scored more goals in a single season in the club's nine-year history. "I think it was the excitement of it all," Ferguson said as to why his rookie year was so special. "Goals started going in during training camp. There was no pressure and no worries. The team had underachieved the year before and finished in last place but my first year there, everything clicked. Ted Hampson, Carol Vadnais and Bill Hicke all had good years too. My first year in Oakland, there were no problems."

On January 25, 1969, Ferguson registered the second hat trick in club history. It came off of one of the game's all-time great goaltenders, Terry Sawchuk at the Olympia in Detroit. Ferguson scored all three goals for the Seals in a 5-3 loss to the Red Wings. The Seals had leads of 2-0 and 3-2 in that game, but allowed four goals in the third period to waste Ferguson's three-goal effort.

Ferguson also had the honor of attempting the first penalty shot in Seals history on November 24, 1968. It was also the first penalty shot in the history of the new (and present) Madison Square Garden. The Seals were awarded the free shot when Rangers defenseman Jim Neilson covered the puck in the crease. "I was chosen to take the shot and I said, 'Uh-oh,' " Ferguson recalled. "I shot the puck on Eddie Giacomin and it trickled through. I don't think it could have broken an egg when it went into the goal." The Seals lost the game to New York 3-2.

Ferguson set a new NHL record for goals by a rookie that season. He was actually tied for that record with Danny Grant of Minnesota, who also scored 34 goals that season. In a close vote, Grant won the Calder Trophy as rookie of the year by a 119-112 margin. New York's Brad Park was a distant third in the voting. "He should have been Rookie of the Year," Seals goalie Gary Smith said of Ferguson. "They gave it to Danny Grant probably because he played more games back East and had more exposure."

One thing Ferguson did earn that rookie season was the respect of his teammates. Brian Perry described Ferguson as "a delight to be with and a fun guy who worked very hard." Gerry Odrowski remembered that Ferguson was "not big but he gave 110 percent and didn't like to lose." Wayne Muloin recalled that the young winger "was hustling all the time."

Ferguson also took a liking to the fans in Oakland, although the lack of attendance did get to him after a while. "We had a great booster club with great people," Ferguson recalled. "We just didn't have enough fans. Some games, we hardly had anybody there. We used to joke around that the guys who couldn't get out of the parking lot after attending Raiders or A's games would be the ones in the stands for the Seals. Bigger crowds put more pressure on you. Seeing just 2,500 people in the Oakland Coliseum didn't put so much pressure on you."

Ferguson was very disappointed with the team's first-round exit in the 1969 Stanley Cup playoffs against the Kings. "I was very sad we lost," Ferguson recalled. "There was very little difference between the two teams, although we finished second and they finished fourth. The series went back and forth. We lost the seventh game in Oakland. We thought we had it made with the seventh game at home, but they shut us down completely." Ferguson played reasonably well for the Seals in that series, scoring one goal and five points in seven games.

In 1969-70, Ferguson admitted the Seals were "a little complacent, although I still don't know why. We expected bigger and better things, but they didn't happen. Maybe it's because we stood pat and didn't make enough changes." The team fell to fourth place and Ferguson fell victim to the dreaded "sophomore jinx." He scored only 11 goals and 20 points in 72 games for the Seals.

In the playoffs that year, the Seals were swept by the Penguins in the first round. "Michel Briere, their rookie, played very well. I thought we would have done better, that we were better than a fourth-place team," Ferguson explained. "I know I didn't play well and not too many other players on our team did either."

Coach Fred Glover now believes he knows why Ferguson was not able to duplicate his rookie success in later years with Oakland. "The only problem with Norm was that he went the same way all the time," Glover said. "He'd deke inside and go outside at the blue line. The opposition caught on and his numbers were never the same."

Ferguson had the unique experience of rooming with Seals goaltender Gary Smith on road trips during part of his time in Oakland. Ferguson called Smith "one of my favorite people in hockey" before adding, "I could write a book about rooming with him." Smith, in turn, recalled that "when Normy had a few drinks, he would fall asleep sitting up while trying to take his shoes off or sitting up on the toilet."

"Some of the road trips were too long," Ferguson admitted. "I remember one year, we left December 17 and didn't get back until January 7. We were away for three weeks at a time. If you're losing, it's a *long* road trip. We were in a different time zone with different weather all the time. We spent a lot of our days flying so we lost days off that way. It creates other habits, too. Guys have a good time."

When asked to describe himself as a hockey player, Ferguson grew thoughtful and answered, "It's hard to say. Strengths—I was a goal scorer and I had a lot of quickness. I never had great size or stamina. I was never going to be a Bobby Orr, but I was proud to fit into a team concept and be one-fifth of a successful team when we were on the ice. I participated in the success of the team. I was more of an offensive player than a defensive one."

Unfortunately, changes were in store for the club that made them less successful on and off the ice. "Before Charlie Finley came in, it seemed like we had a new meeting every month with new owners, Ferguson recalled. Barry van Gerbig started it, then we had George Gillett and Whitey Ford and a few groups. It was very unsettling but for a young player in his 20s like myself, you just don't care." After Finely took over the club, Ferguson believes it "went downhill completely. It took them four to five years to recover from those changes. The players on the team all had bad seasons at the same time and things got very unsettled. We went from standing pat to making too many changes in one season."

One of the changes Finley introduced was the use of green and gold and then white skates for the team to wear. Ferguson was not amused. "I never totally agreed with it but I did it because it was the rules," he said. "We became sort of Barnum & Bailey, like a sort of traveling road show. The onus was more on how we looked than on how we performed on the ice. I remember Gerry Ehman, who was one of the older players on our team, and he couldn't believe we were wearing green and gold skates." Despite disliking the green and gold skates, Ferguson still owns his old pair today.

There were other changes that Ferguson recalled besides the skates, however. "When Charlie Finley came in, he brought in Garry Young [as GM]. He wanted to put his stamp on the team. The players that were already there were suddenly not as important as the ones who were coming in. That had everybody off kilter."

Things were tough on the ice for Ferguson as well in 1970-71. He started the season playing on the new "Battle Line" with center Dennis Hextall and left wing Gary Croteau. The line was very productive, perhaps the only line-scoring goals during the team's early season slump. Just four games into the season, however, Ferguson was felled by a fractured shoulder and missed 21 games. When he came back, Ferguson admitted he had "no confidence. If you don't score, you get down on yourself." The Seals slumped to last place in 1970-71 and Ferguson scored 14 goals and 31 points in 54 games.

Despite the falloff in production, Ferguson's teammates still praised his effort and his role as a veteran on the team. Rookie Tony Featherstone called Ferguson "very down to earth" and recalls that "he was always nice to me as a rookie." "He was very good around the net," Dennis Hextall said. "He was small, but he gave everything he had." Gerry Pinder added, "Fergy was great and was a good goal-scorer. If you looked at him, you thought he couldn't skate. He's not really that big, but all he did was put the puck in the net."

114

Ferguson had one more shining moment with the Seals in 1971-72. On October 13, 1971, he scored another hat trick, this time off of Bruce Gamble of Philadelphia. The Seals lost that game, too 5-4. However, Fergy was unable to regain his consistency and finished the year with 14 goals and 34 points in 77 games.

Ferguson, who played with the Seals from 1968-69 until 1971-72 left his mark on the Seals all-time record book. He is third in Seals history with 73 career goals, 10th in assists, sixth all-time in points and fourth in games played.

After the 1971-72 season, Ferguson left the Seals and the NHL for the WHA. "Mr. Finley wasn't the best payer in the world," Ferguson said. "Oakland didn't protect me in the expansion draft and I was chosen by the New York Islanders. It would have been more losing. I was 27 then and by the time the Islanders would have turned it around, I figured I would have been at least 30. My last year in Oakland wasn't that fun. I actually tripled my salary going to the WHA."

Ferguson signed with the New York Raiders and regained his lost scoring touch in the upstart league. "I had to leave Oakland to get my touch back," Ferguson said. In six seasons in the WHA, Ferguson averaged just over 30 goals per year including three straight seasons of scoring over 35 goals with the San Diego Mariners. His final season in professional hockey was with the Edmonton Oilers in 1977-78.

Despite the less-than-happy ending, Ferguson looks back fondly when discussing his time with the Seals. "The weather was great, the arena was great and so were the people on the team. I loved San Francisco and Oakland. We also had some fine people in our organization like Frank Selke and Bill Torrey."

Today, Ferguson lives in Sydney, Nova Scotia, and is the manager and part owner of Ferguson's Transfer and Storage, a family business previously owned by his father and grandfather. Ferguson and his wife have a son and a daughter as well as one grandson. His son, Craig, made the NHL, playing briefly for Montreal, Calgary and Florida, and is now playing hockey in Switzerland.

Gary Croteau summed up his former linemate by saying, "He was an excellent skater and a good goal-scorer. He played with a lot of heart; a neat guy and a good team man." That was Norm Ferguson, a boy from the Maritimes who made good in the NHL.

Carol Vadnais

"He was our budding superstar. He had a great shot and moved the puck terrifically. He was also a barrel of laughs."

—Gene Ubriaco on Carol Vadnais

Carol Vadnais was the closest thing the Seals had to an elite player during the four seasons he was a member of the club. Vadnais joined the Seals as a young unknown. By the time he left, he was captain of the Seals and had played in three NHL All-Star games. Vadnais left quite an impression on the Seals franchise record book. He stands fifth all-time in scoring, fifth all-time in goals, sixth in assists and holds the Seals career penalty minute mark. He is also third in franchise history in post season scoring with eight points in 11 games.

Carol Vadnais had size, skill and panache on and off the ice. The 6'1", 185-pound Montreal native grew up rooting for the "Flying Frenchmen" and his favorite player, Ralph Backstrom. The Canadiens owned Vadnais's territorial rights, but he was buried in the Habs deep system and could not get enough ice time with the big club. He played 11 games with Montreal in 1966-67, picking up three assists. The following year, Vadnais appeared in 31 games for the Canadiens, scoring his first NHL goal and adding an assist. He spent the rest of the time with the Houston Apollos of the CHL. The Canadiens called Vad up for the Stanley Cup playoffs and he appeared in one postseason contest for Montreal that year. It was enough to get his name on the Stanley Cup.

The Seals selected Vadnais with the first selection in the intraleague draft prior to the 1968-69 season. New Seals general manager Frank Selke Jr. admitted that there was more to the transaction than that. "While the records will show it as a 'draft transaction,' " Selke explained, "Sam Pollack made Carol available to us as part of a long-range deal, which fortunately for the Seals was never finalized as Sam had planned." Selke considered the acquisition of Vadnais as his "best player contribution" of his tenure as GM of the club. Despite the opportunity to play regularly in the NHL, Vadnais himself was not initially thrilled about the prospect of playing in Oakland. "I wanted to stay in Montreal," Vadnais explained. "I was not too charged up. I was born in Montreal and my family was in Montreal. I loved Montreal, but the move to Oakland ended up being the best thing for me."

Vadnais immediately noticed a big difference between the Canadiens and the recently created Seals. "We were an expansion team," Vadnais recalled. "We had a lot of young players and a lot of players who were ending their careers. You can't make a competitive team out of players who are ending their careers."

Vadnais's arrival in Oakland was mutually beneficial to both the team and the young defenseman. Doug Roberts recalled, "The Seals helped Carol take his career to another level. He was stuck behind Serge Savard and those guys in Montreal. He dressed flashy and liked to live good. There was a cockiness to him that was good for our team."

In his first season in the Bay Area, Vadnais scored 15 goals and added 27 assists to go along with 151 penalty minutes. On the ice, it was clear that Vadnais was an emerging star. "He was the best defenseman on our club from day one," Bill Hicke explained. "He was big, he could skate and he could fight. He was just as good on offense as he was on defense."

Vadnais did have some difficulty at first with learning English and adjusting to life in Northern California. Gene Ubriaco recalled an incident in which Vadnais was trying to call his parents back in Montreal from one of the team's hotels on the road. "Vad got on the phone, called the long-distance operator and said he wanted to make a long-distance call to Quebec. The operator asked him what the name was and Carol said, 'Vadnais.' The operator asked him to spell it and Carol said, 'That's V as in Vadnais.'" Wayne Muloin recalled that Vadnais once had to do community work after being pulled over for speeding in his Corvette. "I asked him what he was doing," Muloin said. "He said he was putting a fence around 'dos tings with the long neck' at the zoo. We all assumed he meant giraffes."

Perhaps because of the language barrier, some of Vadnais's teammates thought him a bit aloof at first. Brian Perry explained that Vadnais was "hard to get to know. He wasn't high on himself, but that was the impression you'd get if you weren't his teammate." "You had to get to know Carol to like him," winger Norm Ferguson added, "but he was a very nice guy." Earl Ingarfield recalled that Vadnais was "a good player—the best on the team at that time. He had size and was a tough player who could play either way. He scored as a forward and played well as a defenseman. He really came into his own in Oakland and he got along with everyone."

Vadnais, who was then single, got quite a reputation as a ladies' man among his teammates. "He epitomized the French player from Montreal," Gary Smith said. "He could make great end-to-end rushes, he was flamboyant and good with the girls. I was mad that he used to get all the broads." Vadnais was the team's most "mod" player. He drove a big Corvette, smoked cigars and dressed in style. Coach Fred Glover was always ordering Vadnais to get a haircut. One teammate recalled that Glover once laid down that ultimatum on a Sunday and Vadnais had a very hard time finding an open barbershop. Bob Sheehan later recalled, "He looked good in the white skates with his long, black hair. I used to say to him, 'Vad, if you were a girl, I'd kiss you.' He was a great competitor and a first class guy."

The 1969-70 season was Vadnais's best, statistically, with the Seals. He led the Seals with 24 goals and finished with 44 points and 212 penalty minutes on the season. In mid-December, Glover temporarily shifted Vadnais from defense to left wing and put him on a line with Earl Ingarfield and Bill Hicke. Vadnais promptly went on a seven-game scoring streak in which he scored five goals and five assists. Six of the 10 points came while playing left wing. At the time, GM Selke told Spence

Conley of *The Oakland Tribune,* "Vadnais is about the closest thing to a superstar there is today in the West [division]. He is tough, talented and colorful."

After his 24-goal season, Vadnais's contract expired. Howie Menard remembered that Vadnais was unsure how much to ask for. "I told him to ask for $60,000 because he was the best player on the team and he was young," Menard said. "Vad told me he couldn't ask for $60,000, but I told him you can always come down but you can't go up."

While Vadnais said that both Selke and Bill Torrey treated him well while he was in Oakland, contract signings in those days were anything but fun. "I remember how we used to sign our contracts," Vadnais said. "We were in a hotel. You'd walk into the room and there'd be five or six scouts there. They would tell you 'this is what you're making,' you'd sign the contract and go home."

Vadnais quickly came to enjoy the Bay Area and the Seals fans. "We had good fans," Vadnais recalled. "We sold out when we played good teams like the Original Six, but we'd always lose. Once a year we'd win a game like that. I enjoyed the fans, though. They were really good." Vadnais struck up a close friendship with Ty Toki, who did the club's laundry and was also president of the Seals Booster Club. The two remained in touch until Toki's recent passing.

Despite taking a liking to Northern California, the travel involved with playing in Oakland was something Vadnais never got used to. "It was kind of awful. We'd play nine road games in 18 days," Vadnais said. "Then we'd be home for a long time. Being single, it didn't bother me so much at that time, but for guys with families, it had to be really tough."

The 1970-71 season was a difficult one for Vadnais and the Seals. He appeared in only 42 games, scoring 10 goals, 26 points and 91 penalty minutes. The Seals star defenseman missed 18 games with a fractured thumb before returning to the lineup on February 24, 1971, against Montreal. In his first game back, Vadnais tore ligaments in his knee and was lost for the rest of the season. It was no coincidence that the Seals finished in last place that year. Between the Seals constant losing and the circus atmosphere created by new owner Charlie Finley, teammates began to sense discontent in Vadnais. Dennis Hextall recalled that Vadnais "thought he should have been on a better hockey club. He was disappointed to be in Oakland." Gary Croteau added that Vadnais "hated to lose. He was there game in and game out."

The following season, Vadnais was named captain of the Seals. "I was too young," Vadnais said. He was only 26 at the time. "It should have been given to a veteran. I don't know how I was named captain. I don't think I was the best captain. I was French and my English wasn't too good back then. They made me repeat everything 62 times. It was tough." Being captain of the club also meant getting personal calls at home from Charles Oscar Finley. "He used to call me all the time at home around 3 p.m., which would wake me up because I was taking my pregame nap," Vadnais recalled. "But I was captain of the team so he would call me and ask me how things were going."

Despite his own less-than-rosy assessment of his captaincy, Vadnais's teammates seemed to think he did a good job in that capacity. Bert Marshall recalled that Vadnais "tried hard and competed hard. He was a leader." Gerry Pinder added that Vadnais "was a pretty good captain, and that was not easy with the youth that we had." One of those young players, rookie and fellow Quebec native Gilles Meloche, recalled that Vadnais "took me under his wing the first two or three months I was there. He was a father figure to me for awhile."

As captain, Vadnais also stepped in when Finley introduced white skates to the team. The owner wanted his players to wear the skates in a game the first day they arrived. "He really didn't know the game," Vadnais said of Finley. "When he wanted the white skates to be worn right away, I told him it takes two to three weeks to break in a new pair of skates. Charlie said the skates weren't colorful enough so he wanted green laces. The company didn't make green shoelaces so Finley had the laces dipped in green paint."

On the ice, Vadnais regained his health and scored 14 goals and 34 points in 52 games for the Seals. Off the ice, trade rumors surrounded Vadnais. New GM Garry Young was rebuilding the team in his own image and trading away many of the players Selke had acquired. Vadnais was also the most sought-after commodity the Seals had. It seemed every GM that discussed trades with the Seals inquired about Carol's availability. Vadnais was also frustrated by the fact that Finley was notoriously stingy with his players at contract time. "I was making $33,000 and many of my friends around the league were making $40,000, so I asked to be traded," Vadnais recalled.

Vadnais saved his best performance with the Seals for last. In his final game as a member of the Seals on February 20, 1972, Vadnais scored a hat trick off goalie Jacques Caron during a 4-4 tie with the St. Louis Blues. It was the first hat trick of Vadnais' NHL career and his most memorable game in a Seals sweater. Three days later, Vadnais was traded to the Bruins along with Don O'Donoghue in exchange for Rick Smith, Reggie Leach and Bob Stewart. The Seals slumped down the stretch and missed the playoffs that season while Vadnais helped the Bruins win their second Stanley Cup in three years.

Vadnais played 11 more seasons in the NHL after being traded from California. After three and a half seasons in Boston, he was traded to the New York Rangers as part of the blockbuster deal that sent Phil Esposito to New York and Jean Ratelle, Brad Park and Joe Zanussi to Boston. Vadnais remained with the Rangers for seven seasons before finishing his NHL career with the New Jersey Devils in 1982-83. His career statistics include 169 goals and 587 points in 1,087 NHL games.

Although he liked playing in Oakland and enjoyed the opportunities it gave him in the NHL, Vadnais admitted that "there weren't too many great moments. For us, we were happy to get out with a tie. A tie was like a win for us and a win was like winning the Stanley Cup."

Today, Vadnais lives in Laval, Quebec, and sells commercial and industrial real estate. He and his wife have one daughter.

Gary Jarrett summed up Carol Vadnais and what he meant to the Seals while he was there. "He was a wonderful player, probably our best player there. He was a good friend. He was well-skilled ... and one of the first real offensive defensemen in the NHL. He could skate well, pass well and really move the puck." And he is without question one of the Seals all-time greats.

OTHER EARLY SEALS

Ron Boehm

Ron Boehm opened the 1967-68 season with the Seals. California selected the 5'8", 160-pound Boehm in the expansion draft from the Rangers organization. Boehm played left wing in 16 games with the Seals, scoring two goals and adding one assist. He was sent down to Vancouver of the WHL and spent the rest of the season there. In September 1968, the Seals traded the Saskatoon, Saskatchewan, native back to the Rangers for cash considerations. Boehm never appeared in another NHL game again but spent time with the Omaha Knights of the CHL, the Seattle Totems of the WHL and the Boston Braves of the AHL. He spent his final season as an active player with the NAHL's Binghamton Dusters in 1974-75. Billy Harris recalled, "Bert Olmstead thought highly of him. He was a little winger. He did well in the WHL but had a hard time surviving in the NHL." Center Charlie Burns recalled that Boehm was a "smooth, solid player who had a gift handling the puck."

Bob Lemieux

Defenseman Bob Lemieux also opened the 1967-68 season on the Seals roster. The Seals selected the 6'1", 195-pound Montreal native from the Canadiens in the expansion draft. In 1965-66, Lemieux was awarded the Governor's Trophy as the best defenseman in the IHL when he played for the Muskegon Zephyrs. When he joined the Seals, Lemieux was 23 years old. Tom Thurlby—who also played with Lemieux in Vancouver of the WHL—recalled that Lemieux "was scared to death and didn't know what he was doing here [at first]. Then he did well." Charlie Burns remembered that Lemieux "was smooth with the puck and was a team player." In 19 games with the Seals, Lemieux registered one assist and 12 penalty minutes. "The NHL level was a challenge for him," Billy Harris recalled. Bert Olmstead sent Lemieux down to Vancouver, where he scored 10 goals and 31 points in 44 games. He spent two more seasons with Vancouver of the WHL before ending his playing career. Lemieux was later involved in minor league hockey management and served as the GM of the Fort Worth Wings.

Jean Cusson

Jean Cusson signed a three-game amateur tryout contract with the Seals in March of 1968. The 5'10", 170-pound native of Verdun, Quebec, had played at the University of Montreal and for the Canadian National Team before his brief stay in California. Cusson played in two games with the Seals without registering a point. He took one shot on goal and was a minus one. The Seals did not sign Cusson, and that ended his brief pro-hockey career.

Terry Clancy

Terry Clancy was best known for being the son of Hall of Fame player, referee and coach King Clancy. The 24-year-old right wing opened the 1967-68 season with the Seals after California selected him from the Maple Leafs in the expansion draft. Charlie Burns remembered that Clancy was "a young, strong, fast skater. He still had a lot of skills to learn at that time." Clancy—a 5'11", 195-pound Ottawa native—made his NHL debut with the Seals. He played in seven games without scoring a point. One of those games was the Seals first appearance at the Maple Leaf Gardens, when they faced his father's former team. The Seals led 2-1 after two periods but lost 5-2. Billy Harris remembered the younger Clancy as "a good guy. In the six-team league, he would have been a 10th or 11th forward." Aut Erickson felt that Clancy was "an average hockey player who was stuck in that position because of his dad. He gave what he had." On May 14, 1968, the Seals sent Clancy back to the Maple Leafs for cash. Clancy split time between the Leafs and their minor league affiliates for the next five seasons. His final NHL statistics were six goals and six assists in 93 games. Clancy retired after the 1974-75 season.

Len Ronson

Veteran left wing Len Ronson had a brief tour of duty with the Seals early in the 1968-69 season. Ronson was a great minor league goal scorer who never quite found a home in the NHL. In 1959-60, he led the IHL with 62 goals while with the Fort Wayne Komets. He later twice led the WHL in goal scoring while playing for the San Diego Gulls. Ronson played in 13 NHL games with the Rangers during the 1960-61 season. The Seals acquired the 32-year-old Ronson from the Canadiens in August 1968 in a cash deal. Ronson appeared in five games for the Seals early in the 1968-69 season without scoring a point. In November 1968, the Seals decided they had no place for Ronson and sent him to the WHL's San Diego Gulls for cash. The 5'9", 175-pound Brantford, Ontario, native spent five more seasons in the minors before hanging up his skates after the 1972-73 season.

Barry Boughner

Barry Boughner has the unfortunate distinction of being the Seals skater who appeared in the most games without registering a point. Boughner appeared in 20 games with the Seals over two seasons and registered 11 penalty minutes, but no goals and no assists. The 5'10", 180-pound left wing came to the Seals from the Des Moines Oak Leafs of the IHL. Boughner was only 21 years old when he appeared in four games for the Seals in 1968-69. The following year, he split time between the Seals and Providence of the AHL, appearing in 16 more games with the big club. The Delhi, Ontario, native spent three more seasons in the minor leagues before retiring after the 1973-74 season.

Neil Nicholson

The Oakland Seals selected defenseman Neil Nicholson with the 65th overall choice in the 1969 entry draft. The Saint John, New Brunswick, native never appeared in a regular season game for Oakland, but was called up during the 1970 playoffs against the Penguins, where he played in two games and did not register a point. After two more seasons playing for the Providence Reds, Nicholson was selected by the expansion New York Islanders in the intraleague draft in the summer of 1972. Nicholson appeared in 39 games with the Islanders in parts of three seasons while spending the majority of his time playing for the Fort Worth Texans of the CHL. The 5'11", 180-pound Nicholson scored three goals and four points in 39 career NHL regular-season games. He is the only player in Seals history to appear in the playoffs for Oakland without ever playing a regular-season game for the club. Nicholson later spent four years playing hockey in Switzerland before retiring after the 1984-85 season.

Chapter 2:
The Middle Years: 1970-71 to 1973-74

Dennis Hextall

"A hard-nosed guy who came to play every night. He was not a great skater, but he played with grit. He was the kind of guy I wouldn't want to play against."

—Earl Ingarfield on Dennis Hextall

Dennis Hextall was introduced to professional hockey at an early age. His father, Bryan Hextall Sr., played for the New York Rangers from 1936-37 until 1947-48, and was later inducted into the Hockey Hall of Fame. His older brother, Bryan, also played hockey and later made the NHL. Despite coming from a well-known hockey family, the 6', 175-pound native of Poplar Point, Manitoba, decided to attend college instead of immediately pursuing an NHL career. "My last year of junior I did very well," Hextall recalled. "Still, I didn't think I could make it to the NHL." Instead, he enrolled at the University of North Dakota. "By my second year of college, I thought I had a pretty good chance of playing in the NHL," Hextall admitted.

For the next three seasons, Dennis bounced around the minors, with brief NHL tours with the New York Rangers and Los Angeles Kings mixed in. His rights were also owned by the Canadiens, but he spent all of his time in the Montreal organization with the Voyageurs of the AHL. On May 22, 1970 (the same day the Seals traded the rights to draft Guy Lafleur), the Seals acquired Hextall from the Habs for an undisclosed amount of cash. "I didn't enjoy playing in Los Angeles," Hextall said. "They had a horrible club. I thought, 'Oh, hell, what am I into now?' when I was traded to Oakland, but Frank Selke and Freddie Glover gave me an opportunity. Fred Glover said to me, 'Just go out and have fun.' I had a short fuse so I got some space to skate. I led the team in scoring and penalty minutes. If I didn't have a good year, I was going to do something else. That year, I proved to myself I could play in the NHL. I knew I could do it. Oakland was a stepping stone for me regardless of what the team did."

Hextall appreciated the opportunity and more than made the best of it. In his lone season in Oakland, Hextall led the team in scoring, assists and penalty minutes. He finished the year with 21 goals, 31 assists and 217 penalty minutes. "I had 22 major penalties that season, which was a new league record," Hextall said proudly. No player on the Seals ever received more penalty minutes in a season than Hextall's 217. In addition, Dennis and his brother Bryan, who was then with Pittsburgh, became the first brother combination to lead their respective teams in scoring in the same NHL season.

Hextall took a liking to the Bay Area and to his surroundings. He even appreciated and got along with the Seals flamboyant and controversial owner Charlie Finley. "Charlie Finley was different," Hextall explained. "Anytime there was a function, I went along. I spent four or five evenings with him and I got treated very well. I stayed in Oakland over the summer and I always had tickets to the A's games whenever I wanted them." Hextall also appreciated the gifts Finley gave the players after big wins. "In Boston we beat the Bruins 2-1. After the game, the phone rings. It was Mr. Finley. He said he was buying each player a suit for $300. Back then, that was a lot of money. He also bought us shoes after a win in Chicago. He was trying to get to know the players and to motivate them."

Hextall also respected Seals coach Glover. "He was a player's coach," the redheaded Seals center said of Glover. "Many of the coaches back then were close to management. He was real down to earth. Fred Glover and Fred Shero [who coached Hextall in the minors] both treated me the same way. They treat you like a man if you give them effort. As long as you worked, you got plenty of ice time and an opportunity."

Glover also appreciated his tough center, whose style of play likely reminded him of himself. "He was one of my favorite players," Glover said. "A tough one. I liked him in Buffalo when I played against him [in the AHL]. They traded him away without me knowing about it. Once, when we were in Minnesota, Dennis kept fighting and [NHL president] Clarence Campbell gave me a lecture about Dennis Hextall."

The only major problem Hextall had on the Seals was the club's last-place finish. "We had a few guys there who were just putting in time," he said. "With a poor team, it comes down to a guy's individual character. We had a few guys who didn't care. Harry Howell, for example, really wanted to win. Some other guys didn't have that attitude."

Despite the club's losing record, there were some memorable games for Hextall. "We beat the Rangers twice that year," Hextall recalled. "I wanted to play with them, but they were loaded at center ice. I scored the winning goal both times off of Eddie Giacomin. I also remember in Boston, we won 2-1. I scored the winning goal. We spent the last 18 minutes in our end. That was when the Bruins had the big line of Esposito, Cashman and Hodge. Gary Smith sure came up big."

Hextall was also once a victim of one of Bobby Orr's favorite tricks. "We were on the power play one night and Bobby Orr had the puck behind the net," Hextall explained. "I went behind the goal to get him and he circled the net, and I chased after him, making circles around the goal. Orr was the most dominant player I played against."

Hextall centered the Seals "Battle Line," which consisted of himself, left wing Gary Croteau and either Norm Ferguson or Tony Featherstone at right wing. "We were all scrappers," Hextall said. "Ferguson was small and knew where the net was. Croteau worked very hard. I was physical. When Ferguson got hurt, Featherstone replaced him. He was a tough kid and played well." Tony Featherstone said at the time, "None of us is a smoothie, we just work hard." The problem was that the "Battle Line" was often the only line producing points for the Seals on a regular basis. Linemate Croteau remembered Hextall as "a fiery individual who was great in the dressing room; a good fighter and a tough competitor."

When asked to describe his style of play, Hextall said, "I played physical. It didn't matter to me if I won or lost the fight, I would just get my nose in and get involved. I controlled the corners pretty good. Checking was a strong point. I was an average skater and had an average shot. I think my style got me more room out there."

While all of his teammates recognized Hextall's work on the ice, at times his competitiveness, intensity and quick temper rubbed some teammates the wrong way. "We had a scrap in practice one time," rookie Ron Stackhouse said. "He operated as close to 100 percent as a player could and I respected him for that, but I didn't like his style. I learned to stick up to guys like him by practicing against him." Another former teammate recalled that Hextall always had his stick up, even in some old timer's games.

Still, most teammates regarded Hextall as a valuable asset. Like Dale Hunter 20 years later, Hextall was a guy players loved to play with and hated to play against.

"He was 175 pounds soaking wet but he played like he was 230," said Seals forward Ernie Hicke. "He would fight anybody and was a good fighter. He would back up his teammates and he could also score goals." Team captain Ted Hampson said that Hextall was "ultracompetitive; he wanted to win. He was looking to establish himself as an NHL player. He played well in Oakland. He would battle anyone in the corners or drop the gloves with anybody bigger or smaller than himself. He would also use his stick."

Hextall seemed settled in the Bay Area and with the Seals, but his tenure in Oakland was short-lived. "I had just bought a home in the Bay Area," Hextall recalled. "I was very happy there and had a solid season. I figured the team could only get better. But then management changed. Frank Selke left and Bill Torrey left. Munson Campbell came in and changed everything. Looking back, leaving

Oakland when I did was the best deal in my career but, at the time, I was not sure." On May 20, 1971, Hextall was traded to the Minnesota North Stars for Walt McKechnie and Joey Johnston. Hextall spent four and a half seasons in Minnesota, totaling at least 74 points in his first three seasons there, before playing in Detroit and Washington. His last NHL season was 1979-80. He finished his NHL career with 153 goals, 503 points and 1,398 penalty minutes in 681 games.

Today, Hextall lives in Michigan and works in the manufacturer representation business related to the auto industry. He is married and has four children.

Gary Jarrett summarized a lot of teammates' feelings about Dennis Hextall. "When he was on the ice, there was only one way for him to play: a very, very aggressive and good player. If I were putting a team together, I would want guys like Dennis Hextall on my team." He wasn't the most gifted player or the best skater, but nobody wanted to play against Dennis Hextall.

Ron Stackhouse

"He was a good defenseman who had a better career later. He had a lot of talent, but he was only a rookie when he was with our team and he made his share of rookie mistakes. You could see how good he could become. He also had a great shot from the point."

—Gary Smith on Ron Stackhouse

Ron Stackhouse was a rarity of the California Golden Seals: a high-draft pick who actually played for the team. The Seals made a habit of trading away their top pick in the draft each year. In 1969, they traded their first-round pick but selected 20-year-old defenseman Ron Stackhouse in the second round. "I was pretty naive back then," recalled the Haliburton, Ontario, native. "I didn't even have an agent; almost none of the guys had agents back then. I was happy to be selected by the Seals. My friend Tony Featherstone, who played with me with the Petes, was also drafted by Oakland, so the idea of being able to stay with him and play hockey with him was great. I had never seen a live NHL game before I played in one."

After spending a year with the Seals top affiliate in Providence, Stackhouse was brought up to the big club for the 1970-71 season. He was immediately thrust into the Seals lineup. "I was the seventh defenseman when I got there, Stackhouse recalled. "Then one player had a contract dispute and a few guys hot hurt. Suddenly, I was taking not just a regular shift on defense but also killing penalties and playing on the power play."

The Seals struggled in 1970-71, finishing in last place in the West Division. The attitude in Oakland was a tough one for the 6'3", 210-pound Stackhouse to adjust to. "When I was there, the team didn't do so well," Stackhouse said. "I think we were out of the playoffs by Christmastime. We went into some games hoping just to keep things close. Some guys would mumble, 'Another sellout tonight—5,000.' To be honest, I didn't care if there were 6,000 fans or 60,000 fans there. I just wanted to play hockey in the NHL. Some of the older guys were just going through the motions and some of the younger guys were just happy to be there. I was lucky though. Some doors opened up for me and I was able to take advantage of that situation."

Stackhouse developed a good relationship with coach Fred Glover despite the fact that during the difficult 1970-71 season, many players had become disenchanted with Glovers' coaching. "Freddie had the same practice every day," Stackhouse remembered. "To some people, it was a source of discontent but Fred Glover really liked me. I think he was happy with my attitude. I knew I didn't do some things well, like pass the puck. In practice, we would work on passing and do a sort of "give and go"-type drill. It was the same practice every day, but I volunteered to do the drill because it helped me."

Glover, in turn, sang the rookie's praises. In an interview with John Porter of *The Oakland Tribune,* Glover said, "Since the first month of the season, Stack has improved every game. He gained a great deal of confidence and bides his time, waiting for the right moment to make his move."

Stackhouse spent his rookie year in Oakland with blinders on. He did his best to ignore the distractions both on and off the ice and just tried to make the most of his opportunity to play in the NHL. It paid off, as Stackhouse finished the year with eight goals and 24 assists. He also picked up 73 penalty minutes his rookie season. "Some people perhaps were preoccupied with Charlie Finley's actions, but I didn't know Charlie Finley from a hole in the ground," Stackhouse said. "Being naive was probably a good thing for me at the time. I really didn't care who owned the team; I just wanted to play hockey in the NHL. At the time, I was just awestruck playing against Bobby Orr and Gordie Howe. It was just a great experience."

On one occasion during his rookie season, Stackhouse received a call from Oakland A's third baseman Sal Bando to arrange an interview. "I didn't know who he was," Stackhouse recalled. "Living in Oakland at that time, you should have known who Sal Bando was. I was embarrassed."

Two of Stackhouse's most memorable games in a Golden Seals uniform came against the Red Wings. The first was his NHL debut at the Olympia. "I played against Gordie Howe, who was a legend," Stackhouse recalled. "I remember he headed over the blue line and I tripped him up and said something like, 'Excuse me, sir.' "

Stackhouse also scored his first two NHL goals at the Olympia on December 20, 1970. The first goal was off Red Wings netminder Don McLeod and it helped the Seals defeat the Wings 7-3.

Scouts were high on Stackhouse's future as an NHL defenseman. While the enthusiastic rookie made some mistakes, his teammates also saw the potential was there for Stack to become a top-notch player in this league. Veteran Harry Howell said of the rookie blue liner, "A lot of pressure has been put on Stack, first with [Bert] Marshall injured and then with Vad [Carol Vadnais] and me out. He has really come through. He's got the poise and patience. He's learning all the time and he's got a great shot." Seals captain Ted Hampson added, "He had pretty good size, he understood the game well, positioned himself well and had a good shot."

Other teammates, however, remembered Stackhouse's growing pains. "He was a good player," Dennis Hextall said of Stackhouse. "He was a rookie then. He was going through a learning stage and I think it was a long year for him."

Although he was in Oakland for just over a year, Stackhouse did have a great relationship with the Seals fans. He even had his own fan club that was started by a local hospital worker named Troy Lyon. "I had a big fan club out there," Stackhouse recalled. "They had buttons and I still have one. I got to know some of the fans very well. [They] were always very supportive of me. They had a sense that here's a kid who was working his butt off. The fans in Pittsburgh were very hard. They wanted me to be a goon because I was big—and I am the furthest thing from a goon."

In the summer following his rookie season, Stackhouse learned about the business side of playing in the NHL. "The first contract I negotiated, I made about $12,000," Stackhouse recalled. "I had a pretty good year. I went home for the summer and [general manager] Garry Young came up to talk to me. I was thinking I did well as I went from being a No. 7 defenseman to being No. 3 or 4. Garry Young said he had something to tell me. He said that Charlie Finley had only authorized him to give a raise to three players. He claimed that some guys had to take a pay cut. Then he offered me $14,000. Garry Young had me thinking that any raise was a big deal on this team."

Stackhouse got off to a good start in 1971-72. In the first five games of the year, he had a goal and three assists. Then, just like that, the Seals traded him. Stackhouse recalled the events surrounding the trade. "My second year, I got an apartment not too far from the team's complex. A friend of mine drove my car from Haliburton to San Francisco. My friend arrived on a Sunday night. Just after he arrives, I get a knock on the door. It was Garry Young, who I wasn't expecting. He said he wanted to talk to me privately so my friend said he would go to the bathroom. He said to me, 'I have good news and bad news. We've traded you.' It hit me like a brick. I was thinking, 'Aren't you happy with what I did?' Garry Young said he was not unhappy with me at all but they had to make a deal. 'Where did you trade me?' I asked. 'I can't tell you,' Young replied, 'but you have to be on the plane tomorrow.'

Then he told me that I had to … leave the green and gold suitcase that the team had given all the players behind because it belonged to the team."

Stackhouse was traded to Detroit in exchange for forward Tom Webster on October 22, 1971. Webster had been the Red Wings leading scorer the previous year with 30 goals. "I had to be flattered to be traded for Detroit's leading scorer," Stackhouse said. "At least that's how I rationalized it at the time. I didn't want to leave Oakland. I wish I could have played my whole career there. Now, looking back, leaving there may have been good for me because of what ended up happening out there." Due to injuries, Webster played in only seven games for the Seals in 1971-72. The following year, he defected to the WHA and the Seals had nothing to show for trading their prized defensive prospect.

Meanwhile, after two and a half seasons with the Red Wings, Stackhouse was traded to the Pittsburgh Penguins. He remained an integral part of the Pittsburgh defense for eight and a half seasons and was selected to play in the 1980 NHL All-Star game. Stackhouse finished his career with 87 goals and 459 points in 889 NHL games. He retired after the 1981-82 season. While Stackhouse may have been atypical in that he was a high-draft choice who actually played for the Seals, he was very typical in that his NHL career flourished after he was traded away from Oakland.

Today, Stackhouse and his wife live in Haliburton, where he teaches high-school computer, math and business courses. He has two daughters and participates in a hockey school in Haliburton during the summer.

Ernie Hicke described Ron Stackhouse by saying, "He was a big, tall defenseman—another good one who played a long time. He was about 6'4" and had a really long reach, played on the power play and was great on the point." Glover said, in retrospect, "Ron played better in Pittsburgh than he did for me. He had more confidence in Pittsburgh. He got used to the league and was a hell of a defenseman." For the Seals, he was another one that got away.

Ernie Hicke

"Billy Hicke's younger brother—Billy was instrumental in getting him to Oakland, I think. He was not as good a hockey player as Billy, but he was the same type of player. He could skate well and he had a good shot."

—Gary Jarrett on Ernie Hicke

Ernie Hicke will forever have three issues surrounding his hockey career in general and his tenure with the Seals in particular. He was Bill Hicke's younger brother, he liked to have a bit too much of a good time off the ice and he was the man the Seals acquired when they traded the rights to Guy Lafleur to the Canadiens.

"Playing in the NHL was my ultimate goal. I had been playing hockey since I was 3 or 4 years old," the younger Hicke recalled. "I grew up in a city sponsored by the Canadiens and my brother played for them. I worked as hard as I could. At 18, I went to the Canadiens camp and turned pro." Hicke had some productive years with the Houston Apollos of the CHL and Salt Lake Golden Eagles of the WHL. In his final two minor league seasons, Hicke had back-to-back years with 29 goals. Still, he could not break into the NHL with the talent-rich Canadiens.

On May 22, 1970, Hicke was traded to the Seals along with the Canadiens first-round pick in the 1970 draft (which the Seals used to take Chris Oddleifson) in exchange for Francois Lacombe and the Seals top draft pick in the 1971 draft. When the Seals were beset by injuries in 1970-71 and finished in last place, that pick became the first overall choice in the 1971 draft. The Canadiens used that selection to draft future Hall of Famer Guy Lafleur. To ensure that the Habs would receive the first overall pick and get the chance to draft Lafleur, Montreal GM Sam Pollack traded high-scoring forward Ralph Backstrom to Los Angeles to help the Kings pass the Seals in the standings. It worked and the Seals finished last, giving the Canadiens the first overall pick and the right to select the highly touted Lafleur, who was far and away considered the top prospect available in the draft.

Ernie Hicke was excited to join the Seals. "I had come from the Montreal camp and there were about 320 players there to stock eight farm teams. It was amazing how much talent that organization had. I was called up for the playoffs [although Hicke did not appear in any games for Montreal in the postseason] so I got a taste. When I was traded from Montreal to Oakland, it was a break in the sense that I would get an opportunity to play. I was thrilled to be in the NHL."

Ernie would also be joining his older brother, Bill Hicke, on the Seals. "It was a great opportunity to play with him," Ernie Hicke recalled. "I looked up to him for all those years. He was at the end of his career, but it was still a thrill to play with him. We had our run-ins, as brothers always do, but it was great."

Bill, who was nine and a half years older than Ernie, was also pleased. "I never expected it to happen," Bill Hicke responded when asked about becoming his younger brother's teammate. "He was about 10 years younger than me. I left home when I was 19 and Ernie was about nine. I saw him develop in junior. He was a good skater, had a good shot and was tough. I enjoyed it when he joined our team and it was a good opportunity for him because he would play a lot."

Ted Hampson recalled that Bill Hicke talked up his younger brother. "Billy Hicke was talking about his brother Ernie after he was traded to the Seals. He really talked him up and kept saying he was huge. We were expecting him to be about 6'4". He turned out to be more like 5'11".

The 5'11", 185-pound Ernie Hicke had a very successful rookie season in the NHL. In 1970-71, he led the Seals with 22 goals and seven power play tallies. He finished the year with 47 points, outscoring older brother Bill by 12 points.

Hicke's fondest memory as a member of the Seals came on December 22, 1970. "It was three days before Christmas against Chicago. We were up 2-1 and I had nine goals on the season. The Hawks net was empty and the puck went into their end, and I was in a foot race for the puck. I got there first and scored into the empty net for my 10th goal of the season. I had set a goal before the season started to score 10 goals by Christmas, so it meant a lot to me. Bobby Hull wondered why I was celebrating so much."

Forward Joey Johnston, who joined the Seals prior to the 1971-72 season, fondly remembered Ernie Hicke and his goal celebration dance. "I used to laugh at him. He was quite a character on and off the ice. It was unbelievable, the nerve he had. If he scored a goal, he did a one-minute jig on the ice. I'd say, 'What is that, your last goal?' "

Hicke had another memorable moment on March 7, 1971, in a 3-3 tie in Pittsburgh. He beat Penguin goalie Al Smith to become a 20-goal scorer as a rookie.

In addition to his goal scoring, Hicke also was known as a player who was not afraid to back up his teammates. "I came in pretty cocky, as most rookies do," Hicke answered when asked about his playing style. "My brother was on the team. I could play. I was a fighter and also a goal scorer. I always wanted to win and help the team. I wanted to stand up for everybody." Hicke was known for his good, hard wrist and slap shots and the quickness of his release.

Hicke's teammates also took a liking to the new rookie winger. "He was a great guy and had a great shot," goalie Gary Smith remembered. "He was a sharp dresser. I think he even ironed his underwear."

Veteran Earl Ingarfield recalled that the younger Hicke was "full of mischief and fun to be around. He could really skate and shoot the puck. He was a tough, mean kid. He could have been better than he was, although he was fairly successful in the NHL." Many of Hicke's other teammates also recalled his off-ice activities. "He liked the lifestyle," fellow rookie Ron Stackhouse recalled. "He was always on for a party. He had flashes of brilliance and times when he struggled—and I think the struggles were probably due to his off-ice activities."

Hicke had fond memories of the fans out in Oakland, even if he thought he knew them all by name. "We had about 1,500 loyal fans. The Coliseum was gorgeous, a great arena to watch a game in, especially compared to some of the older barns we played in. The base [of fans] was good, but there just weren't enough of them. I remember, once a friend asked me for tickets to a game and I asked the guys and I ended up with about 115 tickets. We couldn't give them away. It was also tough because we were losing. When you're playing in front of 10,000 to 15,000 people, it gets the adrenaline running more than playing in front of 1,500 people. That's why I think we often played better on the road. We didn't win too many, but we played better. It was nice when we had fans there [in Oakland] when we played against Boston and Montreal, even if they weren't cheering for us."

It was also a different experience for Hicke playing for a team owned by Charlie Finley. "He really liked color," the Regina, Saskatchewan, native recalled. "We wore green and gold warm-up suits on the road while everybody else was wearing suits and ties. We kind of rebelled. The white skates were different, but we had to wear them. The trainers had the biggest problem. They had to paint the skates between periods. The other players probably thought we looked goofy, but we had no choice. We had to wear them and we did."

Ernie Hicke also found out what it was like to enter into salary negotiations with Finley. "After my first year there, I had scored 20 goals and I was talking to Dennis Hextall, who also had scored 20 goals the year before. Well, Dennis told me he was making more money than Finley was offering me and I told Finley I wanted the same amount. He said, 'No way. This is what you're going to get.' Once he called me up while he was brushing his teeth. He was talking to me like a buddy, but he still wouldn't budge on the money. So I went to Montreal to see the arbitrator. We didn't have agents back then, so I had to go at my own expense. Well, the arbitrator gave me exactly what Finley said he wanted to pay me."

Hicke recalled that "Finley didn't want to pay guys but he took care of them. He got us those green and gold suitcases and we always flew first class. One time in Boston, we won 1-0 and Gary Smith made a lot of saves. Finley gave everybody $100 and said we were going to Gucci's tomorrow in New York. The rookies were looking at each other and saying, 'What is Gucci's?' He also gave us all watches around Christmastime. They were nice but, of course, he owned the company."

In his second season with the Seals, Hicke started off red hot. He had a two-goal, one-assist game on October 24, 1971, in Detroit in a 6-3 win over the Red Wings, but was soon struck by the injury bug. He missed 10 games and played hurt in others. With his effectiveness limited, Hicke scored only 11 goals and 23 points in 68 games. Gilles Meloche recalled that when Hicke was injured that season, he "hit the party trail."

Despite his personal struggles, Hicke was fond of new Seals coach Vic Stasiuk. "Vic really wanted to win," Hicke said. "He was a different type of coach and he had younger players. He brought in a system that he thought would help, and it did. It was similar to what they had in Montreal. We had terrific centermen who could really skate so he let them roam around. Getting out of our own zone was a problem for us so they system helped out the younger guys because a lot of us were from different teams and had different systems."

The Seals played better as a team. California was in contention for a playoff spot until the season's final week, when a late-season losing streak ended all chances of postseason play. "We had a lot of injuries and a lot of younger players who hadn't been through [a playoff race] before," Hicke said. "When you get down to the last few weeks of the season and are fighting for a playoff spot, it's like the playoffs in a way. We were young and less focused. I think that if that team would have stayed together just two or three more years, we would have won a Cup on the West Coast and the team would have stayed in Oakland."

But Ernie Hicke wasn't going to stay in Oakland. He was shocked that the Seals didn't protect him in the expansion draft after the 1971-72 season. "I was very surprised," Hicke recalled. "I had signed a contract with [new GM] Garry Young. We had so many young players and Garry Young could only protect so many guys." The Atlanta Flames claimed Hicke in the expansion draft and subsequently traded him to the Islanders late in the 1972-73 season. After a year and a half on Long Island, Hicke was traded to the Minnesota North Stars, where he had his most productive season, a 30-goal effort in 1976-77. One year later, Hicke was out of the NHL after spending half of 1977-78 with the Los

Angeles Kings. He retired as an active player after the 1979-80 season. His final NHL statistics are 132 goals and 272 points in 520 games played.

Today, Hicke is one of the few former Seals who remains in California. He works as the director of hockey operations at the Vacaville Skating Center. He and his wife have a son and a daughter.

Although often overshadowed by the Lafleur trade and his off-ice habits, Ernie Hicke had a productive NHL career and made a positive contribution to the Seals. "He was a good hockey player," Walt McKechnie called. "He could shoot and had a tremendous wrist shot. He was another one of us, one of the group."

Tommy Williams

"A great guy. He was one of the oldest guys on the team. He could still skate, shoot and pass. He would help the younger guys. A team player who really wanted to win."

—*Ernie Hicke on Tommy Williams*

Tommy Williams was one of the first Americans to play in the National Hockey League. For his efforts, he was elected to the U.S. Hockey Hall of Fame. Williams was born in Duluth, Minnesota, and later played for the 1960 U.S. Olympic hockey team that won a gold medal at Squaw Valley, California. The 5'11", 180-pound Williams played one year in the EPHL before making his NHL debut with the Bruins in 1961-62. At the time, he was the only American-born and -trained player in the NHL.

Williams's younger brother Butch Williams, who also played for the Seals, recalled how Tommy Williams ended up in Boston and what it was like growing up with him. "Tom went to Detroit's camp when he was 18," Butch Williams recalled. "Detroit wanted to sign him, but my dad wanted them to guarantee a college education if it didn't work out. We're talking about $5,000 maybe, but he didn't sign with Detroit. Tommy was my hero. He was one of the most likable individuals you could meet. He was always there for me."

Tommy Williams spent eight seasons in Boston, topping the 20-goal mark in 1962-63 and scoring 50 points in 1967-68. He was known for his great skating speed, being very popular with his teammates and for having a good time off the ice. Williams suffered a career-threatening knee injury in 1968-69 and only appeared in 26 games that year. Before the following season, Williams was traded to his hometown team, the Minnesota North Stars, where he scored a career-high 67 points in 1969-70.

The 1970-71 season was a very difficult one for Williams. While he was less effective on the ice, scoring 23 points in 41 games for the North Stars, there was a reason for the falloff in Williams's play. In November 1970, Williams's wife died suddenly. It was never determined for certain whether her death was an accident or a suicide. Regardless, Williams was stunned by her loss. He became moody and fought with his coach, Jack Gordon, who later suspended him before trading Williams to the Seals along with Dick Redmond for Ted Hampson and Wayne Muloin on February 23, 1971.

The next day, Williams made a strong first impression on his new team as he scored a goal and assisted on another during a 5-2 loss to the Canadiens in Oakland. He finished the season with seven goals and 17 points in just 18 games with California, including a game against Pittsburgh, where he assisted on two goals and a one-goal, one-assist performance during a 5-2 win over the Kings on March 21, 1971.

Seals coach Fred Glover acknowledged Williams's superior talents, but also realized that something was holding him back. "He could have been one hell of player," Glover remarked years later. "I thought he could have been a world beater, but he had a few problems that would have driven anybody nuts."

It seems that Williams's penchant for off-ice wildness continued after his trade to the Bay Area. All of his teammates loved Tommy and appreciated him, but they all recognized his problems as well. "He was a fun-loving guy who loved to sing Rod Stewart songs," recalled Gary Jarrett. "He had a great sense of humor and he kept things light." Dennis Hextall added, "He was a wild man off the ice. Tommy had a lot of ability, but his life off the ice controlled his performance on the ice."

In 1971-72, Williams was named an alternate captain of the Seals. He played in only 32 games that season due, in part, to injuries. He scored three goals and 12 points. Despite missing so much playing time, Williams continued to have fun off the ice and to endear himself to his teammates. "He was the best," Bobby Sheehan said of Williams. "He could fly. He was one of the first Americans to play in the NHL. He told me once, 'Nobody skates like you,' then he said, 'You're the best.' And I said, 'No, you're the best,' and we just kept going back and forth. Finally, I said, 'OK, Tommy, you're right, I must be the best.' "

Sheehan also recalled an incident when Williams's fondness for fun-loving pranks got him into trouble. "I called him 'The Bomber,' " Sheehan recalled. "He got his nickname because once, when we were heading up to Toronto, he had a gift he was bringing back for someone. The customs agent asked Tommy, 'What's in the present?' and Tommy answered, 'A bomb.' He was just joking, of course, but they arrested him and he missed the game."

On December 31, 1971, Williams had one more standout game for the Seals. He scored a goal and added an assist during a 6-3 Seals loss at the Olympia in Detroit. Norm Ferguson called Williams "a different guy. He was carefree and footloose. He could skate like the wind. He had played on better teams in the past. He was a character. You never knew what he would do next." Carol Vadnais said Tommy Williams was "an easygoing guy. He could still skate pretty well with the Seals and he had a good shot." Dick Redmond, who roomed with Williams during his time with the Seals, added simply, "He was my roommate and the greatest guy in the world." Paul Shmyr recalled that "Tommy was a fast skater and a leader. Everybody liked Tommy."

On March 5, 1972, during their final playoff drive, the Seals quietly traded Williams back to the Bruins. All they received in return was cash. The Bruins assigned Williams to their AHL farm club, the Boston Braves, where Williams finished out the season. It seemed as though his NHL career was over.

Like many veteran hockey players of that era, Williams's career was revived by the formation of the WHA. He signed with the New England Whalers before the 1972-73 season and scored the very first goal in Whalers history. He finished the season with just 10 goals and 31 points in 69 games, but helped lead the Whalers to the first-ever Avco Cup title. In 1973-74, Williams was healthy again and scored 21 goals and 58 points for New England.

Tommy Williams returned to the NHL in 1974-75 when the Bruins traded his rights to the expansion Washington Capitals. Williams scored 22 goals and 58 points with Washington that season, not bad on a team that set an NHL record for futility by winning only eight of 80 games. In fact, Williams led the team in goals, assists and points. His point total was 33 points higher than the next highest-scoring Capitals player—Denis Dupere, who had just 35 points.

Williams did have one more memorable moment in the history of the Seals. On March 28, 1975, the Capitals won their first-ever road game in team history after an 0-37-0 start. Their victim, of course, was the California Golden Seals as Washington topped California 5-3 at the Oakland Coliseum. Butch Williams of the Seals was named the first star of the game as he scored a goal and assisted on two others. The second star of the game was Tommy Williams, who had two assists for Washington. "After the game was over," Butch Williams recalled, "Tommy marched a garbage can around their dressing room like it was the Stanley Cup." A long, mock celebration ensued in the Washington dressing room as the garbage can was passed from player to player.

Williams retired from pro hockey after the 1975-76 campaign. He was 36 years old. His final NHL statistics were 161 goals and 430 points in 663 games. In the WHA, he added 31 goals and 89 points in 139 contests.

Hard times seemed to follow Williams after he retired from hockey. He remarried and found a new career, and his life seemed to be back on track. Then, tragedy struck again. Williams's 23-year-old son,

Robert, died in 1987. Like his father before him, Robert was a prospect in the Bruins organization. Williams himself died of a heart attack in 1992 at the age of 51.

Wayne Carleton summed up what Tommy Williams meant to many of his teammates when he said, "He was a free spirit. He skated like the wind. He loved life and lived it that way. Tommy was a good guy and a good team player." Everybody liked Tommy Williams.

Dick Redmond

"I grew up with him. He had more confidence than half of our team. He could do everything and he had a lot of talent to go along with his confidence."

—Joey Johnston on Dick Redmond

Dick Redmond was one of the early offensive defenseman who joined the NHL in the wake of Bobby Orr. He could skate, shoot and quarterback the power play very effectively. Growing up, Redmond's favorite players were Stan Mikita and Jean Beliveau. By the time he reached juniors, Redmond knew he had a chance to make the NHL. "I could tell by my overall attitude and desire," Redmond said. In his final season in juniors, Redmond scored 33 goals and 78 points in just 50 games. He was named to the first postseason all-star team in the OHA that year. By that time, Redmond's older brother Mickey was playing for the Montreal Canadiens.

The Minnesota North Stars selected Redmond with the fifth overall pick in the 1969 entry draft. He played 16 games in Minnesota over parts of two seasons, registering three assists. He spent most of the 1969-70 season playing for the North Stars CHL affiliate in Iowa and most of the 1970-71 season with the AHL's Cleveland Barons.

On March 7, 1971, the North Stars traded Redmond to the Seals along with Tommy Williams for Ted Hampson and Wayne Muloin. "I had no qualms about the trade whatsoever," Redmond recalled. "Things were a little different because hockey was new to California. There was an attitude of speculation: What would it be like? What's it like playing hockey in warmer weather?"

Redmond soon found out that in Northern California in the early '70s, hockey was not exactly a high-profile job. "I went to San Francisco one time to buy my wife a long suede coat and one for me," Redmond remembered. "I gave my credit card to the clerk and she said, 'You're one of those entertainers out in Oakland.' That's what we were to these people, I guess." Redmond did admit, however, that the fans who did come to Seals games were good ones. "Those that were there were diehards," he said. "A lot of them were from San Jose. There was a small contingency there who really liked their hockey. Krazy George also did a good job of stirring up the crowd there."

Redmond finished the 1970-71 season with the Seals and made a strong showing. In 11 games with California, he scored twice and had six points. He tallied his first NHL goal off Los Angeles Kings goalie Jack Norris on March 21, 1971, at the Oakland Coliseum during a 5-2 Seals win over the Kings.

Most of Redmond's teammates immediately recognized his talents. Ernie Hicke remembered that Redmond "had the hardest shot outside of Bobby Hull in the game. He was great on the point of the power play with Carol Vadnais." Gary Jarrett called Redmond "as good a skater as I've ever played with. He could also shoot the puck hard."

The drawback to Redmond's flashy style of play was that it was high-risk and high-reward. Fellow rookie defenseman Ron Stackhouse recalled that Redmond "believed in himself and was a pretty good player. He took some chances. Sometimes he got caught and sometimes it worked out well."

As he gained experience, Redmond's play improved and he learned when to take risks. "Dick had good offensive skills," Gerry Pinder recalled. "He just needed to learn to play as a team guy. By the end of the season, he had that figured out." Winger Gary Croteau recalled that Redmond "had a bullet of a shot and was a great skater. He was more offensive-minded than defensive-minded, but he knew how to pick his spots."

The 1971-72 season was Redmond's only one in Oakland. He led the team in assists that year with 35, which set a new team record for assists in one season by a defenseman (the record stood until the final season the Seals were in Oakland). Redmond also added 10 goals for a 45-point season and led the team in shots on goal that season with 254. Many of Redmond's teammates began to take notice of his abilities. "I never realized how good he was until I played with him," Norm Ferguson said of Redmond. "He was good with the puck and had great offensive skills." Lyle Carter added, "He had lots of talent and was beautiful to watch. He was one of the better players on the team."

Redmond did have some memorable games for the Seals. On March 12, 1972, he scored a goal and added two assists in the Seals 7-3 win over the Rangers. It was the Seals sixth season of their existence, but their first win ever at Madison Square Garden. The Kirkland Lake, Ontario, native also had three assists in an 8-1 win for the Seals over Toronto at the Oakland Coliseum. But when asked about his most memorable game with the Seals, Redmond chose a team milestone rather than an individual moment. "We beat Boston once and we were badly outshot," Redmond recalled. "Gilles Meloche stood on his head. After the game, Charlie Finley flew us back to Oakland first class."

"The best thing about playing for the Seals was finally getting to play steadily," Redmond said. "The only way to grow your skills is to play a lot. I finally got that chance in Oakland." Bert Marshall recalled how the experience Redmond gained in Oakland helped advance his career. "He was a talented guy and had a pretty good NHL career," Marshall noted. "When he was in Oakland, he was a young guy at the start of his career."

Still, the confidence Redmond exuded rubbed some of his teammates the wrong way. "He thought he was the superstar of the team," Reggie Leach recalled. "He was one of those guys where it was never his fault when something bad happened to us." Fellow blue liner Paul Shmyr thought that Redmond "didn't come to play every game. I called him 'Twilight.' Sometimes, he'd come to the rink and you weren't sure if he was there or not. When he was on his game, he was a great player."

The other problem Redmond had in the NHL was trying to shine in the shadow of his older brother Mickey. In 1971-72, Dick's first full season in Oakland, Mickey Redmond scored 42 goals and had 71 points for Detroit. He followed that year up with back-to-back seasons of more than 50 goals. "Dick had a great shot and good skill, but he had to live up to his brother's reputation," Carol Vadnais said. "I think that bothered his career." Morris Mott added that Dick Redmond was "a very talented player," but added, "maybe he was disappointed that he was not doing as well as his brother Mickey." Of course, as a defenseman, Dick could hardly be expected to match his brother goal for goal. Still, after the 1971-72 season, Dick Redmond was starting to make a name for himself in his own right in the hockey world.

After the 1971-72 season, there was a mass exodus of hockey players out of Oakland. The Seals lost more players to the WHA than any other NHL team (nine), including some of their best players. Charlie Finley simply refused to believe that the WHA would ever get off the ground so he refused to match the higher salaries the new league was offering his players. Seals general manager Garry Young was told to hold the line on salaries. Redmond was one of the players whose contract was up for renewal. Instead of losing yet another high-profile player, Young re-signed Redmond to a new contract. The only problem was that the contract was above the amount Charlie Finley instructed him to pay. According to Finley, Young never told him what Redmond was actually being paid. There were rumors that there were three copies of the contract with different dollar amounts on them. Finley decided to pay Redmond at the rate he asked Young to sign him at.

When his paychecks arrived, Redmond knew there was a problem. "I wasn't getting paid what I signed for," Redmond said. "Garry Young was trying to keep the nucleus of the team together. There was a rumor that my contract was never registered with the league, but I don't think that's possible."

Fred Glover, who was then working in the Seals front office, recalled what happened from a management perspective. "Dick had a good year in 1971-72," Glover said. "He was supposed to get a raise and I knew what it was supposed to be. An envelope came from Alan Eagleson's addressed to

Dick Redmond Inc. That's when I found the contract. It said $70,000 for the first year and $100,000 for the second year. That was a big raise from $15,000. I knew Charlie Finley didn't authorize that."

The result of the controversy was simple. Young was fired as GM and coach of the Seals and was replaced once again by Fred Glover. On December 5, 1972, the Seals traded Redmond to the Black Hawks for Darryl Maggs. Despite Redmond's fast start to the season (he had three goals and 16 points in 24 games for the Seals), his youth (Redmond was still only 22) and his undeniable talent, he was gone.

Redmond's former teammates, already reeling from the loss of talent to the WHA and a sluggish start to the 1972-73 season, felt betrayed. "Dick was in the top five or six in the talent pool," defenseman Rick Smith said. "Some games, he was like the Bobby Orr of the Seals; he quarterbacked the power play and had tremendous skill. The contract hassle he had with Garry Young and Charlie Finley was a real distraction to the team. It made us feel like ownership was not in our corner." Redmond went on with the Black Hawks to the Stanley Cup Finals against Montreal. The Seals finished in last place, 17 points behind the expansion Atlanta Flames in the West Division.

Redmond played four and a half seasons in Chicago, topping the 20-goal mark in his final season in the Windy City. After splitting the 1977-78 season between St. Louis and Atlanta, Redmond settled in with the Boston Bruins for four more years. He retired after the 1981-82 season. His final NHL statistics include 133 goals and 445 points in 771 NHL games. Despite only appearing in 109 games for the Seals, he stands 25th in club history in scoring.

Today, Redmond is vice president of sales at Hanson International in Toronto. He and his wife have three sons, including one who has played professional hockey in Amsterdam.

Bobby Sheehan summed up Dick Redmond by saying, "He was a good friend of mine. I played with him and Marcel Dionne in juniors. His stick was like a boomerang—he could shoot the puck and he had great moves. He never quit and he was a good man." And he was another talent the Seals let get away.

Tom Webster

Tom Webster stands as one of the great "what ifs" in the history of the Seals franchise, which has a history that is filled with too many of them. Unfortunately for the Seals and their fans, Webster only played in seven games with the Seals during the 1971-72 season. The following year, he was gone, signing with the WHA as part of the mass exodus of talent from Oakland when Charlie Finley refused to enter a bidding war with the new league for players.

Webster was born in Kirkland Lake, Ontario. "Playing in the NHL was something I dreamed about as a kid," Webster said. "Leaving home at 15 and playing junior hockey in Niagara Falls was something I wanted to fulfill. I remember watching 'Hockey Night in Canada.' Both Dick Duff and Ted Lindsay were from my hometown. It was a way to maybe do something with the little talent I had." In his final season in the OHA, Webster scored 50 goals and totaled a league-leading 114 points in just 54 games while playing for the Niagara Falls Flyers.

The 5'10", 170-pound Webster was drafted by the Boston Bruins in the 1966 NHL amateur draft. In 1968-69, Webster played nine games for the Bruins while spending most of the year with the Oklahoma City Blazers of the CHL. The following season, he played two more games for the Bruins and had another successful year in Oklahoma City. Surprisingly, the Bruins did not protect Webster in the expansion draft and the Buffalo Sabres selected him prior to the 1970-71 season. That same day, he was traded to Detroit for veteran goalie Roger Crozier.

"I grew up a Red Wings fan," Webster admitted. "Gordie Howe was my favorite player. I ended up rooming with him in Detroit. That was a tremendous experience for myself. I took a lot of messages. I later played on a line with Gordie and his son Marty with the New England Whalers." Given the chance to play regularly, Webster thrived in Detroit, scoring a team-leading 30 goals and 67 points in 78 games during 1970-71.

Much to his surprise, Webster was traded to the Seals on October 22, 1971, in exchange for second-year defenseman Ron Stackhouse. "I was very disappointed," Webster admitted. "I felt I had a pretty good year with Detroit. They made a lot of changes in management. I was disappointed to leave Detroit. Oakland had a pretty good club, too, though."

Webster had his best game as a member of the Seals on October 27, 1971, during a 6-4 win over the Penguins at the Igloo in Pittsburgh. He set up a goal by Stan Gilbertson and later scored one of his own off Pens goalie Les Binkley.

It was then that injury struck. "Just as I was settling in, I had my first experience with a bad back and I was out the rest of the season," Webster recalled. In seven games with the Seals, Webster scored twice and added one assist and six penalty minutes. Then, he and his bad back sat out the remainder of the 1971-72 season.

After the season was over, Webster was faced with a difficult decision. Should he stay with the Seals, who seemed to be an up-and-coming team in the NHL, or gamble and play for the newly formed WHA? "I was drafted by Jack Kelly of the New England Whalers," Webster said. "They offered me a three-year contract at $50,000 per year and it was guaranteed. I told them, 'I think we have a deal,' but I wanted to be fair to Mr. Finley, so I called him up to tell him about it. He told me to fly out to Chicago to meet with him. He asked me, 'What were you making last year?' I think it was $17,000. 'Well,' Finley said, 'that's a lot of money.' Then he told me what happened when some of his players were threatening to jump to the Mexican League in baseball for more money. He told me the Mexican League folded and those players that had jumped leagues had to come back to him. 'When they came back,' Finley said, 'I offered them less than what they had earned with me before.' So he offered me $15,000 to play for the Seals, saying he had to pay all the medical on my back and what have you. I told him thanks but no thanks, and signed with the Whalers."

Despite the difficult contract negotiations, Webster felt Finley was a competent owner. "We flew first class," he said. "He bought everybody on the team luggage. He was inventive with the white skates and all. I thought he was a good owner."

In 1972-73, Webster was second in the WHA with 53 goals and tied for fourth in the league with 103 points. He added 26 points in 15 playoff games to help lead the Whalers to the first-ever Avco World Trophy, the WHA's answer to the Stanley Cup. He topped 33 goals in his first five seasons in the WHA and played in the first four WHA All-Star games. It is undeniable that the Seals could have used Webster's goal-scoring talents, but he never played another game for the Seals. Webster remained with the Whalers through the 1977-78 season before playing briefly for the Red Wings organization in 1979-80. After that, Webster was forced to retire due to his bad back. He was 32 years old.

Tom Webster remained in hockey after his retirement as a player. He had two stints as an NHL head coach, one with the New York Rangers that was cut short by an inner-ear problem and a successful stint with the Los Angeles Kings from 1989-1992. He was later an assistant coach in the NHL with the Carolina Hurricanes. More recently, Webster coached the Windsor Spitfires of the OHA.

Tom Webster was a proven goal scorer who could have made a difference for the Seals in 1971-72 and beyond. The Seals missed the playoffs by just six points that year and a healthy Webster may have made the difference. Instead, Webster played only seven games for the Golden Seals. Seals fans can only look back and think of what might have been had he stayed healthy and remained in California.

Lyle Carter

"He was a great competitor. We got along very well. He was a nice guy who worked extra hard."

—Bobby Sheehan on Lyle Carter

Goaltender Lyle Carter briefly lived his NHL dream when he was acquired by the California Golden Seals prior to the 1971-72 season. Carter was from the Maritimes. In the '60s and early '70s, very few NHL players came from places like Truro, Nova Scotia. Carter, who grew up rooting for the Bruins, took a roundabout way to get to the NHL. "I had come a long way," Carter recalled. "I played senior hockey, but I always believed I could play. I must have been the only one who believed because I was in the lower senior leagues. I was scouted by Montreal when I was in the Ontario Senior League. I played in the IHL with the Muskegon Mohawks in 1970-71. Gilles Meloche was the backup goalie in Flint and I was the MVP of the league (Carter won the James Gatschene Memorial Trophy as the IHL's MVP that year). When it came time to sign with Montreal, we couldn't agree on an amount. I asked for a $7,500 bonus and $25,000 per year. So I went to University. Four or five weeks later, the Canadiens said they would be interested in signing me and then trading me to the Seals. I started the season three or four weeks late as a result. I remember Charlie Finley called to welcome me. He said, 'Welcome aboard, son.' I was delighted about the trade. Someone thought enough of me to trade for me. They gave up enough for me that I knew they wanted me. I didn't mind playing with Gilles Meloche; he was young."

In early October 1971, the Canadiens sent Carter to the Seals with John French in exchange for Randy Rota. Carter recalled how he found out about the trade and was first contacted by Charlie Finley. "We were in Springfield for an exhibition game," Carter recalled. "A trade was announced by Claude Ruel. Claude said to me, 'Lyle, you were a good fellow and we thought a lot about you. We traded you to the Seals. Charlie Finley wants to speak to you when you get back to the hotel.' I called Mr. Finley and he said he had to take another call. He left me on hold for 14 minutes. He came back on and said to me, 'Are you still there?' "

Carter made his NHL debut on October 17, 1971, against the Pittsburgh Penguins at the Oakland Coliseum. "For me, it was the dream of a lifetime," he recalled. "I knew I could play in the NHL. My timing still wasn't right, though. We lost 4-2 and the last goal was an empty-net goal."

Carter earned his first NHL victory a week later at the Olympia in Detroit. The Seals won 6-3 despite being outshot. Gerry Pinder scored a hat trick and had two assists in the game. "It meant a lot to me to win at the Olympia because Gordie Howe played there," Carter recalled. "We were outshot but we won 6-3." Carter made 34 saves to earn the victory.

The biggest problem Carter faced while with the Seals was staying healthy. Somehow, he just couldn't do it. It started after the Seals 12-1 debacle at Madison Square Garden. Carter relieved Gilles Meloche in the third period of that game with about eight minutes to go. "I gave up three goals in eight minutes," Carter said. "The thing people forget is that I faced 15 shots in eight minutes." The problem arose when some of Carter's equipment was left behind. "The trainer left my belly pads in New York," Carter said. "I was upset. 'Don't worry,' they told me before my next start, 'we'll have one for you tonight.' I used a smaller pad that night and got hurt." Carter also recalled suffering a four-inch cut of his rib cartilage in a game against the North Stars.

On November 28, 1971, the Seals were hosting Buffalo. "We were up 4-2," Carter remembered. "Richard Martin hit a rebound 95 miles per hour and the puck hit me in the rib. I had torn rib cartilage, but the Seals won the game 5-3."

Carter appeared in 15 games for the Seals in 1971-72, finishing with a 4-7-0 record and a 4.16 goals against average. He took pride in his performance and remembers his time with the Seals vividly to this day. "I remember playing against Bobby Orr in Boston in a 5-2 loss," Carter said with pride. "Orr had seven shots on goal but he didn't score on me. I also remember playing against Ken Dryden but

I lost 4-2." Carter also recalled a mini-streak he helped the Seals establish. "Starting on November 27, 1971, I started six games for the Seals and we won five of them. I still derive some satisfaction from that."

Carter was in the minority of Seals players in that he appreciated the team's white skates. "I loved it. I thought it was great," said Carter, who is also an avid baseball fan. "It reminded me of Bill Veeck."

Carter also recalled an incident that took place when the club was in Pittsburgh. "We went to an elite restaurant," Carter said. "We all had prime rib. The chef came out and wheeled it out. Charlie Finley was sitting next to me. He looked at the prime rib and said something about the cut being a little tough. The chef and Finley started to challenge each other and they almost went at it with fists. I don't know to this day if it was a setup."

Another incident Carter recalled took place between coach Vic Stasiuk and Bobby Sheehan. "Once, Vic showed Bobby how to say hello and goodbye with his stick," Carter said, laughing. When it came to Stasiuk, Carter was a bit disappointed in his coaching. "He was a nice man, but he didn't have a long résumé as a coach," Carter recalled. "I just didn't see much of a system. I expected him to design more plays to get the puck out of our end."

The man from the Maritimes did take a liking to playing hockey in Oakland. "The fans were great," Carter said. "We played Boston one game and drew 10,400. They were good fans and they liked the players. They seemed to enjoy hockey, although they weren't as knowledgeable as some of the fans in Canada, but they were good."

Before injuries sidelined him, Carter acted as backup to Gilles Meloche. The two young goalies got along well. Carter said, "Gilles played well and showed he was quite a prospect. You could see he had potential. We got along well and we were roommates. He said he wanted to play in the NHL for 18 years. I wanted to play five. In Pittsburgh once, we decided to walk to the arena from our hotel and we got chased by eight or nine guys who wanted to mug us. It was funny: we got along very well during the 1971-72 season, but the next year, we didn't talk much in training camp." Meloche also recalled Carter fondly. "He is a good man," Meloche said. "He used a stick that was so heavy, I needed two hands to lift it."

Carter called himself "a journeyman minor league goaltender. I kicked around the minors and worked hard. I had a good glove hand. I was nicknamed 'Cat' Carter. I felt I was good enough to play five years in the NHL."

After his injuries healed, the Seals sent Carter down to their farm team in Salt Lake. "I wasn't in shape due to my injuries," Carter said. "They wanted me to get back into shape. I had been written up in the papers so it was a big disappointment." Unfortunately for Carter, the Seals did not call him up to the big club for the rest of the 1971-72 season. Gilles Meloche was playing very well and Gary Kurt had settled in as his backup. The Seals were in the race for a playoff spot and the backup goalie didn't figure to see much action anyway. Carter spent some time in Salt Lake, some in Baltimore and was sent to Oklahoma City for the playoffs.

Carter was back in the Seals training camp for the start of the 1972-73 season. Garry Young, the team's GM, had now also taken over as coach for Stasiuk. "Garry Young told us before the 1972-73 season that whoever wins the backup goaltending job behind Gilles Meloche would stay in Oakland," Carter remembered. "It was basically between me and Marv Edwards in training camp. I played 30 minutes in a 1-1 tie and against Philadelphia in a 4-2 win. I had a 2.70 goals against average and a good record. Marv Edwards didn't play that well. Garry Young comes to me and says, 'Lyle, I have a problem. The problem is that we want you to play every day. We want Marv Edwards to tutor Gilles Meloche.' I asked him, 'Who won the job?' I reached out and grabbed him by his neck. He said, 'Remember what you believe in,' and I let go." Choking the coach/GM of franchise is not a recommended way to move up the team's depth chart.

Carter never played another game in the NHL. He spent the 1972-73 season with the Seals farm team in Salt Lake. The following year, the North Stars took him in the reverse draft and he was assigned to the New Haven Nighthawks. Despite having a winning record and very respectable goals against averages both years, neither team recalled Carter to the NHL. He retired from professional hockey after the 1974-75 season.

Today, Carter lives in Brookfield, Nova Scotia. He runs, owns and manages two automotive radiator shops, manufacturing car heaters and shipping them across Canada. He also writes a weekly column in the *Truro Daily News* called "Sports Scene Replays and Reflections." He and his wife have three sons, the youngest of whom was playing Junior A hockey in Truro. Of course, he is a goalie.

Lyle Carter remains proud of his brief stay in the NHL and still believes he should have had a longer career in pro hockey. He still has his goalie mask, a few pucks and his green Seals blazer and green and gold skates.

Norm Ferguson recalled Carter by saying, "He was a character. He was surprised to be in the NHL. He started a few games but he never got the chance to be a starting goalie in the NHL. Everybody always looked at him as a backup." Marshall Johnston added a fitting postscript on Carter. "He got the most of his abilities," Johnston said. But he didn't get the longest of chances.

Coach Vic Stasiuk

"He was an emotional guy. He loved the game. He played on good teams with great players like Gordie Howe. As a coach, he was enthusiastic. During practices, he'd be out there skating with us."
—*Marshall Johnston on Seals coach Vic Stasiuk*

Vic Stasiuk coached the Seals for slightly less than one season. He arrived on very short notice, just three games into the 1971-72 season and was dismissed after the season ended. As a player, the Lethbridge, Alberta, native played just over 13 seasons in the NHL with Boston and Detroit. Stasiuk scored 183 goals and 437 points and played on three Stanley Cup-winning teams. In Boston, Stasiuk played on the famous "Uke Line" with Bronco Horvath and John Bucyk. The line earned its nickname because all three players were of Ukrainian decent.

At age 33, Stasiuk was put on waivers by Sid Abel of Detroit and went unclaimed. It was the beginning of Stasiuk's coaching career. "Sid Abel asked me to be a player-coach in Pittsburgh of the AHL," Stasiuk remembered. "I said to Baz Bastien, the GM, that it was tough to be a player-coach. I just wanted to coach." Among the players Stasiuk coached with the Hornets were future NHL players Pit Martin, Roger Crozier and Paul Henderson. Stasiuk's next coaching assignment took him to Memphis of the CHL.

When expansion arrived in 1967, Stasiuk joined the Flyers organization. First, Stasiuk coached the Quebec Aces of the AHL. In 1967-68, he was named AHL coach of the year after the Aces finished in second place and made the Calder Cup finals. Later, Stasiuk joined the Flyers as an assistant coach. "Bud Poile was the GM there and I was there when we drafted Bobby Clarke," Stasiuk said. "He was amazing even back then. Bud said, 'We're gonna win the Stanley Cup with this kid.' Of course, he was right. I am proud to be part of the team that drafted and developed him. He was a special player."

In 1969-70, Stasiuk took over as head coach of the Flyers. After a poor showing in his first year behind the Flyers bench, Stasiuk led the team to a third-place finish and a playoff berth in 1970-71. However, Chicago swept the Flyers in four straight games in the first round of the playoffs and Stasiuk was dismissed and replaced by a minor league coach named Fred Shero.

Stasiuk expected to spend the 1971-72 season out of hockey when he was abruptly asked to coach in the NHL again. "I still had a year to go on my Flyers contract when I was let go by Bud Poile," Stasiuk said. "I came home to Lethbridge to my farm. [Flyers owner] Mr. Snider and Mr. Finley had a conference call with me and convinced me to go to the Seals to coach. I wasn't happy taking money from the Flyers for doing nothing and I was happy to be back in hockey. I knew Garry Young from my days in the Boston organization and he was now GM of Oakland."

The Seals were 0-1-2 when Stasiuk took over behind the bench, replacing Fred Glover. Stasiuk had to learn on the job. "I wasn't too familiar with the team before I got there," Stasiuk admitted. The new coach had to pack up and head to Oakland immediately, leaving his wife, Mary, behind. "My wife thought she'd have me all to herself and when I got the job in Oakland, she cried," Stasiuk told *The Oakland Tribune*'s John Porter. It was Stasiuk who probably wanted to cry after his first game coaching the Seals. California blew a 4-0 lead and wasted a hat trick from Bobby Sheehan in a 9-6 loss to the Canucks. Vancouver scored nine goals on only 21 shots.

After losing his first three games as coach, Stasiuk led the Seals to back-to-back wins in Detroit and Pittsburgh. Then came what Stasiuk described as the highlight of his NHL coaching career: The Seals went into Boston and shut out the eventual Stanley Cup-champion Bruins 2-0. Rookie goalie Gilles Meloche earned the shutout in his first game with California. Stasiuk was so emotional about his team's performance, he was literally moved to tears.

"That was the first time I actually cried at a hockey game," said Stasiuk. "I have only cried a few times in my adult life. After the game, I went into our dressing room to congratulate the players. I couldn't stand it. I had to go out in the alley where no one could see me and I cried like a baby. I don't know if I was crying because I was so happy for our young goaltender or selfishly for myself. I guess it was for everyone on the team."

Stasiuk brought emotion and dedication to the team as coach of the Seals. California developed into a fast-skating, young and exciting team in 1971-1972. Attendance was up and for the first time in years, Oakland fans had reason to be optimistic about the team's future. Stasiuk remembered his time in Oakland fondly. "We had a happy club. Nobody had a beef. Garry Young had a way of pacifying the players. Usually on clubs, there were flare-ups between players. We had no problems. It was great."

There were two problems Stasiuk had never faced before: the extensive travel and the weather. "To me, the weather out there was too nice," Stasiuk recalled. "It was not conducive to hockey. There's no doubt the travel affected us. There weren't too many direct flights back then. We'd go to Seattle on the way to Vancouver, for example. We also had some 21-day road trips. It was tough."

The players remembered their coach for his emotion more than anything. "When we were good, he was jovial, but when we were bad, he was not too pleasant to be around," recalled Bert Marshall. "He was old school."

Reggie Leach appreciated Stasiuk's coaching when he looked back at his career. "He tried to teach us, but we weren't mature enough to get it," Leach said of Stasiuk. "He wasn't a yeller and a screamer. He was an old-time coach who often referred back to how things were when he played."

Like any Seals employee, Stasiuk had his moments with Charlie Finley. "He was a stickler for details," Stasiuk recalled. "Once, I remember he was really upset because he couldn't get either myself or Garry Young on the phone. I was back in Lethbridge for a day. Mr. Finley wanted to know every little thing and be on top of things."

Trainer Barry Keast appreciated working with Stasiuk. "Vic treated us like we were on the team. He always asked our opinion. He came in a rush. A TV crew did a story on Vic and they paid him $50 or $100. He gave it to the trainers. He was a super guy to work for."

The Seals were in the thick of the playoff race in 1971-72, but they floundered down the stretch and lost their last six games to barely miss the playoffs. "We were in almost every game," Stasiuk said, looking back. "We were never blown out. Sometimes, it's a three-minute stretch when a game is won or lost." The young Seals were not quite ready for the pressure of the playoff race.

Goalie Gilles Meloche felt that Stasiuk could have pushed his team a little harder at times. "I wish Vic was a little tougher on the team," Meloche said. "Anytime we didn't lose, he was happy. A lot of ties we got should have been wins. We missed the playoffs by a few points."

Garry Young and Charlie Finley dismissed Stasiuk after the season. "They just said it was time to make a change," Stasiuk said. "I thought we had a gentlemen's agreement for a two-year contract, but I said it was fine. I then went to the Blues to assist Jean-Guy Talbot."

Stasiuk never served as a head coach in the NHL again. He had various business interests since retiring from hockey but now lives back in Lethbridge on his farm.

Ernie Hicke remembered Vic Stasiuk fondly. "Vic really wanted to win," Hicke said. "He was a different type of coach and he had younger players. He brought in a system that he thought would help, and it did." Craig Patrick summed up his first NHL coach by saying, "Vic was very enthusiastic and had good ideas about the game. He was good one on one with the players and was a good teacher." As a player and as a coach, Vic Stasiuk loved the game of hockey. While his team fell just short of the playoffs, Stasiuk gave everything he had for the players and fans of the California Golden Seals.

Gary Croteau

"He was a big guy. In fact, we called him 'The Bull.' He came to the rink and played hard every night. He's the kind of guy you like to play with because he was dependable and went up and down his wing. He was a nice guy and he could have played on any team in the league."

—Hilliard Graves on Gary Croteau

Gary Croteau was the epitome of the blue-collar hockey player. He wasn't the fastest skater on the team or the most colorful player, but every single one of Croteau's teammates acknowledged and respected the hard work he put in and the reliability of his game.

Croteau was born in Sudbury, Ontario. Although he recalls being asked to try out for a Canadiens farm team as young as 13, Croteau did not commit to hockey exclusively at that point. "I also enjoyed football, so I played high-school football and hockey," Croteau recalled. "There was no junior team in Sudbury back then." Instead, Croteau attended St. Lawrence University, playing there for three seasons. "I was planning to go to law school," Croteau admits. "When I was a senior in college, I realized I could make it to the NHL. Fortunately, I had a good college coach, George Menard. He was third in the Yankee chain behind Yogi Berra. He said he had a three-year plan to try to get in the bigs and then he would get a real job. I didn't want to be 30 and wondering if I could have made the NHL. I was on the Toronto negotiation list. I went to camp there and was traded to Los Angeles. In Los Angeles, I suffered a knee injury. I had also injured the knee in college, so they sent me to Lloyd Percival for a fitness program to strengthen the knee, but I had to pay for it. If it went well, they said they would reimburse me."

Croteau spent most of the 1968-69 season with the Springfield Kings of the AHL, although he appeared in 11 games for Los Angeles. In just 11 games, he scored five goals and added an assist. The Kings kept him on their roster for the playoffs that year and Croteau had a strong postseason. He scored three goals and five points in 11 games for the Kings, including some key goals against the Seals in the first round of the playoffs. Despite the strong postseason, Croteau spent most of the 1969-70 season in Springfield again, appearing in just three games for the Kings.

Despite his relatively short stay in Los Angeles, it was here that Croteau acquired his nickname, "The Bull." "I got called up late in the season," Croteau recalled. "Red Kelly had the team doing calisthenics in the main level of the arena. Jack Kent Cooke came by and Larry Regan introduced me to Mr. Cooke as the team's newest addition. Jack looked at me and said, 'From now on, his name will be Bull Croteau.' I remember we actually received an interoffice memo from Mr. Cooke saying I was only to be referred to as Bull Croteau. Years later, I was with the Seals and the Lakers just happened to be in the same city. The coach of the Lakers recognized me and said, 'Bull Croteau.' "

On February 20, 1970, the Kings traded Croteau to Detroit. The 6', 205-pound Croteau grew up as a Red Wings fan—and a Gordie Howe fan in particular. "One of the highlights of my career was when I was traded to Detroit and Gordie Howe was the first one to greet me. I even roomed with him on some road trips. He was a great guy." Croteau only stuck with the Red Wings for the final 10 games of the 1969-70 season, adding two assists. The Seals claimed Croteau in the intraleague draft in June of 1970. "In any trade you have mixed emotions," Croteau admitted. "You are disappointed the team trading you doesn't want you and you miss the relationships you had. But the new team *does* want you and it feels as if you can contribute. It was a small community in Oakland and I developed friendships very quickly."

At first, Croteau felt that the situation in Oakland was going to work out very well. "We had four or five players who were new and young and we felt we could make a difference. We were excited about being in Oakland and thought we could build a good team. Charlie Finley owned the team. He treated us very well until contract time came around. We were probably among the lower-paid teams in the league. Arbitration came, but it didn't work well. Charlie Finley had a budget for players and it wasn't very large. We lost between nine and 11 players to the WHA."

Still, Croteau did give credit to Finley for some of his innovations. "He was responsible for putting names on the back of players' jerseys. In some buildings, we weren't allowed to wear them because some teams thought it would reduce program sales. Our trainers had to bring two sets of jerseys on our road trips."

Croteau also remembered the green and gold skates and the white skates Finley introduced to the team. "It was a nightmare for our trainers. By the end of the season, they felt like they were 20 pounds each. They had to polish and shine them before every game. We laughed when we first saw them. I think the green and gold ones looked better than the white. The A's had white cleats made from kangaroo leather. Mr. Finley wanted us to have skates made of kangaroo leather but fortunately somebody explained to him that we needed something stronger on skates. The white skates were silly. They just didn't match the uniforms. People told me that on television, it looked like we were skating on stumps since the skates blended in with the ice. Opposing players didn't say too much to us because they knew we felt the same way about them."

Croteau also remembered Finley's first talk with the team. "He said, 'Boys, I know absolutely nothing about hockey. That's why I have a coach and general manager,' " Croteau recalled. Of course, during the three and a half years that he owned the Seals, Finley fired four coaches and four general managers. Croteau also recalled befriending many of the A's players. "They started telling stories of him calling them in the middle of the night and chewing them out over an error," Croteau remembered. "Thankfully, he never did that to us."

In 1970-71, his first season with the Seals and his first full season in the NHL, Croteau scored 15 goals and had 43 points playing on the Seals "Battle Line." The Battle Line was center Dennis Hextall, Croteau and either Norm Ferguson or Tony Featherstone on right wing. None of these players (with the possible exception of Ferguson) were known for their nifty moves or fancy stickhandling. They played aggressive, physical hockey. Croteau's specialty was digging the puck out of the corners. "Gary was a big, tough guy—not a fighter, but a workhorse," said Ernie Hicke. "He would work the corners and was a solid checker."

Croteau started his career with the Golden Seals with a bang. On October 10, 1970, his very first game in a Seals sweater, Croteau assisted on three goals during a 5-3 loss to the Red Wings at the Olympia. Croteau also managed his first career NHL hat trick on January 27, 1971, during a 6-2 home win over the North Stars. Cesare Maniago was the goalie as Croteau scored three times and added an assist. "Charlie Finley came in after the game and handed me three $100 bills," Croteau recalled. "That started a tradition on the team." Despite these spectacular moments, Croteau was known for his steady and consistent play. Game in and game out, he gave 100 percent effort.

Travel and scheduling were problems that Croteau and his teammates faced while playing in Oakland. "Our building was 500 yards from the football stadium. We played our home games on Wednesday, Friday and Sunday. The Raiders would draw 50,000 fans on Sunday afternoon and we had 1,700 on Sunday night. The following season, all Sunday games during the football season were on the road. As a result, we had a lot of late-season home games, but by then, we were already out of the playoff hunt. The team also made some bad trades. We were putting Band-Aids on major wounds. Guys they acquired would come in and not be able to even contribute."

Recordwise, 1971-72 was the Seals best season while Croteau was with the club. The Seals, led by new coach Vic Stasiuk, were in the playoff race until the final week of the season. They slumped down the stretch and missed the playoffs by a mere six points. Unfortunately, the Bull had an off year statistically, scoring 12 goals and 24 points in 73 games for the Seals. Still, he had the utmost respect of his teammates. "He was strong as an ox, a lot like Terry O'Reilly in that regard," said Bobby Sheehan. "When he was coming down the wing, it was like 'Get out of the way.' He was quiet and businesslike. He was all business." Defenseman Ray McKay added, "Gary was a big guy who had a great shot. He was a hard worker—I mean he really worked. There are guys that worked and then there was Gary Croteau. He used to do pushups until he couldn't do them anymore, then he would go to bed." Paul Shmyr added, "Gary came to play every game. He was a super guy. You couldn't ask for more from a teammate." Croteau's best game offensively that season was a three-assist effort in an 8-1 thrashing of the Maple Leafs in Oakland.

Croteau had a unique take on the efforts of Vic Stasiuk, his coach during the 1971-72 season. "He felt that if we got one point for each game we played, we'd make the playoffs. So he was always playing for the tie. He was basically just opening the gate and saying, 'Go get them guys.' He was old school. Even with a lead, he would just send one guy in on the forecheck. We could be winning 4-0 and he'd still be playing for the tie."

In 1972-73, Croteau was banged up and missed almost half the year with assorted leg injuries. In only 47 games, Croteau scored six goals and 21 points. His best offensive game that season was a one-goal, two-assist effort in a 6-3 win over the Penguins. Another game in Boston also stands out in Croteau's memory of that year. "We had lost a centerman to injury the night before so Marshall Johnston moved up to center and scored a hat trick," Croteau recalled. "We had a long flight back from Boston. The guys bought lobsters and had lobster races in the aisles of the plane." There were other pranks Croteau recalled that his teammates often did on the team plane. "We also used to put shaving cream on guys' heads if they fell asleep on the plane or cut their tie off while they were sleeping. We used to take the tires off of rookies' cars, too."

Despite the constant losing, Croteau did appreciate his time with the Seals. "Playing for the Seals gave me the opportunity to prove myself in the NHL and the opportunity to play regularly. We enjoyed living in the Bay Area. The fans we had were just fantastic—there just wasn't a lot of them. We'd draw well for established teams but we wouldn't play our best. The fans we had would come out to watch us practice at 5:30 a.m. at Berkeley."

The practice facility at Berkeley also held memories for the Bull. "It was awful cold," Croteau remembered. "It was an Olympic-sized rink. We practiced at a weird time in the midafternoon. We took BART [Bay Area Rapid Transit] up there during the gas shortage. It was a pain in the neck to get to. When practice would end, it would be rush hour so we would go to a bar because BART was so crowded."

Croteau said that his style of play changed over the course of his career. "Initially, I was a physical player—a good two-way hockey player who could score goals, but is stronger on the defensive side of the game," he said. "When I was playing with Ivan Boldirev and Craig Patrick, I knew they would take more chances, so I stayed back," Croteau said.

As the Seals franchise fell lower and lower in the standings, Croteau's ability to add stability to the team was appreciated by his teammates. "His work ethic was the best on the team," defenseman Ted McAneeley said. "He was not a great skater, but he was a stabilizing influence off the ice on a team that had a lot of guys who liked to party."

Croteau was paired with Boldirev and Patrick during the 1973-74 season, his final year in California. In 76 games, Croteau scored 14 times and had 35 points. The highlight of the season for Croteau individually was his second career hat trick on October 24, 1973, in a 7-3 pasting of the Red Wings.

Croteau remembered one particular game against the Rangers from that season that didn't quite work out as planned. "It was in Madison Square Garden. Boldirev, Patrick and I were out against the

Ratelle line [the GAG line of Jean Ratelle, Vic Hadfield and Rod Gilbert]. Our assignment was to keep them off the board. The first two or three shifts, we didn't even touch the puck, let alone get it out of our zone. The coach was on us. I decided to stir something up so I elbowed Vic Hadfield into the glass. He hit me on the center of my forehead and like a cartoon character, I fell right down. I didn't even get a punch off."

In February of 1974, Charlie Finley finally sold the Seals back to the NHL. Fred Glover resigned and Marshall Johnston retired as a player and became the club's coach. "He was a technician," Croteau recalled. "He had played at Denver University and for the Canadian Olympic Team. He had a game plan for all the teams we played. He was the most knowledgeable coach with strategy. Other guys would match lines and just tell us, 'Don't let your guy score,' but Marshall would try to take our best scoring line and try to avoid matching it up with the other team's checking line."

By 1973-74, Croteau was also one of the team's more respected veterans and a leader on and off the ice, and was named an alternate captain. Young players like defenseman Barry Cummins recalled that Croteau "wouldn't get too low or too high. He kept an even keel and worked hard and then things would work out OK. He helped you out as much as he could. He tried to help the younger guys." Fellow rookie Paul Shakes added that Croteau "was a great guy off the ice who included us [rookies just called up from Salt Lake] in team activities."

Despite his leadership abilities and steady play, the Seals did not protect Croteau in the expansion draft prior to the 1974-75 season. The Kansas City Scouts selected him and the Bull joined that hapless organization. He played two years in Kansas City and stayed with the franchise when it became the Colorado Rockies in 1976-77. Croteau's final NHL season was 1979-80 with the Rockies. He finished with 144 goals and 319 points in 684 NHL games. Ironically, his fine playoff performance as a rookie in 1968-69 was the only time in Croteau's career that he appeared in the Stanley Cup playoffs. (The one year the Rockies made the playoffs in 1978, Croteau missed the series with an injury.) Croteau also left his mark on the Seals record book. He is the team's 10th all-time leading scorer, is fifth all-time in games played and eighth in assists.

Today, Croteau lives in the Denver area. He and his wife have three children. For the past 20 years, Croteau has been selling real estate.

Rick Smith summed up Croteau by saying, "He was a nice fellow and a strong guy. He personified inspired play. He had a positive approach. He could kill penalties and had offensive abilities. An honest player, he could run right over you when you least expected it." He wasn't flashy or colorful, but the Bull was reliable, worked hard and earned everything he got—on and off the ice.

Gerry Pinder

"A great guy, a real spark plug. He hustled and was a good hockey player. He added a lot to the team."

—Lyle Carter on Gerry Pinder

Gerry Pinder spent only one season with the California Golden Seals, but it was a memorable one. In 1971-72, Pinder led the team in goals, points and shooting percentage and also tied for the club lead in power-play goals. Statistically, Pinder finished the year with 23 goals and 54 points in 74 games.

Pinder was born in Saskatoon, Saskatchewan, the same place as Gordie Howe. As a result, Pinder grew up as a Red Wings fan. He recalled that playing professional hockey "was what I always wanted to do as an 8-, 10- and 12-year-old." In his second year of juniors with the Saskatoon Blades, Pinder won the league scoring title and was named MVP. "That's when I thought I really had the tools to play in the National Hockey League," he said. "There were only six teams then and I still thought I could make it." Pinder later played for Canada in the 1968 Olympics and won a bronze medal in Grenoble, France.

Pinder broke into the NHL with the Chicago Black Hawks in 1969-70. He scored 19 goals and 39 points in 75 games, which was more than respectable considering he did not get a lot of ice time until after Christmas. In 1970-71, the 5'8", 165-pound Pinder scored 13 goals and 31 points for the Hawks. He was disappointed with his lack of playing time and left the team for a few days in midseason as a protest. Although he later returned to the Chicago lineup, things were never the same for Pinder there.

On September 9, 1971, Pinder, left wing Kerry Bond and goaltender Gerry Desjardins were sent to the Seals in exchange for Gary Smith. "I was pretty happy," Pinder said when he recalled the trade that brought him to Oakland. "I didn't have a lot of fun in Chicago. They were loaded with talent and it was hard breaking in with a veteran team. They had their friends and their groups already established. Bobby Hull was helpful in that regard. He said, 'Come with us to dinner,' and would invite me along. Bill Reay was a nice man, but we had some disagreements. I was young and didn't have much patience and I wanted to play. I was happy to go to a team that was lower in the standings but I knew I would be on the ice all the time. I got the call around September 9 while still in Saskatoon, about a day or two before I was supposed to report to camp for the Black Hawks. Billy Reay called me to tell me I was traded and I had to go to Oshawa, where the Seals trained. Other people felt bad for me but I felt good. The Seals had a good young team and I played a lot and led the team in scoring."

When Pinder arrived at Seals camp, Fred Glover was the team's coach. Glover was fired just three games into the regular season. "It became clear during camp that there was friction between Freddie and most of the guys," Pinder said. "He didn't know how to handle younger guys like we had. There was no one guy who got Freddie fired. I never had any problems with him. I always liked him, but I was not surprised he was asked to leave."

Glover's replacement was Vic Stasiuk. "Defensive players were his favorites," Pinder said of Stasiuk. He came from Philadelphia, which had a defensive-oriented system. We had a lot of talent and he favored defense, so I think that was a minus. He was a very, very nice man away from the rink. It was hard not to like him because he was so genuine." Stasiuk called Pinder "a good, smart player and a gentleman. He was not big or forceful, but he was heady."

Pinder was 24 years old when he joined the Seals in 1971-72 and the Seals were one of the youngest teams in the league at that time. "We were young and didn't take care of ourselves off the ice," Pinder admitted. "We would have been fine if we had the knowledge and ability to do that. We were on the road for 18 days at a time. We had a lot of fun, though by the time the year was over, we were tired from travel."

Walt McKechnie recalled that Pinder was "a funny man who wanted the team to do well. He was a good competitor and a free spirit." The team also had a special camaraderie when Pinder was there. "We were a young team and we liked each other," he said. "It was a great experience. I was doing what I really liked and playing a lot. I even played when I broke my hand and had a bad back."

Pinder also appreciated the fans in Oakland. "There was a hard-core group of [8,000 to] 10,000 fans. They loved their hockey," he said. "Even when we lost, they were there. The fan club parties were great. We had really good, hard-core fans—just not as many of them as they had in Chicago. If the team I was on would have stayed together and the franchise had gotten a new rink, the team would never have left." Another difference between Oakland and Chicago was the lack of recognition the players had in Oakland. "We could go out and nobody knew or cared who we were," Pinder said. "I kind of enjoyed that vis-à-vis Chicago."

Pinder and his teammates always found ways to have fun—sometimes a little *too* much fun. Gerry recalled an incident that took place in St. Louis the night before a game. "Some of the guys were drinking too much and getting a bit frisky. The hotel limo was there and some of the guys took it for a ride. Well, the car didn't make it back to the hotel. They hit something. I remember we were woken up later that evening and we sort of pooled our meal money to bail the guys out. The car was damaged and we had to pay for the car."

The young Seals had a lot of cohesiveness the season Pinder was there, which was the best year the Seals had during the Charlie Finley era. Paul Shmyr, who played with Pinder in Chicago, California and with Cleveland of the WHA, recalled an incident in which Pinder was the butt of a prank. "We had just eight or nine crazy guys on our team, real jokesters," Shmyr recalled. "I remember one time we were at LaGuardia Airport and Gerry went to get an ice-cream cone while we were waiting for our plane. I saw two guys dressed in suits and they had a guy in handcuffs between them. They must have been taking this prisoner somewhere. They sat down, so the guy in the handcuffs sat down. I said to him, 'Gerry, there's a guy from Saskatoon who says he knows you.' Gerry looked at the guy but didn't see the handcuffs. He said to the guy, 'Are you looking for me?' Then he noticed the handcuffs and said, 'Oh, I must have the wrong guy.' He still wants to get me back for that one."

Pinder also recalled what happened when Charlie Finley introduced the club's new white skates. "I remember we were in the Hilton Hotel in Detroit or Minnesota. Mr. Finley was there and the skates were delivered to the lobby. Carol Vadnais was our captain at the time. Anyway, Finley said we had to wear those skates *tonight*. We said 'No way,' and Carol had to explain to Mr. Finley that new skates need to be broken in before we could wear them for a game. It takes at least a week. They were stiff and not sharpened—heck, they were still in the box. Vadnais explained that if we would have worn those skates that night, we would have lost 15-0. Finley knew nothing about hockey skates. He knew more about baseball. The skates were pretty humorous but I didn't mind them. Players on other teams laughed and joked about the skates, but it was all in fun. It's just that you didn't want to get injured on the Seals because our trainers were always too busy painting the skates. Mr. Finley wanted them to look perfect. By the end of the season, each pair would weigh something like 50 pounds."

Pinder's best game in a Seals sweater came on October 24, 1971, at the Olympia in Detroit. Pinder set a team record that night by scoring five points in one game. He beat Red Wings goalie Al Smith three times and set up two other goals in a 6-3 California win. "Charlie Finley was at the game," Pinder recalled. "He came into the dressing room and peeled off three $100 bills. I went out to A.C. Lindell's sports bar in Detroit that night. By the time I got back to the hotel, I had no money left."

All of Pinder's teammates seemed to respect him on and off the ice. Wayne Carleton recalled that Pinder was "a good playmaker," while Craig Patrick remembered Pinder as one of the club's many "smaller, skilled guys." Gary Jarrett said Pinder "was confident and played hard. He was my size but he didn't back down from anybody."

Despite enjoying the Bay Area and his teammates, Pinder left the Seals before the 1972-73 season when the WHA made an offer. "I was just about money," Pinder admitted. "I loved living in the Bay Area. The players would all get together and play golf. I wasn't used to that in the winter. I would have been happy to stay, but at three times my salary … I learned that professional hockey was a business and I was never going to make any money playing for Charlie Finley." So Gerry Pinder signed with the Cleveland Crusaders of the WHA. In 1972-73, he scored 30 goals for the Crusaders and had 66 points. He stayed with Cleveland for four seasons before making stops with the San Diego Mariners and Edmonton Oilers. His last active season in pro hockey was 1977-78. An eye injury suffered in his second WHA season limited his effectiveness and contributed to his early retirement.

Today, Pinder lives in Calgary and has his own real-estate development company. He manages projects there. He and his brothers also have an investment company. Pinder and his wife have three sons.

Ernie Hicke summed up Pinder by saying, "He was a little guy with a big heart. He would go into the corners and he could score." Gary Croteau said, "He brought competitive spirit to the team and was a good team guy." And he had fun playing the game. That was Gerry Pinder.

Bobby Sheehan

"He was from Boston and he could skate like the wind. He had an unbelievable slap shot for someone his size—he was slight but he had a big Bobby Hull-type slap shot. The crowd loved to watch him."

—Gary Jarrett on Bobby Sheehan

You could love or hate Bobby Sheehan, the Seals fast, young center—but you could never ignore him. Sheehan was a high-risk, high-reward type of player. One minute, he'd have the fans on the edge of their seats and cheering a move no other player on the ice could have made, while the next minute he'd have his coach pulling out his hair for failing to back-check or pick up his man in the neutral zone—or, worse yet, failing to show up at the team hotel for curfew. Whether he frustrated you or excited you, nobody who played with or against Bobby Sheehan will ever forget him.

Sheehan was born in Weymouth, Massachusetts, but grew up a fan of Gordie Howe and the Red Wings. He was one of the first American-born players to make the NHL, although he went through Canada to do it. "I left Boston at 17 and played junior hockey in Nova Scotia," Sheehan said. "I was one of the better players on the team. I was used to playing 18 games a year—up there we played 88 games per year. You learn quickly to keep your head up."

Sheehan's best weapon was his skating speed. He was drafted by the Montreal Canadiens, a team that based its game on speed, in the third round of the 1969 draft. Sheehan spent most of the next two seasons playing for the Montreal Voyageurs of the AHL, although he was called up for 16 games in 1969-70 and 29 games in 1970-71. Sheehan also played in six postseason games for the 1971 Canadiens team that defeated the Chicago Black Hawks to win the Stanley Cup. "I was with Montreal and we had just won the Cup," Sheehan recalled. "I had that under my belt. With the Canadiens, when you hit 24, they asked you when you were going to get married. I was 22. Sam Pollack asked me when I intended to settle down. I asked him, 'When are *you* getting married?' I would have stayed there [in Montreal]. I loved it. I enjoyed playing with John B. Ferguson and those guys."

Sheehan didn't last too much longer in Montreal. In the off season, Canadiens GM Sam Pollack shipped his speedy 5'7", 155-pound center to Oakland in a cash deal. Sheehan would spend the 1971-72 season in Oakland as a member of the California Golden Seals.

He immediately noticed significant differences between the atmosphere in Montreal and in Oakland. "In Montreal, you've got to win," Sheehan admitted. "Oakland was an expansion team. In Montreal, everybody knew who you were. In California, they didn't who you were. In Montreal, there were always great players behind you and if you didn't play well, you were gone. In Oakland, there wasn't that kind of pressure. You had a lot more room for error."

Sheehan started off the 1971-72 season on fire. In the Seals fourth game of the year, Sheehan scored a hat trick off of Canucks goalie Dunc Wilson. Unfortunately, the Seals blew a 5-1 first-period lead and ended up losing the game 9-6. Sheehan also had three assists in a 6-3 win over the Red Wings later that month. By December 31, 1971, Sheehan had 17 goals to lead the Seals. Unfortunately, after that Sheehan's production fell off dramatically. He finished his only year in Oakland with 20 goals and 46 points.

As fast as Bobby Sheehan could skate, his lifestyle off the ice was perhaps even faster. Sheehan was young, single and loving every minute of living in Northern California. "I got a lot of playing time and I also met a lot of nice people outside hockey," Sheehan said. "I had a great time with the players. I was 22 years old and getting paid to play hockey."

Many of Sheehan's teammates also recalled his lifestyle during his season in the Bay Area. Walt McKechnie recalled that he and Sheehan "would go into bars and Cat would be dancing on top of the bar, doing splits. He could dance as good as anybody." Sheehan earned the nickname "She-Cat," although even today, he wouldn't say how he got that moniker. Gerry Pinder recalled that Sheehan was "a fun-loving guy off the ice. There wasn't a whole lot he wouldn't try." Gary Croteau said that

Sheehan "was one of the fastest skaters in the league. He was a step faster than everybody—a good puck handler and playmaker. He went so fast sometimes he lost the puck. He liked life off the ice, and that reputation followed him."

Many of She-Cat's teammates had stories about him. Tom Webster recalled an incident in practice between Seals coach Vic Stasiuk and Sheehan. "Vic was very emotional and intense. Once he challenged Bobby Sheehan to a race in practice. Vic said, 'I'll race you for $100.' The two of them took off and Bobby won the race by about the length of the rink. Vic skates up to Bobby and says, 'You owe me $100.' Bobby said, 'Bullshit, I beat you by a mile.' Vic said, 'I said I'd *race* you. I didn't say I'd *beat* you.'"

Another ex-teammate recalled that Sheehan kept getting in and out of trouble with the California Highway Patrol. "We had a highway patrolman friend who wanted to help out the guys," the player recalled. "I'd be the intermediary and he'd help us out. Bobby Sheehan got pulled over four times in one month. The patrolman said, 'Tell that idiot to stop doing what he's doing because I can't help him anymore.'"

Ernie Hicke remembered another of Sheehan's eccentricities. "I remember we had a 16-day road trip coming up. We all had the yellow and green suitcases and we were waiting for the bus in front of the hotel. Well, the bus comes and we are ready to pick up the suitcases, and you weren't sure which was yours because they were all alike. So I grab a bag and there's absolutely nothing in it. I look down at the nametag and, sure enough, it's Sheehan's. On a 16-day road trip, he packed absolutely nothing, not even a toothbrush." Gilles Meloche at least gave She-Cat the benefit of the doubt and admitted that Sheehan would at least pack "two pairs of underwear and socks for a two-week road trip."

Gerry Pinder recalled that one on one road trip to Philadelphia, "Bobby Sheehan, Stan Gilbertson and Wayne Carleton all threw a suitcase out of a hotel window. There were clothes all over the place. The general manager of the hotel found out and he had a big meeting but nobody squealed. We were laughing so hard inside, though."

Sheehan also managed to keep his sense of humor when times got a little tough in Oakland. "We played the Rangers and we lost 12-1," Sheehan said, recalling one of the Seals worst defeats. "I missed most of the game with a bruised shoulder. I was laughing on the plane ride home and Vic Stasiuk says to me, 'What are laughing about?' I said, 'Vic, you can't blame me. I was a plus one in this game.'"

Another occasion Sheehan himself recalled warmly was a prank he pulled on Norm Ferguson. "We threw Norm in the pool while he was sleeping," Sheehan said. "The poor guy almost drowned." Another time, Sheehan himself was the victim of the prank. "One night, the guys left me in the St. Louis Zoo and I had to walk home," he recalled.

Occasionally, Sheehan had problems with making it to practice on time. "One time, I was late for practice because one of the bridges went up," She-Cat explained. "Vic didn't believe me. I said to him, 'Vic, come on, you've got to believe me. I'm telling the truth this time.' I was red hot at the time, but he benched me." Despite his occasional run-ins with Stasiuk, Sheehan respected and liked his coach in Oakland. "He was a great guy as long as you produced," Sheehan said of Stasiuk. "He was a comical guy and he knows hockey. He was a good coach."

Sheehan's fast skating made him one of the more popular players on the Seals during his brief stay in Oakland. In fact, actor Tom Hanks, who grew up in the Bay Area and rooted for the Seals, admitted that when he was a young hockey fan, Sheehan was his favorite player. "He sent me a letter and I sent him a signed picture, which he put up on his wall," Sheehan said. "That was great, hearing from him like that."

After the 1971-72 season, Sheehan signed with the WHA's New York Raiders, becoming one of many Seals to jump to the rival league. Midway through the 1972-73 season, the Seals traded Sheehan's NHL rights to the Black Hawks along with Dick Redmond in exchange for Darryl Maggs. "I was sort of uninformed," Sheehan admitted later. "My agent didn't even tell me that I had an offer from the Black Hawks, whcih then owned my rights. It was for the same amount of money I was offered in the WHA. I would have never left if I knew about the offer from Chicago, but my agent never told me about it. He was only interested in making his percentage." Sheehan had a great season playing for the Raiders, scoring 35 goals and 88 points in 75 games, tying him for 10th in the league in points. Sheehan also played in the 1974 WHA All-Star game.

After that, however, Sheehan began the career of a pro hockey journeyman. He had enough undeniable talent to pique a team's interest but, mainly due to his off-ice activities and inconsistency on the ice, he was quickly traded or released. "He could have been a legitimate 40-goal scorer in this league," defenseman Rick Smith said of Sheehan. Paul Shmyr added that Sheehan "could have been a superstar if his heart was really in it."

Sheehan remained in professional hockey until 1982-83, but never stayed in one place for too long. Midway through the 1973-74 season, the New Jersey Knights of the WHA traded Sheehan to the Edmonton Oilers. Sheehan also spent one season with the Black Hawks, part of a season with the Red Wings, part of another season with the Indianapolis Racers and a dramatic playoff-only run with the New York Rangers in 1979. In fact, Rangers coach Fred Shero called up Sheehan from the minors specifically to use his speed in a series against the Flyers. The stint with the Rangers was followed by NHL stops with the Colorado Rockies and Los Angeles Kings in between playing in the AHL, predominantly for the New Haven Nighthawks. Sheehan's career NHL numbers show 48 goals and 111 points in 410 games. In the WHA, he scored 75 goals and 185 points in 241 games.

Today, Sheehan works as an investigator for the Massachusetts State Lottery and has a young daughter. Norm Ferguson, who played with Sheehan with the Seals and the New York Raiders of the WHA, summed up Sheehan by saying, "If he put his mind to it, he was one of the best I ever saw. He had quick feet and a great shot. A great guy and a character on and off the ice." That was Oakland's She-Cat.

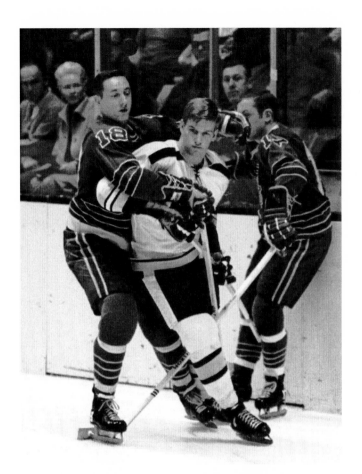

Seals Larry Popein (17) and Bob Lemieux (18) surround Bobby Orr
of Boston. Photo courtesy of Ron Riesterer/Oakland Tribune

Boston's Johnny "Pie" McKenzie slides into the goal behind the Seals Charlie Hodge.
Photo courtesy of Ron Riesterer/Oakland Tribune

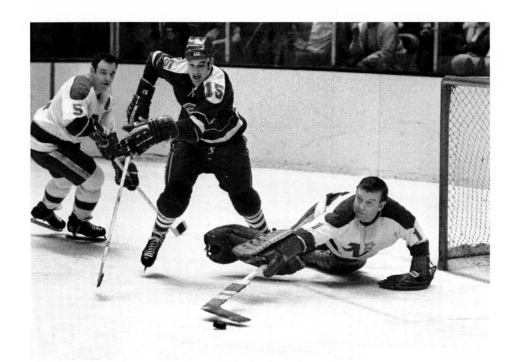

Minnesota's Gump Worsley pokes the puck away from the Seals Mike Laughton while Leo Boivin looks on. Photo courtesy of Ron Riesterer/ Oakland Tribune

Oakland's Billy Hicke puts pressure on Kings goalie Wayne Rutledge. Photo courtesy of Ron Riesterer/Oakland Tribune

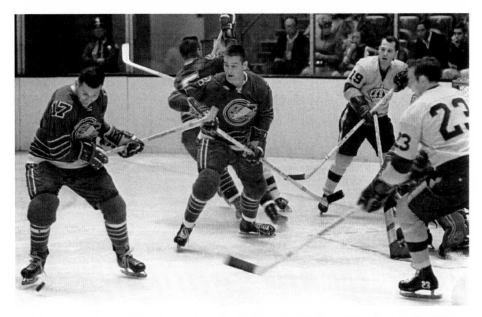

**Larry Popein (17), Bob Lemieux (2) and Larry Cahan (5) take on the Kings.
Photo courtesy of Ron Riesterer/Oakland Tribune**

**Charlie Hodge stops Boston's Johnny Bucyk while Bryan Watson and Carol
Vadnais try to keep Ed Westfall from the rebound. Photo courtesy of Ron
Riesterer/Oakland Tribune**

Mike Laughton is awarded the team's Most Improved Player Award by the Seals Booster Club. Photo courtesy of Ron Riesterer/Oakland Tribune

Bill Hicke and Ted Hampson celebrate a Seals goal. Photo courtesy of Ron Riesterer/Oakland Tribune

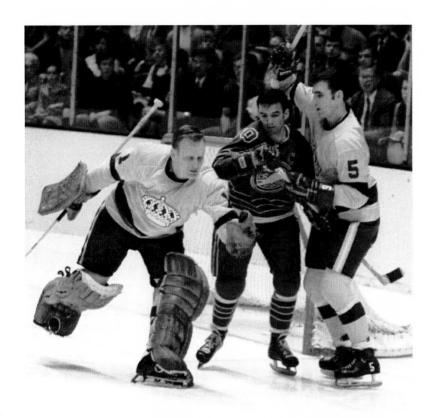

Wayne Rutledge of Los Angeles grabs the puck while Ted Hampson waits for the rebound. Photo courtesy of Ron Riesterer/Oakland Tribune

Goalie Gary Smith, Doug Roberts and Chicago's Stan Mikita follow the action near the Seals net. Photo courtesy of Ron Riesterer/Oakland Tribune

Norm Ferguson accepts a team award at the Oakland Coliseum.
Photo courtesy of Ron Riesterer/Oakland Tribune

Ted Hampson receives an award prior to a Seals home game.
Photo courtesy of Ron Riesterer/Oakland Tribune

Seals owner Charles Oscar Finley Photo courtesy of Ron Riesterer/
Oakland Tribune

Craig Patrick celebrates a goal while ex-Seals defenseman Harry Howell grimaces on the ice. Photo courtesy of Ron Riesterer/Oakland Tribune

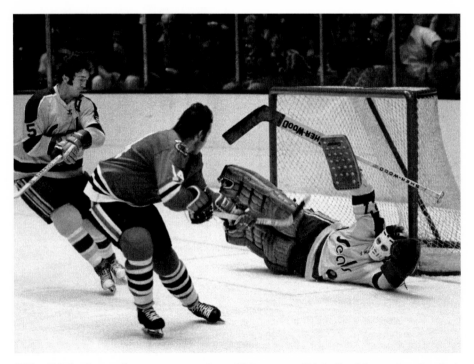

Gilles Meloche makes a save against Chicago as Rick Smith rushes back to help. Photo courtesy of Ron Riesterer/Oakland Tribune

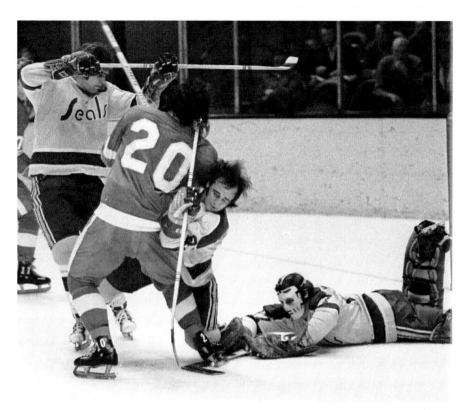

Bert Marshall and Ted McAneeley hold off Detroit's Mickey Redmond while Gilles Meloche freezes the puck. Photo courtesy of Ron Riesterer/ Oakland Tribune

Hilliard Graves watches the action from the California bench. Photo courtesy of Ron Riesterer/Oakland Tribune

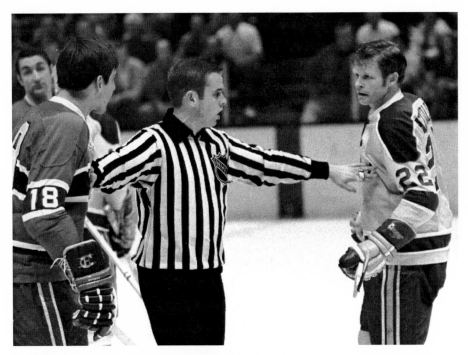

Dennis Hextall has words with Montreal's Serge Savard. Photo courtesy of Ron Riesterer/Oakland Tribune

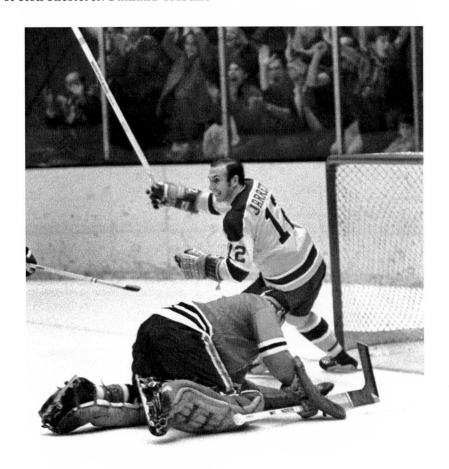

Gary Jarrett scores against Chicago. Photo courtesy of Ron Riesterer/Oakland Tribune

Reggie Leach skates during pre-game warm-ups.
Photo courtesy of Kathy DiPietro

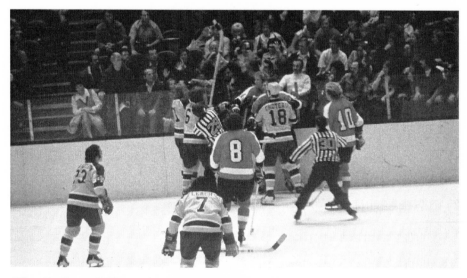

The Seals and Flyers in another scuffle. Bob Stewart (6) is at the center of it. Other Seals include Reggie Leach (7), Ted McAneeley (23), Gary Croteau (18) and Stan Weir (21). Dave Schultz (8) skates in for the Flyers.
Photo courtesy of Kathy DiPietro

Gerry Pinder led the Seals in scoring his one
season in Oakland. Photo courtesy of Kathy
DiPietro

Seals line up for a defensive zone faceoff against in Vancouver 3/30/74.
Seals pictured include Stan Gilbertson (10), Ray McKay (3), Ivan
Boldirev (9), Hilliard Graves (16), Paul Shakes (4) and goalie Gilles
Meloche (27). Photo courtesy of Kathy DiPietro

Ivan Boldirev takes the ice. Photo courtesy of Kathy DiPietro

Goalie Gilles Meloche leaves the ice during his rookie season. Photo courtesy of Kathy DiPietro

Bobby Sheehan and Stan Gilbertson during pre-game warm-ups in Los Angeles. In the background is Norm Ferguson. Photo courtesy of Kathy DiPietro

Future Hockey Hall of Famer Craig Patrick in pre-game warm-ups. Photo courtesy of Kathy DiPietro

Pete Laframboise is ready to re-enter the game.
Photo courtesy of Ron Riesterer/Oakland Tribune

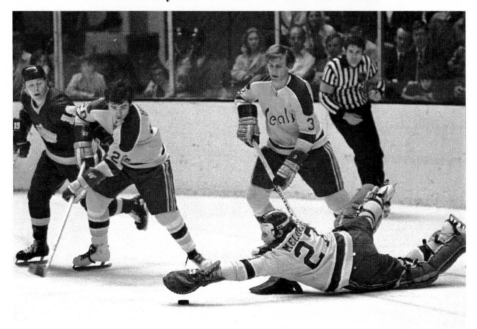

Paul Shmyr and Ernie Hicke move Butch Goring away as Gilles Meloche
gloves the puck. Photo courtesy of Ron Riesterer/Oakland Tribune

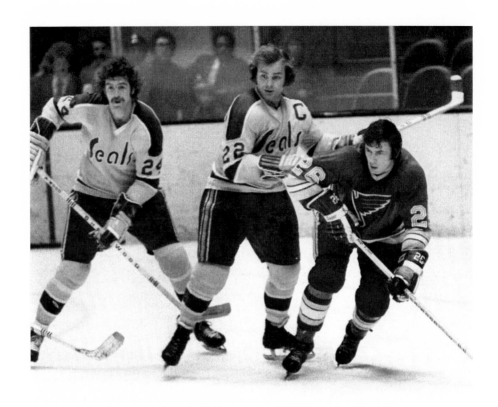

Pete Laframboise and Joey Johnston skate up ice against Don Awrey of St. Louis. Photo courtesy of Ron Riesterer/Oakland Tribune

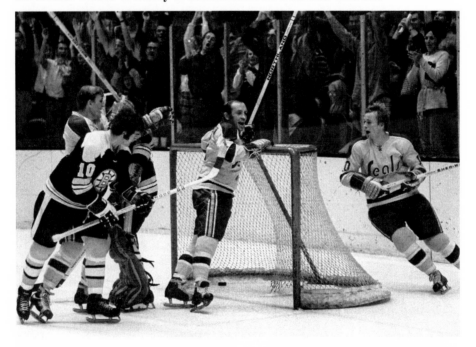

Stan Gilbertson, Gary Jarrett and Paul Shmyr celebrate a goal against Boston while future Seals defenseman Rick Smith watches. Photo courtesy of Ron Riesterer/Oakland Tribune

Speedy Bobby Sheehan crashes the Flyers net while Tommy Williams follows up the play. Photo courtesy of Ron Riesterer/Oakland Tribune

An exhausted Gary Smith after another of his 71 games in the Seals net, 1970-71. Photo courtesy of Ron Riesterer/Oakland Tribune

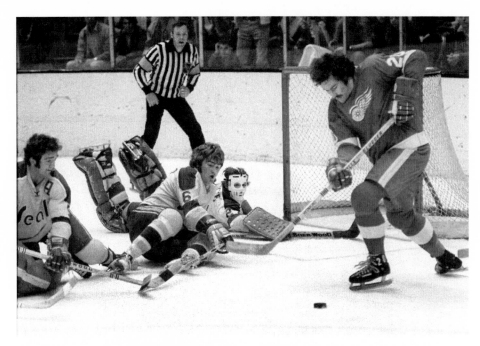

Bob Stewart and Rick Smith watch as Mickey Redmond scrambles for possession of the puck as Gilles Meloche looks on. Photo courtesy of Ron Riesterer/Oakland Tribune

Seals captain Carol Vadnais   Photo courtesy of Ron Riesterer/ Oakland Tribune

Stan Weir and Terry Murray chase after a rebound in front of Gilles Meloche. Photo courtesy of Ron Riesterer/Oakland Tribune

Gary Simmons guards the Seals net in his Cobra mask. Photo courtesy of Ron Riesterer/Oakland Tribune

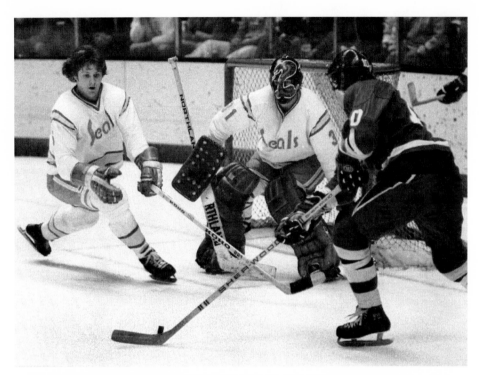

Len Frig helps Gary Simmons protect the Seals net. Photo courtesy of Ron Riesterer/Oakland Tribune

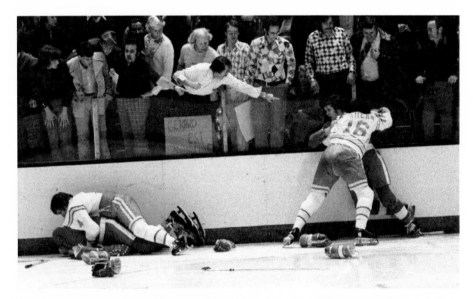

Fred Ahern and Bob Stewart in a line brawl. Photo courtesy of Ron Riesterer/Oakland Tribune

George Pesut angles in against Keith Magnuson of Chicago. Photo courtesy of Ron Riesterer/Oakland Tribune

Bob Murdoch skates behind the goal with Keith Magnuson in pursuit. Photo courtesy of Ron Riesterer/Oakland Tribune

Al MacAdam and Len Frig in the attack zone against Vancouver. Photo courtesy of Ron Riesterer/Oakland Tribune

Rick Hampton skates in behind Chicago's Cliff Korrall. Photo courtesy of Ron Riesterer/Oakland Tribune

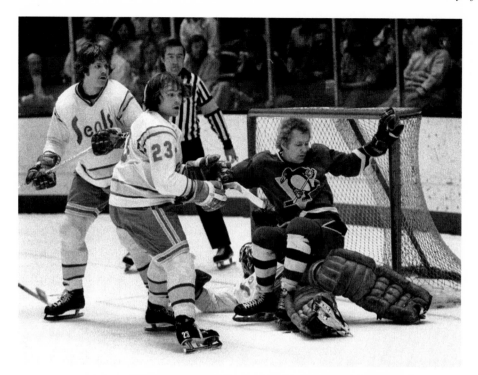

Pittsburgh's Bob "Battleship" Kelly falls down on Gary Simmons as Tim Jacobs and Len Frig follow the puck. Photo courtesy of Ron Riesterer/ Oakland Tribune

Morris Mott Photo courtesy of Ron Riesterer/Oakland Tribune

Wayne King raises his stick in celebration of a Seals goal against Washington.   Photo courtesy of Ron Riesterer/Oakland Tribune

Copies of these and additional Seals photos are available by contacting Ron Riesterer at ronjanr@comcast.net

Wayne Carleton

"Swoop came from Boston. He was one of the better players on the team. He had a difficult time adjusting to the Seals from the Bruins. He had a great shot and was a good skater."

—Gary Croteau on Wayne Carleton

If ever there was a situation where a man was in the wrong place at the wrong time in hockey, Wayne Carleton playing for the California Golden Seals was certainly a prime example. It wasn't that Carleton wasn't a good hockey player for the Seals, it was simply that the set of circumstances he found himself in prevented him from thriving while playing in the Bay Area.

Carleton was born in Sudbury, Ontario, and was the territorial property of the Toronto Maple Leafs after playing for the Toronto Marlboros in juniors. He earned the nickname "Swoop" because of his habit of circling back into his own zone to build up speed before skating down the ice on the attack. Carleton made his NHL debut for the Leafs during the 1965-66 season, picking up one assist during a two game call-up. He then spent the next few seasons splitting time between the Maple Leafs and their various farm clubs in Rochester, Tulsa and Phoenix. He was traded to the Bruins on December 10, 1969, for Jim Harrison—just in time to earn a Stanley Cup ring when the B's swept the Blues in the finals. The following year, Carleton scored 22 goals and 46 points in 69 games for Boston.

Carleton's career looked to be on the upswing and the Bruins were heavy favorites to repeat as Stanley Cup Champions in 1970-71, but they were upset by the Canadiens in the first round of the playoffs. The Bruins management thought changes were needed and, much to his surprise, Carleton was left unprotected prior to the intraleague draft. The Seals, who had ex-Bruin scout Garry Young as their GM, were quick to sign the 6'3", 212-pound Carleton to add proven leadership and goal scoring to a young team.

Carleton admitted it was "disappointing" going from the powerful Bruins of Orr, Esposito, Sanderson and Bucyk to a Seals team that had finished in last place the year before. In fact, rumors started circulating that the 25-year-old left wing was contemplating retirement rather than playing for the Seals. Eventually, Carleton decided to continue his hockey career and reported to the Seals camp.

If going from the mighty Bruins to an expansion team 3,000 miles away wasn't enough to dim Carleton's enthusiasm, what happened next certainly was. Carleton's old contract with Boston had expired and he decided to go to arbitration with the notoriously stingy Charlie Finley. "I went to arbitration and lost my arbitration case," Carleton recalled. In fact, the arbiter awarded the big winger a contract for less money than the Seals were originally offering him. "It just wasn't a good scenario for me," Carleton admitted. "I wasn't as mature as I was later on. My wife was also pregnant at the time" and still living back in Ontario. Carleton grew frustrated before even taking the ice for the Seals.

To add to the string of bad luck Carleton was having, he reported to training camp 10 pounds over his playing weight. Fred Glover, who was then the club's coach, was less than pleased. "You would have thought my stomach was hanging over my belt or something," Carleton said at the time. Glover got on Swoop's case. Gary Jarrett recalled that the coach made Carleton "go back to the Oakland Coliseum football stadium and run around the football field with a big rubber suit on." Needless to say, Swoop was off to a less than auspicious start with his new team.

Carleton's teammates sensed his attitude and also gave him a bit of a hard time when he first arrived. "We were in training camp and Swoop had just arrived from Boston," Bobby Sheehan recalled. "He said, 'Hey, I could kick in 20 goals in this league.' We rode him pretty hard about that. 'Kick in 20 yet, Swoop?' we'd all say." Walt McKechnie added, "He came from the Bruins. Needless to say, we weren't the Bruins. We teased the shit out of him." Joey Johnston felt that Carleton arrived in Oakland with a little chip on his shoulder. "He always said, 'That's how we did it in Boston,' " Johnston recalled. "I'd say to him, 'There's no Bobby Orr here.' I don't think he enjoyed being in

Oakland." Perhaps defenseman Bert Marshall summed it up by saying, "Either he didn't fit us or we didn't fit him."

Carleton also had to adjust to playing hockey in Northern California as opposed to hockey- mad Boston. He also had to adjust to playing for Charlie Finley. "We had those green suitcases," Carleton recalled. "You couldn't miss us on the road unless you were blind, that's how green they were." He also had to wear the dreaded white skates the Seals had that season. "At the time, there was not much we could do," Swoop recalled. "I thought it was eccentric at the time, but we had to live with them." Despite these "eccentricities," Carleton said, looking back, "I think Mr. Finley treated us fairly well."

Three games into the season, Fred Glover was dismissed as coach of the Seals and replaced by Vic Stasiuk. Stasiuk and Carleton didn't exactly see eye to eye, but there was a certain mutual respect between them. "He was a tremendous player with a tremendous work ethic, and he demanded the same," Carleton said of his former coach. "There was a generation gap and he often said, 'Do what I say, not what I do.' Personalities play a part on any team and Vic didn't handle it as well as he could have. You can't use a big stick with everyone because not everyone responds to it." Stasiuk recalled that Carleton was "a big guy who should have been better than he was. He was a powerful skater and big, a main guy on our team. He was aggressive and a good forechecker."

In retrospect, Carleton admitted that the Seals team "came a long way in a short time" the year he was there. What he felt the team needed was more leadership. "We never had a superstar on the Seals to build around. We were molding guys from other teams," Carleton said. "With the travel schedule we had, we needed a leader. There were a lot of characters on that team and a lot of younger players. We had a lot of fun, though."

Eventually, Carleton settled down and accepted playing in Oakland, and his teammates accepted him too. "Swooper had trouble adjusting when he came over from Boston, where he had just won a Cup," Gerry Pinder recalled. "Once he got sorted out, he was an asset and a big, strong guy." Paul Shmyr also recalled the difficult beginning Carleton had in Boston, although that changed after a while. "He was a legend in his own mind," Shmyr said. "He was a good guy, but he came here with an attitude that he was Wayne Carleton and we had to look up to him. That wasn't going to work with our guys. It took awhile to get used to him but it turned out he was a good guy."

Eventually, Carleton even took some good-natured ribbing from his teammates. "We called him 'Jiggy Jog,' recalled Marshall Johnston. "He had trotters and always talked about taking them out for a 'jiggy jog.' Swoop had a lot of talent and was a big guy."

To add to Carleton's frustrations in Oakland, his bad knees continued to act up and affected his play. Although he appeared in 76 games with the Seals in 1971-72, Carleton's achy knees limited his effectiveness. He finished the season with 17 goals and 31 points. "My knees curtailed my career," Carleton said. "I had eight knee surgeries. I had size but I wasn't a fighter. I was a goal scorer and a guy who set them up." Some of Carleton's teammates realized he was playing hurt. "He was the biggest guy in the league," Ernie Hicke added. "He played hurt when he played with us. He was big and strong, but injuries limited his effectiveness." Craig Patrick recalled that Carleton "had the size and the gifts to be a great player, but he got injured too much."

Although he couldn't recall any when interviewed for this book, Carleton did have some memorable moments in a Seals sweater. On November 28, 1971, Swoop scored twice in a 5-3 win over the Sabres in Oakland. He also scored the tying goal in a memorable 3-3 game against the Canadiens. With just 1:26 left in the game, Carleton beat Ken Dryden on a 40-foot slap shot that earned the Golden Seals a draw with the defending Stanley Cup champions.

Since Charlie Finley was a firm believer in the one-year contract, Carleton was once again facing a contract negotiation prior to 1972-73. Instead, he signed with the Ottawa Nationals of the fledgling WHA. "It was closer to home," Carleton said. "We just had a little boy that spring. They also offered more money. People talk about Alan Eagleson, but they should thank the players in the WHA because we caused players' salaries to go up. To me, hockey was just a means to an end. I didn't really want to be in Oakland from the start, so I was happy to get out of there."

In his first season in the WHA, Carleton scored 42 goals and 91 points, placing him in the top 10 in the new league in both goals and points. He was selected to the first WHA All-Star game and was named MVP after scoring one goal and one assist in the East's 6-2 victory over the West. He followed that first season up with 37- and 35-goal years playing for the Toronto Toros and New England Whalers, respectively. After brief tours of duty with the Edmonton Oilers and Birmingham Bulls, Carleton's knees prevented him from continuing his professional hockey career and he retired after the 1976-77 season. He finished his NHL career with 55 goals and 128 points in 278 NHL games and 132 goals and 312 points in 290 games in the WHA.

Today, Carleton and his wife live in Collingwood, Ontario; they have one son. Big Wayne now works in the investment business and hockey is just a memory. His experience with the Seals was clearly not his favorite part of his hockey career.

Norm Ferguson perhaps summed up Carleton best by saying, "He came from the Bruins and it was a letdown for him being in Oakland. He came from a place where hockey was *the* game. A lot was expected of him, but he tried really hard. He was a good guy." But he was in the wrong place at the wrong time.

Paul Shmyr

"He could skate, shoot, pass and check. He was tough—one of the toughest in the league. He could take on the best and win."

—Ernie Hicke on Paul Shmyr

Paul Shmyr always knew what he wanted to do with his life. "I remember in fourth grade we had to write an essay on what we wanted to do when we grew up," Shmyr remembered. "I wrote that I wanted to play in the NHL with Bobby Hull on the Black Hawks. I actually accomplished that and now Bobby Hull is a friend of mine."

Although the Rangers originally owned Shmyr's NHL rights, he was traded to Chicago prior to the 1967-68 season for Camille "The Eel" Henry. After two and a half years playing for Chicago's farm team in Dallas, Shmyr was brought up to the big club for 24 games in 1969-70, in which he had no goals and four assists. He stayed in Chicago for all of the following season, appearing in 57 games while scoring once and adding 12 assists. Still, the 5'11", 170-pound Shmyr was not happy in Chicago. "I wasn't getting a lot of ice time with the Black Hawks," Shmyr said. "They sometimes played three or four defensemen in a game and I was the sixth defenseman on the team. I was on the bench most of the time. I was happy to be traded to the Seals. I was happy to go anywhere then. I got to play a regular shift, kill penalties and some time on the power play. I really blossomed there."

On October 18, 1971, the Black Hawks sent Shmyr and goaltender Gilles Meloche to the Seals in exchange for Gerry Desjardins. Desjardins was originally traded by Chicago to the Seals in the Gary Smith trade, but had a broken arm that did not heal properly and he was not ready to play for California. The Seals cried foul and sent him back to Chicago in exchange for Meloche and Shmyr, the disgruntled defenseman from Cudworth, Saskatchewan.

Although the trade was made on October 18, Shmyr and Meloche did not arrive right away. "Paul and I were in Chicago and we got traded together," recalled Meloche. "Paul said to me, 'They'll want us to fly out to Oakland, but we're driving. Whatever you do, don't answer the phone.' Apparently, Paul wanted to have his car out in Oakland when he moved there. It took us three days to drive out to Oakland. They actually sent the highway patrol out to look for us, but we finally made it."

Shmyr's first game as a member of the Seals came on October 22, 1971. The opponent was the eventual Stanley Cup champion Boston Bruins. "I drove from Chicago with a trailer full of stuff," Shmyr said, recalling that he arrived in Oakland the day of the game. "Garry Young said, 'We don't expect you to play tonight, but it's up to you.' I said, 'I came to play hockey,' so I played. I remember I hit everything in sight and I was named one of the stars of the game."

One thing Shmyr had to adjust to after joining the Seals was wearing white skates. "At first you think it's not manly. After a while though, I sort of liked them," Shmyr admitted. "We got some comments from the other players in the league like, 'Oh, nice skates. Where can I get a pair?' but I think they knew if they said too much, we would take care of them on the ice. We were all in the same boat, really."

Shmyr had a fine year with the Seals in 1971-72. He was a physical defenseman who could also make good passes and skate well enough to make some plays. In 69 games with California, Shmyr scored six goals and had 27 points along with a team-leading 156 penalty minutes. In fact, that total puts Shmyr ninth on the Seals all-time franchise list for career penalty minutes, despite the fact that he played less than one full season with the club.

In addition to playing a physical style of defense, Shmyr was not afraid to take on any of the league's heavyweights when the gloves were dropped. Walt McKechnie remembered Shmyr as "fearless" and said, "He was one tough SOB. In Philadelphia, he had two fights in one game with a cast on his hand. He was a funny man who was always up, never depressed."

Goalie Lyle Carter also remembered Shmyr's skills as well as his toughness. "He was a good skating defenseman," Carter said. "A little guy who was very respected by the opposition. I saw him fight Ed Westfall once and Westfall was bleeding." Bobby Sheehan added, "He was not afraid of anything. I wouldn't mess with him. Paul was a good defensive defenseman who protected his teammates."

Teammates also recall that Shmyr had a burning desire to win. Marshall Johnston simply called Shmyr "the ultimate competitor." Gary Croteau added, "Paul hated to lose. He was not the biggest guy, but he'd battle game in and game out. In the dressing room, he'd let you know if you were letting the team down."

Shmyr instantly won the respect of his teammates. "He had the ability to be a leader on defense," teammate Rick Smith recalled. "He was so good and so strong and tough. I think he was one of the best players on the team."

When asked to describe himself as a hockey player, Shmyr replied, "I came to play every night and rarely took a night off. I wouldn't allow myself to have two bad shifts in a row; 99 percent of the games I played in, I played my heart out. My role in the beginning was based on my toughness. As I matured, I became a very good defenseman. Another thing is that I always stuck up for my teammates. Nobody ever had to tell me to do that—I did it automatically."

Shmyr also got along well with his coach in Oakland, Vic Stasiuk. "I liked Vic. He had a good sense of humor," Shmyr said. "A lot of the players didn't consider him a good coach, but I looked at it from a human perspective. He had a great sense of humor and was a nice man. We were both of Ukrainian descent, which helped a bit. Some guys really didn't want to play for him."

Paul Shmyr was also one of the few Seals players who appreciated Charlie Finley. "I enjoyed him," Shmyr confessed. "I had the entrepreneurial spirit myself. On contract negotiations, he was very strict, but he would come into the dressing room and give us each $300 or $500. He brought the team suitcases and sport jackets—a double-breasted kelly green jacket."

The Seals defenseman also remembered an incident he witnessed between Finley and Oakland A's pitcher Vida Blue. "I remember we were in a hotel in New York that [Charlie Finley] owned. The A's were there and he was negotiating with Vida Blue at the time. Blue was a superstar who brought in a lot of fans. I remember hearing Charlie say, 'No godamned way am I paying a guy $1 million to throw a baseball.' I never had a complaint about Charlie, though. He treated me like gold."

Shmyr saw the Seals as a team on the rise. Although California slumped at the end of the season and barely missed the playoffs, Shmyr knew the potential existed for the Seals to become a very good team if they stayed together. "We came together as a team," Shmyr said. "We were all spare players on other teams and we all wanted to prove ourselves in the NHL. By the end of the year, we were a good team. Some other teams were a bit glad when we didn't make the playoffs. I think we could have done some damage."

Looking back, Shmyr also appreciated the fans in Oakland. "We had very good fans, just not that many of them," he recalled. "We had fan clubs. Ten years later, I remember I was in Los Angeles to play the Kings and the Oakland Seals fan club was at the game. Still, hockey was not too big there. Paid appearances for the players were not that common. In Chicago, there was a lot more. Heck, the sixth defenseman in Chicago could get paid speaking engagements."

After the 1971-72 season, Shmyr was part of the mass exodus of players from Oakland who went to the WHA. "The Seals lost nine players to the WHA," Shmyr recalled. "Nick Mileti of the Cleveland Crusaders offered me twice as much money as Charlie Finley, so I flew out to a hotel in Cleveland. I don't know how he knew where I was staying, but Charlie Finley phoned me in my hotel room in Cleveland. He said he would match the offer the WHA made. He told me this was a renegade league and it wouldn't do so well. I appreciated that, but I told Mr. Finley I had given my word to Nick Mileti, which was true. He told me, 'Anytime you want to come back to the Seals, you're welcome.' It was very nice of him to say that. The move was strictly money. Garry Young tired to keep me in California by saying that everybody wants to play in the NHL. I had already played in the NHL in Chicago and California. I just wanted to make the right business decision and do what was best for my family."

Shmyr thrived in the WHA. He spent four productive seasons with the Cleveland Crusaders before moving on to San Diego and Edmonton. Shmyr was named a first-team WHA all-star three times and a second-team all-star once. He appeared in six WHA All-Star games and played for the WHA version of Team Canada against the Russians in 1974. After the 1975-76 season, Shmyr was awarded the Dennis A. Murphy Trophy as the WHA's best defenseman. There are some hockey experts who say that Shmyr was the best overall defenseman in the WHA's seven-year history.

When the WHA disbanded after the 1978-79 season, Shmyr rejoined the NHL with the Minnesota North Stars. After two years in Minnesota, he played his final pro season with the Hartford Whalers in 1981-82. His final NHL statistics include 13 goals, 85 points and 528 penalty minutes in 343 games. In the WHA, Shmyr scored 61 goals, 309 points and 860 penalty minutes in 511 contests.

After retirement, Shmyr settled in Port Coquitlam, British Columbia. He worked in the construction business and also had some other business interests. Unfortunately, on September 3, 2004, Shmyr lost a valiant 10-year battle with throat cancer. He was 58 years old. Shmyr is survived by his wife, Diane, and their two children, one of whom played pro hockey in the ECHL and another who is in the movie business.

Gary Jarrett, who played with Shmyr in California and Cleveland, summarized Shmyr's career by saying, "Pound for pound, he was the toughest guy in the NHL. Because of his toughness and confidence, he honed his hockey skills. At the end of his career, he was as good a defenseman as any in the WHA." If more valuable players like Paul Shmyr would have stayed with the Seals, there's no telling what the future of the franchise might have been like.

Ivan Boldirev

"He was smooth and saw the ice very well. He was the most talented guy out there. He was low-key and didn't have the up-tempo energy, but he could change a game if he wanted to."

—*Craig Patrick on Ivan Boldirev*

Ivan Boldirev was the first player born in Yugoslavia to make the NHL. Born in Zranjanin, Boldirev emigrated to Canada at the tender age of 2. Growing up in Canada, Boldirev was known as a shy child. He told Bob Verdi of the *Chicago Tribune* that his shyness "probably goes back to when I first came over to Canada and didn't speak any English. My first-grade teacher sent a note home telling my parents that we should speak English at home, but they didn't speak it so they couldn't even read the note."

After arriving in Canada, Boldirev quickly took a liking to hockey. "I liked hockey from when I was a kid," he said. "I always said I would be a professional hockey player when I grew up." His favorite teams were Detroit and Chicago, with players like Gordie Howe, Al Delvecchio and Terry Sawchuk among those he liked best.

Boldirev played his junior hockey for the Oshawa Generals and scored 59 points in 54 games his second year with the club. The Boston Bruins selected Boldirev in the first round of the 1969 NHL entry draft with the 11th selection overall. Boldirev was less than thrilled at first. "I called home to see who drafted me and I said, 'Tell me, please, anybody but the Bruins,' " Boldirev recalled. His dad simply said, "Yup, it's the Bruins." Boston assigned him to their CHL farm club, the Oklahoma City Blazers where "Ike" had 67 points in 65 games as a rookie.

In 1970-71, Boldirev scored 71 points for the Blazers and was selected to the second team postseason CHL all-star team. The Bruins rewarded the 6', 190-pound Boldirev with his first NHL action and he played in two games for the Bruins that year.

In 1971-72, Boldirev played in 11 games for Boston and registered two assists. Still, playing time was hard to come by with the Bruins. "Let's face it, I wasn't playing there and they had Phil Esposito, Fred Stanfield and Derek Sanderson, three pretty fair centers," Boldirev said. The Bruins traded Boldirev to the Seals on November 17, 1971, in exchange for Richie Leduc and Chris Oddleifson. Seals GM Garry Young had scouted Boldirev when he was working in the Bruins organization, so he engineered the trade for the big centerman. At the time, Boldirev was happy about the trade that sent him to the Bay Area. "I knew I'd get a chance to play with the Seals," he said, "and that, more than anything else, is what I wanted."

Shortly after his arrival in Oakland, Boldirev earned the playing time he craved. He tallied his first NHL goal for the Seals on November 18, 1971, during a 7-5 California win over the Buffalo Sabres at the Aud. The Sabres goalie was veteran Roger Crozier and the win helped the Seals end a four-game losing streak. "I had just come to the Seals and it was my first game," Boldirev recalled. "The puck was in the left-hand corner and I took a backhander that beat him to the short side."

Boldirev had a strong rookie season with California, scoring 16 goals and 39 points in 57 games with Oakland. Those statistics look even better when you consider that Boldirev was weakened by a bout with mononucleosis late in the season. Vic Stasiuk, Boldirev's rookie coach in Oakland, had fond words for the big center. "He was a good face-off man and a hard-nosed forechecker," Stasiuk remarked. "A good anchor, he could make a line."

Goalie Lyle Carter said Ivan was "a great team guy, but a quiet guy. He was not an overly fast skater but he was a very good hockey player." Left wing Gerry Pinder, who played on a line with Boldirev, said, "He was loaded with talent. He played in the NHL for, what, 15 years? He was skilled, very strong and could pass the puck well. He was a better playmaker than a goal scorer."

Early in his career, Boldirev was also a good fighter who was not afraid to drop the gloves. Fellow center Walt McKechnie recalled one fight that basically discouraged Boldirev from future forays into hockey pugilism. "He had a fight with Pierre Bouchard of Montreal," McKechnie remembered. "They were going toe to toe and then they got tired. Bouchard sucker-punched Ike and shattered his nose. Ivan said, 'That's it for me with fighting ... Fuck it.'" Boldirev totaled 60 penalty minutes his rookie year in the NHL. He never reached that mark again in his lengthy pro career. "What a talented player he was," Walt McKechnie continued. "He had tremendous skill and with the proper coaching, he could have been a superstar."

Boldirev's playmaking was instrumental in helping Pinder lead the Seals in goals and points in 1971-72. Other teammates appreciated Ike's work ethic and toughness. "He was strong and worked as hard as you could possibly work," recalled Gary Jarrett. Bobby Sheehan remembered that "Ike wasn't afraid to throw 'em. He was very quiet, but he got the job done." Off the ice, Sheehan recalled that Ivan "would tail along with the boys, but he'd leave before we got into any real trouble."

Ike was very fond of his teammates. "We had a good group of guys," Boldirev said. "On the road, we got checked in and said, 'We're meeting in whatever bar in 15 minutes,' and everybody would be there. We were all young guys and we all got along pretty well. We stayed out later than we should have and drank a little more than we should have, but we were a close-knit team without many cliques."

Unfortunately, the close-knit team didn't stay together long, as the WHA raided the Seals roster. "I thought we had a good future," Boldirev said. "We were all young. We lost 11 guys to the WHA. It was a tough year, 1972-73. The attitude changed from the top down and there was chaos. We went from being a potentially good team to being devastated. Nobody wanted to be there. I still wonder what would have happened if there was no WHA."

The Seals expected great things from Boldirev in 1972-73. Instead, he suffered through an injury-riddled season in which he appeared in only 56 games. The biggest culprit was a knee injury that sidelined Boldirev for more than a month. He finished the year with 11 goals and 34 points in what could only be described as a disappointing season. When he was healthy, Boldirev still provided some highlights for Seals fans. On January 3, 1973, he had two goals and two assists during an 11-3 win over Vancouver. Still, the effort was overshadowed by Pete Laframboise's four-goal performance that same game. On February 23, 1973, Boldirev scored twice and added an assist during a 5-3 upset win over the Rangers at the "Jewel Box." Rookie center Stan Weir was impressed by Boldirev's play. "He was smooth and slick and a great player. He was a great stickhandler, passer and skater," Weir said. And "he had a very dry sense of humor."

The slick-skating Boldirev appreciated the fans in the Bay Area who came out to the Oakland Coliseum. "We had a good core of 2,500 to 3,000 people who loved hockey and they were great," Boldirev said. "The rink only seated 12,500. I heard that even if they sold out, they wouldn't make money, but look at San Jose now. With the right management, they made it work."

Boldirev finally enjoyed a year of good health in 1973-74 and had his finest season as a member of the Seals. He played in all 78 games and scored 25 goals and 56 points. It seemed as if Boldirev was finally flourishing as a hockey player. "He was a good hockey player and a smart hockey player," coach Fred Glover remarked. "And he could really skate." Boldirev worked hard during the season and was often one of the last players to leave the ice during practice. He also seemed to be learning how to anticipate players so he would end up at the right place at the right time.

Boldirev had his finest offensive game with the Seals on January 9, 1974, against the St. Louis Blues. He scored four goals in that game to record his first-ever NHL hat trick in an 8-6 Seals win. Shortly after the game, Boldirev described the performance as "his biggest thrill in hockey." He also deflected most of the credit to his linemate Craig Patrick, saying, "He got me the puck in the right places. I could have had five or six goals that night. Things were clicking and I was in the right spot at the right time. The first goal, I remember coming down the right side and taking a pass from Craig Patrick. I took a few steps towards the middle of the ice and shot the puck and it went in."

On February 13, 1974, Boldirev again had a big offensive night, scoring twice and assisting on two more Seals goals in a 9-6 loss to the Bruins in Oakland. Morris Mott noticed that Boldirev "was a good stickhandler who just beginning to establish himself as a solid player" during the 1973-74 season.

Most of Boldirev's teammates appreciated him off the ice as well, although Boldirev did have a reputation of being very quiet and a bit quirky away from the rink. Morris Mott recalled, "Ivan had a very likable personality and a dry sense of humor." Joey Johnston remembered one of Boldirev's idiosyncrasies. "I liked him off the ice," Johnston said. "He liked rainy days or cloudy days. I could never get him out into the sun." Perhaps Rick Kessell put his finger on Boldirev's off-ice personality by describing him as a family-oriented man. "He was a quiet guy off the ice," Kessell continued. "He loved being home with his wife and kids. Ike was a real nice guy." Rookie defenseman Barry Cummins called Boldirev "a class act on and off the ice," adding that despite the Seals poor performance as a team in 1973-74, Boldirev "didn't ever complain."

After the NHL took over the Seals late in the 1973-74 season, management was given a directive to keep costs down. Most of the Seals leading scorers from 1973-74 were traded away that off-season, including Ivan Boldirev. On May 24, 1974, the Seals shipped Boldirev to the Chicago Black Hawks for defensemen Len Frig and Mike Christie. Shortly after his trade, Boldirev admitted that by the end

Brad Kurtzberg

of his tenure with the Seals, he was having problems with the situation in Oakland. "We just got used to losing," he admitted. Then he added, "The problem there was that you never had the fear of being replaced because they just weren't that deep in talent."

The lack of direction from ownership was also a distraction. "After a while, we didn't know who was in charge," Boldirev recalled. "At first, you're there to play hockey. Later, the problem just feeds on itself. As players, we shouldn't have even thought of that. When things go bad, it tends to perpetuate itself. When you played before 1,900 fans, it was tough to get up for games," Boldirev said. "I remember a game against the Islanders where we had 1,900 or 1,600 people in the stands. The Bay Area was not a hockey town. Baseball and football were the big things. Hockey was not considered a major sport back then."

Overall, there were many positives for Boldirev in the Bay Area. "In Oakland I had the chance to play and prove myself," Boldirev said shortly after his trade to Chicago. "It's great weather, a great state and probably could be a great hockey city with the right circumstances. But it wasn't while I was there and I just wasn't happy [at the end]."

Boldirev continued his development in Chicago and became a steady scorer and player for the Hawks. He topped the 60-point barrier his first three seasons in the Windy City before reaching the 35-goal, 80-point mark in 1977-78. That year, he was selected to the NHL All-Star game. Late in the following season, Boldirev was traded to the Atlanta Flames and a year later, to the Vancouver Canucks. In Vancouver, Boldirev enjoyed his greatest team success, as he was a major cog in the Canucks Cinderella run to the 1982 Stanley Cup Finals. In 17 playoff games for the Canucks that season, Boldirev scored eight goals and had 11 points. His best individual offensive season came with the Detroit Red Wings in his next-to-last season in the NHL, 1983-84. The big Yugoslav scored 35 goals and 83 points in 75 games to help the Red Wings reach the playoffs that year. Boldirev retired after the 1984-85 season. His final NHL totals are 361 goals and 866 points in 1,052 games. He remains the NHL's all-time leading scorer among players born in Yugoslavia. He also left his mark on the Seals record books, ranking eighth all-time in career goals, seventh in assists and eighth in all-time points in club history.

Today, Boldirev owns a product-safety business and lives in the Chicago area. He has two children from his first marriage and three stepdaughters with his present wife.

His ex-teammates have fond memories of Boldirev and what he meant to the club. "He was a very strong centerman both offensively and with his physical presence," Rick Smith said. "He turned out to be a great player. He was strong, smooth and a nice hockey player." Defenseman Bob Stewart added, "He was a good playmaker and could also be a tough guy. He was good on face-offs and demanded respect from opponents. He was a good team player."

Stan Gilbertson

"Stan was one of the funniest guys I've ever been involved with. He was a giving person. Like me, he was not the most gifted guy but he came to play each and every night."
—*Stan Weir on Stan Gilbertson*

Every team needs a guy like Stan Gilbertson on their roster, but a struggling franchise like the California Golden Seals probably needed him even more. Gilbertson was a third-line winger who worked hard in the corners and scored 15 or so goals a year when healthy. He was also the Seals locker-room cutup, a guy who kept his teammates loose and smiling even through the most difficult of times. When conducting interviews with former Seals players, Gilbertson's name was mentioned the most whenever humorous stories were told about occurrences both on and off the ice. Sadly, the Seals class clown has hit hard times of late and his whereabouts are unknown. I was therefore unable to interview him for this book.

178

Gilbertson took an unorthodox route to the NHL. For one thing, he is an American, hailing from Duluth, Minnesota, the same town where teammate Tommy Williams, one of the first American NHL players, was from. Gilbertson didn't even start skating until he was 7 years old. Once he started, though, Gilbertson took a liking to hockey and decided to go to Canada to play junior hockey. He played a season and a half for the Estevan Bruins and a season and a half with the Regina Pats. With the Pats, the young American winger had consecutive 40-goal seasons in 1963-64 and 1964-65.

Future teammate Ernie Hicke remembered an incident that took place between he and Gilbertson while they were in juniors that ended up being a most unusual introduction for future friends. "I was the stickboy for the Regina Pats at the time," Hicke said. "Stan was playing for the Estevan Bruins in the Saskatchewan Junior League. It was a big rivalry; one team was sponsored by Boston, the other by Montreal. Anyway, in one particular game we had a lot of fights, including a big brawl. Muggy McGowan was the tough guy on the Pats and he beat up a few guys. I was carrying the sticks back to the locker room after the first period. In this old arena, both teams skated through the same tunnel to get to their locker rooms. McGowan came off the ice last because he knew the Bruins would send guys after him, so he came off with me and I was carrying the sticks. A bunch of Bruins came after him and the Pats players were already in the dressing room. A fight ensued and I grabbed a stick and hit Stan Gilbertson over the head with it; he needed 20 stitches. And a bunch of players, including Stan, were thrown out of the game. The next year, I was on the Pats as a player and Gilbertson was traded to the Pats in the middle of the season. We became good friends after that."

After a half season in the EHL, Gilbertson spent a year and a half playing for the San Francisco Seals WHL club. The Boston Bruins owned Gilbertson's NHL rights and, prior to the 1968-69 season, they loaned him to the AHL's Hershey Bears. The 6', 175-pound Gilbertson spent three productive years in the chocolate capital of the world before the Seals claimed him in the intraleague draft prior to the 1971-72 season. Seals GM Garry Young had acquired yet another player he knew from his time working in the Bruins organization.

Like many rookies, Gilbertson had adjustments to make when he joined the NHL. "They move quicker and shoot harder, and the goalies are tougher, in the NHL," Gilbertson told Hugh McDonald of the *San Mateo Times* during his rookie year. Still, Gilbertson made a respectable showing, scoring 16 goals and 32 points while playing mostly on the Seals checking line. Stan's first NHL goal came off Red Wings goalie Al Smith on October 24, 1971, at the Olympia. At the time, it put the Seals ahead 2-1 in a game they eventually won 6-3. Other rookie year highlights for Gilbertson included a three-assist effort against the Sabres in Buffalo and a two-goal effort in the Seals first-ever win at Madison Square Garden on March 12, 1972.

Gilbertson impressed his first-year coach, Vic Stasiuk, with his willingness to play a physical game and with his effort. "He was light, but big enough, and he mixed it up," Stasiuk recalled. "He wanted to play a physical game, and he did. He struggled a bit skatingwise—he was herky-jerky skater."

Gilbertson found he quickly fit in with his teammates, who took an almost instant liking to him. The blond-haired, fair-skinned Gilbertson was given the nickname "Whitey" by his teammates. "Stan, Joey Johnston and I used to hang out a lot," recalled Bobby Sheehan, who played with Gilbertson during his rookie year in the NHL. "Stan was a good man and a nice guy. He'd do anything for you. He told great jokes and was a solid hockey player. He was not afraid to go into the corners."

Craig Patrick, who roomed with Gilbertson, called him "a hardworking, fun-loving guy. He was gritty and he played hard all the time." Gerry Pinder recalled that Gilbertson "was not really good at any one thing, but wanted it bad and got his nose dirty. He hung tough in the NHL."

The following season was a down year for Gilbertson and the California Golden Seals. The team fell into last place and Gilbertson scored only six goals and 21 points in 66 games. Still, Gilbertson continued his all-out efforts and remained popular with his teammates. Gary Croteau recalled Gilbertson's "crazy sense of humor. He played left wing really well. He was a great team man; he was always there."

Gilbertson was also popular with the Seals fans for his work ethic and his involvement in the Bay Area community. In addition to living in the Bay Area full time, Gilbertson spent his summers working at a hockey clinic teaching the game to young people. He made numerous appearances on behalf of the team, often signing autographs and answering fans' questions in an attempt to sell the game of hockey to the Bay Area masses.

It seems that every former Seals player interviewed had a Stan Gilbertson story. Walt McKechnie recalled, "One time in New York we were being outshot in the first period something like 23-2. The Rangers were beating us 1-0, but Gilles Meloche was playing very well. We went into the locker room and there was dead silence. The shots on goal were announced in the dressing room. Stan Gilbertson looked around the room and said, 'OK, who were the two wise guys?' It broke up the room and I think we only lost the game 4-1." Many different players had similar stories about this quip, although the opponent and the score were often different. It is possible Gilbertson said it more than once.

Off the ice, McKechnie recalled how Gilbertson would just roll with the punches, often poking fun at himself. "Stan was color blind," McKechnie said. "He bought a pair of brown loafers and a pair of black loafers and he would often mix them up, wearing one of each. We would point it out to him and he would say, 'Don't worry, I have another pair at home just like them.' "

In 1973-74, Gilbertson bounced back with an 18-goal, 30-point season for the Seals. He had a two-goal, one-assist game on January 14, 1974, in a 5-5 tie with the Maple Leafs, and a two-goal effort on February 6, 1974, in a 4-2 win over the visiting Vancouver Canucks. Seals coach Fred Glover remembered Gilbertson fondly. "He was a great guy and good to have around," Glover said. "He was a clown, but he kept everyone going." Barry Cummins joked that Gilbertson could be "hotheaded, but he gave you everything he had on the ice. It may not have been the right thing, but he gave you everything he had." Reggie Leach added, "Stan was the class clown. He worked hard. I can still picture him on the ice. He stood out all the time. He skated pretty well, but nothing would really happen when he did."

Late in the 1973-74 season, Glover was replaced by Marshall Johnston as Seals coach. Gilbertson responded to the new regime and finished the season on a hot streak. "From the day Marshall Johnston and Munson Campbell took over the team, I think I was one of the most effective players," Gilbertson said at the time. "I was really working hard and playing both ends of the rink." Gilbertson felt the Seals players really responded to Marshall Johnston as coach. "He's played with us, lost with us and worked hard with us," Gilbertson said of Johnston. "The players think highly of him and I'm sure they're happy to play for him."

Morris Mott remembered that Gilbertson "had a reputation of being a comedian. He was serious when the game was on but in the dressing room he took the role of trying to break the guys up. We were in Los Angeles for the last game of the year," Mott recalled. "Stan Gilbertson got the puck in the slot but he was sort of facing the wrong way and he shot the puck on his backhand. It went between Sheldon Kannegiesser's legs and into the net from about 30 feet out. Kannegiesser still thought the puck was underneath him and Gilbertson tapped him on the helmet and said, 'Hey, the puck's in your net, asshole.' "

Mott also recalled an incident that took place on the team bus. Marv Edwards was talking about Pete Goegan, who was from Thunder Bay, Ontario. Marv said, 'He was so mean, he would take your eye out.' Stan Gilbertson, who was not even involved in the conversation, said, 'The SOB would just do that twice to me.' "

Spike Huston recalled one winter road trip to Long Island. "Stan packed his bag and always said he was going to see his agent. We were at the team hotel around 2 p.m. and relaxing by the pool, which was frozen solid. Stan slid into the pool, but the ice didn't break and he didn't fall in. 'See,' Stan said to me. 'I can walk on water.' "

Despite the obviously humorous times, Gilbertson had a serious side, too. He was a good teammate to all of the players on the Seals, veterans and rookies alike. "Stan was a really good guy off the ice and a real team man," said rookie defenseman Paul Shakes. "He was great to the guys from Salt

Lake. He showed us around and spent time with us." Rick Kessell remembered that Gilbertson was "a happy-go-lucky guy who made me laugh," but also recalled him asking Kessell, who was adopted, about the possibility of adopting a child.

Gilbertson returned to the Seals for the 1974-75 season, but he didn't stay in Oakland long. He played the first 15 games of the year with the Seals, scoring one goal and five points before being traded to the St. Louis Blues on November 11, 1974, along with Craig Patrick. In return, California received fellow Duluth native Butch Williams (the younger brother of Tommy Williams) and Dave Gardner from St. Louis. In February 1975, the Blues dealt Gilbertson to the Washington Capitals, where he finished the 1974-75 season strong by scoring 11 goals and 18 points in 25 games. On April 6, 1975, in the Caps season finale, Gilbertson scored four goals in an 8-4 Washington win over the Penguins. It was the first hat trick of Gilbertson's career and the first four-goal game in Capitals history. Gilbertson split the 1975-76 season between Washington and Pittsburgh. He had his first 20-goal season, scoring 26 goals and 48 points in 77 games.

Unfortunately for Gilbertson, 1975-76 was to be his last full season of professional hockey. Late in the 1976-77 season, Gilbertson was involved in a serious car accident. One of his legs had to be amputated at the knee. His hockey career came to an abrupt end. Fred Glover recalls, "When Stan got into that accident, I was blown away." Gilbertson's career NHL statistics include 85 goals and 174 points in 428 games. Even after his accident, Gilbertson was still trying to help his former teammates laugh. Bob Stewart recalled seeing Gilbertson shortly after the car accident. "He said, 'Hey, Stewie, look at this,' and he showed me his stump. He still had a great sense of humor."

Gilbertson and his wife settled down in Danville, California, where they had purchased a house while Stan was still playing for the Seals. Gilbertson made a living selling real estate in Northern California. Tragically, hard times have hit Gilbertson in recent years. He lost his job and he and his wife got divorced. Many former teammates heard rumors about some serious personal problems and even Stan's family does not know of his exact whereabouts these days. Many former Seals, especially Walt McKechnie, are truly concerned for Gilbertson's health and safety. The NHL Alumni Association is also trying to locate the former Seals wing.

Despite the hard times that have befallen him of late, almost all of Stan Gilbertson's former teammates remember him fondly with a smile and with laughter. Lyle Carter summed up what Gilbertson meant to his teammates by saying, "He was a happy guy who was great to play with. He was a good team guy and a hard worker." And he always kept the team laughing.

Rick Smith

"He was a quiet guy and he was steady. He knew how to win from his days in Boston. He was good for the younger guys; a real stay-at-home defenseman."

—Gary Croteau on Rick Smith

Rick Smith's trade to California on February 22, 1972, came as a shock to him. The 5'11", 195-pound defenseman was in his fourth season with the Boston Bruins. He had already been on one Stanley Cup-winning team with the B's in 1970 and was playing for the 1972 team, which would go on to win another title, when he was traded to the Seals in the Carol Vadnais deal. "It was heartbreaking," Smith admitted. "It was during the playoff run of 1972. [Boston was] in the run for the Cup and we knew we had an excellent team. You hear trade rumors and your name is mentioned, but I didn't think about it. It was an excellent trade for the Bruins—they got a first-class defenseman [Carol Vadnais]. Garry Young got three assets for one solid asset. Reggie Leach was a good caliber player, myself, and Bob Stewart was a solid defenseman and a tough guy."

Smith had grown up a Bruins fan since Boston sponsored a team in Kingston, Ontario, where he grew up. "My hockey heroes were more local players," Smith recalled. "Guys like Orval Tessier and Dick Cherry." The Bruins owned Smith's NHL rights and he made his first appearance with the B's during the 1968-69 season. "I never thought I'd stick there," Smith recalled. "I had a good camp and I stuck with the team. Injuries kept me with the team. The injuries persisted throughout the season. The next year, there were injuries to Ted Green and Gary Doak that got me playing regularly for the first time."

Smith played four productive seasons for the Bruins before his trade to Oakland. It was a big adjustment for him. "The Bruins were the only other team I played for. They were a fun-loving team. There was no other team like them for talent. We were one of the top two or three teams in the league for a long time. The Seals were a young team. In their own way, they had their own character. They had tremendous potential. You could see the signs of potential there, but the team was still young. I don't think the players realized how good they were. The composure hadn't developed yet. I look back with sadness when I think of what could have gone on to be a great team. We had a good combination of youth and veterans; Gilles Meloche was a goalie who could carry a team. We had a strong defense with Paul Shmyr, who was as good as any defenseman in the league. The team was assembled by Garry Young, but it never had a chance to mature."

Smith's first game with the Seals didn't exactly turn out the way he had anticipated. The Seals opponent that night in Oakland was his former team, the Bruins. The Seals jumped out to a 6-1 second-period lead. "On one particular play, I got the puck and put a pass to Wayne Carleton at the red line. He did all the work and scored a goal. I knew I had a small part of it." The Bruins mounted a fierce comeback, however, and tied the game 6-6 in the third period. "The winning goal by Boston, as a matter of fact, the puck hit my ass and went into the net. That is something it took me a long time to get over."

There were other adjustments Smith had to make when he joined the Seals, like playing in front of small crowds at home. "It gave us the impression that this wasn't that important," Smith admitted. "I had just left Boston and everything was hockey there. It was a big thing to be in the NHL. We had to look up and worry about the crowds in Oakland. We could see it wasn't working as a business. The small crowd takes away a bit from your adrenaline. We are all men and all professionals and you want to say you performed your best every night, but there's a human factor. I mean guys like Gretzky and Orr are superstars because they can give 100 percent every night. The rest of us, unfortunately, can't."

Joining a team owned by Charlie Finley was also radically different than playing for the Boston Bruins. "We had those green suitcases," Smith recalled. "We felt like we had joined the circus. We also had the white skates. Back then, I was thinking, White skates, girl's figure skates, sissies. We never got past that. It was so bad, opposing teams didn't say anything. The other players felt so bad for us."

Despite the rather unusual gear, Smith did give Finley some credit for his way of looking at hockey. "I have to give Charlie Finley his due credit. He recognized the finances of the game," Smith admitted. "Economics was a big issue. It *is* a business. He was more in tune with that, but he was not in tune with the economics of the game at that time with the birth of the WHA. He treated the team well. We flew first class and that was a marvelous gesture on his part. We were the only team in the NHL who flew first class. But we didn't treat the honor of flying first class with respect."

The Seals were in the thick of the playoff hunt in 1971-72, but lost their final six games and barely missed the playoffs. Part of the problem, according to Smith, was the coaching of Vic Stasiuk. "He was old school," Smith said. "Vic was a very nice man, but I don't think he was in tune with the team. The team was not working well with him. Sometimes, old-school ideas work, but you have to have respect to get away with it. I didn't see the respect. Our team had a lot of flair and needed to be handled more individually. Vic's approach was more cookie cutter. We all respected him as a player but great coaching never came out. I think he would have done better as a coach a few years earlier, but the game changed a lot between 1967 and 1971." Smith played in 17 games for the Seals in 1971-72, scoring one goal and netting five points and 26 penalty minutes.

Prior to the following year, Stasiuk was fired, but the Seals lost half their roster to the WHA. Garry Young took over as coach of the club. "As a GM he put together a phenomenal group of players," Smith said. "He deserved a lot of credit. He was willing to fight to keep his players. It was like he was the captain of the ship and he was willing to fight to keep the players onboard. He was struggling against Charlie Finley, but there were more players jumping ship then he had arms to catch us with. I thought it was sad at the time he was forced to coach the Seals. He was the general manager, the architect of the team. Charlie Finley would call him at 6 a.m. Chicago time, which was 4 a.m. in California. He would wake Garry up in the middle of the night for a progress report. He was thrown into a bad situation as a coach and he had no NHL coaching experience. Then Charlie Finley brought back Fred Glover to be the GM. Garry Young had been instrumental in Glover's dismissal a few months earlier. It was a bad situation. I remember in training camp, one of the players knocked Garry over and he got hit pretty badly. That was sort of indicative of the entire year there in Oakland." Young lasted only 12 games as coach of the Seals before being replaced again by … Fred Glover.

According to Smith, Glover was placed in the unfortunate position of being Finley's watchdog. "I had heard negative things about Freddie," Smith recalled. "Everybody had painted him black. He didn't do anything to change our minds. In our hotel, his room was always right over the entrance. We got the impression he was writing down when each of us came in every night. He seemed to be the guy who was there on Charlie Finley's behalf to oversee things. When Garry Young was let go, Fred Glover came in and was placed in a thankless position. We respected him. He was a disciplined man. At the end of the year, our team seemed to come together a little bit."

It seemed to Smith that everything about the Seals was different, even practices. "We practiced up at Berkeley," Smith recalled. The rink at Berkeley was an oversized figure-skating rink that was at least as big, if not bigger, than an Olympic-sized surface. This created very different angles than what players were used to in an NHL game. "Because of the rink there, I didn't feel it was serious. The atmosphere at practice diminished. I don't think the players appreciated the importance of practice. The rink worked against it. Even if you did want to do something extra, it didn't feel good. It felt like a circus, not an NHL team. Now professional hockey players should have overcome this, but we were all young."

Smith recalled Joey Johnston's remark one time before a practice at Berkeley: "I don't know why we're practicing our skating. We should be practicing for our ride back home with our trailers attached to our cars." Smith later added, "That spoke volumes about the attitude of the team."

When asked to describe his style of play, Smith quickly answered, "I was a stay-at-home defenseman. I was a dependable defenseman who could stop the play and move the puck up to our forwards. I wasn't a good skater or shooter or stickhandler. I was disappointed I didn't exhibit my strengths in 1971-72. Then, in 1972-73, when all those players were gone to the WHA, I was put in a role I was not ready for. I was playing on the power play and it was brutal. We were all asked to do things we just weren't able to do."

Smith's teammates certainly seemed to appreciate his efforts. Morris Mott described Smith as "a very valuable defenseman. He was intelligent. He wasn't a great skater, but he was reasonably skilled with the puck." Glover saw that Smith "was a good hockey player. He was not that big, but he was efficient and not afraid to hit."

In 1972-73, his only full season with the Seals, Smith had nine goals and 33 points in just 64 games. "He was probably our best defenseman the one year he was there, but a reoccurring injury caused him to miss games," said Joey Johnston. Still, with the loss of talent to the WHA, the Seals sank to the bottom of the NHL's West Division standings.

Despite the dismal record, there were a few bright moments for Smith. On March 18, 1973, the Seals blanked the North Stars 2-0 at Oakland. Gilles Meloche had 20 saves to earn the shutout. The Seals dominated play, outshooting the North Stars 37-20. Although he didn't figure in the scoring, the win gave Smith a real sense of satisfaction. "They were a good team at that time," Smith said of the North Stars. "Really, they were what we should have been."

Smith also gained a real respect for the fans in the Bay Area who followed the Seals. "We had really great fans," Smith said. "Ty Toki was a marvelous guy and the Booster Club was great. The fans were all from San Jose. The base of Sharks fans came from the old Seals. The location of the building where we played was not right."

Despite his positive reaction to the fans, Smith recalls that the Seals were largely ignored in the Bay Area. "They would take the players to a shopping center and nobody would show up," Smith said. "It was like trying to grow something in the desert—at least in the immediate area. We didn't do much promotion in San Jose or other outlying areas. In Boston, when you would speak, you'd get a few hundred dollars and the place would be full. In California, you'd speak for free and nobody would show up."

Despite these difficulties, there were lighter moments during Smith's stay in Oakland. "It was the end of the year, the last game, Smith said. "We were actually playing better. When you win the Stanley Cup, the players would throw everybody in the shower after the game. In our dressing room after our last game, we threw the reporters into the shower. It was a real celebration. It might have been since the season was over. We had beer in the dressing room. Finally, around midnight, Gilles Meloche's wife somehow got in and said, 'Enough is enough. The party's over!' "

Despite his respect of Finley, like many of his teammates Smith did have problems with the owner. "In hockey circles, your reputation often precedes you, and that was true of Charlie Finley," Smith said. "People had the suspicion that he wouldn't pay them much and it all came to a head with the WHA. There was a mass exodus. He just wouldn't pay the going rate. During the 1972-73 season, the WHA attempted to make more raids on NHL rosters. Charlie Finley was in town and got wind of it. There was a bar called Sam's Hoffbrau. It was right near the rink and it was hockey-player heaven. There was a smorgasbord with turkey and beef and we drank bottles of Coors. The Bruins used to say that the difference between winning in the playoffs was the difference between drinking draft beer and bottled beer in the summer. Charlie Finley came in and said, 'Get my boys a pitcher of draft.' I said, 'No, we're drinking bottles.' Charlie and I spoke for about an hour after that. In essence, that was the difference in our contracts that he refused to pay, the difference between draft beer and bottled beer."

Despite all of the distractions, Smith's effort never wavered. "He was always trying to do what was best for the team," Walt McKechnie remembered. "He had talent and played the game the same way every night."

After the 1972-73 season ended, Smith's contract was up. Like many other members of the Seals, he jumped to the WHA and signed with the Minnesota Fighting Saints. "I could see the direction the club was heading in—and it was not up," Smith said. "The WHA offered me $100,000. Charlie Finley's offer was $60,000. The year before, I had made $50,000."

After spending three seasons with the Fighting Saints, Smith returned to the NHL in 1976-77 with the St. Louis Blues before being traded back to Boston early that season. He later played briefly for the Red Wings and Capitals before retiring from hockey after the 1980-81 season. His career totals in the NHL were 52 goals and 219 points in 687 games, while he scored another 20 goals and 109 points in 200 games in the WHA.

Today, Smith is married and the father of two children. He went back to Queens University in Kingston and received his degree in computer science. He works in the computer department there and also does some work in land development and renting lakefront property in rural Ontario.

Bob Stewart recalled Rick Smith as a "good friend. We got traded together and roomed together. With the Bruins, Rick was an unsung hero. He really came on in Oakland. He was an up and down defenseman who stood his ground and moved the puck well."

Reggie Leach

"A talented, free-wheeling guy. It was the best thing for him to go to Philadelphia with Bobby Clarke. He needed somebody to tell him what he could do as a player and what we could have done as a team. He had one of the heaviest shots coming down the right side and he could skate like the wind; he just needed a little more guidance."

—Paul Shakes on Reggie Leach

Nobody could deny the talent of Seals wing Reggie Leach. His goal-scoring ability was unquestioned by anybody who saw him play. However, during his stay with the Seals, Leach's personal problems and the general attitude of the team around him prevented him from realizing his full potential. As soon as Leach left for Philadelphia, he became a prolific goal scorer.

Reggie Leach grew up idolizing the great Gordie Howe. The Riverton, Manitoba, native thrived while playing junior hockey on a line with Bobby Clarke with the Flin Flon Bombers. Leach scored more than 65 goals for three consecutive seasons, including an incredible 87 goals in 59 games in 1967-68. At 16, he realized he had a chance at making the NHL. "I was one of the better players in the league at that time," Leach said. "Bobby Clarke turned pro one year before me and said I would have no problems playing up there. As a kid growing up in Canada, that's what you dream about, but this was when I first had an idea I could really make it."

Leach recalled that as a junior, he had to face some prejudice because of his Native heritage. "When I was playing junior hockey there was a lot of name calling," he said. "Not so much in the NHL—there was hardly anything there. There were not a lot of Natives in the Western Canadian League. There was a lot of yelling and screaming at me in juniors. They called me 'dirty Indian' and stuff like that. I didn't let it bother me. I was one of the best players in the league at that time and I often controlled the puck. I figured, let them try to catch me."

Leach was selected by the Boston Bruins third overall in the 1970 amateur draft behind Gilbert Perreault and Dave Tallon. He split the 1970-71 season between the Bruins and their CHL farm club in Oklahoma City. The following year, he made the Bruins but was struggling to find ice time on a team loaded with talent. In 56 games with Boston in 1971-72, Leach scored seven goals and 20 points. His frustration grew. On February 23, 1972, the Bruins traded Leach to the Seals as part of the trade for Carol Vadnais. "I wasn't playing much for Boston back then," he recalled. "I was practicing and playing the odd shift. I wanted to play so I thought the trade was good."

Leach made an immediate impact on the Seals. In only 17 games with California in 1971-72, Leach scored six goals and had 13 points. Three of his goals were game-tying goals, tying him for the club lead that season.

Leach's first coach with the Seals was Vic Stasiuk. "He was a real nice guy," Leach recalled. "When I was traded, we stayed in the same hotel together. We were like buddies. We took rides through the countryside. When you're a 21-year-old kid and your coach asks you to go with him, you say yes."

Despite Leach's strong play down the stretch, the Seals lost their final six games and missed the playoffs. "My first year in Oakland, we were a pretty good club and we just missed the playoffs," Leach said. "Then came the WHA and we lost something like 15 players. I became one of the older players on the team—and I was about 21."

It was then that playing for the California Golden Seals became tough for the man known as "Riverton Rifle," for his hard shot. In 1972-73, the Seals finished in last place 30 games below .500. The following year, they won only 13 of 78 games and finished last in the league. "We got used to losing," Leach admitted. "We tried our best but we never did that well. There was a difference in coaching from the Seals to the Flyers. We had a very basic system in Oakland. The Flyers had more discipline. In Oakland, if you had a bad practice, nobody really said anything. In Philadelphia, when we practiced poorly, it mattered."

The biggest problem, according to Leach, was a teamwide lack of discipline, including his own immaturity and a general feeling surrounding the team that winning didn't really matter that much. "I was young and playing in the NHL. We didn't have any leadership as a young team," Leach admitted. "It was hard to control the team. We had Walt McKechnie and Joey Johnston, but we didn't really have the talent to compete. Scoring 20 to 25 goals in Oakland was a good year. I basically think we were just a tax write-off for Charlie Finley."

It is a well-known fact that Leach had problems with alcohol during various parts of his NHL career. He has also admitted that while playing for the Seals, he was not in great physical shape. He contends that his drinking did not affect his play while in California. "I don't think it affected my play with the Seals," Leach said candidly. "I know I drank a lot back then; we all did. It affected my career most from 1980-82. I had my career backwards. When I quit hockey, I quit drinking. I haven't had a drink in over 16 years. I was a good player in Oakland. I always played well enough to make the team, but I think it was only at about 80 percent of my capacity. I never did overdo it until I got to Philadelphia. That was just the way I was thinking. I played well enough to get my bonus. It was an easy attitude to get into—to not care if you win or lose. I had to change my attitude when I was traded to the Flyers."

Leach's teammates readily recalled his awesome talent but also believedthat his off-ice activities at times did hinder his performance during games. "He was a great goal scorer with great hands," Barry Cummins said. "He could score from anywhere. He was a little weak defensively. He always had problems with alcohol, even in juniors. Bobby Clarke was able to keep him on the straight and narrow. In Oakland, he had a problem in that he didn't know when to stop. It's not that he drank every night or even close to it. It's just that once he started drinking, he didn't know when to quit."

Former linemate Walt McKechnie added, "Reggie was semi out of control, like we all were. He had the skill in Oakland—you could see it on certain nights." Stan Weir remembered how Leach was a big help to him when he first arrived in Oakland as a rookie. "My first training camp, he took me under his wing. He had a heart of gold but he liked to enjoy life. My first couple of days at training camp in Kingston, Ontario, we had a few drinks after practice and a couple more and a couple more. I couldn't keep up with him."

Still, it was Leach's natural ability and personality that left a lasting impression on his teammates. "What a talent," goaltender Gilles Meloche recalled. "I enjoyed playing with him. Even in practice, his shot was so hard that it hurt you." Stan Weir called Leach "a pure goal scorer with one of the heaviest shots around." Joey Johnston added, "Reggie was a hell of a hockey player. He had a strong upper body. He was amazing, but only when he came to play. He had a lot of talent."

By the time Fred Glover took over as Seals coach early in the 1972-73 season, Leach had earned a reputation as being a bit difficult to coach. Still, looking back, both Leach and Glover—while admitting their occasional differences—developed a mutual respect for one another. "Freddie was a tough player for Cleveland of the AHL and a very nice guy," Leach said. "I liked Freddie. We had our arguments every so often. He came into the wrong situation after we had lost so many players to the WHA. He was basically coaching overage junior players. We didn't give him enough respect for what he knew about the game."

Glover said, "Reggie could score goals like nobody. His shot was tremendous. The problem was that he listened to the wrong people. He would get lost every once in a while."

Leach managed to keep his sense of humor when looking at some aspects of playing for the Seals—like Charlie Finley's white skates. "We laugh about it even today," Leach said. "We were different. We were sort of like a college team. Charlie Finley even bought us outfits to wear on the road; green blazers and black slacks and suitcases to match. It was a little different."

Leach also recalled the problems associated with the Seals main practice arena at Berkeley. "We used to practice at the Berkeley Ice Palace," Leach remembered. "There was no mesh around the boards, the ice was all uneven and the place was very dark. I think it was hard on the goalies. They had low boards, too. It was hard to get there, especially during the gas shortage. We had to take BART.

Back then you could only get gas on odd or even days. I think our practices were run a lot like a junior team would be today. We didn't have weightlifting or training and they never measured our body fat. It was a different world."

In 1972-73, his first full season with the Seals, Leach scored 23 goals and 35 points. It was his first of 10 consecutive seasons in the NHL scoring 20 goals or more. In his first contract, 20 goals was the magic number for his bonus and the bonuses of a lot of NHL players. "We always played a home-and-home series against Los Angeles the last two games of the season," Leach recalled. "We were both out of the playoffs. I remember some guys on the Kings saying, 'I need a goal tonight to get my bonus for 20 goals on the year.' I would say, 'Just come down my side. I don't care if you get your bonus.' That was fairly common back then. The average bonus was $500, which was big money in those days." One of those season-ending contests between the Kings and the Seals ended in a 9-4 final with the Kings winning. Los Angeles' Butch Goring scored three goals to finish the season with 21.

Leach had some very fond memories of playing for the Seals. His favorite was his first NHL hat trick on January 6, 1974, during a 9-4 loss to the Black Hawks in Chicago. Mike Veisor was the opposing goaltender. "We were playing against the Hull boys," Leach recalled. "Dennis Hull also had a hat trick. There was not a lot of defense in that game."

"I also remember Krazy George beating his drum," Leach said when asked about the Oakland fans. "Some of our biggest fans were members of Hells Angels. They had their own little parking area in the back. I think if we were a good team, we would have drawn well. I don't blame the fans for not coming out," Leach added. "We were not a winning team and we didn't give them what they wanted to see. In Boston, we always had sellout crowds. Even in junior hockey, we played before sellout crowds. It's in your mind, 'another 3,000 tonight.' "

In 1973-74, Leach's final season with the Seals, he scored 22 goals and 46 points. Unfortunately, he had a franchise-worst plus minus of -61 on the season. There was also a practice accident that cost the Seals the services of starting goalie Gilles Meloche for two months. "We always had a little contest after practice was over," Leach recalled. "I skated in and tried to deke Gilles. His glove fell off and I accidentally skated over his hand and severed some tendons." It was a rough year all around for the Seals, who finished with 13 wins and 36 points in a 78 game schedule.

Leach does have his regrets about his time with the Seals. "Looking back, I would do things differently," Leach said. "I was too laid back and never took the leadership in my hands like I did in junior hockey. I think I had too much respect for the older players and didn't want to step on anybody's toes. At that point, I also had some issues with authority. My role on the Seals was to score goals and to take a leadership role. When I was there, I was more of a follower than a leader."

Shortly after the completion of the 1974 Stanley Cup playoffs, the Seals traded Leach to the Flyers, where he was reunited with his old linemate from Flin Flon, Bobby Clarke. "I think I could have gotten out of Oakland the year before," Leach said. "Just before the trading deadline, Garry Young asked me if I wanted to be traded. Young knew he was going to be fired at the end of the season. He knew I wasn't too happy there but I decided to stick it out until the end of the season. I was traded two or three days after the Flyers won their first Cup. As soon as I was traded, I went to buy a house. Bobby Clarke always denied being involved in the trade. Clarke said I could get 45 goals easily in Philadelphia. I had around five goals at Christmastime but finished with 45."

Hilliard Graves added, "It took the discipline of the Flyers organization to bring out his talent." Craig Patrick recalled, "Reggie always said, 'Trade me to Philly and I'll play with Clarkie and get 70 goals.' He did." The Seals received Al MacAdam, Larry Wright, the Flyers first-round pick in the following draft and future considerations (George Pesut) in exchange for Leach.

Leach's play really improved in Philadelphia. After his 45-goal season in 1974-75 in which he helped the Flyers win their second consecutive Stanley Cup, he scored a career-high 61 goals the following season. The Flyers returned to the cup finals that year but were defeated by the Canadiens in four straight games. Despite his team's loss, Leach was awarded the Conn Smythe Trophy for his record-setting 19 goals in the playoffs that year. After eight seasons in Philadelphia, Leach played his final NHL season with the Detroit Red Wings in 1982-83. He finished his NHL career with 381 goals and 666 points in 934 games.

Today, Leach and his second wife live in suburban New Jersey, near Philadelphia. They each have two children from their previous marriages. Leach owns a small landscaping company and does work with First Nations, an organization that works with Native children. Leach tells them his story to help keep the children away from drugs and alcohol.

Reg Leach's stay in Oakland did not bring out the best in him on or off the ice. He was young and it showed. Still, his talent came through and his experience with the Seals was a building block for his later success in Philadelphia. "He had so much talent," Rick Kessell said of Leach. "I never saw a guy shoot harder of get a shot off quicker." It was unfortunate for the Seals and their fans that Leach had to leave Oakland to bring much of that talent out.

Hilliard Graves

"He was a tough player you hated to play against. He was small, but he could get his body down so low. A tough body checker, he put a lot of defensemen out with knee injuries. Opponents didn't like him. He was a tough competitor. He played well with Ivan Boldirev; a scrapper and a tough checker."

—Bob Stewart on Hilliard Graves

Hilliard Graves knew what he was up against playing professional hockey. "I'm not a big guy," he said when asked to describe the style of hockey that helped get him to the NHL. "I was maybe 5'10", 165, although my bubble-gum card says 5'11", 175. I never thought I was going to be a player. I was a pretty good skater; the guys couldn't skate as fast as me. I had a mental toughness and a little mean streak that most players have. You do what you have to do. I was physically tough and opportunistic. I liked the physical side of the game and that kept me around. I played the same game every night."

Graves was born in Saint John, New Brunswick, and played his junior hockey in Charlottetown. Although he was not drafted by any NHL team, the Seals invited him to their training camp as a free agent prior to the 1970-71. "I got an invitation to camp and went to see how good they were," Graves recalled. "At camp, I realized I could play there."

After training camp, Graves was signed to a contract with the Seals. He ended up splitting the 1970-71 season between the Seals and the Providence Reds of the AHL. With the Seals, Graves appeared in 14 games but did not score a point in limited action. Perhaps, the Seals rookie wing was a bit too much in awe of his competition. "I was pretty excited," Graves admitted. "I was still in disbelief. I was very excited to make it."

His very first NHL game came against the team he grew up rooting for, the Montreal Canadiens, and his favorite player, Jean Beliveau. "I remember my very first game," Graves said. "I was a 20-year-old kid from Nova Scotia coming out to California. I thought I was going to Salt Lake but they had a lot of injuries in California. My first game was against Montreal and we were facing Beliveau, Cournoyer, J.C. Tremblay and Frank Mahovlich. I went home to Canada and I still had their posters on my wall."

The hockey people in the Seals organization impressed Graves when he first arrived in Oakland, but that soon changed. "When I first got there, they had quality people running the team, like Frank Selke and Bill Torrey," said Graves. "They were excellent hockey people and, at first, Charlie Finley let them run the team. They built up a core of good, young players. Over time, I think Mr. Finley lost enthusiasm for it and just tried to save money. That's when things got out of hand."

During his first season, the Seals were beset by injuries and finished last in the West Division with the NHL's worst record. Graves quickly saw what kind of an effect constant losing has on a team. "I remember in my first year with the Seals in 1970-71, we were playing Boston. That was when they had Bobby Orr, Phil Esposito, Ken Hodge and those guys. We were in one of those situations where we win or we're mathematically eliminated from the playoffs. In between the second and third periods, our radio announcer, Roy Storey, came down to do a between-periods interview. We were losing something like 5-1. The announcer asked Earl Ingarfield, 'What are your chances of winning the game?' Well, Earl answered him seriously and the players all laughed out loud at him. Now this interview was going on live and the announcer had to cut the broadcast."

Then, Graves began a strange journey through the Seals organization. Frank Selke Jr., the club's general manager who signed Graves, was fired. Graves was sent down to Providence of the AHL and the Reds cut him. "They wanted me to sign voluntary retirement papers," Graves said in an interview with Alan Truax of the *Atlanta Journal.* "That way, I would be bound to California for two or three years while I played semipro hockey. But I was only 20 years old so I wasn't going for that." Graves then asked the Seals to put him on waivers. Oakland management was surprised that two teams put in a claim for Graves so they withdrew him from the waiver list. The Seals then sent him down to the Baltimore Clippers of the AHL and Baltimore almost released him as well. He did manage to stay with the Clippers, which was then the Seals top minor league affiliate in 1971-72. In 76 games with Baltimore, Graves scored 14 goals and 32 points.

In 1972-73, Graves was again recalled to the Seals, this time for a full season. He saw regular duty and surpassed almost everyone's expectations. Graves finished his rookie season in the NHL with 27 goals and 52 points, both of which turned out to be career highs. He also set an all-time club record with a 21.1 percent shooting percentage by scoring 27 goals on only 128 shots. The 27 goals was third in the NHL among rookies, behind only Steve Vickers of the Rangers and Philadelphia's Bill Barber. Graves was among the finalists for the Calder Trophy as rookie of the year but the award went to Vickers, who received a lot more media attention playing in New York.

Craig Patrick appreciated Graves's development as a hockey player. "It took him quite a while to make the team," Patrick said. "He was a great skater and had a great shot. He achieved quite a bit." Reggie Leach added, "He could skate like the wind and was one of the tougher little players I have ever seen. He was always in good shape."

Graves still remembers his first NHL goal fondly. "It was the second game of the 1972-73 season and we were in Minnesota," Graves recalled. "Gump Worsley was the other goalie and I was playing on a line with Stan Gilbertson and Ivan Boldirev. I took a pass just over the blue line and took a slap shot. The puck rolled over Gump's shoulder and into the net. We lost the game 5-2. I was excited that I had my first NHL goal but we lost, so you try to tone it down. The next day in the paper, they asked Gump about my goal and he said, 'I should have had it three times. I should have caught it and then I should have stopped it on the way down and I should have stopped it when it was rolling on the ice over the goal line.' Here I was thrilled about my first goal and all the goalie could say was that he should have had it easily."

During his rookie year, Graves adopted a physical style of play that would become his trademark. "Hilly wasn't big but he was quick," recalled defenseman Ted McAneeley. "He was famous for his hip check, which gave him more room to operate." Graves's effective hip check "helped make him many enemies around the league," recalled Rick Smith. Some of his former teammates, who later played against Graves, had problems with his style. "He was a feisty little guy," said Ray McKay. "He had a reputation of going down low when defensemen came around the net. Guys were a little leery of him. He was a tough customer. I remember playing against him in the minors. We got tangled up and I tried to put his head through the ice. He was fast and he had a mean hip check." Gilles Meloche went even further. "He pissed all of his opponents off," Meloche said. "He was a dirty little fucker. You liked to have him on your team, though."

Graves's teammates defended his style of play. Seals captain Bert Marshall called Graves "a legend. He hit and was an open-ice body checker. He hit with his hip and hit guys in the knees. Everybody crucified him because he was with us and was not a 'star.' Denis Potvin used to do the same thing and nobody crucified him."

Early in the year, Garry Young was the Seals coach. Graves recalled Young as "a smart hockey man but he was not a person who inspired trust. He was a good guy, but you could never really believe what he was telling you. Once the guys found that out, it wasn't a good situation." Young was replaced as coach after only 12 games. The Seals hired Fred Glover, a coach who truly appreciated Graves's no-holds-barred physical style of play. "Hilly was a tough, tough kid who played well with us," Glover said. "He wouldn't back down from anything. He could put the puck in the net, too, and that was a bonus."

Graves made a particular enemy of the most hated man in the NHL in those years, Dave Schultz of the Flyers. Due to a few lengthy brawls between the clubs, the Flyers and Seals developed a rivalry, despite the distance between the two cities—and the distance between the two clubs in the standings. The Flyers of the era were the nicknamed the "Broad Street Bullies" and fought their way to two Stanley Cup titles, while the Seals were not exactly known as a physical or fighting team. Still, Graves was one of the few Seals who stood up to the Flyers in general and Schultz in particular. "He fought Dave Schultz every time we played Philadelphia," recalled Stan Weir. "He always held his own." Fred Glover added with pride, "Hilly could beat up Dave Schultz any day of the week."

Glover recalled that in one game between the Flyers and the Seals, the rivalry got so intense that the Seals needed help leaving the Spectrum. "They had Dave Schultz and we had Hilliard Graves," Glover recalled. "They started Schultz so I started Graves and Graves would go out and beat the shit out of [Schultz]. There were fights galore and we needed a police escort to get to our hotel. I told the linesman and the referee, 'Thank God you were here.' "

Despite these particular memories that stood out in his teammates' minds, Graves never accumulated more than 48 penalty minutes in a single NHL season, a mark he set with the Seals during the 1973-74 season.

Although Graves had a fine year in 1972-73, the season was not without its pitfalls off the ice. "We were staying in Montreal at the Mount Royal Hotel and the curfew was 11 or 11:30. We were waiting for an elevator and some guys asked us, 'Are you hockey players?' and we said, 'Yeah,' and they said, 'Where do you play?' and we said, 'The Seals.' They asked us, 'What is Charlie Finley like?' I told them that Charlie liked to get his name in the paper. Another guy said he was 'Mickey Mouse.' We later found out the guy we were talking to was a reporter for *The Montreal Gazette* and he printed [all that in] the article."

Despite the losing teams he played for in Oakland, Graves really took a liking to the Bay Area. "I was 21 or 22 and playing in the NHL," Graves recalled. "Initially, I didn't care where I was playing. When I came back during the 1972-73 season, I had a good year, scoring 27 goals. It was pretty exciting for me. We had 3,000 really good fans. This was my only experience playing in the NHL other than playing at other arenas. Ignorance is bliss. I was just having a good time. The Bay Area is still one of my favorite places in the United States. I try to go every couple of years. I was married in San Francisco and my wife loves it, too. The weather was great; the people were great. The only regret I have about the Seals is that if we ever had a leader and a topnotch hockey player, we might have been able to win. We had a lot of talent."

In 1973-74, Graves returned to the Seals but did not excel like he did the previous year. Due to injuries, he appeared in only 64 games, scoring 11 goals and 29 points. The Seals finished with only 36 points, even fewer than they had during the dismal 1972-73 season. There were still some humorous memories of that season for Graves. "One time during the 1973-74 season we were in Boston. Both Marv Edwards and Gilles Meloche were injured and we had substitute goalies with our team [Ted Tucker and Bob Champoux]. I always liked to follow the goalies onto the ice; that was sort of my superstition. Anyway, the goalie is about to lead us onto the ice and he turns to me and asks, 'Which end do I go to?' I knew right then we were in trouble."

The 1973-74 season also brought the infamous streaking incident to the Oakland Coliseum. "It was done in good fun," Graves recalled. "The girl was one of the fans who came to every game. She had it organized to go down on the ice. Everybody got a good laugh. It was between periods of a game so we as players didn't get a good look at it at the time, but we all saw pictures in the papers the next day. She had three or four Seals decals well-placed, but that was it—she just skated across the ice."

After the 1973-74 season, the Seals traded Graves to the Atlanta Flames for John Stewart. Graves played two and a half seasons in Atlanta and another two and a half in Vancouver before ending his NHL career in 1979-80 with the Winnipeg Jets. He played in 556 games in his career, scoring 118 goals and 281 points. Despite his reputation, Graves's career penalty-minute total was only 209.

Today, Graves and his wife live in Moncton, New Brunswick. They have two children and two grandchildren. Graves owns his own food-brokerage business, which employs a sales force for companies that don't have their own sales department. He has more than 50 people working for him.

Despite his lack of size, Hilliard Graves combined his skating ability and toughness into a solid NHL career. Gary Croteau, who once skated on a line with Graves and Ivan Boldirev, summed up Graves, saying, "He had the best hip check in the game. He would disguise it. He ended some guys' careers because he would get down so low and take guys out at the knees. He was 5'10" and maybe 165 or 170, but he was as tough as any guy in the league"—the kind of guy you loved to play with and hated to play against. That was Hilliard Graves.

Pete Laframboise

"He kept the guys loose. A big, tall, rangy hockey player, he did his best like the rest of us. Off the ice, he loved to party."

—Ray McKay on Pete Laframboise

Pete Laframboise was another in a long line of "saviors" that Seals management tried to sell to the fans. He was the player who was going to bring the team back to respectability once they called him up from the minors. Unfortunately, things never worked out the way management had it planned.

Laframboise played his junior hockey for the Ottawa 67s. In his final two seasons in juniors, he topped 70 points. The Seals made the 6'2", 210-pound Ottawa native their second selection in the 1970 entry draft.

Laframboise was sent down to the Seals top affiliate in Providence in 1970-71 where he had 13 goals and 32 points in 64 games for the Reds. The following year, Laframboise was assigned to the Seals affiliate in Baltimore. It was here that Laframboise showed his enormous potential and that management started raving about their future superstar. Laframboise scored 37 goals and had 81 points in 72 games for the Baltimore Clippers. That placed him seventh in the league in points and fifth in the league in goals scored. He was selected to the AHL's first team all-star squad after the season and expectations were suddenly sky high. Big Pete was called up for five games with Oakland but was held scoreless.

The Seals 1972-73 media guide referred to Laframboise as "this bright star from the Seals' minor league system," and added, "the young centerman could easily mature into a powerful, goal producing player asset for the California Golden Seals."

Rick Smith, who was a teammate of Laframboise in his rookie year with the Seals, called Pete "a fellow I kind of feel bad for. He was an MVP in the AHL. He was going to be the savior when I got there. They were all talking about this guy down in Baltimore who they were keeping in the minors to let him develop. In camp, he suffered an injury and that set him back. He never really developed into the guy they thought he would be."

Hilliard Graves explained why he thought Laframboise had trouble making the leap to the next level. "Pete was one of those guys who was among the best in the AHL but couldn't make the jump to the next level. He was a good AHL player but not a great skater. He needed that extra second to get his shot away. In that extra second in the NHL, the defenseman gets his stick on the puck or the goalie makes the save."

191

In his rookie year of 1972-73, Laframboise had a respectable season. He scored 16 goals and 41 points in 77 games and added 26 penalty minutes. Laframboise scored his first NHL goal on October 25, 1972, against the expansion Atlanta Flames at Oakland. He beat Flames goalie Dan Bouchard twice in a 4-3 Seals loss.

Laframboise had one of the most spectacular games in Seals history on January 3, 1973, against the Vancouver Canucks. Big Pete scored once in the first period, once in the second and twice during a six-goal third period during an 11-3 victory for the Seals. The four-goal game was the first ever in Seals franchise history and would be tied but never broken during the team's nine seasons in the NHL.

After the game, Charlie Finley found his way down to the dressing room and handed the big rookie 20 $20 bills for his performance. "I remember when Pete Laframboise scored four goals in one game," Reggie Leach said. "Charlie Finley tried to get into the arena but the security guards wouldn't let him in. He didn't have a ticket and they didn't believe he was Charlie Finley. He finally got into the dressing room and he gave Pete Laframboise $400. That was a nice little bonus." Unfortunately, only 2,702 fans witnessed Laframboise's record-setting performance at the Oakland Coliseum.

The losing atmosphere around the Seals did not help Laframboise maintain his consistency. Gary Croteau called Laframboise "a good centerman in a tough situation." Defenseman Barry Cummins remembered Laframboise as "moody" but added, "this was because of the attitude of the team. We were going nowhere. Pete had good skills, but he didn't use them all the time."

Laframboise soon developed a reputation for enjoying himself a little too much off the ice. "He lived hard and enjoyed life off the ice," Ted McAneeley recalled. "I don't think he ever lived up to his potential as a result." Gilles Meloche added that Laframboise was "loosey-goosey" and "enjoyed life." Craig Patrick put it succinctly: "He was not a hard worker. Pete liked to have fun."

Laframboise was popular with his teammates and many of them recalled his sense of humor. Unfortunately, sometimes Laframboise didn't always follow his own advice. "We were playing our last game of the season against Vancouver," Morris Mott recalled. "Pete spoke about a small defenseman on their team who checks guys low and takes their knees out. He warned us all to be careful facing this guy. Well, about 10 minutes into the game, who does the guy line up and hit in the knees but Pete. He injured ligaments and couldn't play much golf in the off-season."

"Pete was always laughing and joking," Rick Kessell said. "He had two big dogs similar to greyhounds. Once, we went to the East Coast on a road trip and he had a friend watching the dogs. When he got back, his place was torn apart."

In 1973-74, Laframboise had a rough year with the Seals. He missed time due to injury and his effectiveness was limited. In 65 games, he scored just seven goals and 14 points for the last-place Seals. He had one memorable offensive performance that season, a two-goal, one-assist effort on November 28, 1973, during a 5-1 win over the North Stars at the Jewel Box in Oakland. Unfortunately, there were not many more productive nights for the big Ottawa native.

Walt McKechnie recalled Laframboise's sense of humor and a particular incident that took place before a game between the Seals and their archrival, the Philadelphia Flyers. "Pete was a funny man with a big-time sense of humor," McKechnie said. "We had a lot of bench-clearing brawls against Philadelphia. Hilliard Graves and Dave Schultz always used to fight and Hilliard would drive Schultz nuts. He would pick him up by the pants and put him on the ice. He also had a smile that drove Schultz nuts. We were facing Philadelphia for a Saturday-night game and played Los Angeles on Sunday. Then Monday, since we were out of the playoffs, we were hitting the links. We had a team meeting before the trip. Joey Johnston was our captain and he said, 'Let's keep it cool against Philadelphia.' Well, Saturday morning hits and somebody looked in *The Oakland Tribune* and there's an article which quotes Hilliard Graves as saying, 'I beat up Schultz all year long. If he wants me, he knows where to find me.' Well, Pete Laframboise was on Hilliard's line at that time along with Stan Weir. Pete had a Columbo trenchcoat and he was about 6'4" and had big, bushy hair. He walked into the dressing room like a duck. Pete said, 'Oh, yeah, got to go on the ice today. Did you read the paper?' Then he turned to Graves and said, 'Hilliard, I don't understand you. They got 'The Hammer' [Dave

Schultz], they got 'Big Bird' [Don Saleski], they got 'The Hound' [Bob Kelly] against your fuckin' big mouth and us two chickens."

Laframboise was left unprotected by the Seals in the 1974 expansion draft and was selected by the Washington Capitals. Just when it seemed as if things could not get worse for big Pete, he went from a team with 13 wins and 36 points to a team with eight wins and 21 points, setting the all-time NHL mark for futility. In 45 games for the Capitals, Laframboise scored five goals and 15 points, including a two-point effort against his former California teammates.

Midseason, the Capitals traded Laframboise to the Pittsburgh Penguins. He finished the year in Pittsburgh with five more goals and 18 points in 35 games. Playing for Pittsburgh allowed Laframboise to get his first taste of Stanley Cup playoff action and he scored once in nine games for Pittsburgh in the postseason. He was a part of the Penguins team that blew a 3-0 lead in games to the New York Islanders in the quarterfinal round, marking it only the second time in NHL history a team came back from a three-game deficit to win a best of seven series.

The Penguins assigned Laframboise to their AHL affiliate, the Hershey Bears, in 1975-76 where again, Pete had a productive season, scoring 65 points in 69 games. In 1976-77, Laframboise played 17 games for the WHA's Edmonton Oilers and picked up five assists. He played two more AHL seasons before retiring as an active player after 1978-79. Laframboise's career NHL statistics are 33 goals and 88 points in 227 games.

Today, Laframboise lives in Ottawa and still enjoys playing golf in his spare time. While he never did live up to his advanced billing as the Seals savior, his four-goal game remains one of the few highlights of the Seals snakebitten history. Stan Weir added, "Pete had a great sense of humor and gangly legs. He was talented and a good player."

Reggie Leach remembered Laframboise with genuine affection. "I was a linemate of his with Stan Weir," Leach said. "Pete was a fun guy to be with. We hung around a lot at home and on the road. He was a pretty good hockey player when he wanted to play."

Marv Edwards

"He was the glue that held the team together. He had a great sense of humor and was a competitor. An all-around super guy who kept Gilles Meloche on the straight and narrow."

—Stan Weir on Marv Edwards

The California Golden Seals were a very young team in 1972-73, after so many of their better players signed with the WHA. Perhaps the best asset the Seals had at that time was their young netminder, Gilles Meloche. In 1972-73, Meloche was entering his second NHL season and was just 22 years old. In order to help Meloche's development, the Seals signed 37-year-old veteran goaltender Marv Edwards to be Meloche's backup and goaltending guru.

The 5'10", 155-pound Edwards was born in St. Catherines, Ontario, and started playing junior hockey for the St. Catherines Teepees in 1950-51. In the 1950s, there were only six teams in the NHL and none of them carried backup goalies on their rosters. After finishing his junior career, Edwards began an odyssey that would take him to minor league towns all across North America. He played in the AHL, the IHL, the EHL, a senior league, the CHL and the WHL. Edwards tended goal for, among others, the Johnstown Jets, the Nashville Dixie Flyers, the Milwaukee Falcons and the Minneapolis Millers. Just when it seemed he would be a career minor leaguer, expansion hit and Edwards signed with the Pittsburgh Penguins as a free agent in September 1967. The Penguins assigned Edwards to their WHL farm team, the Portland Buckaroos. In 1967-68, Edwards had a league low 2.36 goals against average. He made his NHL debut with the Penguins in 1968-69, appearing in one game and losing, despite giving up just three goals. He split the rest of the year between the Amarillo Wranglers of the CHL and the Baltimore Clippers of the AHL.

The Toronto Maple Leafs selected Edwards in the intraleague draft before the 1969-70 season. The intention was for Edwards to give the Maple Leafs depth, but Bruce Gamble's play was inconsistent and Johnny Bower started showing his age, so Edwards emerged as the Leafs starter by late December.

"This is something you play your whole life for," Edwards told the Toronto press at the time. In 25 games with the Maple Leafs, Edwards had a 3.25 goals against average and a 10-9-4 record, which was not bad considering the Leafs finished the season five games below .500 and in last place in the East Division. Unfortunately for Edwards, he suffered a knee injury and missed significant time. When he was healthy enough to return to the lineup, Edwards's timing was off and he was demoted to second string.

The following season, the Leafs acquired two future Hall of Fame goaltenders in Jacques Plante and Bernie Parent. Edwards was loaned to the Phoenix Roadrunners of the WHL, where he had two winning seasons. Prior to 1972-73, Seals GM Garry Young arranged for the Seals to acquire Edwards in the intraleague draft. Edwards knew going in that he would only play 25 to 30 games at most and that his main job was to teach the Seals young goalie, Meloche. Still, it was another chance at the NHL—a chance Edwards relished.

Edwards got off to a good start for the Seals. In his first game, he made 32 saves in a 4-1 Seals win at the Spectrum in Philadelphia. Perhaps more importantly to Seals management, Edwards became almost a second coach in the dressing room, providing leadership to a very young Seals squad. "Marv and Marshall Johnston would analyze our defensive mistakes in the dressing room," Joey Johnston recalled. "He was a great, solid guy," Craig Patrick said of Edwards. "He was someone you could always turn to on the bus."

Edwards was always telling stories on the team bus. In fact, Edwards's tales became almost legendary among the Seals players. Defenseman Ray McKay called Edwards "one of the great, old-time goalies. He had stories from everywhere, especially the old Eastern League. He was a really good stand-up goaltender and one of the great guys in hockey." Morris Mott recalled that Edwards "used to sit at the back of the bus. Marv was a bit older and would talk about players he played with or against along the way. He could talk about players all the way back to the 1940s."

Like the Seals themselves, Edwards seemed to be snakebitten when it came time to take the ice. For example, Edwards managed one shutout during his two seasons as an active player with the Seals. It came on November 9, 1972, at the Aud in Buffalo. Unfortunately for Edwards, he didn't even win the game, as Roger Crozier also blanked the Seals and the game ended in a 0-0 tie. Edwards had a tough time during his first season in Oakland, finishing the year with a record of 4-14-2 in 21 games and a goals against average of 4.32. While those numbers hardly sound spectacular, they weren't so awful when you consider the lack of defensive support Edwards suffered through. In the 21 games he played in, Edwards faced 30 or more shots on goal in all but four games. He faced more than 35 shots on goal eight times and 40 shots or more five times. Perhaps Reggie Leach made the understatement of the year when he said, "I think Marv was probably frustrated with us for our lack of back-checking."

If things seemed difficult for Edwards and the Seals in 1972-73, the following season, Edwards's last as an active player, was even worse. Edwards seemingly was handed the starting position, at least temporarily, when Gilles Meloche was the victim of a freak accident in practice on November 28, 1973. Exactly one week later, however, Edwards suffered torn knee ligaments during a 3-3 tie against the Flames. He would not play again until March 3, 1974. The Seals were forced to call up two untested goalies from the minors for the middle part of the season. Edwards finally returned in a crushing 8-2 defeat against the Rangers at Madison Square Garden. As a result of the games he missed due to injury, Edwards played in only 14 games for the Seals, winning just one, losing 10 and tying one. His goals against average was 3.92. Edwards's final NHL win was a 5-1 victory over the Minnesota North Stars on November 28, 1973. He made 19 saves and recorded an assist in the game.

Despite missing so much time to injury, Edwards was still able to provide leadership to a young Seals team and helpful instruction to Gilles Meloche. Meloche, for one, particularly appreciated what Edwards did for him. "He was my tutor," Meloche said candidly. "He really helped me. He taught me a lot of tricks about the game, like how to rebound from a tough game. Most of what he taught me was on the mental side of the game. I used to get down on myself and Marv would put things back together for me."

Other teammates also noticed what Edwards did for Meloche. "Marv was a very good teacher of the game," rookie defenseman Paul Shakes recalled. "He and Gilles Meloche worked well together. Marv helped Gilles with his confidence and with picking things up. He always took the game in."

Edwards also had a certain toughness about him that his teammates and coach appreciated. "I remember, once Marv fought Marcel Dionne," Rick Smith said. "He took off his mask to fight him and he won the fight. He was a nice complement to Gilles Meloche and added that veteran aspect to the team." Coach Fred Glover called Edwards "a good goalie who was around for a long time. He had no temperament at all and didn't like to get beat. In the Western League, he would fight with anybody."

Other young Seals players also respected the team's venerable backup goaltender. "He was the oldest guy on the team," Reggie Leach said. "For a goaltender, he had a lot of sense. Most goaltenders, the elevator doesn't always go to the top floor. Marv was a very nice guy and I enjoyed his company on and off the ice."

Ironically, on a team that won so few games, Edwards earned the nickname "Stinky" for a rather odd reason. "If he won, he never changed his underwear," Rick Kessell recalled. "He was a good guy." Bob Stewart simply referred to Edwards as "Old Man" and recalled him as "a teacher who was great with the younger players."

In 1974-75, Edwards started the season as the team's third goaltender and assistant coach. When Gary Simmons established himself in the goaltending rotation with Meloche, Edwards became a full-time assistant coach for the Seals. He is still seen in the team picture with his goalie equipment on, but he did not appear in any games for the Seals. In 1975-76, when the Seals promoted Jack Evans—who coached the Seals top affiliate in Salt Lake to a championship the previous year to be their head coach—Edwards was given the coaching job in Salt Lake City. He coached there for two seasons and had a 68-74-10 record with the Golden Eagles. After that, Edwards coached in a variety of capacities, most recently as a goaltending coach with the Peterborough Petes of the OHL. Today, he coaches for the Petes part time while enjoying semiretirement.

Marv Edwards's hockey career stretched approximately 25 years as a player and another 25 years as a coach; he has devoted nearly 50 years of his life to the game of hockey. Playing for the Seals had to have been difficult for a veteran like Edwards, but it did extend his NHL career. His final NHL statistics were 61 games, a 3.77 goals against average and a record of 15-34-7.

The influence of Edwards continues to be felt in the hockey world through the many players he coached over the years. Gary Croteau remembered Edwards as "a fun guy. He went out with the attitude that he wanted a shutout every game. He really helped the younger guys." Part coach, part teacher, part elder statesman, Marv Edwards added experience, stability and a colorful sense of humor to the Seals during his stay with the team.

Ted McAneeley

"A little guy and a nice player. He played with a lot of heart. He had great toughness for a small guy."

—Rick Smith on Ted McAneeley

The knock against Seals defenseman Ted McAneeley was always that he was too small. The Cranbrook, British Columbia, native was listed at 5'9", 185 pounds, but as Barry Cummins said, "He was not tall or big-boned." Nobody ever questioned McAneeley's heart and determination but the question that always seemed to be asked was, Is this guy big enough to play defense in the NHL?

From a young age, McAneeley sought to prove the doubters wrong. He recalled that, as a child, "every Saturday at 5 it was a ritual to eat dinner and watch 'Hockey Night in Canada.' " McAneeley grew up cheering for the Canadiens and then the Maple Leafs with Jean Beliveau and "Boom-Boom" Geoffrion as his favorite players. McAneeley played three seasons for the Edmonton Oil Kings. He proved his toughness there, picking up 114, 171 and 92 penalty minutes in his three seasons in Edmonton. By his third year with the Oil Kings, McAneeley's offensive game blossomed and he knew he had a chance to make the NHL. "I saw people I was playing against getting drafted, so I knew I had a shot," McAneeley recalled. He finished the 1969-70 season with 29 goals and 59 points in 60 games for the Oil Kings. The Seals drafted him in the fourth round of the 1970 draft.

After two years of seasoning with the team's minor league affilites in the AHL, McAneeley made the Seals in 1972-73. The rookie defenseman immediately found himself on a losing team with questions being openly asked about its future. "The ownership situation was very unstable and rumors abounded," McAneeley said. "Once we got on the ice, however, we were professionals and we stayed focused. We were a very young team, but I don't think our attitude was different from any other teams'. We wanted to win. I think all the travel we had to do on the West Coast cut into our practice time, and that did have an effect. There was a lot of untapped talent on the Seals teams that I played for that blossomed later on."

In his first NHL season, McAneeley scored four goals and 17 points in 77 games. He also added 75 penalty minutes. He scored his first NHL goal on Boxing Day, December 26, 1972, during a 4-3 loss in Vancouver. McAneeley actually scored twice in that game, beating Dunc Wilson. "I remember my first NHL goal was in Vancouver because my parents were there," McAneeley said. The next night, McAneeley continued his hot play, scoring a goal and setting up another in a 2-2 tie against the Flyers at the Oakland Coliseum.

During the 1972-73 season, the Seals were wearing Charlie Finley's white skates. "It was a bit awkward," McAneeley admitted. "White skates were worn mostly by figure skaters back then but we got used to them. Charlie Finley was a bit ahead of his time. It is true that white paint used to get layered as the season went on because the trainer would have to paint the skates before every game, since they got scuffed."

All of McAneeley's teammates recognized his effort and hard work and, despite his lack of size, they acknowledged he was a good NHL defenseman. Fellow rookie Stan Weir called McAneeley "a small guy with a big heart. He worked his butt off and was a very competitive individual." Morris Mott added, "Ted was a very gritty little defenseman and a terrific passer. He had a very good sense of humor, although he was never the life of the party. He was very supportive as a teammate." Rick Kessell remembered McAneeley as "a hard-nosed little guy. He was always smiling and really friendly and a good checker for a small defenseman."

"I wasn't a big guy," McAneeley conceded, "but I was mobile and agile and I could make the transition from defense to offense. I moved the puck quickly; I think that was my strong point. Plus, I always played hard."

McAneeley played for two coaches in Oakland, Fred Glover and Marshall Johnston. "Fred Glover was an old-school coach," McAneeley recalled. "He expected us to play hard all the time and give effort. He was not a very good communicator, however." Glover who favored a physical style, appreciated McAneeley's play. "He was only about 4'9"," Glover said of McAneeley. "He played well and was a very good defenseman for his size."

McAneeley had a lot of respect for Johnston, his second coach and former teammate. "Marshall Johnston was a great teacher and communicator," McAneeley said. "He really analyzed the game. I think his experience with the Canadian National Team and Father Bauer helped him in that regard. He had the respect of all of his players as a coach."

McAneeley returned to the Seals in 1973-74. Although California sunk lower in the standings, McAneeley improved his numbers to four goals and 20 assists in 72 games. He had two games that season with two assists, one being a 2-2 tie against the defending Stanley Cup Champion Montreal Canadiens at the Oakland Coliseum on December 14, 1973.

Despite having all of these games in which he put up good offensive numbers, the one game McAneeley picked as his most memorable came against the Bruins. McAneeley scored a goal and two assists in the game, while the great Bobby Orr scored twice for Boston. McAneeley was named the first star of the game—ahead of Bobby Orr. "For one game," McAneeley said in an interview with *Sports Collectors Digest,* "on that given day, I was recognized as performing better than Bobby Orr. That's always something I'm proud to say."

McAneeley also enjoyed playing in Northern California. "It was great to be in the NHL and attain that long-term goal," he said. "The West Coast was also a great place to live."

One thing McAneeley wasn't pleased with was the lack of support the Seals had in Oakland. "The fans that came were good. There just weren't enough of them," McAneeley recalled. "I want to say playing in front of small crowds didn't have an effect on us, but looking back, I think it did. We would go to Philadelphia, Montreal, New York and Chicago and the stands are pumping. It would really get your adrenaline going."

The fans also remembered McAneeley fondly. One remembered that Ted drove a fancy sports car that had a California license plate with his jersey number and nickname on it: 23 DUDE.

In 1974-75, change was in the air in California and McAneeley suddenly felt that he was no longer in the Seals plans. "I wanted the opportunity to play," he said. "The Flyers won the Stanley Cup the year before with big, physical players and the Seals were looking for big defensemen. They brought in Len Frig and Mike Christie, so I knew I wasn't going to play much with the Seals." That feeling turned out to be accurate. In 1974-75, McAneeley played in only nine early-season games with the Seals and had two assists. He was then sent to the team's top farm club in Salt Lake City, where he helped the Golden Eagles to the CHL title.

Prior to the 1975-76 season, McAneeley signed with the Edmonton Oilers of the WHA. In 79 games with Edmonton, McAneeley scored two goals and 19 points. The next season, his WHA rights were traded to Houston, but Ted never played for the Aeros and instead spent the next three seasons playing for the WHL's Spokane Jets. His career NHL totals are eight goals and 43 points in 158 games, all of them with the Seals.

After his time in Spokane, McAneeley went to play and coach hockey in Japan. Ironically, the decision to play in Japan led him to his posthockey career. "I played in Japan for six years for a Sabu hockey team," McAneeley said. After his retirement, the company that owned the team offered him a job in the Prince Hotel chain, which they also owned. Today, Ted and his wife live in Hawaii, where he is the general manager of the Hawaii Prince Hotel in Waikiki. The McAneeleys have four daughters.

Hilliard Graves said of McAneeley, "He had to have a lot of talent to play in the NHL with his size. If he were a bigger man, his career would have lasted longer." But McAneeley had a lengthy stay in pro hockey, despite his lack of size, and his hockey experience led him to a successful posthockey career.

Perhaps fellow defenseman Bob Stewart summed up McAneeley best when he said, "Ted was a hard worker. He was a smaller defenseman and I enjoyed playing with him. He gave his best every time he played." What more can you ask of any man, regardless of his size?

Darryl Maggs

"He was traded for Dick Redmond so I guess we all expected him to play like Dick Redmond. He was a really laid-back kind of guy. Talentwise, he had more than 80 percent of the team, but he never did achieve the pre-billing he got."

—Rick Smith on Darryl Maggs

Darryl Maggs had a difficult time in his brief NHL career, but managed to flourish in the WHA. First, the 6'2", 195-pound defenseman from Victoria, British Columbia, was trapped on a deep Black Hawks team and unable to get significant playing time. Then, he was traded to the Seals after the team was depleted of talent by the WHA. The Seals acquired Maggs for Dick Redmond, a very popular and productive defenseman, and that placed unreasonably high expectations on the 23-year-old blueliner.

The Chicago Black Hawks selected Maggs in the fourth round of the 1969 entry draft. After spending one year at the University of Calgary, he signed a contract with Chicago and was assigned to their CHL affiliate in Dallas. Maggs had a productive 1970-71 season for the Dallas Black Hawks, scoring 14 goals and 50 points in 71 games. He also showed his toughness by accumulating 144 penalty minutes.

In 1971-72, Maggs made his NHL debut with Chicago, but he truly lacked a role. The Black Hawks wanted to find playing time for their rookie defenseman but were already stacked on the blue line with players like Keith Magnuson, Bill White and Pat Stapleton already well-established in the NHL. In fact, White and Stapleton played in the NHL All-Star game that year. As a result, Maggs was either the team's fifth defenseman or was rotated in at wing as an extra forward in an attempt to get him some ice time. The rookie struggled with his lack of ice time and produced only seven goals and 11 points in 59 games for Chicago.

Ironically, his first NHL goal came against the Seals at the Oakland Coliseum. Maggs beat Gilles Meloche for the only Chicago goal in a 2-1 win for the Golden Seals. He also grew frustrated because for some unknown reason, many members of the press often mistook him for Keith Magnuson. Due to his lack of ice time and relative inexperience, Maggs lacked an identity with the Black Hawks. Darryl started the 1972-73 season in a similar situation and was pointless in 17 regular-season games with Chicago.

The Seals acquired Maggs on December 5, 1972, in the Redmond deal. Charlie Finley ordered that Redmond be traded after he discovered that general manager Garry Young had signed him for more money than Finley had authorized. Because of Finley's directive and the public scandal that surrounded the trade, the Seals were unable to get market value for their young offensive defenseman and Maggs was given the burden of filling Redmond's large offensive shoes.

In 54 games with the Seals in 1972-73, Maggs scored seven goals and 22 points. He had an eventful debut in a Seals sweater, scoring the tying goal off Denis Herron with just 49 seconds left in a 4-4 tie against the Penguins. Maggs also had an assist in the game.

Seals coach Fred Glover planned to give Maggs regular duty as a right defenseman. "Maggs is young and has a good future," Glover said at the time of the trade. "He is big, solid and strong. We feel he can help our team, particularly because he has the talent to play defense and the knowledge and experience of playing the forward and wing positions."

Unfortunately, the young Maggs never was consistently great as a member of the Seals. "He had all kinds of talent but no work ethic," Hilliard Graves recalled. "It was hard, mentally, to play for the Seals. He played some great games but he made a lot of mistakes, too. I think he gave up at the end of his time here."

Gary Croteau explained, "Darryl was a terrific skater and Bobby Orr-type defenseman—or at least he wanted to be like Bobby Orr. He liked to carry the puck and had a great shot. There were not a lot of guys to back him up defensively on our team so it got him in a bit of trouble with the coach sometimes. He had a great sense of humor and enjoyed the game and the environment." According to Morris Mott, Maggs was "a good guy, but very much a loner off the ice."

Glover appreciated Maggs's ability to carry the puck but, in retrospect, had reservations about his new defenseman. "Darryl was a good player and he could carry the puck, but he was a playboy. I think he slept in his van for months."

Some of Maggs's teammates had a problem with the effort he was putting in on the ice and his off-ice preoccupation with playing golf. "He was just there for the holiday," said Joey Johnston. "I don't know if he lived in his van with his golf clubs. I think he had already signed with the WHA when he came here." Walt McKechnie added, "He worked on his golf swing in the dressing room."

Maggs ended his tenure with California much as he began it, with a great offensive effort. In the club's 1972-73 season finale against the Los Angeles Kings, Maggs assisted on all three Seals goals in a 3-1 California victory at the Oakland Coliseum. After the season was over, Maggs did sign with the WHA's Chicago Cougars. The Seals suddenly had nothing to show for trading Dick Redmond.

Maggs spent the next two seasons with the Cougars and was an integral part of their surprise run to the Avco World Trophy finals in 1973-74. Maggs led the WHA in playoff penalty minutes with 71 in 18 games and also scored three goals and eight points in the playoffs that year. After half a season with the Denver Spurs/Ottawa Civics franchise, Maggs was traded to the Indianapolis Racers. In 1976-77, Maggs had the best offensive season of his career, scoring 16 goals and 71 points in 81 games for Indianapolis. He was named to the first WHA all-star team. Maggs's offensive production fell off the following season and he was traded to the Cincinnati Stingers midway through the year. He played part of the 1978-79 season with Cincinnati before finishing the year playing for a team in Mannheim, Germany.

The Toronto Maple Leafs signed Maggs to a free-agent contract in December 1979. He played in five games for the Leafs before hanging up his skates for the last time. Maggs's final NHL statistics included 14 goals and 33 points in 135 games. In the WHA, he scored 51 times and finished with 228 points in 402 games.

Maggs never really established himself with the California Golden Seals. He was unable to overcome the shadow of Dick Redmond and the unrealistic expectations that went along with being traded for Redmond in a one-for-one deal. Had he stayed with the Seals and been given a chance to develop his skills, his future in Oakland may have been brighter but, like many players, he abandoned the Seals for the greener pastures of the WHA.

Ted McAneeley summed up his memories of Darryl Maggs by saying, "He had a lot of potential and played well at times, but he was not always focused so he never reached his potential." Unfortunately, that was true of a lot of players on the California Golden Seals.

Terry Murray

"We played together a long time. He was with me in Oakland and again in Philadelphia. He was a stay-at-home defenseman, nothing fancy, but he got the job done. He was not very fast on the ice. Off the ice, we were good friends. Every place I went in hockey, he was there."

—Reggie Leach on Terry Murray

Terry Murray was not a flashy hockey player. He played in 90 games for the California Golden Seals over parts of three seasons and scored a total of 17 points, all of them assists. In fact, Murray holds the distinction of playing the most games in a Seals sweater without scoring a goal (excluding goalies). But offensive play was not what Murray was about on the ice. He was about smart, positional play and clearing the puck out of his own zone. The Seals had a difficult time meeting those tasks on the Seals in 1972-73 and 1973-74, so Murray played a valuable role on the team. His teammates respected Murray for his determination, hard work and knowledge of the game.

Murray played his junior hockey with the Ottawa 67s. The 6'2", 190-pound native of Shawville, Quebec, was a defensive-oriented player even then, never scoring more than four goals and 28 points in any of his three seasons in juniors. Still, his size and defensive skills encouraged the Seals to select Murray with the 88th overall choice in the 1970 entry draft. For his first professional season, the Seals sent him down to their AHL farm club in Providence, where Murray scored one goal and 23 points. In 1971-72, Murray split time between the Seals farm club in Baltimore, the AHL's Boston Braves and the Oklahoma City Blazers of the CHL, both of which were Bruins farm teams at the time. He did not seem to figure into California's long-term plans. Fred Glover—who at different times in Murray's tenure in Oakland was the coach and general manager—recalled that Murray "went through a lot of shit" in the Seals organization. "He wasn't at the top of the list when we drafted him," Glover admitted, "but he was a good kid."

In 1972-73, the "good kid" finally got his chance to play in the NHL. Murray played 39 games for the Seals top farm team in Salt Lake City and after injuries hit, he appeared in 23 games for the Seals. He registered three assists in those 23 games and four penalty minutes.

Murray's teammates gave him the nickname "Me Too" because he was always saying "Me too, coach." Craig Patrick recalled the origin of Murray's unusual nickname. "He picked up the nickname in Baltimore," Patrick recalled. "One time, he was late for practice with another player. The two of them snuck onto the ice but the coach told them, 'Leave, I don't want to see you.' Well, Terry was behind the first guy and he asked, 'Me too, coach?' The nickname just sort of stuck." Stan Weir remembered that Murray "was also always saying 'me too' whenever the guys said they were going to a restaurant or something."

On the ice, Patrick appreciated what Murray brought to the team. "He was a steady, solid defenseman," Patrick said. "He was a serious, hardworking guy." Gary Croteau added, "Terry was a stay-at-home defenseman. He gave his all, game in and game out." Rick Smith recalled Murray as "a fifth defenseman-type and he filled the role very well. He was a reliable defenseman." To Morris Mott, "Terry was just a very steady player. Although he was not a great skater, he had great instincts in terms of positional play."

In 1973-74, Murray was a regular for the first time in his NHL career. He played in 58 games for the Seals and registered 12 assists and 48 penalty minutes. Murray continued his strong positional play on the blue line. While most fans wouldn't notice a defensive-oriented player like Murray, his teammates certainly did. Rick Kessell called Murray "a strong defenseman who didn't get the recognition he deserved."

Fellow defenseman Paul Shakes, who also played with Murray with the Salt Lake Golden Eagles, recalled Murray's strengths as a player. "He played the game hard and was not afraid to mix things up," Shakes said. "He cleared the net well and played the basics very well. He did not play a very offensive game, but he looked after his own end and made one pass out of the zone to get things started." Barry Cummins added that Murray's attitude and style were straightforward and simple. "He worked hard and was a strong, young player. He had some shortcomings but he played with the same style as he coaches. If you work hard, you can work through things and improve." Marshall Johnston added that Murray was "quiet and dedicated."

In 1974-75, Murray started the season with the Seals and played in nine games and registered two assists and eight penalty minutes before being returned to the Golden Eagles of the CHL. In 62 games with Salt Lake, he scored five goals and 35 points while picking up a career-high 122 penalty minutes. He helped lead the Golden Eagles to the CHL title that year, adding two goals and four points in 11 playoff games.

The Seals opted not to re-sign Murray after the 1974-75 season and the Flyers picked him up as a free agent in late September 1975. Old "Me Too" spent most of the season with the Flyers AHL farm club, the Richmond Robins. He was named to the first all-star team after the season was over, scoring eight goals and 56 points. The Flyers called him up for three games during the regular season and for the Stanley Cup playoffs, where he appeared in six games for Philadelphia and earned one assist.

The Flyers went to the Stanley Cup finals for a third consecutive year in 1976, but were defeated by the Montreal Canadiens in four straight games.

Murray remained active in professional hockey as a player until the 1981-82 season. He had two tours of duty with the Flyers, a brief stay with Detroit and played his final season with the Washington Capitals. Murray still spent significant time in the AHL and won back-to-back Eddie Shore Trophies as the AHL's best defenseman in 1977-78 and 1978-79. He didn't score his first NHL goal until 1980-81 and finished his NHL career with four goals and 80 points in 302 games.

Murray remained active in hockey and took up coaching shortly after his retirement as a player. He had successful head-coaching stints with the Washington Capitals and Philadelphia Flyers and later coached the Florida Panthers. Murray's 1996-97 Flyers team went to the Stanley Cup finals before losing to the Detroit Red Wings. Ironically enough, Murray was fired after that series, although he later returned to coaching with the Panthers.

Many of his teammates were not sure Murray would coach in the NHL because of his quiet demeanor. "I was surprised he became a coach," Gilles Meloche said. "He never said a word in the dressing room." Ted McAneeley, who roomed with Murray on the road, was also surprised he joined the coaching profession. "He was the last guy I thought would become a coach because he never said he was interested in that as a player. Still, he has been very successful at it."

Bob Stewart seemed a lot less surprised that "Me Too" became a coach. "He was a student of the game," Stewart said. "He would talk more about plays and how to match up against a particular opponent." Joey Johnston added that Murray "was a steady fifth or sixth defenseman, a nice, quiet guy." Johnston didn't seem shocked that Murray became a successful coach, adding, "It seems to me that fifth and sixth defensemen or third- or fourth-line forwards became better students of the game."

Today, Murray lives in Maine and remains one of many former Seals players still active in hockey. After being relieved as coach of the Panthers midway through the 2000-2001 season, he joined the Flyers organization as a scout. In 2003-2004, he became an assistant coach for Philadelphia and works extensively with video and scouting opponents' tendencies for the Flyers. His brother Bryan, who was GM in Washington while Terry was coaching, is now GM of the Ottawa Senators.

Hilliard Graves summed up the kind of player Murray was. "He went a long way with his physical talents," Graves said. "He was a journeyman defenseman—a good one, but not a great one. He has done very well as a coach." Terry Murray, the quiet and unheralded one, has seen his hard work pay off with success.

Craig Patrick

"He was outstanding. Skillwise, he was more of a defensive player, but he added so much to the team. He added dependability and was a great skater. He brought as much to the dressing room as he did to the ice. He was the heart of the team, a central ingredient. He was unsung and he didn't get all the attention he deserved."

—Rick Smith on Craig Patrick

Anyone even vaguely familiar with the history of hockey and the NHL is familiar with the Patrick family. Craig's grandfather, Lester Patrick, is in the Hockey Hall of Fame and was the original general manager of the New York Rangers. He helped lead New York to three Stanley Cups. His father, Lynn Patrick, played for the Rangers for 10 years and later served as coach of the Broadway Blueshirts and GM of the Boston Bruins. Lynn Patrick was elected to the Hall of Fame in 1980. Craig's uncle Muzz Patrick also served as head coach and general manager of the Rangers. Needless to say, the Patrick name carried high expectations around the NHL and Craig Patrick carried the burden of expectations from being part of that famous family.

Patrick grew up rooting for the Bruins because his father was the GM there during his formative years. "Doug Mohns was a favorite of mine because of how he could skate and shoot," Patrick recalled. "Don McKenny was a great skater and playmaker."

Instead of playing junior hockey for an extended time, Patrick attended the University of Denver. It was there that he realized he might have a legitimate chance to play in the NHL. "When I was in college, I went back to St. Louis to watch a playoff game between the Blues and, I think, it was Minnesota," Patrick recalled. "I played against some of the people who were playing in the game so I realized if *they* could play in the NHL, I probably could, too."

The road to the NHL was not an easy one for the 6', 190-pound native of Detroit. After graduating for the University of Denver, Patrick spent two years with the U.S. National Team before signing an amateur tryout contract with the Montreal Voyageurs late in the 1970-71 season. Before the following season, Patrick was invited to the Seals training camp. "I was thrilled," Patrick said. "Over the summer, the Seals made an arrangement for me to go to camp on a sort of tryout. If I made the team, there was a prearranged deal for my rights. If I didn't make the team, I would be dealt back to the Canadiens organization and probably would have played in Saginaw. I could have gone on to the 1972 Olympic Team, but I was 25 and really wanted to play in the NHL."

Patrick made the Seals and appeared in 59 games as a rookie in 1971-72. Used mostly in a checking and penalty-killing role, Patrick scored eight goals and 11 points for the Seals that season. "I killed penalties with him," said Marshall Johnston. "They don't come any better than Craig."

Patrick's first NHL goal was scored on Halloween night of 1971 at the Oakland Coliseum. Patrick beat Roger Crozier of the Sabres during a 2-2 tie between the Sabres and Seals. Still, the predominantly defensive role frustrated Patrick at times. Gerry Pinder, who played with Patrick during his rookie season, recalled that "Vic didn't play Patty as much as he wanted to and he was used in a defensive role. I thought he had good skills. He was a better player than people gave him credit for. He was quiet away from the ice but you couldn't find a better guy."

Coach Vic Stasiuk himself respected Patrick but couldn't quite put a finger on how to best utilize him. "He was an in betweener," Stasiuk said. "He was not a powerful skater, but he sure had the desire." Despite the fact that playing time was scarce under Stasiuk, the rookie wing appreciated his coach's efforts. "Vic was very enthusiastic and had good ideas about the game," Patrick said. "He was good one-on-one with the players and was a good teacher."

Patrick was one of the few Seals who actually appreciated the white skates the team wore in 1971-72. "I liked the white ones," Patrick said, "but they got dirty too fast. It took too much to clean them." Ironically, as despised as the white skates were, they are now collector's items. A sports memorabilia dealer recently listed a pair of Patrick's white skates for US$800.

As for owner Charlie Finley, Patrick was not very critical of him. "I thought he was a good owner," Patrick said. "He treated us well. If we were not playing well, he'd let us know and he didn't spare any words. He could be tough on you when he wasn't pleased with your play."

Patrick's most difficult game as a member of the Seals came on February 23, 1972. "The most disappointing game was when we played the Bruins in Oakland," Patrick said. "We had a good lead, something like three goals going into the third period, and we lost 8-6. There was a lot of hope in that game; things were going so well. Then, we had a big letdown."

While Patrick is known as a quiet person, he was liked and respected by his teammates. "He could fly and put the puck in the net," Bobby Sheehan recalled. "He and his wife invited me to dinner and, as a single guy, I appreciated that. Craig was down to earth." Wayne Carleton recalled Patrick as "serious" and "an executive type," even back in his playing days.

Another thing that Patrick's teammates emphasized was that the young winger rarely mentioned much about his background. "He didn't talk much of his family history," former roommate Gary Croteau said. "He was quiet and respectful of the talent around him. He was a lefthanded shot playing right wing, a great skater and a student of the game." Still, although Patrick rarely spoke of his family legacy, most of his teammates were aware of it and what it meant for Craig Patrick. "It was not easy to accomplish what he did with his family name and the expectations that go along with it," Norm Ferguson said. "There was a lot of pressure on him."

In 1972-73, Patrick's role changed dramatically. Suddenly, he was placed on a scoring line with left wing Joey Johnston and center Walt McKechnie. The JJ-M-P line worked well together and Patrick responded by scoring a career-high 20 goals and 42 points in 71 games. Remarkably, he recorded only six penalty minutes for the entire season. The Seals players voted Patrick their unsung hero that year.

Both of his linemates appreciated what Patrick brought to their line. "Patty, what a great guy," center Walt McKechnie said. "He got 20 goals on a line with Joey Johnston and me. He was a serious guy and a hardworking guy, and he was really dedicated." Left wing Joey Johnston remembered Patrick as "an honest, down-to-earth guy. Not fancy, but steady. He just did his job."

Patrick attributed the success of the line to the varied abilities of all three players. "I provided defense and I could make a play," Patrick said. "Both of those guys could put the puck in the net." Morris Mott thought that playing on a line with McKechnie and Johnston brought out the best in Patrick as a player and added a certain chemistry. "He was a good, smart player as long as he was playing with good players. Craig was a very solid guy. He got along very well with the team characters such as Stan Gilbertson or Walt McKechnie and Joey Johnston, but he was a much less rowdy person than they were."

Patrick certainly appreciated new coach Fred Glover's giving him more ice time and an opportunity to play a regular shift. "I liked Freddie," Patrick said. "He was hardworking and he liked people who worked hard. He preferred to play the game to coaching it. He was a fiery guy and very gruff."

Needless to say, many of Patrick's finest offensive efforts came during the 1972-73 season. He tended to score goals in bunches. Although he never scored a hat trick while with the Seals, he scored two goals in a game five times during the 1972-73 season. His most productive game was a two-goal, one-assist effort on December 22, 1972, against Buffalo.

On March 25, 1973, Patrick notched his 20th goal of the season during an 8-5 win over the Red Wings in Oakland. Despite his fine offensive season in 1972-73, Patrick's teammates appreciated his defensive play. Goalie Gilles Meloche recalled that Craig was "a good, honest hockey player. All he cared about was his own end of the rink, and there were not too many players on our team who were like that."

After the 1972-73 season was over, Patrick admitted that some members of the Seals got demoralized after losing so many games. "Even when things weren't going right last year, we all had our individual pride," Patrick said. "Some of the players didn't seem to care and that made me mad. But most of us didn't like being a joke around the NHL."

The 1973-74 season was one of frustration for Patrick personally and for the Seals as a team. Patrick tore knee ligaments and missed 19 games. His offensive production fell to 10 goals and 30 points in 59 games. Despite the lack of scoring, Patrick still had the utmost respect of his teammates. "Craig knew his role on the ice and developed into a very solid two-way player," defenseman Ted McAneeley said. "He was quiet, but he was always thinking ahead." Patrick still scored in bunches: twice during the 1973-74 season he had two goals in one game.

Patrick recalled the streaking incident during the last game of that season at the Oakland Coliseum with a smile. "I thought it was funny," he said. "I was on the bench so I guess my view was seeing things from behind."

In February 1974, Charlie Finley sold the Seals to the NHL, who ran the club for the remainder of the season. "When the league got control of the team, it was unsettling," Patrick admitted. "I believed something would happen to make it viable. I knew the league had expanded and didn't want to lose this team." When the league took over, Glover resigned as coach and was replaced by Marshall Johnston. Patrick recalled that Johnston had the respect of the players in the locker room. "Marshall was a thinker," Patrick said. "I was very fond of him and he was very well-respected."

When Patrick was with the Seals, he always relished beating St. Louis, where his father was working at the time. "Naturally, I never want to have a bad game—but against St. Louis, I really want to play my best," Patrick said in an interview with Garry Mueller during the 1973-74 season. "My dad likes to kid me a lot so I want to be sure I have something to tease him about—like a victory over the Blues."

Patrick started 1974-75 with the Seals, but on November 11, 1974, he was sent to St. Louis along with Stan Gilbertson for Butch Williams and Dave Gardner. In 14 games with the Seals before he was traded, Patrick scored twice and added an assist. The move to St. Louis wasn't an easy one for Patrick. Craig's father, Lynn Patrick, was the executive vice president of the club and under his father's watchful eye Patrick scored only six goals and 15 points in 43 games.

Prior to the 1975-76 season, Patrick was traded to the Kansas City Scouts, another of hockey's failed expansion teams. In 80 games with Kansas City, Patrick scored 17 goals and 35 points. Patrick split 1976-77 between the "new" Minnesota Fighting Saints of the WHA and the Washington Capitals. He remained active as a player until the 1978-79 season, which he spent most of with the Tulsa Oilers of the CHL. Patrick's career NHL statistics include 72 goals and 163 points in 401 games.

After his playing career was over, Patrick remained in hockey. He was the assistant coach and assistant general manager of the 1980 U.S. Olympic hockey team that shocked the world by winning the gold medal in Lake Placid, New York. Shortly after that, Patrick joined the Rangers organization as general manager and later as interim coach. The Rangers made the playoffs every season during Patrick's tenure.

On December 5, 1989, Patrick was named general manager and interim coach of the Pittsburgh Penguins. He helped build the Penguins team that won back-to-back Stanley Cups in 1991 and 1992 and drafted such players as Jaromir Jagr and Markus Naslund. The Penguins made the playoffs every year of Patrick's tenure until 2001-02, despite the club's persistent and often severe financial problems. Patrick was inducted into the Hockey Hall of Fame in the builder category in 2001.

Craig Patrick's success in management did not surprise many of his ex-teammates. Gary Jarrett remarked that Patrick is "a real student of the game and that's why he's so successful now. He's probably been the best GM in the NHL for the last 10 to 12 years." Stan Weir was also not surprised that Patrick succeeded as a GM. "Craig is a very classy person," Weir said. "He's a hard worker and a solid individual. He is where I thought he'd be today."

Barry Cummins, who only played with Patrick for part of one season, summed up "Patty" by saying, "He used his skills to his advantage on the ice. He was not the greatest player, but he had a great career because he played within himself. He knew his weaknesses and worked to correct them. He knew his strengths and how to use them. He had great wheels and was a good checker." And now, he's a member of the Hockey Hall of Fame.

Walt McKechnie

"Walt was a great centerman and one of the best puck handlers in the league at that time. He was doing things then—like passing the puck between the feet or off the skates—that guys wouldn't do for years. He had a dry sense of humor and was a good team guy."

—Gary Croteau on Walt McKechnie

Walt McKechnie always dreamed about playing hockey as a child. The London, Ontario, native grew up rooting for the Toronto Maple Leafs and was fortunate enough to be drafted by the Leafs in the first round of the 1963 Amateur Draft. After two productive seasons with the London Nationals, McKechnie was traded by the Leafs to the Phoenix Roadrunners of the WHL, where he was named rookie of the year in 1967-68. By the end of that season, the 6'2", 195-pound center had been traded to the Minnesota North Stars and appeared in four late-season games and the playoffs for Minnesota. Although he did not register a point in the regular season, McKechnie scored three goals and had five points in nine playoff games for the North Stars, which was more than respectable for an unproven rookie. The performance earned big Walt a spot with the North Stars the following season, but in 58 games, McKechnie scored only five goals and 14 points in a limited role.

The North Stars even sent him back to Phoenix so McKechnie could regain his confidence. He split the next two seasons between the North Stars and their minor league clubs in Iowa and Cleveland. Despite putting up gaudy minor league numbers, the North Stars couldn't find a spot on their roster for their young center.

Finally, on May 20, 1971, McKechnie was traded to the California Golden Seals along with Joey Johnston in exchange for Dennis Hextall. Hextall had been the Seals leading scorer the previous year, so there was pressure on the two youngsters to produce right away. Still, McKechnie was pleased with the deal. "I was really young and all I wanted to do was play," McKechnie said. "I was not playing in Minnesota, and I wanted to play so I was happy."

McKechnie's first season in Oakland was a frustrating one for the big center. Nagging injuries limited him to just 56 games and prevented him from playing with his usual effectiveness when he was on the ice. He finished the 1971-72 season with 11 goals 31 points. Remarkably, despite the injuries, McKechnie led the team in plus minus that year with a plus two, one of the few times a Seals player had a positive rating in the team's history.

One of McKechnie's roles on the Seals that first season was killing penalties. Carol Vadnais remembered McKechnie as "a good team player. He was good with the puck and a good penalty killer."

Perhaps McKechnie's greatest asset on the ice was his stickhandling. He had a long reach and handled the puck very well. Fellow center Bobby Sheehan said, "This guy could stickhandle through everybody. He had a lot of one-liners and was a real prankster."

Gary Jarrett, who played with McKechnie in 1971-72 likened the big center to "a conductor. He would stand in the middle of the ice and direct everybody where to go. He was a good centerman and puck handler." McKechnie also played some on the power play. Ernie Hicke remembered McKechnie as "a big guy who could pass and shoot. He was great on the power play. He was big and strong in front of the net, a bit like Phil Esposito."

Looking back on his time with the Seals, McKechnie recalled some reasons why the team may not have been as successful as it could have been. "We were a really young bunch and we had a lot of free spirits," McKechnie said. "There were no drugs on our team, at least as far as I knew, but we drank our share of beers and maybe had a few more rums than we should have. We all wanted to win and we didn't win enough. If he had more direction and Charlie Finley would have cared more about hockey, we might have had a chance to do something. Mr. Finley really didn't care about hockey and I think the WHA proved that." McKechnie also felt that the team's refusal to promote the sport in the Bay Area was another problem. "They never spent money," he said. "It was low budget. The Public Relations Department had no budget to work with."

In the off-season after the 1971-72 season, the WHA was formed. Some NHL stars like Bobby Hull and Bernie Parent jumped to the new league. The very existence of the new league caused salaries to go up at an unprecedented rate as teams paid unheard of salaries to their best players to keep them from jumping ship. All NHL teams, that is, except the Seals. California was the hardest hit franchise in the league that first WHA season, losing nine players to the renegade league. The Seals suddenly lost almost half their roster, including their top two scorers from 1971-72 and went from an up and coming young team to a team short on talent and experience.

In 1972-73, the Seals struggled as a team but Walt McKechnie was able to take advantage of the opportunity given to him by the mass defection to the WHA. McKechnie suddenly centered the Seals top line between left wing Joey Johnston and right wing Craig Patrick. The JJ-M-P line worked remarkably well with both Johnston and Patrick topping the 20 goal mark while McKechnie led the Seals in assists with 38 and in points with 54. All three players had career best statistics that season, at least up until that point.

Rick Smith recalled McKechnie by saying, "Walt was as talented as can be, a top scorer. He was on the line with Joey Johnston and Craig Patrick and that was our number one line. He went on to a great career but Walt didn't play as well as he should have in Oakland."

Linemate Joey Johnston appreciated McKechnie's passing skills. "He was an excellent center ice man," Johnston said. "He was an excellent playmaker and not selfish with the puck. I'd tell him, 'I need ten shots to score one goal' and he tried to get me those shots."

The losing did take its toll on McKechnie. "I was so young and had so much energy. We thought we played hard on the ice. We could have been a better team with more discipline and control. We needed some veterans to tell us what to do. Garry Young brought in all these young players and we were his guys. I guess there wasn't a lot of pressure to perform under those circumstances."

Reggie Leach also thought that all the losses the Seals experienced had an effect on McKechnie after awhile. "He hated losing," Leach said. "He tried so hard. He was always talking about other players and how good they were. He was always worried about everybody else. He got mad when we didn't play well. He loved the game and always had his head in the game."

Marshall Johnston, who was both a teammate and later a coach of McKechnie's thinks that part of the problem was that McKechnie "was a good player but he lacked self confidence. He could have been even better than he was."

One person that McKechnie did not always get along with was the Seals new coach in 1972-73, Fred Glover. McKechnie recalled one incident in particular. "I used to like to watch the Montreal Canadiens practice. I suggested we should do some of the things they do in practice in our practices. Well, let's just say it wasn't too well received." Glover, for his part, thought McKechnie had a thin skin. "I worked with Walt when he was a kid in London," Glover recalled. "I ran a hockey school in St. Thomas with Jack Gordon and later I ran it myself. I always thought he would become a good hockey player. I think his temperament got to him. If you got on his back, he thought he was being picked on."

Picked on or not, McKechnie did recall an incident during the tumultuous 1972-73 season in which things came to a boil between players and coach. "A lot of the players were not pleased with the coaching staff," McKechnie recalled. "We had a team meeting and Charlie Finley flew in from Chicago. One player spoke and voiced the opinion of the team. Charlie Finley listened and then said, 'If you don't like my fuckin' coach, you can get off my fuckin' team.'" Needless to say, no changes were being made.

Despite the refusal to address the players' gripes about coaching and his decision to let nine players defect to the rival league, McKechnie did feel Finley treated the players well in general. "I got to see two World Series from behind third base. He bought us all Gucci shoes in downtown New York. He had the store opened for us early on Sunday morning. In Chicago, he took us out for a big roast beef dinner. He could be very generous."

Morris Mott recalled a particularly tough time McKechnie had during a game in Buffalo. "Walt was defending in our end of the rink," Mott said. "As he picked off a pass, he accidentally fired it towards the top corner of our own net. Gilles Meloche saw it and made a great save and held on for a face-off. The guys on the bench all started to laugh. Eventually, McKechnie started to laugh, too."

In 1973-74, McKechnie was back on the Seals top line with Joey Johnston and he had another productive season. Despite appearing in just 63 games, McKechnie topped the 20 goal mark for the first time in his NHL career, finishing the season with 23 goals and 52.

When asked to describe his most memorable game with the Seals, McKechnie hesitated. "We never made the playoffs so it's hard to say," he answered. Despite his failure to pick a most memorable contest, McKechnie had many strong offensive games. Among his finer offensive efforts were a two goal one assist game against the Penguins on October 27, 1972 which helped lead the Seals to a 6-3 victory and a three assist effort in a 7-4 win over the Maple Leafs on March 23, 1973.

Defenseman Bob Stewart recalled many of the attributes that McKechnie brought to the Seals. "Walt was a big, tall centerman. He was a good stickhandler and playmaker. He had long arms like

Phil Esposito and made soft flip passes. He was also great on face-offs." McKechnie was also popular with his teammates. "He would do anything for you," Rick Kessell recalled. "Walt was a good guy." Ted McAneeley recalled that, "off the ice, he knew the right places to go in every city."

Although wins were hard to come by while he was with the Seals, McKechnie did truly appreciate Seals fans and what they meant to the team. "The fans were the best," McKechnie said. "We had 5,000-6,000 hard core fans. They were the best fans you could imagine. They were unbelievable. We would pack the place for good teams but otherwise, it was the same 5,000-6,000."

Late in the 1973-74 season, the NHL took over ownership the Seals and the team tried to get younger and cut payroll. When the season ended, the Seals traded three of their top four scorers from the year before including McKechnie. As part of a complicated three-team deal that involved the intra-league draft, the Seals acquired Rangers defenseman Jim Neilson, the Rangers acquired Bruins center Derek Sanderson and the Bruins received McKechnie. After a half season in Boston with a limited role, McKechnie was traded to Detroit. In 1975-76, he had a career best 26 goals and 82 points for the Red Wings and added 25 more goals the following season. He later played briefly for the Washington Capitals before playing for the Cleveland Barons, Toronto Maple Leafs and Colorado Rockies before returning to Detroit for his final two NHL seasons. McKechnie retired from hockey after spending the 1983-84 season with the Salt Lake Golden Eagles of the CHL. His final NHL totals are 214 goals and 606 points in 955 career contests. McKechnie had the unfortunate distinction of playing on some very bad teams. Despite playing nearly 1,000 regular season contests, Walt McKechnie only played in 15 NHL playoff games and nine of those came as a rookie with the North Stars.

Although he playing only three seasons with the Seals, McKechnie left his mark on the club's record books. He is fourth all-time in assists, tied for tenth in goals and in seventh place overall in points scored.

Paul Shakes summed up the affable McKechnie by describing him as "a big, tall guy who could stickhandle in a watermelon patch. He was a great stickhandler and a good guy to play with. He was a good teacher who had a good eye for putting the puck into the net." And for three seasons, he was one of the best players on the California Golden Seals.

Bob Stewart

"He was a rock on defense. He was a team player and easily the captain of the team. He was a fun loving guy and a great guy. He was the third man in the trade that sent me to Oakland, but Bob Stewart made that trade for Garry Young. He stood up for his teammates. When he was with Cleveland, he was always in demand for trades. I know the Bruins wanted to get him although we never quite did."

— Rick Smith on Bob Stewart

Defenseman Bob Stewart was born in Charlottetown, Prince Edward Island and played his junior hockey with the Oshawa Generals. "When I was 19 and in my last year of junior A, I got feedback from coaches and scouts would talk to me," Stewart said, recalling the first time he thought the NHL was realistically in his future. "I took the game more seriously then."

The Bruins drafted Stewart 13th overall in the 1970 entry draft. His first season of pro hockey was spent with the Oklahoma City Blazers of the CHL where Stewart earned a reputation as a tough guy. He accumulated 270 penalty minutes in just 61 games in 1970-71. In 1971-72, Stewart started off with the Blazers before being promoted to the Bruins top farm club, the Boston Braves. Eventually, Stewart was called up to the Bruins for eight games. He was held scoreless and picked up 15 penalty minutes. Then, on February 23, 1972, Stewart was traded to the Seals with Rick Smith and Reggie Leach in exchange for Carol Vadnais.

Stewart would remain with the Seals for the rest of the franchise's time in the Bay Area. "To me, it was an opportunity," Stewart said about the trade. "It was the break of my career. The Bruins had won two Stanley Cups in three years and were very strong on defense with Bobby Orr, Dallas

Smith, Rick Smith, Don Awrey and Ted Green. On the Seals, I knew I could play regularly." There was a bit of an adjustment for Stewart going from the eventual Stanley Cup champion Bruins to the Seals. "The Seals were an expansion team trying to find its place," Stewart recalled. "The Bruins had a championship attitude. With the Seals, it was more like 'Can we make the playoffs? Can we get by?' We just didn't have the caliber of players that other teams had. When we played Philadelphia, Montreal and Boston, if we weren't on top of our game, we could be killed. Charlie Finley was not building up the team."

The very first thing that Stewart learned about when he arrived in Oakland was that he would be wearing white skates. "I was flabbergasted," Stewart recalled. "I got off the plane in San Francisco after I was traded and the trainer said, 'Give me your skates' and he white washed them. I went to warm-up with my spare skates on and I was the only one wearing dark skates. I ended up getting paint on my gloves and fingers. Other players would make comments to us like, 'Do you ballet in those as well?'"

Stewart finished the 1971-72 season with the Seals scoring one goal and three points in 16 games. He also picked up 44 penalty minutes in that short amount of time. "When you first come into the league, people on other teams want to find out if you will retaliate or not," Stewart told Joe DeLoach of the *Hayward Daily Review.* "After a while, they just tend to leave you alone."

Stewart tallied his first NHL goal on March 12, 1972 in a game against the Blues at Oakland. "I scored on a slap shot from the point," Stewart recalled. Jacques Caron was the goalie and the game ended in a 2-2 tie. Some teammates remember Stewart as a bit green when he joined the Seals. "He was a raw boned, tough kid," Gerry Pinder said. "He hadn't developed his skills yet to a high degree when he joined our team." That quickly changed as Stewart gained experience.

In 1972-73, after the mass defection of players to the WHA, the Seals found themselves losing consistently. Former GM Garry Young took over as coach early in the season and Bob Stewart liked working with Young. "He was a scout in Boston and he drafted me there," Stewart recalled. "He wanted to put a good team together. He was more of a players' coach and was good to play for. Still, he was limited by funds and salaries."

After the defection of so many players, a young defenseman like Stewart got the chance to play right away. Stewart was aware of the benefits of playing for the Seals. "I had an opportunity to play and learn and get a lot of ice time," he said. "It was great playing against great players. I got about 30 minutes of ice time per game, I killed penalties and I took a regular shift. I also enjoyed the dressing room and the people on the team."

In 1972-73, Stewart scored four goals and 21 points in 63 games. He also picked up a career high 181 penalty minutes. Stewart quickly fell into a bit of a policeman's role on the ice. "Bob was a steady defenseman although he was not very mobile," Craig Patrick said. "He was a good guy who took care of his teammates on and off the ice."

Despite the fact that he saw a lot of combat on ice, many of his teammates felt that Stewart did not necessarily relish the role of enforcer on a Seals team that critics felt was lacking in tough, physical hockey players. "Bob was tough when he had to be but he didn't like the tough guy role," Hilliard Graves said. "He had a good career and is a good guy." Gary Croteau said, "It's tough for a young defenseman to break in on a young team. Bob could handle himself really well, though."

Despite his relative youth, Stewart quickly earned the respect of his new teammates. "Bob was a real competitor, he gave 100% every night," Walt McKechnie recalled. "He was blocking shots all the time. He was one of the young breed." Ted McAneeley added, "Bob was very tough, very intense and a good hockey player." Even Seals coach Fred Glover, who took over after Garry Young was fired early in the 1972-73 season, appreciated what he got out of Stewart. "He was a tough one," said Glover, who was known for his toughness during his own playing career. "He played the same way all the time. He could shoot a puck, too, he was not a great finisher but he came to play."

While Stewart was considered a good defensive defenseman, he recalled one time when his opponent made him look foolish. "I prided myself on being tough to go around one on one," Stewart said. "Once, Whitey Widing of the Kings came down on me one on one and put the puck between my feet and beat me. I was on my knees and the puck was in the net and I was thinking to myself, 'God, I can't hide.'"

Stewart also remembered an encounter with Seals owner Charlie Finley prior to the 1973-74 season. "We were at a banquet and the A's had just won the World Series," Stewart said. "Charlie invited us there as guests. Mr. Finley pulled me over and introduced me to Sal Bando, who was then captain of the A's. Mr. Finley said, 'Sal, show them your (World Series) ring.' I had an old school ring on and it also had a green stone so I switched rings with Bando. It took them awhile to figure that out."

The 1973-74 season was a frustrating one for Stewart. Various injuries limited him to just two goals and seven points in 47 games. Although he played in just over half of the team's games, he still led the Seals in penalty minutes that year with 69. Stewart suffered a pulled groin muscle followed later by a separated shoulder. "I never really got going," the big 6'1", 206 pound defenseman said. "Every time I was healthy, it seemed like I would suffer another injury."

It was a tough year for Stewart and the Seals, but it had one highlight for the big defenseman. "We beat Montreal in Montreal," Stewart said. "When we went out there, the comments in the paper were something like, 'We're on a winning streak and Oakland's coming to town.' They figured we were an easy win and it pumped us up real good." The Seals pulled an upset over the defending Stanley Cup champion Canadiens 4-3. It was one of the more satisfying wins for rookie coach and former teammate Marshall Johnson. "He was a defensive defenseman and a sharp guy," Stewart said of Johnston. "It was tough on him making the transition to coaching. He was good. He went from having a few beers with the guys to making sure we only had two."

Off the ice, Stewart liked to have fun with the guys. Stan Weir recalled that he liked to hang out at Arnie's Time Out, a local bar and restaurant a lot. "Bob was tough and a bit of a loose cannon on the ice," Morris Mott said. "He was a good teammate who liked to laugh and liked a party. There was nothing vicious about him off the ice. He really wanted to play well every game." Rick Kessell called Stewart, "a typical Prince Edward Island guy." Nothing scared him or bothered him. He didn't have a mean bone in his body off the ice."

Stewart enjoyed living in the Bay Area and bought a house in Pleasanton, California. It was certainly very different from the Maritimes where he grew up. "It's unbelievable the number of things to do here," Stewart told John Porter of *The Oakland Tribune.* "You can spend every day doing something different—the zoo, Fisherman's Wharf, a football game or a baseball game are just some of them."

Late in the 1973-74 season, the Seals also had a female streaker skate across the ice. Stewart wasn't all that thrilled with the fact that he missed most of it. "I was usually the first person on the ice," Stewart explained. "My ritual was to go out and pick up a head of steam. All I saw was this bare ass heading off the ice. By the time I turned around after skating around, she was gone."

In 1974-75, Stewart was named an alternate captain of the Seals. Despite the fact that he was just 24 years old, he was already one of the more senior members of the Seals in terms of service to the club. Dave Gardner even called Stewart, "One of the elder statesman on our team." Then he recalled the frustration Stewart had playing on the Seals. "We got beat so badly physically and he took the brunt of it," Gardner said. "He played tough but we had nobody on our team to back him up. He was a big guy and one of Jack Evans favorite players."

Veteran Jim Neilson, who was often teamed with Stewart on defense added, "Bob was a good player. He was nothing fancy but he was a hard working, steady stay at home defenseman." In 1974-75, Stewart rebounded to play in 68 games and scored five goals and 17 points. He also added 93 penalty minutes. Unfortunately, the injury bug hit him again late in the season and he missed the last dozen games of the season with an injured knee. Stewart had some big games in 1974-75 including a one goal one assist effort against Boston on February 21, 1975 that helped lead the Seals to a 6-4 upset win at the Oakland Coliseum Arena. "Bob was a good team man," Spike Huston said. "He was hard hitting and he would back anybody up. He was not a great skater, but he got by."

In 1975-76, Stewart had the honor of being named captain of the Seals. A week after Jim Neilson was injured in November the Seals named Stewart captain on December 3, 1975. He was the last captain in Seals history. "Being captain gave me a perspective that everything you do is not just for yourself but for the team as well," Stewart said. "That is both on and off the ice. I tried to lead by example. I tried to get the players to work together and play together. Off the ice, we did charity work with burn victims. I tried to get the name of the team out there more. It makes you a better person. I was captain of my junior team in Oshawa as well."

If Bob Murdoch is any indicator, Stewart did his job as captain well. "He taught me about off ice life," Murdoch said. "How to act away form the ice and on the road. He was a classy guy, the captain of our team and a great guy." Wayne King recalled that as captain, Stewart was "always trying to help you out."

Fred Ahern indicated how his teammates felt about Stewart. "He was the backbone of our defense," Ahern said. "He was a tough kid but a real gentleman. He commanded a lot of respect." Wayne Merrick added, "Bob was a tough intimidating type guy, a stay at home defenseman. He was as good as any defenseman in the league and a good leader."

In 1975-76, Stewart played in a career high (to that point) 76 games and scored four goals and 21 points. He also accumulated 112 penalty minutes. Although he missed only four games during the regular season, Stewart was forced to undergo knee surgery after the season ended. During the off-season, Stewart also got a bit of a shock when he found out the Seals were moving to Cleveland to become the Cleveland Barons. "We read about it in the paper," Stewart recalled. "Then we got calls from other players. Later, there was a press release. It was a rude awakening and a big move from Oakland to Cleveland."

Stewart played two seasons for the Barons in Cleveland and both years he provided steady defense. When the Barons merged with the North Stars after the 1977-78 season, Minnesota protected Stewart in the dispersal draft before trading him to the St. Louis Blues the very same day. After a little more than a year in St. Louis, Stewart was traded to the Pittsburgh Penguins where he finished his career in 1979-80. That year, Stewart also got his first and only taste of Stanley Cup playoff action, scoring one goal and one assist in five postseason games. In 575 career NHL games, Stewart scored 27 goals and 128 points and picked up 809 penalty minutes. Stewart also left his mark on the Seals record book, tying for fifth place in games played with 270 and standing second all-time in penalty minutes with 499.

Today, Stewart lives in the St. Louis area with his wife. He has two children and a grandson. Stewart has been a vice president and branch manager for First Star Bank for almost 20 years working in the mortgage department.

Barry Cummins remembered his former teammate, Bob Stewart by saying, "He was a big man and he was physically strong. Teams did not like to put the puck in his corner. He liked the physical play and got a lot of respect from the other teams." Stewart got a lot of respect from his own teammates as well and he was a major part of the history of the California Golden Seals.

Joey Johnston

"He was a character and he was fun both on and off the ice. He had the ability to play the game; in fact, he was one of our best players. He was a tough player, too. He wasn't that big, but he didn't get pushed around."

—Reggie Leach on Joey Johnston

Peterborough, Ontario native Joey Johnston is the answer to the trivia question: who is the all-time leading scorer in the history of the California Golden Seals. Johnston's name is all over the Seals record book. He is first all-time in goals scored, tied for second in assists, is first all-time in points scored (by one point over Ted Hampson) fourth all-time in penalty minutes and third highest in games played. In some ways, Johnston was the quintessential Seals player: he was immensely talented, was a bit of a free spirit, had a little too much fun off the ice and was very frustrated by losing. Still, Johnston evolved into a leader on the Seals and was eventually named team captain. Had he remained healthy, there is little doubt Johnston would have had a solid NHL career.

Johnston played his junior hockey with the Peterborough Petes. He was not a big goal scorer in juniors, never even reaching double digits in a single season. The New York Rangers selected Johnston with the eighth overall selection in the 1966 entry draft. After a productive season with the Rangers CHL farm team in Omaha, he was traded to the Minnesota North Stars prior to the 1968-69 season. At age 19, he played in 11 games for the North Stars and scored his first NHL goal. "I was with Minnesota and played a few games up there but I lacked confidence," Johnston admitted. "I was busy watching the experienced guys." The North Stars sent Johnston back to their CHL affiliate in Memphis where "Joey the Jet" scored 20 goals. The following year, he netted another 20 goals with the Iowa Stars and in 1970-71, he tallied 27 goals and 74 points for the AHL's Cleveland Barons.

Just after the 1970-71 season, the North Stars traded Johnston and Walt McKechnie to the Seals for Dennis Hextall. "I was happy to go to Oakland," Johnston recalled. "I didn't know Garry Young but the Seals had new management and were rebuilding with younger guys so I knew at least I would get a chance."

While Johnston got a chance as a rookie to play with the Seals, he was limited to third line duty and scored 15 goals and 32 points in 77 games. In his first season with the Seals, Johnston got by on grit and his potential. "He was a tough mother," Gary Jarrett said. "He wouldn't back down from anyone. He played hard every game and got beat up constantly. He was a good player as well as a tough guy." Gerry Pinder, who played left wing on the Seals top line that season called Johnston, "One of the most genuine guys I've ever met. He was tough and strong. He played hard and was a good skater."

Off the ice, Johnston quickly became one of the more popular players on the team. "Joey was a real funny guy," Bobby Sheehan said. "I loved playing with him. If you ever got into trouble, he would always help you out." He also developed a reputation for indulging in a little too much to drink off the ice.

The Seals coach in Johnston's rookie year was Vic Stasiuk. Stasiuk recalled his first year left winger as "A hard worker. He was fast enough although not a speedster. He was an aggressive forechecker and a great team man. He would adjust to any to any shakeup in the lines. He was a good player but not a star."

Johnston appreciated Stasiuk as a coach as well. "I liked Vic Stasiuk," Johnston said. "He talked to us a lot more than Freddie Glover did. He is a good man and he had good ideas. I don't know how they let him go…maybe because he liked me. If the coach talks to you, you feel more a part of it. If not, it takes a few more beers."

"The Jet" remembered the Seals 12-1 defeat at the hands of the Rangers at Madison Square Garden in November 25, 1971. "We had guys who didn't want to go on the ice or wouldn't go on," Johnston recalled. "So I went on. I think I was a minus eight that game, but I didn't care about my plus minus. If somebody wanted to come off, I went on."

A more positive memory from Johnston's rookie year was the night he tallied his first NHL hat trick: March 8, 1972. In that game, the Seals defeated the Sabers 6-3 in Oakland. Johnston scored on both Dave Dryden and Roger Crozier in the game.

Unlike many of his teammates, Johnston never did mind the team's white skates although he recalls fans didn't always appreciate them when the team went on the road. "They were colorful. Charlie Finley had some good ideas. It didn't bother me," Johnston said. "In warm-ups, fans would say 'you sissies' and stuff like that. You expect that, especially in New York and Philadelphia."

During the 1971-72 season, Johnston was pleased to be with the Seals and he recalls the atmosphere around the team as a positive one. "At the beginning, everybody was gung-ho and just happy to be in the NHL," Johnston said. "There were not too many guys there my first year with a bad attitude. But the WHA caused the loss of 10 players. Losing changes everybody's attitude. It was no fun, it was embarrassing."

It was during his second season in Oakland, 1972-73 that Johnston began to develop into one of the team's better offensive players. Johnston was placed on the team's first line with center Walt McKechnie and right wing Craig Patrick. He finished the season with a team leading 28 goals and 49 points. He also led the team in power play goals and tied for the club lead in shorthanded tallies. Craig Patrick recalled his former linemate as, "very talented and a tough individual. He didn't take too much grief from anybody on the ice. He was more talented than he believed he was. If he had more support around him, he would have had a better career."

The 1972-73 season was when problems started to hit the Seals. The losing was hard on Johnston. Garry Young started the season as coach but was quickly replaced by Fred Glover. "I liked Fred Glover because he played me but he didn't teach hockey or didn't know much," Johnston recalled. "I told Fred we needed a system coming out of our own zone and he said, 'They're all three times seven, they should all know hockey.' He didn't communicate well enough and no one had any game plans."

The lack of a game plan both during games and in practices was particularly disturbing to Johnston. "Fred's practices were, 'Let's scrimmage.' Fred scored and we were off the ice. After he scored he would say, 'Twice around and in.' Walt McKechnie and I used to drive to Berkeley for practice together a lot. He would get me charged up. 'We're going to have a good practice,' he'd say. But more or less, you had to do it on your own. The coaches didn't talk to us enough. They relied too much on the players. It's like Freddie said, the players should know hockey but that was not always the case unless you had superstars."

The Seals talented left winger produced his finest offensive effort on November 3, 1972, in a game against the Bruins at Oakland. Johnston put the puck in the net behind Bruins goalie Ross Brooks three times and added two assists as the Seals and Bruins skated to a 6-6 tie. The Seals overcame a 6-3 third period deficit to earn the draw. Johnston scored two of his goals in the third period and then assisted on the tying goal by center Walt McKechnie.

During the 1972-73 season, Johnston suffered a horrible injury during a game with the Chicago Black Hawks. Dan Maloney crushed Johnston and his jaw was broken in four places. "He elbowed me," Johnston said shortly after the incident. "I saw Maloney a fraction of a second before he hit me. He's a hitter but it wasn't dirty. I just didn't see him long enough to get my body ready for the hit. I flew back to Oakland with Mr. Finley and his wife. He was a good old guy but he knew nothing about hockey. He showed me the World Series rings the A's were getting. They said 'S+S=S' which stood for sweat plus sacrifice equals success. I agree with that statement."

Trainer Barry Keast called it the worst injury he had seen in all his years working for the Seals. He also remembered how Johnston didn't miss any time as a result of the injury. "I went with him by ambulance to the hospital and stayed with him," Keast said. "His jaw was wired. We made a mask for him and he played." Although he was eating his meals through a straw after his wife put them in a blender, he showed his toughness and didn't miss a game as a result of the injury. "He played the next game," defenseman Bob Stewart recalled, remembering Johnston's toughness. Johnston played the rest of the season with a special birdcage style helmet and mask to protect his injured jaw.

Seals defenseman Rick Smith, who played with Johnston during the 1972-73 season called "Joey the Jet" "an incredibly talented and very funny guy. He always had humor around the team. He had the potential to be one of the central players on the team and he was but he could have been a Bill Barber or Danny Grant type player."

Gary Croteau, who played three seasons with Johnston in Oakland remembered him as "a tough competitor, a good fighter and a real team player who was there every game." Croteau also remembered an unusual ritual Johnston had between periods. "In the dressing room, he would down two or three coca colas and then throw them back up again."

The 1973-74 season was the most productive of Johnston's NHL career. Despite the Seals lack of victories, Johnston played in all 78 games and scored 27 goals and 67 points. Johnston started the season on fire, scoring in the six straight games; a Seals club record. By the end of the season, Johnston led the Seals in goals, assists, points, power play goals and game tying goals and tied for the club lead in shorthanded goals.

Despite the individual success, "The Jet" was growing frustrated. "I just worked hard and hoped somebody noticed so I could get a job outside this organization. The city was great, the people were nice but I hated playing with a loser." Despite the fact that the Seals were not winning, the league began to take notice of Joey Johnston's play. For three consecutive years (1973-1975), Johnston was selected as the Seals representative in the NHL All-Star game. Among the skills that helped Johnston attain that honor was his ability to shoot the puck from anywhere on the ice. "He was one of the best angle shooters," Bob Stewart recalled. "Joey could move his body and pick it off the post." Morris Mott recalled that Johnston also "took passes in his skates better than anyone."

In February 1974, after Charlie Finley sold the Seals back to the NHL, Marshall Johnston took over as coach of the Seals. "He got the team thinking as a unit when we were out there," Joey Johnston recalled. "A lot of us weren't used to it. We were used to having the coach say, 'Next five up.' If you had the horses back then, you were a good coach."

Another fun memory for Johnston was the streaking incident. "She just came out on the ice," Johnston recalled. "She had skates on but I didn't get a good look to see what size they were. She was noticeable. We didn't have a sellout. I remember once we had less than 1,000 people. I could have called the fans by name. The fans were good, the ones that came were good but there just weren't enough of them. I also remember Krazy George. He was good for the fans out there. He really got the people going. A lot of Canadians lived in the Bay Area but they probably all left Canada because they hated hockey. We should have been in San Francisco. Now, in San Jose, they sell out. We needed a winning team."

Johnston had also earned the respect of his teammates both on and off the ice by this time and despite being only 25 years old, was already one of the Seals more experienced players. "He was quiet but a physical presence," recalled rookie defenseman Barry Cummins. "You knew he would cover your back whether he liked you or not because you were on his team. He didn't look so strong, but he was."

Although he wanted to leave Oakland before the 1974-75 season, Johnston had a year left on his contract. "Finally, I got Alan Eagleson as an agent. Garry Young was fired but I had another year left on my contract so I had to play another year in Oakland. What I thought was good money was not really good. I made $65,000 on my own. Eagleson got me $100,000."

In addition to the raise, Johnston was named captain of the Seals prior to the 1974-75 season after serving as an alternate captain for the past two seasons. "I was surprised to be named captain because my thing was my on ice performance not lecturing the guys and maybe some guys didn't like the way I acted off the ice," Johnston admitted. "I think the guys voted for it although some guys told me they didn't vote for me, which was OK too. I was happy to be named captain. It made me want to work a little harder. The only way for us to win was to have 20 guys go all out on one night. We had too many small forwards and we didn't have defensemen who could clear the puck out of our own end."

Despite being named captain, Johnston's production slumped in 1974-75 to 14 goals and 37 points in 62 games. There was a reason for the diminished production, however. "My final year in Oakland, I broke my wrist," Johnston recalled. "I played 21 games with it. The swelling caused it not to show up on the x-rays. It was very frustrating. My wrist hurt with every pass."

Some of his teammates noticed a shift in Johnston's attitude during his last season with the Seals. "Joey had the best shot I've ever seen," Dave Gardner said. "He shot the puck like a rocket and was quick. When we were playing together, I always tried to look for him. He was just waiting to get traded. It was tough for him to stay in Oakland."

Larry Patey also saw the frustration Johnston was experiencing. "He was a good leader and a tough guy but he was disappointed being with the Seals. He was a tough, talented player. He really could have excelled with any other team."

Gary Simmons said Johnston was "burnt out on losing." Still, his teammates respected him. Charlie Simmer was a rookie with the Seals in 1974-75. He later played on the "Triple Crown Line" with hall of famer Marcel Dionne and Dave Taylor in Los Angeles. Still, he called Johnston, "One of the most talented players I played with. He drank a lot and he got into that car accident which hurt his career. Still, he was a tremendous player."

Even during the difficult 1974-75 season, there were pleasant memories. Defenseman Len Frig recalled one incident in particular that took place on Long Island. "It was the third period and we were losing something like 8-0," Frig said. "Joey Johnston was stuck out there for two or three shifts and Bill McCreary was coaching. He wasn't even changing the lines. Joey skates by the bench and says, 'Anyone else want a turn yet?' Anyway, the Islanders had a breakaway and Joey just sort of stuck his stick out, grabbed the puck and passed to Spike Huston and he went on a breakaway and scored for us."

Wayne King recalled Johnston's sense of humor, which never wavered despite the fact that he was having a difficult season. "He was a joker," King said. "During pre-game warm-ups, he'd put a puck on a string and put it on a stick and then make the guys chase after it. He was always fooling around."

After the 1974-75 season, Johnston finally got his wish. The Seals traded him to the Black Hawks for Jim Pappin and a third round draft choice. Unfortunately, just as "The Jet" was getting his chance to leave the Seals, fate intervened. During the summer of 1975, Johnston was in a serious car accident. He suffered a broken wrist and serious head injuries. His balance was affected and Johnston was never the same player he used to be. He appeared in only 32 games with Chicago in 1975-76 scoring no goals and five assists. The Black Hawks sent him to the minors to see if he could regain his old form, but the lack of balance never improved and ended Johnston's career. After that season, he retired from hockey at age 27, just when he would have been entering his prime. Johnston's final NHL statistics were 85 goals and 191 points in 331 games.

Today, Johnston lives in Peterborough, working in carpentry and other related endeavors. He will be the first to tell you that he drank too much in his playing days but at the time of our interview, he said he hadn't had a drink in 15 years. Johnston is divorced although he has a special woman in his life. He has two daughters from his prior marriage.

Ray McKay described Joey Johnston as "A good hockey player. He could do it all. He had good speed, he could shoot and score goals." Perhaps, more than anybody, Johnston personified what it was to play for the Seals in their later years. He had a lot of potential, got some positive results but left you wondering what might have been had he taken the game more seriously and remained healthy. Still, there is no doubt, Joey Johnston had fun along the way and he left his mark in the memory of his teammates and of any Seals fan who watched him play.

Marshall Johnston

"He was like a father figure to the team; a good defenseman with good instincts. He moved the puck out of our zone. He was a steadying influence on a young team. I knew him from our days on the Canadian Olympic Team. He was a pretty serious guy."

–Gerry Pinder on Marshall Johnston

Marshall Johnston was born in Birch Hills, Saskatchewan and grew up rooting for the Detroit Red Wings. "I was from the Saskatoon area and so was Gordie Howe," Johnston recalled. "Glenn Hall was from a town approximately 50 miles from where I grew up. That made me a Red Wings fan."

The 5'11", 175 pound Johnston attended the University of Denver for four years and played hockey there for three seasons (freshmen weren't eligible to play varsity sports at that time). In his three years on the team, the University of Denver won one NCAA national title and was the runner up once as well. Johnston then joined the Canadian National Team and represented his country in two different Olympic games in 1964 and 1968. In 1968, Johnston scored two goals and had seven points in seven games to help Team Canada earn a bronze medal.

Around this time, Johnston began to realize that maybe he had a chance of playing in the NHL. "I suppose it wasn't until the expansion of 1967 when the league went from six teams to 12," Johnston said. "Playing in the NHL went from a remote possibility to a possibility." The New York Rangers originally owned Johnston's NHL rights but in June of 1967, they sent him to the Minnesota North Stars in a cash deal. Johnston spent four years in the North Stars system, playing a total of 49 NHL games over four years while spending most of his time playing with the AHL's Cleveland Barons or the CHL's Iowa Stars. In 1971, Johnston won the Eddie Shore Award as the AHL's Outstanding Defenseman when he scored 11 goals and 56 points in 69 games. He was also named to the league's first team all-star team.

After the 1970-71 season, Minnesota traded Johnston to the Montreal organization to complete the deal that sent Danny Grant to the North Stars. The Canadiens shipped Johnston to the Seals in August of 1971 for cash. Johnston was pleased with the trade for the most part. "I came as part of a deal from Montreal," Johnston recalled. "Quite frankly, I didn't think I would play in the NHL. Montreal was a powerhouse. I appeared for a few games with Minnesota. I had an opportunity to go play in Europe but to do that, I needed my amateur card and they were reluctant to give it to me. Obviously, my chances of playing in the NHL for the Seals were much better than my chances of playing for Montreal." Johnston joined the California Golden Seals at the age of 30 in 1971-72.

Johnston's first coach with the Seals was Vic Stasiuk. "He was an emotional guy and he loved the game," Johnston recalled. "He played on good teams with great players like Gordie Howe. He was enthusiastic. During practice, he'd be out there skating with us."

Like all new members of the Seals, Johnston had to adjust to the team's new white skates. "We'd go back east and fans would yell," Johnston remembered. "I was never a very physical hockey player anyway, but one fan yelled, 'Hey Johnston, hit 'em with your purse!' Some funny things went on, but I don't remember anybody being upset about them. The trainers hated the white skates though because they had to keep painting them."

The white skates were the product of the fertile imagination of the Seals owner, Charles O. Finley. Despite all the controversy surrounding Finley, Johnston felt he treated the team well. "Charlie didn't interfere with the hockey team. In baseball, he was his own general manager but in hockey, he let the hockey people run the team. We never missed a paycheck while some teams back then were shaky. He flew us first class and bought us clothes and luggage. I was the player rep at the time. I had a meeting with Mr. Finley about getting videotape to help the club. When I told him the cost, he basically said it was wishful thinking."

Johnston established himself as a consistent performer on the Seals in 1971-72. Marsh scored two goals and 13 points in 74 games for California and accumulated only four penalty minutes all year. Gary Croteau recalled, "Marshall was a student of the game. He wasn't real aggressive but he would take the man and would stick his nose in and get involved." Although he usually played defense, Johnston would move up to right wing when needed and could perform adequately there as well.

Marsh's teammates quickly appreciated what he brought to the team. "He was steady," Gary Jarrett recalled. "You wouldn't necessarily notice him much but when you graded him out, you would never find many mistakes he made. He always did his job but in a non-spectacular fashion." Goalie Lyle Carter added, "Marshall studied the game, even then. He was a hard worker. He didn't have all the talent and it wasn't easy for him. He was a very sensible guy." Walt McKechnie remembered Johnston as "a funny man with a dry sense of humor. He had talent but was not a tremendous skater. He was one of us, he was a little talented but not great. He was a great team guy."

Both of the game's Johnston recalled as being the toughest for him to take occurred during 1971-72. The first was a 12-1 loss to the Rangers on November 21, 1971 at Madison Square Garden in which the Seals as a team were flat out embarrassed. The second was 6-3 loss to Detroit at the Olympia on New Year's Eve night. "I think I was a minus four or minus five that night," Johnston recalled. Despite what he recalled as a poor defensive performance, Johnston did have an assist in the game.

Back then, the Seals practiced at the Berkeley Ice Rink, an old Olympic sized rink built back in the 1940s. "I remember driving down the street to the practice facility and there was a girl playing guitar topless on the porch," Johnston recalled. "I think we drove around once or twice more. Berkeley wasn't an ideal place to practice but that's all there was. I can't say it made a difference of ten points per season for our team but it would have been of some benefit to have a better facility. It wasn't an excuse for our play."

In 1972-73, Johnston had the most productive season of his NHL career. In 78 games, Marsh scored 10 goals and 30 points. He was also had the best plus-minus rating on the Seals with a minus one which wasn't too bad on a team that lost 30 more games than it won. Johnston also had the best offensive night of his NHL career on December 10, 1972 at the Boston Garden. Due to injuries up front, Johnston moved up to play forward and ended up scoring his only NHL hat trick. He also added an assist. Although Johnston figured in all four Seals goals that night, the Bruins handily defeated the Seals 8-4.

Like many Seals players, Johnston took a strong liking to living in the Bay Area. "The Bay Area was a beautiful area to live in," he recalled. "I haven't lived in a better place since. Also, in spite of the lack of support, the core of fans we had in Oakland was maybe the best core of hockey fans in the country. They couldn't do enough for us despite our lack of success."

The only major drawback to playing in the Bay Area was the extended travel that went along with playing hockey on the west coast in the early 70s. "No doubt the travel affected us," Johnston said. "We were trying to combat it. Sometimes, we'd practice when we got home and take the following day off. Sometimes, we'd try to leave two days before a game so we had a day out east to practice. I don't think that anybody really solved that problem but again, I don't think it was the reason we were not successful. If you don't have the horses, you don't have the horses."

Johnston has a vivid recollection of Seals coach Fred Glover. "Freddie was a little bit different," Johnston said. "He had been a hard nosed player, a battler. He was a real successful AHL scorer with a Ted Lindsay type of reputation. He brought that with him as a coach. He hated to lose. He probably could have been better than some of us who were playing for the Seals but his timing was off, he missed the expansion by a few years."

To many of his teammates, Johnston added experience and veteran stability to a young Seals team. "He was one of the older players on the team and I had a lot of respect for him from his days with Team Canada," Reggie Leach said. "Marsh was a leader and tried to get us in the right frame of mind. He didn't like losing and he was a friend on and off the ice."

"He was a real disciplinarian and a very solid player," Rick Smith said. "He had great defensive skills, sort of like an Ed Westfall type of player. He was very reliable and extremely effective." Hilliard Graves recalled Johnston as, "a smart, smart player. He didn't have enough physical talent to sustain his career but he is one of the smartest guys I ever played with."

Johnston himself was always modest about his NHL career. "I was a utility player," he said. "I played all forward positions on the third or fourth line and I was used as a fifth or sixth defenseman."

Johnston started the 1973-74 season playing defense for the Seals. In 50 games, he scored two goals and 18 points on the losingest team in Seals history. Then, on February 16, 1974 when the NHL bought the Seals back from Charlie Finley, Fred Glover resigned as coach and the Seals hired Marshall Johnston as his replacement. Johnston immediately retired as an active player. "I was getting tired of playing," Johnston said. "In retrospect, now, I realize I had no business coaching the team. I had no prior coaching experience. It was an opportunity to coach and to see if I had an aptitude for it." Johnston's career statistics in the NHL were 14 goals and 66 points in 251 games played. He only accumulated 58 penalty minutes during his NHL career.

Johnston claims he did not have much trouble making the transition from player to coach. "I tried to do some things to make the team better from a technique and tactical standpoint," Johnston said. "There has to be a good atmosphere and working relationship between the players and the coach and I tried to develop that. I always felt that your personality is your personality. If you try to do something other than that, the players will see right through it in a heartbeat. I was sociable and communicative. I talked to the players."

Johnston also stressed positional hockey, trying to make up for some of the club's physical shortcomings by playing an intelligent style of hockey. In an interview with John Porter of The *Oakland Tribune* late in the 1973-74 season, Johnston offered an example of what he was trying to accomplish. "Our defensemen aren't that big and you're talking about moving guys who are 200 to 210 pounds and have maybe three or four inches in height advantage," Johnston said. "There's no way in hell we can move them out of there, so why be unrealistic? Let's play positional hockey so that if we can't get them out of the way, we can at least make sure we're positioned to that they're not going to get the puck."

Apparently, according to most of the men who played for him, Johnston's attempts at communicating with the players bore fruit. "He was a players' coach," Barry Cummins said of Johnston. "He tried to help you, he talked to you. He was trying to help you see where you could improve or where it might be easier to do something. He always struck me as a guy who looked out for his players."

Ted McAneeley added, "Marshall was a great teacher and communicator. He really analyzed the game and I think his experience with the Canadian National Team and Father Bauer helped him in that regard. He had the respect of all his players as coach."

Despite the fact that he went from a player to a coach during the same season, Johnston seemed to have little trouble earning the club's respect. "Marshall was a thinker," Craig Patrick said. "I was very fond of him and he was very well respected." Rookie Larry Patey called Johnston, "the most sophisticated coach we had. He had a lot of knowledge and could see inside guys' heads and work with them. He had it tough because we had a lot of young players."

The fondest memory Johnston had as coach of the Seals was his first win behind the bench. It came in perhaps the most unlikely of places, the hallowed shrine of hockey, the Forum in Montreal. "Gilles Meloche stopped about 50 shots that night," Johnston said, recalling the Seals improbably 4-3 win on March 2, 1974. The Seals were outshot 41-25 but got excellent goaltending from Meloche and timely scoring. "The players gave me a plaque, which I still have with all their names on it," Johnston recalled. "It had their names in bronze tiles and I put it up on my wall." Unfortunately for Johnston and the Seals, the club finished 2-17-3 that season with the only other win coming against the Boston Bruins in Oakland.

Johnston returned to coach the Seals for the 1974-75 season. He had a team with 10 rookies on the roster including Gary Simmons, Larry Patey, Dave Hrechkosy, Al MacAdam, Jim Moxey, Rick Hampton, Charlie Simmer, Wayne King, Mike Christie and George Pesut many of whom played major roles on the club. At the all-star break with the team falling farther and farther from playoff contention, GM Bill McCreary dismissed Johnston as coach of the Seals. The Seals had an odd schedule in 1974-75 and 19 of their final 27 games were at home. Bill McCreary took over and tried to rally the club but was unable to do so. The Seals finished last in the Adams division and failed to make the playoffs. "GM Bill McCreary took over and fired Marshall Johnston as coach," Gary Simmons said. "We fixed him. He thought he was going to lead the team into the playoffs but we really faded down the stretch." "Marsh really didn't have a chance," Spike Huston recalled. "His hands were tied and Bill McCreary was telling him what to do. He had almost no input."

Given the club's poor record, Johnston was not surprised by his dismissal. "I didn't fall off my chair," he recalled. "I remember a headline in the *San Francisco Chronicle* around Christmas time, 'Johnston Traded, Johnston Fired'. I knew there had been earlier attempts to dismiss me but the league wasn't about to do that." In all likelihood, the league was trying to save money by not firing Johnston.

Even when the league finally agreed to replace Johnston as coach, his replacement, Bill McCreary, was already on the Seals payroll.

Johnston recalled being surprised when McCreary took over the coaching reins himself. He felt his relationship with McCreary started out well but deteriorated as time went on. "We started out OK but relations got strained after that," Johnston said. "I'm not sure why. He replaced me. He didn't hire me, but he didn't have the authority to fire me and bring in his own person. Some things that happened between the general manager and the coach were not necessary. When I was let go, McCreary told me he was hiring [Jack]"Tex" Evans as my replacement. I called Jack to see if he wanted some of my notes on the players and he knew nothing about becoming coach of the Seals since McCreary was taking over himself."

Johnston has remained in hockey after being dismissed as coach of the Seals. In 1981-82, the Colorado Rockies franchise hired Johnston as coach. He lasted 56 games with the lowly Rockies going 15-32-9. Johnston also coached at the University of Denver and later became a scout and director of player personnel of the New Jersey Devils. It was during Johnston's time with New Jersey that many of the building blocks of the Devils first Stanley Cup team were put into place. Johnston later joined the Ottawa Senators organization where he was general manager from 1999 to 2002. Under Johnston's guidance, the Senators became serious Cup contenders, becoming one of the league's best teams. The former Seals defenseman decided to step down as general manager after the 2002 entry draft. He later scouted for the Chicago Blackhawks before retiring during the 2003-2004 season. He is respected around the league for his knowledge of the game and his talent for building up franchises. Johnston now lives in Minnesota with his wife. They have two grown daughters.

Craig Patrick has been teammates with Marshall Johnston, played for him and served as an NHL coach and General Manager with Johnston. "Marshall was a serious guy," Patrick recalled. "He was a thinking man's hockey player and very steady. He was a solid guy in the organization who was always willing to help a teammate out." There's no question as to why Johnston lasted so long in hockey. He knows the game, works well with people and strives for excellence. Through people like Marshall Johnston and Craig Patrick, the influence of the California Golden Seals is still felt in the NHL today.

Morris Mott

"He was a small winger. He would dig, dig and never stop skating. He drove opponents crazy."
                                                                                    –Paul Shakes on Morris Mott

In hockey terms, Morris Mott was perhaps the ultimate example of Andy Warhol's belief that someday, everybody would get 15 minutes of fame. Mott was a third or fourth line wing and a penalty killer who played for a last place team. In two-and-a-half NHL seasons, Mott never scored more than nine goals per year. Yet, Morris Mott was able to develop a cult following in of all places, New York. The city that is known for being hard on opposing players turned the anonymous Mott into a hero and the Morris Mott Fan Club was started with branches in Brooklyn and Long Island. This was Morris Mott's 15 minutes of NHL fame.

Mott came to the Seals via the Canadian National Team. He represented Canada in the 1968 Winter Olympics and scored five goals and six points in seven games to help Canada to a bronze medal finish at Grenoble, France. He then spent two seasons at Queens University where he earned a Masters Degree in History. The Seals signed Mott as a free agent before the 1972-73 season. Mott recalled being very happy about signing with the Seals because it meant, "I had a shot to make an NHL team."

Whenever Mott's name was mentioned to his former teammates, the refrain was similar; he was smart and was always analyzing the game of hockey. Ray McKay recalled that Mott "was always coming from the academic side of things. He analyzed everything." Spike Huston said Mott was "A hard worker and kind of like a school teacher telling us, 'this is how you do it.'" Goalie Gary Simmons remembered Mott often saying things like, "If I were coaching the team..."

Perhaps the one knock on Mott in hockey circles was his size. Although he was listed at 5'10", the Creelman, Saskatoon native weighed in at only 165 pounds. Rick Smith recalled that Mott had "tons of skill but he was a smaller player and that worked against him." Craig Patrick remembered Mott as, "A nifty little player but his size detracted from what he could do on the ice at this level."

During his rookie season in 1972-73, Mott played in 70 games for the Seals, scoring six goals and 13 points. His first NHL goal came on January 24, 1973 at the Omni in Atlanta against Flames goalie Phil Myre. "It was a screen shot along the ice from just inside the blue line," Mott recalled. "I received a pass from Hilliard Graves, I believe, in the high slot. I shot it hard along the ice and it found a hole and went in." Mott also added an assist in the game as California defeated Atlanta 5-2.

Garry Young was Mott's first coach with the Seals. Mott recalled him as a "good judge of talent" but "not much of a tactician."

After Young was fired early in the season, Fred Glover took over again as coach of the Seals. "Fred was not an easy man to get to know," Mott recalled. "I think the players treated him a bit too harshly. He would have done much better as a coach of a real tough team, physically. He did not have the right players in California to play his style of game. Fred had been a very tough and dedicated minor pro player and I know he felt many of the players on the Seals were not willing to pay the price to be good. Maybe he was right. Fred was a fair man but never your friend and you always felt he was aware of your weaknesses but maybe not of your strengths."

Glover, in turn, did see the work ethic he was looking for in Mott's play. "He was a good kid, a scholarly type," Glover recalled. "I don't think he combed his hair the whole time he was with us. He always had a book in his hand. He was a hard worker and a fine penalty killer, he just lacked size."

When it came to Charlie Finley, Mott understood the Seals flamboyant owner better than most of the players because he closely followed Major League Baseball. "I was a baseball fan and I knew that Charlie Finley was always trying or advocating new ideas like the designated hitter or orange baseballs. I really did not mind the white skates. At least I was willing to be a part of the experiment of seeing how they looked. Now, it is true that some people in hockey thought we looked like clowns, but this was not a big deal."

In 1973-74, Mott had the most productive NHL season of his career. In 77 games, he scored nine goals and 26 points for the Seals. It was also the season that Mott had his most memorable game with California, a 1-1 tie with the Chicago Black Hawks on November 7, 1973. With Ted McAneeley in the penalty box and the Seals trailing 1-0 with just over seven minutes left in the game, Mott beat Tony Esposito on a shorthanded breakaway to earn the Seals a 1-1 tie against Chicago.

1973-74 was also the year that the Morris Mott Fan Club was started in New York by Rangers statistician Arthur Friedman. Friedman was known for promoting relatively unknown athletes and Mott became the focus of his attention in part due to his name and in part due to the hustle he showed on the ice in a game against the Rangers. "Here was little Morris Mott, skating around in his green helmet, hustling all the time without anyone really knowing much about him," Friedman told Fran Tuckwiler of the *San Jose Mercury-News*. "And the name Morris Mott was a natural." Friedman was interviewed for Madison Square Garden cable in between periods and told the Rangers broadcasters to look for Mott, touting him as a great third period player. The little man from Creelman, Saskatoon obliged Friedman by scoring a goal and adding an assist in the third period for the Seals. "After that, the camera man started getting close-ups of Mott and we started toasting him with Motts apple juice" Friedman explained. "It was great. Almost overnight, Morris Mott became known."

Shortly after that, Morris Mott Fan Clubs were founded in New York City and on Long Island. Anytime Mott and the Seals came to Madison Square Garden or the Nassau Coliseum, there was a banner hanging from the rafters saying "Morris Mott Fan Club." "Some teenagers in Long Island became attracted to me and started the fan club," Mott recalled. "I remember meeting some of them on a trip to Long Island." At the Nassau Coliseum after a Seals-Islanders game, they even gave their hero a small trophy. "Unfortunately, I had to catch a bus right after the game," Mott said at the time. "I didn't really have time to speak with them. I really wanted to. I mean if somebody starts a fan club for you, you really should speak to them. Especially if it's my fan club."

Mott eventually got to meet Arthur Friedman who worked for the New York Mets in the summertime. "I enjoyed the baseball conversation I had with him," Mott said. "All of this was essentially harmless. I have no idea whey people thought I was worth having a fan club for. Why do people like the Everly Brothers? No one knows why these things happen."

Marshall Johnston recalled the effect the Morris Mott Fan Club had when the Seals came to New York. "I remember the marquee at Madison Square Garden saying, 'The Rangers take on 'MORRIS MOTT' in really big letters and then in small letters 'and the California Golden Seals.'"

The fan club appeared to have a positive effect on Mott's play. He seemed to play his best whenever he was playing against the Islanders or Rangers. After Mott was given the spotlight for his two point effort against the Rangers on December 9, 1973, he scored a goal against the Islanders three weeks later, another goal on Long Island in January and a two assist night against the Islanders at the Oakland Coliseum in March. In nine games against the two New York teams that season, Mott had seven points. He had only 19 points in the other 68 games he played in that season.

Late in the 1973-74 season, Marshall Johnston retired as a player and was handed the coaching reigns of the Seals. "He was the most dedicated coach" Mott said of Johnston. "He was really a student of the game. He was in his first coaching job in California and maybe he was a bit too deferential to the older players but he was a very good hockey man as he has shown with several organizations. He had a great sense of humor. All the players liked him and realized he had a future in hockey as a coach or GM or something." Johnston also appreciated his former teammate with the Seals and the Canadian National Team. "Morris was underrated," Johnston said.

The younger players on the team did appreciate Mott as the voice of experience. "Morris was more than willing to help out defensively and he had great wheels," recalled rookie defenseman Barry Cummins. "He never put you in a bad position when he was on offense. As a young defenseman, that was great for me."

Mott's teammates had some fun with him occasionally too. Bob Stewart remembered teasing Mott about his new automobile. "Morris showed up one day at practice with a Cadillac. He always wanted to own a Cadillac. He showed up in a 1965 model, a huge thing. He was smiling from ear to ear although it was an odd, ugly color."

Since Mott tended to be analytical about the game of hockey, he had more of a problem with the Seals practice facilities at Berkeley than most of his teammates. "It was wider than a hockey rink," Mott recalled. "All your shooting angles were different. It was really a rink in which you could develop bad habits. I think the practices were pretty standard for those days. Nowadays, all the teams have better practices than we had but this is simply as sign that the whole world has changed."

In 1974-75, Mott continued his role as a fourth line player and penalty killer for the Seals. He played in 52 games for California, scoring three goals and 11 points. "Morris was a philosopher and a deep thinker," said defenseman Ted McAneeley. "We called him the professor. He was a great penalty killer and a role player."

Later in the season, when General Manager Bill McCreary replaced Marshall Johnston as coach, Mott was benched and then sent down to the Seals farm club in Salt Lake to make room for younger players. Al MacAdam recalled that Mott was "the doctor of our team. For him, everything was technical. He was an intelligent, thinking player. Marshall Johnston was a Morris Mott type of coach. Bill McCreary sent him down to the minors."

Mott recalled McCreary as "a very calculating man and maybe too manipulative. He did not want me around very much as a player, although I think he felt I was a good influence on the younger players like Stan Weir and Rick Hampton. Bill wanted to go with real young guys and I was 28 by the time he became coach. I will say this though; he did not get in my way when I had other options—Salt Lake City, Sweden. He appreciated the fact that I wanted to play somewhere."

Mott finished the 1974-75 season at Salt Lake and helped the Golden Eagles win the CHL title that season. On the minor league level, Mott had little trouble scoring. He tallied six goals and eight points in 11 late season games for Salt Lake before adding two goals and nine points in 11 playoff contests. "At the NHL level, I was a fringe player," Mott said. "I was a good checker and penalty killer. At lower levels, say Salt Lake City, I was a good offensive player. In the NHL, I found the goalies very hard to beat."

Mott never appeared in another NHL game after that season. He spent the 1975-76 season in Sweden before making a two game cameo appearance with the Winnipeg Jets of the WHA when the Jets had injury problems. His career NHL statistics include 18 goals and 50 points in 199 games.

To this day, Mott has fond memories of his time in the NHL. "I loved the competition," Mott said. "Every night you had a big challenge as a player. In fact, of course, sometimes we had too big a challenge. But it was a real thrill to play against Orr and Potvin and Ratelle and Mikita and Park and other great players."

Mott also appreciated the Bay Area fans. "I thought the fans were great, there were just too few of them," he said. "They were very loyal and I remember that a lot of them came from San Jose. Krazy George was very loud and very entertaining. I appreciated him. Nothing he did was derogatory to the other team or to us."

Today, Mott is an Associate Professor of Canadian History at Brandon University in Brandon, Manitoba. Among the things he writes about is the history of sports in Canada and Mott is a member of the Society for International Hockey Research (SIHR). Mott and his wife have two children.

Reggie Leach remembered Morris Mott as "small, but he could handle the puck well. He had a lot of hockey sense and he worked hard on the fundamentals." And for one, brief, shining moment, he was the toast of New York.

Gilles Meloche

"He was the best goaltender in the NHL when he played. Nobody could take the abuse he took. In Montreal, he'd face 40-45 shots per game. We could have lost a lot of games 10-1 instead of 4-1 if not for Gilles."

–Bob Stewart on Gilles Meloche

Ask most hockey fans to name one member of the California Golden Seals and the player that would be named most would probably be Gilles Meloche, the Seals spectacular young goaltender. Meloche was given an initiation by fire in the NHL and passed every test. It seemed Meloche never had much support in Oakland and while with the Seals, he was facing 30, 40, sometimes, even 50 shots a game. Still, the young goalie never panicked and always maintained the confidence of his teammates. He always seemed to find a way to keep the hapless Seals in hockey games they had no business having any chance to win. Despite the fact that Meloche never won more than 16 games in any season with the Seals and never had a goals against average lower than 3.33, he had the respect of all of his teammates and all of the players and coaches around the league.

Gilles Meloche was born in Montreal and grew up rooting for the Chicago Black Hawks. His favorite goalies were Glenn Hall and Terry Sawchuk. After one all-star season in junior hockey with the Verdun Junior Maple Leafs, the 5'10", 170 pound Meloche was drafted by the Black Hawks with the 70th overall choice in the 1970 entry draft.

"I had a good camp with Chicago," Meloche recalled. "I was sent to Flint, Michigan of the IHL. Near the end of the year, Gerry Desjardins broke his arm. I was called up and played two games for the Black Hawks." In his first game with Chicago, Meloche made 42 saves as the Black Hawks defeated the Vancouver Canucks 7-4. His only other appearance in a Black Hawks sweater came against the Seals on March 19, 1971 in Oakland. Meloche led Chicago to a 5-2 win over California.

After the 1970-71 season, Chicago GM Tommy Ivan told Meloche he was still "two years away" from playing in the NHL. "When I looked at the Chicago goalers," Meloche later recalled, (Tony Esposito and Gary Smith) "I figured it would be more than that."

Meloche remembered how he became a member of the Seals. "Garry Young was the Seals GM," Meloche recalled. "The Seals sent Gary Smith to the Black Hawks for Gerry Desjardins. Desjardins' arm had been broken the year before and when he reported to (Seals) camp, it was still not healed. The Seals suddenly didn't have a number one goalie. They wanted Smith back. For two weeks, the trade was in limbo and then they sent Desjardins back to Chicago for Paul Shmyr and me. I thought it was great, that I had a chance to play at the NHL level. I was going to be a backup for years behind Tony Esposito in Chicago. He was in his prime."

The trade was officially announced October 18, 1971. By then, the Seals had already fired Fred Glover and named Vic Stasiuk as their new coach. California's record was 0-3-2 and the team was desperate to get some goaltending help. The amazing thing was that Seals owner Charlie Finley almost vetoed the trade that sent Meloche to Oakland. "Charlie Finley hesitated," Bob Dunn reported at the time. "He said he'd consider forfeiting some games if the Seals couldn't take the ice with an experienced goalie." Eventually GM Garry Young was able to convince Finley to take Meloche and the trade went through.

There was still the issue of Meloche reporting to the Seals. Meloche and defenseman Paul Shmyr took the long way to get from Chicago to the Bay Area. "Paul said to me, 'They'll want us to fly out to Oakland, but we're driving, so don't answer the phone,'" Meloche recalled. Apparently, Shmyr wanted to make sure he had his car with him in Northern California. "It took us three days to drive out to Oakland. They sent the highway patrol out to look for us." Finally, Meloche and Shmyr arrived in Oakland and reported to the Seals.

"When I got there, the team was on a road trip," Meloche recalled. "They played in Detroit. I forgot the second place (Pittsburgh) and then ended up in Boston. I didn't play the first two games of the trip but we won them both. Vic Stasiuk was the coach and he said, 'Throw the kid in against Boston.' These were the days of the 'Big Bad Bruins.' I was sitting in the hotel, waiting for the bus to take us to the arena and I was shaking in my boots. Walt McKechnie must have seen how nervous I was and said, 'I've been watching you in practice and if you just play your game, you'll be OK.' That made me feel a lot better and we ended up winning the game 2-0." Meloche ended up being the only goalie to shut out the eventual Stanley Cup champion Bruins at the Boston Garden in 1971-72. He made 34 saves to earn the shutout. The win had a profound effect on the 21-year-old rookie. "That first shutout really made me believe I could play at the NHL level and succeed," Meloche recalled. Teammate Marshall Johnston called Meloche's performance "Just about the best goaltending I have ever seen." Coach Vic Stasiuk was literally moved to tears by Meloche's performance.

Meloche's teammates quickly gained confidence in their young net minder. "He was a young, naïve French kid when he arrived," Gerry Pinder recalled. "By the end of the year, he had it figured out. He was a super talent. On a good team, he would have proven how good he was. He had a great attitude. Nothing bothered him. He was a lot like Mike Vernon in that regard."

Meloche recalled the adjustments he had to make after joining the Seals. "We had a talented team with a lot of good young players," Meloche recalled. "We also had a lot of wild players and that was a shock to me. There were a lot of parties. We had Gerry Pinder, Walt McKechnie and Wayne Carleton. All of them had been in the league a few years. We also had two week road trips. We were a loosey goosey team and that did surprise me. Come game time, we played."

Another problem Meloche faced was the language barrier. "Carol Vadnais took me under his wing the first two or three months I was in Oakland," Meloche said. "My English just wasn't too good."

There were also the famous white skates for Meloche to contend with. "I didn't mind, I thought it was funny," Meloche said. "After a few weeks, those things had so much paint on them they weighed a ton. In New York and Philadelphia, opposing fans would yell at us and call us Ice Capades or girlies."

As strong as Meloche's debut was against Boston, he had the worst game of his career 30 days later at Madison Square Garden in New York. The Rangers trounced the Seals 12-1, scoring 12 unanswered goals after ceding California a 1-0 lead. Meloche allowed the first nine goals before being lifted in the third period. During the third period, the Rangers scored eight goals on 21 shots. After he was removed from the game, Meloche buried his head in a towel and cried on the Seals bench. "It was my second or third week with the Seals and I played almost the entire game," Meloche remembered. "I thought it was the last game I would ever play in the NHL and I was crying on the bench. After the game was over, Joey Johnston said, 'I just want to know one thing. Who was the ass hole who scored and pissed them off?'"

Despite the debacle in New York, 1971-72 turned out to be Meloche's finest year with the Seals. He finished his rookie season with a record of 16-25-13 and a 3.33 goals against average in 56 games. He also had a career high four shutouts which tied Gary Smith's Seals season record. Meloche received a $300 bonus for every shutout he registered that season and he quipped, "I'm making more money from shutouts than from my regular salary." By the end of the season, it became quite clear that the Seals intended to build their team around their young goalie from Montreal.

Unfortunately, the Seals lost their last six games that season and failed to make the playoffs. "I wish Vic (Stasiuk) was a little tougher on the team," Meloche said in retrospect. "Anytime we didn't lose, he was happy. A lot of ties we got should have been wins. We missed the playoffs by a few points," Meloche recalled. "The Seals were the team of the future. Then the WHA came in and we lost nine players. I heard we could have kept all nine for about $45,000."

The defection of nine players to the rebel league had a big effect on the Seals in 1972-73. Instead of being a talented young team that played an offensive minded style, the Seals became a team that often lacked the talent to compete with other NHL teams. "My second year in Oakland, my biggest problem was the puck—I think I saw 50 shots per game," Meloche said. "But I didn't say a word. I was 22-years-old. I was playing in the NHL and I would rather play in the NHL than in the minors."

While 50 shots per game may have been a slight exaggeration, Meloche was seeing a lot of rubber. For example, in the Seals first 24 games of the 1972-73 campaign, the opposition registered between 30 and 45 shots on goal 19 times. By mid-season, when it was clear that the Seals would not make the playoffs, the situation got worse. Meloche and Marv Edwards endured a stretch of six games where the Seals allowed 42, 58, 48, 51, 39 and 54 shots on goal. Meloche played in five of the six games, faced 244 shots and allowed just 24 goals, a save percentage of .902! In the second game of the sequence, the Rangers outshot the Golden Seals 58-21 but the final score was 3-1 New York.

"I feel sorry for Gilles," backup goalie Marv Edwards said. "He's a good young goalie but he doesn't always get a lot of help out there." Due mostly to lack of support, Meloche slipped in 1972-73 to a 12-32-14 record and a 4.06 goals against average. That season, he led the NHL in appearances and minutes played.

"Gilles was tops," defenseman Rick Smith said. "The perfect goalie with the perfect attitude and tons of skill. It was sad we couldn't have supported him, he was shell shocked a number of times."

Hilliard Graves remembered some of those difficult games Meloche was faced with. "I remember one weekend we played in New York and Detroit," Graves said. "In New York, we lost 3-2 and were outshot something like 65-17. Then, in Detroit, we were outshot 55-12 and lost 3-1. That's what Gilles had to put up with. He was the best goaltender I played with anywhere. If he were in Montreal instead of Ken Dryden, he would have been an all-star goalie."

Fred Glover took over as coach of the Seals early in the 1972-73 season. Meloche recalled that Glover was an "old school" type of coach. "During his practices, he scrimmaged with us," Meloche said. "When the players were tired, they'd tell the goalies to let Freddie score two or three goals and we'd be out of there. There was not much of a system under Freddie. We'd just send one or two guys in to forecheck and play our hearts out."

Glover had only one minor problem with Meloche. "Gilles was a good kid," Glover said. "The only problem was he was nervous as hell. He wanted to know the day before a game if he was playing. He wanted to prepare but that's not how I did things."

Despite facing so many shots and playing for a losing team, Meloche never lost his confidence. "Every city I would go in, I would read the papers, listen to the radio, etc.," Meloche recalled. "I never really heard anything bad about me. That helped keep my confidence up."

One thing that helped Meloche survive on such bad teams was his outlook on goaltending. "He had a terrific attitude," Morris Mott remembered. "Gilles never blamed anyone but himself if a goal went in on us. He had the capacity to play as well as any goalie in the NHL but he was not as consistent, I guess as Parent, Esposito or Dryden. He was the best player on the team."

Meloche said he always felt, "If I saw the puck, I should stop it. My feeling was that nobody plays the game to make mistakes on purpose. If they don't have enough talent, it's not their fault, so I never blamed my teammates for any goals that I gave up."

Rookie defenseman Barry Cummins recalled how Meloche's attitude helped him as a young player. "He was a great guy and a heck of a goalie," Cummins said. "He never blamed anybody but himself regardless of how much you screwed up but he never blamed himself to the point of getting down on himself. If you went back and apologized to him, he'd say, 'I should have done this or that' or 'I should have had that one.'"

Although Meloche saw many of his former teammates sign with the WHA, the Seals did pay Meloche enough money to stay in Oakland. Still, contract negotiations with Charlie Finely were never easy. "I remember negotiating a contract with Mr. Finley and I was asking for $75,000 per year," Meloche said. "We were on the phone and he's crying to me and saying, 'You're trying to make as much as my baseball players.' He was strange. He wouldn't give you a $5,000 raise but then he'd turn around and take the team out to a great restaurant or bring in a chef to cook for us and spend much more than that."

Another thing was never easy while playing for the Seals was the road trips. "We had some 10-14 days road trips that lasted five games. It was rough and it wears you down," Meloche said. "You hope to win the first or second game of the trip because by the fourth or fifth game, you were just trying to hang in there."

In 1973-74, Meloche would need all the help he could get. The Seals had a shaky start to the season and just when it seemed things couldn't get any worse, they did. On November 28, 1973, Meloche was injured during practice when Reggie Leach accidentally skated over his hand and severed tendons in his arm. "Reggie came down the wing and came in front of the net," Meloche said. "I poked at the puck and I lost my glove. He skated over my hand. I said to him, 'Wait until I get you back.' After I returned, in my first practice back, I poke checked Reggie and accidentally knocked out three of his teeth. That's the last time I opened my mouth like that and I was only joking around."

As a result of the injury, Meloche needed surgery and was out of action for seven weeks. Backup Marv Edwards was injured shortly thereafter and the Seals were without both of their top two goalies. The team won only 13 games all season and finished with the worst record in the NHL.

A special moment for Meloche came on March 2, 1974 at the Forum in Montreal. Meloche made 38 saves and the Seals got two third period goals to defeat the defending Stanley Cup champion Canadiens 4-3. "It was always special playing in the Forum," Meloche admitted. "As a young kid, I used to sneak in to watch the Canadiens. I remember watching Charlie Hodge. It was special. I'd look at the schedule at the beginning of the year and circle the dates we'd be playing in Montreal. As a goalie, I always found it easy to play the Canadiens because I always knew that I've be very busy." Gilles usually played well in his hometown, too. "Some of the best goaltending I've ever seen in my life was Gilles in Montreal," Bob Murdoch recalled. "If he ever played for a contender, he would have had some rings. Gilles kept us in every game. He could beat anyone."

Meloche also witnessed a unique moment in hockey history, the streaking incident. "I was on the bench," Meloche said. "The girl snuck out from behind the bench. She wasn't bad looking although she could barely skate to the corner of the ice."

Despite the occasional heroics, Meloche's record reflected the team's poor play. Meloche played well at times, but he was unable to regain his pre-injury form. "I had trouble getting back in the groove after the injury," Meloche said the following season. In 1973-74, Meloche was credited with nine of the team's 13 wins that season, but sported a disappointing 9-33-5 record and a goals against average of 4.24. Meloche also recorded the Seals only shutout of the 1973-74 season; a 2-0 win over the Sabres at the Oakland Coliseum Arena.

Defenseman Ted McAneeley felt that Meloche's demeanor on the ice helped the Seals. "He was a great goalie who faced a lot of shots. He had a calmness about him on the ice and he had great endurance. He was very classy and had everyone's respect on the team." Teammate and later coach Marshall Johnston called Meloche, "The best goalie I ever played with and there were not many better I played against. He's an absolute number one person."

When asked about his goaltending style, Meloche described himself as "a mix of standup and butterfly. I was mostly a standup goalie but I would butterfly in traffic. I didn't want to go down too much since I was only 5'10". I think I had good reflexes."

Off the ice, Meloche overcame the language barrier and earned the respect and friendship of his teammates. "Gilles and his brother Denis (who played for the Seals farm team in Salt Lake City) are great French-Canadian people," Rick Kessell said. "He invited the single guys to his house to eat. He was a hell of a goalie who never got his due respect." Dave Gardner recalled that Meloche "mingled well with the guys despite the fact that back then, his English was not terrific. He did everything he could to win hockey games."

In 1974-75, Meloche again started to play more consistently in the nets after a slow start. He finished the season with a 4.03 goals against average and a record of 9-27-10 in 47 games. Meloche did set an NHL record in 1974-75 by picking up six assists in a season, then the NHL record for goalies. "I don't get paid for scoring points," Meloche said after he broke the record previously held by Ed Johnston, Ken Dryden, Al Smith and Jim Rutherford. "My job is stopping the other guy from scoring." Meloche also tied Ed Giacomin's NHL record for goalies by recording two assists in a game.

Meloche was teamed with Gary Simmons in goal the last two years the Seals played in Oakland. Gilles was a shy French-Canadian kid and Simmons was a western cowboy type who didn't drink and sold turquoise native style jewelry to player on the opposing teams. If ever there was an odd couple, it was Meloche and Simmons, yet the two of them quickly developed a mutual respect for each other and a good friendship.

In 1975-76, the Seals finally put a competitive team in front of Meloche. Although the Seals finished below .500, they were in every game and seemed to be on the road back from oblivion. Meloche cut his goals against average by over a half goal per game to 3.44 while going 12-23-6 in 41 games. He was 25-years-old and just entering his prime. Meloche had played in the Bay Area for five seasons and was one of the most popular players on the team. Then, the Seals moved to Cleveland. "I got a phone call in the middle of the summer," Meloche recalled. "It was sad. I liked playing in Oakland. I had a couple of really good friends in the Bay Area. We had one of the greatest booster clubs of all time and about 7,000-8,000 loyal fans. I tried to look on the bright side and said maybe a fresh start with less traveling could help the team. After a month in Cleveland, I was crying on my wife's shoulder just remembering how good it was in Oakland."

Meloche had two solid seasons for the Barons although the club never did escape last place. When the Barons merged with the Minnesota North Stars, Meloche was protected by Minnesota and became their starting goalie. His second season in Minnesota was his best statistically as he went 27-20-5 in 54 games with a 3.06 goals against average. Meloche also made his first playoff appearance and celebrated by eliminating the four time defending Stanley Cup champion Canadiens at the Forum in Montreal in game seven of the Quarterfinals. Meloche was on top of his game and gave his team a chance to win. Al MacAdam, another former member of the Seals, scored the winning goal late in game seven.

In 1980-81, Meloche and Don Beaupre split the goaltending duties as the North Stars went all the way to the Stanley Cup finals before bowing to the Islanders in five games. It was the first Stanley Cup finals appearance in North Stars history. Meloche was also named to two NHL All-Star games, in 1980 and 1982.

After seven solid years in Minnesota, Meloche was traded to the Pittsburgh Penguins where he played three seasons before finishing his NHL career in 1987-88. Gilles Meloche played in 788 NHL games and finished with a 270-351-131 record and a goals against average of 3.64. Those are very respectable numbers when you consider the poor quality of many of the teams Meloche played for. Meloche is presently second in NHL history with 351 losses in a career, one less than record holder (and Hall of Famer) Gump Worsley.

Meloche's first wife, Nicole died of cancer in 1993. He has since remarried and is living in Montreal. Meloche is still very involved in hockey, working as a goaltending coach and scout for the Pittsburgh Penguins. His boss is a former teammate with the Golden Seals, Craig Patrick. Meloche has a son and a daughter. His son, Eric attended Ohio State University and played some NHL games for the Penguins. He is now playing with the Philadelphia Phantoms of the AHL. Although his father was a goaltender, Eric Meloche is a forward who tries to put the puck in the net, not keep it out. He wears number 72, the reverse of his father's 27, to honor his father.

Charlie Simmer called Gilles Meloche, "The best. He was one of the top goalies in the league at that time. He kept us in the game every night. He was an honest goalie who always wanted to do better and never complained." Meloche was arguably the best player the Seals ever had and the memory of Meloche making 40 plus saves a game still lingers in the hearts and minds of Seals fans who saw him play.

Barry Cummins

"His nickname was "The Plow." He would plow through you rather than go around you. He would defend you. He was a good team man with the heart of a lion."

–Paul Shakes on Barry Cummins

Sometimes, for better or for worse, one moment can define an entire career. In baseball, for example, Bill Buckner will forever be associated with one ball that went through his legs in the 1986 World Series rather than recognized for a very good major league career. Don Larson on the other hand, is remembered for his perfect game in the 1956 World Series and not for the rest of his mediocre major league pitching career. In hockey, Barry Cummins will be forever associated with a confrontation with Bobby Clarke of the Philadelphia Flyers for better or for worse.

Cummins was born in Regina, Saskatchewan and played his junior hockey for the Regina Pats. He spent two years in the WHL playing for the Portland Buckaroos and the Seattle Totems before the Seals took a chance on him. "I had played in the WHL and it was the best minor league," Cummins said. "We had planes and you traveled first class. It was comparable to the AHL but the AHL had younger players. 50% of the guys in the WHL could have played in the NHL but were past their prime. For example, I played with Andy Hebenton. He was 42 while I was 21. He eventually returned to the NHL a year or two later."

Prior to his stint in the WHL, Cummins was in the Canadiens training camp for three seasons. "They had about 140 people in camp and about 75 guys after they broke camp," Cummins recalled. "They had 21 defensemen and only two of them were out of junior hockey. The chances of making the team were lower than slim to none when Oakland picked me up. I thought it was a good opportunity. When I went to camp with Oakland, I knew I could play in the NHL. The guys who made the Oakland squad were guys I played with or against in juniors. But the powers that be have to like you in order to give you a chance; otherwise they can bury you. If they like you, you can get almost unlimited chances."

In Salt Lake, Cummins was known as a physical defenseman. Although he was only 5'9" and 175 pounds, Cummins was tagged with 190 penalty minutes in 72 games in 1972-73 and 100 penalty minutes in only 37 games with the Golden Eagles in 1973-74. He was also able to contribute four goals and 22 points in 1972-73 and two goals and 14 points in 1973-74. "He tried very hard," Morris Mott recalled. "He was aggressive and worked hard although he was not really skilled at any part of the game."

When injuries hit the Seals defensive corps during the 1973-74 season, Cummins was recalled from Salt Lake. He finished the year with one goal and two assists in 36 games with the Seals. When he was called up, Cummins immediately noticed the Seals had an unusual attitude. "It was a defeatist attitude," Cummins said. "Everybody was trying but the difference between a winning team and a losing team is mostly attitude. You get on a roll when you are winning and everything works. The opposite is also true—when you start losing, nothing works. It's a snowball effect. It wears on you subconsciously. You're afraid to do something because you're afraid it will work out wrong. Hockey is a fast game—you have to anticipate or cheat a little. When you're losing, you're afraid to take that chance."

Both coaches that Cummins played for tried in their own way to combat the defeatist attitude that Cummins saw permeating the club. "Fred Glover was old style," Cummins recalled. "His comment to me at my first practice was, 'Don't listen to the other guys, you play your own game.' I think he was referring to the losing attitude. I <u>think</u> that's what he was trying to say to me. As a teaching coach, he wasn't. Now coaches have to teach. He was old style and tried to emulate the old Montreal style. Marshall Johnston was a players' coach. He tried to help you; he talked to you. He was trying to see where you could improve or where it might be easier to do something. He always struck me as a guy who looked out for his players."

Cummins also had problems with the white skates the Seals and the Golden Eagles wore. "They would have been OK if they were dyed that way, but they were painted," Cummins admitted. "Chunks of paint peeled off all the time. We had to stop the game to pick paint up off the ice. Also, the leather couldn't breathe. It rotted. I didn't mind the color so much although other teams said things just to get under our skin."

When he was called up to the NHL, Barry Cummins appreciated that opportunity he had been given. "It was great getting to play against a lot of the players I grew up watching on TV," he said. "I was watching guys like Frank Mahovlich since I was a young teenager." Cummins received a fairly rude welcome to the NHL courtesy of the Minnesota North Stars. "My first game in Minnesota, I replaced Terry Murray who was injured. My first shift, I got the puck behind the net and Bill Goldsworthy elbowed me. I thought he broke my jaw. I couldn't see after that hit. Three games later, we played Minnesota in Oakland. I had 19 penalty minutes in 39 seconds when somebody gave Goldsworthy a blind pass."

The biggest problem Cummins faced when making the jump from the WHL to the NHL was his confidence. "I always had been a physical player," said Cummins. "I was only 5'10", 180. I didn't know if I could be as physical as I was because I didn't know if I was a good enough skater. My lack of confidence in my own ability hurt me. I realized when I was back in Springfield and Salt Lake that I could use my speed and didn't have to manhandle everyone."

The one issue that dominates any discussion of Cummins' brief NHL career is an incident that took place on December 2, 1973 at the Spectrum in Philadelphia. Midway through the second period in an eventual 5-1 Flyers victory, Cummins found out what happened to players who dared to touch Flyers captain Bobby Clarke. "I got a stick in the eye (from Clarke)," Cummins remembered. "My eye bled and I couldn't see. I reacted. I picked up my stick and did the same thing. When 'Cowboy' Bill Flett came after me, I probably cut him worse than I cut Clarke."

Clarke received about 12 stitches from the incident. Cummins was fined $300 and suspended for three games by league president Clarence Campbell. After he retaliated and hit Clarke, many of the Flyers ganged up on Cummins and started to beat him mercilessly. After the game, in typical "Broad Street Bully" fashion, Flyers coach Fred Shero was quoted as saying, "I think if Cummins could take it back right now, he would."

"There were two or three guys with Philadelphia I had played with in juniors," Cummins recalled. "I was really surprised with the comments I heard from them after the game. The incident probably hurt me because I had never used my stick before. I really questioned my attitude. Was I really becoming somebody I detested? That hurt my confidence a lot, too. It hurt my chances of staying in the NHL. I knew I could play there, I knew I was good enough to play in the NHL."

Some of those comments included Flyers forward Bob Kelly who said, "Cummins deserved whatever he got," and Bill Flett who added, "I don't know who that goon was but you can bet if he stays around, there will be a lot of people taking runs at him."

Joey Johnston recalled what happened in *Hockey Digest*. "Bob Kelly went out with his stick and Dave Schultz and then the rest," Johnston said. "Ed Van Impe was going around jabbing Cummins with his stick—spearing him. There's gotta be six guys pounding him while this was going on; while Van Impe was spearing him. Schultzie was skating around tossing linesmen out of his way."

The Seals players supported Cummins. "He took a swing at Bobby Clarke after Clarke high sticked him," said Hilliard Graves, himself a frequent combatant with the Flyers. "It was Clarke's fault. Barry swung at him like he was swinging a baseball bat and dropped Clarke. I thought he was dead because the entire Flyers team came over the boards and was pummeling him. He covered up his head or they would have killed him. Barry was a tough guy." Rick Kessell added, "You would have thought they killed the president," by the reaction of the Flyers. Joey Johnston said, "Their entire bench came onto the ice and ganged up on Barry." A few minutes later, another fight broke out and three more Flyers were ejected from the game along with Seals forward Hilliard Graves. Referee Art Skov decided to end the second period with 4:04 remaining on the clock and added the extra time to the third period.

Defenseman Ray McKay recalled the incident as well. "We were in Philadelphia and it was never fun going there. Bobby Clarke speared Barry Cummins. I was on the ice at the time, heading up ice and this happened behind the play. Clarke speared Barry and Barry whacked Clarke over the head with his stick. The Flyers bench emptied and they all started chasing Barry around the ice. Then our bench emptied. Those situations are scary. I was tangled up with Tom Bladon. I had him pinned against the glass and we were just holding on to each other. I remember Dave Schultz patrolling up and down the ice. I don't know why he didn't sucker punch me."

A few days after the incident, Cummins called Clarke to apologize and see how the Flyers captain was feeling. "I had a sick feeling when I saw Bobby go down," Cummins told the press shortly after the incident. "It was just a reaction thing. I don't do things like that." Clarke admired Cummins for calling. "Yes, I was surprised he called," Clarke told a Philadelphia newspaper. "I wonder if I'd do it in the same situation. It takes a little courage."

There were bright spots for Cummins in Oakland, however. On January 9, 1974, Cummins scored his only NHL goal during an 8-6 win over the Blues in Oakland. He also added an assist in that game. There were also fun times with his teammates. "We were coming into New York and we circled the airport," Cummins recalled. "The ride was quite bumpy and more than half the guys filled their barf bags. The entire team was either white or green in the face. I slept through it. I came off the plane and felt refreshed."

Another incident Cummins recalled vividly took place in Chicago Stadium in a game with the Black Hawks. "We had a bad line change and I was the only Oakland player on the ice. Stan Mikita had the puck and Dennis Hull was on the ice. Mikita passed to the other winger who passed to Hull and he shot a howitzer shot that went behind the net. Bob Champoux was our goalie. He made the save but his arm was pushed so far back by the power of the shot that it dented the twine. Bob was yelling at the ref, 'I got the fuckin' puck, I got the fuckin' puck.'"

Cummins also witnessed some amazing moments on the ice. "We were playing against Boston in Oakland, Cummins said. "Boston was short two men and Bobby Orr went behind the net. One guy chased him out and he just circles back behind the net. He did that a couple of times. Then, the goalie moved to the top of the crease and Orr went behind the net again. Orr had the puck for 1:45 of a 2:00 disadvantage. Guys were skating full speed and he was by them. A full house at the Oakland Coliseum have him a standing ovation. Nobody came within a stick of him."

Cummins also met members of the then World Champion Oakland A's who shared their stories about working for Charlie Finley. "Rollie Fingers told us about playing seven or eight years for Charlie Finley for about $3,000 per season. He told us getting money from Charlie Finley was like getting water out of a rock."

After the 1973-74 season, Cummins was loaned by the Seals to the Springfield Indians of the AHL for 1974-75. He had a productive season, scoring nine goals and 42 points in 73 games. He also added 151 penalty minutes. Late in the season, Cummins injured his knee and was forced to retire. "I tore up my knee in Springfield and that was pretty much it," Cummins said. "I made the decision to get a teaching degree."

Today, Cummins and his wife live in Kimberly, BC. They have two children and three grandchildren. Cummins works as a steam engineer in a pulp mill and is "looking forward to retirement."

Cummins brief NHL career is almost completely overshadowed by the stick swinging incident with Bobby Clarke. Still, his teammates know there was more to Cummins than that. Gary Croteau said, "He was a good, all around defenseman." Fellow defenseman Ray McKay added, "He always gave his best." Spirited and tough, that was Barry Cummins.

Ray McKay

"He was the tallest guy I played with. A good guy to be associated with, he was very helpful. He played the game well. He wasn't flashy, but he got the job done."

—Paul Shakes on Ray McKay

Ask teammates about Edmonton, Alberta native Ray McKay and the words you would have most often would be tall and quiet. McKay signed a "C-Form" with the Chicago Black Hawks when he was 16-years-old. Tiny Thompson scouted him and signed him to the document that awarded his rights to an NHL club back in the days before the entry draft. McKay turned pro in 1967-68 with the Dallas Black Hawks of the CHL. He spent the next three seasons in Dallas and Portland in between brief call-ups with Chicago.

Prior to the 1971-72 season, the Sabres selected McKay in the reverse draft. In 39 games with Buffalo that year, McKay assisted on three goals and had 18 penalty minutes. He spent only one game with the Sabres in 1972-73, spending the rest of the season with the Cincinnati Swords of the AHL. The Seals then acquired McKay in the reverse draft before the 1973-74 season. "To me, it was a great opportunity to get back into the NHL," McKay recalled. "I had been with Chicago and Buffalo and was playing for Cincinnati of the AHL. We won the Calder Cup that year, but I still wanted to get back to the NHL."

During training camp, the Seals gave McKay one day off to get married. "We had training camp out in Kingston, Ontario," remembered McKay. "In camp, I got married. I left camp on a Thursday, drove to Buffalo, got married on a Friday, had a short evening in Niagara Falls then drove to London, Ontario and played in exhibition game."

What McKay found when he arrived in Oakland, however, was a franchise in disarray. "As the year went on, the Seals attitude was different than other teams," McKay recalled. "It was never a matter of whether we would win or lose but how much we would lose by. The guys that had been there two or three years were so used to losing. You can't play the game that way and be effective. That attitude was always in the back of your mind. In addition, ownership was a mess. Charlie Finley was the owner but he didn't care a lot about hockey. He was really interested in the A's who were in the playoffs when I arrived in Oakland. I also remember passing George Foreman in the hallway of the hotel. He was about 6'2", I thought he'd be much taller but he was wide. Charlie Finley had a donkey outside the hotel with an A's banner on it. The hotel was right across the freeway from the Stadium and the Coliseum. It was bizarre. Later in the year, the league took over the team. That sort of set me up for what was going to happen in the WHA where two franchises folded on me. We actually didn't know if the team was going to finish the season."

McKay did stand 6'4", which made him one of the taller players in the league at that time, but he was very thin, weighing in at only 183 pounds. His teammates called him "The Spider" because of his long thin arms. Barry Cummins noted that the lack of bulk affected McKay's game. "He was a great hockey player. He was a tall man but he had no weight. Playing two or three games in a row just physically drained him. He could be worn down. Ray was a great passer." Bob Stewart recalled McKay as "tall and slender. He was a quiet person and had a good shot." Because he lacked bulk, McKay sometimes had difficulty clearing opposing forwards out from in front of the Seals goal.

Former Seals coach Fred Glover recalled McKay as "a big, tall, SOB. We drafted him out of the AHL. Ray could carry the puck and make a pass. If he were bigger in weight, it would have made a difference in his play." McKay recalled that Glover had a "stand-offish personality" although that, in and of itself was not a bad thing. "The thing was," McKay added, "the players really didn't know if we had a system or not."

Relations between Glover and his players were not always smooth during that difficult 1973-74 season. "I remember one player scrapping with Fred Glover in a hotel on Long Island," McKay said. "Some guys were drinking in the hotel bar and we weren't supposed to do that. Fred came by and said, 'You guys should be leaving.' It got loud and then it went out into the hallway and some punches were actually thrown."

Glover resigned when Charlie Finley sold the team to the NHL and was replaced by Marshall Johnston. "He did his best under really bad circumstances," McKay said of Johnston. "It was hard for a guy who you play with to end up as your coach. There is always a certain separation between management and players. Marshall helped me a lot and showed me some things. He showed me some drills to run that I still use in my hockey schools now."

Despite the problems McKay experienced in Oakland, there were good times as well. "The best part was being given the opportunity to play," McKay admitted. "You always want to play in the NHL. It's always the guys you remember, the personalities more than any one game in particular. I remember we all bought gag gifts for each other over Christmas. I got a pair of the old green and white skates without the blades that had Ted McAneeley's name on them. I found some two by fours and cut them to make the skates look like platform shoes. I gave them to Ted McAneeley as a mock Christmas gift and all the guys just cracked up." McKay also appreciated the fans in the Bay Area. "The Booster Club was good, the fans were good," he said. "Every place has its die-hards, the really good fans that will stick with you."

In his only season in Oakland, McKay scored two goals and 12 assists in 72 games with the Seals. He scored his first NHL goal off of Phil Myre on December 5, 1973, during a 3-3 tie with the Atlanta Flames in Oakland. The announced attendance for that game was only 3,137 fans. His other goal with the Seals was scored on December 23, 1973, off of Fern Rivard during a 2-2 tie against the North Stars.

Perhaps the most memorable game for McKay was a 4-3 win in Montreal on March 2, 1974. McKay had one assist in the game, but being able to beat Montreal was the most satisfying part for "The Spider". He said, "Beating Montreal in Montreal: that was our Stanley Cup right there." It was one of only two road wins the Seals had in 1973-74.

Off the ice, McKay was known as a bit of a loner. Rick Kessell recalled that McKay "kept to himself. He was a good player who worked hard but when the game was over, he was gone." Reggie Leach added, "Ray was one of the straight laced guys on the club."

Those teammates that did get to know McKay well thought highly of him. "He was my roommate," Morris Mott said. "He always had licorice or candy for me in the room. On the ice, he was a good, steady defenseman defensively but not much of a threat offensively."

McKay agreed with Mott's assessment. "I was a defensive defenseman, I didn't rush the puck," he said. "I tried to stop the opposition and move the puck up ice to the forwards." Still, his defensive talents were appreciated. Goaltender Gilles Meloche called McKay "a defensive defenseman and a good hockey player."

The biggest problem McKay faced with the Seals though was the constant losing. "I don't know any hockey player who enjoyed losing," he said. "The number of losses takes its toll. The mental aspect of it is more devastating than the physical aspect. It can really wear you down in a hurry. If you don't want to be on the ice because you don't think you can win, you really shouldn't be there."

The losing was the main reason McKay joined so many former Seals by signing with the WHA for 1974-75. "Losing and the attitude on the team were the main reasons I signed with Edmonton," McKay said. "Also, the money. The WHA more than doubled my salary."

McKay spent four seasons in the WHA playing for Edmonton, Cleveland, Minnesota and Birmingham. Both the Crusaders and the "New" Minnesota Fighting Saints folded while McKay was there. He spent two more seasons in the AHL before going to play in Europe for a few years. In 140 career NHL games, McKay scored two goals and 18 points. He added 14 goals and 58 points in 212 career WHA games.

Today, McKay and his wife live in Ilderton, Ontario. They have two children, a son and a daughter. McKay runs his own hockey schools that are in session from mid-April to mid-August. "I love the game and have stayed in it," McKay said. "The kids need the programs I run and I still enjoy the game." McKay also still has the green and gold suitcase that Charlie Finley gave each of the members of the Seals and a plaque his teammates awarded him for his first NHL goal. Despite the difficulties, he looks back on his time with the Seals fondly.

Gary Croteau remembered Ray McKay simply as "A defensive defenseman, a great guy, a quiet guy and a team player." He was a player who got his best chance to play in the NHL with the California Golden Seals.

Paul Shakes

"A young guy, a good solid hockey player. He gave his all at all times."

–Ray McKay on Paul Shakes

Paul Shakes only got one brief shot at the NHL with the California Golden Seals. To this day, the Collingwood, Ontario native is convinced he was never given an ample opportunity to play in Oakland. Shakes was an offensive style defenseman who like most blue liners of his day, grew up watching the great Bobby Orr. "I still feel he's the best ever to put on a pair of skates," Shakes said. "He controlled a game and he virtually owned the puck. He could play offense, defense and physically." Despite his appreciation of Orr, Shakes grew up rooting for the Toronto Maple Leafs.

Shakes played his junior hockey with the St. Catherines Black Hawks. In his second year there, he scored 71 points while topping 20 goals the following season. It was after his first year at St. Catherines that Shakes realized he had a chance to play in the NHL. "It was more hope than realizing, I think," Shakes conceded. "But my first training camp with Oakland, I realized I could play there." The Seals selected Shakes in the third round of the 1972 entry draft with the 38th overall selection. "I was there at draft day," Shakes remembered. "I was happy to go anywhere. I was 19-years-old and just hoping to be picked by someone. After meeting with Garry Young, I was very excited."

The Seals sent Shakes down to their WHL affiliate in Salt Lake in 1972-73. In 71 games with the Golden Eagles, Shakes scored 11 goals and had 42 points. Shakes sensed early on that there was something different about the Seals organization. "They didn't seem to have the real professionalism other organizations had. It wasn't a high class operation like Toronto, Chicago or Montreal." Shakes recalled an incident that occurred during his stay with Salt Lake City. "Our coach in Salt Lake was Al Rollins. He was told that Barry Cummins was called up to go to Oakland. Al told me that he told the big club I should have been the one going up and that he recommended that to them. They said they were calling up Barry because they already had his name on the sweater."

Even in Salt Lake, the Golden Eagles wore white skates similar to the ones the Seals wore. "At first, I was a little taken back by it," Shakes said. "Once you got used to them, you kind of liked them. By the end of the year, they weighed 10 pounds each because of the paint. The trainer had to chisel the paint off. As soon as Charlie Finley sold the team, the skates were painted black."

In 1973-74, Shakes thought he would be called up to the Seals to start the season. Instead, he started the year back in Salt Lake City. "I thought I would be getting more ice time in my second year," Shakes recalled. "I thought I would get a real chance with the big club. When the team was sold, I was called up. Once ownership changed and Garry Young came back, that's when I got my chance. Guys who deserved a chance finally got one, otherwise, who knows? I would have only played against Philadelphia because a lot of guys on the big club wanted no part of the Flyers and would get 'sick' every time we played them."

Shakes played in 21 games for the Seals during the 1973-74 season, most of them in the final few months of the season. He picked up four assists and 12 penalty minutes. Most of Shakes' games were played under coach Marshall Johnston. "He was upbeat. You knew where you stood with Marshall and what you would be doing. He had more of a plan."

Despite making the NHL, Shakes noticed some oddities about playing in the Bay Area. "We practice at Berkeley," Shakes said. "We had to get dressed at the arena and drive out there in our gear. There was no bus supplied. Driving down the freeway with our hockey gear was weird. We wanted to sort of scrunch down and hide. Of course, in Salt Lake, we practiced at a rink that was three quarters outdoors."

Shakes was also present in Oakland for the streaking incident. "We heard rumblings that it was going to happen before the game and we heard when: between the second and third periods. Back then, there used to be a five minute bell to tell us there was five minutes left before the next period starts. Everybody was breaking down the door to get out onto the ice. She took off after the zamboni got off the ice. We were out on the ice. The girl who did it was around the team a lot."

Shakes found other things to enjoy about his stay in Oakland besides the sight of naked ladies skating across the ice. "I was playing with or against guys I idolized," Shakes said. "It was also interesting seeing the way different people handled themselves, especially the really good players. Going from city to city and knowing you'd play before 18,000 fans. It was a boyhood dream come true to play in Chicago Stadium or the Maple Leaf Gardens and to play against the best players in the world."

Many of Shakes' teammates appreciated his efforts. Fellow rookie defenseman Barry Cummins, who was often fighting with Shakes for ice time called Shakes "a steady defenseman. Nothing flashy but he seemed to do the right thing most of the time. He was never really out of position so that it cost you." Hilliard Graves felt that Shakes could have had a longer NHL career, but not with the hapless Seals. "He was a nice, nice guy. He was tough enough but on the smaller side and he didn't have the physical game. On the right team in the right place he would have been a good player. For example, Paul Coffey would not have been good in California. Guy Lafleur would have been a fall down drunk by his third season with the Seals."

Shakes most memorable game with the Seals was a win over the Bruins at the Jewel Box in Oakland. "It was one of my best games," the 5'10", 172 pound defenseman recalled. "I got lots of ice time and was building more confidence. All of our guys came to play that night and we beat the mighty Bruins."

Another element of playing in Oakland that Shakes appreciated was the cheering of Krazy George. "He kept the place rocking," Shakes said. "We would line up for a face-off and he would come running down the stairs. George kept the crowd into it."

Before the 1974-75 season, Shakes was loaned by the Seals to the Springfield Indians of the AHL along with Tim Jacobs and Barry Cummins. "The writing was on the wall," Shakes said. "I knew I had come to the end of the road in Oakland and I knew I wasn't getting another shot." Shakes scored 11 goals and 43 points in 74 regular season games with the Indians and scored four goals and 13 points in 17 playoff games to help lead the Indians capture the Calder Cup. The following year, Shakes was sent back to Salt Lake but he only appeared in 26 games before he injured his back. Rick Kessell remembered that Shakes needed back surgery in Salt Lake. "They screwed up the surgery and he was never the same," Kessell said. Shakes retired from pro hockey after the 1975-76 season.

"I was always an offensive defenseman who liked to move the puck," Shakes said of his style of play. "I played on the power play and enjoyed killing penalties. I wish I was bigger. I was about 5'10" 185 and I wish I was at least 6 feet tall and 200 pounds."

Despite never getting another shot at the NHL, Shakes had a lot of good memories about his time in the league. Many of his teammates did too. Morris Mott said of Shakes, "He was a move the puck defenseman who was not quite strong enough for the top level of play, but I was surprised by how well he did. He was a very quiet guy and a pleasant personality." All he ever wanted was a fair chance.

Rick Kessell

"Kess was another guy with good skills but with us young guys, he was distracted. He was a real free spirit."

–Walt McKechnie on Rick Kessell

Rick Kessell was a classic case of a hockey player who never reached his full potential. "They had high expectations for him," former Seals goalie Gilles Meloche recalled, "but he never realized them." The 5'10", 175 pound Toronto native had a spectacular junior career in Oshawa, scoring 26 goals and 92 points in just 53 games for the Generals in 1968-69. After that season, Kessell knew he had a chance to play in the National Hockey League. "I was second or third in scoring at Oshawa and then I was drafted by Pittsburgh," Kessell recalled. "Back then, we didn't go to the draft, I got a phone call telling me I was drafted."

Kessell spent most of the following season with the AHL's Baltimore Clippers but played in eight games for the Penguins. He scored his first NHL goal and had three points in his debut stint in the NHL. Kessell had brief stays in Pittsburgh the next two seasons, but spent more time in the CHL and AHL honing his skills. In 1972-73, Kessell finally stuck with the Penguins appearing in 66 games. He scored one goal and had 14 points in a defensive and penalty killing role. "I enjoyed Pittsburgh," Kessell admitted. "I was thinking of moving to Pittsburgh. They told me I would play more next year. I was in Cambodia, Vietnam and Hawaii on a USO tour. I called home from Hawaii and they told me I was taken by Oakland in the reverse draft."

When he arrived in Oakland, Kessell found the Seals franchise in tatters. "We didn't know what would happen next in Oakland because it was a poorly run organization," Kessell said. "One of our trainers was a florist. Management was simply terrible. There was always the question of whether we were moving to another city. I was single so it wasn't so bad for me but it was hell for the married guys. There were always rumors."

With the Seals, Kessell became a fourth line player and penalty killer during the 1973-74 season. In 51 games with California, he scored twice and had six points. He did finish the season with the best plus-minus ranking on a last place team with a minus four rating. The Golden Seals finished the 1973-74 season with a horrific 13-55-10, by far the worst record in the NHL. "I was primarily a penalty killer," Kessell recalled. "Morris Mott and I were good penalty killers. I also played point on the power play. People would ask me, 'How could you play on the power play when you weren't taking a regular shift?' I'd say, 'Ask Fred Glover.'"

As a result of the constant losing, Kessell remembers that coach Fred Glover had his problems. "When you lose that many games, morale falls," Kessell said. "There was a lack of respect. Fred was a great AHL player and was respected as a hard-nosed player. He took that attitude that you didn't have to be coached. He would change lines and the guys would just play. He lost the players' respect over time. I remember once he brought his girlfriend to the airport and they were kissing in front of the team. That wouldn't have happened in Pittsburgh with Red Kelly. I respected Fred as a person, but he wasn't the greatest coach around."

Glover, in turn, recalled that Kessell "was a better player than he showed" in Oakland. "He could really skate," Glover added. "I got shit for picking him up."

Kessell had a better relationship with teammate Marshall Johnston, who replaced Glover as coach in February of 1974. "He took me under his wing," Kessell said. "He must have thought I was spending too much time at the bars. I remember once in Buffalo, Marsh said to me, 'I'm in better shape than you are.' He was about 34 and I was 24 but he challenged me to a race. So we raced around the rink and I just barely beat him. I respected him a lot."

Kessell's two best offensive games in a Seals jersey came one week apart in January 1974. On January 9, Kessell scored a goal and set up another in a wild 8-6 win over the Blues. It was Rick's first goal as a member of the Seals. On January 16th, Kessell scored once and set up two more goals during a 5-5 tie with the Maple Leafs at the Oakland Coliseum.

While on the ice, Kessell saw most of his ice time killing penalties, off the ice, he was known for his sense of humor and as a "free spirit." Ray McKay remembered that Kessell "loved to party" and drive around in his 1955 Corvette.

Morris Mott recalled that "We were in Toronto and we were on a big, two story jet plane flying back to California. One of the levels of the plane actually had a piano bar. Back then the newspapers in Canada printed the lyrics to Christmas carols in their papers right before the holidays. Rick Kessell had the entire level of the plane singing the words to all these carols. He had a pretty good voice, too."

Gary Croteau remembered one time where Kessell was late for a game. "We had to be at the rink an hour before warm-ups. Rick didn't show. The trainer called his apartment, there was no answer. He didn't show up for the first period or the second period. We later found out he ran out of gas in Oakland. He didn't want to leave his car there. He actually got a note from a police officer saying why he didn't show up. The coach just shook his head."

Kessell was often involved in practical jokes in the dressing room. "I was always the last guy to get ready for a game," Kessell recalled. "Once, I was getting ready at the very last minute when I realized Joey Johnston shit in my skates. It was late to start the game and got fined $50."

Kessell did take a liking to the Bay Area and the fans. "Too bad there wasn't better ownership that could have built a better fan base," Kessell said. "The people were loyal even though we were losing and there was no television or radio coverage. The owners wouldn't even pay for reporters to come on road trips. That hurt. The players and their wives were a fun group to be with. The weather was also great although it did snow a couple of times when I was there."

Kessell also was present during the infamous streaking incident. "Marv Edwards and I were sitting next to each other on the bench," Kessell recollected. "She wasn't a very good skater. She had Seals bumper stickers on the lower part of her body. A lot of people had their mouths open. Marv Edwards tapped her on the backside with his stick. I don't think you could do that today, you'd get arrested."

Some of Kessell's teammates feel that the lack of leadership on the Seals really prevented Rick from developing as a hockey player. "He had a lot of talent but needed to be guided down the right path to be ready for games and what to do in between games," said defenseman Paul Shakes. "He needed more self discipline off the ice and I think he started to realize that later."

Kessell split the 1974-75 season between the Seals top affiliate in Salt Lake City and the New Haven Nighthawks. After one more year in Salt Lake, Kessell was playing senior hockey and retired as a pro. His final NHL statistics included four goals and 28 points in 134 games.

Today, Kessell lives in Toronto and owns his own construction company, RK Construction. He looks back at his time in the NHL fondly and recalls his time in Oakland with a smile on his face.

Barry Cummins summed up Rick Kessell by saying, "He worked hard until he got down on himself and then he would kind of float. He was probably his own worst enemy. He was young and hadn't matured to the point where he accepted some things as not being his fault and not letting it get to him." Unfortunately for Kessell, he discovered that too late to prolong his NHL career.

Stan Weir

"He came to Oakland as a top pick. I think they rushed him into the league too early. He was only about 19. I think it also hurt him coming into the league on a losing club. He had the raw ability to become a star in this league."

–Reggie Leach on Stan Weir

The California Golden Seals had high expectations for Stan Weir when they selected him with the 28th pick in the 1972 amateur draft. Weir had been one of the top scorers in the Western League with the Medicine Hat Tigers. His first season in the WCJHL, Weir scored 52 goals and 111 points and was named Rookie-of-the-Year. The following season, Weir was second in the league in scoring with 58 goals and 133 points. "I was second behind my teammate, Tom Lysiak," Weir recalled. He scored 10 points on the last day of the season and beat me by nine or 10 points." Scouts felt that the 6'1", 180 pound center from Ponoka, Alberta seemed to be capable of scoring a lot of goals at the NHL level. "I was happy when the Seals drafted me," Weir recalled. "I didn't know much about the Seals, but I was California bound. I didn't know if I would make the team but they seemed to have a decent organization. They called me up right after the draft."

With the loss of nine players prior to the 1972-73 season to the WHA, the Seals were desperately looking for scoring help. As a result, they placed the 20-year-old Weir with the big club instead of sending him to the AHL to gain some much needed professional experience. Weir quickly noticed the differences between the Seals and his previous hockey experiences. "In juniors, most of the time, you win. In Oakland by Christmas, we were out of the playoffs," Weir said. "It was tough to get motivated. The losing changed the attitude of a number of people, including myself. We didn't go into most games expecting to win."

Weir also felt the beautiful Northern California weather made things tough on him as a native of Western Canada. "Coming from Alberta where it was freezing cold, I think the weather was a problem," Weir said candidly. "I was used to the temperature being minus 25 and now it's 75 and the sun is shining. You've got to get motivated to play hockey."

Another new obstacle Weir had to overcome in the NHL was the Seals rigorous travel schedule. "I think it did have an effect on us as a team," Weir said. "Not so much in the first part of the season but in the second half of the year, when you're mentally tired and the team is out of contention, it got pretty tough."

Other things took Weir some time to get used to as well, like the team's white skates. "Those skates would start out regular black or brown and then they were painted," Weir recollected. "They would just keep painting them and painting them. They each weighed 25 pounds by the end of the season. No wonder we couldn't skate, you couldn't even lift those things up. I would say they looked a little Mickey Mouse. Some players would say stuff like 'nice skates' and fans were just fans. It wasn't a big deal."

Weir also recalled what happened when Seals owner Charlie Finley gave the club their green and gold suitcases to travel with on the road. "Mr. Finley started getting into small details about how they were to be used," Weir said. "Then, when he gave them out, he called everybody by the wrong names. He didn't have a clue."

Weir got off to a decent start with the Seals, scoring his first NHL goal in his fourth career game. "It was a fluke," Weir said, recalling the goal off of Philadelphia's Doug Favell at the Spectrum. "I was passing the puck from the left side and it went through some legs and into the goal untouched." Weir's first NHL goal also turned out to be the game winner in a 4-1 Seals victory over the Flyers. Weir also had a three assist game on January 3, 1973 during the Seals 11-3 thumping of the Canucks at the Jewel Box in Oakland.

Big Stan finished his rookie season with a respectable 15 goals and 35 points in 78 games. Five of his goals were scored on the power play. While the highly touted rookie finished sixth on the Seals in scoring, because of his gaudy numbers in juniors, management expected more offense from Weir. "I felt bad for Stan," defenseman Rick Smith said. "He was a rookie in 1972-73. He was a second pick and he got thrown into deeper water than was fair to him. The talent was there but the situation in California called on him to do more than he was ready to do. He played second line center as a rookie for us."

First line center Walt McKechnie concurred with Smith. "He had talent," McKechnie said. "It was unfortunate he was thrown out there on a team in our situation." Still, as he gained experience, Weir became a solid NHL player. "Stan was a good skater and a good talent," Gary Croteau said. "He was a little intimidated initially about the NHL but he certainly settled down with experience."

The Seals coach for most of Weir's rookie year was Fred Glover. Glover, who was known as a 100 percent effort guy during his playing days, appreciated the effort Weir put forth as a rookie. "He was a big, good hockey player," Glover said of Weir. Weir, in turn, respected Glover but did see some shortcomings in his coaching style. "He knew hockey," Weir recalled. "He was very knowledgeable about the game. He had an easy system that everybody could follow and he was hard nosed. He was also very opinionated. He ran very weak practices, though. We would scrimmage and if we let him score, he'd let everybody go. He wasn't a bad coach, he just wasn't very innovative."

The 1973-74 season was a tough one for Weir. As a result of injuries, the lack of talent around him and perhaps a bit of the dreaded sophomore jinx, Weir finished his second season with just nine goals and 16 points in 58 games. A knee injury caused him to miss the final 15 games of the season. His best game of the 1973-74 season was a two goal effort in the Seals 6-5 win over the Blues in Oakland on November 10, 1973.

Some of Weir's teammates believed that because he was stuck on a hard luck team like the Seals, his confidence needed reinforcing. "If Stan had gone someplace like Philadelphia and had better coaching, he would have been better off," Hilliard Graves said. "He lacked self confidence and needed people to lift him up. He was a great player, he could play center for me anytime." Defenseman Bob Stewart felt Weir was a good all around player but "lacked a little toughness."

Late in the 1973-74 season, Marshall Johnston took over as coach of the Seals. "He was very knowledgeable about the game," Weir said of Marshall Johnston. "He knew it inside out. He had a great game plan and was respected by the players tremendously. He knew how to handle different players; when to pat them on the back and when to kick them in the butt. He was new to coaching and he had a bit of a learning curve."

By 1974-75, Weir was one of the more experienced players on what was now a young Seals team. He was only 23-years-old. Weir started the season off on fire before finishing with 18 goals and 45 points in 80 games. He led the Seals in assists and tied for the club lead in points with Larry Patey.

On the road, Weir roomed with left wing Butch Williams. "Stan was funny, a good player and really pugnacious on the ice," Williams recalled. "One night in Buffalo, I was so tired. We had an afternoon game the next day and we didn't get to the hotel until 3 AM. I threw my suit under the bed because I was so tired while Stan took the time to hang all of his stuff up. Well, somebody went through all his stuff and stole it. Of course, since my stuff was under the bed, they never found my stuff. Stan lost the first dollar he ever made which was his good luck dollar. Another night, Stan lost his teeth. We were looking for them for hours."

The Seals were competitive early in the 1974-75 season but hit a mid-season slump which led to the dismissal of Marshall Johnston as coach. General Manager Bill McCreary took over in a desperate attempt to guide the Seals into the playoffs. Weir was not impressed with McCreary's coaching skills. "He had no strengths," Weir said. "He was an old school type coach who tried to intimidate players. He thought everybody played too much golf. One day, he was trying to be funny and he walked into practice with golf clubs, a golf hat and a golf bag. They guys didn't appreciate it." The Seals slumped down the stretch and failed to qualify for the playoffs in 1974-75.

Off the ice, Weir had a reputation for being a bit quiet, enjoying a few drinks and as a young bachelor, finding time to spend with the ladies. "Stan was a good centerman and a good skater," Rick Kessell recalled. "He enjoyed the women off the ice." Barry Cummins recalled that Weir's "eyes turned for a pretty girl whether he was on the ice or not."

Weir had a few stories about teammates being pulled over by the police after having a few too many drinks. While these went unreported in 1974, they would have been back-page headlines in today's tabloids. "A player on the team got pulled over," Weir recalled. "The cop opened the door and the guy fell out. The cop asked for his license and registration and the player started to look through the glove compartment but he couldn't locate it. He gave the cop the entire contents of the glove compartment and said, 'Here, I can't find it, maybe you can.' Luckily, the officer was a hockey fan and the guy got back OK."

Another incident Weir remembered was, "One time a player had a few drinks and got pulled over by the police. The officer asked him 'have you been drinking?' and they player said 'yeah'. He gave the player a Breathalyzer and it came back .39. The cop said to him, 'You shouldn't be driving, you should be dead.'"

Weir called himself, "a journeyman and a hard worker. If I wasn't digging in the corners, I was not effective. I was a good passer and a decent goal scorer."

Morris Mott, who played three seasons with Weir in California, thought that management had unfair expectations of their young center. "Stan was a young player whose talent, I think, was overrated by management. To my mind, this was less his fault than theirs. He was a good player but no more than that."

Despite the constant losing, Weir did enjoy his time with the Seals. "The area was great, we had a good bunch of guys and I improved my golf game," Weir said laughing. "The fans we had were boisterous. They were loud and they liked their hockey. They were rowdy and got into the game. We just didn't have any direction at the top. With better management and a better coaching situation, we could have been more competitive."

After the 1974-75 season, the Seals traded Weir to the Toronto Maple Leafs for winger Gary Sabourin. Like many players, the year after he left the Seals, Weir had the most productive season of his NHL career up until that point. Playing for the Leafs also gave Weir his first taste of playoff hockey and he went on to score some clutch playoff goals during his three seasons in Toronto. In 1978-79, Weir signed with the WHA's Edmonton Oilers and got to play with a 19- year-old rookie named Wayne Gretzky. The following year, when the Oilers joined the NHL, Weir had his best offensive season, scoring 33 goals and 66 points in 79 games. After another two seasons in Edmonton, Weir was traded to the Colorado Rockies before ending his career with one season in Detroit. His final NHL totals included 139 goals and 346 points in 642 games. Weir retired from professional hockey after the 1984-85 season which he spent with the IHL's Milwaukee Admirals.

Today, Weir lives in Toronto and works for a business to business magazine in the chemical process industry. He is divorced and has one daughter.

Larry Patey was a rookie in Oakland during Weir's final season their. He called Weir, "quiet on and off the ice. We were in a competitive situation," Patey recalled since both were centers. "I looked up to him." Although Stan Weir never lived up the high expectations set for him my management while with the Seals, once he left California, he became a solid NHL player. If the Seals hadn't rushed him into the NHL at age 20, who knows what might have been.

OTHER MIDDLE SEALS

Bob Sneddon

Bob Sneddon had a brief stay with the Seals in 1970-71. Second string goalie Chris Worthy was not with the team so the 6'2", 190 pound Sneddon was called up from Providence to back up Gary Smith. Fred Glover liked big goalies and the Montreal native fit the bill. Doug Roberts remembered Sneddon as a "bright, thoughtful guy." Prior to joining the Seals, Sneddon had played in the IHL, AHL, CHL and WHL. His best minor league season was 1965-66 when he was named an IHL first team all-star and won the James Norris Trophy for having the league's lowest goals against average. Mike Laughton called Sneddon, "a good goaltender who was stuck behind some very good players." Sneddon appeared in only five games with the Seals early in the 1970-71 season. He was 0-2-0 with an unsightly 5.60 goals against average. Lack of work proved to be a problem for Sneddon as it was tough to stay sharp when he rarely got playing time. Center Dennis Hextall remembered that Sneddon, "worked hard" and added, "let's just say goaltending was not our team's problem." Sneddon never returned to the NHL after his brief stint with the Seals. He spent six more seasons in the minor leagues, predominantly in the AHL and NAHL before retiring after the 1976-77 season.

Del Hall

Peterborough, Ontario native Del Hall played in parts of three seasons with the Seals after signing with the club as a free agent in October 1971. The 5'10" 170 pound Hall spent the 1971-72 season with the Columbus Seals and scored 26 goals. He was called up for one game with California that season and did not register a point. In 1972-73, Hall was promoted to the Salt Lake Golden Eagles of the WHL and was called up for six games with the big club but again was held scoreless. In 1973-74, Hall scored the first of back-to-back 30 plus goal seasons in Salt Lake. He was called up to Oakland for two games and finally tallied his first NHL points. Hall scored two goals against St. Louis' Wayne Stephenson on April 2, 1974 during a 5-3 Seals loss in St. Louis. In 1975-76, Hall signed with the WHA's Phoenix Roadrunners and had a fantastic 47 goal, 91 point season. The following year, he was selected to the WHA All-Star game and finished with 38 goals and 79 points. Hall played briefly with the Cincinnati Stingers and Edmonton Oilers in 1977-78 before retiring from hockey. Today, he lives in the Salt Lake City area.

Ken Baird

Defenseman Ken Baird was drafted by the Seals with the 15th overall pick in the 1971 amateur draft. Baird had good size at 6', 190 pounds and the Seals expected great things out of him. Unfortunately, after playing in 10 games for the Seals in 1971-72 and picking up two assists and 15 penalty minutes, Baird was returned to Oklahoma City of the CHL for the rest of the season. Ernie Hicke recalled Baird as a "big red headed defenseman who didn't get to play too much." Bert Marshall recalled being paired with Baird in his first NHL game but that Baird "didn't last long in the NHL." Baird was another Seals player who signed with the WHA prior to its inaugural season. Baird signed with the Alberta Oilers and played over four seasons in Edmonton. In 1974-75, Baird scored a career best 30 goals for the Oilers and had 58 points. He also added 151 penalty minutes that season. The Flin Flon, Manitoba native also played for the Calgary Cowboys and Winnipeg Jets of the WHA before playing two seasons in Germany. His 10 games with the Seals proved to be his only NHL experience but in 332 WHA games, the big red head scored 91 goals and 190 points.

Lyle Bradley

Center Lyle Bradley was a minor league scoring machine who never quite established himself at the NHL level. After playing some junior hockey, Bradley attended the University of Denver before settling in to a very productive WHL career with the Denver Spurs, Portland Buckaroos and Salt Lake Golden Eagles. The Seals acquired his rights in January 1972. The 5'9", 160 pound Lloydminster, Saskatchewan native had his best season in 1973-74 when he was named WHL MVP after scoring 34 goals and a league leading 81 assists for 115 points. "Lyle was a finesse player," defenseman Barry Cummins said. "He was really good with the puck and loved the give and go. He liked playing with speedy wingers who he could feed the puck to." In 1973-74, Bradley was called up to the Seals for four games. He scored his only NHL goal on February 16, 1974 during a 7-3 Seals loss at the Igloo in Pittsburgh. Maskless Andy Brown was the Penguin goaltender. The Barons called Bradley up for two more NHL games in 1976-77 although he did not score any more points. He retired after the 1977-78 season and now lives in the Salt Lake City area. "He was a very smooth centerman," Paul Shakes recalled. "He got a lot of points and skated miles. He worked hard every night and never quit."

Al Simmons

Defenseman Al Simmons was selected by the Seals with the 88th overall pick of the 1971 entry draft. Simmons was tall at 6' but weighed only 170 pounds. He appeared in one game for the Seals in 1971-72. An offensive minded defenseman, Simmons had four shots on goal in his only game with California. He spent the rest of the 1971-72 season in Columbus and was promoted to Salt Lake the following year. The San Diego Gulls of the WHL claimed Simmons in the reverse draft prior to the 1973-74 season and promptly sold him to the Bruins in February 1974. Simmons played in three regular season games with the Bruins that year and one playoff game. In 1975-76, Simmons played in seven games for Boston and registered his only NHL point, an assist. Simmons retired from pro hockey after the 1975-76 season.

Hartland Monahan

Hartland Monahan is an afterthought in Seals history, but like many former Seals, he went on to have a productive NHL career after he left California. The Seals selected the 5'11", 195 pound Monahan in the 1971 entry draft. He remained in the California system for three seasons, playing with Baltimore, Columbus and Salt Lake. The Seals called up Monahan for one game in 1973-74. He had one shot on goal and did not register a point. Prior to the 1974-75 season, Monahan was traded to the New York Rangers for left wing Brian Lavender. Monahan later played for the Washington Capitals, Pittsburgh Penguins, Los Angeles Kings and St. Louis Blues in an NHL career that spanned 334 games. He had one 23 goal season with Washington and finished his career with 61 goals and 141 points. He retired after the 1980-81 season.

Jim Jones

The California Golden Seals signed defenseman Jim Jones as a free agent in June 1971. He would spend two seasons in the Seals organization, splitting time between farm teams in Baltimore, Columbus and Salt Lake City. The 5'10", 185 pound native of Espanola, Ontario was called up to California and played in two games during the 1971-72 season without registering a point. In 1973-74, Jones signed with the WHA's Chicago Cougars and played one WHA game for Chicago before spending the rest of the season with the SHL's Winston-Salem Polar Bears. Jones retired from hockey after the 1975-76 season.

Ron Serafini

Defenseman Ron Serafini was selected by the California Golden Seals with the 50th overall pick in the 1973 NHL entry draft. The 5'11", 180 pound native of Highland Park, Michigan remained in the Seals organization for just one season, appearing in two games for the Seals while registering no points and two penalty minutes. He spent the majority of the 1973-74 season with the Salt Lake Golden Eagles of the WHL where he played well, scoring eight goals and 39 points in 74 contests. Prior to the 1974-75 season, the Seals traded Serafini to the St. Louis Blues in exchange for Glenn Patrick. Instead of joining the Blues, Serafini signed with the Cincinnati Stingers of the WHA where he played 16 games and registered two assists before being returned to the minors. His last season of pro hockey was 1976-77 in which he played for four different minor league teams.

Pete Vipond

Oshawa, Ontario native Pete Vipond played professional lacrosse as well as pro hockey. In fact, the 5'10", 175 pound left wing was probably better on the lacrosse field than he was on the ice. The Seals selected Vipond in the 1969 entry draft after he finished his junior career with the Oshawa Generals. Vipond was finally called up to the Seals in 1972-73 and played in three games for California without scoring any points. That same season, Vipond scored 33 goals and 57 points for the Salt Lake Golden Eagles. "Pete was a finesse player and a good goal scorer," Barry Cummins recalled. "He got a little hot headed at times, probably due to his lacrosse background. A lot of his penalties wouldn't have been penalties in lacrosse." Paul Shakes added that Vipond was "a pure goal scorer who was very fast but didn't like the physical play much." In 1973-74, Vipond played for the Tulsa Oilers of the CHL before playing senior hockey until 1977-78.

Gary Coalter

Gary Coalter was originally a product of the New York Rangers organization but found himself playing three consecutive years with the CHL's Omaha Knights. After the 1972-73 season, the Seals acquired Coalter in a cash deal. The 5'10", 185 pound right wing was assigned to Salt Lake where he flourished, scoring 38 goals and 69 points in 71 games with the Golden Eagles. The Seals called up the Toronto native for four games in which he was held scoreless. "Gary was a tough winger who bore into the corners and caused havoc in front of the net," said Paul Shakes. Barry Cummins recalled that Coalter was "a solid hockey player who was never out of position defensively." The Kansas City Scouts liked Coalter's goal scoring touch and physical style of play and selected him in the expansion draft in the summer of 1974. In 30 games with the expansion Scouts, Coalter scored twice and added four assists before finishing the season with the AHL's Baltimore Clippers. Coalter played in the AHL and NAHL until 1978-79 and continued to be a productive goal scorer at the minor league level. Today, he lives near Toronto and works in the construction industry.

Frank Hughes

Frank Hughes' stay with the California Golden Seals was brief and not exactly happy. The Seals claimed the 5'10", 180 pound left wing from the Maple Leafs organization in the intra league draft prior to the 1971-72 season. The Fernie, BC native who had spent the past two seasons with the Phoenix Roadrunners of the WHL played in five early season games with California without registering a point. In Murray Greig's fine oral history of the WHA, *Big Bucks and Blue Pucks*, Hughes described his frustrations while in Oakland. "I basically sat on the bench," Hughes said. Three games into the 1971-72 season, the Seals fired Fred Glover and brought in Vic Stasiuk to coach the squad. Stasiuk and Hughes didn't exactly see eye to eye. "Stasiuk was a real dinosaur," Hughes said.

"One of those guys who thought you couldn't possibly be a hockey player unless you were built like a brick outhouse." Hughes requested to be sent back to Phoenix so he could get some playing time and he finished the year with the Roadrunners. The following season, the Atlanta Flames selected Hughes in the expansion draft, but Hughes ended up signing with the WHA's Houston Aeros instead. Hughes thrived in the WHA and tallied back to back seasons of more than 40 goals for Houston. He played in the 1974 and 1975 WHA All-Star games. In addition to the Aeros, Hughes played part of one season for the WHA's version of the Phoenix Roadrunners. He retired as a pro hockey player after the 1978-79 season. His final WHA totals were 173 goals and 353 points in 391 games. His five appearances with California were the only games in his NHL career.

Brent Meeke

Defenseman Brent Meeke spent parts of four seasons with the Seals between 1972-73 and 1975-76 but never appeared in more than 18 games in any one season. The Seals selected Meeke with the 118th selection in the 1972 entry draft. After spending most of the 1972-73 season with the WHL's Phoenix Roadrunners, Meeke spent most of the following four seasons in Salt Lake. His most productive season for the Seals was 1973-74 when he scored one goal and 10 points in 18 games. "He had great wheels and took a lot of chances," Barry Cummins said of the 5'11", 175 pound Toronto native. "He wasn't as down as a lot of the guys so the chances he took seemed to work for him. He was not as strong in his own end and was not a big, physical person. He finessed you." Paul Shakes said that Meeke was "a very good offensive player who moved the puck well. He was also a good skater." When the Seals moved to Cleveland, Meeke joined the Barons, playing 49 games for Cleveland in 1976-77. He scored eight goals and 21 points in 49 games. After sitting out the 1977-78 season, Meeke played three seasons in Germany before retiring. His final NHL totals were nine goals and 31 points in 75 games, all of which were with the Seals/Barons organization.

Ted Tucker

Goalie Ted Tucker played in five NHL games with the Seals during the 1973-74 season when both Gilles Meloche and Marv Edwards were sidelined with injuries. Tucker was not a big goalie. The Fort William, Ontario native stood 5'11", but weighed just 165 pounds. Tucker did a workmanlike job for the Seals, finishing with a 1-1-1 record and a goals against average of just 3.39 but he never seemed to gain the confidence of coach Fred Glover who gave Bob Champoux most of the work while Meloche and Edwards were on the mend. Defenseman Ray McKay called Tucker, "a typical goalie. He was a little off center but a nice guy." Seals forward Hilliard Graves recalled that Tucker and Bob Champoux, "had no idea what they were in for. They were facing 30 or 40 shots per game and getting no support." Barry Cummins recalled Tucker as "a good minor league goaltender who was mostly quiet. He didn't challenge shooters enough and in the NHL, the guys shot bee-bees." In the minors, Tucker was a two-time EHL All-Star and played extensively in the IHL after his stint with the Seals with Columbus, Port Huron, Dayton and Saginaw. Tucker retired after the 1980-81 season. His brief stint with California was his only NHL action.

Paul Andrea

Paul Andrea was an athletic right wing the Seals claimed in the intra-league draft from Vancouver of the WHL prior to the 1970-71 season. Andrea was a good goal scorer at the minor league level, twice leading the CHL in goal scoring. The 29-year-old Andrea had previous NHL stints with the Rangers and Penguins before joining the Seals. In nine games with California, Andrea scored one goal against the Penguins in a 3-1 loss at Oakland on October 23, 1970. The expansion Buffalo Sabres claimed Andrea on waivers from the Seals on November 4, 1970, and nine days later, Andrea scored the game winning goal for Buffalo in a 4-2 win over the Seals at the Aud. The North Sydney, Nova Scotia native finished the 1970-71 season with 11 goals and 32 points in 47 games with Buffalo. After a year with the Cincinnati Swords of the AHL, Andrea spent two years with the Cleveland Crusaders of the WHA. He retired after the 1974-75 season.

Gary Kurt

Gary Kurt came to the Seals in the inter-league draft prior to the 1971-72 season. Kurt and Lyle Carter opened the season as the Seals goalies until Gilles Meloche was acquired in late October 1971. Kurt was sent down after Meloche's arrival but was recalled later in the year when Carter was injured and finished the season as Meloche's backup. All told, Kurt appeared in 16 games for the Seals in 1971-72, finishing with a record of just 1-7-5 and a less than impressive 4.30 goals against average. Kurt's only win for California was a 7-3 upset of the Rangers at Madison Square Garden in which the rookie made 40 saves, many of them spectacular. Gilles Meloche recalled that Kurt was often on top of his game in practice but seemed to be unable to play as well during games. "In practice, he could be a really good goalie," Meloche recalled, "but under pressure in a game, he wasn't the same." Norm Ferguson recalled that Kurt, "really didn't have much of a team in front of him but he tried hard and was a good player." Off the ice, Bobby Sheehan said Kurt "liked to hang out in the Winnebago with us after practice and have a few. Like all goalies, he was different." After the 1971-72 season, Kurt signed with the WHA's New York Raiders. Unfortunately for Kurt, the Raiders were another last place team with a porous defense and they gave up more goals than any other team in the WHA's first season. Kurt also played for the Phoenix Roadrunners of the WHA before retiring after the 1976-77 season.

Bob Champoux

Prior to joining the California Golden Seals in November 1973, the only NHL experience Bob Champoux had was one playoff game in 1964 in which as the emergency goalie, he replaced an injured Terry Sawchuk and led the Wings to victory. After that glorious but brief moment, Champoux became a true minor league journeyman, playing minor league hockey in Memphis, San Diego, Pittsburgh, Minneapolis, Kansas City, Dallas and Jacksonville during the next ten years. Champoux even retired from hockey before the 1971-72 season but rejoined the WHL's San Diego Gulls the following year. The Seals signed Champoux when both Gilles Meloche and Marv Edwards were out with injuries. He appeared in 17 games for California and finished with a 2-11-3 record and a less than stellar 5.20 goals against average. Defenseman Barry Cummins recalled that Champoux was "a good goalie but he yelled at his defenseman all the time. Either we were screening him or we weren't screening him, whatever. He had a French temper." Veteran forward Gary Croteau called Champoux's experience with the Seals a "baptism by fire. He played as well as he could. We didn't have the strongest team in front of him." Paul Shakes, who played with Champoux both with the Seals and at Salt Lake in 1973-74 said the 5'10", 175 pound native of St. Hilaire, Quebec was "a very intense goalie. He was wrapped up before a game, a loner type guy who did that to try to prepare. He was very talented and when he was hot, he was very, very hot." Perhaps Champoux's finest performance with the Seals was during a game against the Kings on January 2, 1974. Champoux stopped 35 shots and outperformed Rogie Vachon during a 5-2 California victory. After his 17 game stint with California, Champoux returned to the minors for three more seasons playing in the SHL and NAHL before retiring after the 1976-77 season. Although he was not in the best of situations, playing for the Seals gave Champoux a chance to live out his NHL dream.

Chapter 3:
The Late Years: 1974-75 to 1975-76

Mike Christie

"He was a tough defenseman, you knew he'd stand up for you. He gave his all. A good, steady defenseman with a dry sense of humor."

—*Fred Ahern on Mike Christie*

Mike Christie was born in the hockey "hot bed" of Big Spring, Texas and was the first native of Texas to play in the NHL. It was a technicality, however, as Christie's father was a Canadian citizen working for an oil company in the Lone Star State and he grew up in Canada. Christie grew up a Chicago Black Hawks fan and counted Stan Mikita, Pierre Pilote and Bobby Hull as his favorite players growing up. The 6'1", 190 pound defenseman attended the University of Denver and was a two time All-American selection there before signing as a free agent with his favorite team, the Black Hawks. "I went to camp with Chicago after graduating from the University of Denver," Christie recalled. "I realized I could play with the guys in camp."

The Hawks assigned Christie to their CHL farm team in Dallas. After two seasons in Dallas, Christie was traded to the Seals along with Len Frig for center Ivan Boldirev. Christie recalled he was not surprised about the trade. "The Black Hawks were loaded at that time and in Dallas, if you didn't get called up to Chicago within two years, they traded you," Christie said. "I lost one year there because I tore up my knee. I remember my sister-in-law called and said, 'Why didn't you tell me you were traded?' That was the first I had heard about it. I knew the Seals were looking at me. The former GM Garry Young scouted me during the playoffs the year before. We had about a half-hour long conversation. We won the CHL championship that year. As for the Seals, I was thrilled to go there."

When he arrived in Oakland, Christie found a very different atmosphere than the one he had experienced in the Chicago organization. "It was a strange year. The team had only won 13 games the year before and we were owned by the league," Christie recalled. "We had 10 rookies on our team and not a lot of guys that people had heard of. The team did not have a winning attitude but they changed it around. The leadership on the club was not conducive to winning. I remember my first game in Oakland. After the first period, were getting beat pretty badly. Our captain, Joey Johnston said, 'Well boys, only 239 more periods to go.' The attitude was that things were not going to get better. A lot of guys who were there were towards the end of their careers. There were guys who were just happy to be there and a lot of fringe players. We were not a very physical or tough team and back then, that was the style because the Flyers had won the Stanley Cup the year before mostly through intimidation."

Unfortunately for Christie, he quickly found out about the Flyers intimidation tactics first hand. On October 25, 1974, in just his ninth game as member of the Seals, Christie was placed directly in the path of "The Broad Street Bullies." Christie and Dave Schultz fought just 3:29 into the first period. From then on, the entire game was a tough, physical contest. Finally, at the 8:20 mark of the third period, all hell broke loose and the Seals defenseman quickly found himself fighting four Flyers at once inside the Seals penalty box.

"On the first shift, Dave Schultz came out. He was looking for me because I had won a few fights our first few games," Christie recalled. "It was a very dirty and chippy game. In the third period, Orest Kindrachuk took a penalty. Then we had a fight and Bob Kelly and Don Saleski joined in. Saleski sucker punched me and I was cut. He came over the scorekeeper's bench in the penalty box area. They all got six game suspensions."

At the time, Christie vowed revenge. "I know who it was who hit me even though I never saw him do it," he told reporters after the game. "I'll wait until the next time we play them." The Seals were leading 4-0 at the time of the brawl and went on to win 4-1. The game set a new NHL record (since broken) with 232 penalty minutes assessed including 88 penalty minutes for the Seals and 144 for the Flyers. Five Flyers and three Seals were given game misconducts while the brawl itself went on for approximately 40 minutes and involved all 38 players dressed on both teams. Christie needed 14 stitches when the melee was finally over.

Everybody who witnessed the incident was shocked. "It was the most disappointing night of hockey in the NHL," Seals GM Bill McCreary said. "I never saw anything so cruel and vicious as the Flyers on that night. Mike Christie is a brave person. (NHL President) Clarence Campbell held a meeting afterwards. Len Frig, Jim Neilson, Munson Campbell and myself were there. They had six players, three trainers, lawyers, and accountants. I was disappointed in the officiating and in the NHL. It leaves you to wonder what these people think. Christie was courageous. The fight started in the corner with the center ice man. They fought in the penalty box. I headed down there and a detective grabbed me. By then, two or three Flyers were in the penalty box and two or three more went over the glass. Christie's eyes were shut in the dressing room. The NHL didn't hand down proper sentences. If the NHL had acted then, the McSorely incident [with Donald Brasheer over 25 years later] would never have happened. Some managers feel they need fighting to fill the stands. The incident hurt my respect for the NHL. Two guys held Christie and one guy punched him. They should have been banned for life. It was a cowardly act."

Seals center Stan Weir recalled, "There was a face-off in our end and the Flyers sent five goons over the boards and jumped into the penalty box after Mike. It was the most chicken shit act I've ever seen in hockey."

Even the Flyers most notorious enforcer, Dave Schultz was not pleased with his teammates actions. In his book, "The Hammer, Confessions of a Hockey Enforcer," co-written with Stan Fischler, Schultz said, "I don't like brawls that are one sided. I felt sorry for Christie." And in an interview for this book, Schultz added, "Saleski and Kindrachuk tried to beat up Christie in the penalty box. I had received a game misconduct and I didn't even do anything. Bob Stewart and I were hanging out together and watching this."

Schultz felt that the Seals were responsible for making their games with the Flyers the way they were. "The amazing thing was that the Seals started fights against us," Schultz said. "Why should we start them? We had more fights with those guys than with any other team. I be damned if we were going to take any shit from the Seals. We went there thinking it was an easy two points. Other teams tended to overreact. Guys would drop their gloves with me all the time thinking I wanted to fight. If they wanted to start something, we were tough. We had to live up to our reputation, particularly in visiting buildings."

Seals president Munson Campbell, who was hired by the NHL, lost his cool after witnessing the incident. "We'll bring up the butchers," Campbell threatened. "We'll meet them in the alley or on the ice. We've got guys at Toledo who can tear up ten feet of fence." The Seals farm club in Toledo, the Goaldiggers, had four players who accumulated over 190 penalty minutes in 1974-75 including Paul Tantardini and Willie Trognitz, who had 338 (in just 38 games) and 305 respectively. None of the enforcers who played for Toledo were called up for the next Flyers game. In fact, none of them ever played a game in the NHL.

While he paid a heavy price for it, the brawl and his overall style of play helped earn Christie the respect of his teammates. "Mike was very quiet and a great competitor," Charlie Simmer said. "He worked hard and was good at his job. A real gritty defenseman." Rookie center Larry Patey added, "He stuck his nose in there and did the dirty work. Hockey was a lot different in those days. You had to stand up for yourself and your teammates. Mike would step in and protect his teammates." Gary Simmons said, "What Mike lacked in ability he made up for in desire. If somebody was in a fight and getting ganged up upon, he'd step in. He did a good job and was a good guy off the ice."

Later in the 1974-75 season, Christie tore knee ligaments and missed 37 games. He finished the season with no goals, 14 points and 76 penalty minutes in just 34 games. His first NHL coach was Marshall Johnston. "He was only there a short time and didn't have much of a chance," Christie said. "He was a good guy to play for and he worked you hard. He was a fair person and the guys respected him."

Christie fondly remembered the fun the players had off the ice. "Guys played a lot of pranks," he recalled. "They would light newspapers on fire while guys were reading them either in the hotel lobby or on the team bus. Jack Evans put a stop to it after we had to evacuate the bus because there was too much smoke." He also recalled goaltender Gary Simmons "would sell turquoise jewelry to members of the other teams when we were on the road."

On the ice, Christie recalled an incident that took place at Madison Square Garden. "We were playing the Rangers and we were losing something like 9-1 or 10-1," Christie said. "I was on the ice for something like eight goals that night. They were going in off my stick, off my legs, just about any way they could go in. I remember Marshall Johnston asked the players on the bench, 'Who wants to go out there?' Nobody went."

Bob Murdoch said, "I remember we were on a road trip and Mike Christie got a tooth knocked out and needed stitches. The next game, somebody hit him in the head again. Mike was lying on the ice. Jim Pappin skated over to him and said to Mike, 'I used to be good looking too before I started playing this game.'"

One thing Mike Christie did enjoy about playing for the Seals was the weather. "The Bay Area was a great place to live," Christie said. "You could play golf. It was a great atmosphere and great weather. I think that's why it was such a disappointment when the team moved to Cleveland."

Dave Gardner recalled Christie as, "a great golfer. We had a lot of fun golfing. On the ice, he was tough as nails. He always got in my face and told me, 'You can do it,' and encouraged me. He was a good man and a family man."

Christie also remembered some unusual ways some of the players were sent out into the community to create interest in the team. "Gary Simmons and I road BART in our uniforms. We also did a golf tournament or two."

In 1975-76, Christie was healthy again and played in 78 of the Seals 80 games that season. He scored three goals and 21 points while leading the Seals with 152 penalty minutes. The young defenseman started the season off on a bit of an offensive hot streak, assisting on two goals in a 5-2 win at Detroit on October 11, 1975 and then scoring his first NHL goal off of the North Stars Cesare Maniago on October 22, 1975 in Oakland. The Seals went on to win that game 4-2.

Christie also enjoyed playing for new Seals coach Jack Evans and his style was practically a perfect fit for the man they called "Tex". "He was a former defenseman," Christie said. "He respected guys that stood up for themselves. Jack was good to me. He was from the old school: going up and down your wings, don't get caught in. There were no systems back then or traps. I don't think I had a coach like that until Tom Watt in Vancouver. It was very different back then. The guys really respected Jack Evans."

Some of Christie's teammates were concerned that he was a little too critical of himself at times. "He was a sadist," said veteran right wing Gary Sabourin of Christie. "He was way too hard on himself. He didn't have a lot of talent but he worked hard. He was a depressing player. He always thought he was the worst player in the league and he wasn't. He was also one of the hardest workers on the team."

When the Seals announced they were moving to Cleveland before the 1976-77 season, Christie was philosophical. "I think even if they filled the arena they wouldn't have made money in Oakland," Christie said. "The Oakland Coliseum Arena was a nice rink but it was not as big as some of the other rinks around the league. I think George Gund talked Mel Swig into moving to Cleveland. Just like in Denver, the time was just not right. The owners were also too short sighted. They would lose a half million dollars and think that the sky was falling."

Christie was chosen to represent the United States in the 1976 Canada Cup. In four games, he did not register a point and picked up two penalty minutes. After the tournament, he joined the Barons in Cleveland and had the best offensive season of his NHL career. Christie scored six goals and 33 points in 79 games and was a plus 18 in the plus minus ratings; very impressive on a last place team. Midway through the 1977-78 season, the Barons traded Christie to the Colorado Rockies for defenseman Dennis O'Brien. Christie spent two and a half seasons in Colorado and appeared in his only two NHL playoff games in 1978. In 1980-81, Christie was traded to Vancouver. He appeared in only nine games for the Canucks, scoring a goal and an assist before finishing his professional career with the team he started with, the Dallas Black Hawks. Christie's final NHL statistics include 15 goals and 116 points in 412 games.

Today, Christie and his wife live in the Denver area where he works as a representative for Spalding Golf. The Christies have three children.

Jim Pappin remembered Mike Christie with respect when he said, "Mike was serious. He was a good, tough, smart kid. He was the best looking player in hockey and tough as nails. He hated to lose."

Al MacAdam

"He was strong and he had a great work ethic. I marvel at his self-discipline. He knew what he wanted and where he was going. You couldn't ask for a better linemate. He's a classy guy."

–Bob Murdoch on Al MacAdam

You would he hard pressed to find a former teammate of Al MacAdam who had anything bad to say about him. MacAdam was an unquestioned leader on the Seals despite his relative youth and the fact that he was a fairly quiet man off the ice. MacAdam led by example. Nobody ever questioned his work ethic, his dedication and his desire. "He didn't like to be a leader but he was one," Len Frig said. "He was sort of a quiet leader."

Even coach and general manager Bill McCreary who was not known as a man to spread compliments around lightly, thought very highly of MacAdam. "He was a solid citizen," McCreary said. "He was the type you would want for a son. He was tougher than most people thought he was."

MacAdam was born in Charlottetown, Prince Edward Island. He grew up rooting for Jean Beliveau and the Montreal Canadiens. MacAdam played two years of junior hockey for the Charlottetown Islanders and in his second season, he scored 51 goals and 94 points. Rather than turn pro, the 6', 180 pound MacAdam played one season for the University of Prince Edward Island. The Philadelphia Flyers made MacAdam the 55th player chosen in the 1972 entry draft. He spent most of the next two seasons playing in the AHL with the Richmond Robins. MacAdam was a highly regarded prospect, but the Flyers were on their way to winning their first of two consecutive Stanley Cups and there was little room for a young rookie to break into the lineup. MacAdam appeared in five regular season games for Philadelphia in 1973-74 and one playoff game.

On May 24, 1974, the Seals acquired MacAdam as part of the trade that sent sniper Reggie Leach to the Flyers. "I wasn't sure if I liked the trade," MacAdam admitted. "I was in the minors and then I was with Philadelphia in the playoffs. They won the Cup that year and I was part of it but I was not part of it. A few days after the trade, they called me from California and talked to me about future plans."

MacAdam arrived in camp as a 22-year-old rookie. Immediately, he noticed a difference in the atmosphere in the Flyers dressing room and the Seals locker room. "The attitude I experienced on the Flyers allowed me to survive the next five or six years in California, Cleveland and then my first year in Minnesota when we didn't make the playoffs. I observed what you had to do to win on the next level. I remembered what 'team' was all about and what you had to do to get to the top and how to survive and win in this league. In retrospect, in California and Cleveland, our team was shown disrespect by the other teams in the league. They knew all they had to do to beat us was turn it up a little. Teams were relaxed and jovial when they played us."

MacAdam scored his first NHL goal on October 16, 1974 during a 5-5 tie against the Rangers at Madison Square Garden. MacAdam beat future hall of famer Ed Giacomin with just 2:26 left in the game to give the Seals a 5-4 lead. Unfortunately, the Rangers scored the tying goal with just 1:18 remaining.

One problem MacAdam did have when arriving in California was which position he would play. Although he was a left handed shot, coach Marshall Johnston started him out as a right wing. It took some getting used to for MacAdam. "Early in the season, Al had a lot of good scoring chances that weren't going in," Marshall Johnston recalled. "It was hard to see him come up dry all the time. It was as frustrating for me as it was for him."

Slowly but surely, MacAdam found his scoring touch. He finished his rookie season as the Seals fourth leading scorer, tallying 18 goals and 43 points while playing in all 80 games. Some offensive highlights included a two goal one assist game during a 5-5 tie at the Aud in Buffalo on December 14, 1974, and a two goal effort during a 7-5 loss at the Igloo in Pittsburgh just over a month later. On February 5, 1975, MacAdam had his second three point night of the season, picking up a goal and two assists during a 5-1 win over the Capitals at the Oakland Coliseum.

MacAdam was also one of the more religious members of the Seals. "He was one of the nicest guys you'd ever want to meet," former roommate and teammate Dave Gardner said. "We were both Catholic and we went to church on Sundays. We both sacrificed some sleep to do that."

Because of his hard work ethic, MacAdam earned the respect of veterans and rookies alike. Defenseman Bob Stewart called MacAdam a "tough, no nonsense player. He took his man and was a scrapper and a fighter. He was a real team player and a committed and hard working athlete." Rookie center Larry Patey thought MacAdam was "A dedicated hockey player and a tough player. He was a quiet guy and he was business-like on the ice. He went up and down his wing and did his job. He was a very respected player in the league." "He was always trying to improve," veteran defenseman Jim Neilson recalled. "Every game, he tried to do something to improve his game."

Because of his toughness, MacAdam earned the nickname "Spud". While MacAdam never accumulated 100 penalty minutes in a season during his NHL career, he was considered a fearless player who could more than hold his own when it was time to drop the gloves. "Al was the kind of guy you'd like more of in the NHL," said rookie winger Fred Ahern. "He was hard nosed but he was never a cheap shot artist. He came to play every night and was one of the most underrated fighters in the league."

Morris Mott said MacAdam was "a very solid hockey player and a fast skater. Just a solid citizen type of person, he was also a good fighter although very quiet about it." "He would stand up for his teammates and was one of the toughest fighters in the league," Charlie Simmer said. "It took a lot to get him mad, though." Dave Gardner added, "He was the strongest pound for pound guy I knew. He could do 100 pushups without trying. He was an all around guy who worked really hard."

One fight that many teammates recalled was a standoff between MacAdam and Islanders Hall of Fame defenseman Denis Potvin. "One night on Long Island, he put a good lick on Denis Potvin," Gary Sabourin said. "It was the first time I saw Potvin get hit like that." Goalie Gary Simmons respectfully called MacAdam, "A tough little shit. I remember he beat up Potvin on Long Island once. He could really throw them."

Frank Spring recalled another time when MacAdam got involved with Harold Snepts of Vancouver. "Harold Snepts went after Al in Vancouver once," Spring said. "That was a big mistake. He was respected by everybody."

After his rookie season, MacAdam and his wife headed back home to their cottage on Prince Edward Island for the summer. "After my first year, I took my sweater home," MacAdam recalled. "I got a letter invited me back to camp and at the bottom it said, 'P.S., bring your sweater back." The Seals organization was clearly dollar conscious at that time.

In 1975-76, MacAdam truly began to blossom as a hockey player. A new coach took over for the Seals and the philosophies of Jack Evans and Al MacAdam were seemingly a match made in heaven. "Tex was quiet," MacAdam recalled. "If you worked hard he left you alone. I got along well with him."

In his second season in Oakland, MacAdam was teamed with two rookies, center Dennis Maruk and left wing Bob Murdoch to form "The 3-M Line." The trio quickly became the Seals most dangerous combination and helped bring some excitement to the Oakland Coliseum for the first time in a long time.

"We had some skill and we had some chemistry," MacAdam recalled. "Bob Murdoch had good hands and Dennis Maruk was good with the puck and had speed. I played good defense and worked the corners." In 1975-76, the 3-M line set a Seals franchise record by scoring 84 goals, beating the old club record for goals by one line by 11.

The low-key MacAdam continued to earn the praise of his teammates. "He was silent but deadly," recalled rookie center Ralph Klassen. "He was unnoticeable but got the job done. A quiet guy, but don't get him mad." Wayne Merrick, who joined the Seals early in the 1975-76 season, said, "I had a lot of respect for him. He was a wonderful man who was dedicated to the game and an excellent example as a person. He was a great example to follow. He was tough, he could fight with anybody I know but he didn't go looking for it."

In 1975-76, MacAdam scored 32 goals and 63 points in 80 games. He scored eight goals on the power play and four goals shorthanded. Five of his tallies were game winners. MacAdam led the Seals in goals, points and game winning goals. He was also the Seals player who was selected to play in the 1976 All-Star game at the Spectrum in Philadelphia. MacAdam responded by scoring a goal and an assist to help the Wales Conference to a 7-5 win. The goal was the first and only goal scored by a Seals player in an NHL All-Star game.

MacAdam also picked up his first NHL hat trick on October 11, 1975 by beating Jim Rutherford three times at the Olympia in Detroit. The Seals defeated the Red Wings 5-2. His second hat trick came on February 25, 1976 at Madison Square Garden in a 6-4 win over the Rangers. John Davidson was the unfortunate goalie this time. Despite collecting two hat tricks with the Seals, the most memorable game MacAdam recalled was one in which he didn't score. "I had a breakaway with an empty net in a game at home against Boston," MacAdam remembered. "Bobby Orr was the only guy back. I shot the puck and I hit Orr so I didn't get the empty net goal."

MacAdam's biggest regret during his tenure with the Seals was missing the birth of his daughter. "I remember my daughter was born on a Monday," MacAdam said. "I left the previous Friday for camp so I missed her birth. I didn't see her until she was two weeks old and that was just for a day. I only saw her that one time in the first month. Things are different today."

Al MacAdam stayed with the Seals franchise when they moved to Cleveland for the 1976-77 season. He continued to be a productive player in Cleveland and was later named captain of the team. For the second straight year, MacAdam was the franchise's representative in the All-Star game in 1977. Still, the team's record did not improve in Cleveland and the losing began to take its toll on the hard working winger from Prince Edward Island. "I was young and I wanted to play," MacAdam said. "But by my second year in California or my first year in Cleveland I had enough of losing and I wanted to move on."

While the losing was hard to take, in retrospect, MacAdam appreciated his time with the Seals. "California was good for me," MacAdam said. "They had good fans. It was a great loyal core of fans. Playing in Oakland allowed me to mature as a player. At that point, it allowed me to become an NHL hockey player. In Philadelphia, the team was fixed. I was on the edge; there was no spot on the team for me. In California, we had young, low budget players. The guys were all castoffs. There was something in common about that group. Some of us suffered and moved on. I have nothing negative to say about it."

The Barons were merged with the Minnesota North Stars after the 1977-78 season. MacAdam was one of the players the North Stars protected before the league conducted a dispersal draft. The decision turned out to be a very good one for MacAdam and the North Stars. In his second year in Minnesota, MacAdam enjoyed his finest NHL season, scoring 42 goals and 93 points in 80 games. He also got his first extended taste of playoff action that season and responded by scoring seven goals and 16 points in 15 post season contests. MacAdam also scored the game winning goal in the seventh game of the quarter-final series against Montreal that ended the Habs four year reign as Stanley Cup champions.

The following season, when the North Stars marched to the Stanley Cup finals, MacAdam again was a key contributor, scoring nine goals and 19 points in 19 games. After six productive seasons in Minnesota, MacAdam finished his NHL career by playing one season for the Vancouver Canucks in 1984-85. In 864 career NHL games, MacAdam scored 240 goals and totaled 591 points. He ranks tenth all time in goals scored as a member of the Seals and eleventh in all-time scoring.

Although he has been retired as a player for almost twenty years, Al MacAdam is still very much involved with hockey as a coach. He was hired by St. Thomas University in 1987-88 and later was the head coach of the Toronto Maple Leafs top farm club in St. Johns. He later served as an assistant coach with the Chicago Blackhawks. In the off-season, he and his wife still live in Morell, Prince Edward Island. The MacAdams have three children, one of whom was playing hockey at Wayne State University when this interview with MacAdam was conducted.

All of MacAdam's teammates had nothing but nice things to say about him. Mike Christie called MacAdam, "The Silent Assassin". "Guys didn't know how tough he was," Christie said. "He was the classiest guy I played with. You could count on him. He was a legitimate 20-30 goal scorer and a good two way hockey player." Jim Pappin added, "Al MacAdam was a good hockey player with no bad habits. He wanted to win. He was a hardnosed kid. If we had two or three more Al MacAdams, we'd have been a good team."

Brian Lavender

"He was there to antagonize the other team's players and kill penalties. He was a good player but not a goal scorer."

–Len Frig on Brian Lavender

Edmonton native Brian Lavender defined a journeyman NHL player. Lavender was good enough to play for four NHL teams and was a valuable contributor to each, but he was not a goal scorer on the NHL level and was always seemingly fighting for a job.

Lavender played his junior hockey for the Regina Pats. His second season with Regina, the 6', 180 pound left wing scored 39 goals and 110 points in just 56 games. He was signed by the Canadiens organization and was assigned to their CHL farm team, the Houston Apollos. In Houston, Lavender added grit and occasional scoring, totaling 14 goals and 43 points his second season there to go along with 113 penalty minutes. He then played two seasons in the AHL, one with the Cleveland Barons and one with the Montreal Voyageurs.

On June 8, 1971, Lavender changed teams twice. First, the Minnesota North Stars claimed him in the intra-league draft from Montreal. Then, the St. Louis Blues claimed Lavender in the waiver draft later that same day. Lavender played in 46 games for St. Louis in 1971-72, scoring five goals and 16 points and accumulating 54 penalty minutes. He also spent 27 games with the WHL's Denver Spurs where he scored 14 goals and 30 points in 27 games.

Ironically, Lavender's first NHL goal came on November 30, 1971 against the Seals. He beat Seals goalie Gilles Meloche during a 5-2 St. Louis win over California. Later that season, Lavender added a goal and an assist to help lead the Blues to a 4-1 win over the Seals on March 22, 1972. Lavender made his only career appearance in the Stanley Cup playoffs that spring, accumulating two penalty minutes and no points in three post season contests for the Blues.

Lavender was traded to the expansion New York Islanders in September 1972. In 46 games with the Isles, Lavender scored six goals and 12 points. Again, the gutsy left wing had a strong offensive game against the Seals. On November 21, 1972, Lavender had a goal and an assist in a 4-2 Islanders win over the Seals at the Nassau Coliseum. The win ended a nine game losing streak for the Islanders who finished with the NHL's all-time worst record that season. On January 17, 1973, the Islanders dealt Lavender to the Red Wings in a deal that brought New York center Ralph Stewart. In 26 games with Detroit, Lavender scored two goals and had four points.

The following season, Lavender's tour of the NHL continued. He played four games for Detroit before being sent down to the AHL's Virginia Wings. In February 1973, the Red Wings traded Lavender to the Rangers who assigned the left wing to their farm club in Providence. He never played an NHL game for the Rangers before New York shipped Lavender to the Seals just before the start of the 1974-75 season in exchange for winger Hartland Monahan.

With California, Lavender continued to play his third and fourth line role. He killed penalties and played on the club's checking line when asked to. Lavender played in 65 games for the Seals, scoring three goals and 10 points and picking up 48 penalty minutes. Perhaps his most important goal with California was scored on March 21, 1975, where he got the game winning tally against one of his former teams, the St. Louis Blues, in a 7-4 Seals win. Jim Moxey recalled another of Lavender's goals that earned points for artistic merit. "He scored a goal once in Minnesota where he ran over the puck and both he and the puck slid into the net," Moxey said.

Personality wise, Lavender was a bit of a loner and did not get close with too many of his teammates. "He stayed to himself an awful lot," John Stewart said. "Nobody on the team really knew him." Dave Gardner recalled Lavender as being, "flaky as hell. He drove one of those customized vans. He loved to play golf. He kept himself in great shape and killed a lot of penalties." Gary Simmons called Lavender, "an enigma. He was a funny guy; he had some great lines. He was a good hockey player, not a great one. A university guy, he invested in gold or silver or something like that. He could say things that would piss people off." Al MacAdam recalled that Lavender "could play anywhere" but added that he was "a fringe player."

Other teammates recalled some funny incidents that took place to and with Lavender. "I remember we were in Toronto for a game on Hockey Night in Canada," Bob Stewart said. "The camera was on our bench. They caught Brian picking his nose and looking at it. We never let him live that down. He was a nice guy."

"We were in Philadelphia during a warm-up," Gary Simmons recalled. "Brian Lavender was passing pucks out in the warm-up drills. Soon, there were no pucks left. I asked Brian, 'Where are all the pucks?' They were all down at the other end of the rink. The players were all afraid to go over to the Flyers side of the rink to get them."

Butch Williams was not too fond of Lavender. "He bounced around the NHL," Williams said. "He was a brown-noser who didn't belong in the league." George Pesut recalled that Lavender worked hard and "got the most out of his ability." "Brian was out for a good time," defenseman Mike Christie recalled. "He was a bit of a loner."

In 1975-76, Lavender signed with the Denver Spurs of the WHA. In 37 games with the Spurs, he scored two goals and had seven penalty minutes. When the Spurs moved to Ottawa to become the Ottawa Civics, Lavender moved with the team. That was his last stop in professional hockey. He retired after the 1975-76 season. Lavender's final NHL statistics were 16 goals and 42 points in 184 games.

Today, according to Mike Christie, Lavender is working as a golf pro in the Denver area.

Charlie Simmer gave a very accurate summary of Brian Lavender as a hockey player. "He had a longer career than most," Simmer said. "He was one of the first role players in the NHL. He killed penalties, took a face-off. You'd say, 'Why is he here?' but he'd end up being very valuable." In hockey, sometimes the ability to do little things like kill penalties and check can mean a lot to a team. One player who specialized in this was Brian Lavender.

Larry Patey

"Larry was an annoying and antagonistic player to the other team. He was a ferocious checker, even in practice."

–Len Frig on Larry Patey

Larry Patey was a pleasant surprise for the California Golden Seals in 1974-75. He seemingly came out of nowhere to become a vital player for the Seals and then, seemingly just as quickly, he was traded away. Patey grew up near Toronto and rooted for the Maple Leafs as a kid. "I lived 15 miles from Toronto and in high school, I would watch the team practice sometimes," Patey recalled. "Hockey Night in Canada was the thing to do on Saturdays and then Wednesdays. My second favorite team was the Black Hawks since I played juniors with the Dixie Beehives who were affiliated with Chicago and had the same sweaters as the Black Hawks did. My favorite players were probably Norm Ullman, Bobby Hull and Bobby Orr."

The 6'1", 185 pound red head didn't realize he could make the NHL until the Seals drafted him in the ninth round of the 1973 entry draft. "I remember picking up the *Toronto Star* and reading that I was drafted," Patey said. "I got a call from John Sutherland who was the scout who found me. My first reaction was 'Wow' and then it was 'Where is Salt Lake City?' Being from Ontario, I was not all that familiar with Utah."

Despite being a late round draft choice, Patey blossomed in Salt Lake. Playing on a line with Del Hall and Wayne King, Patey scored 40 goals and 83 points in 76 games for the Golden Eagles and was named the WHL Rookie-of-the-Year for 1973-74. "Other prior Rookies-of-the- Year were Walt McKechnie and Rick Middleton in the AHL. They made it (to the NHL), so I figured I had a shot, too." Patey actually made his NHL debut with the Seals during the 1973-74 season. He had a one game call-up but was held off the score sheet.

In 1974-75, Patey stayed with the Seals for the entire season. As a rookie, he scored 25 goals and had 45 points tying him for the team scoring lead with Stan Weir. Patey also tied for the club lead in power play goals with eight.

Despite the Seals lack of success on the ice, Patey was thrilled to be in the NHL. "I loved every minute of it," he said. "I was charged to be part of the NHL and the Seals. Going into Boston, New York, Montreal, Toronto, Chicago, we got our butts kicked a few times, but that didn't change me. I loved every minute of playing there. The weather was great, too. We went to practice in short sleeves. People would ask, 'How do you play hockey when it's 70 degrees out?' I would say, 'Just watch.'"

There were drawbacks to playing for the Seals, however. "The Seals were not a strong organization so far as character was concerned," Patey conceded. "There was not a lot of leadership and we had a lot of young guys. There were a lot of guys who didn't want to be there and that's not something you wanted to see as a young player. To survive, you ended up doing your job number one and putting the team number two."

Travel was also an issue to the young center. "We would leave early in the morning from Oakland, take a bus to San Francisco to the airport and not arrive in New York or Boston until 8:30 PM that night. I think it did help the team stay together more, though and develop a camaraderie."

Despite the difficult situation in Oakland, Patey's teammates grew to appreciate him. "Larry was an excellent hockey player and a good guy," said Jim Moxey. "He was strong and smart with the puck."

Patey's first NHL goal came against the Red Wings at the Olympia in Detroit on October 13, 1974, in the Seals third game of the season. "I brought the puck out of the corner and beat Jim Rutherford," Patey remembered. "Later, George Pesut fed me with a pass and I got my second goal. I still have the puck from my first one." Patey's two goals were not enough that night as the Red Wings crushed the Seals 7-3.

After scoring his first two goals, Patey went through a slump in November, going 13 straight games without a goal. But, as the season progressed and he gained experience, there were many fine moments for the rookie center. He seemed to play his best against the better teams in the league. On January 5, 1975, Patey scored twice off Bernie Parent during a 5-1 Seals victory over the defending Stanley Cup Champion Flyers at the Oakland Coliseum Arena. He collected four points in a 6-4 win over the Bruins on February 21, 1975. For Patey, this was his most memorable game. "I had a goal and three assists and Bobby Orr played and we won the game," Patey said.

His other most memorable game was when he got to live out every Canadian boy's dream by playing against the Maple Leafs on Hockey Night in Canada. "My family was there and the game was on TV," Patey recalled. "Dave Hrechkosy, George Pesut and I were profiled on TV before the game. I remember taking the opening face-off against Dave Keon and winning the draw."

Patey also registered the only Seals hat trick of 1974-75, beating Chico Resch of the Islanders three times on March 9, 1975, during a 4-2 upset of the Islanders in Oakland. "The Islanders beat us 6-1 and 12-2 in New York," Patey told Norm MacLean of *The Hockey News*. "They were counting the two points before the game and I wanted to show them we could be tough." Three days later, the rookie center notched his 20th goal of the season during a 7-2 loss against visiting Buffalo.

Patey earned his teammates admiration with his determination and hard work on the ice. "He was a wiry type player," Butch Williams recalled. "Larry was a fiery guy, a red head with a temper to match." Gilles Meloche recalled that Patey, "came to play and he loved the game." Fellow rookie Al MacAdam said Patey, "got a chance to play and he ran with it. He was very focused and serious about the game."

In addition to taking a regular shift, Patey played on the power play and killed penalties. Bob Stewart remembered Patey's penalty killing skills. "He was a great penalty killer who scored short handed goals and was a great team guy." Dave Gardner remembered another aspect of Patey's game. "He was so strong on his skates he was almost never knocked over," Gardner recalled. "His skating style was a lot like Wayne and Larry Hillman. He had good hands and shot the puck well. We were young and I think he lost something having to play for our team."

There were tough nights as well, as any member of the Seals would have to admit. One such difficult night was Patey's first trip to the Boston Garden, a 5-0 loss. "We were in Boston, my first time in Boston," Patey remembered. "It was me, Wayne King and Del Hall I think was up at the time. Anyway, they had Bobby Orr, Fred Stanfield, Phil Esposito and Wayne Cashman. We were playing our hearts out. The scoreboard clock in the old Boston Garden was located in the middle and there was a shot clock. I remember looking up at the shot clock and it was something like 55-17 for Boston. I was like, 'Whoa, are we having fun or what?' Looking back, it was hard to believe."

When asked to describe what he brought to the table as a hockey player, Patey recalled, "My strength was my skating. I was also fairly aggressive, I was good at shooting the puck and I was a two-way player. I could play both ends of the ice and I knew what to do without the puck. Of course, I could always work on my passing and shooting a little bit more."

Patey played for two coaches during his first full season in Oakland. "Marshall Johnston was the most sophisticated coach we had," Patey said. "He was a college player at heart. He had a lot of knowledge and could see inside guys' heads and would work with them. We got along well. He had it tough because we had a lot of young players."

Patey was less charitable about Bill McCreary who took over the coaching reigns late in the 1974-75 season. "He had his hands full as general manager and was trying to shake up the club because we weren't doing so well at the time," Patey said. "He had no experience as a head coach and I think it was a lot tougher than he anticipated."

The Seals were building with young players and seemed to at least be heading in the right direction after the 1974-75 season. Still, there was a long way to go if the club was going to realistically compete for a playoff spot. During the 1974-75, Seals President Munson Campbell said, "Gilles Meloche and Larry Patey are our only untouchables." Patey's rookie season in Oakland seemed to bear out Campbell's opinion as the redheaded center tied for the club lead in scoring at age 21.

Patey started the 1975-76 season with the Seals and had little trouble adjusting to new coach Jack "Tex" Evans. "He was stone faced, low key and business like," Patey said of Evans. "The guys respected him and he did a pretty good job. He let you do your job." In 18 games, Patey scored four goals and four assists. Unfortunately, nagging injuries hampered Patey's effectiveness.

Then, surprisingly, the formerly "unavailable" Patey was traded to the St. Louis Blues with a third round draft choice for Wayne Merrick on November 24, 1975. Many of Patey's former teammates were shocked. "He wasn't supposed to be traded," said Wayne King, who was frequently a linemate of Patey's in Salt Lake and again with the Seals. "I remember they said he was untouchable, then he was gone."

Gary Simmons was also irate over the fact that the Seals let their young center go. "Larry was a good hockey player," Simmons said. "He was a good skater and a good playmaker. He was a tough save when I played against him. He was a good player so of course, Bill McCreary traded him."

Mike Christie said, "They should have never let Patey go. He was a two-way player and talented. They didn't give him enough time to develop."

Patey remained with the Blues for eight more seasons, twice topping the 20 goal mark and becoming one of the team's most consistent checking centers and penalty killers. Patey scored a career high 50 points in 1976-77 and went over the 100 penalty minute mark in 1980-81. In 1980-81, he also scored a remarkable eight shorthanded goals for the Blues. St. Louis traded him to the New York Rangers late in the 1983-84 season. Patey retired after splitting the 1984-85 season between the Rangers and their AHL affiliate, the New Haven Nighthawks. His career NHL statistics were 153 goals and 316 points in 717 games. A remarkable 25 of his career 153 goals came shorthanded. Although Patey never matched the 25 goals he scored as a rookie with the Seals, he developed into a very solid and steady NHL player.

Looking back, Patey remembered his time in Oakland fondly, especially his teammates and the fans. He also appreciated the fact that the Seals gave him an opportunity to show what he could do at the NHL level. "The fans in Oakland were good," Patey said. He also appreciated the antics of Krazy George, although he confessed, "It was different then I was used to. They didn't do that sort of thing in Canada, but in the States, they are always trying to market the game and bring in fans. He was exciting and did his job well. The league never really gave hockey a chance in Oakland. Now, they have a very different way of marketing the game. The owners didn't really have a clue about hockey there. Then, when the league took over, they didn't know much about marketing."

After his playing career was over, Patey settled down in the St. Louis area. Today, he lives in Chesterfield, Missouri, with his wife and daughter and works selling real estate.

Seals captain Joey Johnston remembered Larry Patey fondly. "He was a good, honest hockey player," Johnston recalled. "I liked him right from training camp. Game in and game out, he came to play." Charlie Simmer called Patey, "A good young player who wanted to do better. He went to St. Louis and proved what type of player he could be. He worked hard and was a great guy to be around." Unfortunately for the Seals, when he reached his full potential, he was long gone from Oakland.

Butch Williams

"He was a funny guy who was good in the locker room and tough on the ice. He would skate through a brick wall for his teammates."

–Fred Ahern on Butch Williams

Warren "Butch" Williams got the desire to play in the NHL at an early age. "When I was eight years old, I told my dad that's what I wanted to be," Williams recalled. "My brother [Tommy Williams who also played for the Seals] had turned pro with the Bruins after playing on the 1960 U.S. Olympic gold medal team. Tommy inspired me. He was my hero. My dad was also a minor league hockey player. It came naturally to me. At eight, I made up my mind to play in the NHL by the time I was 21. That was my goal and I just made it."

The Duluth, Minnesota, native grew up as a Montreal Canadiens fan. "I liked the skating game they played," Williams said. "Our family prided itself on its skating." Among the players Williams admired growing up included Gordie Howe, Rocket Richard, Bobby Hull, Stan Mikita, Red Kelly and later on, Bobby Orr "because he was opening the game up."

Like many members of the Seals, Butch Williams took an atypical route to the NHL. After two seasons of junior hockey in the OHA, Williams signed as a free agent with the St. Louis Blues. The Blues assigned him to their farm club in the EHL and then to the Denver Spurs of the WHL. Williams was known for his scrappiness and toughness even in the minor leagues. In just 54 games in the EHL in 1972-73, Williams scored 22 goals and 64 points but added 129 penalty minutes. Finally, the Blues called Williams up to the NHL during the 1973-74 season. In 31 games with St. Louis, Williams scored three goals and 13 points. He started the following year back in Denver (now as part of the CHL) before being traded to the Seals on November 11, 1974, along with Dave Gardner in exchange for Craig Patrick and Stan Gilbertson.

"I had a falling out with St. Louis management," Williams recalled. "I was on my way to the WHA at midnight. I got a call at 11 PM telling me I was traded. I was happy because they weren't letting me play in Denver since I had a contract dispute. I thought they traded me to California to spite me because my contract with Cincinnati of the WHA was lucrative. I enjoyed Oakland once I got there."

Williams had an auspicious debut as a member of the Seals. On November 13, 1974, he scored a goal and picked up an assist during the Seals 2-0 win over the Black Hawks in Oakland. The win snapped a seven game winless streak for the Golden Seals.

Shortly after his arrival in Oakland, Seals coach Marshall Johnston placed Williams on a line with Spike Huston and Dave Hrechkosy. Dubbed "The Wrecking Crew Line", it became one of the more effective threesomes on the club. "It was two rookies and me and I was almost a rookie," Williams said. "We had fun together, we even hung out off the ice. They went to the horse races with me. We complimented each other well. Wrecker was not a great skater but he had a great shot. He liked the high corners. I dug the puck out of the corner and Spike passed it to Wrecker. It was a nice group." Spike Huston, who centered the line, said of Williams, "I don't think he had a whole lot of finesse, but he could score goals and he worked hard."

Williams remained with the Seals for the rest of the 1974-75 season, appearing in 63 games for California. He scored 11 goals and 32 points and set a club mark for most penalty minutes by a right wing in a season with 118. Despite the high penalty minutes, Williams said he didn't exactly go looking for fights. "I've been retaliating," Williams told Ken Miller of the *San Francisco Examiner.* "You just can't let a guy know you won't fight back if he hits you. I don't like to be pushed around."

Looking back, Williams described himself as "a power wing with some playmaking ability. I liked to pass more than shoot and score. I was criticized sometimes for that. They liked that fact that I wouldn't back down. I didn't look for fights but I wouldn't allow people to get away with intent to injure my teammates. We had a big rivalry with the Flyers. Moose Dupont speared me right away. I responded immediately and landed some good punches. I got respect from the Flyers after that. I guess I was put in the role of policeman although I didn't seek that role."

Like many of the Seals in the club's last few seasons, Williams was considered a "free spirit." Wayne King remembered Williams as "a good partier." "The camaraderie on the Seals was pretty darn good," Williams recalled. "We got to be good friends with a lot of the Raiders, A's and Warriors. I shot baskets with Rick Barry and later I almost bought his car. We had big parties at Cactus Al's in downtown Oakland." Len Frig also recalled Williams as a "free spirit" adding, "He had an undisciplined style. He could skate like the wind. Even his teammates didn't know what side of the ice Butch would be on."

Williams' "different" attitude caused him problems with Seals GM Bill McCreary. "I was hard for Bill McCreary to handle," Williams admitted. "I wore a beard and I think I was the second guy to do that. McCreary made a big deal out of it. I shaved it off and he said nothing for three or four days."

As the season progressed and the losses mounted, Williams noticed more problems surrounding the team. "Anytime a team isn't doing real well, there is a missing cog in the machinery," Williams said. "It's true what they say about developing the habit of winning. Montreal wouldn't accept losing. There seemed to be a 'well, this is just a job, the score doesn't really matter' mentality on our team."

In addition, Williams felt that the unstable ownership situation also took its toll on the Seals. "There was a sense of not knowing what was going to happen to the franchise," Williams said. "Who were we going to be sold to? Were we going to close up shop? It was very prevalent during my stay with the team. There was talk of the team going to San Francisco as opposed to Oakland. The NHL took the team over, but they were just keeping it afloat until a buyer came along as opposed to making the club as good as it could be. The facilities were not as good as NHL teams were used to since we were always watching out budget. In St. Louis, we flew charters and got unlimited steaks for out pre-game meal with beer or wine. The team sent us to Florida after the season." That was not the case with the Seals.

Butch Williams had some fine offensive games for the Seals. On December 4, 1974, he scored twice off of Phil Myre to help lead the Seals to a 3-1 win over the Atlanta Flames. On March 23, 1975, Williams scored a goal and had two assists but the Seals were crushed by the Sabers at the Aud 9-4.

Still, Butch's fondest memory with the Seals was a very personal one for the Duluth, Minnesota native. "I got to play against the Capitals, my brother's team," Williams recalled. "It was 1974-75 and we had a great night. I ended up with a few points (one goal and two assists). I was the first star and Tommy (two assists) was the second star. They beat us. Our dad was listening to the game over his short wave and that made it special. The game was in Oakland and the Capitals won. Tommy marched a garbage can around their dressing room like it was the Stanley Cup." Ironically, the game was the first ever road win in Washington Capitals history after an 0-37-0 start.

Williams' teammates remembered what he brought to the team. "Butch wanted to play in the NHL bad," Al MacAdam added. "His brother had played in the NHL. Butch had limited talent but was a hard worker. He was emotional and wore his heart on his sleeve."

Williams also recalled an embarrassing moment in which he almost put the puck in his own net. "I took a pass from Jim Neilson and a guy was on me," Williams said. "The puck rolled on edge and I ended up shooting a bullet to the far right corner of our net. Gilles Meloche had to make a kick save. I apologized to Gilles and was being booed by the fans. Gilles said, 'Don't worry, that's what I'm here for,' in his strong French accent."

Williams started the 1975-76 season with the Seals, but under new coach Jack Evans, his role was not the same. "Jack brought players up from Salt Lake (where he had coached the year before) and some of us were sent down to Salt Lake," Williams remembered. "If Jack would have given me the chance to display what I could do on the ice, he would have known I was his type of player. I think he didn't want to take a chance on me because of my brother's happy go lucky attitude. Jack was hard nosed and I liked those kinds of coaches."

In 14 games with the Seals, Williams collected four assists before being sent down to the Salt Lake. There, he went on a tear, scoring 31 goals and 77 points in just 60 games. He also added 171 penalty minutes. Charlie Simmer, who played with Williams both with the Seals and the Golden Eagles recalled, "Butch was funny, a real character. In Salt Lake, he started a brawl. We were winning something like 9-2 in Tulsa. It was ten-cent beer night. He ran the opposing goalie with about ten seconds left in the game and a huge brawl broke out."

In 1976-77, Williams signed with the Edmonton Oilers of the WHA as a free agent. He played 29 games for the Oilers scoring three goals and 13 points. That was to be his last season in professional hockey. He also represented the United States in the Canada Cup in 1976 and at the World and European championships after the season. In 108 career NHL games, Butch Williams scored 14 goals and 49 points while accumulating 131 penalty minutes.

Throughout his career, Williams felt he was mistreated because he was an American. When his hockey career was over, he sued the NHL because of it. "I sued the NHL for discriminating against Americans," he recalled. "It ended up being thrown out of court on jurisdictional grounds. The judge said that although the teams played games in each city, they were not 'doing business' in each city. My lawyer said I would have to sue in each NHL city and that it would cost tens of thousands of dollars to bring. I didn't have the money so I ended up dropping the case."

Today, Williams again lives in Duluth with his wife and two sons. He owns a personal loan business and has begun working on a book about famous hockey players from the State of Minnesota.

Gary Simmons remembered Butch Williams and what he meant to the Seals. "He was a great guy," Simmons said. "He was a hard worker, a real mucker. He was a good player and a good guy." For one brief season, Williams left his mark on the California Golden Seals by playing his heart out and standing up for his teammates.

John Stewart

"We got along well. He was a fiery type and I had a lot of respect for him. We were on a line together and we both had a good year. He helped a lot with pats on the back, he really encouraged me."

–Larry Patey on John Stewart

Most former professional hockey players look back at their time in the NHL as a highlight of their lives and the achievement of a lifelong dream. For former Seals winger John Stewart, however, the dream proved a hollow one and Stewart did not find satisfaction in life until after leaving professional hockey.

John Stewart may have been the typical hockey player of the early to mid-70s that was able to play in the NHL because of expansion. The 6', 180 pound native of Eriksdale, Manitoba, played three seasons of junior hockey with Winnipeg and Flin Flon of the Western League and part of one season with Sorel of the Quebec League. The Pittsburgh Penguins made Stewart their second choice in the 1970 entry draft. Because the Penguins were not among the NHL's elite, Stewart played 15 games for the Pens in 1970-71, scoring two goals and three points. He spent the rest of the season with the Amarillo Wranglers of the CHL and scored 19 goals and 34 points in 57 games there. Stewart split the 1971-72 season between Pittsburgh, where he scored two goals and 10 points in 25 games, and the Hershey Bears of the AHL.

The Atlanta Flames selected Stewart in the expansion draft prior to the 1972-73 season. It was in Atlanta where Stewart finally got the chance to play regularly. The Flames were a respectable club in their first year, managing to remain in the playoff race until the final month of the season. In 68 games with the Flames, Stewart scored 17 goals and 34 points while playing mostly on the third line.

The Flames made the playoffs in just their second year of existence in 1973-74 and Stewart was a steady contributor. He scored 18 goals and 33 points in 74 contests for the Flames. Although hockey was a new sport in the American South, Stewart took a liking to Atlanta. He met and married a Southern woman and began to feel at home in Georgia.

Stewart recalled that while he was with the Flames, a trip to Oakland was viewed as "good weather, a fun trip, an easy two points and a little California living," by most of his teammates.

The Flames surprised Stewart by trading him to the Seals on July 18, 1974, in exchange for Hilliard Graves. At the time, Stewart was less than thrilled about the trade. "It's not that I disliked coming to the Seals," Stewart told Fran Tuckwiler of the *San Jose Mercury-News*. "It's just that we liked Atlanta so much." Despite the disappointment of being traded from the Flames, Stewart refused to blame the Flames management for the trade. "I feel I had a fair shot in Atlanta," he said. "Any problems I had were my own fault."

At least Stewart got to stay in a warm weather climate although he admitted that there was an adjustment from the Deep South to Northern California. Seals GM Bill McCreary was less than resounding in his confidence in Stewart when he took over the team. "We feel Stewart perhaps didn't fit into the program at Atlanta but can fit in here. He can be a strong player on the left side for us." The trade was made by McCreary's predecessor, Garry Young who was replaced by McCreary before the 1974-75 regular season got underway.

When he arrived in Oakland, Stewart saw a franchise in disarray. "Atlanta had good players and we played hard," Stewart explained. "In Oakland, it was a laissez-faire attitude. We were California dreaming. There were a thousand things to do there."

Stewart said it was tough to develop a team spirit under the circumstances. "The team was in maintenance mode and at the NHL level, you can't perform with that attitude. We weren't building towards anything," he continued. "There was no three or four year plan. It was just play out the year and see what happens."

He recalled the club had some gifted players but did not pull together. "Joey Johnston was a gifted player but his heart wasn't there. We had a lot of rookies on the team and guys that didn't have the ability to play at that level. We were out of it by Christmas. You have to find internal motivation when that happens and it's tough to develop an espirit decorps." Stewart himself admitted, "I didn't handle the situation well," and that he was "disappointed about being there."

Still, there were some bright moments. According to his teammates, Stewart's main asset was his skating speed. "He could skate like the wind," said center Dave Gardner who often played on a line with Stewart and Fred Ahern. "He also talked 100 miles per hour. He played with a big hook on his stick and could shoot the puck." Spike Huston recalled Stewart as "a fast winger with good speed and a good shot."

In 76 games with the 1974-75 Seals, John Stewart scored a career high 19 goals and 38 points. While playing on a last place team, Stewart was a minus 42 in plus minus after being a plus three the year before with Atlanta. Stewart did provide the Seals with some solid games, but he failed to produce consistently. Some of his best games included a two goal performance against the Rangers at Madison Square Garden on October 16, 1974, which helped the Seals earn a 5-5 road tie and a two goal, two assist night against the expansion Washington Capitals on February 5, 1975, in which the Seals defeated Washington 5-1 at the Oakland Coliseum Arena.

Big John recalled that he had 19 goals with about 12 games left in the season and was hungry to get to the 20-goal plateau. He never quite made it and a nagging injury didn't help.

When asked to describe his strengths as a player, John Stewart felt that he was "a journeyman. Someone who could play in the league with above average skill in some areas but could not climb above the 18/19 goal range. My strongest asset was my skating. I had too many weaknesses to mention."

Some of Stewart's teammates recognized his limitations on the ice. Morris Mott remembered Stewart as "fast with a good shot. He was friendly and maybe a bit insecure. He wanted approval. He could have great games and then bad ones." Len Frig felt the Seals asked more of Stewart than perhaps they should have. "John was a role player," Frig said. "They expected more of him and tried to make him something he really wasn't. He was a good skater and checker." Still, nobody ever faulted Stewart for a lack of effort. GM Bill McCreary who later also coached Stewart during the 1974-75 season, recalled that John "didn't have a lot of raw talent but he made a contribution to the team."

Although Stewart had decent size, he was not known for his physical play and some teammates questioned his willingness to mix it up. Joey Johnston said that Stewart, "Just skated. He wasn't that brave, although I guess in a lot of those games, none of us was." Bob Stewart (no relation) said John

Stewart was, "An up and down the wing type guy with a good shot. He was not a very tough player." Stewart was assessed 55 penalty minutes that season. Although he was not known for using his fists on the ice, Stewart was one of the few NHL players in the mid-70s who lifted weights and used body building equipment to keep in shape.

Butch Williams seemed to be the only member of the Seals who was not overly fond of Stewart personally. A proud American, Williams recalled that Stewart "made comments about how America sucked," while he was playing for the Seals. "I told him he wouldn't get the opportunity to do this well in Canada." Even now, Williams seemed uneasy about the conversation.

By the time he had joined the Seals, Stewart knew something was wrong with the direction his life has taken. "I was my lifetime goal since I was five to play in the NHL," Stewart recalled. "I was surprised I could play in the NHL, but the emotional fulfillment was not there. I felt a certain emptiness. That year (in Oakland), it accelerated. I started wondering 'is that all there is?' and wondering 'so what if I score 40 goals.'"

Stewart signed with the Cleveland Crusaders of the WHA before the 1975-76 season began. "I did not want to play in a situation where there was no plan to improve the team," he explained. "I was also being pursued by the Cleveland Crusaders and a friend of mine [Al McDonough] who wanted me to come to Cleveland to play with him there."

While the WHA was considered a more offensive minded league than the NHL, Stewart's statistics remained roughly the same. In 79 games with the Crusaders, he scored 12 goals and 33 points. The Crusaders became the "New" Minnesota Fighting Saints the following year and Stewart made the move with the team. In 15 games, he scored three goals and six points. He also played one game for the Birmingham Bulls in 1976-77 before an injury cut his season short. He returned to play with the Philadelphia Firebirds of the AHL in 1977-78 before retiring from pro hockey. Stewart's career statistics in the NHL include 58 goals and 118 points in 257 games. In the WHA, he scored 15 times and had 39 points in 95 contests.

After quitting hockey, Stewart found his calling as a Christian writer/author. In 1977, he became born again and says, "I finally have the meaning and purpose that pro hockey [or anything else] could not give me." He lives in Minnesota and runs an organization called Lamplighters International designed to help people understand God's word. Stewart and his wife have three sons. He travels often as part of his work.

Although he was not a "name" player or a member of the Seals for long, John Stewart worked hard and left a positive impression on most of his teammates. "He was only there a short time," defenseman Mike Christie said of Stewart. "He was a good team guy, a good skater and a blue collar type guy."

Dave Hrechkosy

"He had a super year. He worked hard. After that one year, I don't know what happened to him."

–Joey Johnston on Dave Hrechkosy

Dave Hrechkosy was the Seals ultimate one-hit wonder. Not unlike a singing group that has a song that is on everybody's lips for a few months and then disappears seemingly without a trace, Hrechkosy burst onto the NHL scene as a rookie and then, almost as quickly was out of the league.

Hrechkosy was born in Winnipeg and played junior hockey with the Winnipeg Junior Jets of the Western League. The New York Rangers drafted Hrechkosy at age 19 which surprised the 6'2", 195 pound left wing. "I hadn't had a very good season that year with the Winnipeg Junior Jets," Hrechkosy admitted. "I was having problems on and off the ice that year. By off, I mean with management. The coach had ideas about changing my skating style (and) said I wasn't skating enough. The owner of team would call me in and chew me out every two or three days and ask me why the team wasn't winning. The pressure was getting so hot and heavy for me, I couldn't concentrate on having a good season myself."

The issue of skating style would always remain with Hrechkosy throughout his hockey career. While his critics felt he was not a good skater, some teammates recognized his style was unorthodox but effective. "The Wrecker was like 6'3", 215 pounds and like a teddy bear," Larry Patey said. "His nickname was 'Crazy Legs' because he was a goofy looking skater but when you were skating with him, you realized he could skate pretty fast."

Hrechkosy admitted his skating style wasn't pretty to watch but it got the job done. "It's just that I skate in what looks like an awkward way, not totally smooth," he said. "This is my natural way of skating; no way anybody can change your style."

Hrechkosy reported to the Rangers training camp before the 1969-70 season but wasn't pleased with the way he was treated. "I saw Ed Giacomin and Rod Seiling carrying in some beers and they said, 'Hey, rookie, why don't you carry this stuff in for us.' They just weren't all that nice," Hrechkosy said. Hrechkosy spent the 1971-72 season playing for the New Haven Blades before moving on to the AHL's Rochester Americans in 1972-73. "The Wrecker" scored 15 goals and 39 points in 70 games for Rochester that season.

Big Dave was traded to the Seals as part of the deal that sent Bert Marshall to the Rangers at the end of the 1972-73 season along with Gary Coalter. The Seals assigned Hrechkosy to their farm team in Salt Lake City for the 1973-74 season. It was there that "The Wrecker" began to blossom, scoring 36 goals and 71 points in 78 games for the Golden Eagles. The Seals called him up for a pair of games that season. Although he was held pointless in his NHL debut, his first shift was a memorable one for Hrechkosy. "We played the Boston Bruins at the Oakland Coliseum and coach asked me to go out and kill off a Bruins power play," Hrechkosy said. "Intimidating enough were the road black jerseys but their lineup of Orr, Bucyk, Esposito, Hodge and Cashman could cause any player to experience a flood of butterflies! I almost scored short handed and we killed the penalty off."

In 1974-75, Hrechkosy made the Seals and remained with the club for the entire season. After a slow start, Hrechkosy finally got his first NHL goal on November 6, 1974, during a Seals 7-3 loss against the Rangers in Oakland. Hrechkosy was very pleased that he scored his first NHL goal off of Ed Giacomin. "I picked up a pass at the Rangers blue line, broke in and beat Ed Giacomin high to the stick hand side. I have the picture of the goal in a frame. It was particularly sweet," Hrechkosy admitted in light of the way Giacomin had treated him as a rookie in training camp when he was with the Rangers. "It was great to beat him for my first NHL goal."

On December 3, 1974, Hrechkosy was teamed with the newly acquired Butch Williams and former Salt Lake teammate Spike Huston to form "The Wrecking Crew Line". The line scored 11 goals for the Seals in the next six games, half of the club's total. It quickly became the team's most productive line. "The Wrecking Crew line worked so well because of my unselfish linemates, Ron "Spike" Huston and Warren "Butch" Williams," Hrechkosy said. "We worked so well together as Butch would go into the corners and get the puck to Spike who would in turn set me up so I could light the lamp. We always looked to help each other out!"

"The Wrecker" also attributed to line's success to the fact that all three members of the line had many similarities on and off the ice. "Maybe we've jelled because we're three of the same type of hockey players," Hrechkosy said. "We think alike, do things alike. We're all mild mannered guys; we don't get down on ourselves or each other. All of us seem to make the most of the tools we've got."

Butch Williams noted that Hrechkosy "had a great reach, similar to Phil Esposito and he liked to stay out front (of the net)." The three members of the line also enjoyed shared an interest in horse racing and often went to the track together.

Hrechkosy remained red hot throughout the 1974-75 season. He finished his rookie year with 29 goals and 43 points in 72 games. The rookie left wing led or tied for the Seals club lead in goals, power play goals, shorthanded goals, shooting percentage and set an all-time franchise record with six game winning goals. Center Stan Weir recalled, "Everything he touched that year went into the net."

"The Wrecker" always seemed to save his best games for when the Seals were playing top competition. Some of his best offensive games included a two goal effort against the Islanders and Billy Smith in a 3-3 tie in Oakland; a two goal, one assist game during a 5-3 upset win over the Bruins on December 27, 1974, and another two goal one assist effort against Gilles Villemure and the Rangers on January 7, 1975. Hrechkosy also beat Gilles Gilbert of Boston twice as part of a 6-4 Seals win at home over the Bruins on February 21, 1975.

Hrechkosy enjoyed playing for Seals coach Marshall Johnston. "He was great to play for," Hrechkosy said. "He commanded respect and was very good at analyzing the other team's strengths and weaknesses. He just needed experience and he would have been fine."

"The Wrecker" was looking forward to his first appearance on "Hockey Night in Canada" on December 31st in a game against the Maple Leafs in Toronto but the game ended up being the most disappointing of his career. "I got thrown out of Maple Leaf Gardens just two minutes into the game," Hrechkosy said. "I got tangled with a big Leaf defenseman and we got game misconducts. My family in Winnipeg were huddled around the TV but got little to watch of my play that evening."

Off the ice, Hrechkosy was known as an easy going guy and a practical joker who enjoyed meeting women and having perhaps a few too many drinks. "He once taped me to the trainer's table," Jim Moxey said. "Wrecker was a real comedian." Wayne King recalled some of the pranks Hrechkosy would play on his teammates. "On the plane, Wrecker would put shaving cream on guys (who were sleeping) or cut a guy's tie off. On the plane one time, we got him back. He was sleeping soundly and we cut the crotch off his pants. He had to walk through the airport that way."

Despite (or perhaps because of) the practical jokes he played, Hrechkosy was well liked by his teammates. "He played extremely well and made a good teammate," John Stewart said. "He was not cliquish and cared about everybody."

Eventually, "The Wrecker's" off-ice activities started to affect his on ice performance. "Dave worked hard on the ice but he partied harder off it," George Pesut recalled. "His off-ice activities hurt him," Al MacAdam said. "It slowed him down. He was a big guy and he took the league by storm his first year and then he was out of the league two years later. A good time guy, but like a lot of the guys on our team, he didn't care where he was playing. He would play the same in California, Salt Lake or anywhere." Jim Pappin added, "If he never drank, he would have been an all-star. He was an easygoing Ukrainian kid. He wasn't serious."

In 1975-76, Hrechkosy returned to the Seals with high expectations. For some reason, the results were just not there for him. In 38 games with the Seals, "The Wrecker" managed nine goals and 14 points before being returned to Salt Lake. Bob Stewart felt that Hrechkosy "got involved in off-ice activities that were not conducive to being an athlete. He drank too much." Charlie Simmer summed up Hrechkosy's problem by saying, "He was a great guy and a very talented scorer. He got distracted. If he could do that well while drinking, imagine how well he could have done sober?"

Hrechkosy himself admits he had problems adjusting to life in the NHL and the expectations that were placed upon him. "I don't think I was mature enough to handle the press and outside interruptions that my success caused going into the 1975-76 season," he recalled.

Bob Murdoch, who was a rookie in 1975-76 recalled, "Wrecker took me under his wing. We were both single. The first time I saw him I thought he was the toughest guy in the league. He looked like a big pumpkin and never combed his hair. He was the nicest guy. If he had wheels, he would have scored 50 goals. He had an incredible shot. He was a big guy and the women loved him."

In 1975-76, new Seals coach Jack Evans had a reputation as being a no nonsense kind of guy. Hrechkosy said, "You always knew if you didn't work hard in any game that Jack would get it out of you on the practice ice." Hrechkosy recalled one instance in which Evans did just that. "One time, most of the guys were out late the night before and Coach Evans called an 8 AM practice at Berkeley," Hrechkosy recalled. "We didn't want to get on the ice smelling like alcohol, so we rubbed our chests with Ben-Gay. Well, that didn't work. Tex yelled, 'It smells like a hospital here' and made us do wind sprints for 20 minutes straight."

Due to his lack of production, Hrechkosy's stock quickly plummeted within the Seals organization. On March 9, 1976, the Seals traded "The Wrecker" to St. Louis. All they got in return was two draft choices, a third rounder and a fifth rounder. Hrechkosy finished his season in St. Louis, scoring three goals and six points in 13 games. He also saw action in the playoffs, scoring one goal in three post-season games for the Blues. In 1976-77, Hrechkosy made some cameo appearances for St. Louis, playing in only 15 games and scoring one goal and three points. He spent the rest of the season playing for the Blues CHL farm club in Kansas City. The following year, he was back in Salt Lake. He played two more minor league seasons before retiring from pro hockey after the 1979-80 season. Hrechkosy's final NHL totals were 42 goals and 66 points in 141 games.

Dave Hrechkosy has settled down a lot since his days in Oakland. He has been married to the same woman for almost 25 years and has a son and a daughter. He lives near Salt Lake City and works as the concessions manager for the athletic department at the University of Utah.

Gary Simmons remembered Dave Hrechkosy warmly but admitted his shortcomings. "He had a drinking problem and he'd be the first to admit it," Simmons said. "He had a good shot and he could really snap it. He was a lumbering skater. 'Wrecker' was a great team man and great in the dressing room. He was a party guy off the ice."

Dave Hrechkosy was an NHL star in Oakland for one brief season. Although he was unable to sustain his NHL career, those who saw him play will always have fond memories of "The Wrecker" which will take them back to a simpler time and place, just like hearing a song by your favorite one hit wonder on the radio.

Dave Gardner

"He was a tremendous fundamental hockey player. He had good hands and was a smart player. Dave was a super nice guy. He was one of the best juniors in Canada. He was a good player who wasn't in the right situation."

–Wayne Merrick on Dave Gardner

Dave Gardner was born surrounded by hockey. His father, Cal Gardner, played for the Rangers, Maple Leafs, Black Hawks and Bruins from 1945-46 to 1956-1957. "I grew up in Toronto and was a Leafs fan," Gardner said. "I remember watching them win the Stanley Cup in 1964 and 1967. Dave Keon was probably my favorite player. I loved the way he skated. I also liked Jim Pappin; he contributed and he worked hard. I met some of these guys as a child because my dad was in the NHL. They were more like fathers to me—some of them even changed my diapers."

Gardner was one of the top players in Junior B starring for St. Mike's. "I scored 54 goals in 36 games," Gardner recalled. "I was gearing myself towards college but I was the first guy drafted into the OHL from Junior B." Gardner didn't disappoint when he joined the Toronto Marlboros in 1970-71. In his first season with the Marlies, Gardner scored 56 goals and 137 points in 62 games. The following season, Gardner scored 53 goals and 129 points in 57 games. Both years he led the league in assists while in his second year with the Marlies, Gardner won the league scoring title. He was a second team OHA postseason all-star both seasons.

The 6', 185 pound Toronto native was drafted in the first round of the 1972 entry draft by the Montreal Canadiens. The Habs started Gardner out with their AHL team, the Nova Scotia Voyageurs. In 66 games, Gardner continued to be productive, scoring 28 goals and 72 points. The Canadiens called him up for five games during the 1972-73 season and he notched his first NHL goal and two points during his brief call-up. "Frank Mahovlich had the assist," Gardner said remembering his first NHL goal. "And to think, I used to baby-sit his kids."

Gardner started the 1973-74 season with the Canadiens but was frustrated by his lack of ice time. In 31 games for Montreal, Gardner had one goal and 11 points. On March 9, 1974, the Habs traded Gardner to St. Louis for a number one draft choice. He played 15 late season games for the Blues, scoring five goals and seven points. "I was on the bench in Montreal, then I scored five goals in 15 games after being traded to St. Louis," Gardner recalled. "I was put on the "B" team at training camp the following year." In eight games with the Blues in 1974-75, Gardner assisted on two goals before the Blues traded him to the Seals along with Butch Williams for Stan Gilbertson and Craig Patrick on November 11, 1974.

Gardner recalled his trade to the Seals and his first impression of the organization. "I remember when I was acquired, Bill McCreary called me on the phone and said his team lost 1-0 or 2-1 to Philadelphia and he was looking to bring in young talent. He told me I would be an integral part of that. He said to me, 'Dave, you can help our team. You can get Joey Johnston the puck and he can get 40 goals.'" Unfortunately, Johnston and Gardner never jelled as linemates. Gardner was a finesse player while Johnston was known for being a very physical player. "I don't know what he was doing there," Johnston said. "I don't know who they were punishing Dave or me. He would skate with me Monday or Tuesday and by Wednesday, he would be off my line."

"The Seals had a multitude of talented young guys who were being let go because they couldn't gel," Gardner recalled. "These guys were dispersed around the NHL. The attitude of the team was to try to work our way up from zero. It was surprising. We had a good bunch of guys and I think the travel hurt us the most. The thought was, 'Play well in California and get traded somewhere else.' As an organization, the Seals were weak in a lot of areas. The training staff was weak, accommodations and plane flights were weak. They expected us to fly home to play Toronto the same night while the Leafs were in Oakland waiting for us for two days. The Seals were a minor league organization trying to exist in the NHL. We had major league fans, but the club was just trying to scrape by."

Early in his Seals career, Gardner found ice time hard to come by. "I didn't get to play too much when I first joined the Seals," Gardner recalled. At least one of his teammates felt Gardner deserved a chance based on his play in practice. Gilles Meloche added, "If Dave played like he practiced, he'd have been a Hall of Famer."

The slick-passing center felt that Seals coach Marshall Johnston did not fully appreciate what he brought to the table. "With Marshall if you didn't perform, you sat on the bench. He didn't know as much about the finesse part of the game and that was my strength. He didn't always understand what I was saying. He was more of a college guy. We played hard but we were getting the crap beat out of us all the time. He was able to speak to you and tell you, 'I'm not happy about this' and he knew how to pat you on the back."

Gardner got off to a slow start with the Seals in 1974-75, but once he adjusted to his new teammates and found his niche on the club, Gardner began to thrive. On January 5, 1975, he had his breakout game, a one goal two assist effort that helped the Seals defeat the defending Stanley Cup champion Philadelphia Flyers 5-1 in Oakland. Exactly one month later, Gardner scored twice during a 5-1 win over Washington before having his biggest offensive game of the season on March 23, 1975, when he scored twice and added an assist during a 9-4 Seals loss to the Sabres at the Aud in Buffalo.

Despite the slow start and a limited role early in the year, Gardner scored 16 goals and 36 points in 64 games for the Seals in 1974-75. One issue dogged Gardner during his career with California: he was not a physical hockey player. In fact, in his two seasons with California, Gardner collected a total of just 14 penalty minutes. In the mid-70s, while the Flyers were winning back-to-back Stanley Cups by fighting their way through the league, Gardner's lack of desire for mixing it up stood out, especially on a team like the Seals that lacked many physical players. Teammates appreciated Gardner's obvious puck skills, but also were quick to note that he seemed to shy away from the more physical aspect of the game. "Dave was a quiet man and a great leader," defenseman Len Frig recalled. "He was a smart centerman and he won face-offs left and right but he was scared of his own shadow." Goalie Gary Simmons recalled that Gardner was, "a tremendous talent and the nicest guy you'd ever want to meet. He just didn't like the rough going." Jim Pappin was more blunt. "Dave was a good kid, everybody liked him. His problem was he was too soft to be a good NHL player."

The wings that played with the slick passing Gardner, however, were more than pleased with what he brought to the table. Fred Ahern, who often teamed up on a line with Gardner and Jim Moxey, appreciated what Gardner did for his game. "I gave him a lot of credit for setting up most of my goals," Ahern said. "He was a great puck handler, a good playmaker and a smooth centerman."

Gardner was popular among his teammates off the ice as most mentioned what a genuine and nice individual he was. He did remember some lighter times as a member of the Seals. "One time I had cut my tongue in half," he recalled. "The guys laughed that I could tip the girls with my tongue. We had a lot of good times."

Gardner also made many friends in the Bay Area among the fans, particularly members of the Seals Booster Club. "They were just nice people," Gardner said. "The fan club was very devoted, open and nice. They asked a lot of questions, but they were honest. I'd say there were about 9,000 fans who came to see us." He recalled one specific family who befriended Gardner. "The man's name was Paul. "He and his family were very nice," Gardner said. "They sort of took us in. I drank with him and we sang songs by Three Dog Night. His three kids were great athletes, two boys who were on baseball scholarships and a girl. They were just the ultimate Oakland fans. Then there was Ty Toki who was a great guy along with his wife and daughter. They were just nice people."

While Gardner appreciated many of the members of the Seals Booster Club, he was a bit less kind when speaking about Bay Area sports fans as a whole. "The Oakland fans as a whole were fickle, they loved a winner," Gardner said. "Bay Area sports always had problems. The A's were champs back then and few people were at those games. The beer guy sat down next to me and my brother one time. There were problems with racism. Except for the football team, Oakland didn't really accept their teams." He also recalled a game against the Flyers that the Seals won handily. "We beat the Flyers but the fans were upset as we were coming off the ice because there were no fights," Gardner said.

Gardner also recalled how cheap the Seals organization was, especially at Christmas time. "My brother [Paul Gardner] was playing for Leafs at that time. For Christmas, he got plane tickets to anywhere in the United States or Canada. I got a tee shirt from the Seals."

On the ice, Gardner was exceptionally dangerous on the power play where he often patrolled the blue line. Fourteen of the 32 goals that he scored as a member of the Seals came with the man advantage. By playing point on the power play, Gardner could see the ice better and have more room to work his magic with the puck. "Dave played on the power play a lot and was a good play maker," Bob Stewart recalled. When asked about his own skills on the ice, Gardner added, "I played the point on the power play. My game was stickhandling and making plays."

In 1975-76, Gardner played 74 games for the Seals, scoring 16 goals and a career high 48 points. He still had problems, however, with the new Seals coach, Jack "Tex" Evans. "Jack Evans lacked a lot in all aspects of the game," Gardner recalled. "He didn't understand the power play. He couldn't understand the finesse part of the game. He relied on Gilles Meloche to stop all the pucks. I had a run-in with him but I have no regrets about it. He did not compliment anybody's abilities. I guess he kept certain people happy."

Gardner recalled one incident in particular between himself and Evans. "I was out of the lineup one time and I was screaming at Jack Evans. The trainer had to get me out of the way. The next night, I played and scored two goals and an assist."

Gardner's best offensive game with the Seals came on February 15, 1976, during a 7-3 Seals win at Minnesota. The smooth center scored once and added three assists to lead the California attack. Despite having a number of high scoring games with the Seals, Gardner's favorite moment was an individual play he made against the Los Angeles Kings. "Dave Hutchinson was the defenseman chasing me," Gardner recalled. "I flipped the puck between my legs and over Rogie Vachon's shoulder and into the net. I sat there amazed that I did it and so did everybody else."

There were many teammates who felt that Gardner's talents were not taken full advantage of on a team like the Seals. "Dave was a different kind of player. He was very gifted and a very nice person," Charlie Simmer said. "I think being with the Seals confused him." Al MacAdam added, "Dave was a highly skilled player, a good family man and a nice guy. He was in Montreal before California and he had high expectations. He sensed the difference in the team and how you were treated. As a result, I think he lost focus."

Gardner remained with the Seals organization when they moved to Cleveland. In 1976-77, Gardner scored 16 goals for the third consecutive season and finished the year with 38 points. He scored a career best 19 goals in 1977-78 and had 44 points for the Barons. When the Barons merged with Minnesota prior to the 1978-79 season, Gardner found himself without an NHL job. The Los Angeles Kings acquired him but assigned him to the minor leagues. In 1979-80, the Flyers inked Gardner to a free agent contract. He played only two games with Philadelphia that season, scoring one goal and two points. He spent most of the year in the AHL, splitting time between the Binghamton Whalers and Maine Mariners. Gardner then spent the next five seasons in Switzerland where his finesse style was more appreciated. He retired as a player after the 1984-85 season. Gardner's NHL career statistics include 75 goals and 190 points in 350 games. He accumulated only 41 penalty minutes in his NHL career.

Today, Gardner and his wife live in the Toronto area where he works for Molson as a promotions manager. The Gardners have two sons including Ryan who was playing hockey in Switzerland when I interviewed his father.

George Pesut recalled that Dave Gardner was, "Mr. Lady Byng and played a European type of style. He didn't like the rough stuff, but he was a talented player." Ralph Klassen added, "Dave was a super talent and an excellent play maker. He was a good person on and off the ice."

Fred Ahern

"He was a good kid, an American from Boston who was tough as nails. He would back up anybody. He could skate but he didn't have the talent to keep himself in the league. He would fight anybody and was very tough, pound for pound. He just wasn't big enough to be the type of player he was. If he were two inches taller and a bit heavier, he could have beaten anybody."

–Jim Pappin on Fred Ahern

Fred Ahern was only the second NHL player born in New England to play in the NHL. The first was former Seals center Bobby Sheehan. The 6', 180 pound native of South Boston was a long shot to make the NHL but through hard work and determination, was able to find a way to make the big time.

"Growing up in South Boston, I was a Bruins fan," Ahern said. "It was the Bobby Orr era. I remember falling asleep with the transistor radio on listening to the Bruins. Before Bobby Orr came to town, there was no one player I liked in particular. Then, there were a lot of players I liked...Orr, Johnny Bucyk and Derek Sanderson."

Ahern spent three years at Bowdoin College in Maine and then surprisingly found his way to the Seals as a free agent. He was captain of the hockey team at Bowdoin for three years. "I went to a Division II school back in New England," Ahern said. "I thought I could end up playing in the minors. After my senior year, I was given a walk-on invitation to Seals camp. Bill Cleary, who was then coach at Harvard, spoke to Jim Sutherland who scouted for the Seals and they signed me to a free agent contract. I had a good camp and was sent to Salt Lake City, the Seals top affiliate."

Bob Murdoch recalled how much of a long shot Ahern was at Seals camp that year. "We were both invitees to camp," Murdoch recalled. "The first day of camp, there were 101 guys there and they put us all in order. The guys on the Seals last year were numbers 1-20, the guys on Salt Lake last year were 21-40 and so on. Fred was number 100 and I was number 101. We both made it through the first week of camp. He had a great shot. He as the best looking guy in pro hockey: an American and a college man. The guys called him 'Preppy'. He was a tough guy."

Ahern played well in Salt Lake City in 1974-75. The long shot from South Boston scored 26 goals and 52 points for the Golden Eagles in 64 games. In nine playoff contests, Ahern scored five goals and eight points as Salt Lake won the CHL title.

In January of 1975, Ahern got called up to the Seals for a three game stint. "I was thrilled," Ahern said. "Just being an NHL player was a big thrill for me. I think the day I first stepped out on the ice in the NHL was when I realized I could finally make it. Dave Hrechkosy got injured and I was called up for three games during the 1974-75 season. My first ever game was against Philadelphia. It's a thrill I'll never forget."

Along with his first NHL game, Ahern had the thrill of scoring his first NHL goal. "I was on a line with Larry Patey and he and I had a two on one break," Ahern recalled. "Just as I crossed the blue line, Bernie Parent was sitting back in his net and did not challenge me. I shot the puck into the far corner off the post and just along the ice." The Seals went on to win the game 5-1.

Two days later, Ahern picked up a goal and an assist as the Seals edged the Blues in St. Louis 3-2. In his brief three game call-up in 1974-75, Ahern had three points.

Ahern was fortunate when Jack Evans, who had coached him the year before as Salt Lake, took over as coach of the Seals in 1975-76. "He was a fabulous coach," Ahern said. "He was a hard nosed, demanding coach but fair. If he sat you down for a game, he told you why, unlike many coaches today. He was a hard nosed player who demanded the same from his players. He got that kind of play in Salt Lake. In California, I think he was just a bit shy on talent to get the results he wanted. I think we needed a couple of more 50 goal scorers. We were an expansion team and we had trouble getting that solid base of talent. That was our biggest problem."

Ahern again started the 1975-76 season in Salt Lake City. In 30 games, he scored 12 goals and 26 points. Roughly midway through the season, the Seals called him up to the NHL. With the Seals, Ahern scored 17 goals and 25 points in just 44 games. He also turned out to be a clutch goal scorer as four of his 17 goals were game winners. Ahern also led the Seals in plus/minus with a minus two rating and in shooting percentage, scoring on 19.3 percent of his shots.

Perhaps the biggest thrill Ahern got was scoring the winning goal against the Bruins on March 5, 1976, in Oakland. "It was my first game against Boston and I scored with about five or six minutes left in the game," Ahern recalled. "Gerry Cheevers slid toward the center of the net and I shot the puck to the spot where he was sliding away from. After the game, Jim Pappin introduced me to Cheevers. Gerry said to me, 'You looked like you were going to jump out of the rink after you scored that goal.' I used to do a dance after I scored. I explained to him that I had just scored the game winning goal to beat the team I idolized as a kid." Nine days later, Ahern had the thrill of scoring a goal off of Gilles Gilbert at the Boston Garden. After he scored, the cheers from friends and family in attendance could be heard throughout the ancient arena. The goal pulled the Seals to within a goal late in the game before an empty net tally gave the Bruins the 4-2 victory.

Ahern's toughness and determination earned him the respect of his teammates. "He was a great guy, a prince of a guy," Gary Simmons said. "A good hockey player and a tough little shit. He could throw 'em. He was a good looking guy, he could have been on the cover of GQ." Gary Sabourin felt that Ahern lacked NHL talent, but "he worked hard and was a good kid."

Ahern did have some trouble adjusting to the Seals lengthy travel schedule. "We had two or three week road trips," Ahern said. "It was tough to get up for every game. East coast teams maybe had one long road trip per season. We had them all the time."

Like many players, Ahern was surprised when it was announced that the Seals were moving to Cleveland during the summer of 1976. "We thought we were staying," Ahern recalled. "There was talk of a new arena in San Francisco. By the end of the last season there, we were drawing 10,000-11,000 fans per game. We had some good, young unknown players. I don't know why the San Francisco deal fell through. We got a letter midway through the summer that we were moving to Cleveland. The phone calls started between the players. Most of the guys were not too happy to be moving from California to Cleveland. It was like, 'anybody who owns property in the Bay Area, it's time to sell.'"

At the end of the summer of 1976, Ahern played for the United States team in the Canada Cup. He played in five games for his country in the tournament and scored two goals, one of them coming off Rogie Vachon and the tournaments eventual winners, Team Canada.

Ahern followed the Seals organization to Cleveland but injuries derailed his 1976-77 season. On December 6, 1976, Ahern suffered a broken arm in a game against the Canadiens. "I'll never forget that game, the moment my skate got caught, I hit the boards and my arm snapped," Ahern said. He played in only 25 games for the Barons that year scoring four goals and four assists. Midway through the 1977-78 season, the Barons traded Ahern to the Colorado Rockies along with Ralph Klassen for Rick Jodzio and Chuck Arnason. In 74 games total in 1977-78, Ahern scored eight goals and 25 points. He made his only postseason appearance in the NHL that year with the Rockies. In two playoff games, Ahern picked up one assist. The Flyers swept the Rockies in two straight games in the first round of the playoffs.

After the 1978 playoffs, the Rockies traded Ahern back to the Barons for cash. Unfortunately, the Barons were in the midst of disbanding and merging with the Minnesota North Stars. Ahern was placed on the North Stars reserve list, but he never played another NHL game. He retired as a player after four more seasons in the minors, playing for Binghamton Whalers, Adirondack Red Wings, Oklahoma City Stars and the Cape Cod Buccaneers. Ahern's NHL career totals are 31 goals and 61 points in 146 games.

Today, Ahern once again lives in Boston and works for the mayor's office at the Boston Redevelopment Authority where he helps Boston residents get jobs in local construction projects. He still plays recreational hockey in a league when he gets the chance.

Ralph Klassen recalled the hard work that Ahern used to get to the NHL. "He came to play," Klassen said of his former linemate. "He didn't have a lot of talent, but he made himself into a sniper." Fred Ahern was a sniper from South Boston, who managed to play in the NHL.

George Pesut

"I knew George from Saskatoon. He was off the wall. You never knew what he was going to do or say. You need that kind of person on your team."

–Ralph Klassen on George Pesut

Saskatoon native George Pesut was told at a relatively early age that he had a chance to play in the NHL. "When I was 12, I had my first inkling," Pesut recalled. "My high school principal was a mentor. I was going for stitches and he told me I could go to the NHL one day. I was always a few levels ahead of my age group." Pesut grew up rooting for the Montreal Canadiens. "Where I was from, you were either a Montreal fan or a Toronto fan," Pesut said. "I was a Canadiens fan and Jean Beliveau was my favorite player. I also liked Bobby Orr."

Pesut grew to be 6'1", 205 pounds and spent his final year of juniors with the Saskatoon Blades. In 1972-73, his final year with the Blades, Pesut scored 12 goals and 37 points in 68 games which were pretty good statistics for a defenseman. He was named to the Western League's first team all-star team. The St. Louis Blues selected Pesut in the 1973 entry draft in the second round based on his size, strength and his solid offensive production in juniors. After playing only seven games for the Blues WHL affiliate in Denver, Pesut was traded to the Flyers in November and finished the 1973-74 season with the Richmond Robins of the AHL. Pesut played in 38 games for the Robins, scoring three goals and eight points. He started the 1974-75 season in Richmond, too after being the last player cut from the eventual Stanley Cup champion Flyers in training camp. Pesut appeared in only eight games for Richmond in 1974-75 before joining the Seals, picking up one assist.

"Looking back, I was my own worst enemy," Pesut admitted. "In Richmond, I didn't get along with the coach too well. He didn't dress me for a few games and I was skating circles around the guys on that team. I asked for a trade and was made part of the trade that brought Reggie Leach to

Philadelphia. Looking back, the trade was good for me, but going from Philadelphia to Oakland was a big change. It was like a country club in Oakland." Pesut was sent to the Seals on December 11, 1974, as the player to be named later in the deal that sent Reggie Leach to the Flyers and Al MacAdam to the Seals.

Pesut recalled noticing the difference between the Flyers organization and the Seals right away. "My first game with the Seals was in Kansas City [December 12, 1974]," Pesut recalled. "Marshall Johnston was the coach at the time. Joey Johnston was our captain. I remember Marshall Johnston wanted to talk to the captain. Joey Johnston blew him off and said he was 'busy'. He saw some rookies in the bathroom. Joey went into the bathroom and took a dump at their feet. I couldn't believe the coach couldn't even speak to his captain. It was very different than Philadelphia." Pesut felt that Marshall Johnston "knows his hockey but as a coach, I think he was too good a guy."

If Pesut felt Johnston was too easy going as a coach, he felt his successor, Bill McCreary failed to communicate well enough with his team to be effective. "He was not a great mentor for the younger players," Pesut remembered. "In Philadelphia, Fred Shero wouldn't say two words to you but we had a go between in [assistant coach] Mike Nykoluk. Bill McCreary once taped my glove to my stick to tell me to put two hands on the stick. That was strange. He was sort of in the Joe Crozier category... A bit of a madman."

Pesut played in 47 games for the Seals in 1974-75. He finished with no goals and 13 assists along with 73 penalty minutes. His best offensive game that season was a two assist effort on March 21, 1975, against the St. Louis Blues in Oakland. The Seals won the game 7-4.

Pesut also recalled one of the girls who liked to hang around the team. "We had a girl who we knew called 'The Steel Worker,'" Pesut said. "Each team had their groupies. There was 'Chicago Shirley' for example. But 'The Steel Worker' was at every practice we had. When the season was over, she would go to A's games. She said the Buffalo Sabres were her favorite team because she liked the French Connection. 'The Steel Worker' knew our practice schedule better than we did. I remember once we called a spur of the moment practice and she was there. Once, Joey Johnston stopped in the middle of practice and took the guys to the bench. Joey Johnston told the guys we couldn't go on with the practice because 'The Steel Worker' was late and she had never missed a practice before."

George Pesut remained an enigma to many of his teammates. Many of them felt he was a bit of a loner. Still, the team seemed divided as to whether Pesut was a hard worker who did not have an abundance of talent or a talented player to never applied himself enough to succeed. "He had a lot of potential and could really skate and shoot," Jim Moxey recalled. "But it didn't really happen for him." Len Frig concurred with Moxey. "He had all the tools but never utilized them properly," Frig said. "He could skate and hit but he was so inconsistent. We called him 'Mr. Wonderful' because he was always combing his hair."

Other teammates felt Pesut worked hard and played a gutsy game. "George would stick his nose in anywhere, he wasn't afraid," Fred Ahern said. "He would fight anybody, even if he didn't win." Spike Huston said, "George hung on, I guess. He was not a great talent but he made it."

Pesut took a real liking to Northern California while he was there. "I couldn't understand why guys left in the off-season," he said. "I played golf and tennis. It was a great place to be." Dave Gardner recalled that Pesut could, "play tennis like an SOB." Pesut stayed in the Bay Area in the off-season and even competed in the local Superstars competition (which was run by ABC television in the US). He more than held his own in the regional Bay Area contest. "I wanted to go to the national competition," Pesut said, "but I was not a high profile athlete at the time."

Pesut recalled one single teammate who did so well with the ladies that it made him late for practice. "He could never find the practice rink," Pesut said. "He would always come from a different direction." Eventually, Pesut recalled that the player had to get a separate apartment for himself just so he could get some privacy on dates.

The one thing Pesut did not like about playing in Oakland was the traveling. "We flew something like 90,000 miles in a season," Pesut said. "You got used to it. We played in Washington and that was a seven hour flight. Then we went back to Oakland for a game. Then a few days later, we were in Washington again. We always took the bus to San Francisco, which is where we flew out of. It definitely had an effect on us."

The Seals uniforms were also not among Pesut's favorites. "I think we had the ugliest uniforms in hockey," Pesut said. "I didn't see them as hockey uniforms. Pacific blue, what was that?"

In 1975-76, Pesut returned to the Seals. In 45 games, he scored three goals and 12 points along with 57 penalty minutes. The big defenseman scored his first NHL goal by beating Rogie Vachon on October 18, 1975, during a 5-3 Seals loss in Los Angeles. His finest offensive performance with California came on February 15, 1976, at Minnesota. Pesut assisted on three Seals goals in a 7-3 win over the North Stars. The win ended a nine game winless streak for California.

Goalie Gary Simmons remembered Pesut "sort of the team whipping boy. He'd skate around during warm-ups and look into the glass to see how his hair was. He did his job but he didn't stand out. He was comical."

Again, in his second season with the club, teammates disagreed on Pesut's talent level and how much effort he put into the game. Veteran wing Jim Pappin said Pesut was "All muscle all the time. He wanted to be a good player in the worst way but he didn't have the talent. He had everything but no game." Meanwhile, Bob Murdoch described Pesut as "an average type of guy whose eyes made you wonder if he was asleep or awake." Fellow blue liner Mike Christie had a different view of Pesut altogether. "He was a strange guy," Christie said. "He thought on a different level. He was a smart guy and he thought like a college guy. He spent so much time thinking about how he got there that he lost sight of the result. He had talent but it never really got all the way out."

After the 1975-76 season, Pesut decided to sign with the WHA's Calgary Cowboys. In 17 games with Calgary, Pesut scored twice and accumulated two penalty minutes. He spent the rest of that year in the minor leagues, playing 14 games with the Tidewater Sharks of the SHL and 25 games with the NAHL's Erie Blades. Pesut later went to play many productive seasons in Europe before ultimately retiring from hockey in 1994.

Today, Pesut has settled down in Kelowna, BC with his wife and two sons. After retiring from hockey, Pesut worked for a while in the mining industry. He was later involved with an Internet site for retired hockey players, Icelegends.com.

Perhaps Morris Mott summed up Pesut best by saying, "George was a little insecure. He was a tough player who was always looking for assurance that his teammates respected him. He was a really well motivated guy and not selfish in the least." George Pesut was a bit of a mystery to his teammates. While he never played in an All-Star game or made himself a household name, he was a tough, honest hockey player who was able to make a living playing the game that he loved.

Wayne King

"He was a grinder. He'd go up and down his wing and he would body check, which was a lost art on our team. He was not a big goal scorer but he did his job and was a good guy off the ice."
–Gary Simmons on Wayne King

Wayne King grew up in Midland, Ontario, one of eight children in a Native Canadian household. King played his junior hockey with the Niagara Falls Flyers. Even at the junior level, King was not a big goal scorer. During his most productive season in junior hockey he scored 14 goals. Throughout his hockey career, King's best assets were his smarts and his strength. He was able to use his 5'10", 185 pound frame to his advantage on the ice. The Seals signed by the Seals in 1971 and was assigned to their IHL farm team in Columbus.

In 1971-72, King scored a respectable 22 goals and 51 points in 72 games for the Columbus Seals. The following season, he moved up to the Seals top minor league affiliate in Salt Lake City where he scored 16 goals and 43 points in 72 contests. In 1973-74, King blossomed at the WHL level, scoring

34 goals and 68 points for Salt Lake in 76 games. He got a brief call-up to California that season as a reward but failed to register a point in two games. "The first time I was sent up for only two games," King recalled. "I was very happy. It was not expected but I got an invitation to camp. I got the tryout through friends. There were some big names at camp."

The following season, King made the team as a third or fourth line player. His specialties were checking, penalty killing and defensive play. Immediately, King noticed that that atmosphere around the Seals was a little different than what he was accustomed to. "Well, we never had a winning team," King recalled. "Everybody was pretty loose. The coach once came in with golf clubs and a keg of beer."

Barry Cummins, who played with King in Salt Lake and briefly with the Seals remembered, "Wayne had a hell of a shot but he didn't even know where it was going sometimes. You didn't want him giving you a pass across the ice. One time the puck would land right on your stick, the next time it would hit you in the helmet. He had good wheels and was an up and down winger."

For King, the biggest obstacle he faced at the NHL level was getting enough ice time. "I killed penalties and played on the third or fourth line," King said. "Gary Holt and Morris Mott were my linemates most of the time. We were a checking line."

The 1974-75 season started on a good note for King. While he was not getting a lot of ice time, he did play in almost every game. On November 1, 1974, he scored his first NHL goal. "It was against Detroit," King recalled. "I took a pass from the corner and took a slap shot from in front of the net that beat Jimmy Rutherford." King finished the game with two goals and an assist as the Seals and Red Wings skated to a 4-4 tie in Oakland. That was his finest offensive day in the NHL.

King was beginning to find his niche on the team when disaster struck. On December 1, 1974, in Washington, King tore knee ligaments in a game against the Capitals. He showed his toughness during that game by playing the rest of the contest despite the injury. Dave Gardner remembers saying to King with disbelief, "You played the entire game." King replied, "It hurt a little bit."

The knee required surgery but even that didn't go well for the man his teammates called "The Little Chief" (Veteran defenseman Jim Neilson, the other member of the Seals of Native origin was called "Big Chief" during the 1974-75 season). "While having surgery on his knee, his appendix ruptured," Al MacAdam said. "He went from about 215 pounds to about 160. I don't think he ever recovered emotionally." King's season was over and he finished with four goals and 11 points in 25 games.

King returned to the Seals for the 1975-76 season after a long and difficult off-season rehabilitation. Again, he found himself playing a checking role, often being placed on a line with Dave Gardner and Jim Moxey. New coach Jack Evans was a defensive oriented coach so King fit in with his philosophy. "He was strict," King recalled when asked about Evans. "He was pretty good, but it was his way or you didn't play. He was more defensively oriented."

King's teammates appreciated his effort. "He skated funny but he got the job done," Dave Gardner remembered. "He was a bit like a bull in a china shop." Defenseman Len Frig said, "Wayne was a good checker and a role player. He was a great penalty killer. Offensively, he got his chances but he couldn't score much." Jim Pappin recalled King as "a good minor leaguer and a good kid," then added, "Wayne was an easy going guy. He didn't have any meanness."

Looking back, King understood his limitations as a player on the NHL level. "I wasn't a goal scorer," he said. "I was tough in the corners, took the body and had a good slap shot."

Perhaps King's best scoring chance came on January 10, 1976, in a game at the Boston Garden. "I had a penalty shot," King recalled. "I remember saying, 'I can't hardly score in practice.' I tried a shot but it didn't work. I was happy it was near the net." Gilles Gilbert made the save on the penalty shot and the Bruins held on for a 3-2 win over the Seals.

Off the ice, King liked to hang around with former Salt Lake City teammates like Dave Hrechkosy and Spike Huston. He was known to enjoy himself a little too much off the ice at times. Mike Christie thinks that King's "living habits hurt him a lot. What happened off the ice was more important to him than what happened on the ice." Butch Williams remembered an incident when "The Little Chief" was pulled over on the freeway for driving the wrong way. "The officer asked Wayne is he was drinking," Williams recalled. "He said, 'Oh, yeah, only one or two cases.'"

King had some fun on the ice as well. "We were practicing one day and a photographer wanted to see a slap shot from behind the goal," King recalled. "I took a slap shot and the bottom of the net was loose and the puck went through the bottom of the net and hit him in the nuts. He was OK but they had to take him off the ice."

In 1975-76, King appeared in 46 games for California, scoring a goal and 12 points. He was sent down to Salt Lake City for 20 games and scored nine goals and 17 points there. He was never called up to the NHL again. After one more season in Salt Lake City, King played a year of senior hockey before retiring after the 1977-78 season. His final NHL totals were five goals and 23 points in 73 games. All of his NHL experience came with the Seals.

King truly enjoyed playing for the Seals. "It was a pleasure playing in the NHL," he said. He also appreciated the Oakland fans. "The fans were into it," King said. "The fans were pretty good, there just weren't a lot of them and the rink was not too big to begin with. I also remember Krazy George. He scared the heck out of you waiting for a face-off. He certainly scared the visiting team. We knew he was there, they didn't."

Today, King has returned to Midland, Ontario, where he lives with his wife and two children. He has worked for over 20 years now as a nurse in a maximum security hospital for the criminally insane.

Wayne King was a fringe player in the NHL, but he certainly enjoyed his opportunity to play there. His teammates acknowledged his effort and heart. "All he lacked was spit and polish," Paul Shakes said. "He had a tremendous shot and played his wing very well." Spike Huston added, "'Little Chief' was a hard worker, he would run over anybody. He had to work hard to stay there." His hard work paid off with two brief tours of duty in the NHL.

Gary Simmons

"What a character. He slept all day and watched movies all night. He smoked all the time, had a lot of tattoos and never touched an ounce of booze. He was a good goalie, too."

–Gilles Meloche on Gary Simmons

Gary Simmons is what you would call a "free spirit." "That's why I didn't make the NHL at 22 or 23," Simmons said. The native of Charlottetown, Prince Edwards Island was one of the more unique and unforgettable personalities on the Seals or any hockey team for that matter. Simmons was one of a kind both on and off the ice. His story is too good to be fiction. If you made it up, nobody would believe you.

Simmons became a goalie by accident according to an interview he did with Dick O'Connor of the *Palo Alto Times*. "I was about 15 years old and our goalie didn't show up," Simmons recalled. "I had to do it and I've been doing it ever since."

By age 16, he decided to enlist in the Canadian Navy where he got his first tattoo. Shortly after joining, he changed his mind and convinced the recruiting officer to let him finish school first.

Simmons continued to look for a goaltending position but couldn't find one so he signed up to be a police officer in Lethbridge, Alberta, where he lived as a teenager. He was given his gun and told to return that afternoon to take his oath when he got a call from a team in Newfoundland asking what it would take to sign him as their goalie. "I told him double what he offered me because I really didn't want to go to that place and I figured he would say no," Simmons said. "Well, he said yes and told me to get on a plane that day." Simmons tried to return his gun and badge to the chief of police in Lethbridge and before leaving asked, "Hey, do I qualify for a pension?"

Simmons then bounced around minor and senior hockey, took a year off to travel in Europe and across the United States before eventually settling down with the Phoenix Roadrunners of the WHL in 1972-73 and 1973-74. There, he helped Phoenix to two consecutive league titles.

While in Phoenix, Simmons received the nickname "The Cobra". "I did a lot of scrambling up and down," Simmons said. "A reporter said I looked like a snake. A teammate said I looked like a cobra. One day in Detroit, a guy brought me a real cobra eye. I still have it." Ironically, Simmons was nicknamed "Cobra" because of his fast movements around the net, yet it turned out that the cobra is among the slowest of snakes. Still, the nickname stuck.

It was then that the opportunity to play major league hockey presented itself to the 6'2", 200 pound goalie. "I had a chance to play in the WHA," Simmons recalled since the owners of the WHL Roadrunners were being granted a WHA franchise. "I played in the WHL with Phoenix. I was a Western type and I loved it out there. It was hard to leave Phoenix; California vs. Arizona, two very different lifestyles. But it's 26 years later and I'm still here. But the NHL was always the league so that's where I wanted to be."

Simmons signed on as a 30-year-old rookie with the Seals for the 1974-75 season. In his first game with California, Simmons made 24 saves to shut out the Atlanta Flames at the Oakland Coliseum Arena 3-0. Despite the early success, Simmons realized things were different in California than they had been in Phoenix. "I came from two championship teams to a team that had only won 13 games the year before," Simmons said. "They were owned by the league and the league wasn't spending much money on the club. A lot of this team's good players had jumped to the WHA. I remember after my first season there, I went with Len Shapiro [the Seals assistant director of public relations] on a speaking engagement at the Rotary Club. A man asked, 'What's wrong with the Seals?' I also remember our GM, Bill McCreary saying we wanted to be out of it by Christmas. Our better players were pissed off about having to be there. We weren't supposed to win. Being a goalie, it was a difficult team to play for. It was a job. There was no pressure to win."

Simmons compared his situation in California with other goalies at the time. "I remember talking to Ken Dryden of Montreal and he said, 'If I ever got traded to the Seals, I'd retire.' I told him, 'I face 30, 40, 50 shots a game; you face 13, 14 maybe 15 shots. I have the pressure of facing all those shots.' Also, when a team is out of the playoffs, the players mostly care about scoring points. Nobody is checking. Bernie Parent for example, almost never faced rebounds. Rogie Vachon, who I thought was the best goalie in the NHL back then, was stopping third and fourth rebounds with the Kings. We (the Seals) just weren't geared to win. We'd get a good start on the season and then fade down the stretch. There was just no winning attitude. I came from a winning attitude (in Phoenix). It was in the minors, but it was still a winning attitude."

When asked to describe his style in the nets, Simmons said, "I gave it everything I had in games. I didn't like practicing and I guess I could have worked harder but with the Seals, I worked hard enough in games. I had a fast blocking glove and I was big. I played the butterfly style and I had good anticipation but I was lousy at screen shots. I don't think I had a great glove hand although others said I did."

Simmons easily stood out on the Seals when they were on the road. He stood 6'2", and had about ten tattoos on his body. He also always wore western style clothing including a hat and cowboy boots. "He was a different breed with all of his Indian jewelry," Seals captain Joey Johnston said. "We used to wear a shirt and tie on the road but the jewelry was his tie. I stuck up for him."

While with the Seals, Simmons wore two different masks. "I was the first guy who ever had designs painted on my mask," Simmons said proudly. "In San Diego in 1970, I painted my mask all black. I called it my 'Equal Opportunity Mask'. Howie Young was friends with some Indians. They painted my mask with some things on it." The markings on the mask were supposed to bring the goalie good luck.

"I started in Oakland with the old (Native style) mask. I went to Toronto and Greg Harrison made me the Cobra mask. There were two of them. One I gave to my ex-girlfriend and I never got it back.

Harrison borrowed the mask and I never got it back from him. He sent it to the Hall of Fame. I asked for a replica but Greg Harrison wouldn't make one."

Simmons' cobra mask remains in the Hockey Hall of Fame in Toronto but he did get to wear it one more time in 1997. "I used to cobra mask for the 1997 old timer's game at the All-Star game in San Jose," Simmons said. "But after the game, it was sent right back to the hall." The Cobra mask ended up being strange for a few reasons. First, it was not in Seals team colors. When Simmons was later traded to the Kings who then wore purple and gold, the mask stayed a green cobra on a black mask. In addition, the cobra snake had a rattle on it; something actual cobras do not have.

Those who played with or against Simmons could never forget him. "He'd chew tobacco. He used to go to the opponents side of the ice in warm-ups and put a big chaw in the other goalie's crease," Bob Stewart said. "I used to say, 'Gilles Meloche, you're sane, Gary Simmons, you're crazy.' He was into Indian jewelry and sold it to the players on other teams. He was a big guy. After the first period, he'd smoke a cigarette. He also threw up before a game."

Butch Williams added, "He had a body that was different, he was kind of pear shaped. He was odd and different but he could play." Jim Moxey added, "If you put him in a police lineup, he's the last guy you would pick out as a goalie." Morris Mott seemed mildly surprised by Simmons' abilities in goal. "Gary was a very unlikely athlete," Mott said. "He had no flexibility but he was an effective goalie."

Simmons started the 1974-75 season under coach Marshall Johnston. "He was an awesome guy," Simmons said. "He was a players' coach. He was fired in Pittsburgh during the All-Star game. Marshall Johnston, Gilles Meloche and I were in a sauna. Marshall Johnston said, 'I always treated the players how I wanted to be treated.' The players loved Marshall Johnston. He was a great guy but he was fired."

In February, general manger Bill McCreary took over the coaching reigns himself. "Of our last 25 games that year, about 20 were at home," Simmons said. "Bill McCreary took over as coach. He thought he was going to lead the team into the playoffs but we really faded down the stretch. We fixed him. Bill was just not nice to the players. I remember we had a new player on the team. Bill McCreary wanted a defenseman to show him around. The guy was a marginal player. He told Bill he couldn't show the guy around because it was his wedding anniversary. McCreary responded, 'How would you like to go to Salt Lake?' He just couldn't communicate."

Simmons played in 34 games in 1974-75 and finished with a record of 10-21-3 and a goals against average of 3.67. He led the team in wins, shutouts (two) and goals against average that season. Simmons seemed to save his best games for the better teams in the league. He defeated Boston twice, the defending Stanley Cup Champion Flyers once and the semi-finals bound Islanders once as a rookie.

His worst game was a 10-0 drubbing at the hands of the Rangers at Madison Square Garden on November 17, 1974. Rookie Rick Middleton scored four goals for the Rangers in that game. "Four goals were scored in the first period and three of them went in off Mike Christie," Simmons recalled. "I wasn't mad at him though, he was trying. Giving up ten goals in one game was embarrassing and didn't help the goals against average." Simmons seemed allergic to the New York area as three weeks earlier he lost a game to the Islanders 10-1 at the Nassau Coliseum.

Simmons also recalled a game on January 12, 1975, at the Spectrum in Philadelphia. Although the Seals lost 2-1, it may have been the best performance of Simmons' NHL career. "We were outshot something like 49-13 and lost 2-1," Simmons recalled. "The winning goal was scored by Moose Dupont who shot it from the side of the net, it bounced funny off the boards and back to me. The first goal of the game went in off my hand, I caught it bare handed but it went in." Simmons made 46 saves in the game but yielded the winning goal with just over five minutes left in the third period against the defending Stanley Cup champions.

Most teammates felt the combination of Meloche and Simmons worked well in the California nets. Len Frig said, "Gary was a free spirit but Gilles Meloche instilled a less carefree attitude in him. He sort of realized that with our team, staying close was good but Meloche made him realize he needed to care more about winning. They were a good tandem."

On the ice, Simmons was also not afraid to play a physical game. "I love the game of hockey," Simmons said. "It's a sport for men—the contact is there. I expect to be hit and I'm going to hit people back." Dave Gardner recalled Simmons' attitude towards the game. "He was a tough guy. I didn't think he could play but I know he could play," Gardner recalled. "He once told me that he wasn't afraid to swing his stick at anybody because he has a bigger stick than anybody. He told me not to be afraid out there." Gardner also recalled an off the ice incident. "His Doberman bit me in my pant pocket once," Gardner said laughing.

Off the ice is where Simmons was most unique. There is no shortage of good Cobra stories. "He was off the wall," Jim Pappin said. "You never knew where he was coming from. He was an average goalie—a good backup. He had a tattoo on his leg of a rooster in a hangman's noose. He tried to make a bet with people that he had a cock that hung below his knee." It was a bet Simmons often won.

Bob Murdoch said, "I remember there was a top ten list for various categories in the league and one list was the top ten "flakes." Gary Simmons was either first or second on the list. He was pissed."

Simmons also had a reputation for treating people as equals regardless of their station in life and for always being truthful with people. "He was dead honest," Charlie Simmer said. "He'd tell you to your face whatever he thought. He was a good goalie who never took himself too seriously." Simmons recalled one reason that Simmer, who was constantly being called up from the Seals top farm club in Salt Lake City and then being sent back down always seemed to play the Flyers. "We had one player who would fake an injury every time we played Philadelphia," Simmons said. "It was the 'Philly Flu.' Every time he wouldn't play, they would call up Charlie Simmer from Salt Lake. Charlie said to me once, 'See you next Philly trip.'"

In 1975-76, Simmons returned to the Seals and had his best year of his NHL career. In 40 games, "The Cobra" had a goals against average of 3.33 and a record of 15-19-5 with a pair of shutouts. Again, Simmons led the club in wins and goals against average. He also developed a good rapport with new Seals coach Jack "Tex" Evans. "He was a tough old bird," Simmons said. "I played behind him in San Diego. He played old time hockey. He moved people from in front of the net. He got upset whenever I was sprayed by the other team. The guys loved him and respected him."

Simmons also remembered one quirky feature of the Oakland Coliseum Arena that made things tough for him as a goalie. "It was the only rink in which the dasher boards were blue and that made it hard to follow the puck," he said. "The ice was good but the dressing rooms were terrible. We had road dressing rooms that were better than what we had at home. There was easy access from Highway 17 and there was lots of parking available."

Some of the reporters who covered the Seals felt that Simmons was one of the best interviews on the team and that he could always be counted on to be up front with them. At times, however, Simmons liked to have fun with reporters. "When I first got to the Seals in July of 1974, Joe DeLoach worked for the *Hayward Daily News*," Simmons said. "We met at a bowling alley. He asked me when I was born and I told him, 'February 30, 1944.' He saw me in western dress and asked me if I liked horses. I said I was a jockey. Have you ever seen a 6'2", jockey before? I gave him heck."

Simmons also recalled some incidents on the ice. "Collin LaVallee was our trainer," Simmons said. "He was a referee in Canada and was hired by Garry Young as a trainer. He knew jack shit about medical. I remember a player was cut and bleeding. I froze the puck. We called LaVallee 'Scalp' because he was bald as a cue ball. He came out onto the ice. Joey Johnston said he was going out to follow the trail of blood."

"Another time, we were playing Montreal in Oakland," Simmons remembered. "Jacques Lemaire could really shoot the puck. Lemaire came in front from about 35 feet out and the puck was rolling. He cracks it off my shoulder and onto the roof of the building. Gilles Meloche said from the bench in his French accent, 'I tawt that guy was gonna kill you. I duck, I didn't look.'"

274

While Simmons had a sharp sense of humor at times, he always tried to be accessible for young fans seeking autographs. "I did about 85% of the speaking engagements for the team," he said. "I was getting $50 while in Boston or Montreal, they were getting $500. I gave back the money when speaking for kids or charities. I always thought it was a player's responsibility to sign every autograph and make themselves available. After a hard loss, it was tough. I remember one time Dennis Maruk refused to sign an autograph for some kids and I gave him a hard time. I told him to remember a few years ago when he was 14 and waiting for an autograph from his favorite players. He was good after that."

Simmons remembers how he found out that the Seals would be leaving the Bay Area. "I remember driving over the San Mateo Bridge," Simmons said. "They mentioned that there were four sites that the team might move to: Miami, New Orleans, Denver and Cleveland. I knew it would be Cleveland. Two weeks after Len Shapiro and I bought a restaurant, the team moved. It was tough to go from a place where you could play golf after practice to a place where you threw snowballs. It was depressing. There were a lot of politics involved."

Simmons started the 1976-77 season with the Barons before being traded to Los Angeles for Gary Edwards and Juha Widing. He spent a year and a half backing up Rogie Vachon who was then in his prime with the Kings. Simmons only played in 18 games over a season and a half with Los Angeles. He retired from professional hockey after the 1978-79 season. Simmons' career statistics in the NHL include a record of 30-57-15 in 105 games and a goals against average of 3.56. He also registered five career shutouts.

The restaurant Simmons and Len Shapiro bought turned out to be a very good investment. They became partners in a Round Table Pizza franchise. Today, Simmons is basically retired. He remained in the Bay Area until a few years ago when he moved back to Arizona. Simmons is divorced and has three children.

Simmons looks back at his days with the Seals fondly. "We had about 6,500-7,000 loyal fans and they were awesome," Simmons said. "They made as much noise as 15,000. Over the years, I've had about 30,000 people tell me that they never missed a game."

It is impossible to sum up Gary Simmons in one brief quote. George Pesut said Simmons, "Had the worst physique in the league but was a heck of a goalie." Larry Patey called Simmons, "a funny guy; a different type of guy. We had a mutual respect." Perhaps the best way to describe him is to say that there will never be another quite like Gary Simmons.

Spike Huston

"He was a free spirit. Nobody found him until later in his career. He was smooth. He would have been a better player if he were 10 pounds lighter. Ron made Dave Hrechkosy. He was so smart with the puck and a great passer. He had the longest stick I've ever seen and he was not that big a guy, he was only 5'9"."

–Len Frig on Spike Huston

While many members of the Seals took less traditional paths to the NHL, perhaps Ron "Spike" Huston traveled the most unusual road. He was given the nickname "Spike" by his sister's boyfriend when he was about 12 because he was small. The nickname stuck. "Only my mother calls me Ron," Huston told *The Oakland Tribune's* John Porter.

Huston was a 28 year old NHL rookie in 1973-74. The stocky 5'9", 170 pound center from Manitou, Manitoba, did not sign a pro contract until he was 27 years old. "I was playing in junior at Brandon which was affiliated with the New York Rangers," Huston recalled. "I went to camp one year and you figure you have a chance." The Rangers wanted to assign Huston to their affiliate in St. Paul, Minnesota but Spike balked at the assignment. "Jake Milford, the GM and I didn't see eye to eye, so I didn't report to camp," Huston recalled. "I played senior hockey in Cranbrook." While playing senior hockey, Huston had to get another job to make ends meet. "I started out as a laborer doing pick and shovel work for two months," he recalled. Later jobs included working for the recreation department in Cranbrook. Eventually, Huston settled in as an electrician. As a result of his senior hockey experience, Huston had a trade to fall back on after his hockey career was over.

Huston's experience in senior hockey was the beginning of his long, unlikely journey to the NHL. "I was picked up by Philadelphia in the expansion draft but the Flyers weren't offering me enough money," Huston said. "I later played for the Spokane Jets and we won the Allen Cup in the senior league. A year later, Boston said come to camp. I thought I had the Boston Braves made but they wouldn't pay me what I wanted, so I played senior league in Calgary and we were finalists for the Allen Cup." Twice, Huston led the league in goals and three times in total points. It was clear he could play above the senior hockey level, which was designed for players who were too old to play junior but not good enough to play professionally.

Prior to the 1972-73 season, Huston finally signed a contract to play professional hockey. "Al Rollins was the GM at Salt Lake at the time and he asked me to turn pro," Huston recalled. "I had two good years in Salt Lake and then played 23 games with the Seals at the end of the 1973-74 season." In 1972-73, his first season with Salt Lake, Huston scored 42 goals and 84 points in 72 games. He was named WHL Rookie of the Year and was a second team league all-star at the end of the season. In 1973-74, he scored 20 goals and 52 points in just 50 games with the Golden Eagles before the Seals called him up to Oakland.

Huston was excited about finally making the NHL. "I thought it was great," he said. "You find out when you play against those guys that you're not far behind them. Somebody just had to take a liking to you and give you a chance." Huston was determined to make the most of his chance. In 1973-74, in 23 late season games with California, Huston scored three goals and 13 points. His first NHL goal came on February 6, 1974, during the Seals come from behind 4-2 win over the Vancouver Canucks and it turned out to be the game winner.

Despite his relative success on a last place team, Huston could not seem to satisfy management. "I got a point a game when I first came up there," Huston recalled. "Garry Young told me I should be scoring more. I said to myself, 'How many point a game guys do they have?'"

One of the reasons Huston's NHL debut was delayed was due to his reputation as a free spirit off the ice. "Now there's a character," Stan Weir said of Spike. "He was one of the most talented 30-year-olds who hadn't played in the NHL. He had a great shot and a great sense of humor. He loved to drink and gamble." Rick Kessell recalled that Huston "always had a cigar in his mouth." He was also known as one of the team's more active practical jokers. "He never took himself too seriously," Morris Mott remembered.

While he was considered fun loving off the ice, on the ice, Huston's hard work and skills on the ice were recognized by his teammates, especially his passing ability. "He was really smart, he had eyes in the back of his head," recalled Barry Cummins who played with Huston in Salt Lake and California. "You couldn't hit him because he knew where you were. He had deceptive speed and he looked a lot slower than he really was. He was really smart with the puck." Goalie Gilles Meloche recalled Huston "had good hands and saw the ice really well."

Like many of his teammates, the biggest problem Huston found playing for the Seals was travel. "We were flying to New York every other Friday and playing three, four or five road games. We'd practice in the morning and then take a bus to San Francisco and then a five hour plane ride. We'd get to New York and the day would be over, it would be 9:30 PM there. Of course, I was only 6:30 PM back in Oakland. How could we go to bed at the 11 PM curfew? That's only 8 PM in Oakland. When visiting teams would come in, it would be the opposite. They would often stop off in Vegas as part of their west coast swing and take a few days off. It was rough."

In 1974-75, Huston remained with the Seals all season. He played in only 56 games due to a variety of ailments but still scored 12 goals and 33 points. Beginning in November, Huston was put on a line with Dave Hrechkosy and Warren "Butch" Williams. It was dubbed "The Wrecking Crew Line" by the press. When everyone was healthy, it was the Seals most successful line that season. "'Wrecker' was up and down his wing and Butch mucked in the corners," Huston said when asked about the line's success. "I was the playmaker. I was always more of a playmaker than shooter." Williams agreed that Huston's playmaking was a key to the line's success. "He was a funny looking player because he was so barrel-chested and top heavy," Williams said of his former center. "He was not a fast skater, but he was capable of turning plays." Veteran defenseman Jim Neilson added, "Spike was pretty good with the puck and a good playmaker. If he had more speed, he would have had long career. He was a crafty player."

Huston had some memorable games during the 1974-75 season. For him, the most memorable was a two goal effort against the Canadiens. "In Montreal I got two goals one night and was the second or third star of the game," Huston recalled. "We lost something like 4-3. I didn't have too many two goal games."

On January 17, 1975, Huston had a goal and two assists in a 4-4 tie with the Rangers at the Oakland Coliseum. The three point night was the highest scoring night of his NHL career.

While Huston was happy to make the NHL, his reputation as a free spirit eventually got him into trouble with management, particularly with Seals GM and coach Bill McCreary. One issue Huston always had was his weight. While he weighed only 170 pounds, Huston was not known for his skating speed and was "top heavy" according to many of his teammates. As a result, his weight became a problem for McCreary. George Pesut remembered that Huston "had all kinds of bonus clauses in his contract for weight and other types of obscure things."

While the weight issue continued to be a problem in the eyes of management, Spike Huston's real problem with Bill McCreary began one evening in Toronto. "One Sunday, we were in Chicago for a nationally televised game. We lost 3-1 but we didn't play too badly," Huston said. "Monday, we flew to Toronto. I went to practice and the bus left Bill McCreary at the rink. He wouldn't give the guys their room keys so we all went to the bar. We weren't allowed to drink at the hotel, but what else could we do? The next morning, Bill told me that I missed curfew in Chicago. I told him that I didn't. Wrecker had missed curfew but I wouldn't squeal on him. I never saw eye to eye with Bill McCreary after that and Bill blamed me for everything."

"I also remember in Washington once we were in a bar and it was almost curfew time, around 10 PM," Huston said. "Jim Neilson had a little too much to drink and he sat down at our table so we were all cut off. Well, Jim Neilson and Len Frig started to shout about being cut off and they got arrested. I took a taxi to go get them bailed out. I was told they were sent to Baltimore but they were actually sent to Washington, DC. I didn't get back to the hotel until around 2 AM. The next morning, I ate breakfast and went to our pre-game skate. Bill McCreary said to me, 'You missed curfew'. He fined me, I don't remember how much. 'Who was with you?' he asked me. 'Nobody,' I said. He fined me for bailing the other guys out but nobody else was fined. He had such a double standard." Some players felt that the arrest of these players was the last straw that led to the dismissal of Marshall Johnston as coach.

The final straw between Huston and McCreary came later in the 1974-75 season. "I was hurt," Huston said. "Bill McCreary told me, 'I don't think you're hurt.' From then on, he never trusted me."

Teammate Gary Simmons remembered that Huston was "a great guy and a great playmaker. He lived the high life off the ice. He went to clubs." Simmons also believed that Huston was largely responsible for the success of Dave Hrechkosy. "Spike was out the last 20 games or so of the 1974-75 season and Wrecker had 29 goals. He had a bonus for 30. Guess how many goals he finished with? 29."

Frank Spring remembered that Huston "was a great player. What a talent. He just did things you wouldn't expect. He was a heady player."

After the 1974-75 season, GM Bill McCreary looked to trade Huston. Gary Simmons recalled that McCreary thought Huston "was a bad influence on Wrecker." In a rare interleague deal, the Seals traded Huston's contract to the Phoenix Roadrunners of the WHA along with Del Hall in exchange for the rights to Gary Holt. "Bill McCreary was incredibly stupid for making that deal," Simmons continued. "All the guys liked Spike."

Huston recalled, "Al Rollins, [the former Salt Lake Golden Eagles GM] went to Phoenix of the WHA and asked me if I wanted to go to Phoenix. I ended up playing two years there." Huston was productive in Phoenix, scoring 22 goals and 66 points in 1975-76 and 20 goals and 59 points in 1976-77. Although he enjoyed his stay in the WHA, Spike Huston recalled, "The WHA wasn't even close to the NHL. There was no other league to play for." Huston then went back to senior hockey in 1977-78, leading the league in assists and points with the Spokane Flyers. He retired from senior hockey after the 1978-79 season.

Today, Huston and his wife live in Cranbrook, British Columbia. He has two children and three grandchildren. He works as an electrician, the trade he learned while playing senior hockey. Now, working for an electrical outlet, he works 21 days straight before taking seven days off. He often travels during his 21 days of work, which must seem almost like his lengthy road trips with the Seals. He remembered his time in Oakland fondly and with warmth.

Dave Gardner recalled that Huston, "played great. He was a little pudgy guy who handled the biscuit well. He was a good guy and a very smart player." While it took Spike Huston a long time to get to the NHL, he did it his way. Ask him and he'll tell you the experience was worth the wait.

Len Frig

"Len had a lot of heart and played a tough game. He would stick up for his teammates."
–Ralph Klassen on Len Frig

Lethbridge, Alberta native Len Frig remembered always being around the game of hockey. "I was a rink rat as a kid," he said. "Hockey came naturally to me and I didn't think a lot about it." Frig played his junior hockey for the Lethbridge Centennials. In his second year of juniors, Frig's team went to the Memorial Cup finals and Frig played in the league's All-Star game. "I made the all-star team, which made me think I was good enough [to play in the NHL] but it also almost ended my career. I broke my arm and had two pins put in."

The Chicago Black Hawks made Frig a third round selection in the 1970 entry draft. "I went to camp with Chicago in 1970 and Dan Maloney cracked my arm again," Frig recalled. "I tried to get the trainers to keep it quiet because I hadn't even signed a contract yet." Frig eventually signed a contract and was assigned to the Black Hawks CHL farm team in Dallas. He spent two years with the Dallas Black Hawks and was named a first team CHL all-star in his second season. At the end of the 1972-73 season, Chicago recalled Frig for the playoffs. When defenseman Keith Magnuson was injured, the 5'11", 190 pound Frig was pressed into service. He responded by scoring a goal and an assist in four playoff games for Chicago. In 1973-74, he made the Black Hawks outright and scored four goals and 14 points in 66 games.

In 1973-74, the Seals had the league's worst record and gave up more goals than any other team in the NHL. One problem the Seals perceived was a lack of size on defense. As a result, the Seals acquired Frig and Mike Christie from Chicago in exchange for center Ivan Boldirev on May 24, 1974. Frig was not exactly thrilled with the trade to Oakland. "I was disappointed, really," Frig admitted. "I was sick the last month of the 1973-74 season in Chicago. I think I had something like mono and I lost about 25 pounds. I got shifted from defenseman to forward a lot. I didn't get along too well with Tommy Ivan [the Black Hawks GM]. I negotiated my own contracts. When I walked into his office, he told me to sit down and as soon as I did, he stood up. So I stood up. He had a real short man complex. That was my first meeting with him and it sort of went downhill from there."

"After I was traded, (Chicago coach) Billy Reay called me and said he didn't say much to players but he told me he didn't want the trade to go through." Frig did find playing for the Seals an advantage in one respect. "I tripled my salary when I was traded to the Seals," Frig said. "I threatened to sit out a year and go to Europe or Calgary or Edmonton of the WHA so they tripled my salary. When the WHA came along, the money got much better for the players."

Frig started his Seals career on a personal high note. "I scored two goals off of John Davidson who I had played with in juniors," Frig recalled. "It was against St. Louis, my first home game as a member of the Seals. One of the goals was an end-to-end rush. I thought it would be a good start to my season, that I would score 15-20 goals that year." Frig scored only one more goal all season, finishing 1974-75 with three goals and 20 points while playing in all 80 games for the Seals. All three of his goals that season came on the power play. He also led the team in penalty minutes with 127.

Frig noticed some significant differences between the attitude on the Black Hawks and the prevailing atmosphere in Oakland. "The Seals were more carefree and lackadaisical," Frig said. "We were undisciplined to a certain degree. Our veterans didn't provide too much leadership and the leadership had to come from the middle guys. Jack Evans installed more discipline the second year I was there. It was funny we always played very well against good teams like Boston, Philadelphia, Montreal and Chicago. But the teams we needed to beat, like Toronto who we were fighting for a playoff spot, we couldn't beat them but we'd always keep it close."

One problem Len Frig had on the Seals during the 1974-75 season was coaching. Marshall Johnston started the season off as coach before being dismissed in February of 1975 when GM Bill McCreary took over the coaching reigns himself. Neither of them impressed Frig from behind the bench. "Marshall Johnston wasn't a coach, he was a player. He played a defensive defenseman style as a player and as a coach. He didn't really have the respect of the players because he was so inexperienced at coaching," Frig said. "He was thrown into the job and the team had no real personality. The players mostly did their own thing. They listened up until a point, but that was it."

Frig felt McCreary was also not the most qualified man to coach the Seals. "Bill McCreary was arrogant," Frig recalled. "The league owned the team at that time and I think they sort of figured they were already paying Bill so let's keep him in the organization. They didn't want to spend any more money to hire a coach. The players realized that. The league didn't know what to do with us. We also had a trainer on our team who had never been a trainer before. It was hilarious, to a degree."

One moment that Frig wanted to forget on the ice occurred in a game against the Buffalo Sabres. "I had the puck behind the net and I was all alone," said Frig. "I heard somebody yell for the puck and I thought it was one of our guys. Without even looking, I threw the puck to the guy and it turned out to be Gilbert Perreault. He was all alone and put the puck right in the net."

Despite the occasional blunder, Frig won the respect of most of his teammates both on and off the ice. Dave Gardner recalled that Frig, "Tried to stick up for everybody on the ice. Off the ice, he played a lot of golf with me." Veteran defenseman Jim Neilson recalled Frig as "feisty" and called him "a good defensive defenseman." Al MacAdam recalled Frig very fondly. "He was very emotional and wore his heart on his sleeve," MacAdam said. "Len was a good guy, you could depend on him. If your car broke down at four in the morning a half hour away from his house, you could count on him to come and get you."

Despite playing for a losing team, Frig's work ethic never wavered. "He was a good guy and he played hard," John Stewart said. "He applied himself despite knowing he was not going to win and that there was not much of a future with the Seals."

Many of Frig's former teammates recalled stories of his off-ice exploits. Frig had a unique sense of humor and was prone to exaggeration when describing his latest exploits with the rod and reel. He once told John Porter of *The Oakland Tribune* some real fish tales. "I went fishing at another lake on the Blackfoot Reservation in Montana and I saw a guy in waders catch an eight and a half pound trout on a fly rod. Another time, a bunch of us went fishing and we caught four trout that were so big they fed 16 guys."

Frig was back with the Seals for the 1975-76 season and suddenly found himself among the leaders of the team on defense. When veteran Jim Neilson went down early in the season, Bob Stewart was the only remaining veteran on the California blue line. The team's defensemen held a meeting and Frig was in the middle of it. "We talked about how we'd have to tighten up without Jim Neilson, that we weren't going to be able to sit back and rely on his experience." In 1975-76, Frig played in only 62 games. He was lost late in the season with torn cartilage in his right knee. "They cut my knee open the old fashioned way," Frig said, recalling his season ending surgery. Frig scored three goals and 15 points in 1975-76 for the Seals but added only 55 penalty minutes. His positional play seemed to improve dramatically during the course of the season. Coach Jack Evans recalled that, "Before he got hurt, Len was playing outstanding defense for us."

Frig also admired Evans and what he brought to the Seals as coach in 1975-76. "He instilled discipline, he was respected," Frig said of Evans. "He said something and you listened. He let the players play to a degree. He gave the players options. You know what to do, go out and do it. We had a direction. He installed a system. On the road, we had one forechecker and two forwards who would hang back and clutter the middle. At home, we would have two forecheckers."

Off the ice, Frig continued to do things that kept his teammates off balance. Butch Williams called Frig "the class clown. He was always doing goofy shit. He was a smoker. Once, he walked around the dressing room with a cigarette dangling out of his penis."

Bob Murdoch recalled "One time I was stopped at a road block," Murdoch said. "The officer who stopped me was from Lethbridge. He said, 'You must know Len Frig.' I said, 'Yes, he's a friend of mine,' figuring that I would get off without a ticket. He arrested me. Apparently, Len used to beat this guy up back in school."

Goaltender Gary Simmons recalled Frig once commented to him at a pre-game meal, "One year in Dallas, I had 300 penalty minutes." I said, "Jeez, Friggy, that's 30 misconducts. Len would yap over a lineman's shoulder after tussles. I actually only saw him in one fight," Simmons said laughing. "He was also a very honest guy with the press."

One thing that Frig was honest about was how difficult road trips were while playing in Oakland and how those road trips affected the team. "Our road trips took forever," he admitted. "We flew out of San Francisco so we would take a bus from Oakland to San Francisco and we'd leave early in case of traffic. Everybody drank on our road trips. I think we were one of the top alcoholic teams in the league. Because we were out west, we were on the road for two weeks at a time and we didn't have a lot of days off. We'd lose some close games, get frustrated and then drink some more."

George Pesut said he called Frig "Friggy the Piggy" because "he reminded me of Pig Pen from Charlie Brown. He would do anything to stop the puck," Pesut said. He worked hard." Other teammates felt that Frig was not as dedicated as he could have been to the game. Jim Pappin, who played with Frig in Chicago and again with the Seals in 1975-76 recalled, "Len was a nut. He had a lot of talent, he was good and he worked hard. He didn't have much discipline and wasn't really dedicated. A lot of things came before hockey for Len."

After the 1975-76 season, the Seals announced they were leaving the Bay Area and moving to Cleveland. Frig was less than thrilled with the move. "Going to Cleveland didn't sit too well with us," Frig said. "The fans were finally coming around and we were playing entertaining hockey. We thought we had turned the corner. We had lots of players in their early and mid 20s and that was the nucleus of our team. We had started to play together for a couple of years and we were gelling. The league should have waited one more year. I think we were definitely catching on."

Frig played for the Cleveland Barons in 1976-77. In 66 games, he scored two goals and nine points and had a career high 213 penalty minutes. Frig was traded to the St. Louis Blues for Mike Eaves prior to the 1977-78 season, but he only played 37 games with the Blues over two seasons. He spent the rest of his playing days with the Salt Lake Golden Eagles of the CHL.

Jim Moxey felt that playing for the Seals at such a young age hurt Frig's development as a hockey player. "It was tough to be a young defenseman in California," Moxey said. "Len would have been better off starting on a stronger team and being brought along slowly. He was a good player who didn't play to his potential."

Frig retired after the 1980-81 season but then returned four years later to play another two years for Salt Lake. He hung up his skates for good after the 1985-86 season. Frig's final NHL statistics were 13 goals and 64 points in 311 games. Today, he lives in Salt Lake City, Utah and works for Delta Airlines as a ramp supervisor. He and his wife have two daughters and one granddaughter.

Wayne Merrick, who played with Frig both in California and Cleveland, recalled that Frig, "Was a right-handed defenseman who played on the power play. He was enthusiastic, a winner—he wanted to win. At times, he got a little down on himself because he wanted us to play better as a team." Bob Stewart summed up Frig by saying, "Len was crazy, a real character. He loved the game and was good to have on our team. He stirred things up on the ice and was a good teammate."

Jim Neilson

"He was my defensive partner. He didn't say much, but when he spoke, guys listened. He was our senior statesman and we all respected him. He never played in the minors and was in the league a good long time. A very classy guy."

–George Pesut on Jim Neilson

Jim Neilson grew up in Big River, Saskatchewan. His father was Danish while his mother was a Native Canadian and a member of the Cree Tribe. Hockey was a part of Neilson's life from an early age. "I used to listen to the radio," Neilson recalled. "We could only hear Toronto and Montreal. My favorite player was Rocket Richard. It was harder to know the guys back then because he had no television, only radio."

Neilson played junior hockey with the Prince Albert Mintos, joining the team at age 18. The 6'2", 205 pound defenseman played well for Prince Albert, twice topping the 20 goal mark. "Everything happened so fast," Neilson said. "All of a sudden, I was with the New York Rangers organization. I had only one-and-a-half years of junior hockey and then bingo, I was practically with the Rangers. I came up with Rod Gilbert, Jean Ratelle and Vic Hadfield."

Neilson made his NHL debut with the Rangers during the 1962-63 season. He played 12 seasons for the Broadway Blueshirts and was always a steady contributor. Neilson was selected to the second team post-season all star team after the 1967-68 season and appeared in two NHL All-Star games. His best season offensively was 1968-69 when he scored 10 goals and 44 points in 76 games. "The Chief" could carry the puck and make good passes, but as his career progressed, Neilson became known more for his steady defensive play. While he was not afraid of playing physically, Neilson was known to play a smart defensive game and play the puck more than he played the body.

When Neilson joined the Rangers, the team was struggling, seemingly stuck at the bottom of the standings. Despite the fact that four teams made the playoffs in the six team league, the Rangers didn't qualify for the post season until Neilson's fifth year with the club. Coach and general manager Emile Francis built a strong team by the late 60s and Neilson was a key component of the Rangers success. The club made the Stanley Cup semi-finals in each of Neilson's final four seasons in New York and defeated the defending Stanley Cup Champions for three consecutive years. Still, the Rangers could never win a championship.

In 1973-74, Neilson saw his playing time reduced. Eventually, he became the Rangers fifth defenseman, losing ice time to the newly acquired Gilles Marotte. His 1973-74 statistics were his lowest in his career until that point, as Neilson scored just four goals and 11 points in 72 games. He was not surprised therefore, when the Rangers arranged for Neilson to go to the California Golden Seals in a three way agreement that was done through the waiver draft. The Rangers acquired Derek Sanderson from Boston, the Bruins acquired Walt McKechnie from the Seals and the Seals received Neilson from New York.

"It wasn't bad at all," Neilson said. "I talked to Emile Francis. He let me know I was going to somebody and then that it would be the Seals. I had no trouble with it. I enjoyed it. Heck, better

California than Pittsburgh. It was fun. It's all part of the business. We had nice weather in Oakland and I could play golf."

The Seals were rebuilding yet again in 1974-75 and had one of the youngest teams in the NHL. Bob Stewart was the most experienced defenseman on the roster and he was only entering his fourth season in the league. California acquired Neilson to add a badly needed veteran presence to their defense corps. "He brings the experience we need on the club," Seals general manager Bill McCreary said at the time Neilson was acquired. "He stabilizes our defensive corps. He plays hard and he practices hard and he plays hurt."

Assistant coach Marv Edwards added, "Jim means a lot to the club. He's a leader. He talks to the players on the ice during a game and he settles down our young defense. He's not spectacular, but he is consistent."

Neilson admitted there was an adjustment going from a team that was one game away from the Stanley Cup finals to a team that had won 13 games the year before. "I was going from a team that was a pretty good team to a team that was a little shaky," Neilson said. "You try to bring something with you, how to win. We weren't a great team but we weren't a bad team either. We just only had so much to work with. You do the best you can with what you've got. The guys were playing in the NHL and they did the best they could."

According to his teammates, Neilson also handled the situation well. "He impressed me," John Stewart said. "He came into a situation not near what he was raised with in the NHL. He took it seriously and handled being with the Seals better than I did."

Another obstacle the Seals faced in 1974-75 was that the franchise was owned by the league and rumors continued to circulate that the club would be moved or disbanded. "Ownership was shaky," Neilson said. "It affected the younger guys more than me. I'd been around the block and had been through things. We hung in there and I let the guys know it's a business and you could get traded any moment. They hung in there good."

Neilson scored three goals and 20 points in 72 games for the Seals in 1974-75 and provided the leadership and experience the Seals craved. Along the way, he had some special moments during his initial season in Oakland. On October 16, 1974, Neilson returned to Madison Square Garden for the first time as a member of the Seals after playing a dozen years on Broadway. Neilson picked up an assist as the Seals and Rangers skated to a 5-5 tie. The New York crowd, which often was critical of Neilson for what they perceived to be his lack of physical play, cheered "The Chief" upon his return to New York.

On January 5, 1975, Neilson picked up a pair of assists during the Seals 5-1 win over the defending Stanley Cup champion Flyers at the Oakland Coliseum Arena. Two weeks later, Neilson scored his first goal as a member of the Seals, beating Tony Esposito during a 3-1 loss to the Black Hawks in Chicago. The veteran defenseman also picked up two assists during a 6-4 win over the Bruins at Oakland on February 21, 1975.

Many of Neilson's young teammates were clearly in awe of the veteran defenseman. Rookie Fred Ahern said, "I couldn't believe I was on the same ice with him. He was my first roommate on the road, this all-star defenseman. I was almost too nervous to sleep in the same room with him." Goalie Gilles Meloche added, "Jim was so good defensively it was a dream to have him play in front of you." Larry Patey, who was also a rookie in 1974-75 said, "Jim was a leader. It was neat to see him on my team because I looked up to him as a kid. He was a role model." Seals captain Joey Johnston was also highly respectful of "The Chief". "He was a hell of a hockey player," Johnston said. "He could play hockey. He was still our best defenseman and I don't know how old he was. He did things automatically. For example, he would take a hit to make a pass. The young kids we had didn't do that."

Travel was another aspect of playing in California that Neilson had to adjust to. "I wanted to get out of the house but not for that long," Neilson said. "It did have an effect on us. On a 14-day road trip, you could start the trip with piss and vinegar but it's tough, especially in February when you know you can't make the playoffs. You wish you could just mail in the two points."

While Neilson was highly respected by his teammates on and off the ice, most of his former teammates also remembered his problems with alcohol. "We all looked up to him," Gary Simmons said of Neilson. "He played all those years. When he was seeing things straight, he was a big help but he was not always seeing things straight."

Defenseman Len Frig called Neilson, "an amazing man. He would drink very hard at night and still play well the next day." "When we went to New York, you knew not to skate near him in the morning skate," Butch Williams recalled. "He would stink. He ate snails and he drank."

Despite his problems with alcohol, Neilson was respected and admired by his teammates not only as a hockey player, but as a person as well. "He never said a bad word about anyone," Morris Mott recalled. Dave Gardner added, "He was terrific. He was like a father and an associate with me. He went through a lot of problems but always looked after people."

On the ice, his teammates remembered how well "The Chief" knew the game of hockey. "He was steady," Bob Stewart recalled. "He was like a grandfather. He could pass the puck up and let the forwards do their jobs. He was a smart player who used his head." Ralph Klassen recalled that Neilson was, "very intelligent. He didn't have to work up a sweat because he was so intelligent on the ice."

In 1975-76, Neilson was named captain of the Seals. Although he was never a vocal player in the locker room, Neilson tried to lead by example. "They know if you're working hard," Neilson said. "As long as I'm hustling, a younger player might think, 'If the old guy can do it, so can I.'" Apparently, Neilson was successful. Jim Moxey recalled, "I learned a lot from Jimmy. He didn't say much but he led by example. He played hard."

Part of Neilson's leadership was natural. He knew what to do on the ice. For example, during the 1974 incident in which three Flyers jumped into the penalty box to gang up on Mike Christie, Neilson was the first man who came to Christie's rescue. "I got to him first," Neilson said matter-of-factly. "It had to be done."

Neilson was not overly fond of Seals coach Jack Evans for one reason in particular. "I didn't enjoy his coaching," Neilson said. "I was old. He wanted us to skate for an hour every day. Why? We were leaving our game on the ice. I didn't buy it. He wasn't a bad coach but I couldn't believe he made us skate for an hour when we had a game that night." Neilson then conceded, "He was a pretty good coach."

Unfortunately, Neilson's tenure as captain of the club was short lived. On November 30, 1975, in Atlanta, Neilson was lost for the season with a knee injury. "I was blindsided and there was damage to my tendons and ACL," Neilson said. "My son was at that game. I was rattled good. My son ran down and got on the ice. He went to the hospital with me." Al MacAdam remembered that, "Hilliard Graves nailed him. The injury put him on the decline." Neilson scored one goal and seven points in 26 games with the Seals in 1975-76. "The Chief" is seen in the 1975-76 Seals team picture in a jacket and tie, wearing a large cast on his injured leg.

Even though he was injured, Neilson continued to guide his younger teammates both on and off the ice. Rookie Bob Murdoch recalled that Neilson "was a great dresser and he new the best places to eat in every NHL city."

Neilson returned for the 1976-77 season, although the Seals had moved to Cleveland to become the Barons. Again, injuries limited "The Chief's" playing time but he still scored three goals and 20 points in only 47 games with the Barons. In 1977-78, Neilson returned to the Barons and played in his 1,000 NHL game. He scored two goals and 23 points in 68 games for Cleveland. The following year, he signed with the Edmonton Oilers of the WHA. One of his teammates in that final year of his playing career was a rookie named Wayne Gretzky. Neilson's final NHL statistics include 1,023 games played, 69 goals and 368 points.

Today, Neilson lives in Winnipeg. Life after hockey has not always been easy for "The Chief". "He has had a rough time since retiring," Morris Mott said. A few other ex-teammates concurred. His drinking problems continued and eventually, Neilson and his wife got divorced. Neilson is now basically retired although he still speaks to groups for Native Canadians and appears at an odd old timer's game.

Wayne Merrick summed up what Jim Neilson meant to the California Golden Seals during his two year tenure in Oakland. "He was a wonderful man and a great player. He did things on the ice that you didn't think somebody could do. He was real crafty and could do different things. He was a real pro."

Jim Moxey

"He was the other wing on a line with me and Dave Gardner. We were good friends in both California and Cleveland. He was a tough kid, nothing fancy but a hard worker and a grinder in the corners."

—Fred Ahern on Jim Moxey

Jim Moxey grew up in Toronto so naturally he rooted for the Maple Leafs growing up. "I was a Leafs fan," Moxey said. "I think my favorite players were Bobby Orr and Frank Mahovlich. I was always my dream to play in the NHL. When I was 17-years-old, I went pretty high in the junior draft so that was a hint that maybe I could make it."

The 6'1", 190 pound Moxey spent three seasons with the Hamilton Red Wings in the Ontario League and improved his offensive output each season. By his third year in juniors, Moxey scored 40 goals and 80 points in 59 games. The Seals made Moxey their fourth round selection in the 1973 entry draft. "I was also drafted by Edmonton of the WHA," Moxey said. "I knew Pat Flannery, the Seals scout. I chose the Seals over the Oilers because the WHA was not that stable at the time. It was just starting out and not a sure thing." In his rookie season as a pro, Moxey scored 26 goals and 49 points in 76 games for the Seals top affiliate in Salt Lake City.

In 1974-75, the 21-year-old Moxey was called up to the Seals. He played 11 games for Salt Lake and 47 for California. In his rookie season, Moxey scored five goals and nine points and was assessed four penalty minutes. Overall, Moxey found his rookie experience a bit difficult. "The whole thing was pretty frustrating," Moxey said. "I just wasn't playing with much confidence. I really was disappointed with myself. There was one game in particular that I remember. We were playing the Islanders at home and I had plenty of chances to score. Late in the game, when I finally did score, the officials ruled that it wasn't a goal. They just took one away from me. That game was the kind of year I had. I think it was pretty much the same way for the whole team."

Moxey still fondly looks back at his first NHL goal even if while admitting it was a less than spectacular play. "It was in Washington," Moxey said. "The puck rolled in front and I banged it in past Ron Low. It wasn't pretty, but they don't ask how, just how many."

Moxey also recalled an embarrassing moment that happened to the club during their first trip to Boston in their new uniforms. "Once, in the Boston Gardens, the fans were whistling at us because of our Pacific blue uniforms. That was embarrassing," Moxey said.

While Moxey's offensive statistics were not overwhelming as a rookie, his teammates did recognize the kind of hockey player the young Torontonian was. "Jim was an honest player who came to work every day," Gilles Meloche recalled. Charlie Simmer, who also played with Moxey in Salt Lake thought Moxey was "A fired up right winger who was pretty competitive." Butch Williams, a fellow winger, recalled, "Jim was just a young kid. He was an up and down winger but he could make a few fakes or moves."

Unfortunately, Moxey's season ended prematurely. He suffered a separated shoulder and after it healed, he finished the year in Salt Lake City.

Moxey worked hard in rehab during the off-season. He came to training camp in 1975 10 pounds lighter than the 200 pounds he had weighed the previous year. Len Frig noticed that Moxey "always seemed to be a step behind," during his rookie year. The weight loss helped the young wing improve his play. "It makes all of the difference," Moxey said. "At 190 pounds, I can get a better jump on the ice. I'm more mobile and can do more things."

Although he had a strong camp, Moxey was sent back to Salt Lake City to start the 1975-76 season. Despite the setback, he remained determined to return to the Seals. "I was disappointed about not making the team," Moxey told Joe DeLoach at the time. "But I had a good camp and I knew if I worked hard in Salt Lake, there wasn't any way they could keep me down. I knew I would get my shot."

The Seals did recall Moxey in December after he got off to a solid start in Salt Lake. He scored 11 goals and 28 points for the Eagles in 30 games. "When I was called up, Jack Evans told me to concentrate on every shift," Moxey said. "He told me not to worry about just scoring goals. When you work hard, you can turn things around." Looking back, Moxey felt Evans was the best coach he had while with the Seals. "He was a fair guy, but a tough guy, though. He turned the team around a bit. Jack was a no nonsense guy who ran good practices."

Moxey started to play better hockey with the Seals in 1975-76. He was at his most effective when teamed with center Dave Gardner and winger Fred Ahern. Gardner was the playmaker, Moxey the mucker and Ahern the goal scorer. Dave Gardner recalled that Moxey "got the puck to you when you needed it. We had some good times together." In addition to his regular shift, Moxey also began to kill penalties with regularity. "I was more of a checker," Moxey said. "I killed penalties and was an up and down the wing kind of guy. I scored a few goals, I tried to keep the plus/minus down and I was steady."

Moxey managed some fine offensive games in 1975-76. On February 3, 1976, he scored twice as the Seals tied the Blues in St. Louis 4-4. On February 15, 1976, Moxey scored a hat trick in a game against the North Stars in Minnesota. Cesare Maniago was the victimized North Stars goalie.

Moxey finished the season with 10 goals and 26 points in 44 games with the Seals. His teammates continued to appreciate his hard work and dedication. "He was a hard worker and good as a penalty killer," Gary Sabourin said. Wayne King added that Moxey was "a good fighter and good with the puck." Wayne Merrick also recalled Moxey's toughness. "He was a solid player who was kind of tough, too. He wouldn't take any garbage from anybody. He had a lot of talent, too."

Off the ice, Moxey apparently had one problem as former roommate Bob Murdoch recalled. "Jim was a sleepwalker," Murdoch said. "One time, I was sound asleep and he beat the heck out of me. He thought I was some guy breaking into our room. He tried to kick me out. The next morning, he didn't remember it at all."

Moxey also had a good relationship with many of his young teammates. "He was the same age as Wayne King, his wife and my wife and myself," Al MacAdam recalled. "We all made about the same amount, too, around $25,000 and we all had nothing. We survived together. He was a confident player but a fringe player."

Jim Moxey had some fond off-ice memories of his times with the Seals as well. "I remember we played an intra-squad game at Charles Schulz's rink. We played there when he opened his rink in Santa Rosa and in return, he made "Sparky the Seal" our mascot." Sparky appeared on the Seals final two media guides as well as on Seals t-shirts, bumper stickers and programs.

Moxey also appreciated the fans out in the Bay Area. "They liked rough hockey and they were knowledgeable," Moxey recalled. "They liked to see us play Philadelphia. When we played them, the place was packed. The fans were noisy and good although a better team would have helped attendance. We tried to promote the team at schools and stuff. Now, after Wayne Gretzky, it would have been easier to promote the sport."

After the 1975-76 season, the Seals franchise moved to Cleveland. "We found out about the team move on the radio," Moxey recalled. "Then we got a letter from the team that camp was to be held in Cleveland. It was not a personal notification. I was just thinking, 'Hey, we got a great place to play; a fresh start and we aren't going to fold. It didn't work out though. The location of the rink in Cleveland was terrible."

Moxey started the 1976-77 season in Cleveland and scored seven goals and 14 points in 35 games. Then, he was traded to the Los Angeles Kings along with goalie Gary Simmons in the deal that brought goalie Gary Edwards to Cleveland. "When we were traded, Jim said, 'What the hell do they want me for?'" Gary Simmons remembered. "I told him 'I don't know.' He played two or three games there and was sent down to the minors." Moxey actually appeared in only one game for the Kings. It was the last NHL game of his pro career. The following season, Moxey played with the Springfield Indians of the AHL. In 71 games with Springfield, Moxey scored 22 goals and 56 points. He retired from hockey after that. Moxey's career statistics in the NHL include 22 goals and 49 points in 127 games.

Moxey still looks back at his days with the Seals fondly. "It gave me a chance to play in the NHL," Moxey said. "We played some good hockey and some good games. The Seals were known as the doormat of the league but we played well."

Today, Moxey and his wife live in Erin, Ontario. He is a sales representative for Genie Industries, which is based out of Seattle. Moxey has two children, a son and a daughter.

Ralph Klassen remembered Jim Moxey as "A good guy; a character player who always gave 110%. He was hyper and high strung. He wanted to do well. He tried to overachieve." In that regard, Moxey was a lot like the team he played for, the California Golden Seals.

Gary Holt

"I played on a line with him in Salt Lake. He was tough as nails and never gave less than 110%. You wanted to play with him, not against him."

–Bob Murdoch on Gary Holt

Sarnia, Ontario native Gary Holt was born on New Year's Day, 1952. The 5'9", 175 pound left wing made his living as a tough guy despite his small size. In juniors, Holt did not have a reputation as an enforcer. In two seasons with the Niagara Falls Flyers of the OHA, Holt never scored more than 11 goals and never accumulated more than 48 penalty minutes. Since he was undrafted, Holt signed as a free agent with the Columbus Seals of the IHL prior to the 1972-73 season. In December, Columbus traded Holt to the Port Huron Wings. In 75 total games that season, Holt scored 30 goals and 60 points while accumulating 85 penalty minutes. The undrafted wing seemingly blossomed, at least at the minor league level.

The following season, the California Golden Seals signed Holt as a free agent. Although he didn't make the team in 1973-74, he was assigned to the Seals top farm club, the Salt Lake Golden Eagles. In Salt Lake is where Holt began to find his role as a tough guy. In 71 games, he scored 21 goals and 47 points while being assessed 197 penalty minutes. Holt was called up to the Seals briefly when injuries hit the team. In one game, he took one shot on goal and did not figure in the scoring.

In 1974-75, Holt again played in Salt Lake for most of the season and his numbers improved all the way around. He scored 26 goals and 65 points in 78 games and compiled exactly 200 penalty minutes on the season. The Seals again called him up one game, this time for the last game of the regular season. In his only NHL game of the year, Holt picked up his first NHL point when he assisted on Larry Patey's game tying goal in a 1-1 stalemate against the Kings. After his brief time with the Seals, California sent Holt back to Salt Lake for the CHL playoffs. Here, he truly came through in the clutch, scoring the game tying and then game winning goal in game seven of the CHL Championship to give Salt Lake their first ever title. "He scored the winning goal against the Dallas Black Hawks in the seventh game of the CHL Championship game for Salt Lake," Fred Ahern recalled. "His brother Randy played for Dallas at the time. Gary quietly went out and did his job." It was a moment Salt Lake hockey fans will not soon forget.

Holt's performance with Salt Lake City earned him a chance to play for the Seals in 1975-76. He started the season off in California and scored his first NHL goal on October 17, 1975, off of Washington's Michel Belhumeur. The goal turned out to be the tying tally in a 3-3 draw in Oakland.

For the rest of the 1975-76 season, Holt was up and down between California and Salt Lake City like a yo-yo. Len Frig recalled why this was the case. "Gary never got a fair chance with the Seals," Frig said. "They always sent him down to the minors once he was getting into his groove. He was tough as nails and gave 110%. Management always sent him down because he had a two way contract."

In 48 games with California in 1975-76, Holt scored six goals and 11 points while adding 50 penalty minutes. One of his goals came on the power play. Despite riding the Salt Lake City to Oakland shuttle, Holt was respected by his peers. "We called him 'Baldy'," Gilles Meloche said. "Gary was a good skater and an honest player. He was not overly skilled but he was a very hard worker." Charlie Simmer, who played with Holt both in California and Salt Lake said, "Gary was a real athlete. He was in the best shape of almost anybody I've ever seen." Jim Moxey remembered Holt as, "A wiry tough guy. He was an up and down the wing player and shot the puck well."

The one thing that was working against Holt on the NHL level was his lack of size. At just 5'9", 175, it was hard for him to play the role of enforcer against the likes of Dave Schultz, Jerry Korab, Clark Gillies and Terry O'Reilly. "He was a good, tough little player," veteran forward Jim Pappin said of Holt. "He was too small for his heart. If he were taller, he would have been a terror. He had more talent than his brother and a mean streak." Ralph Klassen also admired Holt's toughness despite his lack of size. "He was a small man but tougher than nails. He brought an attitude that he wanted to play."

To his teammates, Holt was more than just a fighter. "Gary and Randy had different mentalities," Al MacAdam said. MacAdam played with both Holt brothers at various times in his NHL career. "Randy was a tough guy but Gary really wanted to compete."

The Seals lacked a true enforcer in 1975-76 and that is one reason some experts believed the team had trouble against physical opponents. Holt tried valiantly to fill the role whenever he could. "Gary had a vicious temper and was just as tough as his brother," Mike Christie said. "He was kind of like Bob Gassoff, you never knew when he would lose it."

Holt remained in the Seals organization when the team moved to Cleveland in 1976-77 to become the Barons. Once again, however, he spent the majority of his time in Salt Lake City where he scored 17 goals and 38 points in 68 games. He also led the CHL in penalty minutes that season with 226. Holt was called up to Cleveland for a couple of games that season and picked up one assist and two penalty minutes for the Barons.

In October 1977, Holt signed a free agent contract with the St. Louis Blues. In 49 games with St. Louis, Holt scored seven goals and 11 points while adding 81 penalty minutes to his career totals. That would be his final stint in the NHL. After another year with Salt Lake in 1978-79, Holt hung up his skates for good. His final NHL career totals are 13 goals and 24 points in 101 games. Today, Holt has settled in Salt Lake City where he played most of his professional hockey.

Dave Gardner remembered Gary Holt fondly. "He was my linemate for awhile. He had one of those hair transplants. He was in great condition and very strong. He tried to help me with my strength but it never really worked out. He was hard nosed and you did not want to back him into a corner. His brother was very tough but don't underestimate Gary." Those who underestimated Gary Holt did so at their own risk.

Rick Hampton

"I felt sorry for him. He was drafted high, made good money but he made lots of mistakes. It was not fair to him—he had a lot of pressure on him and he was so young."

–Spike Huston on Rick Hampton

If today, every team in hockey is looking for the next Wayne Gretzky or Mario Lemieux, in 1974, every team in the NHL was looking for the next Bobby Orr. Orr had revolutionized the way the game of hockey was played by making end-to-end rushes and dictating the tempo of almost every game he played in. Teams went looking for defenseman like Orr who could take control of a hockey game and provide an offensive threat from the blue line. The Rangers found Brad Park, Denis Potvin joined the New York Islanders and the Maple Leafs acquired Borje Salming.

As of the summer of 1974, the closest the Seals came to a rushing defenseman was Dick Redmond, who was traded away after his contract controversy angered owner Charlie Finley. Finley fired GM Garry Young and quickly dealt Redmond to Chicago. Carol Vadnais, another talented offensive defenseman had been traded a season earlier. California was looking for an offensive defenseman to quarterback the power play for 1974-75.

1974 also marked the first time in three seasons that the Seals had their own first round pick in the entry draft and the first year that 18 year old players were eligible to be drafted. All of these factors combined to result in the selection of Rick Hampton as the Seals top pick (third overall). Hampton had played junior hockey for the St. Catharines Black Hawks and in his final year of junior, scored 25 goals and 50 points in 65 games. He signed a contract with the Seals one day after his 18th birthday. Seals management went overboard touting their newest draftee. Garry Young, the director of player personnel at the time said Hampton was, "the kind of skater you could build a franchise around." Hampton signed one of the first big contracts for rookies—earning over $100,000, a huge sum for 1974.

At the time, Hampton was pleased when he was selected by the Seals. "I was very excited to be drafted by California," Hampton recalled. "I thought it would be a lot less pressure to play for a team like this than say Montreal or Toronto. Also, having never been out of Canada, I thought it might be a pleasurable place to play, considering the sunny weather."

Unfortunately for Hampton, his reception would not be as sunny as the California climate. Many of the veterans on the team were upset about the fact that an unproven teenaged rookie was making much more money than they were before he ever played a game in the NHL. In the long run, of course, the fact that a rookie like Hampton could make more money would drive up the salary structure for all players but the veterans of the time didn't see it that way. To make matters worse, Hampton was immature at 18 and a bit cocky, as many rookies tend to be.

Dave Gardner recalled, "'The Chief' (Jim Neilson) tried to help Rick out a lot but Rick sort of disowned 'The Chief' and was on his own." Butch Williams said, "He was very young, cocky and brash. I disliked him at the time. In retrospect, they were expecting too much of him too soon. They didn't give him time to mature or let him develop."

As a result of his cockiness, most of the rookies and younger players on the Seals were more supportive of Hampton than the veterans. The fans also were expecting Hampton to be the team's savior. Management made matters worse by promoting Hampton as if he actually was the next Bobby Orr. It made for a volatile mix in the locker room and a lot of pressure on an 18-year-old making his NHL debut.

Team captain Joey Johnston recalled, "Rick was too young and very naïve in his first year. We gave him a lot of shit for buying that two-seater Mercedes." Veteran defenseman Bob Stewart remembered the reception that Hampton was given after he was drafted and the pressure that it put on the NHL's second youngest player. "He was our first round pick," Stewart recalled. "I remember the 'Oakland Welcomes Rick Hampton' banner. He was an offensive minded defenseman and a good skater who could move the puck. He was not a team player. He was more interested in what was in it for Rick Hampton. I remember in a restaurant he once asked, 'What kind of fish is the chateau briand?'"

Defenseman Mike Christie was also frustrated when playing with Hampton. "He was my partner," Christie said. "He was a terrible defenseman but a great skater. They paid him a lot and at the time, he didn't give a shit. He didn't have a lot of heart and never really tried to get better. He relied on his skating ability."

Like most rookies, Hampton had to undergo the various initiations and hazing rituals that hockey players have traditionally endured. But unlike most players, Hampton didn't exactly take it lying down. "We had all kinds of initiation rituals for rookies," goalie Gary Simmons recalled. "I never took part in that crap but they had a shaving ritual and when they went to shave Rick, he threw a skate at our captain [Joey Johnston]. He just never fit in."

Hampton realized the problems he had, at least in retrospect. "My biggest problem was my acceptance with the other players," he said. "I was 18, very cocky and making a hell of a lot more money than most of the veterans."

Most of the younger players got along better with the rookie defenseman. Fellow rookie Larry Patey called Hampton, "A good player and a great guy." Wayne King said, "For a rookie, Rick was good. He was laid back and a great skater." Jim Moxey, another rookie, felt that Hampton was, "really thrown to the wolves."

In hindsight, most of the veterans on the team agreed that Hampton was given too much responsibility too soon. "I blame Bill McCreary for ruining Rick's career," Gary Simmons said. "Bobby Orr was 18-years-old when he came up. Rick Hampton was also 18 but he was immature, almost like a 15-year-old. They should have sent him down to develop but instead, they featured the guy. They had a picture of him in *The Hockey News* in front of the Golden Gate Bridge saying, 'Seals Draft the Next Bobby Orr' or something like that."

To make matters worse for the Seals and Hampton, the Seals designated savior got off to a slow start in his first season. "My most embarrassing moment came in my first shift in my first game played," Hampton recalled. "It was against Buffalo and Gilbert Perreault deked me out so bad. He just went in and scored."

For most of the first half of the season, Hampton rode the bench and rarely saw action. "I thought the Seals made too much out of the whole thing," Hampton told reporter Gary Hanlon at the time. "They said at the time they needed the publicity to help build interest in the team. I really think all the publicity put a lot of pressure on me." Despite the slow start, Hampton scored eight goals and 25 points in 78 games as a rookie.

Midway through the season, the club almost sent Hampton to Salt Lake City. "They were going to send me down to Salt Lake on January 30," Hampton recalled. "I was told about it and since we were in Toronto, I went home to see my folks the night before. The next morning at the airport when I walked over to Bill McCreary, instead of a ticket to Salt Lake he gave me one to Boston where the team was going."

Hampton saw action on two power plays that next game in Boston but then began to see regular ice time after that. Because of his offensive mindedness and skating ability, the Seals played Hampton at left wing as well as at defense. "I didn't care which position I played," Hampton said. "Switching did not affect me. Offense was my strength and defense was my weakness."

Hampton's weak defensive play became the butt of jokes among Seals goaltenders. "I remember in 1988 or 1989, the Penguins came to town for an exhibition game and Gilles Meloche was there as goaltending coach," Gary Simmons said. "I was talking to him and I asked him, 'Gilles, does this Coffey look as bad defensively as he looks on TV?' He said to me, 'Cobe, next to Rick Hampton, he's the worst I ever played behind." Overall, however, Meloche felt sorry for Hampton. "He was a really good kid," Meloche said. "Too much pressure was put on him right off the bat. He should have had a longer career but he never really panned out. They were calling him 'The Next Bobby Orr.'"

Hampton remembered his first NHL goal very well. "It was on October 29, 1974, at the Montreal Forum against Ken Dryden," Hampton said. "It was a shorthanded goal, a slap shot from the point which beat him glove side, low." The Seals lost the game 5-1.

Sitting on the bench was difficult for the young rookie. "It was frustrating to watch and not participate," Hampton said. "Even after a playoff spot for the Seals was gone, I was still sitting on the bench. I started having some self doubts, but I knew I wasn't as good a defenseman as the others." Later in his rookie season, injuries hit the Seals defensemen and Hampton saw more ice time. He steadily began to show signs of improvement.

After Bill McCreary took over as coach of the Seals in February of 1975, he did his best to work with Hampton and help him to improve. "Bill McCreary spent a lot of time with me one on one after practice working on refining my skills," Hampton recalled. "He had an unpersonable personality." One of the things McCreary worked on with Hampton was his shoot from the point. McCreary called Hampton "my biggest disappointment. I didn't think he had any confidence in himself whatsoever."

In his second season with the Seals, Hampton's confidence started to come around. Suddenly, the youngster began to find his step and became a solid offensive defenseman. His plus minus rating improved from a minus 40 his rookie year to a minus 12 in 1975-76. He finished the year with 14 goals and a career best 51 points in 73 games. Late in the season, Hampton set a new Seals record for points by a defenseman, breaking Dick Redmond's prior record of 35. He also finished second on the team with eight power play goals.

New Seals coach Jack Evans saw the improvement in Hampton's game. "He's coming along in leaps and bounds, concentrating on his defensive game," Evans told Jack Fiske of the *San Francisco Chronicle*. "We know he can carry the puck and has good speed but he's playing the man more, rubbing him against the boards."

In his second season with the Seals, his teammates became a bit more accepting of Hampton, who they nicknamed, "The Crow." Unfortunately, many of them still felt something was lacking. "He had all the talent in the world," Fred Ahern said. "He could fly, he could handle the puck, he could shoot and score. I guess he lacked a little intensity. He had the potential to be a super star but I guess it never quite worked out."

Veteran forward Gary Sabourin thought a different factor was responsible for Hampton's failure to meet expectations. "He was supposed to be the next Bobby Orr," Sabourin said. "He could skate like Orr, but he couldn't think like Orr. He was drafted number one with great fan fare but he just became an average hockey player."

Len Frig thought that in addition to being so young, a developing young team like the Seals was not the best place for Hampton. "I think that he would have developed much better on an established team where they didn't ask so much of him right away," Frig said. Charlie Simmer concurred. "Rick lost a few years off his career by not having good leadership. A lack of supporting cast hurt him."

Hampton did enjoy living in the Bay Area. He met his future wife there and by his second season in the league, things were getting serious between them. He also liked the Bay Area fans. "Seals fans were the best around," Hampton said. "There weren't many of them, but they sure could make a lot of noise. The Seals weren't given time to grow and develop in the Bay Area. We had the makings of a really good team and like any town, a winner brings out the crowds."

Hampton was not pleased when the team announced it was moving to Cleveland before the 1976-77 season. "I felt terrible about the move," Hampton said. "So, to make me feel better, I married my girlfriend!"

The two seasons Hampton spent in Cleveland were productive. He scored 16 goals and 40 points in just 57 games in 1976-77 followed by a career high 18-goal season in 1977-78. When the Barons folded, the North Stars protected Hampton and then traded him to the Los Angeles Kings over the summer. Hampton played 49 games for the Kings in 1978-79 scoring three goals and 20 points and then appeared in three games for Los Angeles the following year before being sent to the minors. He later played in Switzerland for a few years before retiring from professional hockey. His career NHL statistics include 59 goals and 172 points in 337 games.

Unfortunately for Hampton, he was one of the many NHL players who had issues with NHLPA chief Alan Eagleson. "Rick had real problems with Alan Eagleson," Joey Johnston recalled. "He was a real con artist. The only trouble was that Ted Lindsay was the only competition but Lindsay was such an asshole as a coach and a player that everybody hated him. It's a shame he was right all along." Hampton ended up being a part of a successful lawsuit against Eagleson and he was able to recover some of his lost money. Still, it only added to Hampton's NHL-related frustrations.

Today, Hampton and his wife live in King City, Ontario, near Toronto. They have two children. Hampton is the manager of an ice arena in King City and owns a pro shop. He has also been involved in the invention and manufacturing of a new skate blade system called Quick Blade.

While Rick Hampton ruffled a few feathers in the Seals locker room when he joined the team in 1974-75, perhaps what happened to him is a good example of why the Seals failed both on and off the ice. He did not get treated properly by management, which over hyped him and rushed him into the NHL. He also did not get the support of his teammates both on and off the ice. As a result, Hampton was never able to fully realize his immense talent and the Seals organization lost a golden opportunity to improve itself.

Dave Gardner summed up "The Crow" by saying, "He was one of the most talented skaters I've ever seen. He got a raw deal in Oakland. He was only 18. He could have been a great one if he were nurtured. He didn't have great vision on the ice, but he wasn't really taught anything after he turned 18. They figured if you were in the NHL, you knew what you needed to know. He was a strong and tough kid."

Al MacAdam added, "Rick was the start of the 'new breed' of player. He signed for something like $100,000. The older guys on our team ran him into the ground instead of nurturing him. I think it drove him out of hockey too early. On a good team, he would have played a long time. He became apathetic but he was very talented. For him, it was the wrong team at the wrong time."

Charlie Simmer

"He was a good guy. He was not intimidated coming up to the NHL. He wasn't good enough to play for us full time, but he sure played well enough in Los Angeles."

–Al MacAdam on Charlie Simmer

In sports, there are always famous tales about the superstar that got away. In baseball, Red Sox fans believe their team was cursed because their owner sold Babe Ruth to the Yankees supposedly to finance the Broadway production of "No-No Nannette." Fans of the Atlanta Falcons cringe every time Brett Favre's name is mentioned as they think of what might have been had their team kept the gunslinging quarterback from Kiln, Mississippi, instead of trading him to Green Bay. The Seals had a player like that in their history as well. His name was Charlie Simmer. With the Seals, he was up and down from Oakland to the minors. Later, when he joined the Los Angeles Kings, he became a 50 goal scorer and part of what was arguably the most feared line in hockey at the time: "The Triple Crown Line" which featured Simmer along with Marcel Dionne and Dave Taylor.

Simmer was born in Terrace Bay, Ontario. "Because of Hockey Night in Canada, I was a Leafs fan," Simmer recalled. "My favorite players included Dick Duff, Tim Horton, Johnny Bower and Bobby Hull." Simmer played junior hockey with the Sault-Ste.-Marie Greyhounds and in 1973-74, he scored 45 goals and 99 points in 70 games. The Seals selected the 6'3", 210 pound forward in the third round of the 1974 entry draft. "At first, it was disappointing being selected by the Seals," Simmer admitted. "I was a traditional type guy. Then I realized that it may be a quicker way to the NHL so my disappointment quickly turned to optimism. Playing in the NHL sooner also meant more money and that didn't hurt."

291

Throughout the 1974-75 season, Simmer split time between the Seals and their top affiliate in Salt Lake. In 47 games in Salt Lake City, Simmer scored 12 goals and 41 points. With the Seals, he had eight goals and 21 points in 35 games. Although the Seals finished the season 29 games under .500, Simmer was a very respectable minus two in the plus minus ratings. Despite the fact that he played fairly well every time he was called up to California, the Seals always sent him back down to the minors.

Simmer felt there was actually a better attitude among the players down in Salt Lake then there was with the Seals. "There was an attitude in Oakland I never thought I'd see in the NHL," Simmer said. "I was happy to be there but the Seals were not a well run organization. There was a lack of leadership. We were out of the playoffs by Thanksgiving and nobody really cared. Jack Evans, who coached me at Salt Lake hated to lose and I was very disappointed to get to the NHL and find out how lightly the players took it."

Another thing that surprised Simmer was the lack of assistance from the veterans and the organization itself. "When you turned pro, everybody assumed you knew everything," Simmer recalled. "There was not much guidance there. The attitude was, 'You should know what you're doing, you're a pro.' The old guys didn't take the young guys under their wings. I guess there was a fear that you would challenge them or take a job from one of their friends on the team."

Despite these difficulties, Simmer has some fond memories of his time with the Seals, including his first NHL goal. "It was against Boston and we won the game," Simmer said. The final score was 5-2. "My goal was an empty netter," he said. "I beat Gerry Cheevers by 65 feet. I was taking a face-off against Phil Esposito who I knew from Sault-Ste.-Marie. He was encouraging. Bill McCreary sent me out to take the face-off. I got the puck to the red line and Espo was at the blue line and then he caught me at the other blue line. I was shaking like a leaf, but the puck went in."

Simmer had some other fine offensive moments in his limited tour of duty with the Seals in 1974-75. On January 1, 1975, he scored a goal and added an assist in a 3-3 tie with the Maple Leafs at Maple Leaf Gardens. It was his first appearance on Hockey Night In Canada and Simmer made it a memorable one. Then on March 9, 1975, Simmer had three assists as the Seals defeated the Islanders 4-2 in Oakland. Larry Patey had a hat trick in that game for California.

"Charlie made me in Oakland although he never fully blossomed until he left," Patey said. "He could shoot, he could pass, he was a big guy and he became a superstar. I guess he became a superstar later because I didn't compliment Charlie as much as he complimented me. Of course, in Los Angeles, Marcel Dionne was really able to set him up well. Charlie could shoot really well...We just never knew that in Oakland."

Simmer had a real appreciation for his first NHL coach, Marshall Johnston. "He was great. He got the shaft that year," Simmer said recalling Johnston's mid-season dismissal. "He got caught up in the situation and didn't get any support from upstairs. He was old school and very honest. I mean, if I play shitty, tell me what I'm doing wrong. He did that."

He was less fond of Johnston's replacement, Bill McCreary, although for different reasons than most of his teammates. "Bill McCreary was not as disciplined as Marshall Johnston or Jack Evans," Simmer said. "He was a little bit easy going and the players took advantage."

If Simmer had a weak point in his game, it was his skating. Butch Williams recalled, "I once asked Charlie if he broke his legs as a kid. He said, 'No, why?' I said, 'You don't skate very well.' Still, Charlie was a good scorer. He had a great shot and a great reach. Playing with Marcel Dionne picked up his game."

In 1975-76, Simmer continued to ride the shuttle between Salt Lake City and Oakland. In 42 games with the Eagles, Simmer scored 23 goals and 39 points. With the Seals, he was put in a more defensive role and scored one goal and two points in 21 games. "I remember I was given the role of a defensive specialist," Simmer recalled. "I was the checking center, along with Ralph Klassen, we played defense and killed penalties. Then they said I wasn't scoring enough and they sent me down to the minors. Why didn't they say something to me sooner? Whey didn't they tell me, 'Hey, we need a few more goals from you?' That's how I learned about the business side of hockey."

Veteran wing Jim Pappin recalled what happened to Simmer with the Seals. "Dave Hrechkosy, Charlie Simmer and I were a line for the first two weeks I was in Oakland," Pappin said. "We were the best line on the team for two weeks then they sent him back down to Salt Lake. We were not too well coached and Tex Evans didn't like Charlie. Charlie was a good kid, too."

While Jack Evans may not have been Simmer's biggest fan, Simmer respected what Evans brought to the team. "He was my type of coach," Simmer said. "He was hard nosed. He figured there was no excuse not to try. He wanted effort from all of us."

Despite being given a primarily defensive role in 1975-76, some of Simmer's teammates saw the offensive talent Simmer possessed that remained untapped with the Seals. "He was a great goal scorer and a great guy," center Wayne Merrick said of Simmer. "He got pushed around. He had the hands and was big and strong." Goaltender Gilles Meloche also saw the talent Simmer had. "He was up and down from the minors," Meloche recalled. "He was not much of a skater but he sure knew where the net was."

One former teammate felt that Simmer got caught up in the heavy drinking some of his fellow single teammates were doing at the time. "The talent was there but he lived too hard off the ice," Gary Sabourin said. "I tried to tell him that he could make it but he had to put in more effort. The talent was very evident when he got to Los Angeles."

Another problem Simmer experienced both in Oakland and again in Los Angeles was travel. "It was a big disadvantage," Simmer recalled. "It hurt us in two ways. First, we had less practice time then other teams. Second, we didn't have as much time to recuperate and our small injuries became big injuries. We complained in Oakland and Los Angeles but the league didn't believe us until Wayne Gretzky played for Los Angeles. We had long road trips and when you come home after two weeks of being on the road, you have things to settle. We would always lose our first game after a long road trip no matter who we were playing."

The statistics back up Simmer's memory. In 1974-75, for example, the Seals were 0-4-3 in their first home game after a road trip of three games or more. The Seals finished the season with an overall record of 15-15-10 at home.

While Simmer had his difficulties while playing for the Seals, he has fond memories of the team's fans. "We had a great booster club," Simmer said. "They had the best looking girls of any club in the NHL. Most of the fans were not from Oakland and I think that hurt a little bit. But even if some of the crowds were smaller, the crowd in Oakland was always very loud. The hard core fans were always there."

Simmer also recalled some lighter moments from his time with the Seals. "Rick Dudley of Buffalo used to wear a headband during games," Simmer recalled. "Joey Johnston was on the bench and he starts yelling at Rick, 'Hey Dudley, we got real Indians on our team.' Then he looked at Jim Neilson." Frank Spring also recalled the moment. "Dudley, who was normally a very serious guy, started laughing. That was the only time I saw him laugh on the ice."

Simmer also remembered an unusual habit that goalie Gary Simmons had during games. "Gary Simmons was a unique guy. In the second period, he had two hot dogs and one mustard every game."

In 1976-77, the Seals moved to Cleveland and became the Cleveland Barons. Once again, Charlie Simmer split the year between the NHL and the Barons farm team in Salt Lake City. With Cleveland, Simmer scored twice in 24 games. With the Eagles, Simmer began to show his offensive talents, scoring 32 goals and 62 points in 51 games. Simmer's contract expired at the end of the season and the cash strapped Barons elected not to re-sign him. The Kings picked him up as a free agent in August 1977. So the answer to the question, "What did the Seals organization get in exchange for Charlie Simmer?" is absolutely nothing.

"The best thing that happened to him was that the Seals let him go," Jim Moxey said. "He said he was going to open up a sporting goods store back home when the Kings called him. The rest is history."

After a 42-goal season in Springfield, Simmer made the Kings for half of the 1978-79 season and scored 21 goals and 48 points in 38 games. Then, Simmer caught fire scoring back to back 56 goal seasons and topping 100 points both years. He later played for the Bruins and the Penguins before leaving the NHL after the 1987-88 season. Simmer's career NHL statistics include 342 goals and 711 points in 712 games. He played in two NHL All-Star games, was named to two postseason NHL All-Star teams and won the Masterton Trophy for dedication to hockey in 1986.

Looking back at his hockey career, Simmer admitted, "I think skating was not my strong point. I think my strengths were my size and I anticipated well. I knew how the game was played and had a strong desire to be successful. I enjoyed the game and I still do. I had a desire to keep playing after five years of giving it a try."

Simmer remained in hockey as the color commentator for the Phoenix Coyotes television broadcasts until the lockout. Simmer is married and has three children. He lives in Scottsdale, Arizona.

Dave Gardner summed up Charlie Simmer by saying, "I was not so surprised about his ability. He replaced me when I was hurt. They played him at center, which is where he played in juniors. He had the ability but were we developing our players properly? He got 50 goals playing with Marcel Dionne. He wasn't an NHL centerman but he could play and he was a very good guy." For the Seals and their fans, Simmer will always be the one that got away.

Frank Spring

"He's still a good friend of mine. I wish I had his body. We called him "Gentle Ben" because he was so easy going. He never reached his potential."

–Butch Williams on Frank Spring

Frank Spring was a highly touted player coming out of junior mostly because of his size. The imposing looking Spring stood 6'3", and weighed 213 pounds. He played his junior hockey with the Edmonton Oil Kings and in his first season there, he scored 24 goals and 51 points in 57 games. "When I was in juniors," Spring recalled, "I knew I would be drafted." Although his scoring fell of in 1968-69, his second year with the Oil Kings, Spring was selected by the Boston Bruins with the fourth overall selection in the 1969 entry draft after the Canadiens selected Rejean Houle and Marc Tardif and the Bruins chose Don Tannahill third.

Spring remembered how different the draft was back then as compared to the media circus it is today. "It was the first or second year that the draft was done as we know it," Spring said. "I went to a local radio station and watched the ticker tape. Nobody went to the draft back then."

Spring spent most of the 1969-70 season with the Oklahoma City Blazers in the CHL and in 62 games, scored 17 goals and 39 assists. He was called up for one NHL game with Boston and was held scoreless.

In 1970-71, Spring was promoted to the Hershey Bears of the AHL. Although his season was shortened by injury, he still managed 12 goals and 24 points in just 43 games. At that time, however, the Bruins organization was perhaps the most talented in hockey and Spring was left unprotected in the waiver draft prior to the 1971-72 season. The Philadelphia Flyers selected the former number one pick and assigned him to the their AHL farm club, the Richmond Robins.

Once again it seemed Spring was in the wrong place at the wrong time. Although he had great size, Spring was not an aggressive player. He joined the Flyers organization just as they were transforming themselves into "The Broad Street Bullies". After consecutive seasons with 12 goals and 31 points with Richmond, Spring was on the move once again. In December 1973, the Flyers traded Spring to the St. Louis Blues in exchange for Ray Schultz, the brother of Flyers enforcer Dave Schultz. Spring was assigned to the Denver Spurs of the WHL where he scored 17 goals and 28 points in just 47 games. He earned a two game call-up with the Blues and again was held without a point or penalty minute in NHL competition.

In 1974-75, Spring started the season in the Blues system, again playing for the Spurs. He seemed to find his goal scoring touch in Denver that season, scoring 19 goals and 28 points in 31 games. The Blues recalled Spring for three games and again he was held without a point. On January 9, 1975, the Blues traded Spring to the Seals for defenseman Bruce Affleck. The Seals had selected Affleck in the second round of the entry draft in 1974 but felt they could not afford his salary. *Sports Illustrated* considered the trade a salary dump by the Seals who were still being run by the NHL at that time.

Spring was pleased when the Seals picked him up. "I looked at it as a great opportunity," he said. "Somebody wants you." Still, there was a noticeable difference playing in Oakland as opposed to traditional hockey cities like Boston or Philadelphia. "In Boston or Philly, we were thinking, 'We're gonna win it all,'" Spring said. "In California, we were just trying to get it going, just starting to believe in ourselves. Also, we were playing in a place where hockey means nothing which was very different from Boston or Philadelphia."

After a quick adjustment, Spring grew to like the Bay Area. "I loved California," Spring said. "My family was happy there. We had a home there and we enjoyed the summer."

On the ice, Spring was very inconsistent. He was invisible at times and then at other times, seemed to accumulate points in bunches. Spring scored his first NHL goal on January 24, 1975, at the Oakland Coliseum Arena, putting the puck behind Toronto netminder Doug Favell. The Seals went on to win the game 6-1. "It meant a lot to me to score off the team I rooted for as a kid," he said.

Spring also remembered a nationally televised game against Chicago that the Seals lost 3-1 but he scored the Seals only goal. "Wayne Merrick passed to me in the air, the puck hit the shaft of my stick and went behind Tony Esposito," Spring said. Hockey fans all across America got to see Spring score on the Black Hawks future Hall of Famer.

The big native of Cranbrook, British Colombia, had another big game when the Seals and Maple Leafs met on February 19, 1975. Spring scored once and assisted on another goal in a 3-3 tie against the Leafs. Spring continued his pattern of scoring points in bunches as he set up two California goals in a 7-2 loss to the Sabres in Oakland on March 12, 1975.

Overall, Spring scored three goals and 11 points in 28 games for the Seals. The big winger was forced to sit out the final eight games of the regular season in 1974-75 due to strained knee ligaments.

Spring was well liked among his teammates but his lack of physical play did bother some of them. "He was big but he wouldn't run over people," said Spike Huston. Goalie Gary Simmons, who also played with Spring in Richmond added, "I never saw a guy who could pump iron and lost weight to get into shape. He could score goals but he didn't. He was a big guy but he wasn't mean. He bought a house before training camp in 1975. I told him in camp he had to hit people, but he didn't hit. He was sent to Salt Lake. We called him 'The Saint Bernard.' He was a good guy but he just wasn't mean enough." John Stewart thought something was missing for Spring in the NHL. "He was a huge star is juniors," Stewart said. "When I was 16, I remember watching him play and he was larger than life. He must have lost his confidence somewhere along the way."

Spring was sent down to Salt Lake City in 1975-76. "Jack Evans sent me down to Salt Lake and told me I couldn't score," Spring recalled. "So, in Salt Lake, I led the league in scoring. I figured I'd show him." Spring had the best season of his career. In 75 games with the Golden Eagles, he had a league leading 44 goals and 73 points. The Seals called him up for one game against the Los Angeles Kings and Spring responded by picking up two assists.

When the Seals moved to Cleveland in 1976-77, Spring remained in the organization. He split the season between the Barons and Salt Lake. He was productive in both places. With Cleveland, the gentle giant scored 11 goals and 21 points in 26 games. At Salt Lake, he scored eight goals and 18 points in 19 games.

In 1977-78, Spring signed with the Indianapolis Racers of the WHA and was briefly teammates with an 18-year-old rookie named Wayne Gretzky. He scored two goals and six points in 13 games. After the Racers folded, the Rangers acquired Spring's rights and he spent the rest of the season playing for the New Haven Nighthawks of the AHL. Spring retired after the 1977-78 season and returned to Cranbrook where he still resides with his wife. He works at the family car dealership and has three sons. Spring's career NHL statistics were 14 goals and 34 points in 61 NHL games, hardly what was expected of the fourth overall selection in the draft.

Looking back at his NHL career, Spring acknowledges he would do things differently "both on and off the ice. I should have been rougher than I was. I'm not like that and I didn't want to play like that. I wanted to get to the NHL because I was a good hockey player and I did that. Off the ice, I think it was due to naïveté. I would have more to do with management and coaching. I thought I was just a hockey player so I should go out and play. You have to interact with management. It bothered me for years now but I've come to terms with it. Everything happens for a reason. I'm happy now and maybe I wouldn't have gotten here if things went differently."

Spring's son, Corey, is presently playing professional hockey. After attending the University of Alaska-Farbanks, Corey Spring had two brief call-ups with the Tampa Bay Lightning in 1997-98 and 1998-99. He split the 2000-2001 season between a team in England and the Long Beach Ice Dogs of the WHL. "It meant more to me to see my son score his first NHL goal," Spring said proudly. "I told my son wherever his first NHL game was played, I would be there. Of course, it was in Tampa which is about as far as you can get from Cranbrook." Spring was in attendance at his son's NHL debut.

Jim Moxey summarized Spring's career by saying, "He had lots of potential and was a big kid. He just never put it all together." After his hockey career, "Gentle Ben" did put it all together and he takes satisfaction from that fact.

Bob Girard

"He was one of the best conditioned athletes I've ever seen. He played up and down his wing and was feisty. He used to swear in French during practice. 'Frenchy' was committed to winning. He was older, but he didn't believe he was older. He pushed the limit and wanted to win. He was a funny guy in the dressing room, too."

—Dave Gardner on Bob Girard

Bob Girard was one of many rookies who played for the California Golden Seals in 1975-76. His style of play was exactly what the team needed, a tough winger who skated well and was at home mucking in the corners. The 6', 175 pound Girard was born in Montreal. Although he was not drafted, Girard refused to be discouraged. "Frenchy" played senior hockey in Quebec for the Amqui Aces before signing as a free agent with the Seals prior to the 1973-74 season. After two seasons in Salt Lake in which he played mostly defense, Eagles coach Jack Evans converted Girard into a left wing.

"When I came to Salt Lake we were allowed to carry 11 forwards and five defenseman," Evans recalled. "If you wanted to make up a fourth line, you had to use a defenseman. I put Girard up there one night and his line scored six goals."

Girard helped the Eagles to the 1974-75 CHL championship. In 74 games with Salt Lake, he scored 13 goals and 45 points before adding two assists in 11 playoff games.

Evans became head coach of the Seals in 1975-76. He was familiar with Girard's abilities and after a strong training camp, Girard made his NHL debut with the Seals at age 26. On October 26, 1975, the rookie from Montreal scored his first NHL goal, beating Sabres goalie Gerry Desjardins in a 3-2 Seals loss at the Aud.

"I am proud of the fact that I made the NHL in just three years," Girard said at the time. "I worked hard in training camp and it is a challenge for me to be on this team. It doesn't concern me that this has been a last-place team." Girard wanted to win and in the worst way. "When we lose a game, no guys on this team are happy," he said. "That is a good sign. We try too hard to lose. We came here to win, not to lose."

Girard was placed on a line with Gary Sabourin and Wayne Merrick. This line provided both the ability to score and solid defensive play. Sabourin recalled Girard's ability to check and then added, "He was happy to be there. He couldn't believe he was playing in the NHL. He was a terrific team guy." Wayne Merrick remembered Girard's skating speed the most. "He could fly," Merrick said. "He worked hard, but he just couldn't put the puck in the net."

Girard's abilities and effort were not lost on his teammates. "'Frenchy' was a good person," defenseman Mike Christie said. "He worked his ass off with limited talent. He survived primarily as a penalty killer." Gary Simmons recalled Girard as colorful. "He played his heart out," Simmons recalled. "He could skate fast and he would go into the corners although he was not that big. He was always yapping, half in French and half in English. He was a very likable guy."

Girard was not a flashy goal scorer, in fact, he considered his shot to be one of the weaker points of his game but he proudly did the dirty work required of him to stay in the NHL. "I really love the corners," Girard said half joking. "It is a good place to be. I have trouble scoring, so I like to set up my linemates with the puck because they have a better chance to score. If I want to stay up here (in the NHL), I have to improve my shot. I know my game is defense because I'm a good skater. If I score a lot, that is a bonus. I just have to learn to shoot more. Then, I'll be all right."

Jack Evans was pleased with the play of his rookie left wing. "He's a good skater, gets on the puck quickly and isn't afraid to go into those corners," Evans said of Girard. "That's what we were looking for. We needed Girard's checking ability."

Although he was not known as a goal scorer, Girard did have some fine offensive games while with the Seals. On January 2, 1976, while linemate Wayne Merrick was setting a new club record with six points in a game, Girard tallied three points in an 8-5 win over the Washington Capitals. Girard also had the distinction of scoring the game winning goal in the Seals final game ever, a 5-2 win over the Los Angeles Kings at Oakland. Overall, he finished his rookie year with a very respectable 16 goals and 42 points while appearing in all 80 games for California.

Off the ice, Girard seemed popular with his teammates. "He kept the room alive and he never shut up," goaltender Gilles Meloche recalled with a smile. "He could also skate like the wind." "He was a fun guy in the dressing room," George Pesut said. Fred Ahern, who also played with Girard at Salt Lake, called Girard, "Pound for pound, he was a little pit bull or a Boston terrier. He gave 150% every night and wouldn't back down from anybody." Nobody ever seemed to question Girard's effort and hustle. "He had a great work ethic," Len Frig said, "just like Gary Sabourin."

Girard did have a run-in with one of his teammates, veteran forward Jim Pappin. "He was a good player and a good, tough kid. He was different and the guys bugged him about it all the time," Pappin said. "I called him "Fee-Fee" and he cut my jeans to shreds when I said that."

Like many Quebec born players, Girard also had to work to perfect his English. "He was funny," Wayne King recalled when asked about Girard. "He had an accent and was always saying the wrong words." Eventually, Girard's English improved and he had no trouble communicating with his teammates.

Girard followed the Seals to Cleveland in 1976-77 but his offensive numbers were off. In 68 games with the Barons, "Frenchy" scored 11 goals and 21 points. The following year, after picking up only four assists in 25 games for Cleveland, the Barons shipped Girard to the Washington Capitals for Walt McKechnie. Girard spent a season-and-a-half with the Capitals before spending the 1979-80 season with the Hershey Bears of the AHL. He retired from pro hockey after the 1979-80 season. In 305 career NHL games, Girard scored 45 goals and 114 points. He never did appear in an NHL playoff game in his four-and-a-half year career.

Al MacAdam summed up Bob Girard by saying, "He was a little older, sort of a late bloomer. He played senior hockey in Gasbay. He was physically fit year round which was unusual back then. He had the ability to compete and play at an NHL level and was a good team player."

Bob Murdoch

"He was a good guy. He got along well with the team, sort of just fit in. Bob was a good goal scorer."

—Ralph Klassen on Bob Murdoch

Bob Murdoch came from a hockey family. His younger brother, Don also played in the NHL with the New York Rangers, Edmonton Oilers and Detroit Red Wings. Like many Canadian families, the Murdochs loved their hockey. "I would watch Hockey Night in Canada at 5 PM every Saturday," Murdoch recalled. "Toronto or Montreal would always be on. My dad was a Maple Leafs fan and every Saturday, we watched the Leafs with dad. We were dressed in Leafs blue from September until April. When we played in the backyard as kids, we pretended to be Frank Mahovlich or Dave Keon once in awhile for fun."

Bob Murdoch was a long shot to play in the NHL. When he played junior hockey with the Brandon Wheat Kings, he thought he had a chance to make the big time but nobody drafted him. He spent the 1973-74 season with the Cranbrook Royals of the Western International Hockey League. Murdoch tallied 37 goals in 48 games. He remembers how he first managed to get invited to the Seals training camp in the summer of 1974. "I was scouted by Corky Egar in senior hockey," Murdoch said. "He was looking at goalie Pierre Hamel. I scored three goals in each game that weekend and I was then given an invitation to Seals camp. I was ecstatic and happy to go to the NHL."

Although he was not expected to make the Seals, Murdoch played well enough to sign a free agent contract with California and be assigned to their developmental club in Salt Lake of the CHL. In 76 games with the Golden Eagles, Murdoch scored 33 goals and 63 points. He added another six goals and 12 points in 11 playoff games as Salt Lake won the CHL title. Murdoch's coach in Salt Lake was Jack Evans. Evans recognized Murdoch's goal scoring ability and worked hard with Murdoch to improve other facets of his game. "The only knock they ever had against Murdoch was his checking ability," Evans said during the 1975-76 season. "Well, he worked on that all last year and again this season and now the checking end of his game has picked up greatly."

After Evans helped Murdoch, the young right wing developed a good deal of respect for his coach. "I loved the guy," Murdoch said. "I could always count on him being the same every day regardless of the situation. He was a hard nosed guy. If you worked hard for him, there were no problems. If you didn't, you disappeared. He coached me in Salt Lake and then my game was all offense. He sat me down and told me I had the talent to play in the NHL but I was a liability on defense. He taught me a lot about hockey. He and Lyle Bradley taught me a lot about defense." By his rookie year in the NHL, Murdoch appreciated the importance of playing defense. "I've gone into a more defensive game and I don't take as many chances offensively as I used to," he said. "What good is a player who scores three goals a game and lets in four?"

Murdoch learned his lesson well. In 1975-76, he was promoted to the Seals. He scored the winning goal in his first ever NHL game. "We were in Atlanta and it was late in the second period," Murdoch recalled. "Atlanta took a penalty and Jack Evans put me out on the power play. I scored on a slap shot from the point. We won 4-3 and that was the game winner."

Coach Jack Evans put Murdoch on right wing with fellow rookie Dennis Maruk and second year left wing Al MacAdam to form "The 3-M Line". It instantly became the top line on the Seals as both Maruk and MacAdam had 30 goal seasons in 1975-76 with Murdoch finishing with 22.

"They key guy was Dennis Maruk," Murdoch recalled. "His attitude was not that of a rookie. He was confident and tenacious. It was like he had already been playing in the league for eight years. He had the speed to break open a game. Al MacAdam was so steady, he never had a bad game. We got the puck from the corner, Maruk was always open or trying to get there. We were all young. We could all shoot. We scored a goal a game and were one of the top lines in the league."

In 1975-76, the 3-M line set a new club record for most goals scored by a line in one season. Al MacAdam appreciated what Murdoch brought to the table. "I liked him a lot. He was my linemate. He'd do anything for you. I was always sort of waiting for him to grow up." Charlie Simmer called Murdoch, "a good, opportunistic goal scorer."

Murdoch was always known as a goal scorer and had a booming slap shot. "I work on scoring," he told Hank Masler during his rookie year. "In practice, I take slap shots from all angles and even shoot off the wrong leg. I want to be prepared for any shot I have to take during a game." The practice paid off for Murdoch.

Bob Murdoch had a productive season with the Seals in 1975-76. The 5'11", 170 pound Cranbrook, BC native finished his rookie year with 22 goals and 49 points in 78 games. He led the Seals in power play goals that season with nine. Murdoch and the 3-M Line had many big games for the Seals in 1975-76. Murdoch scored twice against the Bruins in a 6-3 loss in Oakland on November 9, 1975. He also had a pair of goals against St. Louis in a 7-1 Seals route on March 22, 1976. Perhaps his best offensive game was a one goal, three assist effort at the Aud in Buffalo during a 5-5 tie with the Sabres on February 8, 1976.

Despite these and other fine offensive efforts, the game Murdoch remembers most fondly was a close loss against the eventual Stanley Cup champions, the Montreal Canadiens in Oakland on December 21, 1975. "We lost 2-1," Murdoch recalled. "Clarence Campbell, who was still president of the league at that time, was at the game. He never used to come to the dressing room. Dennis Maruk hit a crossbar and I hit a post. We may have even outshot them. After the game, Clarence Campbell came into our dressing room. I felt like we had won the Stanley Cup although we were all disappointed. He shook all of our hands and said it was the most memorable game he had seen at the Coliseum in years."

Perhaps the biggest problem Murdoch and many of his teammates faced was the Seals hectic travel schedule. "Our road trips were huge," Murdoch said. "We had a 17 day road trip, then we had a 12 game home stand in November and December. We came back and your focus was gone from hockey. We all had bills to pay and things to catch up on. I think we only won four of the 12 games at home during that stretch."

Murdoch remembered many off-ice moments as well including a time honored hockey tradition, the hazing of rookies. "We had a lot of rookies on our team," Murdoch said. "I had gone through a horror show with initiation in Salt Lake. I was painted black with shellac. It took three weeks to get that all off and I didn't want that again. I had an idea that the rookies would take all the veterans to dinner and we would pay for it. The veterans said they would think about it. The next morning, they shaved me. It was an initiation. Ralph Klassen's shave was over in less than five minutes because he had almost no body hair. With Dennis Maruk, the only shaved off half of his fu manchu. I think it grew back in like four days."

Another less than stellar memory Murdoch recalled took place during pre-game warm-ups at the Spectrum in Philadelphia. "We came on the ice for the warm-up," Murdoch said. "One of the Flyers skated over to our blue line. They warmed up in a big circle and our circle was small, just around our net. They would have started a brawl if we would have skated near them. That warm-up was embarrassing."

There was also the time that Murdoch ended up fighting Pierre Bouchard of Montreal. "We were losing 5-4 in Oakland and we pulled our goalie," Murdoch said. "Bouchard went into the corner after the puck and I nailed him pretty good so he elbowed me in the head. He laid me out. I was face down on the ice when I saw two red and blue gloves drop. I tried to pull him down on the ice but he got down and started pummeling me." Needless to say Murdoch did not win that fight.

If Murdoch had a problem, it was off the ice. "There were distractions," he admitted. "Suddenly, there was no winter. I remember we had our Christmas party around the pool. I really enjoyed living in the Bay Area. I came from a small town to a big city and there was much more available to you. There was stardom to a certain degree. You needed self-discipline." At 21-years-old, Murdoch didn't always have it. "The Bay Area was a great place to live," Murdoch recalled. "The people were so friendly and not just the people you met through hockey. It was a unique place to be at the time. The Patty Hearst kidnapping happened a few blocks from our practice rink."

Some of Murdoch's teammates felt that his "distractions" took a toll on his play after awhile. Wayne Merrick said Murdoch was "a good player, but not focused." As always, Gary Simmons was direct and to the point: "He was a good goal scorer but he was a partier and it cut years off his career by drinking. He was a good guy and a free spirit. He liked the outside stuff that went along with being in the NHL."

One place Murdoch and many of the Seals players hung out in was an Oakland bar called Cactus Al's. "It was across from the Blue Cross Building and the girls who worked in the building would go there for lunch," Murdoch recalled. "I had a friend who looked like Mark Spitz. I remember a black guy saying to his friend, 'That guy looks like Mark Spitz,' and his friend said, 'Yeah, all those white guys look alike.'"

Murdoch, then 21 and single, was also popular with the Bay Area ladies. "He had a shot and was a tough competitor," Bob Stewart said. "He swore he would never get married. He worked hard on and off the ice." Fred Ahern simply said, "Bob was one of my best friends on the team. We had more laughs together than I call tell you about and some I know I can't tall you about."

Dave Gardner recalled, "Bob and Charlie Simmer lived next door to me in Cleveland. I never had that many girls knocking on my door wondering where they were. He reminded me of a young George Armstrong. He would get the puck to you. He was a free spirit, a young guy away from home. He got things done on the ice but you weren't sure exactly why. He was always worrying about keeping his weight down."

Murdoch stayed with the Seals organization when they moved to Cleveland to become the Barons. He played in Cleveland both seasons the club existed. In 1976-77, Murdoch scored 23 goals and 42 points in just 57 games before his season was cut short by injury. The following year was not as productive as Murdoch scored 14 goals and 40 points in 71 games.

When the Barons merged with the Minnesota North Stars in 1978, the North Stars had a protected list of players and then the rest of the team was available in a "fill-in draft." Murdoch went unprotected and was claimed by the St. Louis Blues. He spent one season in St. Louis, scoring 13 goals and 26 points in 54 games before heading back to Salt Lake. Murdoch's career statistics in the NHL include 72 goals and 157 points in 260 games. He never appeared in the Stanley Cup playoffs.

Today, Murdoch owns a dairy distribution company in Cranbrook. He broke his vow and did get married and now has three sons. Now, Murdoch seems much more mature and can look back at his days with the Seals fondly but from a distance. Gilles Meloche summed up Bob Murdoch by saying, "He could score goals; he loved life and was a good player." And for one season in Oakland, he was part of the most productive and exciting line in Seals history.

Gary Sabourin

"He was my first roomie. I have nothing but respect for him. He played many years on heart. He took me under his wing and told me the right thing to do. I have nothing but admiration for the man. He was kind of silent."

–Ralph Klassen on Gary Sabourin

Gary Sabourin was brought to the Seals to teach younger players how to win. By the time he arrived in Oakland, however, the 5'11", 180 pound Sabourin was already 31-years-old and coming off a major knee injury. Still, the native of Parry Sound, Ontario tried to lead his inexperienced teammates by example.

Sabourin began his professional hockey career as property of the Rangers although he never played in New York. "I was in the Rangers organization for three years, but I was never called up to the NHL," Sabourin said. Finally, with the advent of expansion, Sabourin got his chance. The St. Louis Blues selected Rangers defenseman Rod Seiling in the expansion draft and in a pre-arranged deal, traded Seiling back to the Rangers for Sabourin, Bob Plager, Gord Kannegeisser and Tim Ecclestone. Sabourin appeared in 50 games for the Blues in their first season in the league, scoring 13 goals and 23 points. Sabourin's first two NHL goals came against the Seals on December 13, 1967, when he beat Oakland goalie Charlie Hodge twice as the Blues downed the Seals 3-1.

"After my first year playing in St. Louis, I knew I could play in the league," Sabourin recalled. "The team went to the finals. I never thought I'd score as much as I did. I was not a big goal scorer in the minors; I was always more of a physical player. I played robustly. I found playing in the NHL was easier than playing in the minors. In the NHL, I was not a fighter, the fighters in the NHL were really tough." Even then, Sabourin was working hard to improve his play. "I worked hard on my shot that off-season," Sabourin said. "I put weights on my sticks and practiced. As a player, I had enough speed to get into open areas. That came with experience."

Sabourin ended up staying in St. Louis for seven seasons and topped the 20 goal mark four times while with the Blues. Sabourin appeared in the Stanley Cup Finals in his first three seasons in the league. Unfortunately for Sabourin and the expansion Blues, his club was swept all three times. Sabourin was twice chosen to represent the Blues at the NHL All-Star game in 1970 and again in 1971.

After a sub-par year in 1973-74 in which he scored only seven goals in 54 games, the Blues traded Sabourin to the Toronto Maple Leafs in exchange for goalie Ed Johnston. Sabourin spent one year in Toronto and it was not a pleasant season. "I had missed all of training camp that year with a knee injury," Sabourin said. "I had a rough year. I played in only 55 games and was used primarily to kill penalties." Sabourin rarely saw a regular shift on a deep Leafs team. In 1974-75, Sabourin scored only five goals and 23 points. Many scouts began to speculate that at 31-years-old, Sabourin was washed up.

Still, the veteran right wing wanted one more chance to prove he could still play in the NHL. His former St. Louis teammate, Bill McCreary, was now GM of the Seals. "Once, the Seals were in town and I saw Bill McCreary watching the pre-game skate," Sabourin said. "I yelled up to him, 'Why don't you get me to Oakland?' I was traded later for Stan Weir."

Sabourin immediately noticed a difference in attitude between the Blues teams that he went to the finals with and the young Seals, who had never had a winning season in their then eight year history. Sabourin tried to teach the young Seals a bit of what it took to win consistently in the NHL. "In St. Louis, the attitude was different," Sabourin remembered. "All the players acquired by the Blues were winners in the minors. They came from winning programs. In St. Louis, they brought in Scotty Bowman to coach. He was a great bench coach. He made all the right adjustments between periods and was a great motivator. The dressing room in St. Louis was vibrant and full of winners. We had Dickie Moore, Jean-Guy Talbot and Jimmy Roberts. The attitude in St. Louis was you <u>had</u> to win. I couldn't wait to get on the ice. Oakland had some good, young players like Dennis Maruk and Bob Murdoch, but they were not as dedicated to winning as they were in St. Louis."

In addition to joining a team that had yet to learn to develop a winning attitude, Sabourin faced another problem with California; he was suddenly a "senior citizen" on the NHL's youngest team. "The age difference between me and most of my teammates, it was a bit different, that's for sure," Sabourin said. Also, on a team full of pranksters and practical jokers, Sabourin was all business. When asked if he recalled any humorous stories from his season with the Seals, Sabourin paused and said, "When you're winning, there's a lot of humor but when you're losing, there's not much to joke about. I took losing hard. After losses, some guys were laughing in the shower. I didn't like that and I told them so. Losing makes things sour in the dressing room."

Although he was playing for a losing team for the first time in his career, Sabourin found a lot of positives in joining the Seals. "For me, it was a second chance at my career," he said. "People had already written me off. It was uplifting to be playing regularly again and I had a good season. I felt like I didn't let Bill McCreary down and I tried hard to help the young players."

While Sabourin was glad he came through for GM Bill McCreary, some teammates felt that playing for the Seals put a strain on the friendship between Sabourin and McCreary, who had played together for four years in St. Louis. "Gary grew not to like McCreary," Gary Simmons said. "He was a veteran and a holler guy in the dressing room. He was a sage and a good team player."

Sabourin appeared in 76 games for the Seals in 1975-76, scoring 21 goals and 49 points. Sabourin eventually settled in on a line with Wayne Merrick and Bob Girard. Merrick, who also played with "Sabby" in St. Louis, appreciated his veteran winger. "He was a great human being," Merrick said. "He worked so hard." Sabourin himself thought that Merrick, Girard and he complimented each other's play well. "Girard was a checker and a digger, Merrick was a good passer and shooter and I was a grinder and a shooter," Sabourin said, trying to explain the line's success.

There is little doubt that Sabourin was able to help many of the Seals younger players. "Gary was at the end of his career at that point but he came from St. Louis and knew what winning was all about," Al MacAdam said. "He never lost his focus. He was good at nurturing other players. He was good for me and good for our team."

Dave Gardner concurred with MacAdam. "I met Gary when I was 16 or 17 and I was thinking of going to St. Louis University," Gardner recalled. "When we became teammates, he remembered that time. He had a lovely family and was a straight shooter. He knew what it took to play in the NHL. He worked hard at the game until the day he retired. I thought to myself, 'Listen to this guy, he's already been through it.' So I listened. He was getting older. 'We're only a couple of players away from winning some games,' he would say." Mike Christie added, "Gary was a class gentleman and a good leader. He was on the downside of his career, but he set a good example." Perhaps Jim Moxey went the furthest in showing his respect for Sabourin. "I named my son after his boy, Kevin," Moxey said. "I learned a lot from 'Slappin' Sabby.'"

Sabourin's most memorable game with California was easy to choose. On November 7, 1975, Sabourin scored four goals as the Seals downed the Rangers 7-5 at the Jewel Box in Oakland. The win ended a nine game winless streak for the Seals. "John Davidson was the goalie and it was Phil Esposito's first game as a Ranger just after the big trade," Sabourin said, recalling the deal that sent Esposito and ex-Seals defenseman Carol Vadnais to the Rangers and Jean Ratelle, Brad Park and Joe Zanussi to Boston. "I had played with John Davidson in St. Louis and I knew he was a bit weak on his stick side if you kept the puck on the ice. I remember our line was matched against Esposito, Vickers and Fairbairn. I had four goals that game but I could have had five." Sabourin also had a two goal effort in a losing cause at the Nassau Coliseum on November 4, 1975.

Sabourin was one of the few Seals players who was not overly impressed with Jack Evans as a coach. "Jack was a pretty nice guy," Sabourin said. "He didn't have a lot of strength as a bench coach as far as analyzing a game. He was a very fair guy to play for but I think he was happy just to have a coaching job in the NHL."

Ironically enough, the only player who didn't seem to appreciate Sabourin's presence on the team was Jim Pappin, another veteran brought in to add stability to a young team. For some reason, Sabourin and Pappin just couldn't get along. "He was a bullshit guy who thought he was better than he was," Pappin said of Sabourin. "I tried to get along with him. He was five years younger than me and trying to give me pep talks. He was a good, hard working player but a pain in the ass type."

Like most of his teammates, Sabourin was surprised when the Seals moved to Cleveland prior to the 1976-77 season. "It was not very evident that there would be a move," Sabourin recalled. "We didn't have much to do with moving that season. It shouldn't be used as an excuse. They're paying you to do a job and you should go do it regardless." Still, leaving the Bay Area was a bit disappointing for Sabourin. "My family enjoyed the Bay Area," he said candidly, "and I was happy to play there."

Sabourin started the 1976-77 season in Cleveland, but age and his bad knee finally caught up to "Sabby". He played 33 games for the Barons and scored seven goals and 18 points before retiring as an active player. His career NHL statistics are 169 goals and 357 points in 627 games.

Today, Sabourin lives in Chatham, Ontario with his wife and four children. He now owns his own business, a bakery called "Buns Master" which is also located in Chatham. Just as in his hockey playing days, Sabourin puts in a maximum effort into his work.

Rookie Bob Murdoch appreciated what Gary Sabourin brought to the Seals in 1975-76. "Sabby was a real veteran," Murdoch said. "He brought character and class to the team. He was excellent at helping out the younger guys. We were both right wingers and he really helped me out." Gilles Meloche recalled Sabourin's passion for hockey. "He was near the end of his career when he played for the Seals," Meloche said. "He was good with the young kids. He loved the game and taught it to the younger players." In 1975-76, that was just what the Seals needed.

Jim Pappin

"He was like Jim Neilson, it was nice to have him around. He had done everything and seen everything there was to see in this league. He was a practical joker in the locker room and kept everybody loose. He added experience and we looked up to him. He had been there."

—Fred Ahern on Jim Pappin

Jim Pappin played his junior hockey with the Toronto Marlboros and scored 40 goals in just 48 games during his second year with the Marlies in 1959-60. The Maple Leafs owned his NHL rights and Pappin began a journey to the NHL through Sudbury and Rochester before making his big league debut with the Maple Leafs in 1963-64. It was while in Rochester that Pappin earned his nickname, "The Bird". "Bronco Horvath named me that," Pappin said. "I think I said one time that in my next life, I would come back as a seagull and shit on the people who shit on me." After five productive years in Toronto, Pappin was traded to Chicago where the 6', 190 pound winger really blossomed into one of the games better scorers.

By the time he joined the Seals in 1975-76, there wasn't much the 36-year-old right wing from Sudbury, Ontario hadn't accomplished in the NHL. He had won two Stanley Cups with the Maple Leafs in 1964 and 1967. In 1967, Pappin led the league in post-season goals and points. With Chicago, he appeared in two more Stanley Cup finals only to lose to the Canadiens in 1971 and 1973. Pappin had played in five NHL All-Star games and had four seasons of 30 goals or more. In Chicago, he teamed with Pit Martin and Dennis Hull to form the "MPH Line" which led the Hawks attack in the early to mid-70s. Pappin had even won the NHL's first "Showdown" series on NBC's nationally televised "Game of the Week", scoring the most goals in a breakaway competition between NHL stars that was shown to TV audiences during intermissions.

The year before he joined the Seals, "The Bird" scored 36 goals and 63 points in 71 games for Chicago and still seemed to be on top of his game. On June 1, 1975, the Black Hawks traded Pappin to the Seals in exchange for the Seals all-time leading scorer, Joey Johnston. Seals GM Bill McCreary was very happy with the trade. "We're very happy to have Jim on the team," McCreary told the press shortly after the trade was announced. "We know he'll make a tremendous addition to the Seals."

Years later, McCreary added, "The trade I took the most flak for was the Joey Johnston [for Jim Pappin] deal. I wouldn't want it back though. Joey was going through some problems, especially off ice and I wanted to clean house." McCreary felt that Pappin would add badly needed experience and goal scoring to a young Seals squad starved for leadership.

The trade came as a shock to Pappin who had spent the last seven seasons in Chicago. "I couldn't believe I was traded," Pappin recalled. "I was all done. I was 36-years-old and I think I had only one year left on my contract. I really thought I was all done. I was so used to being in Chicago, I was never going to play again but the Seals kept calling. I had a bad back and skated with the local junior team to get into shape."

As a result of his bad back and his reluctance to report, Pappin didn't play his first game for the Seals until November 7, 1975, the fifteenth game on the Seals schedule. The man they called, "The Bird" found a sharp contrast between playing for Toronto and Chicago on the one hand and life in Northern California playing for the Seals on the other. "It was a whole different feeling," Pappin recalled. "The teams I played for in Chicago and Toronto were experienced teams. We had a few good young guys in Oakland and we had a few goofs, too. When I look back, there were a lot of players who became good like Al MacAdam and Gilles Meloche. Besides Len Frig and Mike Christie who I played with in Chicago, I had to look in *The Hockey News* because I didn't know who those guys were on that team."

According to Gary Simmons, Pappin had a special clause in his contract. "He didn't want to be here," Simmons said. "Jim had a deal in his contract when he was traded to Oakland that when the team went on the road, he would take the last two games of the road trip off to see his wife since she didn't move to Oakland with him. He would insist on that clause even if we had an important game at the end of the road trip. Pappin was comical and could score but it was obvious his heart wasn't in it."

Pappin did admit road trips were particularly hard although he did not confirm the special clause in his contract. "We were on the road two weeks at a time," Pappin said. "There were only two teams out west back then so we'd play six or seven games on the road. We got into some bad slumps as a result."

Although road trips were not easy for Pappin and the Seals, rookie Bob Murdoch recalled that Pappin never overslept. "I roomed with Jim for awhile," Murdoch said. "He was a human alarm clock. He never missed a wakeup call. I'd tell him what time I wanted to wake up and he would get up and wake me up."

Pappin scored his first goal with the Seals in just his second game with the club and it seemed as though he hadn't lost his scoring touch. He also had the satisfaction of scoring against his former teammates, the Black Hawks at Chicago Stadium on December 30, 1975. Unfortunately for Pappin and the Seals, Chicago won the game 5-3. Offensively, the best game Pappin had with California came on January 2, 1976, when "Pappy" scored a goal and two assists during an 8-5 win in Washington. He finished the season with six goals and 19 points in just 32 games for the Seals.

One thing that the veteran winger appreciated greatly was how he was treated by the Seals organization. "Ownership was good," Pappin said. "Mel Swig was a real guy. His partner was Bob Kulvin, a dentist. They treated you really good. I got treated better in California than I did in Chicago. They were first class. We stayed in the best hotels and never had any problem with money. Bill McCreary treated me 100 percent better than Tommy Ivan [the Black Hawks GM]. He said he would retire my sweater but I said no, 'I owe you, you don't owe me.' I felt badly that I couldn't live up to his expectations. I was only able to go for 30-40 second shifts. I could have helped a good team but not a team on its way up, not taking 30-40 second shifts when everybody else was taking one minute to 90 second shifts."

One person Jim Pappin didn't get along with too well was Seals coach Jack Evans. The main reason was that Evans questioned the severity of Pappin's injured back. "He didn't believe I had a bad back," Pappin said of Evans. "He was a minor league coach and when they won the championship at Salt Lake with him the year before, they brought him up. He didn't have a clue. He was a big, tough guy but he had one hour practices the day of the game. I was 36-years-old. Do you really think I could play my best after practicing an hour of heavy practice earlier the same day?"

Pappin also felt Evans embarrassed him in front of his teammates. "We had a road trip just before Christmas and I had a bad back," Pappin recalled. "I couldn't even tie my shoes. Jack Evans thought I just didn't want to go away on Christmas. I couldn't even get on the bus. Jack screamed at me, 'You're letting your team down!' and he yelled it in front of all the players. The bus pulled away. I went to Bill

McCreary and told him what happened. I spent the next two days in traction and came back a week later feeling better. The team got back and Jack Evans said, 'See, I told you that you were faking.'"

Pappin's teammates seemed to break down into two camps when asked about him. One camp really respected Pappin and felt they learned a lot from him, the other felt he was just along for the ride and to pick up his large paycheck from the Seals. Wayne Merrick felt that "it was an honor to play with Jim. He was a great player and an intense guy. He was always nasty, yelling at us on the bench, 'Get your act together.' He was very honest but you don't always want to hear that on the bench."

Charlie Simmer felt Pappin's presence helped him as a young player. "He brought some leadership to the team. I know he helped me out quite a bit," Simmer said. "The problem was, on the Seals, Pappin didn't have anybody to lead." Gilles Meloche admitted Pappin was at the end of his career with the Seals but added, "I just loved watching him play. He was a real old pro."

Some teammates, probably resenting Pappin's high salary and low productivity, questioned his work ethic. "Looking back, he was playing out his time," Dave Gardner said. "He played against my father. At handling the puck and making plays, there were not many better right wings. He was a legend. When he was in Oakland, the money was good but he didn't really want to be there. Despite his status, he was still just one of the guys."

George Pesut, who liked Pappin a great deal, said he used to call Pappin, "'the highest paid scout in hockey'. He was making around $150,000-$175,000 per year. Bill McCreary and he had some kind of connection. He pre-scouted a lot of games for us and was a really good guy." Len Frig felt Pappin was "in California just to play another few years and trying not to get hurt."

Defenseman Mike Christie, who played with Pappin in California and Cleveland, recalled that Pappin "talked five of us into buying a racehorse. All I did was sink more money into that racehorse. When I was traded off Cleveland, I said, 'That's it, I'm out of this.' He was a good guy and a good friend."

Pappin enjoyed playing and living in the Bay Area. "I loved the weather," Pappin said. "I could go play golf. The Raiders had good team and I got to know some of them since they hung out in the same places as we did. The team had good camaraderie. Bill North of the A's also hung out with us. We all lived in the Alameda Beach and Tennis Club. The fans were great, too although we had small crowds until the end of the football season."

Pappin re-signed with the Seals for 1976-77 and followed the team to Cleveland when they became the Cleveland Barons. "I was surprised the team moved because they were just starting to draw," Pappin said. "We found out they were moving to Cleveland which was closer to my home. I got into shape and ready for camp but a week before the season, I caught the flu. Jack Evans thought I was faking again." Pappin's bad back severely limited his playing time. He played in just 24 games for the Barons in 1976-77, scoring two goals and 10 points. He retired after the season was over. In 767 career NHL games, Jim Pappin scored 278 goals and 573 points.

Today, Pappin lives in Palm Desert, California and works for the Western Golf Cart Company as a Key Account Executive. He and his wife have three children and two grandchildren.

Al MacAdam recalled that Pappin "was at the end of his career," when he joined the Seals. "I don't know how badly he wanted to play but he tried to bring some professionalism to the team." Ralph Klassen added, "Jim brought experience. That was his strongest contribution." It was something the Seals were lacking in 1975-76.

Ralph Klassen

"Mr. Versatility, he could play any position; a real defensive player, not a goal scorer. He was a checker and a consummate team player."

–George Pesut on Ralph Klassen

Lanky Ralph Klassen was the Seals first round draft choice in 1975. The 5'11", 175 pound native of Humboldt, Saskatchewan played his junior hockey with the Saskatoon Blades of the Western League. Despite missing over 20 games with mononucleosis, Klassen scored 21 goals and 68 points in just 41 games for the Blades and served as team captain. He also played for Canada in the World Juniors that year and had three assists in four games.

Klassen, the youngest of seven children, said he always longed to play in the NHL when he was growing up. "It was always a dream but I think it became realistic in my second to last year in juniors," Klassen said. "Scouts were talking to me and that sort of made me realize that the dream could become a reality."

Klassen was considered one of the more well rounded players available in the 1975 entry draft and the Seals made his their first round pick, third overall behind only Philadelphia's Mel Bridgeman and Barry Dean who was selected by the Kansas City Scouts. "I was in awe," Klassen said when asked his reaction to being drafted by the Seals. "You dream about it. I had no inclination I was going to go there. I know Chicago was interested in me. I was very surprised [to be selected by California] but not disappointed by any means."

The summer before joining the Seals, Klassen worked at the Orr-Walton hockey camp. "Rick Hampton was there too and we were introduced since we were going to be teammates the following year," Klassen recalled. "Rick told me the home colors were not too bad but on the road with that sort of turquoise color sweaters, people will whistle at you." Hampton, who was an 18-year-old rookie with the Seals the year before, tried to give Klassen some advice. "Just do your job and you'll be fine," Hampton told Klassen.

Although he was a solid two way player in juniors, Klassen took on a more defensive minded role as a rookie. The thing that set him apart as a rookie was his skating ability and his forechecking. "As a center, I enjoy forechecking," Klassen said. "The more physical a game I play, the better overall game I have. If I give someone a good hit early, it makes me feel right in the game."

Because he weighed only 175 pounds, Klassen had some trouble playing a physical style in the NHL. "Ralph was a great skater and a penalty killer but he was too slightly built," linemate Gary Sabourin said. "He couldn't play so well in traffic. He was a terrific kid but a hard liver."

Klassen made an interesting first impression on center Dave Gardner. "He was our number one pick and we had high hopes for him," Gardner recalled. "I don't know if he ever washed his hair but I saw him in the shower so I know he must have. You take a look at him and you say, 'That's what we got for a number one pick?' He could skate forever. He was feisty and he stuck his nose in there. He was very quiet which was good for young kid. He listened and learned. He reminded me of Butch Goring the way he skated. Ralph was a great team guy. He just didn't seem to gel anywhere but that was the fault of management."

Veteran Jim Pappin thought that Klassen contributed to his eventual failure to live up to his status as the third overall pick in the draft. "They thought he could be another Bobby Clarke," Pappin said. "But he had no drive and too many bad habits."

It didn't take Klassen long to get his first NHL goal. "It was in my first game [in the NHL] in Atlanta," Klassen said. "Gary Sabourin had the puck behind the net and I was floating in the slot. He passed the puck out to me. I remember I didn't get much on it, but it went behind Dan Bouchard. I thought to myself, 'Man, this isn't too hard.' I only got five more goals all year."

The rookie center got off to a relatively fast offensive start. He twice picked up three assists in a game, once on October 29, 1975, during a 6-4 loss to the Red Wings at the Olympia and then just over a week later in Oakland during a 7-5 win over the New York Rangers. Unfortunately for Klassen and the Seals, he was unable to maintain that kind of scoring pace. Klassen finished his rookie season in the NHL with six goals and 21 points in 71 games. At one point, the club sent him down to Salt Lake City to give him more ice time and more confidence. In a brief four game stint in Salt Lake, Klassen scored three goals and six points. "Getting sent down to the minors was embarrassing," Klassen recalled. "It was tough when I was drafted in the first round. In the long run, I think it was a good thing. It certainly was an eye opener."

The biggest adjustment Klassen had to make from juniors to the NHL was the quickness of the game. "I've been really impressed by everyone's quickness in this league," the rookie said. "As soon as you get the puck you haven't got time to look around. You almost have to know ahead of time what you're going to do. My biggest adjustment is getting used to the tempo, the quickness of the game."

Off the ice, Klassen fit in well with his new teammates. At times, however, the fans were critical of Klassen because of the success of the Seals second round selection in the 1975 draft, fellow rookie Dennis Maruk. While Klassen settled in to a defensive role and scored six goals, Maruk electrified crowds with his offensive skills and scored 30 goals as a first year man. "Ralph was a good checker and he lasted because of that," Gary Simmons recalled. He also remembered Klassen's nickname was "The Goat". "He killed penalties very well and was a good team guy. The players liked him as much as they disliked Rick Hampton."

Klassen was also known among his teammates for his heavy smoking and heavy drinking. "He smoked three packs a day," Jim Moxey said. Bob Murdoch went as far as to give Klassen the nickname of "Smokescreen". "He would wake up in the middle of the night to have a cigarette," Murdoch recalled. "We had two races in camp in the four minute mile skate; the morning race was won by Ralph Klassen, a heavy smoker, and the PM race was won by Spike Huston. Ralph was a strong and great skater."

As far as drinking, Klassen's ability to put a few away amazed goaltender Gilles Meloche. "He was quiet and never said a word. He came to play every day, drank his 8-10 beers and then worked his guts off every morning." "Nobody could drink like that guy," Wayne Merrick added. Some teammates also recalled Klassen as a bit of a lady-killer. "Ralph could never find the practice rink," George Pesut said. "He was always coming from a different direction."

Klassen got along well with Seals coach Jack Evans and thought he had a good understanding of his first NHL coach. "Jack was a man of few words," Klassen said. "You knew by the look on his face; if things were going well, he'd be a little more relaxed. When his face got red and he walked in the room, you knew you were in trouble. If you didn't work hard, you would hear about it but he came down on the team more than he did on individuals. He taught the importance of effort. The team with the most talent doesn't necessarily win and the team with the least talent isn't necessarily the worst team."

Klassen had the privilege of rooming with goalie Gary Simmons for part of his rookie year. "Gary loved watching movies on TV, sometimes until 4 AM." Klassen recalled. "I was asleep, rolled over and sort of noticed that the TV was on, so I turned it off. Gary says, 'Hey, I was still listening to that,' so I turned it back on."

One of Klassen's responsibilities with the Seals was killing penalties and one of his partners was Charlie Simmer. "I was a penalty killer and face-off guy with Ralph," Simmer recalled. "He was one of the most gifted skaters and stickhandlers in the league and a great penalty killer but he never quite lived up to his talent. I called him 'Snake.'"

While the Seals were not a playoff team in 1975-76, Klassen, like many of his teammates, thought that the team was young and improving. "The team was trying to go in the right direction," Klassen recalled. "They traded some guys to give Dennis Maruk and me a chance to make the club. They were planning for the future. The team had a good rapport and we had a decent year. The travel was tough, but when you're as young as I was, your eyes are open all the time."

According to Klassen, the Seals had great fans in the Bay Area. "We had excellent fans and an awesome booster club," Klassen said. "They were very enthusiastic. Towards the end of the year, we were drawing 10,000-12,000 fans for many games. They were very vocal. You wanted to play harder for them and didn't want to let them down."

Klassen was surprised when it was announced the Seals were moving to Cleveland for the 1976-77 season. "We had no inclination we were moving," Klassen recalled. "I learned about the team's move to Cleveland on the news. We didn't get phone calls from management like that in those days."

Klassen played a season-and-a-half in Cleveland before being traded to the Colorado Rockies midway through the 1977-78 season. Cleveland was not a fun experience for Klassen. "When we got to Cleveland, the attitude changed when we thought the team would fold," Klassen recalled. Colorado was not also a club that was rumored to move many times. After a year-and-a-half with the Rockies, Klassen was selected by the Hartford Whalers in the expansion draft. The next day, the Whalers sent Klassen to the Islanders who in turn, shipped him off to the Blues later that day. Klassen played four-and-a-half seasons with St. Louis and continued his role as a checker and a penalty killer.

"They [the Seals] tried to make him into a scorer," Len Frig said, "but he wasn't a big one on this level. He was one of the best forecheckers in the game and a great penalty killer." That was the role Klassen played throughout his career. Although he played just over eight NHL seasons, Klassen never scored more than 14 goals in a season. He retired as an active player after the 1983-84 season with 52 goals and 145 points in 497 NHL games.

Al MacAdam remembered Ralph Klassen fondly. "He was highly skilled and very low key," MacAdam said. "He had all the skills to play the game a long time. He could skate and handle the puck. Everybody liked Ralph." Although he was never flashy, Klassen turned his skating and checking skills into a productive NHL career. He got his start with the California Golden Seals.

Tim Jacobs

"He was a hard nosed kid who didn't have a shitload of ability but got things done. He loved every minute of being in the NHL; a team guy who knew who to get the puck out of the zone. He stuck his nose in there when he had to."

—Dave Gardner on Tim Jacobs

Tim Jacobs was selected by the Seals in the sixth round of the 1972 draft with the 70th overall choice. Jacobs played three seasons of junior hockey with the St. Catherines Black Hawks. Even on the junior hockey level, he was known as a defensive defenseman. His final year with St. Catherines was his most productive offensively. In 1971-72, Jacobs scored six goals and 25 points in 58 games. He had a reputation of being steady and dependable in his own end.

The Seals assigned Jacobs to their Salt Lake City farm club for the 1972-73 season, his first as a pro. Jacobs scored seven goals and 21 points in 72 games. He followed that up with a two goal, 28 point season with Salt Lake in 1973-74. In 1974-75, Jacobs was loaned to the Springfield Indians of the AHL, an indication that he no longer fit in the Seals long term plans. Jacobs played well for Springfield, scoring three goals and 34 points in the regular season before adding a pair of goals and 15 points in 17 playoff games. He also played a key role in the Indians march to the 1975 Calder Cup Championship.

Jacobs returned to Salt Lake City for the 1975-76 season. In 30 games with the Eagles, he scored four times and totaled 16 points. When California suffered injuries to Jim Neilson and Len Frig, Jacobs was recalled to the Seals for the first time. "He was a small defenseman who moved the puck up and played steady," said Jim Moxey. Jacobs played in 46 games with the Seals and picked up 10 assists. His best offensive game was a two assist effort on February 15, 1976, during a 7-3 win in Minnesota.

Jacobs spent the season being sent up and down from Salt Lake. Whenever the Seals needed a defenseman, he was the first man on call from the minors. When the injured players healed, he was usually sent down. "He was a good team player but a fringe player," Al MacAdam said of Jacobs. "Something was missing for him to be in the NHL."

At the NHL level, Jacobs was a defensive defenseman but he lacked the size necessary to be dominating physically and lacked the offensive skills necessary to quarterback a power play. What Jacobs brought to the table was enthusiasm and desire. "He was a good friend of mine in Salt Lake," forward Charlie Simmer said. "He was a little too small for a defenseman but he worked hard." Fellow blue liner Mike Christie shared Simmer's view. "He was smaller and not very physical," Christie recalled. "He was a hard working stay at home defenseman." "Tim was nothing fancy," Ralph Klassen added. "He was a mucker type in the corners who would quietly do his job."

Jacobs did manage to keep his sense of humor, however. Fred Ahern recalled, "Once a reporter asked Tim Jacobs how to defend Gilbert Perreault, a player who made even an all-star defenseman look bad. Timmy said, 'I fall down in front of him and hope he trips over me.'" Ahern respected Jacobs as a player. "He was not the tallest guy around but he was tough," Ahern said.

When the Seals moved to Cleveland for the 1976-77 season, Jacobs was in camp but was again sent back to Salt Lake City. He was never recalled to the NHL again. In 71 games with Salt Lake, he scored one goal and 20 points. The Barons did not bring Jacobs back in 1977-78. The diminutive defenseman returned to Springfield for two more seasons before retiring from professional hockey.

Gary Simmons recalled the essence of Tim Jacobs on the ice when he said, "Tim was a real tryer. He worked hard and that's why he was here, not because of his ability. He was like Mike Christie in that regard. He was small and stocky. A real good guy." While Jacobs did not have a very long NHL career, his hard work paid off and helped him reach hockey's highest level.

Wayne Merrick

"He was one of the fastest skaters in the league. An all-around player who could kill penalties and play on the power play."

–Jim Moxey on Wayne Merrick

Sarnia, Ontario native Wayne Merrick grew up rooting for the Toronto Maple Leafs like so many other kids from Ontario in the 60s. "My first game against the Maple Leafs was hard," Merrick admitted. "Dave Keon, Frank Mahovlich, Alan Stanley, Red Kelly, these guys made me want to play in the NHL. In my last year of junior, I had a real good year offensively and defensively and I realized maybe I did have a shot to make it (to the NHL)."

Merrick played his junior hockey for the Ottawa 67s and had a spectacular 1971-72 season, scoring 39 goals and 95 points in 62 games. The St. Louis Blues selected the 6'1", 195 pound Merrick with the ninth overall pick in the 1972 entry draft. Although he spent some time with the Blues farm club, the Denver Spurs, Merrick spent most of his first season in pro hockey with St. Louis, scoring 10 goals and 21 points in 50 games. He then put together back to back seasons of 20 goals or more, scoring 20 in 1973-74 and 28 the following season. His point total also climbed each year, first to 43 and then to 65. The speedy Merrick became a favorite with Blues fans for his exciting style of play.

Merrick started the 1975-76 season with the Blues and scored seven goals and 15 points in the season's first 19 games. Then, shockingly, he was traded to the Seals for Larry Patey on November 24, 1975. Seals GM Bill McCreary called the acquisition of Merrick the best trade he made as Seals GM. "We didn't give up anything," McCreary said. "Merrick brought a presence to the team and we had three solid center icemen then."

While McCreary was overjoyed at the acquisition of Merrick, Merrick himself was less than thrilled to be sent to California. "I was pretty disappointed," Merrick recalled. "That was the understatement of the year. I had played so well the year before in St. Louis and wasn't playing bad the year I was traded. It really was a shocker. It was a wakeup call that this was a business. Garry Young, who was then the Blues coach actually told me he disagreed with the trade. There was a little bit of adjusting for me. For awhile, I was in a daze."

Merrick quickly found he actually enjoyed playing for the Seals. "When I went there, they were on a high," he recalled. "They had improved a lot. They were getting some pretty good players and more fans for that sized arena. The Seals weren't great but you could see they were improving. They had some young talent and were doing some things right. I had fun playing out there. In St. Louis there was a lot of pressure. If you lost a few games, it was awful."

Despite the obvious improvement, however, Merrick did see some things in hindsight that kept the Seals from being more successful. "We had some good players and were moving in the right direction," Merrick said. "We didn't have enough guys that were truly dedicated. There were too many guys going in their own direction as opposed to pulling together as a team. On Long Island, guys wouldn't let you leave early from practice. We coached each other to an extent and we pushed each other. The line combinations and chemistry just weren't there in Oakland."

If his trade to the Seals shocked Merrick, you couldn't necessarily tell that by looking at the stat sheet. He produced points at a clip of nearly a point per game all season long. In his first 30 games with the Seals, he scored 16 goals and 31 points. On December 28, 1975, he tallied 10 shots on goal in a game against the Kansas City Scouts, one shy of the Seals franchise record. Three games later, he set a Seals all-time record by scoring a hat trick and three assists in one game against the Capitals, breaking the previous club mark of five points in a game. It was Merrick's first NHL hat trick.

"It was a thrill," he admitted at the time. "I went through three seasons in St. Louis and never got a hat trick. I was beginning to wonder if I would ever get one." While scoring six points against the Capitals was a thrill, Merrick got a bigger sense of accomplishment scoring a hat trick against the team he followed during his childhood, the Toronto Maple Leafs. "I got a hat trick playing against Darryl Sittler and Borje Salming," Merrick said. "We won that night, too (5-3) and I played like I was capable of playing."

Merrick had another special game in St. Louis on February 3, 1976, his first trip back to the home of his former team. The fans gave Merrick a standing ovation upon his return to The Arena and cheered loudly again when he scored a goal for the Seals in a 4-4 tie against the Blues. There were many pro-Merrick banners in the stands that night, including one that said, "Trade Sid Salomon, III for Merrick". Salomon was the Blues president at the time.

There were some low points as well for Merrick. "I got thrown out of a game in the first period," Merrick recalled. "It was the first or second shift against Washington and Yvon Labre. I gave him the finger and was ejected and suspended for a game. I watched the rest of the game with my wife. It's the sort of thing you don't do. It was a learning ground for me. I learned what not to do. You work out, you play with discipline."

Merrick finished the 1975-76 season with 32 goals and 67 points in 75 games. He scored seven times on the power play and added four game winners. Despite playing for a last place team, he was only a minus three in 56 games with California. The goal and point totals were career highs. With the Seals, he scored 25 goals and 52 points in 56 contests.

"Hockey player wise, being traded to Oakland was good for me," Merrick admitted. "I played a lot, played on the power play and killed penalties. We had just a great group of fun loving guys. The fans in Oakland were great; they were one of a kind. They loved hockey and they wanted us to win so badly. We had a great booster club and I remember Krazy George got everybody rocking and rolling. It was neat and it was unique to Oakland."

Despite having his best offensive season with the Seals, Merrick had mixed feelings in hindsight about coach Jack Evans. "He was very quiet and I was kind of intimidated by the guy," Merrick admitted. "He was tough looking and played pretty tough, too. A great coach has a certain personality that puts him above the good coaches. It's unique and they don't come along very often. They just know how to motivate guys. One practice around holiday season, we had been off the ice for a few days. We skated around for about 15 minutes and Jack said, 'You guys go home, you had too much turkey.' He sent us home. That wasn't right. I wanted to win. That's what I was there for. If we were tired, let's skate it out. That would never happen on Long Island. We would come to practice after arriving at 2 PM from a road trip and we would hold a full practice. The key to coaching, and Al Arbour realized this, was getting every player on the roster to play well, not just the superstars, the Bryan Trottiers and Mike Bossy's, but the Hector Marinis and the Gord Lanes. You are only as good as your weakest link and Al knew this."

Upon his arrival with the Seals, Merrick was placed on a line with Jim Pappin and Dave Hrechkosy. About a month later, however, with the team slumping, coach Jack Evans teamed Merrick with Bob Girard and Gary Sabourin. This combination really clicked. "Their style really complimented mine," Merrick said of his new linemates. "A centerman is only as good as his wingers and Bobby and Sabby aren't afraid to go into the corners and get the puck. I like the puck in the slot and my wingers are very unselfish about getting it to me. It is a real good feeling to play with players who work so hard. Bobby had good speed and Sabby was like a centerman on wing. That's what I needed, someone who could set me up and help me score my share of goals."

Many of Merrick's teammates with the Seals were pleased with his acquisition from St. Louis. Bob Murdoch, who played on the Seals top line in 1975-76 remembered what Merrick meant to the Seals at the time. "He was big and fast and he could really play the game," Murdoch said. "I always thought he would have a breakthrough year. He was our number two center. Later in his career, he did very well on Long Island where he became their third center and changed his style of play."

Dave Gardner recalled Merrick as "big, strong and lanky and a phenomenal skater, he was very powerful. He was almost never knocked down. He was a good young kid. We were all young back then." Gilles Meloche went as far as to call Merrick, "One of the best skaters I've ever seen." Len Frig felt that Merrick "Didn't really know how good he was. He was big and had a good reach; he could pass and shoot. I think he was upset about being traded to the Seals and that affected his play here."

If Merrick has a weakness, it was his dislike for high traffic areas. "He was 'Mr. Speed'," George Pesut said. "He had really good wheels but he didn't like the heavy going." In fact, one of the reasons the Blues supposedly traded Merrick was because he wasn't playing a physical enough game. Despite that accusation, the Seals were very pleased with Merrick's play. "Wayne was a big competitor," Charlie Simmer recalled. "He was in good shape and worked hard."

Merrick remained with the Seals organization after it moved to Cleveland in 1976-77 but things were not the same. "I hated the move to Cleveland," Merrick said. "There were no fans and no excitement." Merrick scored 18 goals and 56 points in 1976-77 for the Barons before being traded to the New York Islanders midway through the 1977-78 season. It was the perfect place for Merrick to be. He went from a perennial also-ran to a young team with the best record in the NHL. Merrick played six seasons with the Islanders and won four Stanley Cups as a third line center. His role with the Islanders changed as Merrick centered the Isles checking line. He only scored 20 goals once with the Islanders, but the team success was hard to beat. In 1981 when the Islanders won their second straight Stanley Cup, Merrick scored six goals and 18 points in 18 playoff games. In the finals against Minnesota, Merrick had eight points in five games, tying him for the club lead with Mike Bossy. Merrick retired after the 1983-84 season, just as the Islanders dynasty was ending. In 774 career NHL games, Wayne scored 191 goals and 456 points.

Today, Merrick and his wife live in London, Ontario. They have two children. The ex-hockey player represents Met Life Financial Services in New York, which is quite a commute from Ontario. Needless to say, Merrick does a good deal of traveling these days.

Fred Ahern recalled what Wayne Merrick meant to the Seals in 1975-76. "He was a big strong centerman, our number two center behind Dennis Maruk," Ahern said. "He was a great addition to the team and took the pressure off the 3M line." It seems that Merrick's season in California was mutually beneficial to both Merrick and the Seals. Merrick made the Seals a better team while the Seals gave Merrick a place where he could blossom as a player.

Dennis Maruk

"He was a total competitor. We got along very well. He had a lot of fire in his eyes and was very self motivated. He wanted to prove he belonged because of his size. He was electrifying to watch, a real crowd pleaser and very confident."

–Ralph Klassen on Dennis Maruk

Despite evidence to the contrary, scouts still question whether little men can play effective hockey in the NHL. Since the expansion era, players such as Marcel Dionne, Martin St-Louis and Theoren Fleury have proven that you don't have to be too over six feet tall and 200 pounds to succeed in the NHL. In 1975-76, the Seals found their own little big man, 5'8", 165 pound Dennis Maruk. Although he only played in Oakland for one season before the team moved to Cleveland, Maruk left lasting memories for the fans at the Oakland Coliseum Arena who paid to see him play.

Maruk grew up in Toronto as one of eight children. He played his junior hockey with the London Knights and broke Marcel Dionne's record for goals scored as a junior by potting 155 goals in three seasons in the OHA. In his final season with the Knights in 1974-75, Maruk was third in the league in scoring with 66 goals and 145 points in just 65 games. Still, when draft time came around in the summer of 1975, general managers were hesitant to draft the diminutive speedster. As a result, Maruk lasted until the 21st pick in the draft where the Seals eagerly grabbed him with their second selection.

"We would never have gotten a crack at him in the draft last summer if it had not been for his small size," Seals GM Bill McCreary said during Maruk's rookie year. "Most of the clubs were turned off because they thought he couldn't skate with the big men in the NHL, but he is far better then even we expected. He's got greater potential than any of the best small men I have ever seen in the NHL."

Maruk used being passed over in the draft as a motivational tool. "I was disappointed when it took them so long to draft me," he said during his rookie year. "My pride was hurt. But playing well has put my pride in place. I guess I had to prove to them I could play well up here." He compensated for his lack of size by playing an aggressive hitting style and by using his blazing speed.

Maruk realized he had to play a physical style to make it in the NHL. He established this as quickly as possible by going after Kings tough guy Dave Hutchinson in an exhibition game. Hutchinson stood 6'3" and weighed 205 pounds; meaning he was roughly seven inches taller than Maruk and weighed 40 pounds more. Still, Maruk did not back down and checked Hutchinson hard. He made his point. "Little guys like me tend to grow up being scrappy, all the time having to prove that you won't be pushed around," Maruk said. "The big guys do push me around some, but I can bust right around them some, too. Speed makes up for my lack of size."

Because of his small stature, his teammates gave Maruk the nickname "Pee Wee". "He was a cocky little fucker," Gary Simmons said. "He was good and he knew it. He was like Theo Fleury. He was feisty and a good goal scorer." Gilles Meloche thought that Maruk "played bigger than his size. He was a great little athlete who put up great numbers and really loved the game."

Maruk made the Seals as a rookie and became the center of "The 3-M" line which put him between left wing Al MacAdam and right wing Bob Murdoch. The line set a franchise record for most goals by a line in one season with 84. Amazingly, both Murdoch and Maruk were rookies while MacAdam was just in his second full season in the NHL. Murdoch called Maruk, "the key to the line" adding, "He was one of the fastest four or five players in the league, no one could accelerate like he could. He was loaded with guts and determination." MacAdam added, "When Dennis gets the puck, you know things are going to happen."

Perhaps best of all for the Seals franchise, Maruk gave them a player that could bring the fans out of their seats by his mere presence on the ice. Maruk's small stature, speedy skating, bushy hair and fu manchu made him all the more noticeable on the ice. The Seals fans responded by yelling "Mar-ooooook, Mar-ooooook" every time he touched the puck as the rookie quickly became a fan favorite. The Seals even sold bumper stickers with the fans' chant on them.

"It's exciting to get that kind of fan recognition," Maruk told a reporter while with the Seals. Maruk admitted that the calls of Mar-ooooook gave him a lift when he skated onto the ice at home games. "I like it," Maruk added. "It shows they think I'm doing the right thing."

George Pesut noticed Maruk's ability to bring the crowd to its feet and inspire his teammates. "He was a little spark plug," Pesut said. "A good scorer and a good guy off the ice." The Seals finally had a player who could excite the fans and sell tickets.

The Seals set a club attendance record in 1975-76, averaging over 6,900 fans per game. Attendance picked up as the season progressed. At least one veteran member of the Seals felt that Maruk was largely responsible for the increase in home attendance. "We had 6,000-8,000 fans," Jim Pappin recalled. "All of a sudden, when Dennis Maruk started playing well, we were getting 11,000-12,000 per game. Maruk was the cause of it. He was a large part of it. He caused some excitement." At the end of the season, Maruk was voted the club's most popular player.

The press also quickly took to Maruk, describing his play with a variety of adjectives. One reporter called him a "buzz saw", another said he "looks like a water bug" on the ice. Perhaps the most unique description came from Geoffrey Fisher who wrote, "If you have ever seen a ferret chase a rat you may get some idea of what Dennis looks like in pursuit of the puck." Later he called Maruk, "a surface to air missile on skates." The bottom line for the Seals was the Maruk was colorful, exciting to watch and a real attention getter.

Maruk scored his first NHL goal at the Maple Leaf Gardens on October 25, 1975. He beat Leafs goalie Wayne Thomas while the Seals were shorthanded. The goal gave the Seals a 2-0 lead in a game that ended in a 2-2 tie. In fact, the first three goals of Maruk's career were all short handed goals. By the end of the 1975-76 season, Maruk set a new rookie record by tallying five times while his team was down a man. Howie Meeker set the old record of three back in 1946-47. Because of his speed, Maruk was always a threat to turn an errant pass into a breakaway opportunity.

"I like killing penalties," Maruk told a reporter. "It tires me a little, but I like the extra ice time. It gives me scoring opportunities because the other team is thinking offense. I'm good at stealing the puck and I have speed on skates and I can go one on one."

Dennis Maruk was still a teenager when he started his NHL career with the Seals. To celebrate his 20th birthday, Maruk put on an offensive show at the Igloo in Pittsburgh, scoring four goals as the Seals defeated the Penguins 5-3. "One goal would have been enough for me, "Maruk said after the game. "Then after I got the second goal and the third goal I felt like I was up in the sky. Sometimes, if you start out good, you think that it's really going to be your night and you go crazy. That's what happened that night."

Other big games followed for Maruk. On January 17, 1976, he scored twice at the Pacific Coliseum in Vancouver to help the Seals defeat the Canucks 5-3. Then, on March 22, 1976, Maruk scored once and set up three Seals goals during a 7-1 thrashing of St. Louis in Oakland.

Maruk finished his rookie season in the NHL with 30 goals and 62 points while playing in all 80 games for California. Maruk scored seven goals on the power play, five goals shorthanded and three game winners. He also led the Seals in shots on goal with 233.

Seals coach Jack Evans thought Maruk deserved serious consideration for the Calder Trophy in 1975-76. "When a rookie goes over 30 goals, he usually wins the Calder Trophy," Evans said. "Trottier is good, but I'll take Dennis." Unfortunately for Maruk, the Islanders Bryan Trottier scored more goals than he did (32) and had more points (95) while playing for a winning team. Trottier was the overwhelming choice for the Calder Trophy as the NHL's rookie of the year.

Maruk's teammates quickly recognized the talent "Pee Wee" brought to their team. "Dennis was a great small player," Len Frig said. "I think he was a better small player than Marcel Dionne. He came to play every night and scored even more goals when he played for Washington. He was better than Dionne for his size."

Butch Williams called Maruk "a scrappy little bugger. I played on a line with him briefly. Our passes were off a bit; we just didn't click. We would have over time, I think. He was a water bug type player. He was scrappy, like Marcel Dionne." Defenseman Mike Christie added, "Dennis was a competitor and very talented. He couldn't be intimidated. He had desire and really took care of himself off the ice."

Despite his success on the ice, Maruk rubbed some of his teammates the wrong way. Perhaps his cockiness and persistence weren't always appreciated. "He was outspoken for a little guy," Wayne King said. Although King got along well with Maruk off the ice, not everybody appreciated the outspoken and brash Maruk. A few of Maruk's teammates thought he was not a team player. "I played with him for three years," Al MacAdam said of Maruk. "He was the most selfish player I ever played with. If we lost 12-1 but he scored the goal, he didn't care. He had no idea of team concept. He played eight years in the NHL before he made the playoffs."

Gary Sabourin shared MacAdam's viewpoint. "He was a tremendous player but he wasn't a team man," Sabourin explained. "Only points mattered to him, he was selfish. If we won the game but he didn't score any points, he was pissed." Bob Stewart added, "He would sing in the shower if we lost 4-1 but he scored the goal. He was not a team player."

GM Bill McCreary defended his star rookie, saying that his enthusiasm was often misinterpreted. "He could score in ways nobody else could think of," McCreary said. "He was very self-confident. He always wanted to be on the ice and that rubbed some people the wrong way."

Maruk followed the Seals to Cleveland and spent two years with the Barons. In 1976-77, Maruk scored 28 goals and 78 points in 80 games while the following season, he added 36 goals and 71 points in 76 contests and was the Barons representative in the NHL All-Star game. When the Barons merged with the Minnesota North Stars, Maruk was protected by Minnesota but traded away to the Washington Capitals after only two games in a North Stars sweater.

It was in Washington that Maruk took his offensive play to an even higher level. Maruk had three seasons of 90 or more points, one 50 goal season and a 60 goal season for Washington. Before the 1983-84 season, the Capitals traded Maruk back to Minnesota. Maruk played for the North Stars until retiring during the 1988-89 season. He was the last member of the Seals to play in an NHL game. Maruk's final NHL statistics were 356 goals and 878 points in 888 games. While he only played in 34 playoff games in his career, Maruk managed to score 14 goals and 36 points in postseason play.

Today, Maruk lives in Louisiana and has been involved in minor league hockey as a coach with the ECHL's Baton Rouge Kingfish and the WPHL's Lake Charles Ice Pirates. He also briefly came out of retirement to play for the Ice Pirates in 1998-99.

Dave Gardner recalled Maruk as "A talented kid who created a lot of shit. He was feisty and stuck his nose in there. He was very talented and could score." Although Maruk's emergence proved to be too late to keep the Seals in the Bay Area, his exciting play gave the club a spark that the future could be better both on and off the ice. The Seals fans who saw him play will not soon forget him.

OTHER LATE SEALS

Greg Smith

Big Greg Smith played only one game for the California Golden Seals in the 1975-76 season and he picked up an assist in that contest. It happened to have been the Seals last ever game, a 5-2 win over the Kings in Oakland. The Seals drafted Smith in 1975 after his successful career at Colorado College. The 6', 195 pound Ponoka, Alberta native had two productive seasons with the Seals organization after they became Cleveland Barons in 1976-77 and 1977-78. In 1977-78, Smith had a career best

37 points while playing in all 80 games on the blueline for Cleveland. He later played for the North Stars, Red Wings and Capitals before retiring from hockey after the 1987-88 season. Smith had a very successful career, playing in 829 NHL games, scoring 56 goals and 288 points while accumulating 1,110 penalty minutes. He was also part of the North Stars run to the Stanley Cup finals in 1981. Smith was one of the last former Seals to play in the NHL despite the fact that his California career lasted all of one game.

Bruce Greig

Bruce Greig stood 6'2" 220 pounds. The intimidating left wing played in nine games with the Seals, one in 1973-74 and eight in 1974-75. In that brief time, he recorded one assist and 46 penalty minutes. The Seals selected the High River, Alberta native with the 113th selection in the 1973 entry draft. "He was a tough guy," Paul Shakes said. "He didn't have a ton of natural ability but he was our big guy and he protected the smaller guys." Barry Cummins called Greig, "an honest hockey player who worked hard and played his position very well." Greig paid attention to detail. He actually watched videotapes of his fights to see how he could improve himself. It seemed every time the Seals were ready to bring him up, he had health problems—once a knee injury felled him, another time he contracted mononucleosis. After two seasons mostly with Salt Lake, Greig signed with the Calgary Cowboys of the WHA. He later also played for the Cincinnati Stingers and the Indianapolis Racers of the WHA before concluding his playing career in the minor leagues. Greig playing in the IHL, EHL, CHL and ACHL before retiring from pro hockey after the 1983-84 season. Greig's younger brother Mark was later a first round selection of the Hartford Whalers in 1990. Today, Greig lives in Calgary and is a competitive power lifter.

Glenn Patrick

Glenn Patrick appeared in two games for the Seals during the 1974-75 season and was held without a point. Glenn is the brother of Craig Patrick who had a much longer stay in California. Prior to joining the Seals, the 6'2", 190 pound New York native played one NHL game for the St. Louis Blues. The Seals acquired Patrick from St. Louis during the summer of 1974 for Ron Serafini. After two seasons with Salt Lake, Patrick stayed with the Seals organization when it moved to Cleveland in 1976-77. That year, Patrick played in 35 games for the Barons and scored two goals and five points while accumulating 70 penalty minutes. When the Barons ran out of money and were in danger of folding during the 1976-77 season, Patrick was one of the players the club released from his contract in mid-season as a cost cutting measure. The former Baron quickly found work with the Edmonton Oilers of the WHA where he finished out the season. Patrick played professional hockey until 1978-79. Today, Patrick remains active in hockey with the Penguins organization. He served as head coach of the Pittsburgh Penguins top affiliate in the AHL, the Scranton Wilkes-Barre Penguins until the end of the 2002-2003 season and still works for the Penguins organization.

Larry Wright

Larry Wright came to the Seals from the Flyers organization in the trade that sent Reggie Leach to Philadelphia and Al MacAdam to California. Prior to joining the Seals, Wright played 36 games for the Flyers over two seasons and collected two assists. He spent most of his time with the Richmond Robins of the AHL. Wright was a big center, standing 6'2", but he weighed only 180 pounds. He only played two games with the Seals and was held scoreless, taking one shot on goal. Wright also played 14 games that season for the Seals farm team in Salt Lake before re-signing with the Flyers organization in 1975-76. After playing one season in Germany, Wright joined the Red Wings in 1977-78, appearing in a career high 66 games. Wright retired after the 1978-79 season and scored four goals and 12 points in 106 career NHL games.

Tom Price

The Seals selected Tom Price with the 57th choice in the 1974 entry draft. The 6'1", 190 pound Toronto native spent the next two seasons in Salt Lake while playing three games with the Seals in 1974-75 and five games with California in 1975-76. He did not register a point, received four penalty minutes and was a combined minus 10 during his limited stint with the Golden Seals. Price also spent most of the 1976-77 season in Salt Lake before playing a pair of games with the Cleveland Barons. The Barons released Price late in the 1976-77 season in the same salary purge that cost the team Glenn Patrick. The Pittsburgh Penguins signed Price as a free agent shortly thereafter and he played 19 games with the Penguins over the next three seasons while spending most of his time in the AHL and IHL. Price last played pro hockey for the New Haven Nighthawks in 1985-86. His career NHL statistics include two assists in 29 games and 12 penalty minutes.

Krazy George—Cheerleader

"That SOB. I wanted to grab him. He was a piece of work. He was good and did a great job."
–Flyers left wing Dave Schultz on Seals cheerleader Krazy George Henderson

Take your not so average high school electronics teacher, give him a drum to bang on at a hockey game and presto, the NHL's first professional cheerleader was born. George Henderson, or "Krazy George" as he became known, was a unique part of hockey games at "The Jewel Box," especially during the team's final years in Oakland.

Krazy George's first cheerleading experience started in 1967 at San Jose State University football games and Judo matches. "I went to a game and a friend brought a bugle and a drum," George recalled. "I couldn't play the bugle." But Henderson certainly knew how to bang his drum.

George attended his first Seals game in 1971. The soccer team at Buchser High School (where George was teaching) went to a Seals game and George was invited to come along and bring his drum. "First, I got the entire team yelling and then the entire section," George said enthusiastically. "Pretty soon, I moved around the stands and had them yelling." In the often half empty Oakland Coliseum, it was easy for Krazy George to get noticed. "The next day, somebody told me that a newspaper article said that one player, I can't remember who, said that if they guy with the drum would come back, he'd give me a free ticket to another game," George said. "So I called the Seals and went to another game."

Henderson traveled over 60 miles round trip to attend Seals' games, so being there wasn't always easy. Gradually, however, Krazy George fell in love with the game of hockey and the California Golden Seals. Seals' ticket manager Sam Russo remembered how management quickly recognized how Krazy George could make 4,000 fans sound like over 10,000. "We noticed him at the games and called him into the ticket office and started to give him comps," Russo said.

By 1973-74, Krazy George was a fixture at Seals games. "Originally, I worked for free, although the team did give me free tickets," George said. By my fourth year [1974-75], I was getting paid $17 a game for gas." Eventually, the Seals hired Krazy George as a professional cheerleader.

"I hired George to his first pro contract," admitted Seals PR man Len Shapiro. "We paid him something like $25 per game, all the food he could eat in the press box, tickets to the game and free parking. His contract also said no sex. He was unique and one of the best pro cheerleaders around. Munson Campbell gave me the authority to hire him exclusively to the Seals."

Henderson led the crowd in short cheers, usually no more than three words long. "I also never cussed," George added. Krazy George's favorite cheer was, "Seals, ooh, ooh." "I sort of sounded like a seal, or at least as close to a seal as I could get," George admitted. "We also did 'Go Seals go,' 'Go Seals,' 'Oakland/Seals' which we would alternate by section. I also did, 'We want a goal' a lot late in games when we were losing and needed a goal… or four. I also had a chant, 'Turkey, turkey, gobble, gobble.'"

At Seals' games, Krazy George would wear a "Levi's cutoff, beat up tennis shoes, and either a Hawaiian shirt or a Seals tee shirt with Sparky the Seal on it." Henderson also frequented "Arnie's Time Out," a bar where Seals players and visiting players frequently went after games. "Arnie, the owner, made me a tee-shirt that said 'Turkey' on it," George recalled. "I wore that sometimes [to games] too."

Many times, Krazy George would drive opposing players crazy. Defenseman Paul Shakes recalled a particular incident that occurred during the 1973-74 season. "Once, Greg Polis of Pittsburgh was ready to take a face-off and I'm sure he dirtied his underwear when George ran down the stairs beating his drum. I can still see the look on his face," Shakes said.

His most famous confrontation came with Bruins forward Terry O'Reilly, which resulted in some Bruins fans and players chasing after George. "The Seals beat Boston twice that year," George said, "including this game. It all started when Terry O'Reilly slashed a Seals player in the face. He went into the penalty box and I was nearby and I called him a pimple faced weirdo turkey. Then I called him a coward. Now, at Seals games, we had about 4,000 loyal fans but when a team like Boston came in, we'd get 9,000 fans and half of them would be Bruins' fans. Well O'Reilly cracked when I called him a coward. First, he threw a glove at me. He missed. Then he threw his other glove at me so I moved back a row. Then, O'Reilly stood up and took a swing at me with his stick. The penalty box was pretty full. There were about seven guys there and O'Reilly's teammates started pushing him up into the stands. Then, two Bruins' fans who were both drunk jumped me. Now, you shouldn't jump somebody who is sober when you are wasted. A big brawl started and the game stopped for 15 minutes."

George was a black belt in judo and more than capable of defending himself if he had to. Although the police initially wanted to arrest the Seals loudest fan, things calmed down and Henderson escaped with a scrape on his elbow. He was a hero to the fans and later proudly showed a reporter the "scar" on his arm. George became a crowd favorite. "The crowd and I get along great!" he exclaimed.

Krazy George was also proud to witness what he called "the first ever streaking incident on ice." In fact, George was in on the plot. "This cute young girl had this outrageous plan," George recalled. "She skated naked across the ice wearing only a three inch sticker on her front and one on her back that said 'Seals.' I was supposed to take her picture. I was on the other side of the ice with a camera. As the players were introduced, she skated out from between the Seals players. The crowd was screaming, but I didn't see her until she was near the tunnel when she was skating off the ice. I snapped a picture of her head just then, right before two of her girlfriends were waiting for her with a coat in the tunnel. They weren't very pleased with my picture taking skills."

Krazy George quickly gained a reputation around the league. When the Seals Booster Club paid to send George to a road game in St. Louis, Blues' owner Sid Saloman III took notice. He sent George a telegram saying, "If your drum breaks in Oakland, I've got a bigger one for you here in St. Louis." George called Saloman the next day and was offered a full-time cheerleading position with the Blues if the Seals folded.

"He told me the Seals probably would fold since I was the only thing they had going for them," George remembered. Henderson was offered $12,000 to work all 40 Blues home games, which was more than the $9,200 he was making as a teacher at that time. The Seals did not fold, so Krazy George stayed in Oakland for two more seasons.

Henderson realized cheerleading could be his full-time profession. "I loved the Seals, but I hated teaching," George recalled. "I started to wonder, if the Blues would pay me $12,000 per year, who else would pay me? It made me realize I could do this full time and I've been doing it ever since."

After the Seals folded, Krazy George followed Seals President Munson Campbell to Denver to cheer for the Colorado Rockies. He later worked for the NFL's Minnesota Vikings as well. In 1981,

Krazy George states he invented the wave at an Oakland A's game during the American League Championship Series against the Yankees. George remembers getting entire sections to rise in a synchronized fashion and having fans boo sections that didn't participate. According to George, it only took three tries to get the wave across the entire stadium the very first time he tried it.

Today, George still lives in the Bay Area and works as a cheerleader for minor league hockey and baseball teams all across the country. He still has a special place in his heart for the Seals, where he first found fame.

Krazy George summed up his cheerleading philosophy in a 1974 interview in *Goal* magazine. "I enjoy making people happy, and when I do my cheers, people are happy and they laugh. Everything I do has a humorous approach. I enjoy being out in front of the crowd and getting good responses. All the time out there, I'm having a great time."

Seals' broadcaster Joe Starkey remembered Krazy George as "a good guy with a great gimmick and an extremely colorful style." The story of the California Golden Seals would not be complete without the image of Krazy George Henderson leading the crowd in cheers. Seals fans will never forget him.

POSTSCRIPT

It's been almost 30 years since the Seals played their final game at the Jewel Box. The Oakland Coliseum Arena still stands and has been refurbished and modernized. It remains the home of the NBA's Golden State Warriors. From the outside, it looks similar to they way it did when the Seals played there. An NHL exhibition game is often played at the Jewel Box each September, usually featuring the Sharks. There are only three NHL arenas still in use that the Seals played in: Madison Square Garden in New York, the Nassau Coliseum on Long Island and the Igloo in Pittsburgh.

The Seals Booster Club still exists even though the team has been gone for so long. It still holds monthly meetings and attends the annual NHL Booster Club convention. The booster club made trips to Vancouver and Los Angeles to see the Barons play while they were still in the NHL.

Ty Toki, the founder and multiterm president of the Booster Club, passed away in 2003. He remained in touch with a few Seals players until he died and almost all former Seals spoke highly of the man that did the team's laundry and was one of the club's biggest fans. His widow, Mary, is still active in the Booster Club.

Many former Seals players are often reminded of their time with the club. Hockey fans and collectors send old hockey cards for them to autograph. Ironically, the team is more popular now, almost 30 years after it last took to the ice, than it was when it was still active. Seals memorabilia is very hard to come by and is considered very valuable. A game-used Seals sweater costs between $1,000 and $10,000, depending on the condition, player and year. Fans who remember the Seals recall the team's unique style, colorful uniforms and losing ways.

There were a lot of "what-ifs" in the nine-year history of the Seals in the Bay Area. What if the club had played in San Francisco or at the Cow Palace? What if Mel Swig had been involved in ownership sooner? Could his political connections with San Francisco politicians gotten an arena built on the other side of the Bay Bridge? What if the club had owners with deeper pockets and a stronger commitment to making hockey work in Oakland? What if Rudy Pilous had stayed involved with the team in its first season? What if the league had awarded the Seals to Jerry Seltzer's group instead of Charlie Finley? What if there was no WHA and the Seals were able to keep their young and talented 1971-72 team together? What if the team was marketed more aggressively throughout its history especially in the outlying suburbs where most of the potential fans came from? What if the team had not been forced to trade away future draft picks for quick fix veteran players in an attempt to raise attendance immediately? Could the Seals have drafted Guy Lafleur? Would a player with Lafleur's star power have made the difference or would Lafleur have stumbled in Oakland as many other talented players did? Unfortunately for Bay Area hockey fans, none of these things came to pass. The Seals remained shorthanded both on and off the ice throughout their brief stay in the NHL. The team announced its intention to move to Cleveland in August of 1976. During its nine-year stay in Oakland, the franchise had more names (three) than playoff seasons (two).

NHL hockey would not return to the Bay Area until George Gund introduced the expansion San Jose Sharks in 1991. The Sharks sell out most of their games at the "Shark Tank" in San Jose.

"The climate is so different today," Gund admitted when comparing the Sharks' success at the box office to the Seals' difficulties. "It's hard to imagine the Sharks play in the same area the Seals did."

To prevent a repeat of the Seals' difficulties, Gund took a very different approach when introducing the Sharks, although he was not involved in the marketing of the Seals as a minority owner. "I wasn't sure it would work this time around," Gund admitted. "I was apprehensive. We did focus groups the second time around. We chose a logo and colors before we even had a team. We originally wanted to put a team in San Francisco but we went to San Jose because there are so many other things in San Francisco. It has worked very well in San Jose. Since the 1980 Olympics, hockey has been viewed very differently in this country. We made more of an effort to make people aware of the team. We had a 'Sharks in the Parks' program that helped get the kids familiar with street hockey. We were also one of the first teams to put up a website which was my wife's idea."

Gund held a majority interest in the Sharks from their inception until 2002. Today, he still owns a minority share of the team but no longer runs the day-to-day operations of the Sharks.

Len Shapiro, who stayed in the Bay Area to run a chain of pizza stores with former Seals goalie Gary Simmons admits that more people talk about the Seals now than ever before. "The amazing thing is, now, when I meet people, they all say they went to every Seals game. Well, that's obviously not possible because we never sold the place out."

For those lucky enough to be there, the memories of Seals hockey remain—a time of white skates, long sideburns, streakers, Hells Angels, new opportunities and many frustrating losses. The game had changed significantly since the Seals left the scene. Players make a lot more money and just over 60 percent of the players in the 30-team NHL are from North America now. The game is different now both on and off the ice. Almost all games are televised, the players make a lot more money and are more distant from the fans. Yes, the Seals lost a lot of games, but they represent a simpler and more innocent time, and they did it in their own unique way. They were also a guide in many ways of how not to run a sports franchise.

For those that were lucky enough to be a part of it, the memories of the Seals days in the NHL remain. What a special time it was.

About the Author

Brad Kurtzberg is a freelance writer and a lifelong hockey fan. He has written for Web sites such as packerreport.com, elitestv.com and allsports.com while also working on projects for the Arena Football League and Lelands.com auctions. Kurtzberg graduated the University of Michigan with a B.A. in History and has a J.D. from Georgetown University Law Center. After nine years of law practice, he has devoted himself to writing full-time. This is his first book. Kurtzberg lives on Long Island, New York.